The Short Oxford History of the Modern World

General Editor: J. M. Roberts

The Short Oxford History of the Modern World
General Editor: J. M. Roberts

Endurance and Endeavour

Russian History
1812–2001

Fifth edition

J. N. Westwood

OXFORD
UNIVERSITY PRESS

OXFORD
UNIVERSITY PRESS

Great Clarendon Street, Oxford OX2 6DP

Oxford University Press is a department of the University of Oxford.
It furthers the University's objective of excellence in research, scholarship,
and education by publishing worldwide in

Oxford New York

Auckland Cape Town Dar es Salaam Hong Kong Karachi Kuala Lumpur
Madrid Melbourne Mexico City Nairobi New Delhi Shanghai Taipei Toronto

With offices in

Argentina Austria Brazil Chile Czech Republic France Greece
Guatemala Hungary Italy Japan South Korea Poland Portugal
Singapore Switzerland Thailand Turkey Ukraine Vietnam

Oxford is a registered trade mark of Oxford University Press
in the UK and in certain other countries

Published in the United States
by Oxford University Press Inc., New York

First published 1973
Second edition 1981
Third edition 1987
Fourth edition 1993

British Library Cataloguing in Publication Data

Data available

Library of Congress Cataloging in Publication Data

Data available

ISBN 978-0-19-924617-5

Typeset in Minion and Congress Sans
by RefineCatch Limited, Bungay, Suffolk
Printed in Great Britain
on acid-free paper by
Biddles Ltd., King's Lynn, Norfolk

Author's preface

The opening of long-closed archives, and also more inviting conditions for research in Russia, has resulted in a flow of ground-breaking studies in Russian history. Although the new research has not produced any spectacular revelations, it has added detail, answered some long-standing questions, and uncovered topics and trends whose significance had not previously been grasped.

This Fifth Edition of *Endurance and Endeavour* has been substantially revised to take advantage of the new material. There have been particularly heavy revisions of the chapters covering the early Soviet decades and also those describing the Alexander II and Gorbachev periods. There is also an extra chapter to cover the Yeltsin presidency.

However, the purpose of the book remains the same, to provide as much information as possible, readably and reliably. For those who want more, the Bibliography has been expanded and now mentions over one thousand titles.

Contents

1

Eighteen twelve and after

1812

In his *War and Peace*, Tolstoy portrayed the 1812 war against Napoleon as one of those rare moments in Russian history when almost all people, serfs and lords, merchants and bureaucrats, put aside their mutual suspicions and realized that they were all Russians. The new unity was not quite as flawless as that, but Russia, sometimes called 'a state without a people', did seem to act as one nation for a few precious months, and never quite forgot the experience.

In 1807, Tsar Alexander I had made peace with Napoleon after losing more battles than he could afford and after becoming dissatisfied with his British allies. This peace was made at the celebrated meeting on a river raft at Tilsit, and entailed Russia's desertion of her ally Prussia, as well as her adherence to Napoleon's Continental System. Neither of these elements was approved by Alexander's subjects, and both he and the treaty became unpopular in Russian society. Betrayal of Prussia was regarded as dishonourable, while the Continental System, which meant the virtual cessation of Anglo-Russian trade, damaged many influential merchants and landowners, for Russia was already becoming a grain exporter, and north Russia traditionally supplied the British navy with its masts, rope, and sails.

True, the French alliance enabled Alexander to wrest Finland from the Swedes, and from 1809 until 1917 Finland was part of the Russian Empire, having a semi-independent status as a grand duchy. But the acquisition of this unattractive territory with its equally unprepossessing inhabitants did not mollify Alexander's critics at home, and meanwhile it was becoming evident that the fine sentiments expressed at Tilsit had lost their meaning for both Alexander and Napoleon. Russian breaches of his Continental System especially angered Napoleon, and in June 1812 he led a huge invasion army into Russian territory.

Alexander had chosen to appoint himself commander-in-chief of the Russian armies in the field. But his advisers, remembering his disastrous intervention in 1805 which had given Napoleon his great victory at Austerlitz, persuaded him to go home, leaving the war minister, Barclay de Tolly, in command. Barclay was with the 1st Western Army, and the 2nd Western Army was under Bagration. Bagration was not a Russian, but a Georgian. He had learned the military trade fighting in what were already Russia's traditional battlegrounds. He had fought in the Caucasus against tribes like the Chechens and Circassians resisting Russian encroachment, against the Turks on the south-western frontier, and against Sweden; Russia at the turn of the century was still expanding and meeting resistance as she did so. But Bagration's greatest glory was his outstanding record as a commander under the most celebrated of all Russian generals, Suvorov, in the Italian and Swiss campaigns of 1799. Unlike Barclay, he had the reputation of a fiery and irrepressible warrior, but Barclay's contribution to the Russian army was far greater. Although no stranger to the battlefield, Barclay was more an organizer and thinker. In 1809, after service against the Turks, French, and Swedes, and having attained the rank of General of Infantry, he became governor of the Finland he had just helped to conquer. Then in 1810 he became war minister and immediately began to strengthen the army; he wrote a manual of generalship, tightened army organization, built strong points, and supervised a doubling in size. Like Bagration, Barclay was not a true Russian. His Scottish ancestors had been among the hundreds of skilled foreigners recruited by Russian rulers in the seventeenth century to serve as officers, technicians, or administrators. His family had settled at Riga in the Baltic provinces where the gentry, which was the ruling class and which provided the Russian Empire with many of its most notable administrators, was of German origin. Barclay could speak Russian only badly, although this was less of a handicap than it might seem, for Russia's upper gentry, the class which provided high officers and administrators, regarded Russian as the language of the common people. Top people spoke French, or if not French, German.

Despite his failure to prevent Bagration's army joining with Barclay's, Napoleon still hoped to achieve his original intention of winning an early decisive victory and thereby persuading Alexander to become his ally again. At Smolensk, the westernmost city of Russia proper (as distinct from White Russia), he expected that the Russians would make a real stand. But Barclay merely fought a very stiff rearguard action and then withdrew from the city, having burned much of it.

In the circumstances, the Russian policy of retreating and avoiding a decisive battle was the best course. It would be some time before Russia could convert her manpower superiority into military superiority, and in the meantime withdrawal forced Napoleon either to abandon his enterprise or to push on and thus extend his supply lines. The Russian military leaders were familiar with Wellington's strategy in the Peninsular campaign and realized it was well suited for Russia.

Both Barclay and Alexander had favoured a policy of retreat well before the 1812 campaign started, but neither had anticipated the strength of public opposition to their strategy. In St Petersburg, Alexander was blamed for making peace with Napoleon in 1807, a peace which had dishonoured Russia and had not finally saved the country from French attack, and he was blamed for retreating before Napoleon. Especially was he criticized for entrusting his armies to Barclay, a foreigner who did not understand how precious was every inch of Russian soil. After Smolensk had been relinquished without any attempt at what the St Petersburg gentry considered a proper fight, Barclay's position became untenable. Alexander replaced him with General Kutuzov. However, Barclay continued to serve under Kutuzov and his policy was not abandoned. Kutuzov, a hero of the Turkish wars and a self-styled pupil of Suvorov, was by this time too old for his job. He was 67, so fat that he could hardly walk, gluttonous, in ill health and within eight months of death. But he had the virtue of being really Russian and of enjoying the complete confidence of public opinion. St Petersburg society and the army officers would accept a retreat ordered by Kutuzov more readily than a retreat ordered by Barclay.

Although Napoleon's retreat from Russia would be the more dramatic disaster, it was his advance which caused his army the most damage. Food shortages for both men and horses, heat exhaustion, and large-scale desertions, especially by the non-French components, considerably reduced its strength. Additionally, water was short. The few good sources were usually tainted; occasionally a corpse or an amputated limb would be found in a spring or pond, deposited by the retreating Russians and perhaps recalling to the French soldiers Napoleon's utterance at Smolensk: 'How sweet smells the corpse of an enemy!'

There was never any need for the Russian army to fight a set-piece battle, for Napoleon's forces were disintegrating day by day. However, Kutuzov was persuaded by public opinion, pressure from St Petersburg, and the enthusiasm of his junior officers to make one stand before Moscow. Thus occurred the battle of Borodino, a bloody contest which was strategically quite unnecessary but which was undertaken because to surrender Moscow without a fight was unthinkable. Although Peter the Great had made St Petersburg the official capital, in the minds of Russians Moscow was still the traditional capital. So in early September the Russian army stopped retreating and formed up in a defensive position on high ground near the village of Borodino, commanding the Smolensk–Moscow highway about 70 miles west of Moscow. The Russian forces numbered about 120,000, of whom 10,000 were hastily raised and half-trained militia sent out from Moscow. Barclay commanded the right wing and Bagration the left, with the Russian HQ in the centre. Well supplied with cold chicken and champagne, Kutuzov passed the battle comfortably out of cannon range.

By this time the French army had shrunk from the half-million with which it had begun the campaign to a mere 130,000, and was already slightly inferior to the Russians in artillery. Napoleon decided to make a frontal attack on the opposing positions, probably fearing that otherwise the Russians would be tempted to retreat once more and deny him his long-desired victory. At the end of a hard-fought day, in which positions changed hands time after time, the Russians began a slow and orderly withdrawal. Although the French had won the battlefield they had not won the war, for they had not destroyed the opposing army. Napoleon later regarded Borodino as his most expensive and terrible battle. Bagration was mortally wounded and died some weeks later at his country estate. Barclay, as though conscious of his recent unpopularity, deliberately exposed himself in the battle, emerging a hero and uninjured.

The two armies had been closely matched in strength and Napoleon on this occasion was not able to win a smashing victory by taking advantage of poor generalship on the part of his opponent. There was one critical point in the battle when he could have turned the tide by committing his reserve, the Imperial Guard. However, despite the urgings of his generals, he did not do this and lost his chance. It has to be remembered, too, that Napoleon was unwell at the time. Moreover, the greater part of his army had been afflicted with chronic diarrhoea since entering Russia. This ailment was almost catastrophic for the cavalry, for reasons which do not need to be explained. One French cavalry lieutenant, writing to his wife about the battle, made this comment:

I had again become afflicted by the diarrhoea which had so tortured me at Smolensk, and this day I experienced one of the worst imaginable agonies. For I wanted neither to leave my post nor dismount. I dare not say what I did to get rid of that which was tormenting me, but in the process I lost two handkerchiefs.[1]

By arrangement between the two sides, the Russian army left Moscow through one gate while the French entered it through another. With Moscow in his grasp, Napoleon thought that Alexander would sue for peace. But instead of crowds on the streets and a welcoming deputation, Napoleon met empty streets and silence. Almost all the inhabitants had left, taking the most transportable valuables and food along with them. This was an unusual and unnerving experience for Napoleon, and so was the fire of Moscow which broke out shortly after the French arrived and was probably an initiative of the city's departing governor. Moscow was built of wood, except for a few mansions and public buildings. After four days of burning, during which a puzzling absence of fire pumps and the indiscipline of the occupying troops made fire-fighting ineffectual, about four-fifths of the city was uninhabitable. The difficulty in properly housing his troops, added to the anxiety about his supply lines, forced Napoleon to quit Moscow. He waited a few weeks, hoping that Alexander would negotiate, then gave the order to leave.

The French left Moscow in mid-October. Napoleon ordered the demolition of the Kremlin, but this order was not fulfilled, because the fuses were wet.

---

1. *Vie de Planat de la Faye: Souvenirs, lettres et dictées* (1895), 82.

Another unfulfilled order forbade officers and men to burden themselves with loot; when the *Grande Armée* left Moscow it resembled more a caravan of carpet traders than an army. Some officers had found Russian carts and carriages which they loaded with all kinds of furniture, pictures, and wines.

A week after leaving Moscow there was a heavy engagement with Kutuzov, resulting in both sides retiring to lick their wounds. Napoleon was forced to retreat along the road by which he had advanced, via Borodino with its still-unburied corpses. Although Kutuzov, to the disgust of the British general who was attached to his headquarters, avoided close engagements with his retreating opponent, Cossacks and partisans were quick to bring a bestial death to stragglers or lagging detachments. The first snow fell in the first week of November. At the end of November the Russians were outmanoeuvred for a few precious hours, enabling most of the army to cross the river Berezina, but thousands of stragglers and camp followers were killed at this point, drowned, trampled underfoot by their comrades, or massacred by Russian guns. It was not until early December that the really cold weather set in. Contrary to the impression given by Napoleon's apologists, there was no early winter that year and the French were not defeated by the cold. The cold, when it came, only finished the job. In the final count, probably four-fifths of the half-million men who followed Napoleon into Russia were lost, and relatively few of these died from cold.

The year 1812 had not been good for Napoleon. For Alexander and for Russia, on the other hand, 1812 had been a great year. It was not simply a military triumph; it seemed to be a demonstration of moral strength. Earlier, the government had feared that invasion would spark off widespread peasant revolts, but this had not happened and the people and government had, for once, stood together.[2] Russians called this campaign the Patriotic War, and 1812 was seen as a turning point in Russian history.

The Tsar in Europe

As the French left Russian territory Alexander had to decide whether or not to rest on his laurels. Despite opposition at home, he decided to continue the war, and personally took over his troops at Vilna. This decision was bad for the Russian economy, but Alexander was unable to resist the opportunity of leading his victorious army to liberate Europe from a godless tyrant. It appealed to his vanity, his thirst for military glory, his liberalism, and his newly acquired piety.

The French defeat in Russia, and the incursion of Alexander's troops into central and western Europe, prompted a shifting of alliances, and in 1813 the

2. There were, however, one or two minor revolts, typically by peasants in areas not threatened by the invasion, who resisted call-up.

victorious armies (Russian, Prussian, and Austrian), after winning the battle of Leipzig,[3] triumphantly entered Paris. The subsequent treaty, thanks to Alexander's influence, was not ungenerous towards the former enemy; Napoleon was allowed to exercise his talents as sovereign of Elba, and France was allowed to keep her 1792 frontiers. Before approving the restoration of the Bourbons, Alexander insisted that the latter should grant their French subjects some kind of constitution. After the treaty was signed Alexander visited England, where he received a genuine welcome from the people but not from the ruling class. At the ensuing Congress of Vienna, Alexander was opposed on a number of points not only by the British but especially by the Austrians. At one stage the erstwhile allies, far from organizing a peaceful Europe, were themselves on the edge of war. But unity was restored, and strengthened when Napoleon escaped to France in 1815.

In the ensuing campaign, Russian troops did not participate at the battle of Waterloo, but they made a second entry into Paris, where they were welcomed almost as liberators. The Russians had been preceded by the Prussian army, which was bullying the Parisians and preparing to blow up the Pont d'Iéna (a bridge named to commemorate Napoleon's victory over the Prussians in 1806; the Prussians, insulted, preferred to punish the bridge rather than rename it). The calming effect of Alexander's arrival, his unconcealed sympathy for the French people in the previous year's negotiations, his fine presence, and his ability to please made the Russian Tsar a folk-hero not only in France but in most of Europe. When he went home he took with him a great reputation; and left behind 30,000 Russian troops who stayed until 1818 as part of the allied garrison in Paris and eastern France. It was some of these troops, influenced by their stay abroad, who a few years later would be plotting to murder him.

Russian Society in 1812

The total population of the Empire when Napoleon invaded was 41 million (see table, p. 606). Thus even at this time Russia had seemingly enormous manpower reserves; the population of Great Britain was 18 million and that of the USA 8 million. But the structure of Russian society and of the Russian economy ensured that the human potential of the Empire was not efficiently utilized.

Muscovite Russians ('Great Russians') made up only about half the total. Of the others, the largest group were the Ukrainians (sometimes, to their distaste, called 'Little Russians'). These dwelt in the south-western part of the Empire, with Kiev their major city. At one time they had been under Polish rule, but in 1654 their leaders had opted for allegiance to Moscow. Their language was very

---

3. Of the estimated 50,000 Allied casualties, about 22,000 were Russian.

similar to Russian, and the difference between them and the Great Russians was less in 1812 than it became later. On the northern border of the Ukraine was Byelorussia or Belarus ('White Russia'), similarly one of the eastern Slavic nations, but less populous than the Ukraine.

One other group which was predominantly Slavic was the Cossacks. The name Cossack means 'free warrior', and certainly freedom and warfare were the distinguishing preoccupations of these people. Their territory was mainly in the south of European Russia, around the lower and middle courses of the rivers Don and Dnieper. They were descended principally from Russian ancestors who had fled either from Muscovy or from Poland, from the former to evade serfdom or other hardships, from the latter to avoid oppression from the Catholic Church and non-Russian overlords. The communities they established were on the borders of the Polish and Muscovite lands, and served as a first line of defence against alien peoples, notably the Turks. Apart from fighting off invaders, the Cossacks also found themselves resisting the expansion of Muscovy, but were often compelled either to become subjects of the tsar as the latter incorporated their lands into his own territory, or to move further on. In this situation the Cossacks developed into a tough, savage, and volatile people, jealous of their freedoms, great fighters on horseback, and running their affairs by a riotous form of democracy with elected headmen. In the rebellions of the previous two centuries Cossacks had played a leading part, but in the eighteenth century they had begun to lose their autonomy. The Russian government allowed them their land and did not impose serfdom, but it did demand military service. One by one the Cossack communes in the Empire were converted to military units; each Cossack male was required to serve in the army, providing his own horse. Contrary to the general belief, the Cossacks did not provide outstanding cavalry units, but they excelled in pursuing a beaten enemy and in looting. From the political point of view they changed during the nineteenth century from an independent and vaguely hostile people into one of the most loyal and ruthless supports of the regime.

Of the non-Slavic peoples, the Germanic, Jewish, and Finnic were the most important; Jews (see p. 124) were rare except in the western borderlands. Essentially there were two Finnic groups; the Finns of Finland (and their kinsmen in Estonia), and the remnants of the Finnic tribes which had originally inhabited Muscovy. The latter had been mainly absorbed by the incoming Slavs to whom they passed on some of their physical features, but there remained isolated pockets of them. The Germans, who like the Cossacks played a role in the Empire out of all proportion to their numbers, could also be divided into two groups. Of little political importance were the German settlers who had moved with governmental approval and privileges to the lower Volga and south Russia, where by hard work and intelligent methods they became prosperous farmers, arousing the envy of their neighbours. The Baltic Germans were an entirely different group. They had settled during medieval times in what is now Estonia and Latvia, and had become the ruling class of landowners while the original inhabitants became an inferior labouring class. With their knightly origins, or at least a tradition of social superiority, and their German method and diligence, they supplied the Empire with many of its leading figures: soldiers, sailors, governors, and administrators. They tended to be unpopular among true Russians, partly because of envy but partly because in the eighteenth century several ruling empresses had employed them on a large scale as favourites, advisers, and tax-gatherers, and many of them had abused their responsibilities.

There were numerous Mongols residing within the Empire. They were mainly the remnants of the Tatars who, in the thirteenth century, had invaded the early Russian settlements and held the Russian people as tribute-paying subjects for two centuries. The Tatars had not settled within the Russian borders, but they had established communities outside, notably Kazan and Astrakhan, which had later fallen into Russian hands as Muscovy expanded in the fifteenth and sixteenth centuries. Other non-Europeans lived in Siberia which, although not highly valued by St Petersburg and largely unexplored, was part of the Empire and contained a variety of pagan tribes, including Red Indians,[4] of whom little was known at this time.

Only about 4 per cent of the population lived in towns; and the definition of town included hundreds of settlements which were little more than villages. Only St Petersburg (308,000 inhabitants) and Moscow (270,000) were genuine cities, the next most important towns having populations of less than 60,000. St Petersburg had been the capital of the Empire for a hundred years, and by 1812 most of its public buildings were complete. Architecturally, it was European, in accordance with the westernizing tastes of its founder, Peter the Great. Moscow, on the other hand, was traditionally Russian, with its Kremlin and old churches. This difference was reflected in the inhabitants of the two cities. The people of St Petersburg considered the Muscovites to be a trifle primitive, while the citizens of Moscow regarded St Petersburg society as slightly alien and vaguely suspect. Many regarded Moscow as the 'real' capital, certainly the spiritual capital, and the habit was developing of referring to 'the two capitals'. Tsars were crowned in Moscow.

Of the total population, less than 2 per cent belonged to the nobility, a term which embraces a wider range of status than in the west, and can usually be best translated as gentry. Another 2 per cent covered the priests and emergent middle class, leaving the peasantry as 96 per cent of the total population. The nobility included a small aristocracy, but consisted mainly of average and small landowners, and at the beginning of the nineteenth century was at the peak of its privilege. The aristocracy was mainly families which could trace their ancestry back to Rurik, the reputed founder of the Russian state ten

4. *Arctic*, 22: 71.

centuries previously, or to one or two other ancient rulers of lands since absorbed by Russia. These used the title of prince, but because titles were inherited by every child of a family, princely rank lacked exclusiveness. Close relatives of the tsar were called grand princes, usually translated as grand dukes.

Up to the time of Peter the Great the majority of the gentry inherited their land and title, and performed state tasks. But the tsars did distribute state land, and the peasants on that land, to non-nobles who entered their service as officers or administrators. Possession of this land made the new owner one of the gentry. Because in Russia land was plentiful but labour scarce, it became the practice to tie peasants to the land they worked. On privately owned land they would work both for their own subsistence and also for their owner, who would thereby be sustained while he attended to his state duties. Thus, depriving the peasants of their freedom to move (that is, making them serfs) had some justification originally.

Peter the Great, with his insatiable need for more soldiers and administrators, effected a change in the nature of nobility. For a time it seemed that whereas previously the state had obtained most of its servants from the ranks of the nobility, henceforth it would fill the ranks of the nobility with its servants. Peter insisted that merit and not nobility should determine a person's role in government service, and that when commoners reached responsible positions (that is, a rank) they should automatically receive gentry status. To this end, and to make his civil service as prestigious and attractive as his military service, he introduced his celebrated Table of Ranks. With amendments, this remained in force until 1917 and gave a man precedence not because of his blood, but because of his job. Henceforth, every rank in the administration would be equivalent to an existing rank in the army so that, for example, a provincial secretary would have equal status with an army second lieutenant, and top civil servants could style themselves 'general' and wear an appropriate uniform. There were fourteen ranks; the upper eight automatically conferred hereditary, and the lower six non-hereditary, nobility. (Under Nicholas I the non-noble but privileged title of 'honoured citizen' would be introduced as a reward for achievement, especially in commerce, learning, and the arts.)

Thus by the time Alexander became tsar there were six types of gentry: the aristocrats; nobles of inherited title; nobles holding foreign titles; nobles created by royal patent; nobles who had obtained their title by attaining a rank in the bureaucracy; and those who had been ennobled on gaining an officer's commission. The aristocrats tended to regard the last three groups as upstarts, and also looked down on the barons included in the nobles of inherited title; the title of baron, like that of count, was Germanic, and introduced by Peter mainly to reward merchants or industrialists. It was the aristocracy which, towards the end of the eighteenth century, set the fashion of speaking French rather than Russian, of sending its children to French-oriented schools, or hiring French tutors, cooks, and dressmakers. This Frenchification, and the wearing of European-style instead of traditional Russian clothing, soon spread to the middle ranks of the gentry.

By Alexander's time the gentry had been relieved of the obligation to serve the state, but the serfs had not been relieved of the complementary obligation of serving their gentry. Hence much of the rural discontent of this time. But most of the gentry did in fact serve, although usually for shorter periods, partly out of habit and partly because those who had never entered state service lost important privileges. Most gentry had only small estates; about one-third possessed fewer than ten male serfs, and another third between ten and thirty. Although small in numbers, the gentry were the dominant force in political life. In the eighteenth century it was palace revolutions carried out by Guards officers, themselves from the upper ranks of the gentry, which deposed and imposed the succession of unlovable characters who occupied the throne. It was Guards officers who had murdered Paul and installed Alexander. Obviously, as even the tough Catherine discovered, it was unwise to antagonize the gentry. This is why both Catherine and Alexander failed to fulfil their wish and promise to do something for the serfs.

There were two main types of peasant: privately owned peasants (serfs), who comprised rather more than half the total; and state peasants, who lived on land which had not yet been distributed to private owners, being still the property of the state. (By mid-century state peasants would outnumber serfs.) All lived hard and unrewarding lives, but the serfs were usually the worst off. A serf was simply the property of his owner, virtually a slave. He could be bought or sold, made to work in a factory, had no meaningful legal rights, and in the worst cases was completely at the mercy of his owners, who could have him flogged to death, sent to Siberia, or conscripted for twenty-five years' service in the army. Most of the gentry were not brutal, a few for moral or economic reasons actually gave their serfs freedom, yet most treated their serfs rather as they might treat their domestic animals. Sometimes serfs were compelled to work six days a week on their lord's land, leaving only Sunday for work on their own allotment; and at some periods and places they could be flogged for working on Sundays. Somewhat more fortunate were those who, instead of providing labour, paid a regular rent in cash or kind. Others were compelled to work in factories; they might be attached to workshops established by their lord on the estate, or they might be hired or sold to factory-owners elsewhere. Some were taken as domestic servants by their owner. Others, luckier, were allowed to seek their fortunes as hired workers in the towns, remitting part of their wages to their landowner.

Peasants' lives were organized by their own local communes, and there was little connection with the state. The commune paid its taxes and supplied its army recruits, and expected to be left alone. The peasants were slow to see themselves as Russian nationals; their allegiance was to the commune and any outside allegiance they felt was to the world of Orthodox Christianity. Constrained by the climate, aware of their vulnerability, they relied on ways and routines that had worked in the past. They were dimly aware that the state existed, but did not see themselves as part of that state. The state, for its part, saw that they existed, used their taxes and their conscripts, but regarded them as 'the dark people'. They were nine-tenths of the population, and unremarked except at times of crisis.

There were economic as well as moral reasons why serfdom was undesirable. Alexander took few positive measures, and those he did take (like his ban on newspaper advertisements of serfs for sale) were easily circumvented. But he did forbid the extension of serfdom to his recently acquired territory in Poland and Finland. This was a considerable step forward, because serfdom had been extended to the Ukraine only a few decades previously. Later, Nicholas I similarly forbade the spread of serfdom to Siberia; any serf who could escape and settle in Siberia unapprehended became a state peasant. Yet Alexander continued the practice, which he acknowledged to be wrong, of giving state land to favourites and supporters, thus converting state peasants to privately owned serfs. But his gifts were never quite as generous as those of his grandmother Catherine, who gave away peasants by the thousand to her various lovers.

The gentry and the clergy were exempt from personal taxation, but the peasants were not. In 1825, the government's revenue of 393 million roubles included 115 million derived from the peasants' poll-tax, while the 118 million from indirect taxes on alcoholic beverages also came mainly out of the peasants' pockets. On the other hand the peasants benefited little from the corresponding 393 million roubles of government expenditure. Fifty-four million of this went on state debts, and 18 million on court expenses. The army took 152 million and the navy 21 million. The ministry of finance took no less than 88 million, of which much was no doubt expended on tax-gathering administration. After deducting 15 million for the ministry of the interior, 5 million each for justice and foreign affairs, which had little business with the peasantry, and 12 million for contingencies, there was left about 17 million for services which might directly or indirectly benefit the peasant: transport, education (4 million), and posts.

An additional 4 million roubles went to the Orthodox Church and could be regarded as money spent on behalf of the masses. For the Russian people was a religious people. The tsar (the 'Preserver of the Dogmas') and most Russians belonged to the Russian Orthodox Church, although the Baltic gentry usually remained Lutheran. Foreign brides of sons of tsars adopted the Orthodox faith. At times in Russian history the Orthodox Church became a great patriotic force, symbolizing the common tradition and experience of the Russian people. Together with serfdom, autocracy, and the army, the Church was one of the great forces which made Russia what it was, shaping Russian attitudes and behaviour over many centuries.

The Church

The Greek Orthodox faith was adopted by the Kievan Russians in AD 989, by order of their Grand Prince Vladimir. This was the most important event in the history of the Russian people. Among other things, it cut Russia off from Catholic Europe; Russia never had a real Renaissance, although certain of her rulers tried to impose one. Nor did she experience an intellectual exercise like the Reformation; she did have a major religious schism but this was intellectually primitive.

At first, Greek priests and teachers supervised the affairs of the Russian Church, but after the fall of Constantinople the native Russian clergy, aided and abetted by the tsars, asserted itself. Under one ambitious tsar Moscow was proclaimed the 'Third Rome' ('and a fourth there shall not be'), and a century later the Metropolitan of Moscow was elevated to the dignity of patriarch. Some historians see in the concept of Moscow as the city of God, and in the Russians' belief that only they held the true faith, a spirit of messianism which persisted into the Soviet period. Certainly the Russian Orthodox believer felt that somehow God liked him better than he liked other Christians, and in the nineteenth century the defenders of the principle of autocracy exploited this feeling by emphasizing that the tsar was God's favourite lieutenant on earth. The expression Holy Russia conveyed all this. The philosopher Soloviev would later observe that whereas a Frenchman, wishing to express all that was best in France, would speak of *La Belle France*, and an Englishman would talk of Old England, Russians would speak of Holy Russia. This was not a political or aesthetic ideal, but moral and religious. Dostoevsky, speaking through Shatov in *The Possessed*, went further:

A nation only remains a nation when it has its own God and uncompromisingly rejects all the other gods in the world, and when it believes that with its God it will conquer and drive out all other gods from the world . . . But there is only one truth, so only one nation can have the true God, even though other nations may have their own great gods. The Russian people is the only 'God-bearing' nation.

In the early sixteenth century there had been a struggle between those priests who deplored the Church's rich landholdings and its role in temporal affairs, and the official leadership of the Church. The latter, relying heavily on the concept of heresy for moral strength and on the tsar's forces for physical strength, suppressed the dissidents, only to fall victim to a permanent schism in the seventeenth century. This schism, which created the problem of the Old Believers, was provoked by Patriarch Nikon, who enforced the correction of rituals which, according to Greek scholars, had become corrupted either through time or during their transfer from the Greek to the Russian Church. Among the questions which became burning issues was whether two or three fingers should be used in the blessing, and how Jesus should be spelled in the Cyrillic alphabet. The Old Believers were those who, despite persecution, insisted on keeping the old practices unchanged, and violently opposed foreign interference in Russian tradition. They claimed (and still do) that they were therefore more Russian than other Russians. Over the succeeding centuries, the persecuted Old Believers established their own communities which, according to foreign travellers, were cleaner, better kept, and more prosperous than the villages of the Orthodox. For the Orthodox Church, the schism meant not only the existence of a rival faith, but a loss of power; before Nikon the Church was frequently dominant in affairs of state, but his reliance on the state for help in chastising his priestly opponents led to a weakening of the Church's influence. This weakening was followed a few decades later by Peter the Great's abolition of the office of patriarch and the creation of the Holy Synod. The latter, headed by an Over Procurator (a layman appointed by the tsar), enabled the government to keep a close eye on the Church. Catherine the Great further increased state influence by taking much of the church land and, in partial substitution, giving state salaries to the bishops; that is, bringing the higher clergy into the pay of the state.

The subservience of the Church to the state, and the corresponding willingness of the state to serve the Church, seemed to intensify in the nineteenth century. The Sermon on the Mount well expresses the philosophy which the Church taught its members. Some of this teaching was not open to misinterpretation. 'Blessed are the merciful for they shall obtain mercy' is a concept which underlies the charity of the typical Russian; not simply the easy charity of alms-giving but the readiness to regard, say, a criminal as unfortunate rather than evil. The influential writings of Makarenko, the Soviet educationist, on the possibilities of social redemption for hardened criminals would be well within this tradition. On the other hand, 'Blessed are the meek, for they shall inherit the earth' was a text easily misused to persuade the flock that sufferings imposed by an arbitrary state were in accordance with God's scheme. The place of the Church in Nicholas I's ideology of 'Orthodoxy, Autocracy, Nationality' will be described in Chapter 2. For emphasis, here is an extract from the catechism used in the schools and churches of Nicholas's Russia:

Response. . . . God commands us to love and obey from the inmost recesses of the heart every authority, and particularly the Emperor.
Question: What examples confirm this doctrine?
Response: The example of Jesus Christ himself, who lived and died in allegiance to the Emperor of Rome, and respectfully submitted to the judgement which condemned him to death.

After the death of Alexander II in 1881, the Orthodox Church, with Pobedonostsev as Over Procurator, would eagerly support the autocracy and obtain state aid to persecute Jews, Old Believers, and the various sects. Although some nineteenth-century revolutionaries were priests, sons of priests, or seminary students, most of the clergy preached submission.

The Russian Orthodox clergy was divided into two classes, the white and the black. The black clergy were monks, occupied with various monastic works (including the preservation of what learning the Church possessed), and provided the bishops and other high dignitaries. The white clergy were the parish priests. Unlike the celibate black clergy they were required to marry (but could not remarry) and, in imitation of Christ, wore long hair and beards. Ideally, they were expected to possess a good strong voice: the more leonine the priest, the more his parishioners respected him. The priest was attached to one church for all his working life and received a negligible salary. In the villages he lived almost like a peasant, keeping his own livestock and regarding the local landowner as a very superior being. His income depended on how much he could squeeze from his flock for baptisms, marriages, burials, blessings, and devil-exorcizings. Although he was a graduate of a seminary or theological school, he did not have much learning, but he knew by heart the holy texts and it was these which he retailed, without interpretation, to his congregation. Most parishioners, even the most ignorant, regarded the priest as a church functionary, someone who performed necessary services, rather than as a spiritual guide. This meant that the Orthodox tended to decide for themselves what was good and what was bad: few Russians, for example, took seriously all the admonitions of their priests, but they did celebrate with great fervency such meaningful ceremonies as Christmas and, especially, Easter.

The holy man (*starets*) who was such a feature of Russian spiritual life was not necessarily a monk, although he would settle in or alongside a monastery. A top-class holy man would typically be a rough, ascetic, semi-literate, eccentric, pious, speak-his-own-mind-to-anybody character. Because of his evident spirituality and understanding, all kinds of people would come to him with all kinds of problems. However, the Russian Orthodox masses, which frequently failed to distinguish ignorance from holiness and naivety from purity, did not always discrminate between the genuine holy man and inferior imitations.

A really famous holy man would bring both fame and riches to the monastery which harboured him. Many were canonized. The creation of saints was simpler in the Orthodox Church than elsewhere. Later, under Nicholas II, canonization became so common that it lost part of its glory: it was sufficient for leading figures in a locality to clamour loud and long enough for a defunct bishop or holy man of that locality to be promoted to sainthood. The favoured corpse would then be disinterred and placed on public view in some kind of glass case. Traditionally the strongest claimant for sainthood was a revered holy man in the vicinity of whose corpse miracles were observed.

Theologically, the Orthodox Church was characterized by its denials of the issuance of the Holy Ghost from the Son of God, of papal infallibility and primacy, of the concept of purgatory, and of indulgences. It was cautious in its use of the word transubstantiation. In the 1839 catechism this word would be regarded as only one of several alternatives, and the catechism, while maintaining that the bread and wine were truly of the body and blood of Christ, refrained from explaining how they were thus transformed; this was a secret which only God could understand. Outwardly, the Church approved the worship of relics, and accepted pilgrimage as a significant act of worship. These characteristics continued into the Soviet period. Half a century after the Bolshevik Revolution, pilgrims in their thousands would still be ambulating each year all over Russia, depositing their kisses on the glass cases containing the remains of saints.

Apart from the Old Believers, there were numerous sects. Among them were the *Doukhobors* ('spirit-wrestlers'), hard-working and quite prosperous, whose refusal to acknowledge the temporal government and its works (including military service and state education) led to government persecution. Towards the end of the century, with the help of Tolstoy and others, many Doukhobors emigrated to western Canada, where their relationship with officialdom was as thorny as it had been with St Petersburg. Then there were the *Skoptsy* ('eunuchs'), who had excavated from St Matthew's Gospel their belief that voluntary castration was the key to eternal life. Other sectarians were the *Khlysty* ('whips') who liked to flog each other, and enjoyed the union of eroticism and mysticism offered by group sex; the 'gapers' who prayed with open mouths so that the Holy Spirit might enter into them; the 'wanderers', who were always on the move in search of God's truth; and the 'jumpers', who prayed while jumping so that their prayers would be closer to God. Alexander I was more tolerant of religious eccentricity than his successors; he liked to regard himself as enlightened.

Alexander I

Napoleon called Alexander 'the Northern Sphinx' and 'a real Byzantine', and it is true that Alexander was easy to misunderstand. Domestically, much of his apparent inconsistency was due to a conflict of two consistencies, his fear of disorder and his wish for improvement (a conflict which plagued his successors too). Additionally, his ideas and his thoughts tended to lead their own lives independently of what he happened to say at any particular time. Superficially, he seemed at different times to be an ardent liberal or a reactionary militarist. In conversation he was usually charming and agreeable. To some he seemed a complete diplomat, and to others a complete hypocrite. Physically he was most handsome: tall, of fine bearing, and with attractive blue eyes. These characteristics were presumably inherited from his mother, a German princess. All the later Romanovs were graced, more or less, with the same physical appeal.

Alexander's liberalism was a result of his education and of his earlier friends. His grandmother Catherine the Great had provided him with a Swiss tutor who was sympathetic, among other things, to the ideals of the French revolutionaries. The young Alexander was quick to adopt the feelings of his tutor, although he probably did not think about them very deeply. As a young man he acquired friends of progressive outlook, including one who had actually worked among the Jacobins in Paris. In the early years of his reign he discussed with these friends the best means of translating intentions into practice: how to end the brutalizing institution of serfdom without losing the support of the landowning and serf-owning gentry, how to give freedom to the Poles while keeping them attached to Russia, how to give some political rights to the people while maintaining the principle of autocracy.

Alexander at one time had toyed with the idea of renouncing his rights to the succession and going with his wife to live an idyllic life on the banks of the Rhine. However, as soon as he was tsar he showed no interest in relinquishing his authority and this, basically, was why his liberal intentions were so disappointing in realization. Towards the end of his reign, influenced by pious advisers, he dropped some of his liberal pretensions, but not all of his liberal friends. In general, although historians may have treated Alexander too kindly, he was one of the better tsars even though his improvements rarely touched the heart of a problem.

It is not hard to suggest where Alexander's militarism originated. Both Tsar Peter III, his officially presumed grandfather, and Paul I, his father, had been admirers of all things Prussian, and especially of the Prussian army. Peter III was never happier than when drilling and manoeuvring and inspecting his miniature army of wax soldiers; he even organized a proper field court martial and ceremonial hanging for a palace rat which had been discovered nibbling one of these toys. Paul, to the dismay of his generals, had Prussianized the Russian army, introducing his own drill manual on Prussian principles, and designing Prussian-type uniforms and hairstyles for his troops.[5] As a young man Alexander, fearfully assisting his tyrannical father on the parade ground, learned to stage meticulous inspections, enjoy military bands, and appraise marching regiments.

Alexander acceded in 1801, at the age of 24. There seems little doubt that he had throughout his twenty-four-year reign two burdens on his conscience. Like his grandmother Catherine, he came to the throne as a result of violence,

---

5. Words of command were likewise Prussianized, and are still in use in the Russian army; *Marsh!* (March!) for example, replaced the more homely *Stupai!* (Get going!)

for his father had been murdered by Guards officers wishing to enthrone Alexander in place of the demented Paul. Alexander had acquiesced in the conspiracy, persuading himself that his father would be merely deposed, not killed. Secondly, it is quite likely that Alexander had no more right to the throne than had his grandmother; the inheritance of Paul, Alexander, and the subsequent so-called Romanovs depended on whether Paul had really been the son of the feeble Peter III, husband of Catherine. Paul could claim to be Catherine's son, even though she showed no maternal interest in him, but Catherine by blood had been merely a German princess. She had numerous lovers, and one of these was probably Paul's father. Thus the claims of Paul and subsequent tsars to a divine right to rule were based on a very questionable past.

The Tsar's advisers: Golitsyn and Arakcheyev

In his early idealistic years as tsar, Alexander had relied heavily on Mikhail Speransky. Son of a village priest, doting father of a daughter born of his short-lived English wife, Speransky was highly intelligent and saw things as they were (he once commented that Russians were unproductively divided into two classes, those who were the slaves of the nobility and those—the nobility—who were slaves of the tsar: 'there are no really free people in Russia, apart from beggars and philosophers'). He visualized a regime based on law rather than arbitrariness. He was not a sociable type and was not well regarded; one commentator described him as having the face of a dying calf. But Alexander listened to him in the early years, and agreed that future government officials should be properly educated for their jobs. Denying young aristocrats the privilege of skipping the lower ranks of the state service made additional enemies for Speransky, and the process of blocking the upward progression of incompetent bureaucrats was never completely achieved, then or later.

After 1812 the two most influential advisers of the Tsar were Golitsyn and Arakcheyev, both of whom had been long acquainted with Alexander and held responsible posts. In the difficult days of personal unpopularity and French invasion it was Golitsyn who had led Alexander to the tranquillity of Bible-reading. Alexander, who regarded Golitsyn as an old friend, had appointed him Over Procurator of the Holy Synod in 1803, following which the previously dissipated Golitsyn underwent a born-again transformation into piety. This government post was one of the most influential in the Empire, and Golitsyn soon enhanced the office by making himself Alexander's unofficial spiritual adviser. On Golitsyn's urging, in 1812, the Tsar approved the foundation of the St Petersburg Bible Society by Scottish members of the similar British society. This soon became the Russian Bible Society; its first president was Golitsyn and its most important achievement was the translation of the

Old Church Slavonic Bible into Russian. Since Bible-reading could never become popular among illiterates, many of those who had formerly opposed education of the common people changed their minds, and the Bible Society was able to establish several schools for the poor. Because Alexander was known to favour it, all official doors were opened for the Society, and by the time it ceased operations in 1824 it had 289 branches in the Empire.

In 1817 Golitsyn became head of a new ministry of spiritual affairs and education, while remaining Procurator. In this post, while managing public education in a spirit of religious fanaticism, he showed great tolerance towards the many minor religions and sects of Russia (except the Jesuits, who had converted his nephew into an ardent Catholic, and whom, for ostensibly educational reasons, he then expelled from Russia). For the dignitaries of the Russian Orthodox Church such tolerance was unpardonable, as was Golitsyn's reputed sympathy for freemasonry. Arakcheyev, ever jealous of the Tsar's ear, was also seeking ways to unseat his rival. In 1823 an unsavoury and secret alliance was formed between Arakcheyev and the Metropolitan of St Petersburg. A monk, Photius, whom Golitsyn had once dismissed from the chaplaincy of a cadet unit, was unearthed and groomed for the role of holy man. Photius was brought to the capital, was said to have performed one or two satisfactory miracles, and, like Rasputin ninety years later, made a great impression in St Petersburg society. His new friends brought him into contact with the Tsar, who was evidently impressed by his eloquence. Soon there came a ban on secret societies and freemasonry, which Photius had described as enemies of the true faith. Later, Photius assured the Tsar that there were all sorts of plots afoot, and that the Russian Bible Society was at the centre of them all. The result was the replacement of Golitsyn and the end of the Bible Society.

Arakcheyev had been a loyal servant of Paul, helping him to Prussianize the Russian army. He had sheltered the young Alexander from his father's wrath on the parade ground, and the young heir had developed a trust in him. In the early part of Alexander's reign Arakcheyev was inspector of artillery, and his improvements did much to prepare the army for its encounter with the French. From 1808 to 1810 he was minister of war. He claimed to be absolutely devoted to Alexander, but it was a very jealous devotion. He was reputed to be of great integrity, an unusual quality among Russian officials. His first care was Alexander's military colonies, which he organized and managed. At the time of his rivalry with Golitsyn he was only content when the Tsar seemed to be paying more attention to the military colonies than to Golitsyn's Bible Society.

Justification for the military colonies was primarily economic. The government was heavily indebted at home and abroad. Yet Russia was intent on playing the role of a great power, with a correspondingly great army. The military colonies consisted of selected villages whose active male inhabitants were householding peasants (who worked the fields) and soldiers (who were billeted on the householders). The householders, like everybody else, were under military discipline and, in addition to their economic functions, were drilled and given elementary military training. The soldiers were similarly expected to help in the fields or village workshops. In this way a large standing army could be made economically self-sufficient, and it also enabled soldiers to become family men.

The troops in these colonies were, at first, veteran soldiers, and were billeted on householders who were chosen from men of good character aged from 18 to 45 years. Other inhabitants became a reserve. Young children were enrolled, uniformed, and separated from their parents as 'cantonists' to undergo education in military schools. Men over 45 were required to serve as auxiliaries. Villages thus militarized were on lands belonging to the state, and despite the colonies' unpopularity with the peasants (who in effect found themselves conscripted, together with their families), by 1825 they provided over one-quarter of the army's soldiers. Neither Alexander nor Arakcheyev would tolerate resistance, even though several revolts indicated that the draftees were unhappy.

The villages were often provided with new huts and good furniture, as well as hospitals and churches, all at government expense. Nevertheless they were hated, for they combined the hard labour of agricultural life with the harsh discipline and lack of leisure of army life. In some colonies agricultural work was neglected by uncomprehending commanders, but in others, modern and efficient farming was pursued. This efficiency, and perhaps the open and hidden subsidies, enabled the colonies to become, on average, quite prosperous. In a sense they were a primitive form of planned economy. Girls were directed to marry prescribed bachelor soldiers, for example, and Arakcheyev at one point fixed a production target of one baby per year per family. (Wives who failed to fulfil this plan were fined, as were those who miscarried, gave birth to dead babies, or produced daughters instead of sons.) The colonies made an important contribution, in both men and supplies, to the wars of the late 1820s, but because of disaffection they lost favour subsequently. They were finally abolished in 1857, having in their final decades provided labour gangs not only for local factories but also for railway-building. Nicholas I established several new colonies, mainly in vulnerable border areas, before he became disillusioned with them.

One reason for the unpopularity of the colonies was the character of their chief. Arakcheyev was virtuous, religious, and honest, but he was also uneducated and sadistic. He tended to appoint men of similar character to command the individual colonies, and the result was a regime of savage and brutal repression. Arakcheyev described himself proudly as 'a truly Russian uneducated gentleman', which was true but did not reveal that he was also decidedly eccentric. He was known to weep on hearing a sad story, yet draw satisfaction from ordering the whipping of an errant little girl. He would melt into sentimentality on hearing nightingales sing, and then order all cats to be hung for fear that they might silence this music. In Paul's time he had torn off with his own hands the whiskers of a defaulting soldier. He had a maniacal passion for orderliness and cleanliness, and also a collection of pornographic material. A doctor in one of the military colonies later testified that Arakcheyev had a twisted psychology and suffered from a 'deep disturbance of the whole nervous system'. When, in 1819, he suppressed a serious revolt in one of his colonies, he wrote to Alexander that he had been torn between two courses. On the one hand he had to act 'decisively' and on the other hand he had to decide what he should do as a good Christian. Having 'called on the help of Almighty God' he decided to run the offenders twelve times each through a gauntlet of 1,000 men. As a result, 25 of the delinquents died, which is not surprising since each was entitled to 12,000 blows. Alexander replied, 'I know exactly how your sensitive soul must have suffered in these circumstances.' At the end of the reign the normally dutiful Arakcheyev was adrift in a sea of depression following the death of his long-standing and devoted mistress. This lady enjoyed the relaxation obtained from beating her inferiors, and two of her ill-treated servants finally killed her. Believing this event to be part of a large-scale conspiracy, the court sentenced no fewer than twenty-four servants, including a pregnant woman, to public beating. The two teenage killers, sentenced to more than 100 blows each, died in the course of punishment.

Russia and the world

Under Alexander, Russia attained a position in Europe which was not to be regained until 1945. She was victorious in war, had extended her frontiers almost into central Europe, enjoyed the reputation of liberator, and had the most powerful army in the world. Yet before Alexander died Russia's reputation as champion of the oppressed had evaporated, for the Tsar by his actions proved to be the champion of the oppressors.

Having settled the Polish question as well as his allies at the Vienna Congress would allow, and having earlier in his reign consolidated the territorial gains which his grandmother had made in the Black Sea area at the expense of Turkey, Alexander felt free to play the role of arbiter of Europe. The foundation for his policy had been laid in 1815 by the Quadruple Alliance and the Holy Alliance. The Quadruple Alliance, signed by Britain, Austria, Prussia, and Russia on the morrow of their triumph over France, contained an article foreshadowing the concept of the 'summit conference': periodic meetings of rulers and foreign ministers were proposed to discuss problems which might threaten the peace of Europe. Five such meetings (congresses) were held, the last being in 1825, by which year the British had dropped out and the French had been admitted. As for the Holy Alliance, this was a product of Alexander's new piety. He had reached the conclusion that peace, justice, and charity in Europe could be preserved only if rulers would allow themselves to be guided by the principles of peace, justice, and charity. A document enshrining this Christian platitude was prepared and circulated. Most of the European sovereigns signed it, although without treating it quite as reverently as did Alexander.

The Holy Alliance has been blamed for the suppression of the rebellions against oppressive rulers in Spain, Portugal, Naples, Piedmont, and Greece. In reality, it was the system of congresses introduced by the Quadruple Alliance which enabled Alexander and his fellow-rulers to coordinate their actions against what were genuine liberation movements. As he grew older and holier, Alexander came to believe more and more strongly in a worldwide revolutionary conspiracy, working to overthrow the monarchs whom God had appointed to watch over the interests of the peoples. The wave of revolutions of 1820 and 1821 were discussed at the congresses, and Alexander not only urged his fellow-rulers to intervene but, undeterred by an 1820 mutiny in his own elite Semeonov Guards, offered Russian troops to help them. Making grateful use of Alexander's approval, but tactfully declining his troops, Austria and France marched, respectively, into Italy and Spain, suppressing the revolutionary governments and restoring the former rulers. However, because of opposition from Britain, Alexander's wish to dispatch troops to restore Spain's disintegrating South American empire was not fulfilled.

The Greek rebellion against the Turks was not so easily dealt with. It was begun by a former Greek officer of the Russian army, and Alexander was torn between his sympathy for the Greeks and his anti-revolutionary fervour and promises. He chose the latter, condemning the Greek rebels and thereby making himself very unpopular at home, for Russia was a traditional friend of the Greeks and traditional enemy of the Turks. Eventually Greece would win her freedom in 1830, with some help from Alexander's successor. Alexander's foreign minister at the time of the Greek revolt, Capodistrias, was himself a Greek and later became Greece's first elected president.

Although the western frontier was stable, a Russian army of 50,000 men was kept busy in the Caucasus. The 'pacification' of this region, stubbornly resisted by mountain tribesmen, would continue for many decades. In Central Asia the great period of Russian expansion was yet to come, while in North America there was a regression. Russian settlers had been in what is now Alaska, Oregon, and California long before the United States became interested in these territories. Tsar Paul I had chartered the Russian America Company (and bought his family some shares in it), and by 1812 an armed trading settlement, Fort Ross, had been established about 50 miles north of San Francisco. However, the Russian fur trade in this area was threatened by Yankee traders, who not only collected furs, but brought shiploads of rum and guns for the local Indians. In 1821, under pressure from the Russian America Company (and perhaps to protect his own investment), Alexander issued an order granting a monopoly to the Russian traders. Even when Russia sent a warship to enforce this order, there was little immediate reaction in the USA; the Pacific still seemed remote to Americans of that time. However, it was not long before lobbying by those New England traders who had most to lose from the Russian monopoly whipped up a semblance of popular indignation. Because relations between the two nations were friendly, an agreement was negotiated which protected the rights of existing Russian trading posts but acknowledged that the territory surrounding them was 'unclaimed'. It was while studying this problem that the secretary of state, Adams, evolved the principle of reserving future American colonization for the Americans. This principle, somewhat elaborated, was inserted in President Monroe's address to Congress, and became known as the Monroe Doctrine.

Alexander had always been sympathetically interested in American affairs. The US Constitution had inspired some of his own constitutional dreams, and the American failure to eliminate slavery discouraged him in his scheme to free the Russian serfs. He corresponded with Jefferson, and met Adams when the latter was American minister in St Petersburg. But original American respect and admiration for Alexander diminished when the latter seemed to discard his liberal sentiments. By 1821 Jefferson was describing Alexander as 'the very leader of a combination to chain mankind down eternally to oppressions of the most barbarous age'.[6]

Alexander the constitutionalist

There was a big difference between the constitutionalism which Alexander preached abroad, and the autocracy which he practised at home. But in the case of Poland Alexander did demonstrate a willingness to transform promises into realities.

The history of Poland has always been closely tied to that of Russia. Though both are Slavic nations, their relationship has usually been more baleful than brotherly. Their differences are rooted in Poland's link with the west (and hence with the Renaissance and Reformation) through the Roman Catholic Church; this drew her apart from Russia, whose traditional cultural links were with Byzantium through the torpid Orthodox Church. Lacking indisputable natural frontiers, the shape and the size of Poland have been continuously variable. At its peak the Polish Commonwealth contained an enormous territory stretching from the Baltic to the Black Sea and including Lithuania, White Russia, and the Ukraine. It was the two latter lands, where an Orthodox

---

6. From a private letter, quoted in M. M. Laserson, *The American Impact on Russia 1784–1917* (1962), 134.

and Russian population was ruled by a Catholic and non-Russian gentry, that caused most of the Russo-Polish wars until in 1795, by the last of the Polish Partitions, Poland was divided between Austria, Prussia, and Russia. But although the state of Poland had been thereby eliminated, the nation of Poland lived on, and until 1918 patriots were struggling for a reunited and independent Poland. Moreover, among what until 1945 could be termed the Polish ruling class, there were many who dreamed not simply of an independent Poland, but of a reconquest of the old Polish Empire, preferably by means of a heroic cavalry charge at sunset.

Alexander felt that the dismemberment of Poland, over which his grandmother Catherine had presided, had been a shameful act. One of his closest friends, Czartoryski, was himself Polish, and sustained Alexander's sympathy for the Poles. At the Congress of Vienna, Alexander had been thwarted in his wish to 'reunite' the Poles, although Russia had been granted the Duchy of Warsaw, which Napoleon had earlier created from Prussian Poland. Towards the end of 1815, while at the peak of his popularity, Alexander presented his Poles with a constitution. This made the former Duchy of Warsaw a kingdom (the tsar of Russia being the king of Poland) with a bicameral parliament. Thus, those Poles who were now in the Russian Empire were politically better off than their compatriots in Austria and Prussia, although they had neither true independence nor a truly popular assembly. It was a promising start, especially after the creation of a Polish army, commanded by the Tsar's brother and viceroy Constantine.

Alexander regarded his Polish constitution as a pilot project for an eventual constitution for Russia proper. He had instructed Speransky to prepare a draft constitution, but little came of this apart from the Council of State. This was a gathering of appointed elder statesmen whose job it was to advise the tsar on legislative projects; it remained influential under later tsars. This innovation, and the proper organization of ministries, was about as far as Speransky's constitutional ideas progressed. Alexander was persuaded to dismiss Speransky in 1812 (Speransky's admiration for the French was not an asset in that year), but a few years later the Tsar was again thinking in constitutional terms. Another draft, incorporating some American-style federal features, similarly fell by the wayside. Probably Alexander felt that the prerequisite for a constitution was the abolition of serfdom and, not feeling strong enough to antagonize the gentry, he could do little in this direction.

So effective power would remain in the hands of the tsars, who took advice from friends and family as well as from their recognized advisers. Tsars could issue laws single-handedly, although in practice they usually worked through the Committee of Ministers, whose members were appointed and dismissed by the tsars. Over the next century, Russia would remain an old-fashioned benevolent despotism, enduring a chronic shortage of first-rate benevolent despots.

Education

The course of Russian education had been eccentric, and would remain so. Some of the early tsars of Muscovy, realizing how geography and history had retarded the intellectual development of their people, had imported foreign teachers and sent Russian students abroad. Some, like Peter the Great and Catherine, had allocated substantial funds for opening schools in Russia. But other rulers, like Paul, considering education subversive, took an exactly opposite line, expelling foreign teachers, banning the import of foreign books, proscribing the teaching of certain subjects, and allowing no students to go abroad.

Alexander's education statute of 1804 generated the growth in numbers and quality which would be a feature of Russian education throughout the nineteenth century. The statute divided Russia into six educational districts.[7] Each educational district would be administered by a curator, in close touch with the ministry of education which Alexander had established. In each district there was to be a university, which would supervise the educational activities in that district. Each university would train teachers for, and derive students from, higher four-year secondary schools (gymnasiums) which would serve the main towns. In their turn the gymnasiums would be linked with the next level, the district two-year schools. Finally, at the base of the educational pyramid, were the parish schools, providing a one-year elementary course.

The six universities were to be Moscow (founded 1755); St Petersburg (founded 1819); Dorpat, an old institution promoted to university status and devoted to instruction in German for the benefit of the Baltic provinces; Vilna, which was in formerly Polish Lithuania and was doing for the local Poles what Dorpat was doing for the Baltic Germans; Kazan and Kharkov, both of which were established almost immediately. Each university was to have attached to it a teachers' training institute, the students of which were required to sign a pledge that they would teach in the state system for six years after graduation. University regulations were quite liberal, and there was provision for sending the very best students abroad for postgraduate study. Some of the precepts included in the statutes were also progressive. Teachers were told to rely on their own diligence and method rather than on 'the excessive labour' of their pupils, to concentrate not on fact-cramming but on imparting understanding and curiosity, to make their lessons entertaining and never to give way to anger. In the curricula, practical and technical subjects were emphasized. A higher status for education was achieved not only by improving teachers' salaries, but by finding, in 1819, a place in the Table of Ranks for qualified persons; a degree student was in the 14th Rank (one rank below an army ensign) and could rise successively to the 8th Rank granted to holders of

7. By 1914 there were fifteen educational districts.

doctoral degrees (equivalent to an army major, and conferring hereditary nobility).

While on the university level the plans were achieved, not all the proposed schools were opened. By 1825 the main towns had their gymnasiums, about fifty of them, but the district and especially the parish schools were well below their targets. In fact parish schools, which depended mainly on the charity of landowners and the Church for their funds, probably numbered only about 600. In terms of pupils, there were about 5,000 students in the gymnasiums, 30,000 in the district schools, and perhaps 30,000 in the parish schools. As for the six universities, these had nearly 1,700 students. All these figures were an improvement on those of 1804, but compared to the total population were still tiny. However, if schools outside the supervision of the ministry of education were included, the total number of pupils would be at least trebled.

In the universities teachers and researchers were of a high quality, and in Alexander's time were largely recruited from foreign, especially German, institutions. Although some of the best-known professors took the trouble to learn Russian, most did not because it was the practice to conduct lectures in Latin. This caused resentment among the students, who needed to study Latin to enter university, but rarely knew it well enough to gain maximum benefit from the lectures, and there was a certain weirdness, for example, in using Latin to instruct gentlemen-farmers in scientific agriculture.

That the schools directly under the ministry of education only accounted for about one-third of the total pupils is evident from the following figures: in 1825 there were about 265,000 pupils in Russia; of these, almost 70,000 were in the ministry's institutions, over 100,000 in military schools, another 50,000 or so in church schools, and more than 40,000 in specialized schools. The military schools total was composed predominantly of the 7- to 18-year-olds born to parents in the military colonies and taken for education and training at the age of 7. Among the special schools were those providing secondary education for orphans and girls, which were supervised by the Tsar's mother. In addition, there were already a few factory schools, financed by progressive industrialists (private funds played their part also in the state system; Kharkov University was financed by a local landowner).

In higher education the universities were supplemented by purely techno-logical or professional institutions. These were the responsibility of the appropriate ministries, but, as time passed, the ministry of education began to interest itself in them. Some of the best known were founded before Alexander's time. Peter the Great on his visit to England, for example, had recruited two teenage students of Christ's Hospital to found a Russian school of navigation. The Mining Institute, which like several other specialized colleges of that period still exists under a different name, was founded in the reign of Catherine. In Paul's time were founded the first medical school (the Military Medical Academy), and the Institute of Transport Engineers. Among institutions founded in Alexander's reign were a second forestry institute, several provincial military cadet schools for the nobility, the Main School of Engineering, the Mikhail Artillery School (whose first director was a rocket expert), and also the Corps of Pages to educate sons of the elite. With the exception of the cadet schools, these were all at St Petersburg, helping to make that city the undisputed academic centre of the Empire. Alexander's reign was marked also by a flourishing of scientific societies and journals. The Academy of Sciences was reformed, making it a purely research and disseminating body with no teaching responsibilities. To existing learned associations, like Catherine's Free Economic Society, were added several similar organizations, including the Physics-Mathematics Society, the Moscow Naturalist Society, and the Moscow Agricultural Society. These held meetings and published journals to discuss and spread the latest advances in their fields.

After 1815 Alexander had an understandable but regrettable desire to transform education in the same way that he imagined his Holy Alliance had transformed international relations. He found no lack of helpers, for the war had caused many besides the Tsar to turn towards religion and away from secularism and liberalism. Apart from those of genuine religiosity, there were those who had always been against education, and others who were only too anxious to jump on the most promising bandwagon. It was henceforth from the pious and the careerists that ministers of education and educational district curators were appointed. In 1817, so as to make the educational system dependent more on the Church than on the state, the ministry of education under Golitsyn was enlarged to become the ministry of spiritual affairs and education. Golitsyn's policy was to intensify at all levels the study of the Bible and of dead languages, usually at the expense of technical and commercial courses. With his approval, purges were carried out in the universities; professors who had trained abroad were excluded, students and teachers were forbidden to study abroad, the Jesuit establishments were closed and the Jesuits expelled from Russia. More important still, obsessed pious conservatives were appointed to the educational district curatorships. Because the educational system was well coordinated and centralized, these few men were able to dominate education in their districts from the university down to the parish school.

The most celebrated of these devoted reactionaries was Magnitsky, who earlier had been sent to inspect Kazan University. After a week's sojourn there he had produced a report for the ministry, alleging that the university was infected 'with the repugnant spirit of deism', and that all the professors deserved exemplary punishment. Magnitsky had no doubt that the university should be destroyed, but his report did give two choices: 'This destruction can be done in two ways: (a) by stopping the operation of the University or (b) by publicly demolishing it. I would prefer the latter.' The ministry decided not to kill Kazan University. It prescribed instead a fate worse than death, appointing

Magnitsky curator of the Kazan educational district. He at once settled down to his task which was, as he described it, 'the purging and humbling of the University, in my capacity as a Russian and Christian'. His first step was the removal of most professors, and the hiring of new ones on the basis of their moral credentials. The first part of this programme he easily achieved but, because news travels fast in academic circles, he was unable to find replacements who were willing, virtuous, and qualified. He finally abandoned academic qualifications and appointed a collection of pharmacists, country doctors, schoolteachers, and governesses. To rule Kazan University Magnitsky devised a system which is suggestive of the commander-and-commissar dual leadership of the Red Army a century later. The rector was retained, with responsibility for the academic programme, but alongside him was appointed a director, responsible for political and moral affairs. This director became a sort of watchdog, and forced the rector into a more-or-less insignificant role. In the university's regulations, composed by Magnitsky, the director was enjoined to examine students' exercise books, listen to their conversations, observe their prescribed daily prayers, introduce them to religious literature in their spare time, remind them that virtue is rewarded not only in heaven but also by the government, and above all root out any freethinking. Students who would not conform wore a label on which was written 'sinner'; they were put in cells ('solitude rooms') whose walls were decorated with paintings of the Day of Judgement. During incarceration, fellow-students would pray for the delinquents each morning before lectures. Care was taken to shield the students from harmful lectures. Magnitsky divided the sciences into two categories: 'positive science' (religion, law, natural and mathematical sciences), and 'visionary science' (philosophy, political science, ethics). The first group had an unchanging content, whereas the visionary sciences, according to Magnitsky, changed their content every twenty years, although not simultaneously in each country. Efforts were made to protect the first category from contamination by the second, and teachers of the latter were ordered to emphasize the frivolity and insignificance of their subjects; a notice overhung the chair of the professor of philosophy, bearing Paul's words 'Beware lest any man spoil you through philosophy and vain deceit'. Lecture notes were inspected and had to conform with Magnitsky's requirements. In geometry, the triangle was represented as a symbol of the Trinity and the hypotenuse was described as 'the expression of the union of heaven and earth'. Subversive books, including those advancing the theories of Newton and Copernicus, were removed from the university's library.

Around Magnitsky there grew what would in modern times be called a personality cult. He was awarded an honorary degree whose parchment proclaimed him 'the celebrated guardian angel of the Russian church'. At university ceremonies the rector would praise the genius and piety of 'the beloved Mikhail Leontevich Magnitsky'. The other educational districts did not have curators of quite this calibre, but the pattern was similar. Enrolments fell. The universities lost respect among the public. After his fall Golitsyn was replaced as minister by Admiral Shishkov, who regarded literacy as a first step towards subversion. Nor did he have a high regard for education in general. He compared it to salt: too much spoils the taste.

The Decembrist Revolt

Apart from occasional revolts in the military colonies, and the normal frequency of small-scale peasant disturbances, Alexander reigned untroubled by serious rebellions. Thus he was luckier than his grandmother Catherine, who had faced the peasant revolt of Pugachov, which at one stage had seemed to threaten the regime. If he had lived a few months longer he would have had to deal with the Decembrist conspirators (so called because their revolt occurred prematurely in December 1825 during the confusion caused by Alexander's death).[8]

Catherine at first had encouraged progressive ideas, but had lost her enthusiasm when the French Revolution showed that liberal thought could be dangerous. In intellectual circles, however, liberal ideas were kept alive, and a few Russians of the gentry class were familiar with the works of west European philosophers and political economists. Freemasonry, though banned from time to time, flourished in Russia, and the masonic orders had a wide range of members. The concept of service and charity which they usually emphasized could not fail to prompt criticism of the state of affairs in Russia. The masonic lodges, where men were treated as equals irrespective of their official rank, in effect were semi-secret societies where those of similar views could meet and exchange ideas. Although Alexander in 1822 banned all freemasonry, it was too late to prevent some of the masons forming new and completely secret societies with revolutionary aims.

Prominent among those who realized that drastic changes were needed were Russian army men, especially officers of the army of occupation in France, where there were no serfs, where there was relative freedom of speech and of the press, where there were regular judicial processes, where there was a constitution of sorts, and where new ideas circulated and were openly discussed. When these Guards officers and other military men returned home to the cruelties and arbitrariness of Russian life their bitterness was sharpened by the patriotic posturings of reactionaries who were playing the role of war heroes while praising traditional Russian society and describing the French as barbarians. One returning veteran later wrote:

8. Alexander was aware of their impending plot, largely from information provided by an English soldier serving in his army.

Seeing the insipid life in St. Petersburg and listening to the babblings of old men praising the past and deprecating every progressive step was unbearable. We were a hundred years from them.[9]

By 1825, through a series of foundings, dissolutions, and amalgamations, there were two significant conspiratorial societies, the Southern and the Northern. The aspirations of these two were not quite the same; the southerners were more radical than the northerners of St Petersburg. For geographical reasons contact between the two societies was only intermittent. Their aims included the replacement of the autocracy by a representative type of government, the abolition of serfdom, and judicial reform. The Southern Society, the nucleus of which was made up of army officers serving in the Ukraine, produced a programme composed by its leading member and intellectual, Colonel Pestel. This envisaged a republic, the abolition of class differences, and the division of land into 'social' and 'private' segments. A leader of the Northern Society, N. Muravyov, advocated a constitution somewhat similar to the American; the emperor would have similar powers to those of the US president, there would be civil liberties, police officials would be elected, classes and titles would be abolished, but property would be a prerequisite for office-holders.

Inside the membership of each society there was a variety of attitudes and aptitudes. On one extreme were those who felt that the Tsar could be retained and persuaded to carry out the necessary reforms. On the other extreme was a handful of men with a thirst for violence. There were romantic hotheads seeking martyrdom, and cautious intellectuals hating the idea of bloodshed and counselling a step-by-step programme. Most members, as the complement of their love of Russia, had at least a trace of chauvinism, and had been hurt by Alexander's grant of constitutions to the Finns and Poles but not to the Russians.

Alexander died unexpectedly, and had fathered no heir. Earlier, he had decided, with his brothers' agreement, that the younger brother Nicholas, not the older Constantine, should be his successor. Constantine was a strange character with a strange mind, but he recognized that he would not be a happy choice of tsar, and was quite content to remain as viceroy of Poland. This decision had not been published, so some confusion was inevitable when Alexander died. Constantine made things worse by neither claiming nor renouncing his succession. Nicholas felt obliged to swear allegiance to Constantine as a temporary measure. It was two weeks before Constantine could be persuaded to renounce his succession formally, and in the meantime the members of the Northern Society, well informed of palace secrets, decided that they would never again have an equally good opportunity. They hastily

9. I. Yakushkin, *Zapiski* (1925), 11.

planned a revolt to take place when the capital's regiments were summoned to swear allegiance to Nicholas.

The plan adopted was to persuade the capital's garrison that an oath of allegiance to Nicholas would be an act of treason, that Constantine was the true heir and the report of his renunciation false. This argument was a betrayal of the aims and purity of the Northern Society, for not only was it a lie, but it also portrayed the conspirators as defenders rather than enemies of the autocracy. The plan also meant that the whole action had to be carried out in the interval between the anticipated announcement of Nicholas's accession and the ceremony of swearing in the soldiers. Nicholas, who expected trouble, acted intelligently and courageously throughout. After stationing some of the more reliable troops at strategic points, he arranged to have the announcement of his accession (the reading of a formal manifesto to the assembled Senate) made early in the morning. The sleepy senators were collected before sunrise and the ceremony finished well before eight o'clock. The troops were to swear their new allegiance before noon, so the conspirators had only a few hours in which to act.

The plotters persuaded some units to march to the Senate Square and clamour for Constantine. This was according to the plan, but had been made pointless since the Senate's part in the accession had already been played. Despite this, the conspirators kept their men outside the Senate, where they were joined by a trickle of additional soldiers and sailors. There were occasional mild clashes between the insurgents and loyal troops. Crowds, which soon gathered, showed some hostility to Nicholas, but the conspirators, who after all were of the gentry, did not encourage them for they had no intention of letting their revolution fall into the hands of a common mob. The previously appointed leader of the revolt never turned up, being occupied in wringing his hands in private. Many of the loyal troops would have joined the revolt if the rebels had shown more activity, but on-the-spot leadership was provided by a high-voiced officer with a lisp, who failed to change the rebels' plan and seize the initiative. By late afternoon there had been few casualties, although the governor of the city had been killed by one of the more blood-thirsty of the conspirators. Nicholas, wishing to clear up this dangerous situation before nightfall, gave the insurgents one more chance to surrender and then called on his artillery. After three salvos the revolt of the Northern Society was over. After the revolt those members who had fled, and members of the Southern Society, began to be arrested. Pestel had been arrested on the eve of the revolt, thanks to informers' reports. Some of the Southern officers aroused their troops and for a week tramped ineffectively about the Ukraine at the head of a semi-revolutionary semi-army. Then, after a bloody confrontation with loyal forces, they surrendered.

The Decembrists failed because they were divided among themselves, had made no real preparations for their revolt, refused to make use of discontent among the masses, and were mentally prepared in advance for a glorious failure. Yet the respect in which they were held by later revolutionaries was justified. Despite the pathetic course of their rebellion, it was the first of a series which in less than a hundred years was to topple the regime. It was unprecedented for the gentry and the army to make a rebellion not for themselves but for a better society and to ally themselves with intellectuals. It was also the end of a tradition, for never again did the Guards officers stage a revolution. In the past they had engineered many palace revolutions, overturning one tsar or tsarina in favour of another. In this, their last coup and one of their few failures, they had aimed at something higher.

2

Zeal conquers all

Nicholas I and his reign

THE three decades of Nicholas's rule came to be regarded as a particularly dark period of Russian history. But even at its worst, in the last seven years of his life, most Russians accepted his way of doing things as quite appropriate for Russia. Strong tsars had always been preferred to weak tsars, and the state of the Empire was such that intensification of the autocratic system seemed just as viable a way forward as any other. But Nicholas, despite an almost maniacal attachment to the idea of duty and zeal, was only human; he insisted on having a finger in every pie but had only ten fingers like everybody else. Even if he had been adequately educated, he would have been unable to cope with the regimental-style system of rule which he evolved.

The decisive event of his long reign was the Decembrist Revolt. This shook him, and was a main cause of his irrational nervousness in subsequent years. The later 1820s were the honeymoon years: there were some steps to improve government, to codify the laws, to help the state peasants; there was a successful war against Persia, support of Greek independence, and another successful war against Turkey; there were relatively good relations between the regime and the intellectuals, relaxed censorship, and a political police concerned with public welfare as much as with security. Then came 1830 and the overthrow of the King of France. Then 1831, when cholera struck Russia for the second successive year and Poland rebelled against the Tsar. From 1830 the honeymoon was over. Fear of revolution brought growing internal repression. Poland was Russified. Jews and other minorities were hard pressed. After 1848, when revolutions in Europe were again accompanied by a murderous cholera in Russia, the pressure grew heavier. Nicholas not only stood firm, unlike his fellow-rulers in Austria and Prussia, but sent his army into Europe to help suppress revolution: to Wallachia in 1848 and Hungary in 1849, thereby relieving the hard-pressed Ottoman and Habsburg dynasties. Then came the unwanted war in the Crimea, and Nicholas's Russia, whose claim to greatness rested almost entirely on its enormous army, was shown to be, if not a giant with feet of clay, at least a very ineffective giant.

Nicholas was said to be 'two feet long' at birth, and grew into a tall and exceedingly handsome young man. He was probably of average intelligence, but his upbringing negated this. He received his first toy musket at the age of 2, and wore the uniform of a Guards colonel at 3. His first teachers were army officers' wives. That his mother was disturbed by his later fascination for all things military says, perhaps, as much about his mother as about him; like his younger brother Mikhail, he had grievously little contact with his parents. The main influence in his formative years was his nurse. Like Pushkin, Nicholas learned from his nurse how to be a Russian: how to write Russian, how to pray in Russian, how to feel like a Russian, how to dislike the Poles like a Russian. (But whereas Pushkin's nurse was Russian, Nicholas's was Scottish.) When Nicholas was 7 he was transferred to the care of male tutors, supervised by a general who, apart from being a Baltic German, had the additional disadvantage of believing that education was a process of forcing young men to do things against their will, using the whip if necessary. With this inauspicious start, Nicholas's unusual personality is hardly surprising. He insisted on order, neatness, and regularity, and was uneasy when these were disturbed. He grew up to feel most at ease among army officers, and as a boy the only subjects for which he showed any academic interest were the military sciences, although later in life he showed a certain intellectual curiosity in theology and history. But his tutors' methods simply made him stubborn, less open to new ideas, hostile to learning. His formal education ended when he was 15. His brother the Tsar refused to allow him to take part in the 1812 campaign, but in 1814 Nicholas, as a young officer, was with the Russian army in Paris, where he derived great enjoyment from the endless ceremonies and parades. After this, Nicholas travelled in Europe; in England he was unimpressed by Parliament but deeply impressed by the Duke of Wellington. Then, at the age of 20, he returned home and was appointed commander of a Guards brigade, where he played an agreeable role in restoring discipline to its pre-war level.

In later life Nicholas surrounded himself with army officers. These were the type of men that he felt he could understand and trust, believers like him in an orderly chain of command, with each link accepting and demanding complete subservience of inferior to superior; participators like him in a life which was organized, regular, and capable of perfection; proud possessors of a lightning grasp of the superficial. Nicholas emphasized that his profession was the army by wearing uniform more or less permanently. When necessarily out of uniform at night he consoled himself by sleeping on an army bed. On one visit to Windsor he surprised his royal hosts by requesting, immediately on arrival, straw from the stables to fill his army mattress.

By marrying a Prussian princess, Nicholas added one more German element to the regime, and ensured that he would have frequent and friendly contact with Prussia in later life. That this marriage was, and remained, a love match was not entirely due to the bride's enthusiasm for all things military.

Although towards the end of his life, with his wife in a frail state of health, the Tsar allowed himself the luxury of one or two mistresses, he was a loving husband and good father. Only at home did he remove the mask of the iron autocrat and become a warm personality. He always found time for his children and ensured that they would not have the kind of education he had suffered.

Nicholas spent much of his reign travelling through his Empire, inspecting not only his troops but all kinds of institutions. But these progressions were so rapid, and the foreknowledge of his arrival so sure, that local officials were usually able to conceal the evils and abuses which such visits were intended to reveal. As his trusted advisers were slowly diluted by a later generation, more and more of them flourished by telling him what he wanted to hear. For his top-down system of personal government, prompt and accurate information was essential, but he did not get it.

He did not enjoy his life. He considered that the office to which God had called him was a crushing burden. He was sustained by a strong sense of duty, which enabled him to plod on until the end, which was a bitter end. He died, aged 58, with great dignity, perhaps sustained by anticipation of the ceremonies and parades in the better world to come.

Nicholas's subordinates and their duties

Nicholas soon dispensed with the services of men like Magnitsky and Arakcheyev, but other advisers of Alexander were retained. These included some of the bright young liberals of a quarter-century earlier, now grown older and less liberal. In a secret committee formed at the start of the new reign and containing many of Alexander's counsellors, possible governmental reforms were discussed, but few of them were carried out. One overdue reform, the codification of the laws, was executed by Speransky with his usual technical efficiency. In the past, Russian laws had often been obscure. There had been a codification in the mid-seventeenth century, but since then many laws, in the form of decrees, had been promulgated and then filed away in the recesses of government offices. The few bureaucrats who had access to these decrees (which sometimes contradicted each other) could quite arbitrarily declare what the law was on a given issue, providing great opportunities for legal bullying and, sometimes, fraud. By digging out past decrees, collating them, and publishing them, Speransky and his colleagues after some years of hard work provided an agreed and accessible body of law. Not only did this speed the legal process but it also greatly reduced bureaucratic caprice. It also revealed certain duties, like those of nobles towards their serfs, which had been conveniently forgotten.

One of Alexander's advisers retained by Nicholas was Kiselev, who reorganized and improved the life of the state peasants. Kiselev was a veteran of 1812, and therefore very acceptable. Another ex-soldier was Kankrin, a German in Russian service who had been an excellent quartermaster-general in 1812 and later served as minister of finance under Alexander and Nicholas for twenty-one years. He was a capable man, though sometimes ultra-conservative, and his work will be mentioned in Chapter 3. As time passed, Nicholas's inner circle included an increasing number of military men; one such was Kleinmikhel, a trusted colleague of the Tsar, whose energy and ability to see the heart of a problem was accompanied by a certain ruthlessness. He had been a protégé of Arakcheyev, and succeeded the latter as supervisor of the military colonies. Kleinmikhel was a man who got things done at whatever cost. Supervising the construction of the St Petersburg–Moscow Railway, he would belabour an officer's nose with a pencil and allow workers to die from hard driving with equal unconcern. He earlier had attracted the Tsar's admiration by the speed with which he carried out the rebuilding of the Winter Palace after a disastrous fire; for this he received a gold medal inscribed 'Zeal Conquers All'. Later, Kleinmikhel was a useful go-between for Nicholas and his mistresses, and he provided a good home for the resultant offspring.

Another ex-officer, a cavalry officer of the worst type, was Protasov, who became Over Procurator of the Holy Synod. He concentrated on outward appearances, expecting his department and the Church to function in the smooth way that military organizations were believed to function. He neglected both high matters, such as questions of theology, and low matters, like the upkeep of parish schools. He did, however, broaden the curriculum of seminaries and prescribe Russian instead of Latin as the language of instruction. Uneasy in the presence of learned dignitaries, he preferred the company of the simple-minded. He refused to approve the publication of a commentary in Russian on the Bible, recommending that future priests should not be taught the dangerous habit of appraising holy texts, but should simply learn them by heart, and in Church Slavonic, as had always been the practice. The Church under Protasov played a great part in the Russification of the Empire's non-Russian nationalities. In Poland and the western Ukraine the Uniate Church[1] was gradually dissolved by Orthodox proselytizing and administrative pressures. The Catholic Church continued to be tolerated, as were the Armenian, Protestant, Muslim, and Buddhist religions, and all these came under the authority not of the Holy Synod, but of the ministry of the interior. Those Russian intellectuals who were attracted to Catholicism had little opportunity for propaganda inside the Empire, but several went abroad; one Moscow professor went to Ireland to combat Protestantism. Protasov, with the approval of the Church, exerted his main pressure on the Old Believers and on the various sects which had grown out of the Orthodox faith. In some respects

1. The Uniate Church had been founded in 1596 to attract, towards Poland and Roman Catholicism, the Slavic and Orthodox inhabitants of the Ukraine and Byelorussia. It recognized the authority of the Pope but kept Orthodox rites and language.

these were treated by the Orthodox authorities rather as the Soviet government would later treat the Orthodox. While they were granted freedom of conscience, they were not allowed to proselytize. Their communities, chapels, and cemeteries were attacked, sometimes fiscally and sometimes physically. They reacted by becoming more stubborn and did not diminish. By the 1850s there may well have been 10 million such dissidents, although the figure published by the government was less than 1 million.

General Paskevich had been Nicholas's commander when the future Tsar was starting his army service. The respect which the young Nicholas had felt for him remained and, despite his faults, Nicholas supported him in the intrigues which were continuously simmering in the army and war ministry. As a result, Paskevich rose to be commander-in-chief, even though better generals were available. He did have some organizing talent, but in his campaigns he emerged victorious only because his opponents were more incompetent than he. His critics claimed that he was only at ease when in retreat; he retreated when enemy troops advanced, believing that they would not dare to do so unless they were certain of their superiority; he retreated when the enemy was out of sight, anticipating an attack from an unexpected direction; he was even known to retreat when the enemy retreated, fearing a ruse. But he did win victories from time to time, and his courage was undisputed. Later, in charge of Poland, he helped Russia lose the Crimean War by his reluctance to release troops under his command to reinforce Sevastopol. He was one more example of Nicholas's crucial failing, the elevation of men who were loyal and hard-working, regardless of competence.

Perhaps the characters who did most to shape Nicholas's reign were Uvarov and the two loyal Germans Nesselrode and Benckendorff. The latter, as originator and head of the Third Section, will be described later. Nesselrode was Nicholas's adviser on foreign affairs. It was Uvarov, the intellectually gifted minister of education, who first used the slogan 'Orthodoxy, Autocracy, Nationality' in a report he wrote. Evidently the Tsar liked it, as did Uvarov himself, and thus was born the ideology known as 'Official Nationality'.

Orthodoxy

'Official Nationality', as expressed simply in the three-word slogan 'Orthodoxy, Autocracy, Nationality', provided the ideological justification for the ambitions and actions of the government, and was supposed to be a guideline for the ambitions and actions of the people. Most Russians were indeed comfortable with it. It was popularized by a host of journalists, professors, courtiers, and priests. Most of these popularizers were not hacks or opportunists, but did believe in the concept they were expounding, although not all interpreted the concepts the same way. Their arguments, though one-sided and in retrospect mistaken, were not an insult to the intelligence of their audiences.

Their opposition to democracy, to revolution, and to nationalism was not irrational, but the dangers they saw in change could not be evaded simply by avoiding change. The error of the ideologists was that at a time when the world was in a state of rapid transformation they chose, not to guide the forces of change, but to block them.

It was appropriate that Orthodoxy was listed first. When ideologists during Nicholas's reign talked of Orthodoxy being the foundation of the Russian state, they had in mind several factors, apart from the comforting conservatism of the Church. At its simplest, Orthodoxy implied firm faith in God and the concept of a divine will; it was this faith and this concept which bolstered Nicholas throughout his unsought and unhappy reign. On another level the Orthodox Church was shown as something peculiarly Russian, as the special gift which Holy Russia possessed and wished to share with Christians and non-Christians. For Russians, including Nicholas, Russia's God was special. The messianic trait of the Russian character, the desire to do good to the rest of the world, has been often noticed. The idea of Orthodoxy was perhaps the most powerful message the Russians had in tsarist times, but it was never well received, although it was transmitted energetically in Poland and the western borderlands, where Nicholas's government and the Church strove to drive out the Catholic and Uniate churches as part of the Russification policy.

Thirdly, there was Orthodoxy as a standard of behaviour. Nicholas took this seriously, his habitual severity frequently being mitigated by his appreciation of Christian charity. There were other responsible personages who followed the Tsar's example, but most of them were far more interested in another of Orthodoxy's attractions, its function as a solid prop of the regime. For them, just as the tsar was the defender of the faith, so the Church should be defender of the tsar. It was the Orthodox priests who, once a year and in every church until the reign of Alexander II, publicly and emphatically pronounced a curse on 'those who do not believe that the Orthodox monarchs have been elevated to the throne thanks to God's special grace, and that from the moment they are anointed with the holy oil, are infused with the gifts of the Holy Ghost'.[2] And it was an Orthodox metropolitan who proclaimed to Catherine the Great that God 'hath seen Thy pure heart . . . and Thy sinless ways',[3] a testimonial which would seem to cast doubt on God's all-knowingness.

Autocracy

The second string in the bow of the ideologists was Autocracy. This had several implications, but its essence was that the tsar expected the willing and total submission of his subjects, just as God expected the tsar's willing and total submission. From this, historians and journalists developed other

---

2. J. S. Curtiss, *Church and State in Russia* (1940), 28.   3. Ibid. 27.

justifications of autocracy. The Christian autocrat was the Christian conscience of his people; with absolute power, the ruler was able to soften the
impact of the law in individual cases, thus humanizing something which
would otherwise be impersonal and standardized; all his subjects in his presence were equal; he could reward the deserving and break the undeserving.
The autocrat was also entrusted by God with the task of keeping the people
down; the Russians were great as a people but were dangerous if not kept
under tight control. The people had sometimes to be forced to do what was
good for them; they needed a father who would love them even while punish-
ing them. The tsar was also the great coordinator; only a strong one-man rule
could cope with a phenomenon like Russia with its immensity, diversity, and
potential wealth. Other nations, especially Protestant nations, might prosper
with representative governments, but this was not true of Slavic or Latin
countries, whose peoples' volatility required strong and concentrated direction. Thus the tsar and his executive were very necessary and they had to be
severe. One journalist compared the tsar's ideal harshness with the pepper
which every good salad needs. In foreign affairs, the concept of autocracy was
associated with that of legitimacy; any attempts to overthrow the 'legitimate'
(that is, dynastic) rulers of foreign states were felt to be threats to the principle of autocracy, hence directly or indirectly opposed to Russia's true
interests.

All these arguments in favour of Russian autocracy contained, despite some
wishful thinking, their grain of truth. When Nicholas and his publicists talked
of autocracy, Peter the Great was never far from their minds: Peter, the super-
autocrat, who drove his people hard to create a new empire and a new Russia.
Peter's shortcomings were ignored, as was the possibility that his real
achievements were a long way short of his intentions, and that in the long run
he might have achieved more by encouragement than by harshness. Many of
Nicholas's publicists were historians, and it was easy for them to justify autocracy by drawing on historical examples. They showed how great peoples like
the Romans had declined after rejecting hereditary autocrats, and how strong
rulers like the Ivans and Peter had brought Russia far from its beginnings as an
obscure village on the banks of the River Moscow. Nicholas admired the more
despotic tsars, especially Peter, and identified himself with them, just as did his
successor exactly a century later. In view of what came later, it is also interesting that from adulation of the office of tsar there grew, on the part of the more
tasteless and opportunistic publicists, a 'personality cult' around Nicholas
himself, although this was against his wishes. One historian even proposed
that Russia should be renamed 'Nicholaevia'.

Nationality

Whereas Orthodoxy and Autocracy were terms easy to define and defend, Nationality could be, and was, interpreted in several ways. At its simplest, Nationality signified the union of Orthodoxy and Autocracy: Orthodoxy plus Autocracy equals the Russian nation. But perhaps a better translation would replace the word Nationality with the word Russianism, for this is what the ideologists usually meant. They claimed, rightly, that Russia was not just one of the European states, but that it was something special, something different from other European countries because of its history. Many arguments were advanced to bolster this idea. Some of these were interesting (e.g. Russia's rulers were always closer to the people than in the west because a shortage of stone meant that princes could not build castles); some were twisted (e.g. western states were created by conquest, whereas Russia grew by absorption, hence western nations are based on hate whereas Russia is founded on love); others were exaggerated (e.g. the Russian language has subtleties which give its users a great advantage over other peoples in the formation and exchange of ideas). Yet despite distortions and exaggerations, the essential truth was there, that Russians, because of their unique history and geography, have a different character and temperament, different beliefs, ambitions, and fears, and a different outlook. Shevyrev, who taught Russian literature at Moscow University, warned against western cultural influence; the west was like a man with a lethal infectious disease, enveloped in poisonous vapours, whom Russians embraced at their peril. Others, like the conservative poet Tyutchev, claimed to see a polarization, and like Shevyrev used concepts and language which would be echoed in the 1940s:

In Europe for a long time already there have existed just two real forces, revolution and Russia. These two forces are now opposed to each other and tomorrow they may enter into combat. No negotiations or treaties between them are possible: the existence of one means the death of the other! . . . Russia, country of faith, will not lose her faith at the decisive hour. She will not shrink from the greatness of her calling, she will not shirk her mission. And when could this mission be more clear and obvious? One could say that God has written it in fiery characters across the storm-darkened sky; the west is disappearing, all crumbling and perishing in this general conflagration . . . And when over this enormous ruin we see rising up like a Holy Ark this still vaster empire, then who will doubt its mission, and shall we, its children, lose faith and spirit?[4]

From the acceptance of Russia as a unique phenomenon other ideas followed, varying according to the character of their proponents. Those of messianic temperament felt that the Russian idea was so good it should be shared with the rest of the world. Those whose thinking was more in accord

---

4. F. Tyutchev, *Polnoye sobraniye sochinenii* (1913), 295, 306. These lines are taken from an article written during the European revolution of 1848.

with that of Nicholas pointed out the virtues of Russian life, rooted in Autocracy and Orthodoxy, and warned against any changes; why change something which is already fundamentally perfect? Many went further and claimed that the concept of serfdom was something essentially Russian, the complement to autocracy, the keystone of Russian society which must not be tampered with.

The messianic upholders of Russianism were often in disagreement with the government. Although the Tsar pursued a policy of Russianizing the non-Russian parts of his Empire he did so more for purposes of obtaining a good military-style standardization than for ideological reasons. When the Russianizers began to demand, in print, the Russification of the Baltic provinces, whose German nobility provided Nicholas with his most trusted executives, they were condemned by the Tsar. After all, as Nicholas remarked, whereas the Russian nobility merely served the Empire, the Baltic nobility served the Tsar. Many of the Russifiers shared the spirit of nationalism, the more romantic kind of nationalism, which was abroad in western Europe. They in no way wished to impose Russianism on other countries, upholding the right of peoples to form their own states. Rather illogically, however, they denied this right to non-Russian peoples inside the Empire; these people should Russify themselves, or be Russified by others.

This was the beginning of that period in which intellectuals liked to classify each other as either Slavophils or Westernizers. Westernizers were those who believed that the traditional Russian ways of life could be a handicap, and the sooner Russia caught up with the west the better. The Slavophils, influenced by the German Romantics, opposed westernization and idealized Russia's distinctiveness. Some Slavophils later embraced Panslavism, dreaming of a united Slavic world led by Russia and with its capital at 'Tsargrad' (Constantinople). Westernism, Slavophilism (and Panslavism) should be regarded as useful generalizations for attitudes, rather than for clear-cut groups. A person holding Slavophil views might also hold a few Westernizer views, or be a former or future Westernizer, and vice versa. Only later, at certain times, would there be animosity between the spokesmen of the two trends; they were agreed about much (for example, that the existing regime was unsatisfactory) and their most essential differences concerned religion and history. Westernizers admired Peter the Great and tended to be atheists, while Slavophils worshipped the Russian God and believed that Peter had taken the wrong road. Although the controversy between the two trends of thought was perhaps overdramatized and over-personalized, it did reflect the eternal question which faced philosophizing Russians: was Russia of the east or of the west, or could she be simply Russia?

The Panslavists' brand of patriotism was not always welcomed by Nicholas. Their ambition to use Russian power to liberate the Slavic peoples living under Austrian, Turkish, or Prussian rule was considered not only dangerous, but incompatible with Nicholas's opposition to the overturning of traditional regimes. The Slavophils also had their demerits in the opinion of Nicholas and the proponents of Nationality, even though some of the Tsar's ministers had Slavophil sympathies. The Slavophils, openly or by implication, belittled Peter the Great when they advocated a return to the purity of old Russian society and its traditions. Their opponents, the Westernizers, were in this respect more palatable. Nor did the Westernizers hint, as did some Slavophils, that Nicholas was not a true Russian, but three-quarters German, and therefore not capable of properly appreciating the Slavs. However, the Westernizers were distasteful in other ways, for they implied that Orthodoxy and Autocracy and Nationality were not quite the virtuous necessities portrayed by the regime's publicists.

Government

Although one of Nicholas's first acts as tsar was to entrust a secret committee with the examination of governmental institutions, no fundamental changes were made. At first, Nicholas seemed to enhance the importance of the Committee of Ministers by insisting that its members put duty first and attend sessions regularly and punctually. One secretary was dismissed for tampering with the messages passing between the Committee and Nicholas. However, the slowness of the official channels, and Nicholas's desire to have all strings in his own hand, caused him to bypass the regular processes. He did this by setting up secret committees to discuss specific problems, and by expanding the functions of his own Imperial Chancery. This he organized into sections, each dealing with a particular field which otherwise would have been in the purview of a ministry. The head of each section was answerable to him, not to any minister. The best known of these sections was the Third Section, which administered the political police and gendarmerie, but that had been preceded by the Second Section, entrusted with codifying the laws. Nicholas's insistence on participating in all important decisions meant that he was overloaded with work, for, despite his protests, minor matters also came before him, because few officials had the courage to decide what was important and what was not. Not surprisingly, his method of government meant that some departments or ministries were often unaware of what was going on in their own fields.

Because of its diversity and size Russia has always been difficult to govern, and this was especially so in Nicholas's time, when the Empire was almost at its greatest extent and railways and the telegraph were only just appearing. Continuing centralization of control meant that increasing amounts of provincial paperwork were submitted to St Petersburg, so much so that senior men in the interior ministry were overloaded. Thus it could happen that an important question sent by a provincial governor would be decided by some junior official or clerk of the ministry in St Petersburg.

Dishonesty and corruption, always common in the tsarist bureaucracy, flourished under Nicholas, even though he punished severely in those cases which came to his notice. Laziness and large-scale dishonesty were found mainly in the upper and middle ranks; the minor officials and clerks, overloaded with paperwork and underpaid, had to be content with small bribes. This bribery was well established and regarded almost as normal; citizens requiring a service had to give a tip of a standard amount (if they forgot, they were sternly bidden, 'Don't forget to say thank you!'). But although the bureaucracy had more than its fair share of crooks and bullies, the majority of its officials were perhaps more to be pitied than resented, and this should be remembered when reading the many writers who complained about them. Herzen, who at one time worked in a provincial government office, had this to say:

One of the saddest consequences of Peter's revolution was the development of the official class. An artificial, hungry, and uneducated class, capable of doing nothing but 'serving', knowing nothing apart from official forms, it is a kind of civilian priesthood, celebrating divine service in the law-courts and the police forces, and sucking the blood of the people with thousands of greedy, unclean mouths . . . There, somewhere in sooty offices which we hurry through, shabby men write page after page on grey paper, and make copies on embossed paper—and persons, families, entire villages are outraged, terrified, ruined. A father is sent to exile, a mother to prison, a son to the army—and all this breaks over their heads like thunder, unexpected and usually undeserved.[5]

Herzen also described the local governor, one Tyufyayev:

A governor's power tends to increase in direct ratio to the distance from Petersburg . . . Tyufyayev was a true servant of the Tsar. He was well regarded, but not well enough. Byzantine servility was unusually well combined in him with official discipline. The annihilation of self, the renunciation of will and thought before authority was combined with harsh oppression of subordinates.[6]

The bureaucratic attitude, the subordination of the individual to the requirements of officials' convenience, routine, and obsessions, has been a constant theme in Russian history and a constant trial to the ordinary people of Russia. In the Soviet period this 'bureaucratism' would persist, despite sporadic efforts to eliminate it.

One other feature of the bureaucracy was its role in bringing the euphemism to a fine art. Among the thousands of reports and surveys laboriously composed by officials, penned by clerks, and annotated by superiors, there were few in which a spade was called a spade. Unpleasant facts were not

---

5. A. I. Gertsen, *Byloye i dumy* (1946), 134. The provincial bureaucracy was markedly inferior to the central bureaucracy, with fewer nobles, fewer educated men, and poorer promotion prospects.

6. Ibid. 126, 134. Herzen's *My Past and Thoughts* is available in English. The first two of the four volumes describe his Russian experiences and are good bedtime reading, but a pinch of salt should be kept handy.

described as such, although an experienced official was able to read between the lines of fancy and obscure prose. Thus, as a source of information, the bureaucracy was imperfect. Its statistics were also questionable, especially those supplied by small provincial departments.

Conservative though it was, the bureaucracy in mid-nineteenth-century Russia was in reality a great force which got things done, even though inefficiently. Its social composition was changing; whereas at the beginning of the century its leading officials tended to be former army officers, by 1850 about three-fifths of the two capitals' top bureaucrats had been in the civil service all their working life. German officials had lost some of their preponderance, although they still held about 15 per cent of the upper posts in St Petersburg. Taking the central and provincial offices together, about two-fifths of the bureaucrats were sons of nobles, and about one-third sons of junior officers or of junior bureaucrats. Sons of priests, especially evident in the provinces, accounted for about one-fifth. It was the sons of nobles who tended to rise to the most influential positions. This was not because of their wealth; money helped, but about half the sons of nobles in the service possessed no serfs (serf possession being a measure of wealth and corresponding roughly to land possession). The key to success was education, especially since a specific degree of education now entitled an entrant to join the service at a specific rank. But of course the sons of nobles had better access to education; about one-third of them had higher education and another tenth could claim some elite education such as a lycée or the Corps of Pages.

Internal enemies, and the Third Section

When the western press referred to Nicholas as the 'Royal Gendarme' it was not without cause. Nicholas's Russia, especially after 1848, did resemble a modern police state, with strict censorship, numerous informers, arbitrary arrests, preventive punishments, and frequent denunciations of allegedly subversive citizens. But it should be noted that, because the regime's repression hit literary, and therefore vocal, circles in particular, its impact was probably exaggerated.

The apparatus of a police state was mobilized to sniff out and crush conspirators who were believed to be active all over Russia, but who in fact simply did not exist. Yet Nicholas had no way of knowing that during his rule there would be no serious plot. His reign started with the Decembrist Revolt, which was rooted in that part of society believed most loyal, the army. That the end of the Decembrists was also the end of serious conspiracy could not be known; Nicholas feared that the Decembrists were a beginning rather than an end. Immediately after the revolt there had been a wave of arrests in the capital, involving people who for one reason or another were under suspicion. In all, 121 accused came before the special court. Only 4 per cent were

executed, yet because the hangings were the first held in public in St Petersburg for many decades the sentences seemed unduly severe. Not only were
there five hangings (actually eight, for stretched ropes meant that some of the
condemned had to be hanged twice), but long terms of penal servitude and
exile were inflicted on those considered less guilty. Because of Nicholas's interference, some of the most guilty received light sentences, while at least one of
the hanged was relatively innocent. In time, public opinion, which among
older people at least had been against the rebels, moved to the side of the
victims. This change occurred after it became clear that Nicholas would never
grant amnesty to the exiles, and after the wives of the prisoners had dramatic-
ally given up their comfortable lives and followed tradition by going to Siberia
to share their husbands' hardships.

Despite countless arrests of groups and individuals during Nicholas's
reign, the Third Section suppressed only two major dissident groups, neither
of which was a threat to the regime. In 1847 a Ukrainian society, which was
partly an expression of Slavophilism and partly of Ukrainian nationalism,
was suppressed, and the opportunity was taken to sentence the Ukrainian
nationalist poet Shevchenko to ten years' exile as a common soldier. Articles
on Ukrainian history or in the Ukrainian language disappeared, and even the
adjective Ukrainian became suspect. This suppression of Ukrainian national
feeling aroused no great protest from the St Petersburg and Moscow intellectuals; their concern for the freedom of peoples did not extend to the Little
Russians. The second alleged conspiracy was unearthed by the authorities
in 1849, and thus coincided with a renewal of Nicholas's alarm that the
revolutionary spirit might spread from the west into Russia. This was the
Petrashevsky circle, which discussed current affairs from a reformist and
sometimes radical viewpoint. The Petrashevsky circle was in no sense planning rebellion, but fifteen members received the death sentence, including the
novelist Dostoevsky. At the place of public execution the death sentences were,
at the last possible moment, commuted to exile. This carefully planned drama
was popularly regarded as an act of cruelty rather than an act of mercy, but it
was neither. It was a reflection of Nicholas's view of himself as father of the
Russian people: a 'let's teach them a lesson they'll never forget and then let
them go' attitude.

The Third Section, administering the 'higher police', was established in
1827, and carried out the investigations and arrests of suspected subversive
elements. Political police were not new to Russia. As early as the seventeenth
century, Russian embassies abroad included a clerk who reported secretly to
the tsar on the activities of the mission's leading officials. Under Peter the
Great especially, it was the duty of every citizen to inform the authorities of
any overheard abuse of state or tsar, and this led to an increasing flow of
denunciations. The number of false accusations increased, particularly after
rewards were offered. The investigators had too little time to deal with all

these cases and, since they were afraid to release suspects without proper investigation, many innocents languished and died in gaol. The secrecy surrounding these government operations encouraged negligence; nobody was held publicly responsible for the death of long-held suspects, or for their expiry under torture. Alexander I ostentatiously abolished the political police, but in fact continued to use it under a different name. He later established a ministry of police, whose agents spent many of their working hours defending their role against the ministry of the interior, which continued to regard internal security as its own affair. Alexander, probably fearful of a plot against his life, had many of his associates watched, including Speransky and the virtuous Magnitsky. At one period Alexander even had the minister of police watched by a team of informers. Double agents, intriguers, and power-seekers flourished, which was one of the reasons why much information about the Decembrists' conspiracy never reached responsible officials until it was too late. With so much doubtful information arriving daily, the report of conspiracy in the army was not given the prompt attention it warranted.

Benckendorff, who became the first chief of the Third Section, submitted to Nicholas the plan on which this new political police organization was based. Familiar with the French secret police, which had a high reputation at that time, Benckendorff wished the new organ of state security to be loved and respected by the population. Thus a great effort was made to separate the gentlemanly side of the organization from its more squalid informing and shadowing departments. Incorporating the civil and military gendarmerie, the Third Section offered promising careers to gentlemen-officers. For these, public respect was to be one of the main inducements to join the service. For the undercover operatives, on the other hand, high rewards would be offered, and it was hoped that these inducements might bring forth a larger number of aspirants, so that the lowest types of character could be dispensed with. To emphasize the freshness and purity of the Third Section's better side, bright blue uniforms and white gloves were prescribed. Thus attired, the new gendarmes were sent out, not only on security work, but on behalf of the public welfare. Some, especially in the provinces, unmasked bullying and thieving local officials who had been exploiting the people. Such efforts did for a few years convince many Russians that the Third Section's gendarmerie was a genuine friend of the people.

Its main tasks were the shadowing, investigation, arrest, and punishment of people considered dangerous; observation and documentation of foreigners in Russia; investigation of 'heretical' religious communities; preliminary investigations of counterfeiting; supervision of prisons, camps, and other penitentiary institutions; and provision of general information, especially on the state of public opinion. After its early years, the welfare functions of the organization were overshadowed by its repressive and underground operations. Well before the alarming year of 1848 the Third Section was shadowing about 2,000 persons annually. At times it insisted on participating in censorship and also acted as the regime's public relations organizer, placing unsigned articles favourable to Nicholas in compliant newspapers both at home and abroad. It received petitions addressed to Nicholas, investigated them, and sent both the petitions and the comments on to the Tsar (Nicholas insisted that he should see all petitions addressed to him). With these petitions, plus denunciations and reports on suspected persons, the Third Section in some years dealt with more than 15,000 cases. Even though it expanded, its officials were overloaded, and more and more suspects were arrested, detained, or exiled, not because they were known to be guilty, but because conceivably, in the future, they might become guilty. Third Section officials, who were always polite to their victims, on occasion assured the latter that, although they might be innocent, they should be grateful for their detention for it protected them from temptation. Several false rumours or denunciations were started by government officials, wishing to damage their rivals; sometimes the Third Section helped in the fabrication of such cases and sometimes it was the victim of them. Ordinary people had every incentive to invent accusations, for a denunciation upheld by the investigators could bring the denouncer freedom if he were a serf, promotion if he were a soldier or official, land and title if he were of the middle class. Even after Nicholas ordered that false denunciations should be punished, the flood of accusations continued. Because only a few of the more gifted or experienced investigators could tell intuitively whether a denunciation was in good faith, because punishment was simpler than investigation, and because no chances could be taken, a victim of a denunciation had all the odds against him unless he knew influential people who could intervene on his behalf. But once a victim had served his sentence, he could return and take up his life again with no discrimination against him.

The Third Section, but not the secret police as such, was finally abolished by Nicholas's successor Alexander II. By that time the Third Section obviously had failed to keep the promise of its early years when, among other things, it had attracted officials of good character, had advocated the freeing of the serfs as a contribution to public order, and had recommended the amelioration of censorship. Especially after 1848, it was primarily a repressive organization. Its officers knew that promotion depended on results and therefore eagerly inflated any rumour into conspiracy. It employed agents provocateurs to lure people into unwise utterances. It never succeeded in eliminating from its ranks the incompetent and odious whom the 'higher police' tend to attract in all countries, and this in turn led to dishonesty, false accusations, adulterated evidence, bribery, and an atmosphere of suspicion and fear among the population, the government, and the Third Section itself. That it could put under surveillance Nicholas's own son without informing the Tsar is evidence enough that it was escaping control. While it hardly approached the mechanical ruthlessness which would characterize the secret police of several regimes in the next century, it was certainly a step in that direction.

Towards the end of Nicholas's reign there was a half-hearted 'Red Scare', when the Third Section fanned fears of communism. As in such scares in other countries a century later, socialists of all persuasions were tarred with the same brush, being accused of communism even when they opposed it. For a period it became a common tactic to describe any unwelcome ideas (or persons) as communist.

Education and scholarship

After the death of Alexander, men like Magnitsky lost their influence and were replaced by others who, though reactionary, had certain positive qualities. Uvarov, who was minister of education for most of the reign, was a genuine scholar, and his passion for the classics, and for oriental studies, was reflected in the curricula of the gymnasiums and universities. The European upheavals of 1830–1 and 1848 had as damaging repercussions on education as in other fields. In 1831 there was a drop in university enrolment of about one-third, followed in 1835 by new regulations which made the educational curators directly subordinate to the minister of education, thus bypassing the university councils. At the same time new professorial appointments became subject to prior ministerial approval. In 1849 it seemed at one point that all the universities would be closed down. A new university statute was introduced, student numbers were cut (there were 4,006 university students in 1848, but only 3,018 in 1850), tuition fees were raised (partly to make it harder for commoners to receive a higher education and thus raise themselves above their 'proper station'), inspectors of morals were attached to all universities, and students were added to the growing list of professionals required to wear a uniform. Students were also required to have a special style of haircut, apparently so that they could be easily recognized in any civil disturbance. It was at this time that Uvarov felt himself forced to resign, being replaced by a man rather more reactionary and considerably less cultured.

The departure of Uvarov was followed by a pruning of his beloved classics courses, giving more time for practical and technical subjects. (But Greek was not finally eliminated until the early twentieth century, and Latin only after 1917.) There were further encroachments on academic freedom. Professors not only had to hand in for approval their lecture notes, but there were informers who would denounce them if they departed from their text in the lecture itself. Philosophy could be taught only by a priest. There was a similar stiffening of control in the schools, to each of which, earlier, had been appointed a school inspector to watch over morals and political opinions. In gymnasiums, additionally, monitors were appointed to supervise the dormitories, and these reported any dangerous tendencies to the inspector.

The propagation of new ideas was what the authorities particularly wished to avoid; Uvarov himself had stated that his ambition was to build dams to stop the flow of new ideas into the Empire, and thus 'prolong Russia's youth'. Yet intellectual life was by no means dead. New ideas refused to be suppressed. Perhaps the most advanced in the exchange of ideas was Moscow University, which was, and would remain, the biggest (with 1,200 students in 1855, and 10,000 by 1909). Perhaps because it was in a culturally sophisticated city, 400 miles from the St Petersburg bureaucracy, this university seemed less restricted than others. Even when philosophy was in 'safe' hands, the ideas of the German philosophers, so fascinating to that generation of students, could be imbibed from friends, from banned foreign books (which scholars were usually allowed to obtain), or from teachers in other fields. Herzen, who studied science at this university, later wrote that he learned from the professor of agronomy more about German philosophy than about agricultural science. Moscow University, though academically the responsibility of its rector, was also the concern of the city's governor. He, however, was an easygoing army officer and was probably genuinely disturbed when students were arrested by the Third Section. He also believed that a university was organized like an army, according to Herzen:

It was long before he could get used to the impropriety of there being no lecture if a professor was ill; he thought the next on the list should step in, so that Father Ternovsky sometimes had to lecture in the clinic on female diseases and Richter, the gynaecologist, had to lecture about the Immaculate Conception.[7]

By the mid-nineteenth century the predominance of Germans and other foreigners in the higher teaching posts began to wane, except at Dorpat. A typical university teacher would have had German instructors when a student, would have studied in Europe for his doctorate, and then returned to teach in a Russian university. Despite interference and restrictions, the Russian university teacher had a better life and more opportunities than most other Russians. The lot of teachers was improved by the introduction of a new rank, the Dotsent. This rank, which still exists, gave status to those who had the qualifications for a professorship, but had not yet obtained it.

In the humanities, philosophy was perhaps the subject which suffered most under Nicholas. In fact, the chair of philosophy at Moscow University was abolished in the late 1820s. History, on the other hand, flourished. Nicholas himself was keenly interested in Russian history, and chairs in this field were first established under his influence. One of the most intelligent supporters of the regime and its ideology, Pogodin, even felt able to write that the historian represents the 'crowning achievement of a nation, for it is through the historian that a nation learns to understand itself'. This eulogy would have carried even more weight if Pogodin had not been himself a professor of history.

---

7. Gertsen, *Byloye i dumy*, 57.

But despite the emphasis on history, and the scope and excellence of oriental studies (which remained a permanent characteristic of Russian universities), it was in the sciences that Russian teachers and researchers were mainly distinguishing themselves. Moscow had its chairs of technology and of farm management. St Petersburg had courses on magnetism and electricity which were unmatched in the outside world. Kazan had the mathematician Lobachevsky who, apart from rescuing his university from the damage done by Magnitsky, is recognized as one of the great names in non-Euclidean geometry. It was in this period that the Pulkovo Observatory, which would play its part in the Russian space programme a century later, was established by the Academy of Sciences. The St Petersburg chemist Zinin was making discoveries useful for the production of aniline dyes, and experimenting with nitroglycerine. One person who benefited from his work was Alfred Nobel, who subsequently developed dynamite (the Nobel family was working in St Petersburg during the Crimean War, but returned home in relative poverty when the ending of that war resulted in the termination of their weapons contract). By the mid-nineteenth century, too, Russian mathematicians were very advanced in their studies of the theory of numbers and probability. Mechanical computers were being successfully constructed in St Petersburg. In the new field of electricity, four St Petersburg professors, of whom Lenz was the best known, were leading the world in the evolution of electric motors and the telegraph. Contrary to popular belief, Russian scientists deserve credit for laying the world's first practical electric telegraph; this was the St Petersburg to Kronstadt link of 1835, followed by the much longer St Petersburg–Warsaw line of 1839. Both of these were for military purposes.

One of the best-known names in Russian education and science at this time was that of Pirogov, pioneer surgeon and educator. Known in the west, when known at all, as the doctor who dressed Garibaldi's wounds and the experimentalist who persisted painfully and unsuccessfully in inducing anaesthesia by anal injection of ether, Pirogov's real achievement is obscured. In 1836 he was professor of surgery at Dorpat, and already contributing, through experimentation and publication, to the solution of many problems faced at that time by surgeons and anatomists. He then became an army doctor, and in the Caucasus campaign of 1847 became, apparently, the first person to use ether for battlefield operations. In the Crimean War he became famous for bringing, against all the odds, some degree of organization into the chaotic and deadly military hospitals. In this he was assisted by the first female nurses to enter active service with the army (Russia, too, had her Florence Nightingales). From 1858 to 1861 he was curator of the Kiev educational district, and brought a fresh and broad mind to work on the problems of public education. Some of his ideas were incorporated in Alexander II's educational reforms. He also started the first Russian Sunday school, at Kiev. This taught reading and writing to adults for whom Sunday was the only free day. These Sunday schools were very successful, with about 300 being founded before their popularity aroused suspicion during the reign of Alexander II; they were then put under governmental and church control. As for Pirogov, he fell into official disfavour and was transferred to a lesser position in the early 1860s, probably because he was too imaginative and too popular.

Literature and the arts

During the eighteenth century, common spoken Russian developed into a literary language, but it was the poet Pushkin who marked the transformation of Russian into one of the world's great languages. Since it is the language rather than the content of Pushkin's work which is so exquisite, he is difficult to appreciate in translation. But he did for Russian what Shakespeare did for English and Dante for Italian. He gave poetic meaning to the simplest Russian words and phrases, showing that the language of the common people was as rich and as flexible as any other vernacular. Of noble, but not rich, family, Pushkin achieved some fame during Alexander's reign through his *Ode to Freedom* and his authorship of some of the most witty and cruel epigrams about Arakcheyev. These circulated in St Petersburg society and resulted in his expulsion from the capital. Nicholas allowed him as an act of grace to return to St Petersburg, but his relationship with the Tsar and government was uneasy. He was killed in a duel at the age of 37. In his relatively short life he had written, among many others, *Evgenii Onegin*, a novel in verse; the Shakespeare-style play *Boris Godunov*, a novel, *The Captain's Daughter*, about the Pugachov Rebellion; and the poem *The Bronze Horseman*, celebrating the awesome greatness of Peter the Great. He also composed a multitude of epigrams and a few works which, because of their content, were not widely distributed; his *Gavriiliada*, for example, portrayed the seduction of the Virgin Mary by, almost simultaneously, the Holy Ghost, the Serpent, and the Archangel Gabriel.

Almost within hours of Pushkin's death, verses entitled *The Death of a Poet* were circulating in manuscript. In this indignant and very talented poem, scorn and revulsion was heaped on the moronic and idle young nobles who, unable to appreciate the damage they had done, were responsible for Pushkin's death. An old lady, fearful of revolution, sent a copy to Nicholas, and an investigation was ordered. The author was a 23-year-old Guards officer of Scottish ancestry, Mikhail Lermontov. Nicholas, irritated not only by the poem but by the thought that a Guards officer should waste his time writing poetry, ordered Lermontov's reduction to the ranks and transfer to the Caucasus. When he returned to the capital after this first expulsion, Lermontov's experiences fighting the Caucasian tribesmen and seducing the Caucasian tribeswomen provided the material for a stream of superb poems, stories, and songs written in the Romantic spirit. Lionized by St Petersburg society, writing erotic poems for fellow-officers, dancing, drinking, and seducing, Lermontov led a short and reckless life before being killed in a duel. In his best-known prose piece, *A Hero of our Time*, Lermontov portrayed what later would be called a 'superfluous man'. In this story the hero is a highly talented young officer who seems to have already experienced everything which life has to offer. He runs recklessly after all kinds of diversions, usually involving women or violence or both. He finishes by asking himself why he, talented and courageous as he is, could not have done something better with his life. The superfluous man, whose life is futile because society gives him no scope for his talent, was destined to be a favourite subject of Russian novelists.

Gogol, a Ukrainian writing in Russian, first attracted attention with his semi-humorous, semi-fantastic tales of Ukrainian peasant life, but his best-known works were the novel *Dead Souls* and the play *The Government Inspector*. In the latter, which the censor wished to ban but which Nicholas liked and allowed, bitter fun is poked at corrupt officials of provincial government. The characters, the liars, hypocrites, posers, swindlers, bullies, and other official types, were familiar to the audience but had never before been portrayed so exactly or so amusingly.

In this period Romantic painting superseded the school known as Russian classicism. Bryullov's enormous canvas *The Last Days of Pompeii* was probably the first Russian painting to attract worldwide acclaim; it was sadly overrated by the fashionable public and soon forgotten, except in so far as it inspired Bulwer-Lytton's famous novel. Of greater permanent interest, especially to historians, are those painters who depicted scenes from Russian life. Of these, Venetsianov and the former Guards officer Fedotov were the most important; they led Russian painting into the age of critical realism. Fedotov's painting *The Decoration, or a Bureaucrat the Morning after Receiving an Honour* appears to have been the first painting to be cut by the censor. It portrayed an official, brutalized, soulless, and arrogant, standing in his dressing gown and hair-curlers, trying on his new medal. To the public which flocked to see it in 1848, this picture seemed to express the essence of heartless decoration-seeking officialdom. The censorship appeared to share this impression, for when prints were made it insisted that the medal be taken out of the picture.

Music did not escape the attention of the censor (at one period musical scores were suspect, as potential secret codes). But there was a blossoming of Russian talent in the person of Glinka, who based his work on traditional church and folk music, rejecting the imitative and foreign-inspired work of his less distinguished contemporaries. In general, music was highly appreciated in St Petersburg and Moscow. Guest artists from the west were often heard, and in the capital there was a permanent Italian opera company. The richer nobility maintained their own orchestras and Russian choirs were already being praised by foreign critics. Glinka came to favourable notice when he produced an opera about how a Russian peasant sacrificed himself to save the tsar from malevolent Poles. At first titled *A Death for the Tsar*, on Nicholas's request it was renamed *A Life for the Tsar*, which seems to confirm that beneath his militarist shell Nicholas had at least a sensitive ear for the subtleties of language. Glinka was a principal formative influence on the Russian music that came later in the century, but his reputation varied with the tide of politics. By the turn of the century it approached a cult, with so many of the new national composers acknowledging their debt to him. But his monarchism was held against him after the 1917 Revolution, until Stalin revealed his liking for him, after which Glinka became another kind of cult figure, so much so that young musicians secretly loathed him. But for much of the 1990s Glinka's *Patriotic Song* would serve as Russia's national anthem. There is some poignancy here, because he had been disappointed when his music was not chosen for the new (and first) Russian national anthem, which was introduced in 1833. Hitherto, on ceremonial occasions abroad, the Tsar had been greeted with the British anthem, which Nicholas found mildly humiliating. Apparently the new anthem proved popular, for at the coronation of Alexander II two decades later it was sung three times over during the fireworks display, the first time modestly with 1,000 voices, the second time somewhat louder with the addition of massed choirs and military bands, and the third time more emphatically, accompanied by cannon salvos 'fired by means of an electro-galvanic apparatus'. But the words seemed little more advanced than those of the British anthem formerly used:

> God, save the Tsar!
> Mighty and strong reign for our glory;
> Reign for the dread of our enemies,
> O Tsar of the Orthodox Faith!
> God, save the Tsar!

The critics and commentators

Literary criticism began to flourish under Nicholas, its most noted practitioner being Belinsky. Probably Russia's most influential critic, Belinsky had been excluded from Moscow University after his professors had decided he lacked sufficient intellect. He then became one of the very few Russians who made their living by writing (almost all Russian writers were landowners). It was he who recognized that a specifically Russian literature was emerging, worthy of comparison with the literary heritage of western nations. It was he, too, who, towards the end of his thirty-seven-year life, popularized the description 'critical realism' as a feature and as a standard of judgement of Russian literature. By realism he meant simply the description of things as they are. By critical he meant socially responsible; the writer had a duty to illuminate the seamy side of life in the hope of encouraging dissatisfaction and hence improvement. Critical realism therefore implied that a writer was to be judged above all by the content, the social implications, of his work. Belinsky wrote that Russia's 'salvation' lay neither in mysticism nor piety nor asceticism but in enlightenment and humanity, in sharing the successes of western civilization.

A key work was Chaadayev's *Philosophical Letter* (actually there were eight of these, but only the first was published). Chaadayev, a former Guards officer and participant in the 1812 campaign, published this article in 1836, startling governmental and intellectual circles. He was declared to be mentally defective, the editor of the newspaper which published it was exiled, and the overworked censor who had passed it was expelled from government service. Chaadayev took a distinctly pessimistic view of Russia's past and present. He cast doubts on the assumption that Russia, though behind the west, would eventually go through the same processes as the west had undergone. He pointed out that since Russia had a quite different history, with no Renaissance, no Reformation, and no Roman Law, there was no guarantee that she would pass through the same stages as the west. He later implied that Russia's future lay in following the west, but modifying western experience so as to fit Russian realities. Thus Chaadayev was in a certain sense the harbinger of those Russian revolutionaries, like the Populists and Lenin, who saw the need to modify western concepts before applying them in Russia, as opposed to others, like the Decembrists and the Mensheviks, who seemed content to imitate the west.

The question of Russia's destiny was the preoccupation of minds other than those of Chaadayev and those who thought like him. In a sense, Russia was the Superfluous Man of Europe; so much power, so much capability, but unable to find the opportunity of using these advantages for the general welfare. Proponents of Official Nationality, as already mentioned, thought that Russia should remain as she was in order to serve as a shining example for the rest of the world. When Chaadayev, in his *Philosophical Letter*, wrote that Russia's past was empty, her present intolerable, and her future non-existent, Benckendorff replied that 'Russia's past is admirable, her present more than magnificent: while so far as her future is concerned, it cannot be grasped by the most audacious imagination'. This was a very eloquent eulogy of Russia, especially as it came from a Baltic German writing in French.

At this period discussion groups and literary circles were the only effective way of circulating and developing new ideas. Friends of intellectual bent would join together regularly for a partly social, partly instructive, meeting. The most fruitful of these circles, where not only ideas, but banned books and handwritten manuscripts, might circulate, were usually quite informal. German philosophy, including Hegel, was very fashionable, as well as French socialist thought. Intellectuals were very few in Russia at this time, and were concentrated in the two capitals. For most intellectuals, their most important audience was themselves. As might be expected, the Third Section was not slow to insinuate its informers into these circles, and many participants were arrested. Among them was the young Herzen who, after release from exile, emigrated in 1847. Already known as a gifted and persuasive writer and journalist, he became the inspiration of the left-wing of the Westernizers. He claimed that Russia would only move forward after power had been transferred from the upper classes to the people, and after science, socialism, and freedom had replaced repression. After witnessing the 1848 revolutions, and personally discovering that western democracy meant the replacement of one big tsar by a multitude of little tsars, Herzen changed his views somewhat. He advocated the inclusion of truly Russian features, like the commune, in the society of the future, so that the dangers inherent in western democracy might be avoided by drawing on Russia's experience. From 1856, Herzen was in London, publishing his Russian newspaper *Kolokol* ('Bell'). This included items received from correspondents inside Russia describing, among other things, bureaucratic frauds and injustices. It was smuggled into Russia and attained an influential, though necessarily limited, circulation there. But after 1863, when Herzen supported the Poles in their rebellion against Russia, he lost influence among Russian radicals; when Russian intellectuals talked of freedom they usually meant freedom for themselves, not for the Poles. Nevertheless, and despite the widening gap between Herzen and the younger revolutionaries, he may be said to have been the forerunner of later revolutionary movements. In particular, his advocacy of blending modern western civilization with the old Russian elements inspired the emergent Populists.

Bakunin, one of Herzen's contemporaries, was also discomfited by the fate of the Polish revolt, and henceforth devoted himself to European affairs. Regarded as the inspirer of modern European anarchism, Bakunin was originally simply a revolutionary democrat. Sometimes classed as one of Russia's 'repentant nobility', he had participated in the European revolutions of 1848–9, and had been extradited to Russia and exiled to Siberia, whence he escaped abroad in 1861. It was not until after this, his final departure from his homeland, that he became a real anarchist. Bakunin's ideas reached Russia through returning émigrés and through his *People's Cause*, an anarchist periodical smuggled into Russia and read largely by students. Although his excitable personality hindered the development of an anarchist movement in Russia, most shades of revolutionary opinion absorbed anarchist ingredients. Bakunin never had a strong organization, but he became the inspiration of young revolutionaries; he was something of a hero, having participated in so many glorious failures, while his advocacy of the destruction of the state was congenial to those many Russians who resented the rigidity and repression of the government.

Censorship

The strict censorship under which writers worked during most of Nicholas's reign was by no means an innovation. The last years of Alexander's reign witnessed a stricter control than the early years of Nicholas. It is true that a censorship law introduced in 1826 enabled the authorities to ban almost anything if they so chose, but it was not applied as strictly as it could have been, and in 1828 new and lenient regulations were introduced, reflecting the short-lived honeymoon between the Tsar and literary circles. The censors were instructed not to interfere with certain kinds of publication; most of the censors were themselves either part-time writers or at least in sympathy with writers, the latter being usually in favour of some kind of censorship, and the new law, which made the censor, not the writer or publisher, responsible once approval had been given, was regarded as a measure of protection against post-publication prosecution. But the Third Section gradually encroached on the censorship preserves of the ministry of education; after the upheavals in France and in Poland in 1830–1, and especially after 1848 and the Petrashevsky affair, censorship was strict, unfair, and often absurd.

The atmosphere in which writers and publishers worked in the worst periods can best be conveyed by some examples. Thus, under Alexander's censorship, a work mentioning that certain mushrooms were poisonous had to be changed when the censor pointed out that, since mushrooms were habitually eaten by the peasantry during Lent, they were therefore sacred and to claim that they might be poisonous was sacrilegious. Under Nicholas a poet who referred to his 'divine muse' was told that divinity was not an earthly quality. A cookery book was not allowed to refer to free air in the oven, because 'free air' sounded revolutionary. Medical textbooks could not show diagrams of the body. In fiction the bad end awaiting the villains had to be clearly shown. The newspaper editor who wrote and printed a rather critical review of the play *The Hand of the Almighty Saved the Fatherland* found himself detained and his newspaper (and hence his livelihood) suppressed; Nicholas had liked the play so much that he had seen it several times, and was therefore insulted by the review. Articles on serfdom were not allowed, and even the word itself was banned for a time. Descriptions of poverty in Russia were not permitted. Information on events in Poland and Finland could only be printed if it had first appeared in official government publications. Similarly, news of western Europe, after 1848, could only take the form of reprints from the Prussian newspapers. Magnitsky, fighting the good fight in his enforced retirement, wrote *Instructive Extracts from the history of contemporary West Europe, Revealing the True Cause of the Catastrophes tormenting it, as an example for Young People and for Minds not yet infected with the Foreign Cholera of the Spirit of the Time*, but even with this title the book was banned by Benckendorff, who said its publication would mean the printing of a number of harmful opinions. Writers and people suspected of writing 'harmful' works could be shadowed, detained for days or weeks in the nearest guardhouse, imprisoned, exiled, or, like Chaadayev, certified as insane.

Only three periodicals were banned in Nicholas's reign, but the publication of a far larger number of proposed newspapers and monthlies was not allowed to start. To such requests Nicholas typically replied that there were already enough on the market. The two best periodicals, *The Contemporary* and *Notes of the Fatherland*, were never banned, even though their articles were by no means as uncritical as the Third Section wished. The latter believed that the respect in which these journals were held by a reading public athirst for good commentary would cause a very undesirable public indignation in the event of their suppression. On the other hand, the owner and writers of the subservient newspaper *Northern Bee* were not immune from suspicion, shadowing, and incarceration in guardhouses, even though its publisher was a proponent of Official Nationality, offered to serve as an informer, would always give space to unsigned propaganda articles produced by the Third Section, and forwarded to the latter denunciations against competing editors, publishers, and writers.

Because serious discussion of issues was so limited by censorship, new ideas tended to harden into dogma, being insufficiently criticized and analysed; this would remain a regrettable feature of intellectual activity inside Russia. On the other hand, the situation presented important opportunities for novelists. It was in fiction that, in the nineteenth century as in the twentieth, Russian writers presented, frequently obliquely, new ideas which otherwise would never have reached a large audience. In modern Russian history there is often more truth to be found in fiction than in non-fiction, and the novel had a more important influence on public opinion than in other countries. This meant extra responsibility for novelists; entertainment and virtuosity were not enough, as Belinsky had emphasized. The 'thick' monthly periodical with long, thoughtful, and solid articles in its chosen field was becoming popular, and it was in literary journals of this type that most serious fiction was first published; successful serializations would later be published in book form. In Nicholas's time, periodicals (and newspapers) were reaching a wider audience, but circulations were still small. Because costs were low and prices quite high, books and journals could be published in small editions. Many good periodicals had fewer than 500 subscribers.[8] In intellectual circles, censorship was mitigated by the hand-copying and circulation of original works, some of which remained unprinted for decades. Chaadayev's *Philosophical Letter* circulated in this way among hundreds, if not thousands, of readers for seven years before its appearance in print.

---

8. In 1846, under unenterprising editorship, *The Contemporary* had 233 subscribers. After becoming more radical, it increased this to 3,100 (plus street sales) in 1848. After the death of Nicholas, journals were allowed openly to discuss current affairs, and *The Contemporary*'s subscribers reached a peak of 6,500 in 1861.

The army

The Russian army, with about 1 million men, was the largest in Europe. Although it called up only 1 to 2 per cent of eligible males each year, the conscripts served for twenty-five years. Thus to be selected as a conscript was a tragedy for the individual, and also for his family, which was unlikely to be ever reunited. A man could be chosen at any age between 20 and 35. Land-owners could send their serfs as recruits if they gave trouble, village communes could send men who were unpopular or did not pay their proper share of taxes, courts could sentence men to army service, while richer peasants could bribe the selectors, or hire substitutes. Men exempt from poll-tax (nobles and others) were likewise exempt from conscription.

Two incentives were used to create good soldiers: corporal punishment and Christianity. It was believed that perfection in drill could only be obtained by beating almost to death any soldier who was less than perfect. Christianity was an asset in terms of morale rather than of training. Church services were frequent, regular, and compulsory for all except certain minorities. After the horrors of the parade ground they were a great relaxation, providing with their ritual and music a real inspiration and sense of togetherness, while also promoting patriotic feelings. In wartime, the priests who blessed the bayonets preached that to die fighting for the Holy Tsar was a joyous experience. But most soldiers died not in battle but from disease, aided by negligence, malnutrition, and hardship. In the quarter of a century preceding the Crimean War, Russia lost more than 1 million soldiers through causes other than battle.

Unlike Japan a few decades later, Russia took from Prussia only the superficial features of military excellence. It therefore steadily fell behind other powers in the war-fighting capabilities of its forces. Whereas other armies switched promptly from the flintlock musket to percussion rifles with their faster rate of fire and greater range and accuracy, Russia entered the Crimean War with most of its infantry equipped with Napoleonic-era weapons. And even those were in poor shape because, in the interests of smart drill, parts had been loosened or filed down to make them rattle more emphatically.[9] Nicholas was aware of Russian technical shortcomings, but financial considerations and the poor advice of his military advisers won the day and lost the war. One argument was that, with quicker-firing weapons, the Russian soldier would shoot off all his ammunition in one go; evidently, in their obsession with drill, the generals had forgotten what drill was for.

Until the Crimean War, the Russian army was trained to fight battles like Borodino. The potential battlefield was vaguely envisaged as an immense ballroom, over which bodies of troops in close order would perform a

---

9. J. Bradley, *Guns for the Tsar* (1990), describes how Colt and other US manufacturers were called upon to supply Russian deficiencies.

complex minuet as they prepared for the climax, a decisive bayonet charge. The main event in the peacetime Russian army was the annual manoeuvres, which traditionally took place in the training grounds of the western border-lands. Manoeuvres, however, is an inaccurate term, for under Nicholas the emphasis was on parades and inspections. Units marched and evolved under the eyes of the Tsar, who was quick to detect a line which was not quite straight, a turn which was not quite ninety degrees, or a soldier whose spine was not quite rigid. This spirit spread downward so that officers of all ranks were judged, not by the fighting qualities of their men, but by their perfection on parade. But such parades were regarded as good training for war, for it was laid down that in battle the advances, assaults, and other movements would be carried out in the same way, with the same close order, the same symmetry, and the same rigidity.

The mass bayonet attack was regarded as the supreme battle-winning tactic, which is one reason why musketry training was neglected. It was believed that in battle a cavalry charge would put to flight an enemy softened up first by artillery and then by bayonet attack. The cavalry officers, especially the senior officers, were almost entirely to blame for the poor showing of their men in the Crimean War. Like the infantry officers, they had concentrated on performing brilliantly at parades. Their horses, fed on oats and beer, were magnificently glossy and plump but when, at one annual manoeuvres, Nicholas ordered the cavalry to do everything at the gallop, hundreds of horses died from unaccustomed exertion. The engineers and the gunners were excellent by any standard, and this excellence remained a feature of the Russian army both before and after the 1917 Revolution. The artillery was expected to play a decisive role in the opening stages of a battle. The engineers, in fortification and in sapping, were superior to those of other armies and already made use of electric detonators in the 1850s. A Russian textbook of fortification was translated and used at this time by several European armies.

The engineers and gunners recruited the more intelligent men, both as officers and as other ranks. Infantry and cavalry officers were usually of poor quality. Certainly, there were some good, or potentially good, officers, but it was usually not these who reached the top. The innovator was regarded with hostility, and so was an officer who read too many books or who trained his men for war rather than parades. Anti-intellectualism was the ruling characteristic of the officer corps, which conformed with Nicholas's wish to steer the army away from politics. Many Russian officers were former officer-cadets (junkers). These were youths of noble birth and of doubtful education who would serve in the ranks and then receive commissions after two or more years' service. Although it is true that a fraction of these had some kind of higher education, the majority were dull, spoiled children for whom the army seemed to offer the only suitable respectable employment. A better officer was produced by the various four-year cadet corps establishments which had blossomed under Alexander, and continued to flourish under Nicholas.

In any army there can be found corruption and peculation. In the Russian army these were on a grand scale. It was not a case of the occasional cook, say, who would issue less than the rations and sell the surplus to traders. It was a case of the regimental commander who would spend less than his approved food budget and pocket the difference. It was a case of high officers who would use their men as workers in their own private projects. It was engineers who would inflate cost estimates for proposed structures. It was medical officers who would keep patients in bed as long as possible, prescribing fancy diets and wines for them which they would consume themselves. In all cases it was the officers, sometimes the sergeants, who profited, the ordinary soldier who suffered. The regimental cash box, containing soldiers' savings as well as supply funds, was a frequent victim. Leo Tolstoy, who as a young officer saw active service in Chechnya, included this passage in 'Hadji Murat', one of his short stories:

After they finished smoking the soldiers began talking.
'They say the commander has been at the cash box again,' one of them remarked lazily. 'He lost at cards, you know.'
'He'll pay it back,' said Panov.
'Of course he will. He's a good officer,' Avdeev agreed.

The scale of the Russian army's inadequacies was attributable to the nature of Russian society, and to the army's misfortune that for fifty years it never lost a war. It was only the Crimean War, when Russia found herself fighting against foes stronger than the Poles, Persians, and Turks, that revealed the rot to a wide public. Nicholas was ultimately responsible for this failure, because he claimed to be an autocrat and a professional soldier. Yet he saw further than his high officers (whom, admittedly, he selected). It was Nicholas who ordered the better treatment of recruits, who urged the investigation of the medical and supply services, who released after only fifteen years' service conscripts with unblemished records, who pointed out that soldiers should be trained in fieldcraft, and who tried to instil some common sense among the cavalry officers. That his urgings were largely ineffective was due, not so much to his own shortcomings, as to the traditional difficulty faced by Russian rulers of ensuring that instructions were carried out in their absence.

Russia at war

A short victorious war is the temptation of many regimes, especially of those which feel unsure of themselves. Nicholas was blessed with two such wars at the start of his reign, against Persia and against Turkey. The Persian war was purely and simply a result of Russian expansionism in the Caucasus. Not content with the previous conquest of Georgia and Azerbaizhan from the Persians, Russia claimed still more territory from the Shah. The latter's 1826 counter-attack was defeated, and in 1828 a peace treaty brought Persian Armenia into the Russian Empire. The central, mountainous part of the Caucasus would be outside Russian control for several more decades. However, some progress in the 'pacification' of this region was made during the reign. By cutting down the forests which sheltered the villages of dissident tribesmen, the hostile territory was reduced, while new forts helped to contain sudden attacks sweeping down from the mountains. But one of Nicholas's favourite projects, the securing of the Black Sea coastline by a series of forts, was defeated by malaria.

Nicholas's second short war involved the settlement of the Greek problem, bequeathed by Alexander I. Russia in 1827 agreed with Britain and France to impose a treaty whereby the Turks would acknowledge Greek self-government. The Sultan was slow to agree, and a combined fleet of Russian, French, and British ships attacked and destroyed his fleet at Navarino. Despite this, the Sultan remained obstinate. Nicholas, with tacit French and British approval, sent his army into the Turkish Danubian possessions. The Tsar himself joined his troops, but was honest enough to leave the army after the first campaign, openly admitting that his presence did more harm than good. A further campaign was more successful, although losses from disease and negligence were high. There were also Russian advances in Transcaucasia. The end result was a treaty giving Russian ships free passage on the Danube and through the Straits. Greece was declared independent in 1830. After this war Russia became a friend of Turkey, for Nicholas did not wish to see the fall of the long-established dynasty in Constantinople. When the Sultan was threatened by his own Egyptian vassal, Nicholas sent the Black Sea fleet to help him; the result was the retreat of the vassal and an even more favourable Russo-Turkish treaty. Despite ups and downs, partly caused by British intrigues, Russo-Turkish relations remained peaceful. In 1841, Turkey, Russia, and four other European powers signed the Straits Convention, which specified that Turkey would allow no foreign warship to pass the Straits, except when Turkey was at war. This gave Russia as much security as she could reasonably expect without herself occupying the Straits.

When, in 1830, the King of France was overthrown, Nicholas feared the spread of revolution. And not without reason, for just as the Tsar was contemplating the dispatch of Russian troops to put down the revolt of the Belgians, itself sparked by the events in Paris, he found himself faced with insurrection within his own Empire, in Poland. Nicholas had hitherto accepted the Polish Constitution, although he did not like it. He was justified in accusing the Poles of ingratitude when they revolted, because they enjoyed higher living standards than did the Russians, and had somewhat greater political freedom. Most of the conspirators were young officers, for whom promotion was irksomely slow and who had been reading German Romantic writers to ease their boredom. This reading implanted not only dreams of freedom, but also aspirations to restore the glories of the old Polish Empire. Their revolt should have been easily suppressed but, as is traditionally the case with Polish revolts, irrationalities supervened.

One feature of Polish revolts is that the transition from resentment to revolt typically results from threats to the Polish palate. In twentieth-century communist Poland it would be meat that would provide the spark, and in Nicholas's Poland it was beer. Increased bread prices resulting from a poor harvest had been patiently borne, but a hefty increase of beer prices was too much to bear. So the disturbance engineered by intellectuals and young officers was unexpectedly inundated by a working-class surge of revolt. Virtually the first act was an attempt to burn down a brewery. This did nothing to reduce the price of beer, but confused thinking was characteristic of this revolt. On the Russian side Constantine Pavlovich, the viceroy and Nicholas's elder brother, was equally muddled. He had effective Russian troops at his disposal but did not send them in to quell the initial disturbances. He did not want them to soil their uniforms and doubted whether it was constitutionally proper to send in Russian troops to quell a Polish riot when there were Polish troops also available. These hesitations, which gave time for the transformation of a gentlemanly insurrection into what looked like a 1789-style revolution, meant that Nicholas was in no mood for compromise when moderate Polish leaders, representing the views of most Poles, turned up in St Petersburg.

Czartoryski, Alexander's old friend, was among those who joined the rebel government. The Russian army moved in, but faulty tactics and inherent deficiencies robbed it of an early victory. Moreover, its commander and thousands of soldiers (and also Constantine) died of cholera. After Paskevich took over command, a slow advance was achieved, but Russian successes were due more to quarrels among the Poles than to Paskevich's generalship. After Warsaw was captured some rebels, including Czartoryski, emigrated to Paris, where they carried on propaganda against Russia and for Polish independence. As for Russian Poland, its constitution was abrogated, it was ruled more and more by St Petersburg bureaucrats, its universities were closed, and the Russian language was imposed in official institutions.

In 1848 there was another revolution in France which led to upheavals so widespread that Nicholas was sufficiently alarmed to issue a strong warning to the revolutionaries of Europe: 'Give heed, O ye peoples, and submit, for God is with us!' When his friend and ally the King of Prussia had to compromise with the rebels, he was pained, and announced that if Prussia became a republic he would consider it his duty to send in Russian troops to restore the throne. He did send in the Russian army to enable the Emperor of Austria to suppress the revolt of the Hungarians under Kossuth, the Tsar's zeal on this occasion being heightened by the knowledge that among the ranks of the Hungarian rebels were many Poles. The Russian army lost 10,000 men in this campaign, of whom about 9,000 died from disease; Paskevich was partly to blame for these deaths, as he had failed to provide adequate medical services. Earlier, Russian troops had entered Romania to help the Turks suppress a revolutionary government there.

Nicholas had anticipated, and dreaded, the break-up of the Turkish Empire, and had earlier tried to agree with other powers on how to deal with this when the time came; he thought he had made it clear that Russia did not want Constantinople, but could not tolerate any other power establishing itself there. But there was a strong anti-Russian element in the British foreign office which preferred to disbelieve him.

After a French-inspired quarrel about the respective rights of Orthodox and Catholic priests in the Holy Places under Turkish rule had been settled to France's advantage, Russia demanded the right to 'protect' Christians in the Holy Land. Despite diplomatic efforts, and with the Sultan of Turkey sure of French support and half-sure of British support, a war began. The Russian fleet annihilated the Turkish navy at Sinope (having attacked when the incompetent and unsuspecting Turks were at anchor, the Russian admiral Nakhimov was immediately accused in the British press of committing an atrocity). French and British ships moved in to prevent a possible Russian landing near Constantinople, and then, in 1854, France and Britain declared war in support of Turkey. Nicholas had repeatedly misunderstood the British, mistaking smiles for commitment and silence for agreement.

The Anglo-French leadership selected the Crimea as the best place to fight this war, although there was some naval activity in the Baltic and Pacific. The deficiencies of the Russian army proved to be more crippling than the deficiencies of the Allied armies. The Russian officers were usually more incompetent than their French and British opposite numbers. Back in Warsaw, the apprehensive Paskevich persistently opposed the sending of reinforcements to the Crimea, in case the Austrians should decide to attack the western frontier. Even when specifically ordered to do so by Nicholas, he only went through the motions of obeying. In some other respects he opposed Nicholas's suggestions, although in retrospect it seems that Nicholas had a sounder appreciation of what was needed than either Paskevich or the other leading generals. The best Russian generalship was provided by the handful of admirals who assumed commands on land. Nakhimov virtually took command of the defence of Sevastopol, during which he was killed.

The Allied landing in the Crimea was followed by a Russian defeat at the battle of the Alma (1854). The war then developed into a costly contest over the possession of Sevastopol, whose value was more symbolic than strategic.

After a year's siege the Russian army withdrew from this fortified base, and peace followed in 1856. The Treaty of Paris was not excessively burdensome to Russia; her bargaining position had been improved by military successes against Turkey in the Caucasus, and by Anglo-French differences. The greatest sacrifice was the acceptance that the Black Sea should be neutralized; this meant that Russia could not have a fleet there whereas Turkey, similarly restricted, in wartime would have no difficulty in bringing in her own or her allies' warships from the Mediterranean. Russia also lost influence in the Danubian region, which was soon to see the creation of a new state, Romania. Even though the war had demonstrated the incompetence of its generals, the inefficiency of its officials, and the dishonesty of its army supply merchants, the autocracy was in no danger. All the same, Russia could no longer be regarded, as she had been since 1812, as the dominant power of Europe.

Nicholas had died before this, in 1855. Appropriately, he died from over-inspecting; already having a cold, he insisted on carrying out a military inspection in February and was rewarded with pneumonia. Being worn out and disappointed, he did not show much resistance and died calmly some days later, having apologized to his heir for his failure to leave the affairs of state in proper order. Decades later, the celebrated geographer and anarchist leader Prince Kropotkin recalled Nicholas's death:

On February 18 the local police distributed bulletins among the houses informing us of the Tsar's illness, and inviting the population to go to church to pray for his recovery. Actually the Tsar was already dead and the authorities knew this . . . but because right until the end nothing had been said of the Tsar's illness they considered it necessary to gradually prepare 'the people'. We all went to church and prayed very fervently . . . [two days later] we did learn of the death of Nicholas I. When the news spread, our own and neighbouring households were gripped with fear. It was said that at the market 'the people' seemed very suspicious-looking, and not only expressed no regret but on the contrary expressed dangerous thoughts . . . the landowners expected a serf rising at any minute, a new Pugachov revolt.

At this time in the streets of St. Petersburg intellectuals hugged one another, telling each other the good news. All forecast that there would be an end to the war and to the terrible conditions which had been created by 'the iron tyrant'.[10]

But not everybody rejoiced at the Tsar's death. Among those who were saddened was Queen Victoria, who wrote that she had not forgotten friendlier times. The Queen's opinion of the Tsar, written in 1844, still seems perceptive:

He is stern and severe – with fixed principles of duty which nothing on earth will make him change; very clever I do not think him, and his mind is an uncivilised one; his education has been neglected; politics and military concerns are the only things he takes great interest in; the arts and all softer occupations he is insensible to, but he is sincere, I am certain, sincere even in his most despotic acts, from a sense that it is the

10. P. Kropotkin, *Zapiski revolyutsionera* (1966), 60.

only way to govern; he is not, I am sure, aware of the dreadful cases of individual misery which he so often causes, for I can see by various instances that he is kept in utter ignorance of many things, which his people carry out in most corrupt ways, while he thinks that he is extremely just.[11]

11. A. C. Benson, and Viscount Asher, *The Letters of Queen Victoria 1837–1861* (1908), ii. 14.

3

The Tsar Emancipator

Alexander II

WITH the possible exceptions of Khrushchev and Gorbachev, no Russian ruler brought so much relief to so many of his people as did Alexander II, autocratic and conservative though he was. Born in 1818, bombed in 1881, Alexander II at his accession was 36, and was destined to reign for twenty-six years. Nicholas I had ensured that his son and heir was better prepared than he had been for the high office which awaited him. From the age of 6 to 16, Alexander's education was supervised by a broad-minded army general. Beating was not considered the best way to instil knowledge; the tutors were expected to be tolerant and to gain Alexander's interest. The academic side of the heir's education was supervised by the poet Zhukovsky, whose concern for the well-being of the common people is presumed to have been the source of Alexander's own sensibilities. Thus his upbringing not only equipped him with such essentials as a knowledge of languages, of history, and of the duties of a ruler, but also with a perceptive and humane attitude towards the world in general. At the age of 19 he started on his travels. He was the first member of the royal family to visit Siberia, where his encounter with the lives of convicts and exiles led to a certain improvement in their lot after he became tsar. Then to Europe, where he became engaged to a German princess, the marriage taking place in 1842. Some years later he visited the Caucasus, and won a St George Cross for bravery when mountain tribes launched an unexpected but unsuccessful attack on his party.

Nicholas I had groomed Alexander for the succession by appointing him to a number of committees and councils, including the Council of State and committees dealing with serfdom, railways, and others. In Nicholas's many absences, Alexander was left in charge of routine state affairs. Thus when he came to the throne he was already familiar with procedures and problems, and he knew much of his Empire at first hand. Although not immune to the superficial attractions of military life, he was not quite so passionate a soldier as his father. He inherited from his father and his tutors an honesty of character and loyalty to subordinates, but he was milder, more sensitive, and more patient than his father. He was still, however, an autocrat rather than a leader.

The main events of his reign were, first and very foremost, the freeing of the serfs; then, and partly in connection with this reform, real changes in local government, justice, education, and the army. As so often happens, reform and relaxation were followed by protest, manifested notably by a revolutionary movement. The 'Tsar Emancipator' also had to cope with two burdens that had afflicted his father: cholera and the Poles. These trials led to reaction, and there was a partial return to tactics of repression. However, just before his assassination and having, as he thought, succeeded in calming the Empire, Alexander was considering a new series of reforms to relieve political pressures. Throughout the reign there was steady economic progress, expansion in Central Asia, some attempt to overcome the financial consequences of the Crimean War, and a continuation of railway-building. In foreign affairs there was a rather unnecessary war against Turkey, but Alexander was able to avoid other large-scale conflicts.

Alexander's younger brother Constantine Nikolaevich had made an early contribution. Groomed by his father Nicholas I to head the navy, he had developed into a perceptive intellectual who at the same time was a man of action. Seeing how government offices were devoted more to the production of documents than to any real achievement, he realized that a completely different type of official was required to head departments. He attracted a group of young, well-educated men who were not afraid to accept responsibility and saw the need for change. Subsequently these men, matured by their navy work, migrated to other departments of state, where they helped to design the reforms that Alexander would sanction. The navy department's journal *Morskoi sbornik* ('Naval Review') had begun to publish articles by non-naval thinkers that were quite hard-hitting in their emphasis on the need for change in the Russian state and society. For most of the 1850s this journal was not even censored, and made good but not extravagant use of that freedom.[1] However, the Third Section spied on Grand Duke Constantine; many of Nicholas's advisers saw him as a dangerous man, but he subsequently became chairman of Alexander's Council of State.

The reformist administrators of the kind encouraged by Constantine accumulated data and developed ideas for the future whilst Nicholas was alive, and were ready to formulate their proposals when Alexander became emperor. This sector of the bureaucracy allied with the autocracy to constitute a force for change (there was no western-style middle class to perform this role, and most of the nobility was not interested). The result was the 'Great Reforms' of Alexander II.

---

1. This journal, which is still published in an emaciated form, remained more open to debate than others right up to the 1920s. In the 1850s the term *glasnost'* was often to be found in its pages. The word means openness or transparency; the reformers realized that changes needed to be discussed by those who would feel them most.

The Russian peasant at mid-century

First among the priorities of the would-be reformers was Russia's shameful and harmful tradition of serfdom. But the landowning nobility, on which the tsarist state depended for its administrators and officers, had been opposed to any radical social reconstruction in the countryside. The nobles had a generally free hand in supervising their serfs so long as they did not abuse their privileges too notoriously, while that other large group, the state peasants, was similarly the affair of those appointed to administer them. Thus official Russia could ignore the real Russia; only when the peasantry flared into revolt was it noticed. It lived its own life. It had few cultural links with the urban classes. It was the 'dark people', sometimes described as being alienated from 'society' although it was the latter which was alienated from the peasantry, and thus from traditional Russia.

Discussion of the Russian peasantry can only be generalized because, although there was much that was typical, there was little which was invariable. One broad distinction will be made, but to give a complete and true description of peasant life would require a volume for each province. The broad distinction is geographical: European Russia can be divided into the wooded, clayey north and centre on the one hand, and the fertile and almost treeless south on the other. The latter includes the region of the Black Earth, which stretches from the south-western borderlands into Asiatic Russia, narrowing as it does so. While very fertile, it has unreliable rainfall and hence fluctuating harvests. The distinction between the grain-surplus south and the grain-deficit north and centre was always important; industrial goods and timber moved south, while grain moved north.

The rationale of serfdom, that is, the tying of the peasant to the land he tilled, was that it ensured labour (and hence income) to the landowning noble, enabling the latter to devote himself to serving the state. The enserfment of the peasants had been gradual, but by the middle of the seventeenth century the peasant and his descendants were legally obliged to remain on the land of their master. When the state granted land to new or old nobles for services rendered, the peasants on that land were transformed from state peasants into serfs.

Thus the serf served the noble and the noble served the tsar, a formula having some apparent justice, since serving the tsar was no light matter. But no sooner had serfdom become a fact than the nobility began seeking ways to alter the formula. For most of the eighteenth century the tsars felt dependent on the nobility (there was hardly a middle class to whom they could appeal, and the peasants did not count), and in 1762 Tsar Peter III was persuaded to acknowledge that the nobility was no longer obliged to serve. The formula was fractured, and the serfs expected release from their own corresponding obligations. But the anticipated *ukaz* was never issued and peasants, believing that it had been promulgated but had been concealed from them by the landowners, became resentful. Hitherto, peasant revolts had been localized though frequent, but in the reign of Catherine the Great the intensified discontent expressed itself in Pugachov's rebellion, which lasted two years and threw official Russia and the nobility into a panic. Of the several impulses which drove later tsars to seek better conditions for the peasantry, fear of a repetition of Pugachov's rebellion was the strongest.

In 1850 almost half the peasants were serfs. State peasants outnumbered them, and usually led a better life. After Catherine and Paul, the practice of making gifts of thousands of state peasants to favourites (that is, transforming them into privately owned serfs) more or less ceased, while the confiscation of church lands by Catherine had converted the Church's serfs into state peasants. The state peasantry was administered by crown appointees, some of whom were as bad as the worst landowners, but for most state peasants life was bearable. Serfdom was most prevalent around Moscow and in the south. North and north-central Russia were still largely inhabited by state peasants, and there was no serfdom in Siberia (a century later this was still reflected in the more independent character of Siberian and northern peasants).

Serfs cultivated the land allotted to them, and in recompense for the use of this land they were required to work also on the land reserved for the use of the landowner. Three days a week was about the average requirement but in the worst cases, and in busy weeks, this might be doubled (which meant that the serf could not properly look after his own production). There were no fixed rights or obligations for the peasantry. A landowner could increase his serfs' dues and duties, he could seize their property, he could forbid their buying from, selling to, or working with persons outside the estate, he could make them into domestic servants, sell them either separately or with their families, force them to marry so as to breed more serfs, or forbid them to marry disapproved partners. Except in cases of murder or banditry, the landowner administered rural justice and could send troublesome serfs to Siberia or into the army. Whipping was commonplace. Although there were many landowners who were kindly, educating and sometimes liberating favoured serfs, there were others who were indifferent or even brutal; social isolation and almost absolute power led some landowners to excesses which in other circumstances they would have found revolting. Probably the worst-off peasants were those with an absentee landlord. Some nobles had never even seen their estates, and many more only visited them rarely. Such estates were entrusted to bailiffs who all too often were dishonest and tyrannical.

Some nobles were very poor. For a nobleman and his family to live entirely off servile labour, at least a hundred male serfs were needed, but four-fifths of the nobility had fewer than that. Some possessed no serfs at all. There were villages divided between a dozen or so nobles. On the other hand, 4 per cent of the nobles had enough serfs to let them live as absentee landlords; the richest 20 per cent of the nobles accounted for about 80 per cent of serf ownership.

At that period the wealth of a landowner was measured by the number of 'souls' he possessed. 'Souls' meant male serfs, women did not count. My father was a rich man, he had more than 1,200 souls in three different provinces . . . in our family there were eight persons, sometimes ten or twelve; fifty servants in Moscow and sixty or so in the country did not seem too many . . . the dearest wish of every landowner was to have all his requirements supplied by his own serfs. All this was so that if a guest should ask, 'What a beautifully-tuned piano! Did you get it done at Schimmel's?' the landowner could reply, 'I have my own piano-tuner.'[2]

Englishmen travelling through Russia often compared Russian peasant life, not always unfavourably, with the condition of the Irish. But many foreigners were shocked by the condition of the poorer peasants. An American wrote that the village poor,

generally wanting the comforts which are supplied to the Negro on our best-ordered plantations, appeared to me to be not less degraded in intellect, character, and personal bearing. Indeed, the marks of physical and personal degradation were so strong, that I was irresistibly compelled to abandon certain theories not uncommon among my countrymen at home, in regard to the intrinsic superiority of the white race over all others.[3]

Some landowners tried to help themselves and their serfs by introducing better methods. But the peasants would listen to their new instructions, nod their heads gravely, and then go away to perform their tasks in exactly the way they and their forebears had always performed them. This passive resistance to change was the despair of the improving landowner, who tended to relapse into apathy after a few years of vain effort.

Serfdom might have deprived industry of a labour force had not more and more landowners allowed their serfs to substitute regular money payments for the labour obligation. Even though such serfs still belonged to their master, who could recall them if he wished, this did enable them to seek factory work afield, or stay in the village and devote themselves to handicraft or local industry. Also, many landowners started their own estate factories, using serf labour and local raw materials. Others sold batches of serfs to city industrialists, while state peasants could be drafted to factory work.

Although landowners in the private lands and officials in the state lands had virtually full administrative power over their peasants, in most parts of Russia they delegated authority to the peasant commune (*mir*) and its assembly of heads of households. For urban Russians the *mir* was 'discovered' in the nineteenth century by the German traveller and writer von Haxthausen, who

2. P. Kropotkin, *Zapiski revolyutsionera* (1966), 60.
3. J. Stephens, *Incidents of Travel in the Russian and Turkish Empires* (1839), ii. 38.

declared that it was not simply a village institution but also an object of veneration; the *mir* was the voice of the people gathered together, and Orthodox Christians believed that when they were in congregation they were in close relationship with God. How ancient was the commune, and whether it was unique to the Slavs, was hotly disputed in the nineteenth century. But certainly it was a democratic and egalitarian institution, even if, somehow, the richer members had more influence than the poorer. The peasants' preference for egalitarian collectivism was shown in one of the most important functions of the *mir*, its allocation of the peasants' land. It was the *mir* which decided who should get what. The basic principle was fairness. The amount of land allotted to a household depended on the size of that household. The quality of the allotments had to be equal, and this was usually achieved by dividing each of the various qualities of land into strips, and ensuring that households received strips of each quality. Pastureland and meadow were kept for common use, because animals could not be expected to stay on particular strips. For some peasants, especially in the south-west, their strip allocation had become permanent and hereditary, but for the majority of Russian peasants there were periodic redistributions to allow for changes in the size of households.

From the point of view of justice, this system was excellent. From the economic point of view it was pathetic. Where there were periodic redistributions, peasants tended to exhaust their strips rather than improve them. Everywhere, the uncultivated boundaries between strips occupied a considerable area of the fields, sometimes as much as one-fifth. Strips were often so narrow that there was not room to turn a plough. Peasants might walk hundreds of extra miles each year because their strips were so scattered. Each arable operation had to be identical and carried out at the same time on each strip; for example, it was impracticable for cattle to be grazed on the stubble of a harvested strip if other strips were uncut or planted with cabbages. Thus there was little scope for an enterprising peasant to experiment with improved methods.

The *mir* fixed the dates for the main arable operations and also allocated the burden of taxes and labour services among its constituent households. Sometimes, too, the commune would rent or purchase additional land from the landowner or from the state. After Emancipation many functions formerly belonging to the landowner were transferred to the *mir* or its elected elder. That it was possible for the *mir* to dissolve an unsatisfactory marriage, despite the Church's cherished monopoly of divorce, shows how far the peasantry was allowed to lead a life of its own, largely outside state law and social convention.

But communes were dominated by factions of the older peasants, and these dominant elders not only resisted change, but also found ways to punish those who were reluctant to conform. One of their functions was to select conscripts for the army, which in effect gave them the power to make or break families. The commune could be a model of cooperation and mutual support, but also could be the scene of conflict in which murder, house-burnings, animal-poisonings, and pitched battles would decide an issue. That issue might be a matter that in other societies would be settled in court, like theft or fraud. Neighbours' quarrels and wife-beating were not such matters. They were a fit and proper component of daily life; a peasant was less likely to be accused of beating his wife than of not beating her.

At meetings of the *mir* assembly decisions, typically, were unanimous; a dissenting minority would eventually allow itself to be persuaded, thus creating a consensus. Everyone would then work to implement the decision. Subsequent Russian attitudes to democratic procedures would be influenced by this tradition.

Except in the Black Earth south the peasantry relied heavily on non-agricultural income. Apart from animal husbandry, agriculture, and fishing, there were local handicraft industries, while many males left home in the quiet season to seek temporary jobs afield. Almost everywhere the land was farmed on the three-field system (fallow; winter grain; spring grain). In the Black Earth region wheat was the predominant winter crop, with rye elsewhere. Oats was the usual spring crop. The peasant staples were rye bread, and porridge made from oats, buckwheat, or wheat. The traditional cabbage soup of the north and centre was less common in the south, where *borshch* (beetroot soup) was typical. Little meat was served outside soup, but fish was common. The traditional drink was *kvas*, a rye-based beer, although towards the end of the century tea was becoming popular, with a few of the better-off families possessing a samovar.[4] At festivals and celebrations vodka was drunk, and relative delicacies like pies and pancakes were served.

Russian villages were typically situated near the bank of a lake, river, or stream. Usually the village was a line of unpainted wooden huts along each side of a main street that was unpaved and undrained. Traditionally, the household consisted of the 'big' family, which included the two parents, grandparents, and the sons, daughters-in-law, and grandchildren. But at mid-century the big family was giving way to the small, as sons preferred to start their own households, even though this was less economical. The oldest non-senile male was head of the family, the registered householder, and as such a voter in the *mir* assembly. Children began to help with the work not long after they learned to walk. In the big family the least enviable status was that of daughter-in-law, who was dominated by the mother and often treated like a slave; if her husband was conscripted for twenty-five years' service she had little reason to continue living, but usually stayed on to lead a dog's life with

---

4. Later in the century tea rooms were to be found in town and country, and were regarded as a means of drawing workers and peasants away from alcoholic beverages and bad company.

her in-laws. The tradition still survived of the father-in-law assuming the conjugal rights of a conscripted son. But despite the low status of women (reflected, among other ways, by entrusting the pigs to their exclusive care as well as by numerous proverbs and sayings, like 'The hair is long but the brain is short'), efforts were made to help widows. Villagers might work on a holiday to help someone unable to help herself. When food became short, as it often did after Christmas, those who had food might share it with those who had not. Life was brutish, but not lacking compassion, and everybody had the assurance of knowing their place.

The 1861 reform and after

Many forward-looking state officials met and talked about possible reforms at the premises of the Russian Geographical Society. Some of them also met under the auspices of the Grand Duchess Elena Pavlovna. She was a Württemberg princess who had benefited from a somewhat unorthodox French education, only to find herself married off to Mikhail, Nicholas I's younger brother. In his militarism, abuse, and fetishes Mikhail set remarkable standards even for that time and place, and his intelligent, handsome wife sought diversion by immersing herself in Russian arts, society, and tradition. In due course she was maintaining a salon to which she invited young, talented, would-be reformist, state officials. After the merciful demise of her husband in 1842 her activities became less camouflaged and in the 1850s she was involving herself in the serf problem. Her progressive friends worked out schemes for freeing the serfs on her own extensive lands, thereby developing ideas that would stand them in good stead when they were called upon to devise a general emancipation of serfs.

Alexander I had done little for the serfs, although he knew that something should be done.[5] Nicholas I issued some decrees to help them, which were mainly ignored. But Nicholas did succeed in helping some state peasants, giving the poorer more land, taken from the richer. Nicholas also pointed out that if the peasants' lot was not ameliorated they would rebel and take what they wanted. After the Crimean War the nobles could not deny that the Russian social structure was archaic and inefficient. A few nobles were beginning to have doubts about the ethics of serfdom. A few others had realized that serf labour was less productive than freely hired labour. Many no doubt recalled that Pugachov's rebellion of discontented peasants had resulted in the cutting of numerous noble throats; when, in 1856, Alexander II told an assembly of nobles that it would be better for serfdom to be abolished from above, rather than from below, they knew exactly what he meant.

---

5. But he showed the world that his heart was in the right place by manfully condemning, at the Congress of Aix, Negro slavery.

Nevertheless, the average landowner did not welcome the Emancipation Statutes which were promulgated five years later.

Not for the last time in Russian history, the government, having decided on the measure, instructed those to whom it was distasteful to discuss the best manner of its implementation ('a dialogue of cook and chicken', whispered the nobles in their clubs). Throughout Russia, committees of nobles were formed to evolve their collective opinion on how emancipation should be achieved. It is doubtful whether their opinions were accorded much attention in St Petersburg, but the committees made it easier for their members to accept the idea of emancipation. For the average noble, watching from afar the debates of his representatives, the whole affair was alarming and mystifying. Anna Petrovna, a landowner in Saltykov-Shchedrin's novel *The Golovlov Family*, was not at all untypical:

> The first blow to Anna Petrovna's power was not so much the abolition of serfdom, but rather the preparations which preceded it. At first just rumours, and then the landowners' assemblies with their petitions, then the provincial committees, then the editing committees. All this wore her out and confused her. Anna Petrovna's not infertile imagination played with innumerable petty details. For example, she was suddenly struck with the question, 'what do I call Agashka in future? Agafyushka perhaps? Or perhaps I'll have to be very respectful and call her Agafeya Fedorovna.'
>
> ... At the time the committees were dissolving, Vladimir Mikhailich died ... His last words were, 'I thank God for calling me now, so I won't have to stand before Him among a rabble of serfs!'

Like most compromises in Russia, the 1861 Emancipation Statutes were received with great displeasure by those affected. But the autocracy succeeded, where transatlantic democracy failed, in ending bondage without civil war. That the Tsar's intention had been announced in 1856, with the legislation appearing in 1861, was not proof of foot-dragging, but a reflection of the enormous complexity of the problem. The attempt to be fair to all, despite the innumerable variations and special cases and local circumstances throughout Russia, meant that the legislation was extremely detailed. Only the basic principles will be mentioned here.

The fundamental principle was that the serf was to have not merely his freedom, but also land to go with it. There was no intention of creating a landless proletariat by a stroke of the pen. This fundamental principle led to the fundamental problem of the reform, which was the unavailability of enough land to satisfy everybody, and the consequent failure to reconcile the peasants' beliefs regarding land ownership with the legal facts of land ownership. Whereas legally the land belonged to the landowners in areas of serfdom, the peasants, ignorant of the law, had always believed that the land rightfully belonged to those who worked it. In Nicholas I's time, when his minister of state domains had been studying the problem of the state peasants, it had become accepted that the state would need to finance the transfer of land when the serfs were freed. But because of Alexander's railway-building pro-gramme it was clear in 1861 that the state would not have the money to help purchase the land allocated to the peasants. So under the 1861 statutes serfs were freed and their communes were to receive in trust the land they habit-ually worked for their own account, with the landowners receiving treasury bonds in compensation for the land they were ceding. For this the ex-serfs were required to recompense the Treasury by a series of forty-nine annual redemption payments.

The average area per peasant varied according to the locality and was worked out by local committees. Usually the peasant received slightly less than the land he was working before emancipation. To the peasants, who believed that the land was rightfully theirs, it seemed that they were being compelled to buy their own property. Many believed that their true protector, the Tsar, had ordered that they be given their land without payment, but the nobles were concealing this instruction. Moreover, the valuation placed on the peasants' land allocation was often higher than the product of that land justified. To the nobles, especially of the centre, land overvaluation seemed logical because it was not so much the land as the labour of the serfs living on that land which had been of value to them. The government knew that the peasantry would resent the terms of emancipation, but it was the best it could do without turning noble resentment into noble antagonism. It took the precaution of reading the Emancipation Statutes to the peasants during Lent, when they could be expected to be sober and submissive. Nevertheless, although peasants were grateful for their freedom, there were some serious disturbances in 1861, one involving about 10,000 peasants and another in which 200 peasants were slaughtered by the military.

The Emancipation was not an instant settlement; it took years to put into practice. Many peasants were in no hurry because they anticipated that the land to be received would be more of a burden than an asset; it was too small to support them but entailed heavy tax and redemption payments. The Stat-utes did provide that, with the landowner's agreement, a peasant could obtain exemption from the redemption payments by accepting one-quarter instead of a full land allocation, but not many took advantage of this. Village com-munes were generally held responsible for the redemption payments: through their right of issuing or withholding passports for travel exceeding about 20 miles they could hold back peasants who were in arrears. It was intended that the *mir* should hand over the allotted strips to a peasant when his redemption payment was complete. State peasants were not forgotten; in 1866 they were given the option of purchasing their land in the same way as the former serfs or of remaining as they were, as tenants.

Most nobles, especially in the less fertile regions, felt that they were badly hit by the Emancipation. In the Black Earth region, however, their committees had succeeded in reducing the peasants' allocations to well below the national average, so that a peasant, to make both ends meet, had to work for much of the year as a hired labourer on the noble's remaining land. Many nobles, unable or unwilling to make the required adaptation to a system of hired labour, began to live permanently in town, renting out their land to the peasants and thereby demonstrating that they were nothing but parasites in the agricultural economy. Other nobles did adapt themselves; some worked large estates with modern methods and provided much of Russia's increasingly important grain exports. Some of the shrewder peasants followed their example, buying the lands of poorer neighbours and farming it individually. But the *mir* still limited the freedom of most peasants to experiment, or to develop their holdings before redemption payments were completed.

Despite its imperfections the Emancipation was an enormous step forward. In succeeding decades additional changes were made to remedy some of its inadequacies. But peasant dissatisfaction, expressed in periodic disturbances and, sometimes, refusal to accept the land allotments, was never eliminated. The widespread failure of the peasants to make their redemption payments on time is hardly surprising in view of the general poverty. On certain occasions, such as the birth of a royal heir, tax and redemption arrears were cancelled. The redemption period was extended and finally, in 1906, the payments still outstanding were written off. Meanwhile, to help the more prosperous peasants to buy more land (often from the nobles), the Peasant Bank was established. By the turn of the century the richer peasants were acquiring land rapidly, while the poorer were selling their holdings and becoming wage-earners. After the bad famine of 1891, the ministry of agriculture was set up, and one of its functions was to encourage better methods. On the other hand, because the peasantry was alleged to be resentful, indolent, disrespectful, unruly, and intoxicated, Alexander III approved the appointment of so-called land captains to maintain discipline in rural areas. These, often retired army officers, varied widely in character, but their function everywhere was to replace the authority which before the Emancipation had been wielded by the landowners. Answerable to St Petersburg, they could override the decisions of the *mir* and keep the countryside under control. Policemen were rarely seen in the villages, but the *volost'* (community) courts established at the time of Emancipation, with their often illiterate judges bidden to act according to their consciences, worked quite well. Highly informal, blessed with the absence of lawyers, attentive to tradition, they brought an element of justice into peasant disputes.

The 1905 Rebellion was preceded by several years in which peasant disorders were more widespread than usual. Especially in the Black Earth region there were risings, sometimes planned by the *mir*, in which peasants burned the local noble's buildings and divided up among themselves his stock and implements. Long after the urban rebellion of 1905 had been suppressed, the countryside was still inflamed. The hangings and floggings of Stolypin only brought peace to the countryside in 1907. In 1905 itself it was not so much the urban disorders as the peasant risings which most alarmed the government. One minister, at least, toyed with the idea of compulsorily buying out the landowners, so as to provide more land for the peasants. For Russian governments there was nothing sacred in private property. The land had been distributed by the tsar, and what one tsar had given another could take away. Catherine's nationalization of church lands, Alexander II's forced purchase of landowners' land in 1861, as well as the subsequent expropriations of the Soviet period, shared a common background.

Industry and railways

The 1861 Emancipation can be considered as the loosening of a chronic logjam. Many improvements which serfdom had prevented were now not only possible, but seen to be urgent. There were also effects which were not immediately perceptible. One such effect was the new possibility of Russia overcoming her industrial backwardness as peasants were slowly drawn into new patterns of life and work.

For most of the reign of Nicholas I, financial and economic policy had been in the hands of Kankrin. The latter was a genuine self-made man, a German who had arrived penniless in Russia after dropping out from a little-known university. Having no influential friends, knowing no Russian, he received noble rank from Paul I, but no job. But by making himself an expert on successive current problems he attracted attention and climbed high. As minister, he was characterized by a quiet determination to do nothing. This quality, all too common among students but rather rare among finance ministers, meant that Kankrin felt the economy would develop steadily as it had in the past, and there was little the government could do about it. Nicholas had more faith in government intervention and sometimes overruled his elderly minister. This was especially evident in the question of railway-building, with Nicholas pushing through a construction programme over the opposition of Kankrin.

Apart from railways, the main economic questions in Nicholas's reign had been the stabilization of the currency and the problem of raising enough money from taxes to pay for government expenditure. Both these seemed to be on the verge of solution until the Crimean War broke out. In retrospect, it is clear that what Russia needed was industrial development, for with growth and prosperity taxes would have yielded more, yet seemed less burdensome. But the spontaneous industrial revolution which was transforming western Europe had not spread to Russia; if it had, it would not have been welcome to a government which foresaw the dangers of an emerging proletariat. Private enterprise was usually reluctant to engage in industrial undertakings; whereas foreign entrepreneurs were eventually persuaded to invest their capital and knowledge in large-scale industry, the natives preferred the field of commerce because trade and speculation in Russian conditions seemed to offer higher profits with less risk. It was more profitable to use capital to build up a stock of imported products for resale than to produce those products at home. It was this lack of industrial enterprise that had persuaded previous rulers, like Peter the Great, that the only way to ensure a supply of strategically necessary goods (such as iron for cannon and textiles for uniforms) was for the state to set up its own factories, or to subsidize private producers. Thus the concept of state intervention in Russian industry was well established. By the end of the nine-teenth century, with military expenditure directed largely to state-owned industry, it could be argued that the dominance of the state, rather than lack of enterprise, explained the relatively slow development of private industry. Additionally, most of the state's bureaucracy found private industry (and industrialists) somehow distasteful. Top administrators with any experience or special knowledge of industrial life remained rare.[6]

Towards the end of his reign, Nicholas felt he had to respond in some way to the benefits which Russia was receiving from the move towards free trade in the west. The result was the tariff of 1850, which included some significant reductions. However, some industries remained highly protected; notably, there was a total prohibition of iron imports to protect the technically back-ward Urals industry. One feature of the new rates was that they favoured Russian cotton weavers but not cotton spinners. Unlike weaving, which was still a domestic industry, spinning was Russia's nearest approach to the indus-trial revolution at this time; around St Petersburg and Moscow there were numerous spinning mills with all the characteristics of factory industry, including an emergent proletariat that was badly fed, badly housed, and therefore dangerous.

It would not be until 1882 that a small and overworked factory inspectorate would be established. Under Nicholas I and Alexander II, badly treated work-ers did occasionally send petitions to the tsar. In most cases the response was in keeping with the concept of the benevolent autocrat: punishment of the signatories, arrest of the ringleaders, but also government persuasion of the management to improve conditions.

Under Alexander II, Russian industry underwent a notable expansion, in both old and new branches. The textile industry continued to develop, and very large factories were founded. Many of these were owned and run by the British; the interest of Lancashire in the Russian industry began in the 1840s, when Britain relaxed her controls over the export of textile machinery. When the American Civil War cut cotton supplies, the area under cotton in Turkestan was enormously extended, and henceforth Russia derived most of

---

6. Prince Khilkov, who worked in a British locomotive factory and then drove locomotives in America before becoming transport minister (1895–1905), was a shining exception.

her raw cotton from within her own imperial frontiers. Foreign entrepreneurs were also largely responsible for the transformation of Russian metallurgy. The old Urals ironworks, which had produced high-quality but expensive iron by the charcoal process, were dwarfed in the 1860s by the iron and steel industry of the Donets Basin. It was John Hughes, aided by technicians and workers from his South Wales homeland, who showed what could be done by modern methods. Apart from the local ore, he exploited the hitherto-untouched coal seams of the Donets region, helping to create what would become Russia's richest source of high-quality coking coal.[7] Another fuel, oil, was also becoming practical. The Nobel brothers established a modern oil industry around Baku in the Caucasus. Hitherto the local oil had been dug by hand and transported in leather pouches on camelback but, after a few decades under the Nobels, the region was covered with mechanically bored oil wells, there was a local refinery, and river and rail tankers were carrying the products all over European Russia. In engineering, Russia noticeably lagged behind the west, and it was only through import restrictions and tariffs that the home products could compete with imports. However, there did exist some state and foreign-managed works producing a reliable range of products; railway equipment was often home produced.

Russian railway-building had started under Nicholas I. The first public railway had been the 15.5-mile Tsarskoye Selo Railway from the capital to Pavlovsk, where public entertainments were promoted in order to encourage passenger traffic. The builder of the Tsarskoye Selo Railway was Gerstner, an Austrian whom Slavophils claimed was a Slav. His railway, finished in 1837, was an immediate success, even though the native birchwood used as fuel produced showers of sparks and complaints by smouldering passengers.

Nicholas I had a better appreciation of railways than his advisers, who preferred to develop further the inland waterways. He was especially impressed by the speed with which the Liverpool and Manchester Railway had carried troops to suppress rebellion in Ireland, for he had his own Irish problem in Poland.[8] For the most important railway project, the St Petersburg–Moscow railway, the American engineer Whistler was invited to Russia as a consultant. Although the Tsarskoye Selo Railway was of 6-foot gauge, Whistler recommended for future construction a 5-foot gauge. The Russian railway gauge thereby became 3.5 inches wider than the European standard. The St Petersburg–Moscow railway was opened in 1851, having been built by army engineers and serf labour to very high technical standards. Rolling stock was built in a state engineering works leased to American entrepreneurs.

---

7. For more on Hughes and the city he founded (Iuzovka, later Donetsk) see T. Friedgut, *Iuzovka and Revolution*, vol. i (1989).

8. He began building the St Petersburg–Warsaw Railway, in 1851, mainly for strategic reasons.

Under Alexander II the government drew up successive plans for railway construction; like most of Europe, but unlike Britain and the USA, the railway network was planned, and there was no duplication of lines between any two points. At first, when the government offered concessions to build the lines it wanted, there were few takers. Foreign investors had doubts about Russian financial stability, while domestic capitalists knew they could make higher profits in trade. Thus the practice developed whereby the government guaranteed the annual dividend on the shares of new private railway companies. In this way investors, assured of dividends whether or not the lines were profitable, were encouraged to put their money into railways. But this and other devices left wide loopholes for the sharp practitioner, and fortunes were made by some of the railway 'kings', at government expense. In some cases a railway company was better off making a loss than making a profit.

Foreign investors, especially French, and foreign engineers played a large but not exclusive role in building early Russian railways. Foreign equipment was also imported, for although the government granted various concessions to encourage the domestic production of rails, rolling stock and steelwork, Russian entrepreneurs were reluctant to engage in this business. Nevertheless, in the long run the railway programme did much to stimulate the fuel, metallurgical, and engineering industries. In the 1890s, more than four-fifths of new locomotives were home built.

Growth of Russian common-carrier railways

	Mileage	Freight traffic (millions tons)
1866	3,000	3
1883	14,700	24
1903	36,400	76
1913	43,900	158
1956	74,600	1,371
1990	91,600	3,872
1999	54,150	845

Note: The figures cover the respective territories of the Russian Empire (excluding Finland), the Soviet Union, and (1999) the smaller Russian Federation only.

Sources: J. N. Westwood, *A History of Russian Railways* (1964); *Jane's World Railways* (2001).

The government fluctuated in its preference for private or state railways. In 1867 it sold its St Petersburg–Moscow railway to private interests, and Alaska to the USA, to raise money for more railways; it was a heavy investor in private lines, for frequently the latter could not raise enough capital from private sources. By 1900 the preference was definitely for state-owned and state-managed railways, and by 1917 only a few lines were still in private hands.

4

Reformers and revolutionaries

Towards popular government?

THE optimistic and relaxed decade which followed Alexander's accession could well be described as a thaw following Nicholas's winter. Although discussions about serfdom dominated the early years, time was found for other matters; Russians were even permitted to smoke on the streets of St Petersburg. After the question of serf emancipation had been settled, other major reforms followed which did not, however, fully satisfy the optimists. Especially over-optimistic were those landowners who, envying the political rights and responsibilities of the English squire, sought to popularize in Russia the ideas of British liberalism. These men, an active minority of the nobles, felt that Russia needed a more popular form of government (in which, of course, they would play an important role), and that the nobles' traditional privileges were outmoded. In 1862 an assembly of the nobility of Tver province in an address to the Tsar announced their rejection of the idea that nobles should remain free from taxation or continue automatically to hold the key positions in the state service. Thirteen of these nobles, meeting separately, called for a classless elected popular assembly, and were duly rewarded with incarceration in the Peter-Paul Fortress at St Petersburg. One of the earliest acts of Valuev as minister of the interior was to forbid assemblies of nobles commenting on anything but local matters.

Nevertheless, the government in 1864 introduced a measure of self-government in local affairs. It organized in many provinces local assemblies called *zemstva* (singular: *zemstvo*). There were two levels of these. At the lower level were the district *zemstva*, containing the separately elected representatives of the nobles, the townsmen, and the peasants. Because of the electoral arrangements the nobility held about 40 per cent of the seats and the peasants, vastly more numerous, slightly less than 40 per cent, with townsmen and clergy holding the rest. This disproportion was even more marked at the superior level of *zemstva*, those at provincial level. The membership of the provincial *zemstvo* was elected from the district *zemstva* of that province. Both types of *zemstvo* had as chairman the local marshal of nobility, and both elected an executive for day-to-day decisions.

The government seemed to regret its creation of *zemstva* from the very start. Just 19 provinces had them at first and by 1914 37 of the 70 provinces were still without them, and they were closely supervised by the local bureaucracies. It was not long before restrictions were placed on the *zemstva*'s powers of local taxation, and in addition they were required to carry out with their own funds some of the tasks formally reserved for the central government. But despite these and other restrictions, the institution flourished until the October Revolution, and was an important step towards decentralization. In public education, public health and welfare, local economic development, road-building (and in at least one case, railway-building) the *zemstva* did good work. Their knowledge of local conditions and of local people enabled them to do a good job where a St Petersburg official would have failed. Much of their work lived on after 1917. In the early twenty-first century, for example, local hospitals built by the *zemstva* could still be observed, fulfilling their original function. In 1870 a somewhat similar system was granted to the cities, which were provided with a town council elected by property-holders. These city governments were never allowed to control the city police, which remained under the ministry of the interior, but many of them did good work in such spheres as urban roads and transport, street lighting, garbage disposal, drainage and water supply. The success of the *zemstva* demonstrated that the people were indeed capable of looking after their own affairs. That Russians could make a success of new, untraditional institutions, provided they could see the benefits, was demonstrated not only by the *zemstva* but also by the new judicial system of 1864.

Judicial reform

The debate on law reform appears to have been opened by the lightly censored *Naval Review* journal publishing a long article on French naval law. Probably the blackest aspect of Nicholas's reign had been the virtual impossibility for the ordinary Russian of obtaining justice in the courts. It is true that Speransky had codified Russian laws, but the way those laws were administered and applied was haphazard. This was a situation which Nicholas had inherited from two centuries of neglectful rulers. The Decembrists had placed reform of the judicial system high on their list of priorities, and rightly so. Even amid the inherent injustices of a society based on serfdom, there was no excuse for the wrongs and the cruelties inflicted on innocent citizens by an institution which in theory was intended to protect them.

Under Nicholas there was an amazing number and variety of courts, and cases could be transferred from one to another almost endlessly. It was quite common for a case to drag on for two or three decades before being settled. In any judicial system it is difficult, if not impossible, to avoid favouring members of a particular class, usually those who can afford to wait and can afford to try every loophole the law offers. But in Nicholas's Russia the dilatory procedures alone made recourse to law ruinous for any-one who had no strings to pull. The supreme judicial body was the Senate, which could hear final appeals. Below this there were various courts of appeal, and on the lowest level a multiplicity of courts of first instance. Most judges were quite untouched by legal training, and more than half were illiterate. This illiteracy was in fact assumed in the regulations, which stated that if all the judges of a court were illiterate the court secretary was empowered to write down their decision. This placed power in the hands of the secretary, especially as all evidence was written. The police were also granted great power under the system. Apart from carrying out preliminary inquiries, they had the right in some cases to levy fines. Since both the court secretaries and the police relied on bribes to maintain the standard of living to which they considered they were entitled, it is evident that the majority of court decisions depended on the respective financial resources of plaintiff and defendant. A particularly glaring example of the tempta-tions to abuse police power was the provision that, if a murderer was not found, the police could levy a collective fine on the inhabitants of the locality.

The most obvious feature of the system was its devotion to formality. There was a certain procedure for every circumstance, and every procedure was based on bureaucratic rather than human considerations. This was especially evident in the way judgement was made. An accused never saw his judges, nor they him. All evidence was written. It was presented to the judges as a pile of documents, and they assessed these according to the rules of evidence. The most weighty evidence was a confession. In the absence of a confession, mutual corroboration of two independent submissions was considered especially strong evidence. Then, in descending order of reliability, the rules detailed the other kinds of acceptable evidence. A litigant under these rules was well advised to present evidence of an educated male noble, or, if a noble was unobtainable or unbribable, of a priest of the Orthodox faith. The prefer-ence given to the word of a male over that of a female, of a nobleman over a priest, and of a priest over a layman was accepted as natural and traditional, but could only lead to abuses. In his memoirs, Aksakov mentions the case of a landowner whose main interest was raping his female serfs. He had only progressed through the first fifteen years of his programme when he was strangled by some of his victims. When the case came to court, neighbouring nobles testified that their late lamented friend was 'of decent behaviour, as was to be expected of a noble Russian gentleman', and this testimony, according to the rules, was the strongest presented.[1] So the women were convicted, and their sentence, 100 lashes and Siberian forced labour for those who survived,

1. S. Aksakov, *Polnoye sobraniye sochinenii* (1886), iv. 657.

was particularly harsh because in the scale of punishments it was more serious for a serf to kill a noble than vice versa, even if the vice was versa.

The whole procedure of justice, which was inquisitorial and secret, meant that even a wise and well-intentioned judge was no guarantee of a fair decision. The documents which reached the judges, and which would accompany the case as it went from court to court and from judge to judge, were unreliable, being the product of police methods of persuasion or of venal secretaries. Since the judges never met the accused, the evidence was unlikely to be challenged.

Military courts were sometimes used to try civilians. They were faster, and a more convincing deterrent. Under Nicholas I this practice became widespread; arson, crimes by civilians in the company of soldiers, and riotous behaviour by peasants in the presence of military guards were among the cases handled by the army courts.

The Judicial Reform, enacted in 1864, ensured that the public welfare would henceforth be the main concern of the Russian courts and of Russian law. The Reform introduced several concepts quite new to Russia, and apparently out of keeping with Russian tradition and with the autocratic regime. Yet despite the opposition of conservative circles, the changes were readily accepted and proved a great success right from the start. In brief, the Reform simplified the organization of the court system and introduced the principles of separation of powers, public and oral proceedings, and the jury system.

The reorganization of the courts entailed the replacement of the multifarious existing institutions by a system which, in general, meant that a case started in a lower court could be transferred on appeal to only one, or sometimes two, other courts. Each province was to have its court, and appeals from this were to be heard in one of the ten Palaces of Justice. The final court of appeal was the Senate, although not all cases could go that high. Some courts remained outside the new system, and this was to prove a weakness. These included church courts (which among other things had exclusive jurisdiction in divorce cases), military courts,[2] and the special local peasant courts which tried minor offences. After 1872 a special department of the Senate was entrusted with 'crimes against the state', which gave the government better opportunity to deal with political enemies in a way it considered fitting. Two provisions of the new code provided additional loopholes for arbitrary action, or inaction, against the whole principle of the Reform. One article gave the 'administrative power' the right to 'take measures . . . in order to prevent and limit . . . felonies and misdemeanours'. This gave the authorities the power of 'administrative' arrest or exile: under this provision a person could be exiled, without court intervention, in order to prevent him committing a crime.

---

2. Military courts were confined to military cases. But from 1878, in the face of revolutionary activities, they were used to try civilians who used force against the authorities.

Another article, while allowing officials to be tried for abuses of their powers, insisted that their superiors' approval was a prerequisite for a case to be brought. This meant that a miscreant official could be protected from justice by the head of his department. However, even in the worst periods of reaction in the next two reigns, the government was unable to use these loopholes as much as it wished. The principles of the 1864 Reform became so firmly and so rapidly ingrained in the Russian consciousness that failure to observe them always aroused protest.

In the new courts, while documentary evidence was not excluded, the parties were expected to present oral evidence. Moreover, in criminal cases, not only the evidence but the testimony of witnesses and experts had to be given orally, so that all aspects of the case put together in the preliminary investigation could be challenged and tested in open court. Preliminary investigation, supervised by a magistrate, was to remain hidden from public view, but the new provision for full publicity of court proceedings gave substantial protection to the accused. Even though the latter was unrepresented while the police collected evidence and witnesses against him, he could challenge such testimony in court and could, at his own expense, summon witnesses in his defence against any unforeseen evidence. As further safeguard, voting on the verdict by juries was kept secret, so as to protect them from threats of violence.

The first public session of the civil courts appears to have taken place in the Senate in October 1865, in the presence of the minister of justice. On this occasion the available seats were by no means filled by the public. However, in the provincial courts, which faced fewer competing entertainments, there developed a great demand for seats. It was not long before the simple fact of public access began to result in speedier trials, more business-like judges, and less frequent attempts by the police or administrators to pervert the course of justice. Full publicity, oral testimony, and the controversial procedure made the fabrication of false evidence a risky enterprise.

The controversial principle, the arguing out of a case by prosecutor and defender, would have meant less if at the same time the jury had not been introduced for major criminal cases. In most respects the jury functioned as in the Anglo-Saxon countries, but not always. The new code stipulated that the jury would decide not on the unanimity principle, but according to a majority. In those cases when the vote was equal there would be a not guilty verdict. Decision by majority was by many considered un-Russian, for there had been a centuries-old tradition (in the village commune, in ancient Novgorod, and elsewhere) that only a consensus could justify an action or decision. However, the reason for rejecting the unanimity principle was itself very Russian; it was argued that one juryman should not be allowed to thwart the will of eleven others. Jury members recorded their vote by secret ballot, and their decision was conveyed to the court in writing in response to a written question from the judges. If all three judges believed that the accused was innocent they could, if the jury found him guilty, hold another hearing with a fresh jury; but only once.

An interesting and sometimes criticized feature of the juries in Russia was that they regarded themselves as representing, not only the public interest, but also the public conscience. Once an accused was found guilty the judges enjoyed little flexibility in sentencing. The Russian jury sometimes overcame this problem by finding an accused not guilty, if it believed that the penalty in the given circumstances would be too great. It would do this even if the accused had admitted his guilt and there was no doubt at all that he had committed the crime; for the Russian jury there was a distinction between legal guilt and moral guilt and the latter sometimes had priority. In some rare cases the jury might even contrive to change the offence.[3] For example, if it was presented with incontrovertible evidence that an accused had been stealing horses yet felt that circumstances gave him some excuse, it might, in answer to the judges' question 'Do you find the accused guilty to the charge of horse-stealing?' reply 'The accused is found guilty of stealing rabbits'. In this way an accused could be found guilty but the severity of his punishment reduced.

Judges were appointed for life and were normally irremovable. When special circumstances made the disciplining of a judge essential, the process was in the hands, not of a government agency, but of the judges of a superior court. Also, so as to discourage the re-emergence of a bribable judiciary, salaries were high. Although judges were appointed by the tsar, the list of candidates from which he chose was compiled by the judiciary. Thus the reform did represent a real, if small, weakening of autocracy.

The introduction of the controversial procedure obviously entailed the provision of a pool of trained men to fill the positions of defending and prosecuting counsel. In other words, Russia had to have a Bar. Despite opposition to the creation of a recognized new professional class of lawyers, Alexander gave his consent to the establishment of the Russian Bar. In this way not only the supply of counsel was ensured, but also their supervision and standards of professional conduct. Those who opposed this innovation were correct, in so far as the Russian lawyers became the most effective and vocal body of liberally inclined men in the Empire. The profession not only worked intelligently and effectively for reform, but also provided several revolutionary leaders. Trained in the art of persuasion, professionally involved with both officialdom and the seamy side of Russian life, the lawyer was a natural leader in the movement towards reform. Shortly before the class was extinguished by the Revolution, it began to supply from its ranks some of the better parliamentarians of the Duma. In the courts, high-handed administrators were frequently humiliated by defending lawyers.

3. S. Kucherov, *Courts, Lawyers, and Trials under the Last Three Tsars* (1953), 70.

Another innovation of 1864 was the justice of the peace. This likewise was an immediate success. Elected by the local *zemstvo*, the justice of the peace dealt with small cases where the parties desired a quick, comprehensible, inexpensive, and on-the-spot decision. For the humble worker or peasant who demanded justice but was afraid to get himself entangled in the courts, the justice of the peace provided exactly what was needed. It was not long before these men, or at least most of them, became a firmly rooted and respected institution in their localities. They were so successful, especially in their protection of the small man against local officials, that they were eliminated by Alexander III's government and not reinstated until 1912. The justice of the peace, like the jury, like irremovable judges, like the Bar, was resented by those who regarded justice as something dispensed by rulers rather than something administered by society for the benefit of society.

Not only the ultra-conservatives but, later, many of the revolutionaries deprecated the new judicial system. Some revolutionaries no doubt did so on the principle that reforms to make life more bearable were harmful because they made revolution less likely. Others, placing exaggerated emphasis on the few occasions when justice was seen to be dispensed in favour of a particular class, proclaimed that the system was simply a new system of exploitation devised by and for the bourgeoisie. But the Judicial Reform of 1864 introduced not only a great innovation accepted as a blessing by the vast majority of Russians, but also one of the world's better judicial systems.

It was not long before the restraining force of the new system made itself felt, particularly by those officials who had hitherto scorned individual rights in their quest for convenience, bribes, or power. As this class of person found itself checked by the courts, resentment developed, but remained largely ineffective. With a few exceptions, for the remainder of the Romanov dynasty, lawyers had complete freedom of speech in the courts and their words were reported in the newspapers. Since so many of the accused were directly or indirectly the victim of government action, defence counsel could hardly avoid pointing out the injustices inflicted by the regime. The effect of this was heightened by the eloquence of many lawyers, and the tolerance of many judges; the latter would permit discussion of government actions in court if these were at all relevant to a case.

The Vera Zasulich case of 1878 demonstrated how, by introducing the Judicial Reform, the government had cut a great deal of ground from under its own feet. This was the *cause célèbre* not only of the reign but of the century. It was the practice to try 'crimes against the state' in the special courts prescribed. These courts were part of the regular system, and were public, but defence and prosecution argued their case not before a jury, but before five judges from the local judiciary and four elected 'class representatives' (in a provincial court these would be two leaders of the nobility, a town mayor, and a peasant elder). To avoid publicity the government also made great use of its power of 'administrative arrest' to exile those regarded as potentially danger-ous. However, since both these practices had been highly criticized, the Vera Zasulich case was referred to a regular St Petersburg court.

The accused, the 28-year-old daughter of an army officer, had shot and wounded the governor of St Petersburg, General Trepov. When the case came up, the minister of justice asked the presiding judge to obtain a conviction. The latter, however, rejected this interference, secure in the knowledge of his irremovability. At the trial, defence counsel pointed out that Vera had shot Trepov because she had been greatly upset and moved by a recent incident reported in the press. Trepov had visited a prison and ordered the flogging of a political prisoner who had refused to remove his hat in his presence. As well as pointing out that flogging in general had been banned in Russia, except for prisoners and a few other categories, and that this particular flogging was illegal because the victim had not yet begun his sentence, defence counsel, despite the protests of the prosecution, described Vera's past life. How, being vaguely associated with various revolutionaries, she had spent periods in prison and exile. How, despite being cleared in court, she had still been subject to police supervision and exile. How she had developed a feeling of great sympathy for others who were in gaol for political reasons and how her sensitivities had been thus outraged by Trepov's illegal violence. Defence counsel was enabled to summon witnesses under the terms of the 1864 Reform, and presented to the court other political prisoners who had seen the flogging. The appearance of these young men, pale and worn from months of incarceration, but obviously men of good breeding and education, produced its due effect not only on the jury, but on the public, which burst into applause at several emotional speeches of the defence. The jury brought in a verdict of not guilty. The spectators, who included many persons of high birth, broke into prolonged cheering, and defence counsel was carried out on the shoul-ders of his admirers. The government never again risked an important polit-ical trial in the regular courts. The presiding judge could not be removed, but he lost any immediate chance of promotion, and the minister of justice was dismissed. Although most of St Petersburg society was overjoyed, many had subsequent second thoughts. Vera emigrated, became a marxist revolutionary, was admired by Lenin, but died in 1919 a Menshevik. In the 1890s she wrote several articles condemning assassination as a revolutionary tactic.

Military reform

The Russian state was essentially a militarized autocracy, its military strength maintained by high taxation and compulsory state service. It might well be argued, too, that the huge Russian army was less a deterrent than an encouragement of war. Increases of armed strength made to satisfy genuinely felt needs of defence could lead to greater self-confidence in foreign policy, then to risk-taking, and then to wars in which the real losses outweighed the gains originally sought, and the gains themselves, if any, took the form of vulnerable territorial additions open to attack and therefore demanding additional defence expenditure. A study of nineteenth-century Russian arms provides a good example of that state of mind which regards the army, no matter how big, as too small. At one time the Russian ministry of war was content with merely the biggest army in Europe. Then it required an army equal to those of Austria and Germany combined. Finally it began to doubt whether even a two-power standard was enough, but the progression was broken by the First World War, in which Russian society and the Russian army devoured each other.

This does not mean that the war ministry was blindly pursuing its own interests. Its anxieties were justified, for defence of the long frontiers against more developed neighbours, and defence of the interior against possible rebellions, demanded more men and equipment than the Empire was willing or able to provide. Lack of resources would become increasingly felt in the last tsarist decades. On the one hand, re-equipment became more expensive and was required more frequently as technology accelerated, and on the other, the ministry of finance became less willing to recommend allocating to the army money that it reckoned could be used for more productive purposes. In the 1860s the army was reckoned to consume one-third of the government's income, but failed to provide the armed strength proportionate to this input. By the end of the century the military budget was about double that of France or Germany, but because the army was so big[4] the money spent per soldier was no more than that of the industrial powers.

The generally acknowledged failures of the Crimean War led to the military reforms of 1863–75, initiated by the war minister, Dmitri Milyutin. Apart from changing the conscription system, Milyutin reorganized the army's administration (so that the basic administrative unit became the military district), and put life into the moribund general staff. Also, he phased out the old cadet corps that had provided a free, somewhat brutal, and certainly mediocre education for sons of the nobility entering the army. In their place he established military gymnasiums providing a broad education, whose graduates proceeded to a military school where academic subjects were taught alongside military. Civilian teachers were appointed to these schools. A few of them, as well as the less prestigious junker schools for future officers, were opened to non-nobles. Henceforth education was to be a prerequisite for a commission; in the Crimean War less than a third of the officers had possessed a military education. Wider and better education and more opportunities for

4. In 1900 it numbered about 1 million men, almost double the German army. One reason for the large size of the peacetime army was that conscripts served longer than in France or Germany. Rightly or wrongly, it was felt that the Russian conscript was an ignoramus who needed several years to become a trained soldier.

non-nobles were Milyutin's two aims, aims that were not philanthropic but absolutely necessary for an effective army.

In line with this emphasis on the intellect, he established a staff college with very high standards of both entry and work; officers successful in the difficult entrance exam might still fail to graduate because admission to the third and final year was limited to those who had done well in the first two. Graduates went on to accelerated promotion and in course of time occupied most of the key posts, including those in the war ministry. Milyutin also established three specialized officer schools of similarly high standard, for the artillery, engineers, and military lawyers. Although some of these reforms were diluted after Milyutin's departure, their spirit persisted (the military districts were retained right through the Soviet period). Although the Russian officer corps for the remainder of the tsarist period was numerically dominated by the unprivileged, unintellectual, underpaid officers of the numbered[5] infantry regiments, there was a sprinkling of highly professional officers who had a broader view of how an army should fit into society.

The abolition of serfdom, and the growing railway network which facilitated mobilization and deployment, made a new conscription system desirable. During most of the 1860s the conscription levy was around four per thousand eligible males, providing an annual intake of around 100,000, of whom four-fifths went to the infantry. The standard length of service had been reduced *de facto* to fifteen years' active service and ten years' 'leave'. Increasingly, soldiers were allowed to end their active service after from seven to thirteen years. By 1870, and especially after the triumph of the Prussian army over the French, others in addition to the war minister were concerned about the size and professionalism of the Russian army. In liberal, and even in some conservative circles, opinion moved in favour of a Prussian-style conscription system. Milyutin had long hankered for such a change, and with this new support was able to introduce it despite opposition.

The essence of Milyutin's proposals was the extension of military liability to all social classes, which would raise the pool of eligible males by a small fraction; the registration each year of males reaching the age of 21, of whom about one-quarter would be chosen by lot to serve; the period of military service to be set at fifteen years, of which only seven would normally be full-time active service; men doing their eight-year reserve stint would be subject to occasional calls to summer camps or refresher courses to maintain their effectiveness; only medical evidence could relieve a young man of his liability,

---

5. Numbered regiments were those that lacked one of the inspiring names accorded to regiments of ancient lineage or of distinguished battle record. Some of their officers were good and capable of independent thought; generalizations are perilous because there was among the officer class an enormous range of intellect and view. But with Milyutin's reforms the way was opened for a professionalization of the officer corps, despite the tsars' continuing power, copiously exercised, of appointing and promoting their protégés.

but in practice deferments would be granted to students completing their studies, and exemptions granted to the only sons of widows, or other young men who could claim they were the sole support of their families.

During the discussion stage of the proposals there was strong opposition, which all but defeated them. This was expressed most forcibly by Dmitri Tolstoy, the minister of education. This opposition centred on, and was largely provoked by, Milyutin's intentions in respect to officering and to the privileges to be offered to educated recruits. Milyutin realized that the educated would be trained quicker than the uneducated, and that their withdrawal from civilian life represented a larger social and economic loss to the nation. He therefore proposed reduced lengths of service for these recruits, pointing out that this would encourage young men to remain students as long as possible, thus adding to the intellectual capital of Russia. Those with university education, suggested Milyutin, need serve only six months, while those with a secondary education would serve eighteen months, and even graduates of district and of primary schools would have only, respectively, a three-year and four-year term. These concessions were paralleled by the arrangements envisaged for supplying the increased number of reserve officers which would be needed. This question, too, would be treated with reference to educational levels. A university graduate who volunteered before he was conscripted would pass a simple examination and become an officer, with only three months' active service. Those with secondary or district school education would have the same privilege, but serve one and two years respectively.

Opposition to the reform by the landed gentry, in these circumstances, could hardly have been a surprise. Hitherto, when the sons of the nobility entered the army they did so as volunteers, and provided the service with almost all its officers. Now it was proposed that 21-year-old nobles who had not volunteered should be liable to conscription just like others. Not only this, but noble conscripts might have to live and work together with sons of peasants and workers. Moreover, because of the privileges granted to the educated, an increasing number of the army's officers (and especially reserve officers) would be of non-noble origin. Many merchants, too, were unhappy, being especially resentful of Milyutin's insistence that the hiring of substitute conscripts be banned. But despite all this opposition, which was expressed not only in open discussion but in the press, and by influential men in private discussion with the Tsar, the reform eventually won the royal assent in 1874, becoming law in 1875. Because it was such a great step towards the abolition of archaic class privileges, it ranks with the Emancipation and the transformation of justice as one of the three most significant reforms of the reign.

Serving as minister for seventeen years, Milyutin was able to see his reforms firmly established. The next tsar, Alexander III, promptly removed him but allowed most of the changes to remain in place. However, the military gymnasiums were replaced by cadet corps, entry to which was again restricted virtually to nobles, and the use of civilian teachers in army schools, which Milyutin had favoured as a way of broadening officers' minds, was discontinued. The future General Obruchev had worked out most of the military reforms, and he remained in the war ministry, protecting the innovations as best he could. General Kuropatkin, who later became war minister, carried on this role. Both generals struggled hard against 'grand-dukism', the tsars' practice of appointing untrained family members as heads of the various services. Professional officers at the head of such technical services as artillery, military engineering, and the navy were obviously desirable, but they implied less control by the tsar.

Education, censorship, and publishing

How to advance the state by educating the people, without educating the people to question the state? This is a dilemma not unknown elsewhere, but has often seemed more acute in Russia, especially during and after the reign of Alexander II.

For the universities the late 1850s and early 1860s were unhappy years. Due to Nicholas's virtual ban on foreign teachers, the low salaries, and the generally low status of the universities, the standard of instruction was poor, and many chairs were empty. The students still found themselves inadequately prepared by their gymnasiums for university work, and expressed their dissatisfactions by demonstrations and disorders. These, and their equally disliked criticism of the government, were only intensified after Alexander's first steps in increasing public liberties. The result was the appointment of a former admiral as a 'strong' minister of education, and of a Cossack general as head of the St Petersburg educational district. In 1861 new and restrictive regulations were introduced. Student organizations and even unauthorized student gatherings were banned, and impecunious students lost their privileges, including their exemption from fees. The students responded with large demonstrations of protest which, in the two capitals, were suppressed by police and troops.

In 1861 and 1862 it seemed to many that Russia was approaching a new crisis; dangerous situations seemed to be developing everywhere. In Poland, what was to become the Polish Rebellion was already manifesting itself; the putting into effect of the Emancipation Act was expected to ignite disorders all over Russia: the example of Garibaldi and other factors were encouraging would-be revolutionaries; and to all this was added discontent and disorder in the universities. The incarceration of 300 students in the Peter-Paul Fortress, and the beating-up and expulsion of hundreds more, did not satisfy those among the public who regarded the students as a dangerous, immoral, and unholy threat to Russian society. When in May of 1862 a succession of fires broke out in St Petersburg, it was not long before some newspapers and some influential personages began to suggest that the fires were the work of resentful revolutionary students. But an investigating commission found nothing more conspiratorial than three students who had started one fire when in an almost unconscious state of intoxication. Evidently the almost daily outbreaks of damaging conflagrations at that time were a consequence of a period of hot, dry weather, the prevalence of wooden housing, and the absence of water for quelling fires in their initial stages. Similar fires had devastated parts of the capital two years previously. On that occasion, however, they had been blamed on the Poles.

Alexander, disliking harsh measures, in 1863 approved a new set of university statutes. The planning of these, in which he had shown great interest, included consultation with the universities and their professors, and the dispatch of several of the latter to the better European universities to seek out useful ideas. The new statutes adopted the German practice of giving the universities autonomy in administration, and the French practice of the ministry of education prescribing the curriculum for all the universities, with annual examinations. University administration was placed in the hands of a council at each institution. Each of these university councils supervised teaching, degree awards, and had the right to censor the university's publications, thus freeing the latter from the general censorship. Rectors, deans, and other high positions were filled by faculty elections. Student miscreants were tried by a court of three professors. Previously abolished chairs in philosophy and constitutional law were reinstated. Teaching salaries were raised, and stipends were made available to two-fifths of the students. But the Tsar insisted that those teachers who did not hold the degree stipulated for their particular rank should start working for it immediately. Despite the subsequent appointment of the conservative Dmitri Tolstoy as minister of education, the universities did not lose the advantages of the new statutes until the following reign. At the time of Alexander's death in 1881 there were eight universities. To the seven universities of St Petersburg, Moscow, Kazan, Kiev, Vilna, Kharkov, and Dorpat had been added Odessa, and in Siberia the University of Tomsk was well on the way to establishment. In addition to new universities, in Alexander's reign seven more specialized institutions of higher learning were created.

The *zemstva* administered local primary schools through school boards, the membership of which, however, was heavily weighted in favour of the nobility, the clergy, and government officials. By about 1900 the church schools would be left behind both quantitatively and qualitatively. In 1915 there would be 34,000 primary schools under the Holy Synod, but the ministry of education, with the *zemstva*, would be supervising nearly 81,000, totalling 6 million pupils. In secondary education, a new code confirmed the division between the classical gymnasiums and the more vocational secondary schools, where no dead languages were taught but attention was paid to modern languages, science, and mathematics. The latter became known, German-style, as real gymnasiums. Thanks to the government's interest in schooling there was a doubling of the number of pupils in the first decade of Alexander's reign, 800,000 being reached in 1865. Only the district schools failed to benefit in this period; it was decided to abolish this category, converting some to an improved type of primary school and others to 'pro-gymnasiums', providing gymnasium-type courses on a four-year cycle instead of the classical gymnasiums' eight-year curriculum.

A pistol shot which missed the Tsar in 1866 was fired by a former student of Kazan University, D. Karakazov. This brought to a head the misgivings of some officials about the spread of education:

Nothing harms our independence of thought as much as the passion for reading that is spreading so powerfully among us. Reading decisively kills decisiveness, and the power of acting according to one's reason. This latter gets used to the mainstream of the river of alien thoughts which carries it along, not permitting it, or hardly permitting it, amid the movement of words, to use its own strengths.[6]

Karakazov supplied all the evidence needed by those who had long been eager to castigate educated young men as revolutionary, immoral, and the product of a misguided ministry of education. The first head to fall was that of the minister of education, who was replaced by Dmitri Tolstoy. The latter was already Over Procurator of the Holy Synod, so once again the two offices were held by the same man. Tolstoy believed that the spirit of revolution originated in the schools and universities, and especially in the science courses. He accordingly withdrew science from the schools, replacing it with larger doses of the classics. The real gymnasium courses were reduced to a six-year cycle; hitherto, like the classical gymnasium, they had offered an eight-year course. At the same time entry to universities was limited, more strictly than previously, to those who had graduated from the classical gymnasiums. This last restriction meant that fewer middle-class and more noble youths would attend universities, because the sons of merchants and artisans usually went to the real gymnasiums, which offered the technical and commercial subjects they needed. At the same time, difficult final examinations in the gymnasiums ensured that only those capable of absorbing and regurgitating an enormous quantity of facts and quotations would ever receive their leaving certificate. It became usual for only about one-third of those entering the gymnasiums to succeed in graduating; university entry thereby tended to embrace those students who had kept their noses to the grindstone and lost the dangerous habit of looking around them.

6. This diary entry is remarkable in that it was written by a professor and goverment censor who had been born a serf and won his freedom and a good job solely because he had been a brilliant pupil. It would be hard to find a clearer case of a climber wanting to pull up his ladder behind him. A. V. Nikitenko, *Dnevnik* (1956), iii. 31.

Tolstoy did not take serious action against the liberties of the universities, apart from transferring certain disciplinary functions from the universities to the police, a move which led to the renewal of student demonstrations in the 1870s. He did, however, impose greater ministerial control over the primary schools. The school boards set up in 1864 were tending to be dominated by their *zemstvo* representatives, largely because the latter were more energetic than their colleagues. Tolstoy in the early 1870s therefore transferred such decisions as teachers' appointments and the opening and closing of schools from the local school boards to inspectors from his own ministry. Thus by 1877, although the *zemstva* and town councils were providing about two-thirds of the funds for primary schools, the ministry had effective supervision. The ministry's inspectors, who were always too few to be as effective as Tolstoy had anticipated, were encouraged to be vigilant over such matters as the choice of books, the nature of the political and moral views conveyed by teachers, and the eating habits of the latter on fast days. However, because the inspectors were quite often competent in pedagogic matters, they did also bring positive benefits.

In the mid-1860s, the proportion of army recruits (almost entirely peasants) who were literate was about 7 per cent, and this rose to about 30 per cent by 1890. Inside the army, the ministry of war since the 1850s had encouraged units to teach their men to read and write, and some officers gave not only their time but also their money to this task. By 1870 the army had a literacy rate much higher than that of the general population; about half the soldiers could read, and about a quarter could read and write. In the first twenty years after the 1874 reform, probably 2 to 3 million men were taught by the army to write and read. Thus the army remained Russia's greatest single educational institution. The ministry of war also attempted to mitigate the ruling by Tolstoy that only classical gymnasium graduates could continue to higher education. The ministry found that this meant that insufficient candidates came forward to train as army surgeons in its medical school. The minister, Milyutin, therefore waived the requirement. But Tolstoy, who was always glad of an opportunity to attack Milyutin, persuaded the Tsar to reprimand the latter for this. However, Milyutin's failure here did not prevent his offering medical training to female students.

There were already a few girls' schools, traditionally supervised by the empresses, and in 1870 some gymnasiums and pro-gymnasiums were established for girls, together with teacher-training courses. The university statutes of 1863 excluded women from universities, but public pressure persuaded most of the universities to offer extra courses on holidays and weekends for female students. However, it had already become a tradition for the more adventurous girls to go to foreign universities, and this continued until 1914.

The spread of education, the relaxation of censorship, and the increasing interest in public discussion created a growing demand for the written word.

In 1855, 1,020 book titles were published, 1,836 in 1864, and 10,691 in 1894. The 1894 total was about equal to the output of new titles in the USA and Britain combined. The Imperial Library at St Petersburg with its million titles ranked third in the world after the Bibliothèque Nationale and the British Museum, and the St Petersburg Public Library had almost half a million volumes in addition. Periodicals flourished in the second half of the century. In 1855 there were about 140 periodicals in circulation. Of these about sixty were 'official'; they were published by one or other government department but often only part of their contents was related to that particular department. (Pirogov published several of his advanced educational articles in the navy's journal.) A similar proportion of the periodicals was scholarly or specialized journals, leaving less than twenty dealing in general terms with literary or current affairs. Periodicals dealing with current affairs, literature, and other general interests did not multiply under Alexander III; the total remained more or less constant, with the number of new ventures equalling the number of those periodicals which ceased publication. In 1894 Russia had 89 newspapers and 32 general-interest 'thick' periodicals. In Alexander II's reign the practice (continued in the Soviet period) of government departments publishing their own newspapers for general distribution became widespread. Especially noteworthy among these was the *Russkii Invalid*, published by the ministry of war. This became especially popular among the public during the Polish Rebellion, because it was able to give the latest (and most reliable) news about the military situation. Milyutin used the paper not only to publicize his own strong anti-Polish and anti-Catholic sentiments, but also to popularize his views on the army reforms he was planning. Milyutin's possession of a news-paper, in which he could dispute the views of the conservative press, caused his political enemies to persuade the Tsar to issue an order compelling departmental newspapers to publish only 'official' items. This order robbed Milyutin of his most valued weapon, but it did not permanently affect the departmental newspapers.

One of the factors encouraging the public to read more books and period-icals after 1855 was the relaxation of the censorship. When Alexander suc-ceeded his father, there was not so much a formal relaxation as a completely new atmosphere, in which newspapers and journals freely criticized those aspects of the government which had been proven shameful or ineffective during the Crimean War. However, even at this time there were certain topics which could not be mentioned. In 1860 censorship was removed from the ministry of education and later came into the purview of the ministry of the interior. The multitude of separate censorships, which in Nicholas's time had meant that a publication had to be approved by several offices, was almost eliminated, although the Church and the army insisted on maintaining their own separate right to censor material dealing with their own fields of interest. 'Preventive' censorship (the submission of publications before distribution), which enabled and encouraged censors to interfere in all kinds of details, was largely replaced by 'punitive' censorship, which simply involved the punishment of publishers and writers and editors if they broke the rules and published material of a type known to be forbidden. Under this system both the authorities and the publications knew, in theory, just how far they could go. But within two weeks of the 1865 law formalizing these concessions, an unsuspecting newspaper was served with an official warning for discussing a financial question; it was claimed that this article was against the interests of the state, for it might harm Russia's international credit. Soon, other newspapers received cautions, and their editors were aware that if they received too many of these they would become eligible for stronger measures. Later, after Valuev had been thwarted by the courts in his efforts to punish delinquent editors, he issued an instruction removing censorship cases from the provincial courts. In the succeeding years of mild reaction, further changes hampered the development of a healthy press. Some papers could be sold only to their established subscribers, some journals were returned to preventive censorship, and the minister of the interior could arbitrarily forbid the discussion of certain questions of state. In the reaction following the 1866 attempted assassination of the Tsar, Valuev even suppressed the well-established journal *The Contemporary*. Nevertheless, for writers and publishers the reign of Alexander II was an interlude of freedom separating the repressive years of Nicholas I and Alexander III.

The arts

The reign of Alexander coincided almost exactly with what is called the golden age of Russian literature, the age of Turgenev, Dostoevsky, and Tolstoy. It was also the golden age of Russian realism, although that term is misleadingly broad; it might be more meaningful to say that writers preferred to write about their own country and their own time, and that they had a deep seriousness and sense of responsibility towards society. For the historian, their novels have great value in conveying the atmosphere of the time; they should be read, rather than read about. For their original readers, too, they were more than entertainment. Because Russians so often have been prevented by censorship from discussing issues openly, fiction has frequently been a unique medium for presenting unpleasant truths and original solutions. Turgenev's *Sportsman's Sketches* (1847), for example, presented portraits of Russian peasants and thereby suggested to its readers the novel truth that the peasants were real suffering individuals, not just insensible and indistinguishable components of a grey mass.

In other novels Turgenev dealt sympathetically but sadly with the young radicals. In *On the Eve* (1860), the only radical character is a Bulgarian, suggesting that Russia is not yet producing the energetic young men she needs.

Then, in *Fathers and Sons* (1862), the Russian nihilist appears in Bazarov, who denies the worth of everything that cannot be justified scientifically, is unable always to practise as he preaches, and dies before achieving anything. Later, *Virgin Soil* (1877) portrays the idealism, naivety, and pathos of the young men and women who 'go to the people' to educate and radicalize the masses.

Dostoevsky condemned Turgenev's sympathy for the radicals. He put his faith in Christian humility and the 'Russian soul'. His novels present a wide range of complex psychological types, and were of great interest to psychologists and philosophers; Freud and Nietzsche were but two who were influenced by them. It is not easy to decide which characteristics of Dostoevsky's heroes are specifically Russian, and which universal, but it is widely accepted, for example, that the three brothers in *The Brothers Karamazov* (1880) represent three salient Russian types. Ivan is an atheist intellectual who hankers for the west, even though he knows the west is alien. Dmitri exemplifies the extremism of the Russian character, which can shift in a flash from generosity to swinishness, from caution to recklessness, from kindness to cruelty. The third brother, Alyosha, a disciple of the local holy man, represents Russian love, humility, and self-sacrifice.

Tolstoy was revered by many as the greatest Russian ever. He was not simply a writer, but in his later decades a moralist and philosopher who influenced, among others, Gandhi. His condemnation of violence and wealth, of government repression and church hypocrisy, brought him administrative pinpricks and excommunication. After his two best-known novels, *War and Peace* (1869) and *Anna Karenina* (1877), were completed, Tolstoy underwent a spiritual crisis. This affected his subsequent works, which tended to reflect whatever mental torment their author was passing through at the time. The novel *Resurrection* (1889), for example, dealt very harshly with the workings of the judicial system, and was written after Tolstoy discovered by experience that Alexander II's reforms meant that nobles like the Tolstoys could no longer influence verdicts in the local court. Again, *The Kreutzer Sonata* (1889), a diatribe against feminine sexuality, reflects Tolstoy's failure to adapt to monogamy. *War and Peace*, which was written between 1862 and 1868, is regarded as *the* Russian novel. Describing the events of 1812, it did much to restore confidence lost in the Crimean War. By depicting 1812 as a time when all Russians were comrades with a single goal, it expressed the idea of Russian nationality without arrogance or chauvinism. Tolstoy, himself an old soldier, described the battles of 1812 with an absence of heroics and a lack of respect for Napoleon; whereas the wise old Kutuzov realizes that history will take its course irrespective of what so-called great men may do, Napoleon imagines that he is controlling events, and thereby the destiny of the world.

Among writers less well known in the west, although available in translation, Goncharov, Leskov, Saltykov-Shchedrin (see p. 73) and Chernyshevsky are especially rewarding for historians. The hero of Goncharov's *Oblomov*

(1859) is an extreme example, both of the 'superfluous man' and of Russian inertia; while he sits around in his dressing gown, apathetic and opportunity-wasting, his energetic friend (who, not by coincidence, is of German origin) gets things done. Leskov specialized in the holy, corrupt, comic, and superstitious lives of the provincial clergy. Chernyshevsky perhaps belongs more to the history of the revolutionaries than to the history of literature, for his novel *What Is to Be Done?* became an inspiration for generations of revolutionary intellectuals. The son of a priest and educated at St Petersburg University, Chernyshevsky became one of the editors of *The Contemporary*, the favourite journal of the radical intelligentsia. In this position, and in so far as the censorship permitted, he advanced his theory that most unhappiness in the world had economic causes, and that society could only be perfected through socialism. In the student disturbances of 1862 the authorities decided to arrest him as a precautionary measure. This precaution lasted two decades, and after his return from Siberia he was not in a condition to make much further contribution to Russian letters. However, in 1862, while in gaol, he wrote *What Is to Be Done?* This novel had an enormous public success, especially among the young, many of whom tried to model their lives after those of the heroes. A main theme of the novel is the emancipation of women, as expressed by the heroine, whose initial marriage enables her to escape from grasping and unperceptive parents,[7] and who then marries a second time for love, the first husband having generously faked his own suicide. The heroine, by establishing humane but profitable seamstresses' cooperative workshops, shows how socialist ideals and female self-sufficiency are complementary. Generations of revolutionaries, including Lenin, were impressed by the only-too-perfect hero, devoid of humour, hard-working, self-controlled, and putting the cause above everything else.

Chernyshevsky, in his role as critic, did much to further the concept of critical realism as a standard by which literature should be judged. In this he was aided by his friend Dobroliubov, who is regarded as one of the most influential Russian critics, even though he died at the age of 25. Like Chernyshevsky, Dobroliubov was the son of a priest and a contributor to *The Contemporary*. However, the influence of the radical critics of the Belinsky tradition was not always positive. For example, in the early nineteenth century there had flourished in Russia native novels of the Tom Jones genre, but after Belinsky's condemnation these fell rapidly out of fashion. Thus Bulgarin's *Ivan Vyzhigin* was a best-seller in 1830 but forgotten by 1840; Bulgarin was a proponent of Official Nationality and this may have given Belinsky's criticism extra venom. Again, radical critics were inclined to invent a cause when running short of genuine issues. When the progressive educationist Pirogov, an

---

7. This feature later inspired many real-life 'fictitious marriages' of young women seeking freedom from parental control.

opponent of corporal punishment, wrote an article recommending the limitation of birching to a few specific circumstances, Dobroliubov immediately
attacked him as an advocate of birching. Corporal punishment, being applic-
able only to non-nobles, was an issue too much imbued with class distinction
to be treated rationally by the radicals.

Although literature was reaching a wider audience, among the educated
there were still loyal subjects of the Tsar who distrusted contemporary writers.
The mathematician Sofia Kovalevskaya, whose father was a retired general
living in a remote village, described a childhood experience of 1865 in her
memoirs:

Our father, as I have mentioned, regarded with great mistrust anything which originated from the literary world. Although he did give permission for my sister to make the
acquaintance of Dostoevsky he did so with a shudder and inward trepidation.

'Remember that you are responsible, Liza,' he told our mother as we said goodbye
on leaving our village. 'Dostoevsky is not from our kind of society. What do we know
about him? Simply that he is a journalist and was once in gaol. That's a fine recom-
mendation! What more is there to say? You must be on your guard with him'.[8]

In the theatre, foreign plays remained the most numerous, but Ostrovsky's
work was popular. This playwright illuminated the naive and petty side of the
Russian middle class. That the characters he portrayed were types well
entrenched in Russian society is suggested by the continuing popularity of
his works. Like the ballet, Russian theatre would not attain worldwide
appreciation until the turn of the century. Until 1881, city theatres were state
owned, and there was a tendency to refuse the staging of truly original plays.
In the absence of privately owned public theatres, the only other performances were in the private theatres of the greatest landowners. The actors,
designers, musicians, and playwrights of these were often former serfs, a
few of whom rose high in the theatrical world. However, until Ostrovsky
founded various theatrical associations, the social status of the actor was very
low in Russia.

During the reign of Alexander II, most Russians would have named Anton
Rubinstein as their best-known musician. A child prodigy as a pianist, he
had later written operas and done much to encourage Russian musicians by
helping to found the St Petersburg Conservatoire. The latter and the Imperial
Russian Musical Society were distrustful of the group of musicians known as
the 'Handful of Five'. Of these, Balakirev was the inspirer and Cui the publicist
while Borodin, Rimsky-Korsakov, and Musorgsky wrote music that appealed
to worldwide audiences. For most of these composers music was a part-
time interest. Cui was a military engineer of French descent who wrote
standard texts on fortification. Balakirev was touched by religious mania
and later became a not-quite-sane anti-Semitic railway stationmaster.

8. S. Kovalevskaya, *Vospominaniya i pisma* (1951), 103.

Rimsky-Korsakov had initially followed family tradition by becoming a naval officer, while Borodin was a renowned professor of chemistry who helped to establish a medical school for women. Being amateurs, they largely relied on each other for technical advice, and pieces ascribed to one of them could be influenced or perfected by another. One of their best-known creations, Borodin's *Prince Igor*, was finished by Rimsky-Korsakov and Glazunov after Borodin unexpectedly died in his fifties.

Sometimes called the 'Mighty Five', these composers produced a markedly Russian music. As their supporter the eminent critic Stasov put it, unlike in western Europe the old folk songs in Russia were still part of daily life and were part of the childhood background of the emerging musicians. To this national element was added the experience of travels in the Caucasus, which had its own distinctive eastern elements. By absorbing these influences, and treating with some suspicion the 'universally recognized authorities', the new composers had created a true Russian school, if not a completely new musical system.

For Stasov, 'universally recognized authorities' was a euphemism covering the rival, if not hostile, musical establishment based on the St Petersburg Conservatoire. Here, under Rubinstein, classical western music was the inspiration of new works. Thus in music, as elsewhere, the lure of the west competed with assertion of Russian individuality.

However, Tchaikovsky showed it was possible to make the best of both worlds. One of the first students at the Conservatoire, he went on to worldwide acclaim. While finding ideas in Russian folk music, he maintained a generally European approach. Early in his career he sought friends among the 'Mighty Five', and his *Romeo and Juliet* grew from a suggestion by Balakirev. But Tchaikovsky differed so much from the Five that a lasting alliance was impossible, and there was deep antipathy between Tchaikovsky and Musorgsky; the latter's *Boris Godunov* was apparently described by Tchaikovsky as 'musical excrement'. Musorgsky, whose inner contradictions lay at the base of exceedingly complex music, was largely unappreciated in the outside world until well after his death (which came early, when he decided that a large dose of cognac would be a good way to convalesce from a minor stroke). Tchaikovsky, on the other hand, was immediately acclaimed, partly because his European foundations made his music more assimilable and partly because despite his western inclinations he was imbued with Russian patriotism. Tsar Alexander III considered him loyal (unlike the suspect 'Five') and rewarded him well. Works like *Year 1812* were obviously patriotic as well as moving. In 1891 he conducted his music in the USA amid popular acclamation, returned home via Britain, and finished his *Nutcracker* suite. His death in 1893 was said to be a consequence of the cholera epidemic, but there were rumours of suicide occasioned by problems stemming from his homosexuality.

Composers were not excused from open or discreet censorship. Nicholas I allowed the depiction of pre-Romanov royalty in drama and tragedy, but not in opera, as Rubinstein discovered when his *Dmitri Donskoi* went to the censor:

It's true what you wrote about the opera. Caution was needed, as the censorship returned the libretto with the instruction that Prince Dmitri Donskoi must not sing![9]

Rimsky-Korsakov had to remove references to medieval Pskov's republican form of government from his opera *Maid of Pskov*. Musorgsky's opera *Boris Godunov*, with its anti-militarist undertones, suffered from royal disapproval. The same composer also had a work banned outright. What happened was that the distinguished artist Vereshchagin, having dragged himself through a campaign in Turkestan, put his paintings on show in the capital. One of them, titled *Forgotten*, showed vultures appraising the body of a Russian soldier, abandoned as the troops marched on. Savagely abused by generals and critics who were incensed by this picture, the artist burned it, whereupon Musorgsky composed his own *Forgotten*, transferring picture to music. It was a minor masterpiece; after it was banned the composer went on to produce *The Field Marshal*, which also hurt the military but was less of an artistic triumph.

The Russo-Turkish War

The end of the Crimean War had enabled Russia to reassert itself against the Caucasian peoples. These were of various religion and language. Some of them accepted the Russian presence while others violently resisted it. Among the resisters were the Circassians in the west and the Chechens and Dagestanis in the east, all Muslims. Under Alexander I there had been a successful campaign against the Dagestanis and Chechens and a Russian base was established at Grozny. The Russian commanders conducted themselves with great savagery, burning villages and killing their inhabitants. They set out to teach these people a lesson they would never forget, and succeeded only too well. In the 1830s under the soon-to-be-legendary Shamil, an expert in mountain and forest warfare, these nations hit back and in 1845 inflicted heavy losses on a Russian expeditionary force. But in the decade following the Crimean War Shamil was defeated, and the Chechens and Dagestanis subdued. The Circassians, also defeated, were subjected to an ethnic cleansing; being co-religionists with the Turks, and on the Black Sea, they were regarded as dangerous in a future war, so most were driven out to Turkey.

Fighting in the Caucasus had become a traditional ritual for the Russian army, but in Alexander II's one major war, against Turkey, the main field of activity was in the Balkans. However, it was not the Russo-Turkish War but the

9. Letter from Rubinstein to his mother, Dec. 1850. The opera was finished in 1850 but, renamed *Battle of Kulikovo*, was not performed until after Nicholas's death.

emergence of a united Germany that was the main event in Russia's foreign relations during Alexander's reign. Bismarck's work was to have as damaging an effect on Russia's position as it would have on France. Whereas Russia's relations with the German states had been successfully managed in the post-Napoleonic period, helped by royal marriages and common interests, there was now a completely new situation. For a time, cordiality between the Romanovs and the Hohenzollerns persuaded the former that the old relationships might continue. But the underlying reality, which emerged plainly in 1914, was quite different. With a new and militant power established in central Europe and determined to make its mark, an additional and often unhelpful voice was heard as the great powers strove to accommodate peacefully the political and social upheavals of the time.

Bismarck was familiar with Russia, having been the Prussian minister in St Petersburg. He had no great regard for the Russians and, like several of his successors, tried to encourage them to turn their attention towards expansion in the east; if kept busy in Asia, Russians would be less concerned with the Balkans, where Austrian ambition, British anxieties, Ottoman decline, and local nationalisms promised perilous changes. In fact, Russia no more needed encouragement in her military excursions into Central Asia than she did in her continuing 'pacification' of the Caucasus. But despite these preoccupations she was unwilling to turn her back on the Balkans. Alexander was anxious to avoid trouble, yet even the Tsar-Autocrat had to heed the outcry from those of his subjects for whom the tribulations of Orthodox Christians under the Turks was a burning wrong. Among these subjects of the Tsar it was the Panslavists who were the most vocal, and they were influential not only in Russia but also in the Slavic lands of the Ottoman Empire. In 1875 a revolt started in Herzegovina and spread to Bosnia and Bulgaria. Despite British reluctance to intervene, the 'Bulgarian Atrocities' perpetrated by the Turks precipitated interference by the great powers. A European conference was summoned at Constantinople, but its decisions were rejected by the Turks, as were subsequent proposals by the powers. In 1877 Alexander declared war on Turkey in defence of the Slavic peoples.

The war, fought mainly in what is now Bulgaria and Romania, occurred while the Russian army was still in the period of transformation following Milyutin's reforms. Thus many of the deficiencies of the Crimean War reappeared. Only the engineers and the sailors distinguished themselves. The engineers brilliantly executed the initial crossing of the Danube, and made possible the eventual capture of the Turkish stronghold of Plevna. Bold young naval officers, including the future Admiral Makarov, commanded steam launches whose torpedoes defeated the Turkish navy. Early in 1878, his army threatening Constantinople but with Russia under British pressure, Alexander signed an armistice which was followed by the Treaty of San Stefano. This was highly favourable to Russia, and included the establishment of a large Bulgarian state which would be independent but under Russian influence. Alexander was not surprised when Britain and other powers made strong objections and at Bismarck's suggestion agreed to a congress of governments in Berlin. The result was the Treaty of Berlin (1878), which superseded the Treaty of San Stefano; the provisions of the latter were partly retained, but the new Bulgaria was reduced in size and Britain received Cyprus. Ordinary Russians saw this as a diplomatic defeat, and the Panslavists were infuriated at what they regarded as Russia's humiliation; their agitation was one of the main factors in Alexander's loss of popularity at this time.

The revolutionaries

There were to be no more honeymoons of tsar and people after the mid-1860s; for the next half-century revolutionaries and unnecessary wars wore down the state, while the state wore down its peoples. Alexander II found that relaxation and reform led not to contentment but to increasing demands for concessions which he had never been prepared to grant. This, and the attacks of revolutionaries, eroded his reforming zeal.

The informal circles of intellectuals of the late 1820s and 1830s had devoted themselves mainly to the idealistic philosophy then in fashion. At that time, questioning young men like Belinsky and Bakunin were buried in German metaphysics and in the study of Schelling and Hegel, placing the pursuit of truth and beauty before the problems of Russian society. But there were others, of whom Herzen was the outstanding representative, who were beginning to care about social problems, were acquainting themselves with the French socialist thinkers, and were adopting the view that, instead of the political revolution which had proved so disappointing in France and Poland, what Russia needed was a social revolution; if the economic advantages held by the property-owning class were eliminated, political privilege would automatically disappear. The intensification of the Westernizer versus Slavophil discussion in the 1840s also indicated a growing concern in intellectual circles about whether Russia should follow the path of industrial and liberal western society, or should build a unique society on the basis of her traditional institutions and concepts. After emigrating in 1847, Herzen began to accept that the Russian peasant commune might well be the factor enabling Russia to bypass the capitalist phase of development. The commune, with its implication that the land belongs to those who collectively cultivate it, had prepared the people for the principles of socialism; hence the latter would be more easily accepted than in western Europe, where the capitalist mentality was well entrenched. Like many of his generation, Herzen did not exclude the possibility of the tsar himself introducing the needed reforms; the centuries-old acceptance of the autocrat as the agent of revolutionary change was slow to disappear.

When the long-repressed revolutionary movement emerged after the death of Nicholas, it was largely in the hands of students, or recent students. Alexander II had soon removed many of the previous restrictions on university entry, and this had led to an increase of student numbers, especially of students from poorer backgrounds. More than half the students relied on state financial help. Many were undernourished and diseased. Student cooperatives, organizing communal kitchens and libraries, emerged as a form of self-aid, while a student *esprit de corps* developed in reaction to poor teachers, absurd discipline, and the police actions which were the authorities' all-too-frequent response to complaints. In 1861 there were large-scale disturbances, and the government's response was a reduction of scholarships and a ban on student meetings. At St Petersburg University the students retaliated by breaking into a locked lecture room to hold a protest meeting, marching through the city, and boycotting lectures. Several hundred were gaoled for a couple of months and the university was closed until 1863. In Moscow there were similar disorders and several injuries, inflicted by local inhabitants who had been persuaded by the police that the demonstrators were either young landowners demanding the retention of serfdom or, worse, were Poles.

Student and peasant disturbances, with growing governmental repression, persuaded many that peaceful transformation was no longer likely. Those who, like Herzen, still shrank from a violent revolution found themselves criticized as old-fashioned and ineffective. The younger generation increasingly gave its adherence to Chernyshevsky and his like-minded colleagues on the editorial board of *The Contemporary* who, within the limits of the censorship, were advocating the imposition of socialism by revolution if necessary. Chernyshevsky was well aware of the price of revolution but many of those whom he inspired were not; the futile violence advocated by some of his followers led to public alienation and his own imprisonment.

The more realistic dissidents perceived that 'the people' did not yet want a revolution, and that the successful revolutionary must spend years, even decades, preparing people's minds. Notable among such thinkers in the 1860s was Pisarev who, apart from his aversion to revolution-at-any-price, had great faith in the scientific method as the solution to all problems. The good society he envisaged was a kind of technocracy, with an educated elite providing the leadership. Pisarev was described by conservatives as a 'nihilist', a word which became popular among those seeking derogatory generalizations for those who were against tradition, against authority, and against hypocrisy. With the help of conservative journalists, 'nihilism' soon became associated in the public mind with young people who were alarmingly immoral, godless, freeloving, subversive, treasonous, indecent, dirty, and with menacing hairstyles:

According to popular opinion the Nihilists were a band of fanatical young men and women, mostly medical students, who had determined to turn the world upside down and to introduce a new kind of social order, founded on the most advanced principles of social equality and Communism. As a first step towards the great transformation they had reversed the traditional order of things in the matter of coiffure; the males allowed their hair to grow long, and the female adepts cut their hair short, adding occasionally the additional badge of blue spectacles . . .

This was the ridiculous side of the movement, but underneath the absurdities there was something serious. These young men and women, who were themselves terribly in earnest, were systematically hostile, not only to accepted conventionalities in the matter of dress, but to all manner of shams, hypocrisy, and cant . . . while ridiculing romanticism, they had romantic sentiment enough to make them sacrifice their time, their property, and sometimes even their life, to the attainment of an unrealizable ideal . . . I must say that, without at all sharing or sympathizing with their opinions, I could not help respecting them as honourable, upright, quixotic men and women who had made great sacrifices for their convictions . . .

In a satirical novel of the time a little girl is represented as coming to her mother and saying, 'Little Mamma! Maria Ivan'na, our new schoolmistress, says there is no God and no Tsar, and that it is wrong to marry!' Whether such incidents actually occurred in real life, as several friends assured me, I am not prepared to say, but certainly people believed that they might occur in their own families, and that was quite sufficient to produce alarm even in the ranks of the Liberals, to say nothing of the rapidly increasing army of the Reactionaries.[10]

The reading public, regaled with the real and imagined superficial characteristics of the nihilists, rarely noticed that these young people did not merely reject the old but also sought a better alternative, even though they had not yet agreed on the latter. Certainly many of those who called themselves nihilists did so uncreatively out of a desire to be fashionably radical, but for the sincere dissidents the misrepresentation of their views was a factor driving many of them to extreme forms of revolutionary activity.

Of the varied groups meeting in the 1860s, Land and Liberty was notable. It was very radical, and against reformism. Bakunin, who was a heroic figure for the young revolutionaries, gave his blessing to this organization, although Herzen disapproved of it. Another revolutionary circle was the Committee of Russian Officers in Poland. The latter prepared a rising in Poland, hoping to persuade fellow-officers and soldiers not to fire on the rebels. But the Polish Rebellion of 1863 was premature. The troops remained loyal to the Tsar, and there was much bloodshed. Herzen reluctantly gave his approval to the rising, but was probably not surprised when his *Kolokol* immediately lost readers; even Russian radicals were not immune to 'Great Russian chauvinism', especially when the Poles were involved. Like dissidents at other times and places, Herzen had to admit that the public can be worse than the government, and the journalists worse than the public. Land and Liberty was crushed by the wave of arrests which followed the Polish Rebellion, but other revolutionary circles continued. These represented a variety of opinions, and inside

10. D. Mackenzie Wallace, *Russia* (1961), 449–52.

each there was again a difference of views. One circle, generally devoted to Chernyshevsky's socialism, harboured an extremist wing calling itself Hell, which attracted romantic young men anxious to become instant martyrs, and obsessed with all kinds of ill-thought-out schemes of violence. In 1866 one of them, Karakazov, a sickly youth believing that he was suffering from a progressive and incurable mental disease, sought to win a glorious place in history by murdering the Tsar. But his bullet flew wide of its august target. He was immediately arrested and found to be carrying a list of the members of the circle. One arrest led to another, and one circle led to others, including those of the moderates. The latter were now unable to carry out their plans for on-the-spot propaganda and study in the provinces; this delayed for some years the revolutionaries' discovery of what 'the people', on whose behalf they were acting, were really like.

Apart from intensified censorship, the banning of some periodicals, and the arrest of genuine or suspected revolutionaries, Karakazov's shot also led to closer supervision of higher education because he had himself once been a student. Student cooperatives were banned because, although recognized as an aid to poor students, they provided good places to exchange revolutionary opinions and leaflets. But police action inside the universities continued to radicalize students whose indignation overcame their reluctance to break the law.

Students were too young to remember what life under Nicholas I had been like, so they seemed ignorant and ungrateful to administrators who had struggled under Nicholas to develop their reforms. Most newspapers blamed 'outside agitators' for student troubles, choosing to ignore the factors which made the students receptive to subversive ideas. One such agitator was Tkachev. Like many other revolutionary ideologists, he was of the 'penitent nobility'. He was a journalist and one of the first Russians to be interested by Marx, although his ideas came mainly from Chernyshevsky. He was as opposed to the moderate reformers as he was to the regime itself. For him, violent revolution was the only solution and revolutionaries, being entrusted with so high a task, were absolved from the bounds of conventional morality. He formed a group to radicalize the students; that is, to convert the wide-spread student grievances against their universities into a hostility towards the regime. After renewed student unrest in 1869 he was imprisoned, but soon escaped abroad.

One of Tkachev's admirers was Nechayev, a student of proletarian origin. It was probably he who presented the police with a list of students sympathetic to the radicals, hoping that the resulting arrests would convert the 'liberals' into real revolutionaries. Nechayev also fabricated and planted evidence that he had been arrested but had succeeded in escaping from the hitherto prisoner-tight Peter-Paul Fortress. Having with this and other tales made himself into a student hero, in 1869 he paid a visit to émigré revolutionaries in

Switzerland and convinced Bakunin that he controlled thousands of revolutionary students. In return for this fictitious asset, he received a certificate signed by the great anarchist himself, declaring that Nechayev was a representative of an émigré organization controlled by Bakunin (equally fictitious, unknown to Nechayev). During his stay in Geneva, Nechayev published several leaflets calling for a destructive revolution. Some of these were smuggled into Russia, but others were sent through the mails in the hope that the addressees would be arrested and thereby radicalized.

When Nechayev returned to Russia, the prestige of Bakunin's alliance brought enough supporters to at last turn his fictitious organization into a real one. The ideology of the movement was expressed in the *Catechism of the Revolutionary*. This declared that a revolutionary should be totally dedicated, should not allow himself to be distracted by questions of survival or by noble feelings, should be absolutely vicious and selfish for the sake of the new benevolent society to come. The aim was to kill the intelligent and the influential, who might hamper the ruthless course of the revolution. However, hated or corrupt figures of the regime were to be spared, because their acts served to incite the people. Liberals were to be enticed into conspiracy by working on their consciences and then, once they had broken the law, blackmailed into doing the dirty work of the revolution. The *Catechism* drew the conclusion that since the masses would not revolt unless they were desperately miserable, and since they could be made happy only through revolution, it was the duty of the revolutionary to ensure long-term social happiness by intensifying short-term social misery. Nechayev's post-revolutionary society (ridiculed by Marx as 'barracks communism') was to be communistic, with a controlling central committee, and various compulsions: compulsory physical labour for all, including mothers, compulsory membership of a workers' organization, and compulsory utilization of communal dining halls and dormitories. Nechayev organized his membership into small cells which were unknown to each other. He insisted on the strictest secrecy and obedience. This enabled him to send on suicidal missions those members whom he distrusted, to set one member to spy on another, and to convince his handful of members that they belonged to a vast underground organization. In his dealings with the cells he spoke as the representative of an all-powerful and highly secret central committee. This in reality had but one member, Nechayev himself.

When Nechayev was opposed by one of his doubting comrades, he had him murdered. The discovery of the body led to the discovery of the organization. Murder was not a political crime, so Nechayev's flight to Switzerland in late 1869 ended in extradition and imprisonment for life. The trial of his comrades, who had not fled, and especially the reading of the *Catechism* in court, enormously damaged the whole revolutionary movement, even though Nechayev represented only an anarchistic fringe. Many who had been sympathetic to radical thought came to believe that all revolutionaries resembled these cold-blooded conspirators, whose only achievement had been the savage murder of one of their more scrupulous members. Dostoevsky's novel *The Possessed*, inspired by the Nechayev episode, perpetuated this disquiet.

Circles and groups normally had short and undistinguished lives, but some developed through successive stages to play an influential role in the revolutionary movement. One such was the so-called Chaikovsky circle which, like so many others, originated in a student commune, where young people joined together with the aim of self-education. Gradually becoming radicalized, it then started to distribute books and left-wing literature among interested workers. This radicalization was largely the result of the persecution of students after Karakazov's assassination attempt. All kinds of anti-student incidents had occurred. In one city women with cropped hair had been banished, on the grounds that they looked like nihilists, while in St Petersburg such women had been handed yellow tickets, the ultimate insult.[11]

But the Chaikovsky circle, though it was visited by Nechayevites, was of moderate disposition. A St Petersburg women's circle soon merged with it.[12] That circle, which included the subsequently celebrated Sofia Perovskaya, was interested in self-education but also in sexual equality and the provision of higher education for women. It was one of many which was moving from an interest in purely female questions to participation in the radical, and then revolutionary, movement as a whole. The Chaikovsky circle was soon much more than a circle, having branches outside the capital. Perhaps under the influence of the anarchist Prince Kropotkin, its programme began to resemble that of Bakunin and the anarchists, but by 1873 it was disappearing, thanks largely to successive arrests of its leading members.

The 1870s was the great decade for revolutionaries seeking a socialism based on the peasantry. These revolutionaries were called Populists (*Narodniki*), but later the term Populist was applied misleadingly, and often against their will, to all those from Herzen to the anarchists who sought a revolutionary change enabling Russia to escape the capitalist stage of development. The true Populists of the 1870s idealized the traditional agricultural commune, and the traditional cooperative workshop (*artel*); many believed that these two institutions would provide a base on which economic development could be built without recourse to capitalism with its big factories, centralized control, unequal distribution of wealth, and reduction of the individual to a cog in the

---

11. After long discussion, under Nicholas I the prostitution problem had been tackled by compelling prostitutes to carry a yellow registration card. This lasted until 1917.

12. This group, like others, came originally from women following 'Alarchin' courses, which were higher education courses, somewhat informal, which women were allowed to attend and soon almost monopolized. Other women had gone for education abroad, especially in Zurich, where they were often influenced by Russian émigrés.

economic machine. Two ideologists of Populism were Mikhailovsky and Lavrov, both of noble birth and both journalists. Lavrov's *Historical Letters* of 1868 had added a new element to Populism by arguing that only the intellectual elite, united in a party, would be able to assure the people's welfare. It was, moreover, the intellectual's duty to serve the masses, for it was their labours which in effect had paid for his education. The new Populist circles, distrustful of Nechayev-type central committees, were uncoordinated. Wary of Nechayev's cold-blooded violence, they stressed a clean-hands policy. They were more interested in propaganda work among the workers and peasants. In 1874 and 1875 there was a 'going to the people'. Perhaps as many as two or three thousand young men and women, dressed as workers and peasants,[13] settled in the villages and industrial cities. The ever-hopeful Bakuninists anticipated that their arrival would ignite an instant rebellion, while the Lavrovites regarded it as the start of the long process of winning people's minds. But the results were disappointing for all. The peasants, perhaps recalling that 'the egg does not teach the hen', were unconvinced and unimpressed by their young visitors.

Many of the young missionaries were arrested. The subsequent trials only strengthened the will of both the arrested and the survivors. Two notable trials were held in 1877. At the 'Trial of the Fifty' the idealism and the honesty shown in court by the defendants made a great impression on the public; the Russian Christian mind was not slow to see saintliness in the accused. The long prison sentences which were imposed gained the victims additional sympathy. At the 'Trial of the 193', involving almost 200 defendants (some of whom died in prison before the trial opened), the prosecution presented the scattered activities of the various individuals and circles as though they were all part of one gigantic conspiracy. This attempt to make the prisoners appear more dangerously subversive than they really were did not, apparently, impress the court, for sentences were light and there were many acquittals. Those acquitted, however, were immediately deported to Siberia by the so-called administrative procedure. Of the eighty condemned, twenty-eight were described as being of the nobility, seventeen were sons or daughters of priests, ten were middle class, five were children of government officials, five were peasants, and three were foreigners.

The failure of the 'going to the people', and the arrests, encouraged the extremists among the revolutionaries. They argued that the people were far from revolutionary and that government-encouraged capitalism with its ethic of private property and free enterprise was making the people ever less receptive to socialist ideas. It would be better to make the revolution first and win people's minds afterwards. Many of those who had not been arrested

13. There were even reports of young Jews converting to Orthodoxy so as to be closer to 'the people'.

joined a resurrected Land and Liberty. This reverted to a strong central organizing committee, in reaction to the ineffectiveness and muddles of the post-Nechayev unorganized circles. Its programme (with which not all its members were in agreement) included the allocation of all land to the peasants and the abolition of the state apparatus, to be achieved by a revolution which would take place as soon as possible. Its central organization possessed the two essential tools of the revolutionary, a secret press to print its leaflets and a section skilled in the forgery of passports and other documents. It also owned a prize horse.

With great caution, Land and Liberty formed cells in town and country. Its first big manifestation was in St Petersburg, where a demonstration, organized by and on behalf of discontented workers, was taken over by radical students. There was a particularly violent speech by a student named Plekhanov, and then a procession formed, soon broken up by the police with the help of hooligans. Land and Liberty had a section devoted to violent action, whose task was the freeing of imprisoned members, and the murder of informers or of key or despotic administrators. Among others, the head of the Third Section and a high official of the Kiev police were killed, the former in broad daylight with the two assassins escaping with the aid of the society's light-footed horse. The government was alarmed, but in some quarters the revolutionaries' daring and success earned admiration. The government decreed that cases of political violence would be tried henceforth by military courts. Within the society there was a widening split between those who wished to develop the terroristic branch and those who did not. Attacks on some men could be justified as defensive measures against official illegality and brutality, but indiscriminate murders seemed likely to alienate the masses. Vera Zasulich was among those who opposed unrestricted violence, and so was Plekhanov. These differences came to a head when a would-be regicide appealed for assistance from the society. Several members of its central committee pointed out that attacks on the Tsar could only lead to mass arrests of the innocent, and would bring the society into disrepute since the masses, especially the peasants, still revered the monarch and believed simply that his good intentions towards them were being thwarted by the gentry in the administration. The society compromised, simply refusing to make available its horse. The attempt was made. All five shots missed, the assassin failed to poison himself as planned, was hanged, and Land and Liberty was blamed. Many arrests followed.

Disagreement on the uses of terrorism in 1879 caused a formal though amicable break between those like Plekhanov, who wished to concentrate on propaganda, and those who were devoted to violence. The latter became the People's Will, while the former took the name of Black Repartition (referring to their proposed redistribution of the land). The People's Will had a strong executive committee, organizing a membership which was probably in the region of four or five hundred. It was probably the biggest of the nineteenth-century Populist organizations, but its members never agreed on a common ideology and tactics; although it was called Populist, it inclined towards the anarchists. By this time the revolutionary movement included fewer gentry; the People's Will was largely composed of young men and women from the middle class or from the educated lower classes.

The declared aim of the People's Will was the destruction of the state, followed by the taking of power by the people and a redistribution of economic power on socialist lines; only the people could fill the post-revolutionary vacuum because there did not exist any organized force in Russia that could usurp the leadership. The People's Will had no intention of becoming an elite governing party. Its chosen role was to ignite the revolution by a campaign of necessary but regrettable terrorism. The group became mistakenly obsessed with the supposed necessity of killing Alexander II, persuading itself that the murder of the Tsar would alone cause revolution. A plan to dynamite the royal train was adopted. Tunnels were dug under the rails, and dynamite placed in readiness. But of the three mines, one was laid under the wrong route, one failed to explode because the battery had been wrongly assembled, while the third was successfully detonated under the wrong train. A well-planned scheme to blow up a St Petersburg bridge as the Tsar passed over it came to nothing because one of the pair entrusted with the detonation arrived too late, not having a watch. Yet another attempt in 1880 demonstrated the same courage, determination, and technical incompetence. Dynamite was secreted under the dining room of the Winter Palace, but the conspirators fired the charge before enough had been accumulated; some guards were killed but Alexander was unhurt.

The government, picturing hordes of revolutionaries busily tunnelling like moles all over Russia, was driven to unusual measures. Loris-Melikov, soon to be minister of the interior, initiated a programme of short, sharp repression, to be followed by a new leniency. Some students were hanged merely for distributing leaflets, but Tolstoy, the much-disliked minister of education, was dismissed. Fact-finding missions were dispatched to the provinces and Loris-Melikov persuaded Alexander to agree to the establishment of a 'General Commission', including some members elected by the *zemstva* and city councils, as a consultative body. This commission would have fallen far short of a national assembly, but it would nevertheless have been a short step towards popular participation. The Third Section was also abolished at this time, although its functions were transferred to a department of the ministry of the interior. Loris-Melikov improved its organization and tried to ensure that it interested itself only in genuinely dangerous persons (more than 31,000 citizens were by this time under surveillance). The apparent government concessions reduced the appeal of the People's Will, and the group was further weakened by the arrest of a conspirator who turned informer. A last, desperate almost, conspiracy to kill Alexander was therefore hurriedly devised. The attempt was to be made when the Tsar was passing down a main street in St Petersburg. More by luck than good management this attempt was successful. Two bombs were thrown and the second mortally wounded the Tsar (1881).

5

Alexander III

Violence and counter-violence

THE coming of railways and of the telegraph alarmed custodians of law and order, fearful of how these technological innovations could make work easier for criminals. As things turned out, railways and telegraphy made things easier for the police, too. There was no such consolation with the invention of dynamite in the 1860s; it was a godsend for terrorists. No longer was an assassination dependent on a lucky revolver shot, or on a knife-man evading the bodyguards. As the murder of Alexander II had shown, all that was needed was a couple of bomb-throwers, each accompanied by a 'spotter' to signal the target's approach. The new technology did, perhaps, demand a new kind of assassin, who was prepared to kill a score or so of innocents in order to make sure of the target.

What was certain was that enhanced police protection was required. The assassination of Alexander II was followed immediately by the 'Decree Concerning Measures for the Protection of State Order and Social Tranquillity', which strengthened the gendarmerie and established the *Okhranka*, or Okhrana.

While the ordinary police (dealing with minor crimes and disorderly behaviour) were regarded with some justified contempt by the ordinary Russian, the Okhrana soon gained a sinister reputation. In theory, its arrestees had to be released within a month or placed on proper trial, but this did not always happen. Moreover, with the assent of the interior minister, suspects could be dealt with 'administratively', providing the sentence did not exceed five years of exile.

The Okhrana employed thousands of informers, both 'outsiders' and 'insiders'. The latter were those who were members of suspect groups and kept their superiors informed of what was happening. If it seemed that a group was, or might become, a danger to the state, then its members were arrested and exiled. No doubt genuine revolutionaries, and terroristic conspiracies, were broken in this way, but so were many innocents, and non-violent dissident opinion was suppressed. The insiders were sometimes professionals who worked their way into the confidence of those they would betray. Many actually planned and encouraged terroristic crimes so as to disarm suspicion and, in some cases, help their careers. Others had been genuine conspirators who had been blackmailed or bribed to change sides, or who had undergone a real change of heart and were ready to spy on their friends. In 1914 three of the seven members of the Bolsheviks' key Central Committee in St Petersburg were police informers. It was acknowledged that the insiders were often shady characters, but the outsiders were the pride of the organization. To ensure that only men of high character were employed in this side of the Okhrana, great pains were taken: Poles and Jews were excluded, and recruits were sworn-in before an Orthodox priest The outsiders were masters of disguise, and were entrusted with the observation and tracking of suspects and listening to the conversations of ordinary citizens. Many of them masqueraded as city cab drivers, for this occupation gavé the best opportunity for eavesdropping. Others specialized in the opening, reading, and skilful resealing of suspects' correspondence, or in code-breaking. By 1917 special security sections of the Okhrana had offices in all major cities, and also an office in Paris to watch émigrés. Major post offices had 'dark rooms' where mail was read, and all foreign mail was scrutinized. The first phone-tap was in 1910. There were about 1,000 insiders and 2,000 outsiders, and the Okhrana card-indexes were said to contain millions of names. Despite all this, in 1906–9 about 6,000 state officials were assassinated.

After the murder of Alexander II, one of the bomb-throwers made a full confession, betraying his comrades. Five of the conspirators were hanged, including one woman, Sofia Perovskaya, who was the daughter of a former governor of St Petersburg. The army mutiny and civil disorders which the assassination had been expected to ignite did not take place; soldiers and citizens resented the murder. Meanwhile a law (destined for a long life) was passed which made it possible for the ministry of the interior to declare states of emergency in provinces or regions. Among other things, this enabled civilians to be tried by military courts according to wartime regulations, bringing swift verdicts and a restricted audience for stirring speeches by the accused.

Arrests weakened the People's Will, which never regained its previous strength, but neither the government nor its supporters realized how weak it had become; it was at this time that the short-lived Holy League, an unofficial counter-terrorist organization, was set up by a group of reactionaries intending to meet violence with violence. Count Tolstoy, who became interior minister, was convinced that terrorists were lurking behind every corner. He refused to participate in police matters, appointing a deputy minister to do that part of his work and frankly acknowledging that he wanted somebody else to be shot at. This proved only a short-term comfort, and within a few years Tolstoy was a bag of nerves, finally expiring in 1889. Meanwhile the improved police methods, notably the Okhrana's success in turning arrested revolutionaries into police agents, and the ability to banish suspects, was keeping violence under control. But the greater the success of the Okhrana in uncovering plotters, the stronger became the belief that would-be assassins were everywhere. Alexander III carried a loaded revolver, and ordered that officers attending him on inspections should be unarmed.

The weakened central committee of the People's Will, in view of the failure of its terrorism to spark a popular revolution, soon inclined towards the possibility of a revolution made by a small conspiratorial minority, which would impose a socialist system before handing over power to the people. Its supporters abroad opposed this change, accusing it of seeking power not for any cause, but for the sake of power itself. There was a split in the group, and it was further weakened by the presence on its central committee of a police informer. At times it sank to anti-Semitism, welcoming the pogroms as a form of popular rebellion and condemning those police forces which intervened against 'the people' to protect the Jews.

Subsequent historians, partly for the sake of clarity, identified different groups by the name of their supposed leader, even though most groups did not acknowledge such leadership, seeing themselves as bands of equals. Similarly, a kind of false clarity was obtained by presenting movements like Land and Liberty, Populists, and social democrats as though they were already parties. But they were not, and individuals might not only float from one to the other but also at a given moment be possessed of beliefs coming from one or more groups. It was the revolutionaries in emigration who built ideological walls around themselves and engaged in feuds against other revolutionary groups, frequently evolving dogmas in order to protect their positions. Inside Russia, revolutionaries of different groups often worked together and almost always had some sympathy for each other. From several accounts, one of the noblest of these broad-minded revolutionaries was Alexander Ulyanov, destined to be best known as Lenin's older brother.

Ulyanov and friends from Kazan University were drawn into a plot to assassinate Alexander III. Ulyanov gradually emerged as the most effective of these conspirators and, with considerable help from Polish revolutionaries, he manufactured the bombs. One of the plotters was picked up by the police in connection with another offence and in custody, for no apparent reason, told all. The conspirators were arrested red-handed, and at the trial Ulyanov did his best to concentrate the blame on himself. He was hanged, together with four others. Subsequently his younger brother Vladimir and his sister tried to reconstitute his political thoughts as the basis for their own development as revolutionaries. Vladimir, as Lenin, became an activist very different from his brother, jealously guarding his dogmatic purity and excoriating revolutionaries who differed from him. The execution of his brother, his long spells in emigration, and the failure of the old-type revolutionaries all contributed to this difference.

The powerful Socialist Revolutionary party (see p. 148) eventually developed from the remnants of the People's Will, but the other wing of the Populists, Black Repartition, turned to marxism. The great age of Russian Populism was finished. Populism had more viewpoints and outstanding individuals than can be mentioned here. But typically Populists were educated men and women attracted to radicalism while students, who would join a circle and, during their lifetimes as their views changed, proceed from one circle to another, often via prison. Thus circles which were almost unknown to anybody, or which due to arrests or dissension had a brief existence, could nevertheless be influential in moulding or changing the views of those who passed through them. Most Populists were against violence on principle. But the supposed need for an early revolution did persuade many to accept violence as a temporary necessity. Non-violence increasingly seemed to be a dead-end; opening the eyes of the ignorant masses was a slow process and, it seemed, would not be accomplished before the last propagandist died in gaol. Savage penalties imposed on young idealists whose only crime was to express their views in public predisposed more and more Populists to accept violence as a last resort.

Violence was a reflection of weakness as was, essentially, the violence practised by the government. The terrorism of the revolutionaries was understandable but counter-productive. The reason most frequently given for this conclusion is that Alexander II was on the point of introducing the beginning of a constitution at the time he was assassinated. But this presupposes that the reforms would have developed in the way the optimists expected, which seems doubtful. However, terrorism produced several other negative results. It alienated that part of the public which accepted the criticisms made by the Populists but could not tolerate their methods. It was excessively expensive in terms of money (which was never plentiful) and also in terms of personnel; almost every terroristic act was followed by a wave of arrests, and it was the outstanding members who tended to be caught first. While achieving nothing in the long run, this expenditure of money and members held back the less dramatic but less unpromising propaganda work among the people. Violence also reduced the influence of those state administrators who believed in reform, although for the more extreme revolutionaries this was a positive result.

Although in 1917 the heirs of the Populists, the Socialist Revolutionaries, failed to exploit their potential strength, it is wrong to belittle the movement simply because it never gained power. It was the Populists who made a start in developing the political consciousness of ordinary people. Moreover, their actions inspired, and their ideological discussions informed, later generations of revolutionaries, including the marxists. Above all, those Populists who distrusted western industrial society may have been right. As Peter the Great had discovered, and as subsequent tsarist and Soviet governments would discover, the Russian masses did not relish westernization, especially when the fruits of westernization were not immediately apparent. Yet western modes of production to be fully effective required western attitudes to life and work. For underdeveloped countries the westernization of technique is relatively easy, but imposed westernization of culture is difficult and perilous because it threatens the soul of a nation.

On the eve of the 1905 Rebellion the working-class component of those arrested for revolutionary activities was approaching 50 per cent, a rise from around 16 per cent in the 1880s. This was despite attempts to improve the workers' lives at a time when fast industrialization was creating obvious problems of urban housing, low wages, and worker militancy. Plehve, head of the police department, chaired an 1880s committee to review labour laws and discovered that, for example, up to half a worker's pay was taken back in the form of fines, and another proportion disappeared through the compulsion to buy the necessities of life from company stores. Managers could oblige workers to do overtime above the twelve-hour day without compensation. When the government decided to eliminate night work for women and children it was opposed by Moscow (but not St Petersburg) industrialists who urged that night work kept women off the streets at night.[1] The government did legislate to improve conditions and reduce hours for women and children, but it never went far enough. Many within the government opposed such legislation, fearing that foreign capital would flee if labour costs rose. Some were unable to see workers as part of a working class, but only as part of the peasantry. It was only a big strike in 1897 that won an eleven-and-a-half-hour working day (and small workshops were not covered). Plehve was wise enough to oppose the use of troops against strikers. The factory law of 1886 increased penalties for striking but also increased the number and powers of factory inspectors.

Alexander III and his ministers

Alexander III's intellect was far from scintillating, although this judgement has to take into account the alcoholic fog in which he seems to have done most of his ruminating. Nobody denied his honesty, nor his loyalty to subordinates. His hatred of war aroused mixed feelings; it may have been at the root of Alexander's growing preference for the views of the finance ministry against those of the war ministry, and therefore a factor in Russia's economic development. But war ministers did not see it that way. In the Russo-Turkish War Alexander commanded 70,000 men in battle and knew what a battlefield really looked, sounded, and smelt like. Perhaps because of his experience,

1. Moscow industry consisted largely of small enterprises producing consumer goods, whose owners claimed that long hours and low pay were essential to beat off competition from Poland. St Petersburg industrialists, who liked to think of their premises as factories (*zavody*) in contrast to the workshops (*fabriki*) of the Muscovites, tended to be more progressive in their labour policies, but not out of altruism.

unlike other tsars he loathed military pomp and was adept at finding reasons to miss parades.

His suspicion of liberalism may have come largely from his education, but he had, after all, seen how his father's reforms had been followed by terrorism. One of his first acts, prompted by his adviser Pobedonostsev, was to reject the constitutional proposals which his father had been ready to introduce. This rejection, and Pobedonostsev's apparent dominance, was followed by the resignations of the more progressive Loris-Melikov and Dmitri Milyutin. The reign was notable for the persecution of national and religious minorities and the partial reversal of several promising reforms developed during the reign of Alexander II. However, Alexander III's administration has been credited with two successes: it kept Russia out of war, and it helped industrial development. The first achievement is perhaps over-praised; after all, Alexander only reigned thirteen years, and moreover he laid the foundations of the Russo-Japanese War. His achievement of a French alliance certainly changed the international situation, but not necessarily for the better. More sustainable is the economic achievement of Alexander's minister Bunge. As finance minister (1881–6) and chairman of the Committee of Ministers (1887–95), Bunge helped several industries by tariff protection and railway-building, established the factory inspectorate, reduced peasants' redemption payments, established the Peasant Land Bank to help peasants buy additional land from the nobles, abolished poll-tax, and envisaged a universal income tax; he introduced Russia's first income tax in 1885, but this was on businesses only. It was his successor as finance minister, Vyshnegradsky, who started collecting peasants' taxes immediately after the harvest, forcing them to sell their grain when prices were low, which meant they had to place more on the market. This in turn ensured that they had nothing in reserve, so the famine of 1891 became a major tragedy.

The finance minister from 1892 was Witte, one of tsarist Russia's most notable ministers. The son of an official and of Germanic ancestry, Witte had graduated from Odessa University and soon entered the administration of a then-private railway company. He appears to have attracted Alexander III's attention by indiscreetly warning other railway officials, despite the Tsar's displeasure, that their timetables for the imperial train were likely to break the imperial neck. In a subsequent derailment (1888), caused by excessive speed over neglected track, Alexander was unhurt, and in 1892 Witte became minister of transport. The same year he was promoted to minister of finance. During his eleven years in this office he developed the expansionist economic policies favoured by Bunge. Large-scale railway construction, more protectionist tariffs, the securing of foreign capital, and high taxation of the peasantry were his chosen methods of fostering home industry. Alexander had great faith in his advice, and so had foreign investors after he succeeded in elevating the rouble to the Gold Standard. Nicholas II had less confidence in him, and dismissed him in 1903, although he felt obliged to rely on him as prime minister in the critical year of 1905. Bunge and Witte were Alexander's best advisers but unfortunately, outside economic affairs, the Tsar was most influenced by Pobedonostsev.

Pobedonostsev's published works on Russian law and acquaintance with the right people had earned him appointment as tutor to the heir in 1865. Earlier, he had helped in the preparations for the 1864 Judicial Reforms, but this was his last participation in a liberal endeavour; by 1873 he was condemn- ing the jury system and had become a complete though intelligent reactionary. In the 1860s he gained great influence over his pupil Alexander. The latter was far from brilliant and therefore tended to respect the judgement of those who appeared to speak with intellectual authority. Pobedonostsev began to fear that the future Tsar was too inclined towards westernism and liberalism, but soon his prescribed reading changed Alexander's outlook. During the Russo- Turkish War, they became very close. This was unfortunate for Russia because Pobedonostsev, although he abandoned his Panslavist fervour, remained reactionary and was inflexibly devoted to the official Orthodox Church. Since Pobedonostsev was not only tutor and adviser to Alexander III, but later to Nicholas II, he was able to ensure that just when Russia needed continuing reform, the next two tsars would be implacably against change and, like Pobedonostsev, devoted to the principles of autocracy, Russianism, and Orthodoxy.

One year before the assassination of Alexander II, Pobedonostsev was appointed Over Procurator of the Holy Synod. This was on the recommen- dation of Loris-Melikov, whose views were very different from those of Pobedonostsev. Loris-Melikov had calculated that this appointment would gain him the favour of conservative and religious circles which otherwise would have resisted the new set of reforms which were being prepared. He also believed that Pobedonostsev would be less dangerous in this position, but was proved wrong; the Over Procurator not only had influence in the Church (which in turn influenced the population), but also was concerned with such matters as education and social welfare. Moreover, Pobedonostsev enhanced the importance of his office by persuading the Tsar to give it ministerial status, enabling him to participate in the Committee of Ministers. Pobedonostsev's earlier work in the Senate had taught him about the inefficiency of the bureaucracy, and it was this experience which led him to advocate government by a small body of well-informed and intelligent men surrounding the Tsar. He had no sympathy for democracy, which he termed 'the biggest lie of our time'. Pobedonostsev not only desired that all citizens of the Empire should become Orthodox Christians but also believed that the non-Orthodox must inevitably be disloyal. This attitude, that anybody who is different is necessar- ily hostile, was demonstrated in other actions, and was often a self-fulfilling allegation: Pobedonostsev treated loyal nonconformists so badly that they did become hostile to Russia, Orthodoxy, and autocracy. He died in 1907, having placed the regime firmly on the rails which would lead to 1917. In his last decade he was less influential for, in attacking the Lutherans of the Baltic provinces, he aroused powerful and influential enemies who succeeded in reducing the trust which Nicholas II felt for his former tutor.

The nationalities

Non-Great-Russian minorities accounted for 55 per cent of the Empire's population in 1897. To some extent all had been subject to a degree of Russification, but until the reign of Alexander III they had, in the main, retained their privileges and individuality. But after 1881 all this changed, and Russification remained the policy of the government up to 1917. This change in attitude was probably a combination of several factors. First there was the quest for standardization on the part of the bureaucracy. Then there were the dignitaries of the Orthodox Church. These had always sought the conversion of the non-Orthodox, both Christian and non-Christian, but in Pobedonostsev they had found a powerful supporter. The war ministry, too, was in favour of Russification, partly in the interests of a good military-style standardization, and partly because of the presumed security risk posed by the non-Russian borderland areas. By this time, too, many Slavophils had degenerated to a condition in which they no longer simply believed in the superiority of the Slavs and the Orthodox Church, but insisted that the Great Russians had a duty to impose their virtues on those brother Slavs who had not yet seen the light.

The Empire's nationalities could be divided into three groups: the mainly loyal, the mainly disloyal, and the Jews. The loyal, those in which a majority of the population was in favour of the relationship with the Russians and of carrying out the obligations imposed by such a relationship, included the Finns, the Baltic Germans, and the Armenians. These nationalities, however, were treated just as insensitively as were the potentially disloyal Ukrainians and Tartars, and the really disloyal Poles. Thus by 1917 the Finns in particular, and the Armenians, and some of the Baltic Germans had been driven into opposition to St Petersburg. In terms of security, Russification only weakened the Empire.

The administration, like so many of its successors, underestimated the strength of nationalism. There was some excuse for this, because much of what passed for national consciousness was artificial, fabricated by the intelligentsia. The latter was the sector most incommoded by Russianization, for the kinds of jobs it fancied required good command of the Russian language (and sometimes, officially or unofficially, Russian birth). Peasants had little concept of nationality at first, although in the Ukraine they would form the basis of local nationalism. The development and even creation of new national languages was a first step towards full-fledged nationalism, and intellectuals worked hard at this, when necessary combining real or imagined remnants of old discarded languages. In Estonia and Latvia the new languages were designed to oppose German, whereas in Lithuania the new language was directed against Polish. Elsewhere, new languages were to supersede Russian, the nationalists hoped. In course of time, the most successful nationalist parties proved to be those of left-wing inclination, which could combine class appeal with nation appeal.

In Poland, Russification had intensified earlier than elsewhere, following the abortive 1863 Revolt. The Warsaw educational district was absorbed into the Russian system, and in 1869 Warsaw University was closed, to reappear as a genuine university only during the German occupation of 1915. Under Alexander III the Polish language was prohibited as a language of instruction in all institutions, including primary schools, except for Polish language and scripture courses. Only for a few months was this prohibition lifted, as a temporary concession after the 1905 disturbances in Poland. The state service was more and more reserved for Russians, although some Poles found insecure positions in the bureaucracy outside Poland. When the Warsaw–Vienna Railway was nationalized, Polish executives and engineers were replaced by Russians, and Polish railwaymen had to perform their duties, like announcing train departures, in Russian only, even though they themselves and perhaps all the passengers were unfamiliar with that language. With rapid social change and urban growth there came a movement towards socialism, and this inspired a majority of the revolutionary groups. Poland being divided between Russia, Austria, and Germany, there was a multiplicity of noncooperating revolutionary groups. They achieved little. Many were arrested and executed. Others, including the socialist Pilsudski, were exiled to Siberia. But in 1914 Poles were still Poles. A famous general expressed the dislike felt by an influential section of Russian society towards not only the Poles, but Finns and other 'privileged' peoples of the Russian Empire:

I do not refer to those Poles who have begun to regard Russia as their Motherland, and the Russian language as their mother tongue; I refer to those Poles who inside Russia talk loudly, demonstratively, in Polish, even in official relationships, in buffets, and on railway platforms . . . Accepting this kind of Pole in the Russian railway service and in judicial or other departments is a big mistake. We have already paid for our trust in such Poles, notably on the Transcaucasus Railway and other lines in 1905.[2]

In the Ukraine the situation was somewhat similar to Poland, except that the nationalist movement was much weaker; probably a majority of the Ukrainian people were not greatly interested in the concept of an independent Ukrainian nation. There had been an influx of Russian and other non-Ukrainian people into this area, and many of them were in key positions; the

2. A. Kuropatkin, *Rossiya dlya russkikh* (1910), iii. 73.

local officials, for example, were mainly Russian. On the other hand repression and Russification were less intense, repression being directed only at the comparatively small intelligentsia, which included most of the nationalist movement. In 1863 the publication of a Ukrainian Bible had been forbidden, and until 1905 there were very few Ukrainian-language publications.

Although in Central Asia there was little overt Russification, in the Tatar areas of Russia the Orthodox Church carried on an intense and mainly forcible conversion campaign. By the end of the century well over 100,000 Tatars had become Christian. However, a large number, perhaps one-third, of these relapsed and, moreover, Muslim missionaries were simultaneously and less obtrusively converting neighbouring Christian peoples to Islam. Among the Crimean Tatars there also developed a strong and mainly secular nationalist movement. This, devoted to the regeneration and eventual union of the Turkic peoples, published its own newspaper and soon gained adherents among the Tatars in other parts of Russia. In 1905 an All-Russia Muslim League was established. After the 1905 Rebellion Muslim members of the Dumas had a forum in which to voice their complaints of the way Russian officials and Orthodox clergy put pressure on the Tatars and other Muslims, and of the official encouragement of Russian settlement in Central Asia and traditional Tatar areas, in many of which Russians had become a majority. But these remonstrations had no result; by 1914 the Muslim leaders were looking to Turkey as a source of inspiration, while the Muslim masses, who if left alone might have been loyal subjects, were becoming more and more resentful of Russian domination.

The situation in Armenia was complex. The Armenian nation was divided by the Russo-Turkish frontier, and those Armenians inside the Russian Empire considered themselves lucky and did what they could to help their compatriots, who from time to time were massacred by the Turks. The Russian government in the early twentieth century was anxious to improve relations with Turkey, and was embarrassed by the anti-Turkish activities of its Armenian citizens. Accordingly it encouraged the Azerbaizhani neighbours of the Armenians to harass the latter, and for several years there were civil disturbances, sometimes engineered and usually encouraged by the Russian local authorities, in which Azerbaizhanis would beat up, loot, and kill their traditional Armenian enemies. It was only the appointment of a relatively wise governor, who realized that one day the Armenians might be needed in a new war against Turkey, that prevented this nation turning completely against the Russian regime by 1914. However, as in neighbouring Georgia, there were many revolutionaries among the townspeople.

In Georgia, too, fear of the Turks was a strong factor in the acceptance by the local population of Russian domination. Yet here again, the unholy alliance between the Russian administration, the Russian Church, and the landowning class transformed what might have been a loyal domain into a hostile and strongly revolutionary nation. The serfs of Georgia on various pretexts had not been truly emancipated in 1861, as had the Russian serfs. This naturally had led to discontent, which would manifest itself in the initial success of the Georgian rebels in 1905. The Georgian Orthodox Church was alienated by the claim of the Russian Orthodox Church to supervise its affairs. After Russian troops were called in by the Russian Orthodox to chastise the local clergy, there was an outbreak of ecclesiastical assassination, in which church dignitaries of both persuasions were the victims and the instigators. Although on the eve of the First World War the peasants received more land and administration became wiser, Georgia was one of the least loyal and most revolutionary parts of the Empire.

Finland, like Poland, was becoming an industrial nation in the last half of the century. When Finnish products began to compete in Russian markets, new arguments were provided for those Russians who resented the continued existence of so-called privileged minorities living under the Tsar's protection. Not only were tariff barriers raised against Finnish products but at the turn of the century, under the auspices of Governor Bobrikov, various standardizing and Russianizing measures were introduced, despite the Finns' contention that, under the terms offered by Alexander I at the time of annexation, they were legally entitled to their privileges. Hitherto, Finns had been virtually free from military service, but now they were compelled to serve. The Finnish post office, and later the railways, became part of the Russian system. Russian laws were given precedence over laws passed by the Finnish Diet. Russian officials had to be brought in to replace recalcitrant Finns. Russian became an official language of the administration. In 1903 Bobrikov suspended the Finnish Constitution and in 1904 he was assassinated by a Finnish revolutionary. After the 1905 Rebellion the government was forced to make some concessions; the conscription law was rescinded and a new Diet established. The latter, in which the Social Democrats were the largest but not predominating party, was remarkable at the time because it was elected on a franchise which included female suffrage. But the new situation was not regarded as permanent by either the Finnish revolutionaries or the Russian nationalists. The Russian prime minister Stolypin, in particular, was determined to return Finland to what he considered its natural position, that of a Russian province. With the support of Russian nationalists and the unimpressive remnants of the Slavophil movement, and with the interesting slogan 'Russia for the Russians', the government in 1908 embarked on a new campaign to repress 'the separatists and traitors' of Finland. The Diet's powers were reduced, it was dissolved, re-elected, dissolved and re-elected again, then abolished. Russian police were introduced, partly to limit the refuge which Finland provided for Russian revolutionaries hardpressed in their own country. By 1914 there were very few Finns who openly advocated maintenance of ties with Russia.

In the Baltic provinces, the Russian government again failed to win the support of the local population. Nicholas I and Alexander II had resisted the campaign waged by certain Slavophils to Russianize these areas, but with the ascendancy of Pobedonostsev the Russifiers had their opportunity. With the encouragement of Pobedonostsev, the Orthodox Church, helped by government funds, campaigned against the local Lutheran Church. In Riga a huge Orthodox cathedral was erected, an object of resentment for most of the inhabitants. In the schools Russian replaced German, the University of Dorpat became the University of Yuriev (Yuriev being the Russian name of Dorpat) and its student body was no longer primarily German but mainly Russian. But while the German upper class was thus humiliated, the native lower classes were not appreciative, even though they disliked the Germans. For them it was a case of one alien dominating class replacing another. At this time native Estonians and Latvians were beginning to settle in the towns, and from this new class there emerged nationalist and revolutionary groups. After the shock of 1905 the pressure on the Germans was relaxed, for they had remained mainly loyal in that year. In neighbouring Lithuania the situation was less acute; there the Polish ruling class was not quite so obnoxious to the local inhabitants, and after the stern 'pacification' following the Lithuanians' participation in the 1863 Polish Rebellion, this area gave little trouble.

The Jews in Russia

When Alexander III became tsar there were about 5 million Jews in the Empire. They were officially regarded as an eccentric and undesirable part of the population. In 1835 new legislation had clarified the various laws and ordinances relating to them. The Pale, that area in which Jews were allowed to settle, was redefined; henceforth it consisted of Lithuania, Poland, the south-western provinces (including the Ukraine), and White Russia. In most of these areas Jews were not allowed to live in rural localities, and a few cities were also prohibited. In the Baltic provinces old settlers could remain but no Jews could enter as new settlers. Also, no Jews were permitted to settle along the western frontier. Other restrictions introduced or confirmed at this time were the prohibition against building synagogues close to Orthodox churches, on Jews employing Christian servants, and on the use of Hebrew in public documents. In the first part of Alexander II's reign, some concessions were made to the 'useful' Jews. Jewish merchants of the First Guild (those paying more than 1,000 roubles in taxes each year) were allowed to trade and reside anywhere in the Empire, university graduates had the same right and could henceforth enter government service, while incorporated artisans could obtain documents allowing them to work and live outside the Pale. But after the Polish Rebellion of 1863 (blamed in some quarters on the Jews), liberalization was halted. The rebellion intensified Russian nationalism and renewed anti-Semitism followed naturally. Influential newspapers forgot their sympathy for the Jews, and anti-Semitic literature of both intellectual and obscene content appeared. One book, forecasting a Jewish takeover of the Empire and the enslavement of its Christian population, was printed at state expense and distributed to government offices. Many Jewish schools were closed. The reorganization of town government in 1870 limited the participation of Jewish citizens; no Jew could become mayor, and Jewish representation on town councils could nowhere exceed one-third of the total.

It was in the reigns of Alexander III and his son Nicholas II that the situation of the Jews changed from uncomfortable to unbearable. In those thirty-six years, officially sponsored anti-Semitic hooliganism and brutality not only shocked the outside world, but brought forth the protests of foreign governments. The murder of Alexander II in 1881 was ascribed in some quarters to the Jews, and scarcely had the late Tsar expired before the first of a series of pogroms was launched against them. Essentially, a pogrom consisted of the assembly of a mob which would throng into the Jewish parts of a town, break into houses and shops, to loot, beat, rape, burn, and frequently kill the inhabitants. Local police, and even sometimes the local troops, seemed reluctant to intervene except against those Jews who were successfully defending themselves. In the 1881 disturbances, the minister of the interior was still Loris-Melikov, who was not the kind of man to instigate this sort of action. Yet the 1881 pogroms were well organized, with bands of hooligans brought in by train, well primed with alcohol and anti-Semitic indoctrination. Local authorities knew of planned pogroms in advance, and made preparations. It would seem that the force behind these disturbances was the Holy League, consisting of extreme nationalists and anti-Semites. Pobedonostsev was a supporter of this organization, and many high and middling officials were members. When Loris-Melikov was replaced by Ignatiev, a member of the Holy League, these 'spontaneous demonstrations of an outraged people' were intensified. However, it seems that the Tsar disapproved of this unseemly way of dealing with the Jews. Ignatiev was soon replaced by Dmitri Tolstoy at the ministry of the interior. Tolstoy, though disliking the Jews, certainly did not favour brutal civic disturbances, and for a time they ceased.

There were other ways to deal with the Jews, even after the dismissal of Ignatiev and the banning of the Holy League. Just before his departure, Ignatiev had issued what were called Temporary Regulations, which in fact lasted until 1917. Among the provisions of these was a ban on new Jewish settlers in all rural areas of the Pale, a ban on Jews either owning or managing land, buildings, and farms outside the towns of the Pale, and a ban on Jewish trade on Christian holidays, including Sundays. Under cover of the latter regulation, as was no doubt anticipated, Jewish traders lost business to their Christian competitors, because they henceforth closed on both Christian and

Jewish holidays. Many Jewish businesses had to be sold at giveaway prices in the countryside because they had become illegal, and many Jewish settlers were turned out of their homes. It sometimes happened that a Jew who had made a trip outside his own locality would on his return be defined as a 'new settler' and ejected; in 1905 this even happened to wounded Jewish soldiers returning from the Manchurian front. Those Jews of the upper category who resided outside the Pale were harassed, and the thousands of Jews who were illegal residents were expelled, even though hitherto their presence had been ignored. Finally, in 1891, the governor-general of Moscow (Grand Duke Sergei) celebrated Passover by issuing an Edict of Expulsion which announced the ejection of legal as well as illegal Jewish residents. This edict was itself of doubtful legality, for it revoked an 1865 law, but was signed by the Tsar on presentation by the minister of the interior. Legal residents were given a few months' grace to settle their affairs, offering bargain sales of possessions and businesses to Muscovite Christians, and glorious opportunities for the police to gather bribes in exchange for time extensions. For the illegal or semi-legal residents, execution of the order was immediate and brutal. Other measures taken during the reign of Alexander III were the limitation of Jewish university students to 10 per cent of the total enrolment in universities within the Pale, 5 per cent outside, and 3 per cent at Moscow and St Petersburg universities; parallel limitations on gymnasium entries; the limitation to 5 per cent of Jewish military surgeons in the army because, as the official order alleged, of their bad effect on hygiene.

The Jewish reaction was mass emigration, especially to the USA and South America, and a strengthening of the Zionist movement. More important, with the Jews forming an urban and oppressed community it was natural that they should be attracted to the socialist and revolutionary parties. Thanks to official policy, the Jews provided a strong flow of ideal recruits for the revolutionaries: intelligent types hardened by circumstance and having little to lose. In 1897 the Jews' own social democratic *Bund* (union) was formed.

Under Nicholas II there was no likelihood of improvement. Pobedonostsev remained the Tsar's spiritual adviser, and Nicholas had imbibed his tutor's anti-Semitism. It is probably true that, whereas Alexander III merely strongly disapproved of Jews, Nicholas had a well-entrenched hatred of them. Sensing this, many provincial officials were encouraged to take actions which Alexander would have found excessive. Pogroms began again on a large scale, and existing restrictions were tightened. As in most fields of Russian official life, the application of anti-Semitic laws and policies was never absolute or complete; there were some officials, high and low, who were ashamed of the government's policy and would make exceptions wherever possible, and there were others who would make the same concessions for a bribe. Thus in reality there were usually Jews illegally resident outside the Pale, and Jewish students in excess of the legal proportion. Under Nicholas, however, such exceptions were rarer.

Pogroms, which typically took place as part of the Christian Easter celebrations, reached a new peak in the Kishinev outbreak of April 1903. The ground was laid for this by a local newspaper which for several weeks printed fantastic and frequently obscene anti-Semitic stories. It was probably sanctioned by Plehve, the minister of the interior, who, though himself no great anti-Semite, was anxious to please the Tsar. The army was slow to respond, possibly because the district commander was an avowed anti-Semite but also because the police and army commanders were at loggerheads. There were about fifty deaths and hundreds of injuries in the two days of the outbreak. It caused an outcry not only in Britain and the USA, but in Russia itself, with Leo Tolstoy openly accusing the government of complicity. In 1905, when the war against Japan was going badly, there were fresh outbreaks, and these were intensified after the 1905 Rebellion, in which Jews took a prominent part. In October a pogrom was organized, with the assistance of the local police, at Odessa. Probably about 500 lives were lost in this, which lasted four days. Further outrages followed in later years, despite the efforts of many members of the Duma to investigate them. Moreover, there were mass executions of Jews by the army, during the 'pacification' of the Baltic states and Lithuania.

It was at this time that a new organization, similar to the old Holy League, was formed to unite anti-Semites and nationalists for propaganda and pogrom work. This was the so-called Black Hundred, and the Tsar himself patronized this. It was the Black Hundred which established in 1905 the Union of the Russian People, a political organization in many ways a precursor of subsequent fascist parties and which was intended to be the overt instrument of the movement. In 1908 Nicholas received a delegation of the Union and agreed with a proposal to allow army chaplains and officers to join right-wing organizations; on this occasion Nicholas's much-condemned readiness to change his mind had positive results, for he soon backtracked in response to a war ministry presentation about the non-political status of officers. In fact, inside the army there was, as usual, a great variation of attitudes. On balance the war ministry, at least after 1905, favoured opening the officer corps to Jews, but the engineer generals were horrified by the idea of Jews or Poles[3] becoming officers, whereas the artillery strongly welcomed the proposal.

The reputation of the Empire abroad was badly damaged by its anti-Semitism, especially in the United States. Reacting to the pogroms which followed the assassination of Alexander II, Congress passed a joint resolution, nicely pointed:

To request His Imperial Majesty to exercise his august power . . . to protect the Jewish subjects from the violence of their enemies and to extend to them his protection as the

---

3. Nationalists and aggressive Panslavists usually put Jews and Poles at the top of their list of undesirables. As for Polish Jews . . .

late lamented sovereign, his father, did over the Christians of Bulgaria at a time when said Christians had been the victims of a like persecution.[4]

In 1911 the USA terminated the commercial treaty with Russia. The immediate cause of this was that foreign Jews, unlike other foreigners, had no clear right to visit and reside in Russia; thus there had been discrimination against Jewish US citizens. The termination caused a great stir in St Petersburg. The administration explained that if American Jews were given new rights, then Jews of other nations would demand the same treatment (which would enable them to settle in Russia outside the Pale). This nightmare vision of the world's Jews clamouring to settle in Russia did not seem very convincing, except perhaps to right-wing members of the Duma, who accused the American press, 'almost entirely owned or controlled by Jews', of trying to stir up hatred against Russia.

In 1913, the widely reported Beilis Case persuaded many that the tsarist administration was incorrigible. Beilis, a young inoffensive Jew, lived in Kiev near the scene of a murder in which a young Russian was murdered. The boy had in fact been killed on behalf of a woman who feared he might reveal her criminal activities. Two policemen who deduced this were dismissed. A court heard accusations against Beilis by bribed witnesses; he was said to have murdered in order to obtain Christian blood for one of those totally secret Jewish rituals that everyone knew about, but the result of this show trial was an acquittal, and a retrial produced the same result, although the retrial contrived an implication that unknown Jews had indeed been doing something nasty. The unsuccessful prosecutor and judge were rewarded afterwards, because they had clearly tried hard.[5]

A long-term success of official Russian anti-Semitism was the concoction of *The Protocols of the Elders of Zion*, produced in 1902 inside the police department. This fabrication, purporting to be a programme of conquest and corruption leading to a Jewish takeover of society, has been used worldwide by anti-Semitic propagandists ever since. A copy was found among Nicholas II's belongings after his death.

---

4. *Congressional Record*, 47th Congress, HR Res. 151, 1647.
5. Beilis subsequently emigrated. The woman who had arranged the killing was herself killed, by a lucky misfortune, in the Bolshevik Red Terror of 1918.

6

Russia in Asia

Grand duchy to empire

HELPED by its location on a river network, Muscovy had expanded over centuries. Under Peter the Great the growth continued, mainly in the north and west, and under Catherine it was towards the Black Sea. Because of the lack of natural frontiers, there was always an urge to expand one more stage, so as better to protect the most recently conquered zone. Alexander I had thought it necessary to conquer barren Finland from the Swedes simply to help protect St Petersburg. In the east and south-east, the preserve of nomads, it sometimes seemed that there was litle alternative to constant expansion because those nomads, descendants of the Mongols, delighted in raiding Russian settlements for plunder and slaves. The last successful raids on Moscow by Tatars were as recent as the late sixteenth century. In the Caucasus, Russia's links with Orthodox Georgia and Armenia seemed threatened by the mainly Muslim nationalities of the north Caucasus, and this invited territorial aggrandizement.

The expansion process finally produced what could be called an empire, and the Russian tsars began to call themselves emperors. Other countries took it for granted that the aim of the Russian emperors was to expand still further, although this was not always the case and, when it was, it was expansion for safety's sake as often as for gain. Britain's entry into the Crimean War had been stimulated more from a desire to check Russia's empire-building than from sympathy for the Ottoman Empire (Lord Palmerston toyed with the idea of throwing the Russians back from the Black Sea entirely). In due course the Russian Empire became the pride and joy of the tsars, the Slavophils, and many other Russians, but a problem for the foreign, interior, and war ministries (and later, even more so, for the navy ministry). It was unusual among empires in that it was a continuous land empire, so there was not a rigid division in people's minds between the motherland and the 'colonies'. On the whole the Russians felt good in the east, where they could persuade themselves that they were a superior people entrusted with the care of the natives.

Conversely, in the western borderlands, where the regime, helped by the Orthodox Church, was consciously engaged in protecting the native

Ukrainians and Byelorussians from Polish influence, Russians felt less assured, having a sneaking feeling that maybe Polish culture was more advanced than Russian. Apart from a late and hesitant move to extend the *zemstva* to the western borderlands, there would be no intention of allowing any form of local self-government. One of the more intellectual generals, Kuropatkin, would candidly observe that equality and freedom gave an advantage to people of the stronger culture over those of the weak culture. In the east, although in Siberia there was a more liberal kind of society, self-government was equally unthinkable.[1]

However, there were people who, in dark corners, might think the unthinkable. Describing the rule of Count Muravyov, the outstanding governor of East Siberia in the 1860s, Prince Kropotkin had this to say in his *Memoirs of a Revolutionist*:

[The Count] . . . had succeeded to a great extent in getting rid of the old staff of civil service officials, who considered Siberia a camp to be plundered, and he had gathered around him a number of young officials, quite honest, and many of them animated by the same excellent intentions as himself. In his own study, the young officers, with the exile Bakunin among them (he escaped from Siberia in the autumn of 1861) discussed the chances of creating the United States of Siberia, federated across the Pacific Ocean with the United States of America.

This idea would crop up again. In the late nineteenth century a Siberian autonomy movement was suppressed. It surfaced again after the Revolution, and yet again in the 1990s.

Russia in Central Asia

Russian interest in Asia dates back to at least 1469, when Nikitin visited India and wrote an account of the wonders he encountered. In the next century an Englishman employed by the Tsar visited Central Asia, and this was followed by the dispatch of emissaries to the various khanates of the region. Peter the Great sent expeditions to the Kazakh steppelands and to the khanate of Khiva. The latter expedition was instructed to steal the Amu-Darya River by diverting it into the Caspian Sea, but was massacred before it could achieve this. By 1800 the Kazakh nomads had acknowledged Russian sovereignty but this was hardly felt, even though Russian forts were maintained in the steppes. More alarming to the natives were the independent Cossacks who settled in the vicinity of those forts.

Alexander I decided to enforce his nominal rights over the Kazakhs. Russian military government with mainly Russian administrators was imposed. The Kazakhs were not allowed to grow crops, thus giving the Cossacks a monopoly

1. For a deeper understanding of the Russian Empire, a good place to start, and the site of a full bibliography, there is D. Lieven, *Empire* (2000).

in grain production. These measures, plus the burden of taxes, caused a number of revolts and an expansion of Russian territory as rebels were pursued into non-Russian lands. Throughout the century, campaign followed campaign as the Russians established a new frontier, built forts, pushed on to make those forts less vulnerable, and again established a new frontier. There were bigger campaigns in the reign of Alexander II, during which the last three major khanates were defeated. These conquests added big Muslim cities like Tashkent and Samarkand to the Russian Empire (see Map 4). The major part of this huge territory became the new Russian province of Turkestan, the defeated khans becoming vassals of the Tsar. Another province, Transcaspia, was set up in 1881 after General Skobelev had massacred a considerable part of the male Turcomans as a precautionary measure. The building of the Trans-Caspian Railway eastwards from the Caspian confirmed the Russian possession of this territory. As Russian influence neared the Himalayas, there was disquiet in London, largely baseless but not unwelcome to the Russians, who regarded British anxiety about India as a useful bargaining weight to set against their own vulnerability to a possible Anglo-Turkish threat from the Black Sea.

Although it was the government's intention to interfere as little as possible with the lives of the original inhabitants, this could not be reconciled with the intended development of the new territories. In agriculture there was an upheaval after a new direct railway brought Moscow to within three weeks of Tashkent by freight train. This enabled existing cotton cultivation to expand rapidly, supplying the textile industries of European Russia. The region became dependent on outside sources for its grain but, on the whole, the shift was beneficial, especially after the government embarked on a big irrigation programme. Much more serious in its effect was the Russian immigration. To find land for peasants arriving from European Russia, the original inhabitants were dispossessed, often by military force (the official euphemism was that the land was 'surplus'; the original owners did not really need it). The 1891 Steppe Statute allowed about 40 acres per family, which was enough for a settler but useless for a native nomad. Expropriation became more and more common as immigration increased, especially after Stolypin in 1910 decided that the region was ideal for his programme to relieve land hunger in European Russia. Although it is probably true that the new settlers used the land more efficiently, this was little consolation for the dispossessed who, typically, moved to less desirable land or to the towns. It was this virtual expulsion of the natives by the Russians which was, and remained, the prime grievance of the Muslims of Russian Central Asia. It was this resentment that underlay the savage conscription revolt of 1916 (see p. 213). In the 1950s Khrushchev's 'Virgin Lands' campaign would bring in more Slavic immigrants, making the Kazakhs even more of a minority in their own land.

The settlememt of Siberia

Not long after Ivan the Terrible captured the Tatar city of Kazan in 1552, Russian freebooters acting in the Tsar's name began to penetrate beyond the Urals. The big lure was furs, but the prospect of adding territory in the east was also an incentive. The pioneers, who later included Cossacks and regular soldiers, used the rivers as far as possible, constructing wooden forts at key points along them. Local tribes sometimes resisted, but in the long run were subdued and subjected to tribute, usually in the form of so many skins per year, the sable being especially sought. Tyumen, later an important Siberian town, was the first permanent settlement, being founded in 1586. Yakutsk was reached in 1637, and two years later a band of Cossacks reached the sea. Regular settlers were not far behind although, in contrast to the settlement of the American west, there was a generous sprinkling of state employees among the new inhabitants. Fur traders predominated, but the tsars sent administrators and soldiers to guard the interests of the state. Later, the fur traders were joined by cultivators, peasants coming east to seek freedom and land. In the eighteenth century, Russia's explorers discovered the Bering Strait and established settlements in Alaska, Oregon, and California. Later, there were expeditions to Japan and to Hawaii. With the foundation of the Russian America Company it seemed that the Pacific might well become a Russian lake.

In general, the Russians refrained from turning southwards to annex territory in which the Chinese Empire had an interest. Russian penetration into the Amur Valley had earlier led to conflict between the two empires, regulated by the Treaty of Nerchinsk in 1689; in this the Russians agreed to leave, and to recognize a frontier more to the north. But in the mid-nineteenth century, when China was weakened by the Opium Wars and when her territory was being divided by the powers into spheres of influence, Russia took advantage of the situation and forced on China a series of new treaties. The first of these, the Aigun 'Treaty of Friendship' in 1858 and the Peking Treaty of 1860, transferred extensive territories from China to Russia, including the northern shore of the Amur and the Maritime province east of the Ussuri River. It was in this latter acquisition that Russia established her new naval base of Vladivostok. The new territory also meant that Russia henceforth had a frontier with Korea. In 1875 Russia acquired Sakhalin from an unwilling Japan.

Although Russian expansion in the east at this time was inspired by a desire for expansion as such, and for military and commercial advantage, there were several nobler reasons which received more publicity. The Slavophils, and especially those who had progressed to Panslavism, emphasized the civilizing role which God had prescribed for the Russian people in the Orient. Others began to claim that Russia was indeed an Asian nation and therefore had much more moral right than the western powers to assert itself in Asia; later, the British imperialist Lord Curzon would disdainfully agree, describing Russian expansion as 'the conquest of orientals by orientals'. A world-famous Russian professor of international law justified the breach of treaties with the claim that, when dealing with uncivilized peoples, human rights could not be considered as having their usual force. Under Alexander III Russian officials began to dream not only of Manchuria and Korea, but also an eventual conquest ('liberation of subject peoples') of the moribund Chinese Empire and even the annexation of India. The more level-headed, such as Witte, were more cautious but nevertheless favoured a strong policy in the east, largely because the latter might provide that mass market which Russian industry seemed to need. Alexander's eastern policy had two prerequisites, a strong navy in the Pacific and a railway to supply Russian Far Eastern forces. These he set out to achieve.

Russian naval policy

In the 1880s Russia was the fifth largest naval power in terms of battleships, but ranked lower in terms of effectiveness, for her battleships were small, her ports iced up for several months each year, and her two fleets separated. On the other hand, she led the world in torpedo craft. The main preoccupation of her navy was the protection of cities like St Petersburg and Odessa from seaborne attack, and her myriads of small torpedo boats seemed a cheap way to achieve this. But although torpedo boats might defend the capital, they were of no account in an expansive foreign policy; it was battleships and bases which were needed. Just before his death Alexander II had sanctioned a new naval programme aimed at making Russia a real naval power. As approved by his successor in 1882, this programme covered twenty years and anticipated an expenditure of eighteen million pounds sterling (battleships at that time cost from half a million pounds apiece). By the late 1880s new ironclads built under this programme were joining the navy, although their impact was diluted because Russia, unlike the other powers, had to divide her ships between two fleets which could not be united; by treaty her ships could not move freely to or from the Black Sea.

The 1882 programme had stipulated that the hulls of the new ships should be built in Russia (engines continued to be imported, mainly from Scotland, and guns were usually Russian made but of foreign design). Complete self-sufficiency in shipbuilding was never attained, but the shipyards of St Petersburg expanded and were kept busy. Russian-built ships cost about one-third more than imports, and took longer to build. The ships were enclosed in enormous barns so that work could continue in the winter, but a hull which was not launched in the autumn had to wait six months for the thaw; the cruiser *Avrora*, which fired a famous shot in the 1917 Revolution, took six years to build. In 1898 a follow-on construction programme reflected increasing tension in the Far East and envisaged an expenditure of £51 m. over the period 1898–1904; eight new battleships with attendant cruisers and destroyers were to be built so that Russia would remain the world's third naval power.

After the Russo-Japanese War it was often said that Russian warships were of inferior design and construction, that Russian officers were incompetent, and that Russian sailors were dull. To some extent these criticisms could have been applied to any of the world's navies, and the Russian navy was not glaringly bad by the standards of that time. In some respects it led the world; for example, in mine and torpedo warfare, in the design of armour-piercing shells, and in the application of oil fuel. In the adoption of the watertube boiler, Russia was second only to France. As for her officers, there were indeed very many bad ones and some were corrupt. The Sevastopol trial of 1900 revealed that high officers of the Black Sea Fleet had been bribed by contractors to accept inferior supplies for their ships at superior prices, and this trial probably only revealed the tip of an iceberg. It is true also that there were many autocratic denizens of the quarterdeck whom a speck of dust would render apoplectic, but who were not in the least interested in accurate gunnery. But as in other navies, this type was slowly dying out. As for the sailors, these were mainly conscripts, and they had plenty of cause for dissatisfaction. They were bawled at rather than instructed, they were badly fed, during their seven-year active service they were not allowed to marry or to go home, and they had scant chance of promotion. Training was a slow process because the ships were activated only during the summer; ice prevented ship movements in winter, in both the Baltic base of Kronstadt and the Black Sea base of Sevastopol. Thus for half their service the crews lived ashore in barracks. Towards the end of the century ships of the Baltic Fleet were detached to form a Mediterranean squadron, much to the disgust of the British, and it was this squadron, and the Pacific Squadron, which provided the best training for officers and men. The Pacific Squadron had grown from the former Siberian detachment, based on Vladivostok. The latter port was also iced up in the winter, but the ships went south each year on long cruises. Before relations with Japan deteriorated, the Russian navy had a base near Nagasaki and here for a few months each year the ships would anchor and their officers settle ashore with temporary Japanese wives.

The Pacific Squadron was maintained with ships sent out on rotation from the Baltic. When war became more likely in the east the Baltic freeze-up became a serious problem, because if war broke out in November reinforcing ships could not be dispatched until April. This was why a new ice-free port was started at Libau, in Lithuania, in 1893. However, by the time it was completed the Russian navy, prompted by Admiral Makarov, had already acquired its first icebreaker. Vladivostok was also developed, being provided with a battleship-size dry dock in 1897, one year before the ice-free base at Port

Arthur was acquired. The latter was not quite so valuable a prize as the Russian government imagined. It was separated from Vladivostok by 1,500 miles of sea, much of which was Japanese home waters. In a war against Japan it would be exceedingly difficult to unite the Vladivostok and Port Arthur forces.

Siberia as a planned economy

The great period for Russian railway-building was the last three decades of the nineteenth century, and the Trans-Siberian Railway can be regarded as the culmination of this period. It ran from Chelyabinsk in the Urals to Vladivostok, and at Chelyabinsk connected with lines to European Russia. It was a state enterprise, and was started in 1892, construction being carried on from both ends and in the middle at the same time.

The transport ministry had been making proposals for a railway-based development of Siberia since the 1870s, but had been consistently opposed by the finance ministry. The latter's wish to be the dominant influence in railway construction, daggers-drawn relationships between the ministers of the two rival bureaucracies, and the finance ministry's distrust of any proposal that might increase state indebtedness, all contributed to delay in approving the line. As so often in Russian history, there was also a conflict of nightmares; some dreamed of a Yellow Peril threatening underpopulated Siberia, others of an economically developed Siberia feeling strong enough to follow the example of Britain's American colonies. In the end, development tied to a railway planned, controlled, and operated from St Petersburg seemed the best answer to both fears.

Witte, railwayman, finance minister, and born manipulator, was well placed to convert the idea into reality. Persuading the astonished Alexander III to appoint his callow heir Nicholas as chairman of Witte's Siberian Railway Committee was a clever move. It assured royal enthusiasm for the project during two reigns, it gave the young Nicholas useful experience of decision-making, and, as so often with Witte's dabbling in appointments, it gave the latter a colleague whose will was conveniently weak.

Once approval was given, construction proceeded fast to make the most of the warm months. Witte's overriding aim was to create a fact as soon as possible and engineering considerations, accounting, and honesty had lower priority. In the feverish atmosphere he created, sections were built before they were properly surveyed, green timber was used for track and bridges, costs consistently overran estimates, and bribery, speculation, and misappropriation were widespread even by Russian standards.

But the line was built. So far as western Siberia was concerned it had great economic advantages, but its eastern sections were through difficult and unproductive territory. In fact its entire eastern half could be regarded as simply a strategic railway intended to supply Russian forces in the Far East and to confirm and extend Russia's interest in that part of the world. This political aspect was emphasized when it was decided to take the final sections through Chinese Manchuria rather than over the longer but all-Russian route along the Amur River. The Chinese government was in no position to resist Russian requests, and leased a strip of land across Manchuria on which the Russians could build their railway and maintain troops. This line was built by a Russian-controlled and subsidized private company, the Chinese Eastern Railway, which made enormous losses. However, the consequent drain on the Treasury was considered well worth while, for not only did the Manchurian routing of the railway cut several hundred miles from the distance to Vladivostok, but it also promised to be an excellent first step towards acquiring more territory from the Chinese Empire. By 1904 rail transport between Europe and Vladivostok was a reality, even though Lake Baikal for a time was crossed by ferry. After the Russo-Japanese War, in which the Chinese Eastern Railway was shown to be vulnerable, the Amur line was started, to provide an all-Russian route. This was finished during the First World War, in the expectation of one day 'having another go' at Japan. The Trans-Siberian Railway had an enormous political effect although, at the time, the world was most impressed with the passenger service. By 1912 there were regular arrangements for round-the-world tours using the line, and its 'International' train with marble-tiled bathrooms and grand piano was world-famous, even though it only averaged about 20 m.p.h.

The building of the railway was not the beginning of economic development in Siberia. For decades previously, enterprising peasants had been moving eastwards. Rural overpopulation in European Russia, expressing itself in frequent famine, caused many villages to dispatch a 'scout' to look for land across the Urals. If the scout returned safely (and often he did not) villagers might move to the land he had inspected and found good. But moving hundreds of miles over tracks and waterways entailed a high casualty rate; only about four-fifths of the migrants survived the journey. The railway project, largely through the influence of Witte, was regarded as only the most important part of a plan to transform the economy of Siberia through government planning and participation. As feeders for the railway, rivers were made suitable for navigation. Peasant scouts were given low rail fares, and land settlement was made easy. Government medical and sanitation points reduced the casualty rate to about 1 per cent. Schools, churches, and prisons were built in anticipation of needs. The government provided agronomists and encouraged cooperatives. The incoming peasants responded both to official encouragement and to the free atmosphere of Siberia. Siberia was, and remained, the least controlled part of Russia; there had never been serfdom there, and government officials tended to be less repressive. It was natural that the settlers would be the more enterprising peasants of European Russia, but nevertheless the speed with which they adopted new techniques surprised many who believed that Russian peasants possessed an inbuilt inertia. In the first decade of the century there were several years in which immigrants into Siberia (mainly western Siberia) exceeded a quarter of a million. By 1910 the railway served about 10 million inhabitants. Although grain was grown, the new lands specialized in high-value products; by 1914 half the meat consumed in Moscow and St Petersburg came from Siberia, while a fleet of white-painted refrigerator-car trains plied between Siberia and the ports with butter for the markets of England and Germany. Arctic ports were developed, served by Siberia's great north-flowing rivers. Other projects were under way in 1914, like the Turkestan–Siberia Railway and the Yakutsk Highway, both completed by the Soviet government.

Given the centralized control, the breakneck speed of construction, the ramshackle result, and Witte's concept of Siberia as a planned economy, it is legitimate to regard the Trans-Siberian Railway as a precursor, even a dress rehearsal, for Stalin's industrialization of the 1930s. Many similarities can be noted, including Witte's use of convict labour to speed construction and reduce costs. This device was enthusiastically developed under Stalin, although with different incentives: under Witte good work brought pecuniary rewards, whereas under Stalin bad work brought reduced rations.

The Russo-Japanese War

The accession of Nicholas II coincided with the Chinese–Japanese War. The basic cause of this was Japan's desire to expand her territory, or at least her influence, at the expense of China. The field of battle was Korea, which China regarded as her own, and the result was a Chinese defeat. The victors imposed a hard treaty which included the payment by China of a war indemnity and the cession to Japan of the Manchurian territory around Port Arthur. None of the other great powers welcomed this strengthening of the Japanese position, for they had their own ambitions in China. At the suggestion of St Petersburg, France, Germany, and Russia diplomatically forced Japan to return Port Arthur to China. At the same time, in a bid to buy Chinese goodwill, Russia raised a loan in France to enable China to pay off her war indemnity. It was at this time that China agreed to the building of Russia's Chinese Eastern Railway across Manchuria, thus extending Russian influence in that region.

China's faith in Russian friendship was misplaced. In 1897 Germany occupied Kiaochow and other powers demanded their own fair share. Russia demanded the most; she leased Port Arthur and its peninsula and built a railway southwards from the Chinese Eastern Railway to link the latter with her new acquisition. Port Arthur, ice free, became a Russian naval base. This caused great indignation in Japan, where the forced relinquishment of Port Arthur after the Chinese–Japanese War still rankled. More humiliated than

Japan was China, and this showed itself in the Boxer Rebellion of 1900. When the European legations were besieged in China's capital it was the Russians, with their garrisons and ships close at hand in Port Arthur, who did most in the raising of the siege. It was Russian troops who first broke into the city, battering down the ancient gates with their artillery. In Manchuria, at this time, a war was fought between China and Russia. The Chinese Eastern Railway was attacked not merely by rebels but by regular troops. The city of Blagoveshchensk on the north shore of the Amur was bombarded by the Chinese, as were many Russian settlements along the route of the railway. Fighting was often savage, but the Russian army was better equipped and better trained than its opponent. Russia then used the presence of her armies in Manchuria to demand stiff peace terms, but with Japanese backing the Chinese resisted these. Finally, Russia agreed to withdraw her troops by the end of 1903. The victory over the Chinese army convinced most Russian officers that their army could easily beat any other oriental enemy, a dangerous conclusion.

With both Japan and Russia insisting on expansion at the expense of China, tension was inevitable. It was in Korea that the crisis arose. At first Russia and Japan managed to coexist uneasily in Korea, and Japan would have been willing to concede Russian supremacy in Manchuria in exchange for Japanese supremacy in Korea. But the Russian government seemed to want both, although in this connection the term Russian government was, even more than usual, an imprecise term. At the time the crisis was developing neither the minister of finance (Witte) nor the minister of war (Kuropatkin) nor the foreign minister (Lamsdorff) wanted a conflict with Japan, though they certainly wanted to strengthen Russia's presence in the east. According to Kuropatkin, Plehve, the minister of the interior, avidly wanted 'a little victorious war', believing it would calm discontent at home.[2] More important, there was a group of Guards officers, admirals, and courtiers with access to Nicholas who were intent on an aggressive policy.

When in 1901 Japan sent a distinguished negotiator to St Petersburg, he languished in the capital making no progress. At the time it seemed to be a case of insulting procrastination, but in retrospect it seems that the conflict of views around Nicholas prevented any decisive response being made. Japan, impatient, then secured the Anglo-Japanese Alliance of 1902 which, among other things, would make it risky for France to assist her new friend Russia in the event of a Russo-Japanese conflict.

The Russian troops in Manchuria were not withdrawn as promised. Tension built up. To the surprise of Nicholas, Japan commenced hostilities

---

2. Even if Plehve never actually said this, the anecdote expresses his thoughts. Theodore Roosevelt had used almost identical terms in his sponsorship of the Spanish–American War. Roosevelt's little war was a great step forward in a career which would bring him the presidency and a Nobel Peace Prize. Plehve's little war would bring him only a bomb. Problem: find the moral.

prematurely in February 1904. Prematurely for Russia, that is; for Japan it was a carefully timed attack. The line capacity of the Trans-Siberian Railway was still limited by the Baikal ferry crossing; Russia had seven battleships in the Pacific in 1904 but five new ones could be expected in 1905, and by February the weather was suitable for a Japanese landing in Korea.

Before Japan declared war she landed troops at Chemulpo (Inchon) in Korea, and her torpedo boats made a surprise night attack on the Russian Pacific Squadron at Port Arthur. Some officers of the latter had been on shore attending a ball given by their admiral's wife, the ships were lit, and there were no torpedo nets. Despite this, most of the torpedoes missed. Three Russian ships were damaged but none sunk. However, this was a serious blow to Russian morale and the next morning the main Japanese naval forces appeared on the horizon to block any sortie. Command of the sea was crucial, because Japan's expeditionary force depended on the sea route from the homeland. When Russia's only competent admiral, Makarov, took command, it seemed that the Russian squadron would take some damaging initiatives. Makarov took his dispirited ships to sea, exercised them and occasionally exchanged shots with the Japanese, all in preparation for a subsequent decisive action. But Makarov was drowned when his flagship struck a mine outside the harbour, and his successors were timid characters. There was one occasion when Russia could have won the war in a day. This was when two of Japan's six battleships struck mines off Port Arthur and sank. But instead of issuing forth to finish off the demoralized Japanese squadron the Russian ships remained safely in harbour.

The minister of war, Kuropatkin, was appointed to command the Far Eastern land forces and, no doubt familiar with *War and Peace*, adopted a strategy of retreat. Since he was outnumbered, this had much to justify it but many, for reasons of officerly honour, proved reluctant to carry out his orders. Kuropatkin was further embarrassed by the earlier appointment by Nicholas of a viceroy for the Far East, who could override Kuropatkin's orders, and frequently did so. The first big battle, at the Yalu, occurred when the Japanese army, moving northwards out of Korea, encountered the Russian army defending south Manchuria. The Russians were outnumbered by three to one, but their defeat astounded world opinion, which had not expected a European army to be beaten by orientals. In fact the defeat was unnecessary; if the Russian commanders had obeyed orders and withdrawn in good time Russian dignity would have been preserved. But so many officers insisted on fighting that when the retreat did begin it was disorganized; one Russian commander even retreated in the wrong direction. This Japanese success enabled her more easily to raise loans to continue the war, and had the opposite effect on Russia's credit; this was a 'fight now, pay later' kind of war. Also, inside Russia, discontent and angry humiliation developed, not the loyal patriotism on which Plehve had counted. It was not long before Port Arthur was besieged, isolating its 60,000-man garrison from Kuropatkin's main forces (at the beginning of the war Russia had only 100,000 men in the Far East, and the single-track Trans-Siberian Railway was delivering about 35,000 reinforcing troops each month). The Russian defences at Port Arthur were excellent, as were the engineering troops, who won great successes with their sapping and mining. But these advantages were wasted in the hands of the commanding officer, Stoessel, a man of breathtaking incompetence. The Pacific Squadron, uneasily anchored in the besieged port, made one attempt to break out to Vladivostok but in the fleet action which followed an unlucky shot killed its commander. The next in command panicked and the ships fled back to the comparative safety of the harbour they had just quit. Meanwhile the Baltic Squadron was dispatched to link up with the Port Arthur ships and thus form a fleet considerably stronger than that which the Japanese Admiral Togo could muster. The voyage of this squadron halfway across the world was an epic in itself. It had the use of no bases and few anchorages en route (and its ships needed to take coal every several days), its sailors were hastily recruited reservists, defaulters, or new conscripts, and it had a disproportionate number of incompetent officers. It was commanded by Admiral Rozhestvensky, a favourite of the Tsar. With its repair ship, colliers, and hospital ships, it was a forerunner of the Task Force concept used four decades later in another war against Japan.

Russian secret agents abroad had sent fanciful reports of Japanese torpedo boats lurking in the North Sea, so it was not surprising that when the squadron was crossing the Dogger Bank at night the unexpected appearance near the battleships of the cruiser *Avrora* was greeted with a hail of shells. Some British trawlers fishing the Bank were fired at during the confusion and this killing of innocent fishermen caused an international crisis. Much of the British press did what it could to stir the public into demanding war with Russia, and Rozhestvensky did not help the cause of peace by blaming the trawlers for wilfully obstructing the Russian shells. However, the British government had no wish for war, and the matter went to international arbitration.

At the end of December 1904, when the Baltic Squadron was off Madagascar, Port Arthur surrendered. It could have been defended for several more weeks, but for reasons best known to himself Stoessel gave up the struggle. He did send a telegram to Nicholas, beginning 'Great Tsar, forgive me . . .', and he did, like the Japanese general commanding the siege, receive a military decoration from the Kaiser (for whom the war was a great excitement), but this did not save him from being indicted as a traitor after the war. With Port Arthur the Japanese acquired the scuttled remnant of the Russian Pacific Squadron, but nevertheless Rozhestvensky was ordered to continue with the Baltic Squadron to Vladivostok. To reach that port he had to pass through Japanese-controlled waters, and in May 1905 he was met by Togo's experienced and faster fleet in the Tsushima Strait. Here the Russian squadron was annihilated. Meanwhile Kuropatkin was continuing his retreat northwards. By this time he had more men than his pursuers, but they were of low quality because the best troops were kept in European Russia in case of rebellion. At Mukden, his headquarters, he unwisely made a stand, and after a two-week battle was forced to retreat. The fall of Mukden, and Tsushima, made peace almost inevitable. The Tsar sent Witte to negotiate with the Japanese, under the auspices of President Roosevelt. In the resulting Treaty of Portsmouth, Witte succeeded in gaining moderate terms; Russia would not pay a war indemnity but agreed to withdraw from Port Arthur, southern Sakhalin, southern Manchuria, and to acknowledge Japanese supremacy in Korea (see Map 5).

This war had shaken the tsarist regime, and shocked the world. Russia had been regarded as a great power and Japan as a minor power; David had defeated his fellow-imperialist Goliath. The traditional comment is that this was the first full-scale war in which an oriental nation defeated a western, but since Japan's warships were built in England, her admirals trained in England, and her armies similarly built on the Prussian model, it is perhaps relevant to ask which of the two belligerents was western, and which oriental.

7

1905

Nicholas II

To say that Nicholas II lacked the personal defects required of an effective leader would be excessively kind. All the same, this was a man of great courtesy and consideration for others, a man of modesty, an exemplary father, and a good husband. But family happiness has never yet saved a dynasty. The lives of Nicholas and Alexandra were tragic because both had endearing qualities and both found themselves playing roles for which they were quite unfitted.

To be the son of Alexander III and the pupil of Pobedonostsev was a bad beginning. Nicholas had genuine charm and simplicity but was unable to overcome attitudes imbibed at an early age: belief in an absolute holy autocracy, chauvinism, anti-Semitism, and a touch of militarism. He had not studied hard in his youth, although he could speak French, English, and German as well as Russian (with his wife, who had been brought up by Queen Victoria, he spoke English). He showed little interest in learning about Russian politics and as a young man preferred to spend his time with fun-loving officers from superior regiments.

His father, apparently, had little confidence in his intelligence, but nevertheless allowed him to participate in various committees to familiarize himself with his future duties. Chairmanship of the Trans-Siberian Railway Committee was one of these duties. He also toured India and Japan, unsuccessfully hunting tigers in the former and having his forehead sliced by an assassin's sword in the latter.

As emperor, he distrusted the bureaucracy, partly because of its habit of suggesting reforms and partly because it seemed to interpose itself between him and his people. He was reactionary in the sense that he vaguely yearned to return to the imagined good old days before Peter the Great, when the tsar was close to his people and there were no clever bureaucrats around to spoil things. On fancy-dress occasions, he liked to appear with the Empress in sixteenth-century garb. He preferred to talk of *Rus'*, the traditional, almost sacred, term, rather than of the modern, imperial, *Rossiya*. Naturally, therefore, he preferred the true-Russian Moscow to western-style St Petersburg;

he showed this by visiting Moscow whenever he could. Like his father, he favoured the dumping of Muscovite architecture into St Petersburg's classical townscape; the more onion domes the better, even if long-established residents hated them.

Many instances have been pointed out of his political naivety: his open approval of the extreme right-wing and demagogic Union of the Russian People: his taking of advice from his palace commandant and not from his prime minister in 1906, just when Russia was supposed to be making a new start in representative government; and his faith in holy men, of whom Rasputin was not the only example.

He acceded in 1894. His Moscow coronation was marred by the death of hundreds of common people massed for the ceremonial distribution of royal gifts. These deaths by crushing could have been avoided if only commonsense precautions had been taken by the authorities; Moscow's governor, Grand Duke Sergei (Nicholas's uncle), was responsible, but was not blamed. Although big disappointments were suffered by those who had hoped that Alexander's death would mark the beginning of a more liberal era, in general the first years of the reign were not disastrous. This was partly because several of Alexander's ministers, including Witte, stayed in office and gave good advice. Later, Nicholas tended to appoint ministers who knew how to please him, and to take council with advisers who, at best, were talentless and, at worst, dishonest. Throughout the reign both the ministry and the court were riven by intrigues, intrigues which flourished on the Emperor's lack of will and reluctance to make the intellectual effort to get to the bottom of a situation.

The Hague Conference

Resentful after the Congress of Berlin, which had seemed to deprive her of the fruits of her 1878 victory over Turkey, Russia seemed to lose interest in European affairs. This perhaps was why Alexander III's reign had been peaceful. Apart from some intrigues in Bulgaria and Romania, which included the kidnapping and murder of figures hostile to Russia, the government concentrated its attention on the east. Alexander disliked the Germans and his reign coincided with a loosening of the bonds which had previously existed between the three monarchies of Russia, Austria, and Germany.[1] To avoid isolation, a mutually satisfactory alliance was concluded with France. Russia at this time benefited from French investment, so better relations were desirable on both economic and political grounds. There were military staff conversations, and the navies exchanged visits, Alexander politely keeping his thoughts to himself as the revolutionary 'Marseillaise' was played at Kronstadt.

1. He had married a Danish princess, unlike his predecessors who had married Germans.

Relations with Germany improved after Nicholas became tsar. He had a fairly close, though not devoted, relationship with his kinsman Kaiser Wilhelm, with whom he corresponded on 'Dear Willy'–'Dear Nicky' terms. Wilhelm was anxious to turn Nicholas's attention towards Russia's civilizing mission among the inferior yellow races, and his telegram to Nicholas, 'The Admiral of the Atlantic greets the Admiral of the Pacific', was notorious for its blatant appeal to the Tsar's vanity. In 1905, when Nicholas was thoroughly embroiled in the Far East, Wilhelm induced him to sign a Russo-German treaty at a private meeting off Björkö in the Baltic. However, the remonstrations of his ministers and his reluctance to behave dishonourably towards France persuaded Nicholas to back out, and henceforth Willy and Nicky were less intimate.

An unusual initiative with permanent consequences came from St Petersburg in the beginning of Nicholas's reign. This was no less than a call to the nations of the world to gather together and discuss a halt to the arms race, and kindred subjects. The genesis of this move came when the Russian general staff realized that Austria was re-equipping with quick-firing field artillery. Austria was Russia's potential enemy, but the Russian economy could not afford new guns. Or, rather, the finance ministry preferred to invest in railways than in guns, and could argue that the former did more to strengthen the Empire.

With the encouragement of Witte, what started as a proposal for a rearmament moratorium with Austria developed into a full-scale peace conference at The Hague. Many ridiculed and resented the notion of abolishing war, and cast aspersions on the Russian motives. In fact Nicholas's proposal was for arms limitation rather than the abolition of war, but despite this Kaiser Wilhelm condemned the idea because, he said, it would mean the disbandment of ancient sacred regiments and would place monarchs at the mercy of democrats and anarchists. Rudyard Kipling gratified the always-strong Russophobic segment of British opinion by penning some verses about how especially dangerous is the bear 'When he veils the hate and cunning of his little swinish eyes'. Many governments, including the British, sent men known to be bellicose as delegates. However, it was realized that some positive measures should emerge from the Conference, which had raised great hopes among the common people of Europe (that is, those who would do the fighting in the next war). So a few agreements were made, of which the most progressive was a five-year ban on balloon warfare. More permanent than these agreements was the general acceptance of arbitration as a means of settling international disputes. One of the earlier cases to be thus passed to international judgement was the dispute between Britain and Russia after the latter's ships had fired on British trawlers in 1904. In this case, at least, the possibility of arbitration made it easier to avoid war.

Marxism comes to Russia

The relative decline of Populism after the murder of Alexander II was mainly due to exhaustion, repression, and a feeling that nothing had been gained. There were also the attractions of a rival revolutionary movement, that of the marxists. Marx's theories had been known and appreciated since the 1840s by Russian radicals, but the Populists, devoted to the idea that Russia, because of her backwardness, might skip the capitalist phase of economic development, naturally could not accept Marx's declaration that every society inevitably passes through that phase (Marx subsequently acknowledged that Russia might possibly escape capitalism). Nor did early Russian revolutionaries approve of the post-capitalist society implied by Marx: Bakunin, for example, said that marxism would merely replace the capitalist with the bureaucrat. On the other hand, Marx's forecast of the post-revolutionary withering away of the state was attractive, or could be made attractive, to most Russians, so great was the alienation of the people from the state apparatus.

By the 1880s it was obvious that, despite the wishful denials of Populists, capitalism was firmly entrenched in Russia. More and more intellectuals turned towards marxism for an explanation of society more in keeping with reality than Populism. The tsarist regime and its police had always been relatively lenient towards the marxists,[2] whom they regarded as a small group which not only did not advocate terrorism like the Populists, but might even weaken the latter movement. In 1872 the first volume of Marx's *Capital* in Russian translation passed the censor. Publication had been sponsored by Populists, and proved to be the first commercial success for the work.[3] Populists liked it because it portrayed the horrors of the capitalist system which they wished Russia to avoid. Slavophils liked it because it condemned western society. Even St Petersburg industrialists liked it because it condemned, they said, the kind of factory system which their rivals, the Moscow industrialists, were trying to imitate.

But although sales were good it took about ten years for the book's political significance to become plain. According to Marx, production was society's main function, and social institutions reflected, with some distorting time-lags, the nature and ownership of society's means of production. In western Europe capitalism had replaced feudalism after commerce and large-scale production had created a social class more powerful than the nobility, whose land was no longer the dominant means of production. Under capitalism

2. Towards the end of the century many marxists (the 'legal marxists') operated on the basis of what the government would tolerate; for example, by confining their writing to permissible publications.

3. Marx rather ungratefully ascribed the high sales to Russian intellectuals' notorious enthusiasm for any extremist fashion originating in the west.

workers were dehumanized, and more and more exploited and impoverished. But growing monopoly, increasing industrial depression, and workers' discontent would eventually cause a collapse and a revolution in which the owners of the new dominant means of production (the labour of their own hands) would take power. After this inevitable proletarian revolution, existing institutions (political, judicial, economic, cultural) would be refashioned, because such institutions always reflected the requirements of the dominant class.

By the 1880s, with Plekhanov's allegiance transferred to marxism, Russian radicals were increasingly discussing *Capital*. Some became marxists, and passed on their opinions to some of the more thoughtful workers. But few working men had the time and inclination to master marxist theory, and there was a wide cultural gap between them and their instructors. The marxists had more success when, in St Petersburg, they introduced an idea which one of their members, Martov, had borrowed from the Jewish socialists of Lithuania. Instead of devoting time to explaining the intricacies of marxism to a chosen few, Martov advocated offering help to the masses of the workers in the struggle for higher wages and better conditions, thus winning their trust and providing an opportunity to transmit a few of the most appealing principles of marxism. Among the marxists of St Petersburg there was strong opposition to this idea, because it implied that it was possible for the workers to improve their lot under capitalism. However, the idea was eventually adopted (Lenin, a friend of Martov, was one of those supporting it) and it did enable the Social Democrats to take off as a real political force. The marxists played a small but noticed role in the St Petersburg strikes of 1895, 1896, and 1897, which extracted concessions from the industrialists and brought publicity and a few worker-members to the Social Democrats. At the end of 1895 the police at last took action against the marxists of St Petersburg, many of whom were arrested and given light sentences of exile in Siberia. Thus in 1898, when the Russian Social Democratic Workers' party was founded to unite the marxists, its main strength consisted of young activists like Lenin and Martov confined to Siberia, and a handful of veterans in Switzerland gathered around the revered figure of Plekhanov, one of the first Populists to turn to marxism.

Marxism because of its breadth attracted a great variety of adherents, all of whom seemed to find what they were looking for and tended to ignore other aspects of the ideology. There were Social Democrats who had abandoned the idealism of the earlier French and German socialists in favour of the more 'scientific' marxism. There were ex-Populists, often people whose main interest was revolution. There were those who had great faith in technology as a solution for all social problems. There were the born bureaucrats, drawn to a doctrine which seemed to promise a new, orderly, and well-organized society. And there were the ill-at-ease intellectuals, who idolized the 'pure' worker just as the Populists had honoured the primitive peasant. With such variety among its members it is not surprising that the history of Russian social democracy was largely a succession of doctrinal disputes and consequent splits and 'deviations'. Presumably the first marxist deviationist was Marx himself, who made substantial changes in his ideas during his lifetime. A dangerous schism in the Russian party developed with the emergence of the view known as Economism. This advised the party to acknowledge that some of Marx's prognostications were apparently not being fulfilled, and to devote itself henceforth to obtaining better conditions for the workers while supporting the liberals' campaign for a constitution through which socialism might eventually be achieved. Lenin and his supporters bitterly resisted this deviation.

Lenin

Lenin, whose real name was Ulyanov, was born in 1870 in Simbirsk (later Ulyanovsk). His father, the son of a serf, had been a schoolteacher but had risen to the rank of schools inspector, an office which carried a title of hereditary nobility. His mother was the daughter of a doctor. Thus Lenin grew up in a cultivated, liberal environment. The death of his father and, soon afterwards, the execution of his brother (see p. 115) shook the young Lenin, but did not affect his school work. He won the gold medal for the best graduate of his gymnasium and, highly recommended by the director of the latter (who was the father of the Kerensky whom Lenin was to displace in 1917), he proceeded to the University of Kazan to study law. In the meantime, however, he had taken over the political beliefs of his late brother, so it was not long before he was expelled, in company with forty-five fellow-students, for taking part in a demonstration. Because he was the brother of an executed terrorist, his several petitions for readmission were refused. So for three years, from the age of 18, Lenin lived with his family at Samara, occupying himself with reading. It was apparently when he was 19 that he embraced marxism; he had been a great admirer of the Populists and Chernyshevsky, but an acquaintance with Marx's *Capital* and a persuasive work by Plekhanov convinced him that only revolutionary socialism offered a genuine solution to Russia's inadequacies.

Lenin's mother pulled strings on his behalf, and the ministry of education agreed that although he could not be allowed to attend any university, he would be permitted to take university examinations. Thus, through private study, he was able to pass the law finals of St Petersburg University. After spending more time in Samara, he returned to the capital and joined a law firm in 1893. His employer, a liberal, was quite content for him to devote most of his energies to revolutionary activity.

In Samara Lenin had had experience of marxist discussion groups, and his legal training, combined with a naturally logical way of thinking and speaking, soon helped him to become a leading figure among the socialists in the capital. With many others he was arrested in 1895, spent fifteen months in gaol, and was then sent to Siberia for three years' 'free exile'. This sentence meant that he was confined to a certain area, but was free to move about and do what he liked there. His mother was again able to influence the authorities on his behalf and he was sent to one of the warmer parts of Siberia, being allowed to travel there as an ordinary passenger, not under escort. During his exile he married Nadezhda Krupskaya, one of his socialist associates in St Petersburg. He spent much of his time reading, carrying on correspondence with other socialists, both free and unfree, and writing.

After release in 1900 Lenin soon went abroad to carry on the struggle for what he considered the correct interpretation of marxism. He brought to the socialists a hitherto rare hardness in discussion. He could be scurrilous about his opponents. He would not compromise, would not admit that his ideological enemies might be partly right. His friends, like Martov, were only friends so long as their views coincided. And yet, although in politics Lenin was devious and unpleasant, there were a few who found him an enjoyable companion in private. In his later years, Lenin suffered progressive arterio-scelerosis of the brain. There were signs of this before 1917.

Revolutionaries and reformers

The Social Democratic party was eventually cured of its Economism deviation, thanks largely to Lenin's persuasiveness. After his exile, Lenin emigrated in order to confer with the elders of Russian marxism and to help edit a new periodical. The latter, called *Iskra* ('Spark'), was smuggled into Russia and was intended to unite the marxists inside Russia, to encourage them to reject revisionism, and to give them a sense of belonging to a big international organization. The six-man editorial board included Lenin and Martov as well as the veterans Plekhanov and Vera Zasulich.

After about 1895, marxism was in competition with a revived liberal movement and with the new Populism expressed by the Socialist Revolutionary party. The liberals attracted those in favour of non-violent change while the Socialist Revolutionaries (who had a terrorist section) attracted those who believed that revolutionary goals should be centred on the peasantry rather than the workers. It was to reassert the Social Democrats, and to attack those members who, relying on Marx's predictions, were content to wait while history took its predetermined course, that Lenin produced his *What Is to Be Done?* (1902). This, distributed inside Russia by *Iskra*'s agents, expressed Lenin's idea of what the Russian Social Democrats should be and do.

Superficially, it was a one-sided and sharp attack on Economism, but really it marked the beginning of what was later to be called Marxism-Leninism. That is, it was a substantial revision of Marx, although its author took care to claim that it represented orthodox marxism. It admitted that the workers were not really capable of spontaneous socialist thought, because their horizon was limited to trade unionism, improved conditions, and higher wages. Thus, since the workers did not see where their real interests lay, they had to be protected by a socialist party which would act on their behalf. This party could no longer be a collection of well-meaning amateurs, but had to be a tightly knit group of full-time, well-trained, devoted professionals, controlled by a strong central organization. It was this latter small group which would do the conspiratorial work of the revolution. Lenin was not against open organizations, like trade unions, for the masses, but these could only be of secondary importance. Terrorism was rejected. The organization of the party was to consist of a supreme organ abroad (the *Iskra* board) with a subordinate Central Committee inside Russia which would organize secret local committees throughout the country.

This did seem a possible path towards socialism. But the ordinary party member did not relish the proposed strong organization, with its implied stress on obedience; this was quite the reverse of the traditional free discussion which had hitherto preceded all actions and which was one of the most-valued features of the revolutionary movement. However, when in 1903 a party congress met in London, most delegates seemed willing to accept the ideas of *What Is to Be Done?* But perhaps because revolutionaries are by nature contentious and intellectuals disputatious, it was not long before the 1903 congress was riven with disagreement, which developed into dissension and animosity. The delegates of the Jewish socialist union walked out, feeling that they had little in common with the white-handed radical intellectuals who knew nothing of the practical side of the Jewish workers' miserable lives. This exodus changed the balance of votes, so when Martov opposed Lenin's proposal to reduce the *Iskra* board from six to three members he was defeated by five votes. It was this vote, much more important as a symbol of division than the issue itself warranted, which resulted in Lenin's faction being termed the *Bolsheviki* ('those of the majority') and Martov's supporters the *Mensheviki* ('those of the minority'). Underlying the split lay a distrust of Lenin's personality and methods, and his uncompromising demands. Martov refused to cooperate with him. Those delegates who had come, furtively, from Russia had to return home and tell their appalled comrades that the movement was split. Martov persuaded Plekhanov to withdraw his support from Lenin. Lenin then resigned from *Iskra*, and thereafter resisted conciliatory moves to mend the Bolshevik–Menshevik split.

Among the Socialist Revolutionaries there was also a diversity of views; some of the members were inclined towards marxism, some had spent their entire revolutionary lives working among the peasants in the Populist tradition, and others were addicted to violence. The Socialist Revolutionaries never became a highly centralized and disciplined group as did the Bolsheviks, nor at first did they have a large membership. But in time, and especially after their participation in several peasant risings, they attracted much support among country people; in the nationwide and relatively free election of 1917 they and their associates gathered a majority of the votes. In the early years of the century their terroristic organization gained them much publicity after a number of successful assassinations. Among their victims were two ministers of the interior in 1902 and 1904. The 1904 success, killing the unpopular Plehve, brought not only public renown but public acclaim.

Although it was not until 1905 that the Constitutional Democratic (KD or 'Kadet') party was formed, the liberals had been growing more active since the death of Alexander III. In Russia the term 'liberal' was avoided, perhaps because Russian liberalism embraced viewpoints as far apart as those of marxists who accepted Marx's interpretation of society but preferred non-revolutionary solutions, and those who wanted merely to temper autocracy with the ancient practice of the tsar taking council with his people through a consultative assembly. Preferring to call themselves the 'social movement', or even 'public opinion', Russian liberals were predominantly *zemstvo* members[4] who were impressed with their own effectiveness and wished to extend their sphere of influence, or paid specialists employed by the *zemstva*, or urban professionals. Almost half the Kadets' central committee were professors.

When Alexander III died the liberals had great hopes of a future in which people's representatives (that is, themselves) would have some influence in the decisions of the government. In its loyal address to the new Tsar, the strongly liberal *zemstvo* of Tver province even mentioned the need for public opinion to be expressed and heeded. Nicholas, newly installed, ill at ease, and under the influence of Pobedonostsev, responded with his own public opinion about *zemstvo* representatives 'intoxicated by senseless dreamings' about participation in government. 'Let it be known that I will maintain the principal of autocracy as strongly and as firmly as my late memorable father.'

This was not a good beginning for the liberals, and subsequent concessions never included the granting of real power. When *zemstvo* members' advice was needed in the agricultural committees set up to examine Russia's pressing rural problems, care was taken to see that they were not elected, but selected by the provincial governors. In such an atmosphere the more radical liberals, who were demanding not only moves towards constitutional government but also universal primary education and a higher legal status for the peasantry, began to turn towards illegal activities. One of their acts was the foundation of the Union of Liberation, an illegal, largely liberal, political organization. In 1904 the Union emerged from the underground and held a series of banquets which were advertised as celebrations of the fortieth anniversary of the 1864 law reform. Banquets were a form of public gathering permitted by the police, but at these particular celebrations speeches were made, and reported in the

---

4 But by no means all *zemstva* were predominantly liberal. Many were strongly conservative.

press, demanding such things as a constituent assembly, social justice, and better schools. Meanwhile those liberals for whom the Union of Liberation was too radical weathered the discouragements of Plehve, and were allowed in 1904 to hold a national congress of *zemstva*, but only in private.

Luckily for the government, three waves of rebellious dissidence had not coincided. From 1899 to 1902 the rebels had been the students, whose crowning hour had been the assassination of the minister of education. Then, in 1902, a poor harvest superimposed on existing land hunger set off a series of peasant attacks on landowners' estates, actions that were suppressed by troops whose purpose was as much to teach the peasants a lesson as to restore order. Then, in 1902–3 many industrial workers staged strikes. Meanwhile the government was split between repressors and reformers. Plehve believed in repression, Witte in reform, and Plehve prevailed. But, in the old tradition, widespread arrests of actual or suspected troublemakers were followed by a few concessions: the students were allowed to hold meetings so long as they were properly supervised by their professors, peasants' debt arrears to the state were cancelled (outstanding redemption payments would be written off after 1905), workers injured at work were allowed pensions. This last measure was supported by Plehve, as also was the law enabling workers to elect 'elders' to negotiate with employers. Yet Plehve's interior ministry, with its officials placed all over the country, could often work against what it regarded as policies of appeasement, and its repressive measures did much to ensure that in 1904 the government was facing a revolutionary situation. The war against Japan was going badly, and the government was blamed for its handling of the armed forces. Many began to feel that the proved administrators of the *zemstva* organizations should be given more executive responsibility, for the official bureaucracy was obviously deficient. All this strengthened the cause of the liberals, and the government could hardly have failed to notice that, among the guests at the liberal 'banquets' being held to further the cause of a constitution, there was a sprinkling of army generals.

The Socialist Revolutionaries were active. Plehve was murdered and so, in 1905, was the equally disliked Grand Duke Sergei, the Tsar's uncle and governor of Moscow. In many localities the Socialist Revolutionaries were successfully persuading local peasants to expel the landlords and take over their land. To contain these threats, the war ministry felt obliged to keep the most reliable troops in European Russia and to send mainly reservists to fight the Japanese.

That the police had agents in all the revolutionary parties was no longer of great help, for while an agent could recommend the arrest of key conspirators he could do little to prevent popular manifestations. A dramatic police scandal, which subsequently damaged both the regime and the Socialist Revolutionaries, was that involving the murder of Grand Duke Sergei. Azev, the leader of the Socialist Revolutionaries' terrorist organization, was himself a police agent. It was he who organized the murder of Plehve and several police officials, but there was an understanding between him and his official paymasters that he would prevent any attacks on the royal family. Obviously, if he was to play the part of a good revolutionary he would have to carry out some murders, and perhaps those who employed him had their own quarrels with some of the victims. However, it seems that he felt unable to refuse the revolutionaries' suggestion that Sergei should be killed. For some people, therefore, Sergei's death came as a double shock, but it was not until 1908 that Azev's activities were publicly denounced. By that year Azev had been five years in control of the Socialist Revolutionaries' terrorist section, and the revelation that he was a police agent took away much of its hard-won glamour.

Even the outwardly respectable Kadet party was slow to condemn assassinations. The state was so oppressive and immovable that violence sometimes seemed the only way forward. Among Socialist Revolutionaries, anarchists, and some Social Democrats there was an enthusiasm for violence which sometimes verged on terrorism. Violence became a creed, and those parties which practised it did attract numbers of psychopathic young men. Murders and attempted murders of state officials became almost routine, preoccupying and slowing down state administrators and inviting reprisals or, at least, harsh policies. In creating a pool of experienced killers the revolutionary parties facilitated the 'Red Terror' of the early Bolshevik years; the understandable failure of intellectuals to set an example of respect for the law likewise left a defective heritage.

Free trade unions were not permitted, and to divert the workers' desire for unions into safe channels the police, through its agents, had set up its own legal trade unions. The originator of this idea ('police socialism') appears to have been Zubatov, formerly a poor student on the fringe of revolutionary groups who had been 'turned' into a police agent. He became an efficient and fairly scrupulous chief of the Moscow security police before Plehve appointed him head of the Special Section, handling undercover agents. It was in 1902 that he obtained permission to establish an association for engineering workers. With the help of mostly unsuspecting university professors and some former Social Democrats, this was a great success, and the idea spread to other industries and other cities. The membership, which was large, was regaled with lectures and community singing, but to maintain its support the union leaders had to produce clear gains in terms of wages and working conditions. Since most employers favoured this kind of union, for fear of something worse, some real concessions were negotiated. But it was not long before the unions felt obliged to take strike action, and the spectacle of police-organized strikes and demonstrations was too much for the administration, especially as foreign capitalists were beginning to drop hints that Russian industry was perhaps after all not a good investment. So police socialism, whose success for some time had alarmed the Social Democrats, came to an end. Zubatov went into exile for a while, finally shooting himself in 1917 when he heard of the Emperor's abdication. The St Petersburg members of his disbanded union for the most part joined a church-based union, organized by an Orthodox priest, Gapon.

Bloody Sunday

Gapon organized, with police support, a union for industrial workers. Like other such unions, it was penetrated by Social Democrats who used its gatherings for agitation. However, Gapon made great efforts to weed out the marxists (and also, as a loyal citizen and good Orthodox Christian, Jews). The strikes and demonstrations into which he led his members were probably not instigated by workers fired by socialist propaganda, but were embarked upon because Gapon was impressed by the misery of the working class and rather fancied himself in the role of saviour. In January 1905, after the news of the fall of Port Arthur reached the capital, discontent intensified among all classes. There were more workers' protests, and Gapon organized a Sunday march of the St Petersburg workers to present a petition to the Tsar at the Winter Palace. In fact the Tsar was not in residence at the time, but the thousands of marchers had no opportunity to discover this, because before they reached the palace they were shot down by troops who had been brought to the capital in anticipation of trouble. How many were killed and wounded is unknown, for unofficial and official counts differed widely. The fact remained that a peaceful column of workers' families, singing hymns and the national anthem as it marched to present a petition to the sovereign, had been fired on. When a new governor of the capital was appointed in haste to sort out this crisis, his main initiatives were to arrange a deputation of 'good' workers to ask the Tsar's pardon for their misdemeanour, and to send many of the surviving demonstrators out of the capital. These expellees, scattered all over Russia, spread the news of the massacre and it was this which, on the one hand, led to a wave of sympathy strikes throughout the Empire, and, on the other, discredited the traditional belief among the simple masses that all the evils they suffered could be remedied if only they could reach their 'little father', the Tsar, to tell him what was really happening. As for that other little father, Gapon, he denounced the Tsar and fled abroad to be lionized by European society, canvassed by the revolutionaries, and to write *The Story of my Life*. He eventually joined the Social Revolutionaries, who hanged him in 1906 on discovering that he still had contacts with the police. At one stage Lenin declared Gapon was a Social Democrat, because in 1905 great public prestige attached to the group which could claim Gapon's favour. And after all, Gapon had succeeded in doing something which the revolutionaries had long failed to do: he had aroused the workers en masse. That he had done this was probably because he had much of the reputation of the holy man, a class of person traditionally able to work on the emotions of simple Russians of all classes. Probably as a holy man he was only second-rate, for he was a great drinker and gambler, but with his holiness there was also a real sympathy for simple workers and, at first, an inspiring optimism.

The *Potemkin* Mutiny

Bloody Sunday was followed by a general strike in the capital, and an outbreak of protest strikes throughout the Empire as the news spread. Apart from the capital, most rebelliousness occurred in the non-Russian parts of the Empire. Disgust and discontent were not confined to the traditionally dissident; even the industrialists' association showed its disapproval by voting a sum of money to aid families whose breadwinners had been killed on Bloody Sunday. Early in February came the assassination of Grand Duke Sergei, and that same month the Tsar publicly conceded that some kind of elected consultative (but only consultative) assembly was desirable. At about the same time localized peasant revolts became more numerous, especially in the south. In the following weeks the liberals, expressing themselves through the *zemstva* or through professional associations, became more bold in their demands; that summer Nicholas spoke to a delegation of *zemstvo* figures, and a joint meeting of *zemstvo* and city council delegates was held in Moscow, despite a police prohibition.

Especially unnerving was the mutiny on the battleship *Potemkin* in June; for a regime which seemed unlikely to survive without the use of troops, this first substantial demonstration of disloyalty in the armed forces had great significance. *Potemkin* was a fairly modern battleship of the Black Sea Squadron, which after the recent loss of the Pacific and Baltic squadrons was the only fleet still in being. As hostilities with Japan had revealed, there was a certain rottenness in the Russian navy, and part of it was in the officers. The majority of officers were not brutal and incompetent, but many were. Brutal treatment of seamen had been a traditional feature of all navies, but whereas in most navies a kinder atmosphere prevailed in the twentieth century, this was not always the case in Russian warships. Arbitrary corporal punishment was officially forbidden in the army and navy, but not all officers conformed. This is what one of the seamen who survived Tsushima thought of his officers:

These noblemen's sons, well cared-for and fragile, were capable only of decking themselves out in tunics with epaulettes. They would then stick their snouts in the air like a mangy horse being harnessed, and bravely scrape their heels on polished floors, or dance gracefully at balls, or get drunk, in these ways demoralizing their subordinates. They didn't even know our names. Corporal punishment was forbidden on paper only, for decency's sake: the sailors were beaten for all kinds of reasons, and often. It was considered the natural order of things. There was no way of complaining . . . We were compelled to eat rotten biscuits and stinking decaying meat while our officers fatted themselves with the best food and drank the most expensive wines.[5]

Potemkin was an unhappy ship, and there were no perils of war service to distract the men from their grievances and hatreds. So the crew, which included several revolutionary agitators, killed many of the officers, took control of the ship, and cruised around the Black Sea. Other ships were close to mutiny and it was thought unwise to order their crews to open fire on the errant battleship. At one point, later celebrated on film and canvas, *Potemkin* steamed unscathed past the warships which were, theoretically, hunting her down. However, after bombarding Odessa and threatening other southern ports, she was compelled to steam off and seek asylum in Romania. She had shaken the nerve of the regime, brought the navy ministry into even more disrepute, had excited the revolutionaries (who had at first thought she would ignite a full-scale revolution in south Russia), and had destroyed much of the Empire's remaining prestige in foreign capitals.

The strike and the Moscow Rising

Taking advantage of the government's confusion and indecision, labour unions and political parties were busily establishing themselves during the summer of 1905. The various professional organizations set up a coordinating body known as the Union of Unions. This was a third and radical liberal body, supplementing the Union of Liberation and the *zemstvo* group; its first chairman, Milyukov, was also a leader of the Union of Liberation. Only a few weeks passed before the Union of Liberation and the majority of the *zemstvo* group jointly founded the Constitutional Democratic party (usually referred to as the Kadet party). Its main demand was for a freely and fairly elected constituent assembly to sort out the Empire's political problems.

In August a proposal for a consultative assembly had been published (the 'Bulygin proposal'), but by that time half-measures were no longer acceptable; almost all politically conscious citizens expected something more. A further government concession, the granting to the universities of that autonomy which the students had long sought, did bring to an end the students' strike. But now that the lecture rooms were open they provided almost the only place where meetings could be held without police permission, and it was not long before socialist students in St Petersburg took advantage of this to hold anti-government meetings, attended in the evenings by the city's workers. General dissatisfaction culminated in the railway strike of October.

The railwaymen's union was effectively organized throughout most of the Empire, and, since the latter was dependent almost entirely on the railways for moving troops and feeding the cities, it was clear that the regime was now in

---

5. A. Zaterty, *Za chuzhiye grekhi* (1907), 19.

really mortal danger. When strikes spread to other industries, when the peasant revolts seemed to be on the increase, and when disturbances occurred among troops in transit from Manchuria, it was clear that extraordinary decisions were needed. Thus, after toying with the idea of a military dictatorship, Nicholas accepted Witte's advice and issued what later became known as the October Manifesto. This conceded the principles of freedom of speech, conscience, and association, freedom from unwarranted arrest, and accepted the calling of an assembly (*Duma*), which would be elected (though not by direct or equal voting). But the ministers would not be responsible to the Duma, and although it could block a law going into force, it would not have the right, alone, to enact legislation. Thus, although an improvement on the Bulygin proposal, it seemed inadequate to those parties which had been demanding a constituent assembly. Only those liberals who found the Kadet party too radical rallied behind the Tsar's October Manifesto, calling themselves the Octobrist party.

Just before the October Manifesto appeared, leading workers of St Petersburg had established the St Petersburg Council (*Soviet*) of Workers' Deputies. This was a body to coordinate the strikes and other activities of the various factories, each of which was to elect its own delegates. The Socialist Revolutionaries and the Bolshevik and Menshevik factions of the Social Democrats all realized the potential significance of this ultra-democratic workers' assembly and soon had their own delegates on its executive committee. There were similar soviets in other cities, and in many, including the capital, the soviets became virtually the local government for some weeks.

Although the political parties varied in their attitudes to political change, they were more united in their demand for civil rights. This probably reflected the attitude of ordinary people for whom, ultimately, civil rights were the great goal. The term 'personal inviolability' had become almost a slogan, not least among workers, and reflected long-standing resentment at the powerlessness of the ordinary person, both at the workplace and in society as a whole.

In general, committed revolutionaries played a small part in the 1905 upheaval. The Socialist Revolutionaries were more interested in the countryside, while the Social Democrats in exile were too busy with their own feuds to pay full attention to what was happening in Russia. Many of them no doubt also felt that there was no hope of the socialists taking power at this stage. Eventually some of the exiles returned to Russia to participate in events, but of them all only Trotsky won great distinction. Trotsky had met Lenin in 1902, during the latter's stay in London, and had won his respect as a great intellect and a great speaker. However, he had stayed with the Menshevik faction after the 1903 split and it was as a Menshevik that he became the leading figure of the St Petersburg Soviet. His skill as an orator was unmatched by any of the other socialists. For Lenin and his friends the 1905 Rebellion was a rude awakening; the workers had revolted spontaneously and were conducting their affairs in their own way. Cultured Russian gentlemen like Lenin, skilled in fine arguments, seemed unable to find a way to arouse the proletariat so that it would follow their leadership along the true path to a socialist society. Only Trotsky, it seemed, had the oratorical skill to set his listeners on fire, and even he achieved a smaller response among the masses than had Father Gapon. Only the anarchists could congratulate themselves; spontaneous revolts, and soviets, seemed to confirm their belief in grass-roots democracy.

From October, Witte was virtually prime minister, being the chairman of the Council of Ministers, whose powers had been strengthened. His first task was the pacification of the country. Not only was there trouble in the cities, but there were mutinies among the troops returning home from the war and nationalist demonstrations in Poland, the Caucasus, and other non-Russian parts demanding more independence from St Petersburg. At one stage the Trans-Siberian Railway was in the hands of rebellious troops and workers, and much of Transcaucasia fell from government control. To clear the Trans-Siberian Railway a trainload of loyal troops was dispatched from east and west under 'firm' officers. With frequent halts, to disarm mutineers and execute their leaders, the trains met halfway, and the railway with its vital telegraph line was declared reopened for traffic. In St Petersburg, the Soviet called a general strike in November, but its indifferent success only encouraged Witte to dissolve the Soviet and arrest its leaders. But in Moscow a parallel strike developed into a full-scale rising which lasted almost two weeks and was savagely suppressed by loyal troops. Durnovo, the interior minister, then undertook reprisals, not always directed at the appropriate targets. Thousands of socialists were sentenced to long exile, and sometimes death. In the Baltic provinces, where armed bands of workers and peasants were fighting armed groups of the disliked German landowners, the pacification was brutal, many innocent suspects being hanged to set an example to others. How many hundreds or thousands of executions took place is not known. Soldiers additionally indulged in shooting, robbery, and rape. Meanwhile there were mutinies in the naval bases of Kronstadt in the Baltic and Sevastopol on the Black Sea.

In early 1906, in the breathing space between the quietening of urban rebellion and the not unexpected surge of rural violence in 1906–7, the autocracy engaged in a purge of the faint-hearted and the recently dissident. Unreliable officers, and sometimes their units, were dispensed with. Newspapers and their editors were suppressed. Professionals of radical inclination lost their jobs in local government and were sometimes exiled. An international loan, raised with the help of French bankers, helped the government through this difficult period. Meanwhile, as the country seemed to become more stable, a new political life was being born as the promises of the October Manifesto became a temporary reality.

Russian government before and after 1905

Autocracy, in theory, meant that all the power of the state was exercised by one person; the monarchy was absolute even though it had chosen to be ruled by law.[6] In practice, no tsar exercised his powers alone. He entrusted authority to men of his own choice and it was not always clear where the real power in Russia lay. As a generalization it might be said that the tsar could and did intervene in any matter he chose, but many day-to-day decisions, which were not always minor decisions, were made by the bureaucracy. Since the tsar had the final word, those persons who could influence him also had great power. He tended to take the advice of aristocratic confidants, often with more opinion than knowledge, rather than that of state servants.

Until 1905 the bureaucracy was headed by the State Soviet (Council), whose members were nominated by the tsar. Legislative projects were handed down for study to the relevant ministry (or to a special commission) and were then returned for discussion by a general meeting of the Council. The opinion, often divided, of the Council was transmitted to the tsar and he made his own decision, which became law. His verdict was not necessarily in accordance with the majority or even minority opinions, and moreover he could, independently of the Council, promulgate a manifesto or *ukaz* at will (some notable reforms were effected thus). In 1906 the State Council was transformed into an upper house to balance the new Duma. Its nominated members were supplemented by elected representatives of the towns, Church, guilds, universities, *zemstva*, and nobility. As was intended, it became a conservative though quasi-parliamentary body which considerably restrained the more liberal and energetic Duma; all proposals had to be passed by both the Duma and the State Council before being submitted to the tsar for approval or disapproval.

Until 1905 the Soviet (Council) of Ministers was moribund, but there was a Committee of Ministers which discussed current questions involving several ministries. The four most weighty members of this were the ministers of the interior, finance, and war, and the Over Procurator of the Holy Synod. In the 1890s there were ten ministries: foreign affairs, imperial court, war, navy, interior, education, transport, finance, agriculture and state domains, and justice, plus departments with ministerial status (state control, charities of the Empress Maria, state horse-breeding, and the Procuracy of the Holy Synod). Of these the ministry of war had by far the biggest budget: two-fifths of the total for all ministries, ten times more than the ministry of education and 200 times more than the horse- breeders. By 1917 the ministry of agriculture had become a department, and a new department of health had been introduced.[7]

6. In Finland the Russian tsar was still a constitutional monarch (but not in Poland after 1832).

7. Ministers' competence varied, and there were some who were far from being the privileged and unperceptive intriguers that are sometimes portrayed as the norm. D. Lieven's *Russia's Rulers under the Old Regime* (1989) provides a fair picture.

Neither before nor after 1905 were the ministers responsible to anyone but the tsar, and it was the tsar who chose them. Thus they were bound by no sense of ministerial solidarity. Vying for the favour of the tsar, they were often divided by jealousies and intrigues. The minister of the interior had perhaps the most influential office, for he controlled the police and censorship, and supervised provincial governors. But the minister of finance could also make himself felt, for not only did he administer taxes, tariffs, and the vodka monopoly, but he could also set back the proposals of other ministers simply by saying no funds were available. Only the minister of war could sometimes count on getting funds over the opposition of the minister of finance; the military strength of the Empire was regarded by the tsars as their overriding priority. But no minister had total authority in his own sphere. That there were powerful figures in the tsar's entourage was well known, and strikingly confirmed when the Russo-Japanese War was provoked against the advice of both the minister of foreign affairs and the minister of war.

In 1906 the Committee of Ministers was abolished, its functions being divided between a revived Council of Ministers, the Duma, and the State Council. The Council of Ministers had been formally established in 1861, coexisting with the Committee of Ministers and the State Council; Alexander II did not favour his father's system of private chanceries. Under Alexander it consisted of ministers and nominated officials, chaired by the Tsar himself. It discussed project-laws and other measures, which might receive prompt royal assent or be sent to committee for further study. Through the Council passed Alexander's great reforms, but its functions ceased in 1882. Then, in October 1905, it was transformed into the supreme legislative and administrative body. Its chairman (prime minister) was selected by the Tsar from trusted officials. It gave preparatory study to projects which would later be debated by the Duma and State Council. However, the ministers of foreign affairs, war, and finance frequently bypassed these channels by reporting to the Tsar privately. According to Article 87 of the Fundamental Laws of the Empire, promulgated in 1906, between sessions of the Duma or State Council proposed laws could be submitted directly to the Tsar for his approval. As it was difficult for the assemblies to undo such laws, this provision provided a loophole whereby the government could pass measures that would have been rejected by one or other of the houses; that is how Nicholas obtained his first beloved dreadnoughts. In the World War the Council's functions diminished, although its four special committees for defence, supply, transport, and fuel were important.

The supreme court after 1905 remained the Senate, which by 1914 had nine sections. It was not only a court of appeal, but was also the promulgator of imperial *ukazy*, the confirmer of titles of nobility, and the settler of landowners' boundary disputes.

Each of the ministries had its own offices in the provinces, and these offices would often act under direct orders from St. Petersburg without reference to the local governor. At the turn of the century there were seventy-eight provinces (*gubernias*), together with eighteen regions which, because of their remoteness or other special features, were considered unsuitable for division into provinces. A province was headed by a governor (*gubernator*), responsible for the observance of the laws of the land and directly answerable to the minister of the interior. His province was subdivided into districts and the latter into towns and cantons. Largely subject to the will of the governor were the provincial and local *zemstva* which, despite limitations[8] imposed in the reign of Alexander III, had considerable influence in economic, agricultural, and social matters. The towns were administered by the town councils, elected by the wealthier citizens; Moscow with over a million inhabitants had about 10,000 electors. The peasantry had its village commune (*mir*), and sent representatives to the *volost* (canton) assembly. Each village elected its elder, an office which was more a burden than an honour because its holder was personally liable for the conduct of his electorate. Each *volost* had a three-man magisterial bench to try petty crimes. Between 1889 and 1912 rural self-government was restricted by the supervision of 'land captains', appointed from the local nobility; among other things, these could order peasants to be flogged if they trespassed on nobles' land. Nicholas sometimes seemed to regard them as his direct link with the peasants, bypassing the bureaucracy. The peasantry hardly took part in the *zemstva*. Stolypin wanted to institute *zemstva* at district level, with peasant members, but was frustrated, so once again the chance of bringing the peasantry into normal society, as normal people, was lost.

Bureaucracy and bureaucratic practice were (and remained) a pervasive and depressive feature of Russian life. The officials not only preferred to place administrative convenience before the interests of the individuals they allegedly were intended to serve, but in Russia they had exceptional opportunities to do so. This was partly because the ordinary citizen had no channels of effective complaint. The police were part of the bureaucracy, and in any case complaints against the bureaucracy were investigated by the bureaucracy. Ordinary Russians seemed to accept injustice from above as something which had always been and always would be. Moreover, the traditional Russian emphasis on the common good in preference to individual rights worked in the same direction; most would not find outrageous, for example, the arrest of ten men in the hope that one of them might be a criminal.

For many Russians the bureaucracy seemed an alien imposition, an internal colonialism almost. In the sense that public power and noble status were

---

8. Peasant representation in the *zemstva* had been limited, the provincial governor had been given the right of veto over the *zemstva*'s staff appointments, and the local bureaucracies continued to stifle spontaneous initiatives of the *zemstva*.

linked, the bureaucracy was behind the times. The pedigrees of the most exalted office-holders sometimes revealed imposing titles but no really relevant training for their responsibilities, although it is true that there were institutions like the Corps of Pages and the Institute of Jurisprudence to train the sons of the wealthiest nobles. Possibly the slavish relationships between upper and lower ranks in the government offices were merely a reflection of this feudalistic remnant, reinforced by the regulation that the higher officials could dismiss the lower with no cause given. Corruption and bribery were still normal. It was said that the low pay scales of public officials were a reason, and excuse, for this, but it was the worst-paid officials (abacus and copy clerks) who received the least in bribes. While this clerical proletariat was literally starving towards an early death, the better-paid officials could enrich themselves with bribes, book-cooking, and plain theft; the higher the salary the higher the bribe. But nevertheless it was not the dishonest official who was the most harmful. It was the zealot, sitting behind his desk, ignorant of the real life outside, virtuously formulating new regulations or new schemes for the common good, who aroused the most resentment.

The Dumas and the parties

Witte, whom Nicholas was beginning to blame for the concessions made in 1905, was dismissed before the Duma met. His successor was Goremykin, whose only distinction, according to Witte, was his whiskers. The election results showed that the hope that the peasantry would choose conservative candidates was ill-founded; both town and country elected a preponderance of radicals. The Kadets and their allies won 179 seats. The Socialist Revolutionaries boycotted the elections as a party, but their sympathizers, thanks to rural support, were the second largest group in the Duma: they won 94 seats and called themselves the Labourists (*Trudoviki*). The Social Democrats had also decided not to participate in the elections, except in the Caucasus, where they knew they were strong: they elected 18 members, mainly Mensheviks from Georgia. The Octobrists, near the centre of the political spectrum, won 17, while right-wing parties won 15. From the non-Russian parts of the Empire came strong groups of Polish and Ukrainian nationalists and weaker groupings from the Baltic provinces. There were also 30 Muslims, most of whom allied themselves with the Kadets.

Some half-hearted negotiations were started to persuade moderate party leaders to enter the government, but these produced no results, largely because such leaders had no intention of sitting side by side in the Council of Ministers with reactionary colleagues chosen by the Tsar. In the Duma, intelligent debates were staged on some of the main problems of the Empire (land distribution, the rights of Jews and religious dissenters, the Polish question), but since the government gave only perfunctory attention to the opinion of the chamber these discussions had no immediate effect on policy. They did, however, have some effect on public opinion, because the debates were reported in the press. This, the First Duma, did not last long. Angered by a governmental announcement that compulsory redistribution of landowners' land was absolutely out of the question, which was not the Duma's opinion, the latter issued its own statement on the rural crisis. The government was able to describe this as a revolutionary and certainly an illegal action, and with this excuse troops were sent to occupy the chamber. The Duma was thus dissolved only two months after its first meeting.

Under Article 87, the ensuing period before the election of a new Duma provided an opportunity for the government to pass measures by decree. By this time Goremykin had been replaced as chairman of the Council of Ministers by the far more energetic and perceptive Stolypin. When the Kadet and Trudovik members of the dissolved First Duma crossed into Finland and signed a proclamation (the 'Vyborg Manifesto'), urging the Russian people to resist the government by refusing taxes and conscription, Stolypin retaliated by arresting them on their return. They were put on trial (automatically barring them from election to the new Duma) and were sentenced to short terms of imprisonment. In December 1905 Witte, dissatisfied with some army officers' softness toward disturbances, had obtained the Tsar's support for a more trigger-happy policy, which the war ministry unwillingly passed on to its commanders. Regular military courts were trying hundreds of alleged civilian rioters but, because of their usually quite high standards of procedure, were taking more time and acquitting more accused than the government wanted. So in summer 1906 Stolypin and the interior ministry, despite the distaste of the war ministry, decided to introduce field courts martial. Great care was taken to appoint officer judges who had not been tainted by training as army lawyers, and in general the courts martial achieved the aim of fast trials and fast executions. They aroused great protest in the Duma and also undermined Stolypin's aim of encouraging popular respect for the law.

Stolypin was himself the target of a Socialist Revolutionary bomb at this time, and throughout Russia there were assassinations, sporadic peasant revolts, and more naval mutinies at Sveaborg and Kronstadt. Not all these plots were the work of anarchists and Socialist Revolutionaries. By this time the extreme right-wing groups had their own terrorists, and one of these succeeded in killing a Kadet leader; the assassin had his death sentence commuted by the Tsar.

Distaste for 'Stolypin's neckties', the hundreds of hangings authorized by courts martial, was one of the reasons the Octobrist leaders refused his offer of a place in the government. In February 1907 the Second Duma was elected; the Kadets, damaged by the arrest of so many candidates after the Vyborg Manifesto, won only 92 seats, while the Trudoviki won 101. The Social Democrats, who this time participated wholeheartedly, won 65 seats, and even the Socialist

Revolutionaries won 34 although that party still claimed to be boycotting the election. On the other hand, while the right-of-centre Octobrists increased their seats to 32, the extreme right-wing parties rose to 63. The government was still reluctant to cooperate in any real way with the Duma, although Stolypin himself was perhaps more flexible than his colleagues. Right-wing confidants of the Tsar were horrified by the Duma's criticism of the way the Russian army was managed, while Stolypin himself was riled by the Duma's opposition to his land reform. The police soon came to the rescue of those clamouring for a dissolution, using a tactic which they would still favour half a century later. A document, in the form of an appeal to soldiers to mutiny, was obtained. This was then handed to a Social Democrat member of the Duma, who before he had time to read it, was arrested and accused, together with his Social Democrat fellow-members, of sedition. A similar action was taken against a Socialist Revolutionary. Stolypin believed the police evidence to be genuine, but the Duma refused to lift the socialist Members' immunity without a thorough examination of the charges, and this provided an excuse for dissolution. Troops were brought into the capital in case of trouble, the Tsar issued a manifesto accusing the Duma of subversion, and it was announced that the next Duma would be elected under quite a different system.

The new electoral system was an infringement of the Fundamental Laws by which the Duma had been established in 1906. It gave great weight to the country gentry and to the urban rich, thus ensuring that the resulting chamber would be dominated by those in favour of the status quo. At the same time it contrived to reduce the influence of the nationalists from the non-Russian parts by a similar gerrymandering. Warsaw, for example, was to send an equal number of Polish and Russian members, even though Warsaw's Russian electorate was small. When the Third Duma met in late 1907 it had, not surprisingly, a preponderantly right-wing complexion. It was now the Octobrists who were the largest party, with 120 seats. To their right were 145 members of various affiliations, but to their left comparatively few; the Kadets were down to 52 seats and the socialist parties had been reduced to much below their level in the previous Duma.

Nevertheless an unrepresentative Duma was not necessarily an ineffective Duma. Although its members were predominantly of right-wing inclination, they were mostly able and sincere. The government was anxious by this time to show that it really did wish to cooperate with the Duma, and Nicholas and his personal advisers found the composition of the new chamber not entirely distasteful. Thus little by little the government attached more and more importance to gaining the Duma's approval for its measures. Ministers went to the Duma and were expected to give genuine answers to the criticisms, often searching, voiced by members. Stolypin's tampering with the electoral system had not affected the field of competence of the Duma, and the latter, especially through its discussion of the annual budget, discovered that few fields of inquiry were closed to it. Duma committees were largely responsible for the improvements in the army and navy which occurred at that time; if the navy ministry and the war ministry had not been forced to respond to Duma criticism, the Russian armed forces would have been in a very bad state indeed by 1914. During its term the Third Duma also succeeded with two reform projects of its own. The justices of the peace, introduced under Alexander II and replaced by land captains under Alexander III, were reinstated and the land captains abolished, and health and accident insurance programmes were established for industrial workers. This Duma served its full term to 1912. Towards the end its relations with the government deteriorated, due largely to Stolypin's inability to understand its rights and sensibilities; faced at one stage by difficulty in getting a measure passed by the upper chamber, Stolypin prorogued both chambers for three days, in which period he employed Article 87 to put his measure into effect. This action destroyed the trust which had been built up between the Duma and the ministers, and the leader of the Octobrists in the Duma, Guchkov, in protest resigned from his office of Duma president. It had been the mutual respect of Stolypin and Guchkov which had enabled this Duma, despite its bad beginning, to do better than its predecessors and to demonstrate to the people, as well as to Nicholas, that some kind of interaction between rulers and ruled was indeed workable.

The measure which Stolypin had passed into law with Article 87 was for the extension of the *zemstvo* system into the western borderlands. This had aroused intense dispute because Russian landowners in that region feared that excessive numbers of Poles and peasants would be elected. The electoral regulations did seek to minimize this danger, but in the course of the lengthy argument the Nationalist party organized itself. Among its principles were loyalty to both the autocracy and the new representative institutions, financial help for the peasants, strong armed forces, support for the Orthodox Church and its educational institutions, the promotion of the Russians as the leading people of the Empire, and the impossibility of granting full citizenship rights to Jews. It was a well-organized party and Stolypin began to rely on it. It seemed likely to replace the Octobrists as the leading party, but it did less well in the election to the Fourth Duma than it had hoped. That election, held in 1912, produced the final Duma, whose leaders would supervise the abdication of Nicholas in 1917. Of the 432 members, 91 were of the Nationalist party, but they did not dominate the right because the Octobrists managed 95 and various other rightists 63. But it was very much a right-leaning assembly and subject to successive bouts of manoeuvring as the prime minister of the day strove to coax two or three parties into a supportive majority. The Centre party had 31 seats and the Kadets 53, but the left had only 10 Trudoviki and 15 Social Democrats. However, by 1914, after many disappointments, the various rightists were in no mood to give automatic support to the government.

Stolypin

Undoubtedly the outstanding Russian statesman of the last Romanov decade was Stolypin. He was a man of many enemies, and these enemies were to be found in all political camps. Like many others of unimpeachable integrity and definite views, he did not hesitate to take strong action, and it was probably this which created the hostility towards him. His field courts martial with their high-speed death sentences earned him the hatred of the revolutionaries. His abuse of Article 87 and his interference with the electoral process earned the dislike of the liberals. He caused offence among the minorities, especially among the Finns, whose liberties he curtailed. Above all, perhaps, he was hated by the right extremists, those who resented any dilution of autocracy and found offensive Stolypin's executive power.

Unlike so many other ministers, Stolypin did not rise through the ranks of the central administration, but first attracted public attention as governor of Saratov province. In this office he distinguished himself by personally, and at some risk, intervening in peasant disorders; instead of sending troops he sent himself, talked to the peasants, and avoided bloodshed. He was called to St Petersburg as minister of the interior, and his elevation to chairman of the Council of Ministers soon followed. He could perhaps best be described as a progressive conservative. His actions were often repressive and uncompromising, but he was contending not only with left-wing revolutionaries, but with extreme right-wing radicals also. Regional governors and some of the St Petersburg administrators found ways to frustrate his endeavours. He had no control over the police; the Okhrana opened his mail and channelled money to right-wing opponents. His wish to extend primary education and to protect the Old Believers and Jews was frustrated by the Church.

Apart from the right-wing parties there also existed from 1905, outside the Duma, the Union of the Russian People. This, which was intelligently led, aimed at appealing to the emotions of the masses and enlisting their support for a return to the traditional autocratic regime. Playing on the theme of 'Great Russia', it was anti-Jew, anti-left, and anti-intellectual and, when it had time, anti-Kadet, anti-Finn, and anti-Ukrainian. Money was channelled to it by the interior ministry, and it had sympathizers in the police, who on occasion assisted in its arming. It was involved in street violence and later in the pogroms. Called the 'Black Hundred' by its enemies, it was favoured by the Orthodox Church and also by Nicholas. The latter, at times, seemed to welcome the violence and murders perpetrated by the Black Hundred as evidence of a loyal backlash.

There were also those, often in close touch with Nicholas, who spent much of their time devising ways to abolish or emasculate the Duma, so that power could be returned to where it traditionally belonged. Compared to some of their schemes, Stolypin's tampering with the electoral system was mild indeed. Among the ambitious men seeking to replace Stolypin was Witte, embittered by his own dismissal in 1906 and not averse to consorting with the rightists if that would improve his chances.

Witte, however, never got back. But he wrote his memoirs and outlived Stolypin. The latter was bombed in 1907, but although his house was damaged, his daughter crippled, and about twenty-five persons killed, he emerged unhurt physically if not emotionally. In 1911 he attended a Kiev theatrical performance in the presence of the Tsar. During the interval, Nicholas wrote later to his mother:

we heard two noises . . . I thought a pair of opera glasses had fallen on somebody's head and ran back into the box to look . . . women shrieked, and right in front of me stood Stolypin in the stalls. Slowly he turned his face towards us and made the sign of the cross with his left hand in the air. Only at this point did I notice that he was very pale and that his right hand and uniform were bloodstained. He sat down quietly and started to unbutton his tunic.[9]

Stolypin died a few days later. His assassin was a romantic revolutionary acting mainly to satisfy his own needs. A police informer as well as a revolutionary, and finding in neither activity a cause to which he could belong or contemporaries who would respect him, he sought to win appreciation by a glorious deed. As an Okhrana agent, he had secured a pass into the theatre and got to within three paces of Stolypin. His first shot ricocheted into the leg of a violinist sitting in the orchestra pit, but his second was fatal. His association with the police later led to rumours that the assassination had been arranged with the complicity of highly placed officials.

The Stolypin Reform

Lenin later described 1905 as a dress rehearsal for 1917. This was a dress rehearsal that demanded substantial rewriting of the plot, for the revolt took a course that surprised both the regime and the revolutionaries. Hitherto the latter had supposed future revolution to be on the lines of the European upheavals of 1848, but events had shown that the Russian workers could spontaneously organize themselves into soviets and that the peasants were not the inert conservative mass that had been supposed.

Certainly nothing would be quite the same after 1905. Peasants became less deferential. In the towns, middle-class people began to fear the masses. The *zemstva* tended to become more conservative. The United Nobility was formed to protect the interests of landowners, but many nobles moved permanently to the towns. The scattered peasant revolts of 1906–7 had taken many forms, beginning with invasion of private and state forests or grazing

9. *Krasnyi arkhiv*, 35 (1929), 210.

land, or refusal to pay taxes, and progressing to robbery of warehouses, arson, destructive attacks on the property of local landowners and often on the landowner families. Although landowners were the main target, government officials, and especially the police, were also attacked. Contrary to official descriptions, these risings were not coordinated with each other and were not instigated by a small minority or by outsiders. What typically happened was that the peasants of a *mir* (commune) decided that enough was enough, found their own leaders from among themselves, and deliberately and with forethought set out to wreak their havoc. Some of them joined together to form independent 'republics' in which no government official dared to tread until the army had been brought in to restore the situation. The richer peasants seemed the keenest to participate, while the poorer tended to hang back. Neither had revolutionary or even socialist goals, but they had a strong feeling for social justice. They were cruelly punished. Many, including teenagers, were hanged with virtually no trial.

This unexpected display by the peasants was noted, each in his own way, by Lenin and Stolypin, and each absorbed its lesson. Lenin, while continuing to underestimate the strength of the peasant *mir*, nevertheless began to think of a democratic dictatorship of not just workers, but workers and peasants. Stolypin was strengthened in his belief that the autocracy could not survive unless it solved the peasant problem.

The far-reaching and fundamental peasant reforms introduced piecemeal between 1906 and 1911 are called the Stolypin Reform, although they were worked out by a Danish agricultural expert and other government officials. Because Stolypin hoped that they would create from the 'best' peasants a class of prosperous smallholders with a stake in the status quo, the reforms were sometimes called a wager on the strong (or, more realistically perhaps, a wager on the sober). Instead of easing the land shortage by expropriating the landowners (as many Duma members demanded), the reforms promised a solution at the expense of the *mir*.

In the official view, the *mir* seemed harmful and, with the end of redemption payments, superfluous. It still imposed the traditional methods of the majority, and its strip system of land division by which a peasant landholding might be divided into thirty or more strips could never be efficient. It is true that since the Emancipation it was possible for peasants to withdraw from the *mir*, and to consolidate their strips, but all too often the *mir*'s opposition prevented such action. It is also true that most peasants wanted to keep the *mir*, partly because it protected them from the winds of change; it was only a minority which had the will and the ability to be independent. It was this minority of shrewd, perhaps selfish, farmers which the government wished to increase and encourage; the less enterprising would, it was thought, eventually either quit agriculture or begin to imitate their more advanced neighbours.

In the beginning, release of unused or underused land[10] for sale on easy terms to the poorer-than-average peasant was the most publicized feature of the legislation, but the planners were also hoping to spread better farming practice. The new legislation established a land settlement commission, whose officials were to confirm peasants in the ownership of the strips which they cultivated at that time. Then, in the many communes where there had been no complete land redistribution since Emancipation, any householder wishing to convert ('consolidate') his strips into one integrated landholding could request the survey officials to suitably rearrange all the strips of the commune, whether or not his neighbours desired this. In other communes a two-thirds majority vote could enforce consolidations for the whole village. The cherished hereditary household plot of each family, which traditionally had not been subject to redistribution, was not included in consolidation plans. It was hoped that eventually the new peasant farmers would transfer their homes (which stood on or near their household plots) to a site on their new consolidated land area, but this was a slow process. The legislation included a prohibition of the sale of peasant land to non-peasants, and a maximum allowable landholding: it was not intended to create a few big peasant landowners.

The above paragraph is a simplification of a highly complex scheme for a highly complex situation. Unfortunately some of the complexities would emerge only later. The legislation, and especially its local application, was very much a play-it-by-ear process, peasant reaction to the earlier measures affecting the later decisions. After the first few years, consolidation on behalf of individual peasants declined, but more and more peasants collectively demanded village consolidation. Thus officials began to deal with villages as collective units rather than with individuals; their task virtually became village redevelopment.

Some poorer peasants sold their land as soon as their ownership was confirmed, and then went to the towns in search of work. Many more stayed on, eking out a meagre and often resentful existence; resentful because often their familiar way of life and work was changed by land rearrangements desired by their better-off neighbours. Village elders tended to oppose the reform, and there could be intimidation and violence directed against those who wanted to take advantage of the scheme; such violence could include beatings, cattle-killing, and home-burning. The land captains, entrusted locally with the reform, more often than not tried to block it. Governors and local administrators likewise were lukewarm or opposed. The central agricultural region was the least receptive. There, surveyors were best advised to take an armed guard

10. In 1905 in European Russia about 25% of the agricultural land was privately owned, 35% was peasants' strips, and about 40% state owned. Of the private land 62% was owned by the nobility (as against 80% in 1877), 15% by merchants, and 15% by peasants (6% in 1877). See P. Khromov, *Ekonomicheskoye razvitiye Rossii* (1967), 495–6.

with them. Separating peasants were often given the worst land; some did remarkably well with it but others failed.

The reforms added fuel to the already smouldering social tension in the countryside. But, given a few decades of peace, there might have developed a prosperous and loyal peasantry. In the immediate pre-war years there were indeed higher yields, increased use of machinery and fertilizers, and a burgeoning of farmers' cooperatives. When peasants became soldiers in 1914 the reform had to stop, because the possibility of changes in the home village was demoralizing for soldiers at the front. By that time about 2.5 million households (of an eligible total of about 12 million) had had ownership of their strips confirmed and were thus outside the authority of the *mir*. Of these about one-half had reached the second stage of consolidating their holdings. In the wheat-growing south almost half the households had broken away from the *mir*, and commercial farming was well established.

One of the first consequences of the 1917 revolutions was a partial reversal of the process, with the resentful majority of a village forcing the independent minority to replace their land at the disposal of the *mir*. But this reversal seems to have been prevalent mainly in areas where extensive individual consolidations had taken place, or where outsiders had bought consolidated plots; whole-village consolidations appear to have been reversed only rarely.

8

Russia in 1914

The population

RUSSIA's first really comprehensive census was undertaken only in 1897, and it was not perfect. According to this, the Empire contained 125 million inhabitants (excluding Finland, which had about 2.5 million). Both the birth rate and the death rate were higher than in most other parts of Europe, and the fourteen per thousand excess of births over deaths promised a fast population growth. What this increase amounted to by 1914 is disputed, but a conservative estimate for the 1914 population is 155 million,[1] of whom 125 million were in European Russia, 13 million in Central Asia, 10 million in Siberia and the Far East, and 6 million in Transcaucasia. The most densely populated part of the Empire was Poland, followed by the notoriously overpopulated wheatlands of the Ukraine (which had 150 persons per square mile in 1897). Six per cent of the Empire's territory (Poland, Ukraine, Lithuania, the Moscow region, the central agricultural region) contained two-fifths of the population. In 1897 15 per cent of the population was classified as urban,[2] but there were only nineteen cities of more than 100,000 inhabitants. St Petersburg approached 1,250,000 and Moscow had recently reached the 1 million mark, while Warsaw, in third place, had 684,000.[3] By 1914, thanks to high birth rates and rapid migration to the towns, St Petersburg had 2,118,000, Moscow 1,762,000, while Riga and Kiev had doubled their populations and passed the half-million mark. There were over half a million villages, averaging 200 inhabitants each in 1897. Urban returns indicate that by 1911 the towns of Russia (many of which were little larger than villages) contained almost 2 million residential buildings, of which a little more than half were wooden. Of the 1,082 communities classified as towns, 886 claimed to have some street lighting (usually kerosene, but seventy-four had electric and thirty-five gas lighting). One hundred and ninety-two towns had piped water systems, and thirty-eight some kind of piped sewage, although these facilities rarely covered

1. Some reputable estimates go as high as 170 million or more. In any case, the Russian population was roughly one and a half times greater than the American, and more than treble the British.
2. Compared with four-fifths in Britain and two-fifths in the USA.
3. See table, p. 611.

the whole urban area; St Petersburg water was tainted in 1911, worse than it was ninety years later, and cholera outbreaks happened there about once every three years. Fifty-five towns had tramways and 182 had telephone systems. Moscow's telephone system dated from as early as 1882; the city council of St Petersburg took great pride in its Central Telephone Exchange, opened in 1905 soon after the local system had been taken over from Bell Telephone.

Compared with the figures for the beginning of the nineteenth century (see p. 606), the most striking change is the absolute growth of the population and the growing importance of the non-Russian nationalities. According to the 1897 census, there were 92 million Slavs in the Empire, of whom 57 million were Great Russians, 22 million Ukrainians, 6 million Byelorussians, and 8 million Poles. Among the other nationalities were 5 million Jews, about 15 million Germans, and 13 million Turkic and Tartar peoples. Seventy per cent of the population was classified as Orthodox (including Old Believers), 11 per cent as Muhammadan, and 9 per cent as Catholics. Of the Empire's males 0.2 per cent, and of females 0.01 per cent, had had some form of higher education. In Finland and the Baltic provinces the literacy rate was over 75 per cent, but in Russia proper much lower; only the Moscow and St Petersburg regions exceeded 40 per cent, the rest of European Russia ranged from 10 to 40 per cent. Thanks partly to the growth of primary education after 1905, about 30 per cent of the population were literate by 1913, with a much bigger percentage for young urban males. Another source records that only a third of Russian conscripts were illiterate in 1913 (compared to a quarter of US army recruits in 1917, although the tests may have differed).

Seventy-seven per cent of the population in 1897 was classified as peasant, 10 per cent was 'middle class', and 0.5 per cent was of the Christian priesthood. The hereditary nobility amounted to 1 per cent, and non-hereditary nobles plus non-noble officials added another 0.5 per cent to this. Cossacks were 2.3 per cent, and foreigners 0.5 per cent. Emigration was small, but increased in the early twentieth century. In the first decade of the latter about 1.5 million emigrants left, mainly for the New World; nearly half of these were Jews, and one-quarter Poles. Seventy-five per cent of employed persons were engaged in agriculture. Nine per cent were in manufacturing and mining, and this increased to about 10 per cent by 1914, by which year about 1.5 per cent of the total population were non-agricultural workers, compared to 12 per cent in the USA.

With a pervasive bureaucracy there was a correspondingly large output of official statistics. These were of varying accuracy and relevance; two returns which throw some light on Russian society are the medical/mortality figures, and the annual state budget. Mortality figures depended largely on the records kept by priests, who had little medical knowledge but abundant discretion. According to the 1897 statistics, one-tenth of all Russians died of 'old age'. Infantile mortality was very high, but after this the most common cause of death was unhelpfully defined as 'convulsions', accounting for 14 per cent. The traditional scourge of the intelligentsia, tuberculosis, was not confined to that class, for it caused 10 per cent of all deaths. Cholera took 4 per cent, and strokes 5 per cent. The 'English disease' (rickets) took less than 0.5 per cent. Murder was responsible for almost 0.1 per cent, and accidents 2 per cent. Suicides at 1 per cent were low compared to more urbanized nations. These categories obscure the incidence of two causes of death which were causing much anxiety, vodka[4] and syphilis. In 1913 in Russian towns 1.8 per cent of the inhabitants were registered syphilitics. In the famous Moscow Foundlings Hospital there was a ward devoted to syphilitic babies, who were fed by specially recruited syphilitic wet-nurses.

Until 1894 the government farmed out the right of selling and manufacturing alcoholic beverages, but in that year Witte introduced a state liquor monopoly. This was designed to reduce drunkenness and also to divert to the Treasury funds which had previously swelled the fortunes of the liquor merchants. Deaths attributable to alcohol did fall but, after the Russo-Japanese War dislocated the state budget, revenue needs took precedence over temperance. Higher sales were encouraged and temperance measures were half-hearted. One such measure was the regulation that liquor could not be consumed within fifty paces of the place of sale, presumably in the expectation that only the sober would find their way back for more. That the death rate from alcohol was four or five times higher than in western Europe was largely because Russian imbibing was concentrated in a few drinking bouts, rather than spread evenly through the year. Drunkenness was especially widespread on holy days, which are generously distributed throughout the Orthodox calendar. In winter, a drunken sleep could mean a frozen death, unless the victim was picked up by one of the special police patrols organized in some districts. In 1908 an anti-alcohol exhibition was held for the first time in Russia, and there was a strong temperance movement in the Duma. Prohibition of strong spirits was achieved in 1914.

Whereas Russia in 1913 could take pride in her veterinary services, medical services were still inadequate, though improving. For several decades the *zemstva* (which, however, only existed in about half of the provinces) had organized rural medical services, and it is indicative of the advanced social consciousness of the Russian professional class that the ruling principle of these services was that a free medical service was a right, not a privilege or charity. The doctors who practised under the *zemstva* were a particular type, hard-working and idealistic. In the cities it was different. There the medical services were usually paid for and, apart from factory medical services, little was done for the poor. In all, there were about 25,000 doctors in 1913; more than ten times more, and better prepared, than a century earlier. Among the

4. Convulsions?

wealthy the belief persisted that German doctors were better, and few would admit to their friends that they had a Russian doctor.

By 1910 the state budget was back to normal after the upheavals of 1905. Direct taxes accounted for only 8 per cent of income, whereas indirect amounted to 21 per cent.[5] Indirect taxes on sugar, matches, kerosene, tobacco, and cigarette paper were proportionately more burdensome for the poor, although as the range of taxed items widened the urban classes began to take a fairer share of the tax burden. Various internal duties accounted for another 6 per cent, but the biggest sources of income were state investment (29 per cent, including 22 per cent from state railway receipts) and 31 per cent from state monopolies. Of the latter, almost all was accounted for by the liquor monopoly which, unlike the state railways, had low operating costs. The liquor monopoly income, plus taxes on various beverages, accounted for 29 per cent of the state revenue in 1910. Compared with 1901, when the state liquor monopoly was still only partially in force, this income had doubled; even when the operating expenses were deducted it still amounted to 25 per cent of state revenue. On the other side of the budget, operating costs of the state railways accounted for 22 per cent of expenditure, the ministry of war for another 20 per cent, and the ministry of finance for 17 per cent. Interest on government loans had reached 16.5 per cent of the total expenses. The ministry of the interior (which besides security was responsible for a host of services: fire brigades, some roads, telegraphs and posts, map publishing, etc.) took 7 per cent, and the ministry of education 3 per cent. (The latter figure was only a part of the Empire's educational expenditure, for other organizations made their own contributions.)

Society

For the landowning nobility, the portents were not good. Long before the Emancipation many had been leading lives far in excess of their incomes. On the eve of Emancipation two-thirds of their property had already been mortgaged to government banks. Over the century, in effect, state funds had been diverted as mortgage loans to landowners who used them less for productive investment than for maintaining their standard of living. For many of these improvident gentry, Emancipation meant the paying-off of their mortgages through the indemnities which the government allotted for the land transferred by the nobles to the peasantry. But in the long term, Emancipation only made things worse for the average landowner. A few saved themselves by marrying into rich commercial families, while others did weather the storm and learned to farm their estates on commercial principles. But many had

---

5. Personal income tax was not introduced in Russia until 1916, and even then was at a rather low graduated rate, which excluded half the population.

recourse to the Nobles Land Bank, founded in 1885 to advance mortgage loans, or sold their land to peasants and cut their links with the countryside. Whereas in the mid-1870s the gentry possessed about 200 million acres, by 1910 this had diminished to less than 140 million, of which about nine-tenths was rented out to peasant farmers. Although about two-thirds of the senior state offices were held by landowning nobles, this proportion was diminishing as educated non-landowners made successful careers in the bureaucracy. The landowning gentry was not at all homogeneous. It had, for example, a liberal component anxious to extend its role in local government, and an enterprising component that dabbled in industry and intellectual pursuits. But what might be called the traditional, or provincial, nobility was still very influential. It did not like change and did what it could to hinder progressive innovations like the *zemstva* and Stolypin's reforms.

Much of the country's new wealth, the industry and commerce that had developed since the freeing of the serfs, belonged not to the nobles but to a developing middle class which by 1914 exceeded 2 million people. This was small by European standards and its effectiveness was further diminished by its divisions. The Jews and foreigners, who were prominent in trade and industry, were certainly 'middle class' but were hardly of the Russian middle class. There was also a division between the commercial class on the one hand and the intellectuals on the other. Of the latter, the professionals were growing fast and probably amounted to a million workers by 1914, although only about 130,000 of those had higher education. Primary-school teachers and doctors multiplied especially fast, and may have doubled between 1900 and 1914. Both the creative intellectuals and the more numerous professionals tended to scorn the capitalist and the merchant. This is probably why the capitalists were ignored or treated negatively by Russian writers, even though many of their names were household words, and even though their works determined the shape of Russia's economic life.

The best-known industrialists of the nineteenth century were the Morozovs, whose four establishments employed 54,000 workers by 1914. The founder of their fortune was a serf born in 1770, Savva Morozov, who secured his landowner's permission to start a dye-works on the estate, and made a fortune. He purchased his freedom in 1820, and died forty years later. His son Timofei was an innovator too. He imported foreign specialists, encouraged the domestic production of textile machinery, established scholarships for technicians wishing to study abroad, and invested in banks and railways. But his passion for efficiency drove him to extract the last ounce of production from each worker. He introduced a fining system which not only penalized obvious misdemeanours such as lateness, but any failure to achieve what Timofei considered was achievable. The very best worker could expect to pay back about 10 per cent of his wage in fines. Timofei was so ruthless towards his workers that he spent tearful hours before his icon, asking for forgiveness.

However, his prayers did not avert the famous Morozov strike of 1885, when his 8,000 workers protested against the fines. The strike was broken by armed force and its leaders imprisoned, but Timofei was never the same again, and neither was the Russian labour situation, for the strike encouraged other workers to resist their managements. Timofei's son Savva was deeply affected by these events, and when he succeeded his father his reaction took the form of improving working conditions, workers' housing, and medical services. He was also interested in the arts, financing the new and soon-celebrated Moscow Art Theatre, much of whose stage equipment he designed himself. He became a friend of Chekhov and Gorki. The latter portrayed him in one of his works, and was bailed out of gaol by him in 1905. Savva, on Gorki's invitation, also contributed to the Social Democrats' funds, including the budget of Lenin's journal *Iskra*. But when in 1905 he proposed a plan for profit-sharing among his workers, his mother persuaded the board to dismiss him, and he shot himself.

Men like the Morozovs were exceptional, but they were the leaders of a whole class of capitalists which did much for Russia. If the breed disappeared in 1917, certainly the bricks and mortar of their works lived on. Often Jews or Old Believers, they were notable for their quiet lives; apart from their work and their families they had few interests outside the arts, which they encouraged by their patronage of native talent. But despite their common sense and enterprise, they did not understand that the transformation of Russian economic life which they were engineering was producing the social and political tension which in 1917 would engulf them.

By most standards, the status of women was at least as good in 1913 Russia as elsewhere. The revolutionary movements, which tended towards a natural sexual equality, had included female liberation in their aims and these ideals had spread among the educated classes. Advanced Russian women were more interested in sexual freedom and careers than in voting and property rights. Many girls had gone abroad to study, and returned, hoping for a better Russia. By the turn of the century it seemed that their hopes might be justified. In 1908 the first all-Russia women's conference was held, at which it was claimed that although there was much to be done, the opportunities available to a woman outside the home were less restricted than in western Europe. There were already female teachers, doctors, and architects working in *zemstva* and town council organizations. In 1904 the first women's agricultural college had been opened. In 1905 university co-education was won. For those interested in the 'woman question', and for those actually working for sex equality in the 'women's movement', educational equality was regarded as a commanding height whose capture would eventually change the structure and attitude of society. But despite middle-class sympathy, despite literary and journalistic successes by women, the women's movement was less strong than it might have been. This was largely because the conventional radicals expected militant women to fight for the general cause rather than the female cause; once the regime was overthrown, they promised, women would get their rights. Those women who gave priority to female emancipation they castigated as 'bourgeois', or worse.

As for the peasants, the casual observer might have noticed little external change in the villages since 1861. There was still very little direct contact between the administration and the peasantry. Although many peasants had acquired extra land from bankrupt gentry or from poorer neighbours, there were others who were dissatisfied and receptive to revolutionary propaganda which they incompletely understood but often found convincing. The Stolypin reforms had done little to remove the tensions between landowners and peasants. On the other hand, tension between rich and poor peasants was by no means as great as marxists liked to believe. A characteristic of the period was the increasing number of peasants who became industrial workers, either in local enterprises or in the towns. Those who went to the urban factories usually maintained their ties with the village, returning home to help with the harvest. Others, more independent, moved about Russia seeking temporary work; most of these would also go home at harvest time, taking with them whatever they had managed to save. The elite among them were the specialists, who often grouped themselves into a cooperative (*artel*) whose elected leader would seek short-term contracts in such trades as house-painting or stonemasonry.

Artels were also important in industry. They were formed by workers who capitalized themselves by paying an entrance fee. Because the members knew and trusted each other, and cherished the reputation of their group, the *artels* were noted for their reliability and good workmanship. In a sense an *artel* member was a privileged member of the proletariat, but he was found only in small-scale enterprises. The bulk of Russia's industrial workers worked in factories. These were often situated far from towns, and frequently were much larger than their western counterparts. Their owners were usually responsible for the housing of their workers, providing barracks nearby. The barracks, though making little demand on the workers' pockets, were hopelessly over-crowded and insanitary, with each man having barely the space of his own bunk; with a two-shift system two workers might be expected to take turns with one bunk. Workers' families also inhabited the barracks. But on working days the men were too tired to notice discomfort, and on holidays too drunk. Moreover, conditions were much worse in the smaller enterprises, where workers and their families might live alongside their workbench in cramped, slimy, and stinking conditions unmatched in the most primitive village.

As industry developed, there appeared a small but growing nucleus of skilled workers. These tended to live outside the factory in private rooms, and gradually broke most of their ties with the villages. They lived in overcrowded conditions, but in several respects they were privileged. Especially at times of boom, enterprises had to make some effort to attract and keep them, so they enjoyed better wages and working conditions. They had a high literacy rate and were ready to listen to revolutionary propaganda. It was from their ranks that the Social Democrats drew much of their strength.

Although trade unions were not permitted (except, with many restrictions, after 1905), the existence of workers' mutual aid associations did foster some sense of solidarity among the proletariat. In the last fifty years of the tsarist regime, there were many strikes which, in part at least, led to government intervention to improve working conditions. The first law came in 1882, and limited the industrial employment of women and children. After the Morozov strike it was made illegal for an employer to benefit from workers' fines; the practice of fining continued but the proceeds went to a fund to help the workers themselves. In 1896, after the St Petersburg textile workers' strike, the government imposed the eleven-hour working day (with ten hours on Saturday). By 1914 most enterprises worked a nine- or ten-hour day, which, in view of the ninety-eight Sundays and religious or statutory holidays each year, was not arduous.[6] But wages were low. Although strikes were illegal even after 1905, with instigators liable to imprisonment, they intensified in the prosperous years preceding the outbreak of war. The most notable strike was that at the Lena goldfields in 1912. Their workers, mainly peasants, were badly treated and finally erupted after the discovery of disgusting parts of animals in their stew. The management might have calmed the situation but the police exacerbated it by arresting the leaders. Troops were ordered to open fire, killing an estimated 200 workers. Although the interior ministry showed no remorse for the actions of its police, this massacre of workers employed by a notoriously mean British-owned company aroused angry reactions throughout Russia. The Lena goldfields massacre took its place alongside the 1891 famine and Bloody Sunday as an event after which nothing seemed quite the same:

There has never been so much tension. People can be heard speaking of the government in the sharpest and most unbridled tones. Many say that the 'shooting' of the Lena workers recalls the 'shooting' of the workers at the Winter Palace of January 9 1905. Influenced by questions in the Duma and the speeches which they called forth there, public tension is increasing still more . . . It is a long time since even the extreme left has spoken in such a way, since there have been references in the Duma to 'the necessity of calling a Constituent Assembly and overthrow the present system by the united strength of the proletariat'.[7]

Large enterprises were held responsible for providing medical services, including hospitals and sometimes maternity homes, for workers and their families. Workers' accident insurance, hitherto neither generous nor widespread, was systematized in 1903 and 1912 by new regulations, the most

---

6. The industrious Dutch had only 57 Sundays and holidays.
7. From a Moscow Okhrana agent's report published in *Istoricheskii arkhiv*, 1 (1962), 178–9.

important of which acknowledged employers' liability for work accidents, with no necessity for the victim to prove negligence. Many factories provided schools for the children of their workers. There were many ruthless employers, but some did more than the law required. Individual consciences were as important as the government's factory inspectors in setting standards.

In contrast to its attitude towards trade unions, the administration did little to hinder, and even encouraged, the cooperative movement which flourished after 1905. Producers' cooperatives in the form of *artels* were already part of Russian tradition; what was new was the sudden popularity of marketing and purchasing cooperatives. There was also a blossoming of the savings bank movement. By 1918, after doubling their membership during the war, the cooperatives' membership was equivalent to about one-third of the total population. The biggest cooperative retail store was Moscow's *Kooperatsiya*, which had 210,000 members. There was a cooperative wholesale union (*Tsentrosoyuz*), and in 1911 a People's Bank had been founded. The latter, the Moscow Narodny Bank, was 85 per cent owned by the cooperative movement. All this does not mean that Russia in 1914 was well on the road to socialism, but it does suggest that Russians, and especially rural Russians, had not become as individualistic as some commentators assumed.

Day-to-day control of the population was aided by the internal passports which citizens had to carry, and by the registration with the police of all travellers staying overnight outside their home districts. The janitors of dwelling houses kept lists of arrivals and departures which were sent to the local police. In towns the police kept a list of all the inhabitants' addresses (and by applying on a special form a citizen could obtain the address of any individual he was seeking). Scant attention was paid to individual rights. For example, on May Day 1912, men without collars were chased off St Petersburg's main streets, because this seemed the most convenient way to prevent a workers' demonstration.[8] Despite occasional outrages such as this, and the feeling that everyone was being watched, it is probably true that police repression was accepted by Russians as a necessary evil. Most citizens had been shocked by the murder of Alexander II: many regarded the revolutionaries as enemies of reform, and knew that violent protest only strengthened the position of the reactionaries.

Freedom of the press was one of the 1905 guarantees frequently evaded by the administration. It could happen that particular issues of a newspaper were impounded, but more frequently newspapers appeared with white spaces where material had been deleted. Arbitrary (and illegal) attacks on press freedom were most blatant in the provinces:

The newspaper report concerning the small Kiev kopek-newspaper *Ogni* is arousing

---

8. Six years later it was men who did wear collars and ties who were at risk in revolutionary Petrograd.

deep indignation. It has been fined 1,200 roubles each month and now the present editor, Madame Prokhasko, has been put under administrative arrest despite her illness. They wanted to make her keep quiet about three things: about the Jews, about the workers, and about the priesthood.[9]

The Russian talent for euphemism was well exploited. For example, when newspaper criticisms prompted the administration to ban mention of Rasputin, the term 'dark forces near the throne' was substituted. In 1913 there were about 1,000 newspapers published in the Empire (excluding Poland and Finland). Since the combined circulation of these was about 3.25 million, it is evident that in Russia small-circulation newspapers could survive, especially since one-third of the combined figure was contributed by just three papers: the *Russkoye Slovo* of Moscow (750,000), the right-wing *Novoye Vremiya* of St Petersburg (200,000) and the liberal prefessionals' paper, *Russkiya Vedomosti* (100,000). By contrast the St Petersburg liberal paper *Rech'* sold only 17,000 copies. *Novoye Vremiya* was sufficiently monarchistic and chauvinistic to become daily reading for Nicholas II. But it was not unenlightened. At the other end of the scale was *Gazeta-kopeika* of St Petersburg, which when it appeared was the first 'kopek newspaper', highly illustrated, tabloid-style, and costing only a kopek. It began with a print-run of 10,000 but within a couple of years was selling a quarter-million copies daily and had been imitated in other cities.

The economy

Russian output grew fast but unevenly after the end of the Crimean War. In terms of industrial production, there was a doubling of output between 1860 and 1880, and a doubling again over the following twelve years. The 1890s were a decade of boom, thanks largely to the 1891 protective tariff and renewed railway-building sponsored by Witte. Despite a recession in 1894 there was a further doubling of production in the eight years 1892–1900. After 1900 there was a slower growth, but only 1905 produced an actual decrease. Overall economic growth (measured by net national product) averaged 5 per cent annually from 1909 to 1913, with large-scale industry growing by an annual 7 per cent and even the inefficient agricultural sector (favoured by a run of good weather) by around 3 per cent. On a per-head basis, overall growth would have been about 3.5 per cent, because of the rapid population increase, but that was still a fast rise. However, 1913 national income per head (a rough indication of prosperity) was still only one-fifth of Britain's and one-eighth of the USA's. In terms of production (and especially consumption) Russia was far behind the other great powers. In 1913, in absolute terms, Russian coal production was only one-tenth of Britain's and one-seventeenth of the United

States'. Oil production, in which Russia occupied first place in the world in 1900, was only one-third that of the USA in 1913. In steel, Russia produced one-half the British output and one-eighth the American, in cotton textiles one-quarter and one-third respectively. The picture would only be marginally changed if Polish and Finnish output were included in these calculations.

The main industrial areas were the St Petersburg and Moscow regions, Poland, and the Ukraine. The first two were primarily manufacturing, whereas the Ukraine had supplanted the Urals as the Empire's metallurgical base, using the first-rate coal of the Donets Basin and the iron ore of Krivoi Rog. Cartels, in which ostensibly rival companies joined to share contracts and fix prices, were strong in the coal, engineering, and textile industries. Factories tended to be large; labour productivity was so low that to produce the same output a Russian plant might be double the size of an equivalent American plant. Although there were many big factories, some well-equipped, small-scale and handicraft industry still provided a high proportion of the Empire's needs. By 1914 output classified as workshop or artisan occupied about two-thirds of the industrial workers, although it accounted for only one-third of total production.

Witte, when minister of finance, tried with some success to solve the same problem faced by Stalin in the late 1920s, how to bring backward Russia to the same industrial level as the more advanced nations. Taxing the peasants hard to raise money for state investment was one policy, but most of this tax revenue was spent on other things. Much more effective, because they produced profits and savings for investment, were the unequal terms of trade (low grain prices and high prices for manufactures) which transferred wealth from the peasants to industry. Witte's protective tariffs, discouraging low-priced imports, were part of this process, while his gold-based stabilization of the rouble encouraged foreigners to invest their capital in Russia. By 1913 one-third of the capital of private companies was foreign owned. Since the economy was developing quite rapidly, this still left wide opportunities for the Russian investor; although foreign investment was growing faster than domestic, the latter was increasing rapidly, aided by a favourable balance of trade after 1908. About one-third of foreign investment was French capital, which was especially strong in mining and metallurgy. Britain and Germany accounted for about one-fifth each, Belgium for about 5 per cent. The USA share of about 5 per cent included, notably, the Russian establishments of the International Harvester Corporation. Apart from direct foreign investment in companies, Russia also benefited from the sale of government bonds abroad. Witte was very successful in persuading the capitalists of Europe to subscribe to Russian government loans. By 1914 probably 45 per cent of the state debt was held abroad. But as the total of foreign investment grew, so did the problem of servicing it. By 1914 interest on foreign loans and investment equalled a quarter of export earnings. This was why balance of payments problems, as well as balance of budget problems, frequently dominated the deliberations of the government.

Foreign investment brought with it much-needed foreign technology. Although there was some home-grown technical innovation, designs and equipment obtained from the west were the usual basis of the new industries. When factory production of aircraft began in 1911 the designs were French, and this was still substantially the position in 1913, when 280 machines were produced by the three companies involved, although one of the latter, the Russo-Baltic railway car works which had diversified into automobiles and aircraft, was building Sikorsky's novel designs. But in 1917 the Russian aircraft output of 1,900 units was less than a tenth of the French. With automobiles the picture was similar, the French De Dion Bouton being built from 1900 and an Oldsmobile design (known as the *Duksmobil*) from 1904. The First World War spurred the development of new car plants, one state owned and the others private. Other advanced industries, like those producing machine tools and bearings, were painfully emerging but were at a low technical level. The optical industry was sponsored by the navy, which needed good rangefinders, and other defence needs were a spur to the government in its encouragement of foreign investors.

By 1914 Germany was the Empire's main trading partner, with Britain far behind in second place. Russia's need for German colliers to supply her naval squadron en route to Tsushima had been a lever enabling Germany to obtain a favourable trade treaty in 1904; the previous treaty, according to the Prussian landlords, had ruined German agriculture. In 1913 one-half of Russia's imports came from Germany, and only one-seventh from Britain. British consular officials complained that British firms would not supply on credit and would not modify their products to meet the customers' wishes. The Germans were more obliging, and of the major British exports only Scotch herrings and whisky seemed safe from German competition. Russia's main export was grain, for which there was a ready demand in the industrial nations of north-west Europe. Several of Russia's railways had been built simply to carry grain from the producing areas to the ports of the Baltic and Black Sea. However, Russian grain lost some of its attraction when grain from the Americas entered the world market. Luckily, the expansion of wheat production in the north Caucasus region enabled Russia to gain substitute markets in the Mediterranean nations, for the new wheatfields produced a hard grain ideal for spaghetti and macaroni.

In 1914 agriculture was still the weakest part of the Russian economy, although since the turn of the century it had been showing definite signs of progress; the 1913 harvest was the best ever. Grain production per head of population had risen appreciably over the previous decade, although not in the overpopulated central agricultural region. While most peasant farmers still used primitive methods, harvesting by sickle, the formation of large and medium farms using modern knowledge and equipment was accelerating. In many areas small farmers were uniting themselves into producer, consumer, or credit cooperatives, and almost everywhere newly trained agronomists were at work. As both Witte and Stolypin realized, Russia's main economic problem was how to shift part of the agricultural population from the land to the factories. Rural overpopulation meant that there were too many mouths, and a surplus of hands, on the farms. Thus millions of peasants consumed more than they produced, relying on loans, charity, or casual work to tide them over the hungry months. A peasant who ate all, or more than, the food he produced was an economic liability: transferred to a factory the value of his work would be greater than the value of his consumption, and he would become an asset. But Witte's policy of taxing the peasant hard, and Stolypin's policy of helping the strong peasant squeeze out the weak, intensified rural discontent and rural hatreds.[10] Moreover, when the taxed-out or squeezed-out peasant moved to the insalubrious factory barracks, he became part of an ill-paid, unhealthy, unskilled, and uneducated proletariat which was a social problem in itself.

The army

Although in the Russo-Japanese War the army had not suffered any crushing defeats, the very fact that it had surrendered territory aroused enormous and often wild criticism after the war. Really the performance of the army in Manchuria had been limited mainly by the supply problem: neither munitions nor men arrived at the front in sufficient quantities. Nevertheless, it was true that even the munitions and men which were available were not handled efficiently. Post-war reforms were therefore almost inevitable, especially as public opinion had a new way of expressing itself, through the Duma.

In the war ministry and among commanders there were many who had drawn their conclusions from the late war and were eager to make changes of organization and tactics, but they faced several handicaps. One of these was Nicholas, who regarded the army as his, loved the superficialities of military life, and took advice from officers of the elite regiments, officers whom in many cases he had appointed himself from regiments unsullied by the recent war. In 1905 Nicholas placed the general staff directly under himself, so the war ministry often did not know what the staff was recommending. Nicholas believed that duelling was beneficial for *esprit de corps* (and failed to see that this much-vaunted *esprit* was only a euphemism for a caste system). Although

10. Witte's policy as minister of finance meant that the peasant still had to sell his grain immediately after harvest in order to pay his taxes. That is, to sell when prices were low. This boosted grain exports, but also meant that peasants were impoverished and, frequently, undernourished. Witte's fall from power was not unwelcome to the minister of the interior, alarmed at the discontent caused by his economic policy.

during his reign only about thirty officers died from duelling, a larger number were discharged from the army by their regiments when they refused to duel, or staged a sham duel, after some alleged insult. He appointed and promoted incompetents and caused great damage by putting grand dukes (nephews, cousins, uncles) in high positions. The Tsar's distrust of the Duma and of reform in general was also a great handicap. Many officers wanted to cooperate with the Duma which, they saw, had a better grasp of military realities than the government. But one reforming war minister was dismissed largely because Nicholas distrusted his cordial relationship with Duma leaders. As for reform, the contrast between the allegedly high morale of the Japanese soldier and that of his Russian opponent had impressed on many high officers that only by creating a better society would it be possible to create a better soldier. This view was also unpalatable to many of those influencing the Tsar.

Another handicap was the continuing lack of resources, made worse by the war. Lastly, there was the long-continuing controversy over the army's interior role. Continuously, but especially in the disturbed years after 1905, considerable numbers of troops were engaged in internal security. Most of these were on guard duty outside banks, prisons, or railway stations and were rarely called upon to open fire. But these units had to take their orders from the despised local police, whose deficiencies they were making up, and this was as bad for morale as their exposure to dissident influences. Most important, with so many troops engaged it was difficult to stage the field manoeuvres that the war ministry realized were so essential for training. But despite these burdens, successive war ministers did introduce some useful changes.

To end justified complaints that staff officers frequently had little understanding of real life at the front, a rule was introduced making it obligatory for such officers to spend periods actually in command of units. Just before the First World War another blow was struck against incompetent higher officers. This took the form of a Supreme Control Commission, chaired by the minister, which would examine the competence of any general officer and, if necessary, retire him. How well this measure would have worked in the prevalent conditions of favouritism is questionable, but it at least showed an awareness of the problem of incompetent senior officers; other armies had the same problem, but did not yet know it.

Artillery had always been a strong point in the Russian army, but in the war against Japan it had not distinguished itself. This was because it was unused to indirect firing in close cooperation with the infantry, because it was ill-provided with weapons suitable for the Manchurian terrain, and because ammunition was not only scarce but also defective: a creeping barrage fired over the heads of the infantrymen was perilous. These defects were remedied after the war, and rearmament by Germany and Austria caused the Duma in a closed session in 1913 to approve an increased investment in artillery. The war began before this could bear fruit, which meant that Russian divisions had significantly less artillery support than their opponents. Lack of gun-making capacity, and especially of gun-repair works, would be a serious handicap in the war. Such deficiencies, as well as the rather small stocks of ammunition, resulted more from financial stringency than lack of foresight.

The infantry was still equipped with the .299 inch rifle of 1891, with a five-round magazine. This was a sound weapon when properly made and maintained. After 1905, the so-called Suvorovite reliance on the bayonet was discredited, and both officers and men spent more time on marksmanship. But in the World War many of the older infantry officers still relied on the bayonet charge. The Russian bayonet was a fearsome four-edged blade which, when attached to the rifle, formed a weapon five and a half feet long. Machine guns had been used in the Russo-Japanese War, but only in small numbers. They had been treated as artillery rather than infantry weapons and their main advantage, local intensification of fire-power at short notice, was thereby lost. After the war more machine guns were issued, but their significance was never quite grasped before 1914, when it was realized that infantry units needed many more than the approved allocation. Officers were still uncomfortable with the idea of positional warfare. When war came they were not only reluctant to construct trenches, but had little idea of how to set about it.

The 1874 conscription system implied that the army was to be the nation armed, yet the soldier was still considered as a being apart from society; or rather, a being beneath society. Successive reformers and critics had pointed to the necessity of treating the soldier as an individual, of educating him and stimulating his initiative, but the army always found it easier to treat him like a sheep. Russian military law gave the lower ranks fewer rights than in other armies: as critics liked to point out, a soldier who defended his wife from violation by an officer thereby committed a crime. Nor could a soldier refuse to carry out an illegal order. When civilians addressed a soldier, they did so in the second person singular, as to a child or pet. If a soldier met a general in the street he had to stand to attention so long as that officer was within three paces of him. He was not allowed to ride in a private carriage, and on a public carriage was not allowed to sit inside. On the railways he was forbidden to enter the first and second class. On a steamship he had to occupy the lower deck in the bow. In the two capitals a soldier was not allowed to sit in the theatre stalls, nor lower than the third row of the balcony. He could not enter restaurants or cafés apart from third-class railway and steamer buffets.

The soldier lived on soup, tea, and black bread; which, according to a British war correspondent, was why he smelt like a horse. His pay was negligible. Yet he was loyal, and not dispirited. His term of active service had been reduced after 1905 to three years in the infantry and artillery, or four years in the other arms (five years in the navy), with a further fourteen or fifteen years in the reserve (and then a final five years in the *opolcheniye*, a kind of elderly territorial army). In 1914 the standing army was about 1,400,000 men, and mobilization produced almost 4 million more. During the war over 15 million men were absorbed by the army, peak strength being reached in January 1917 (about 6,900,000). However, it was not easy to equip or officer so large a force. The 1874 reform had prescribed shorter periods of service for educated conscripts, which meant that the men who had become reserve officers in peacetime had served less than the two years regarded as the minimum required to train good officers. Another drawback of the 1874 scheme was the large numbers of exemptions; with nearly half of each age group able to claim exemption, the 'Russian Steamroller' would soon run short of steam. By 1917 the proportion of over-forties in the army would be high, and minimum physical standards would be lower than those of other belligerent armies. The high proportion of the population exempted from service is evident from the following approximations, indicating the number of men (in millions) called up for army service by the belligerents:

	Peacetime army	After initial mobilization	By end of war	Total population	Per cent called
Russia	1.4	5.3	15.23	180	8.8
France	0.8	3.8	7.9	39	19.9
Britain	0.2	0.6	5.7	45	12.7
Germany	0.8	3.8	14.0	68	20.5

Source: P. Lyashchenko, *Istoriya narodnogo khozyaistva SSSR* (1956), ii. 613.

The navy

The Russo-Japanese War was painful for the army, but catastrophic for the navy. Of the three main pre-war squadrons, two had been destroyed ignobly and the surviving Black Sea Squadron was mutinous. The navy ministry was openly accused not only of inefficiency, but of gross corruption. The ministry and the naval general staff (founded 1907) wished to rebuild the fleet, but for several years they mishandled their case, failing to convince the public (and especially the Duma) that they were capable of producing a good return from any budgetary appropriations.

Like other nations, Russia had its naval lobby, but instead of one Navy League, as in Britain, the USA, and elsewhere, she had two. The League for the Renewal of the Navy, which numbered two grand dukes among its leadership, was the advocate simply of a big navy. The Russian Naval Union, financed largely by industry, wanted a big navy, but built in Russia. These two organizations were in frequent opposition because the domestic shipyards had longer deliveries and higher costs than foreign companies. However, this weakening of the naval lobby was compensated by Nicholas's emotional attachment to its cause; one general lamented that the usually polite Nicholas would shout and thump the table whenever he heard criticism of his beloved fleet. The Duma's Defence Committee could be circumvented by appealing directly to the Tsar. This was done, and four dreadnought-type battleships were laid down for the Baltic. They were to be built at home, although with technical help from a Scottish company. But opposition from the Duma was an inconvenience, and a threat to further developments, so its demands for the reform of the navy ministry and the appointment of a better navy minister were satisfied. The new minister, Admiral Grigorovich, was sympathetic to the Duma's criticism. The powers of the minister were strengthened so that he was no longer bound by the decisions of innumerable committees which had been established to control almost every detail of naval administration; the chief of naval staff henceforth reported to him, and not directly to the Tsar. With the reduction of the role of committees and the introduction of one-man control, decisions became speedier and better coordinated. The Duma, mollified, approved a five-year plan for the navy, which envisaged the construction of four big battlecruisers for the Baltic and three battleships for the Black Sea, with appropriate additional investment in smaller ships and dockyards. A long-term naval programme was subsequently drawn up and approved. This specified the construction for the Baltic of two capital ships each year until 1931, by which time the Empire would be the world's third greatest naval power, with twenty-four battleships and twelve battlecruisers in that sea alone (the Baltic Fleet was also the source of the Far East Squadron). In the Black Sea the aim was to construct a fleet one and a half times bigger than the combined navies of the three other Black Sea states. Foreign participation was envisaged: some smaller ships, especially prototypes, would be built abroad, and the British Vickers and John Brown companies would help to reorganize the government shipyards on the Black Sea and Baltic respectively. Vickers were also to build a new ordnance works at Tsaritsyn. Attention was also paid to undersea operations. Russia was ahead of other countries in mine warfare: it had built the world's first successful minelaying submarine and in 1914 supplied mines to the British navy. Radio was also well advanced, and a series of radio-direction stations on both sides of the Gulf of Finland enabled the navy to locate any vessels which broke radio silence. The *Novik* was so far in advance of other countries' destroyers that even in the 1990s some naval historians, unwilling to believe that tsarist Russia was capable of successful innovation, were still claiming that it was really built in Germany.[11] By 1914, although the ambitious capital-ship programme was far from complete, the quality of the officers, of

---

11. *Novik* was also remarkable in that it was one of twenty-three warships built by public subscription, a charity having been registered for that purpose just prior to the war against Japan. It was a gift to the navy ministry, which neither ordered nor specified it.

whom one-fifth were Baltic Germans, and the morale of the seamen, were vastly superior to their 1905 condition.

Education

In 1914 there was still an imbalance between the developed university system and the rather inadequate primary and secondary schools. Nevertheless, elementary schooling had been greatly extended since the 1860s by the work of the *zemstva*. By 1896 there were nearly 79,000 primary schools, compared with nearly 23,000 in 1880. These 79,000 schools were attended by about 3 million males and 850,000 females. Thirty-three thousand of them were the direct concern of the ministry of education, being mainly *zemstva* schools and Sunday schools (the latter, about 1,000 in total, were usually financed by benevolent citizens to teach basic subjects to adults). The Holy Synod supervised about 34,000 parish schools, and another 10,000 primary schools were the responsibility of the ministry of war. The typical (one-class) primary school taught religion, Church Slavonic, Russian, calligraphy, arithmetic, and singing, but there were superior town, district, and two-class schools where geography, history, drawing, and geometry were also offered. Secondary education at the turn of the century remained divided on class lines, with the gymnasiums providing an eight-year course concentrated on the classics and leading to the attestation of maturity. The latter enabled its possessor to enter a university or to obtain preferential treatment if entering state service. The real schools provided a six-year course of more practical subjects, and their graduates could, by taking an entrance examination, continue studying at a higher technical institution. Higher fees, and limitations on non-noble entry (with quotas for Jews), ensured that rather more than half the secondary students were of the nobility. Many sons and daughters of the richer non-noble classes were sent abroad for their education. In 1899 there were 191 gymnasiums, plus 53 pro-gymnasiums and 115 real schools. In addition, there were secondary schools for girls, with about 130,000 pupils.

By 1914 there were 120,000 schools of all types, with 8 million pupils (of whom 7 million were in primary schools). In the gymnasiums the classics were beginning to lose their predominance and more practical subjects were increasingly favoured. Despite the efforts of the ministry of education, the lower classes were making headway in the gymnasiums; even in 1902 nearly 10 per cent of gymnasium students were from peasant families. Most of the one-class primary schools offered an extra, fourth, year, while most of the real schools had an extra, seventh, year to prepare students for higher technical education. However, Stolypin's ambition to extend the primary-school system was frustrated by opposition from the Church.

The peasant saying 'Education is an ornament in good times and a refuge in bad' well expressed the attitudes of most Russians, but not of the ministry of education. Under the last Romanov, the history of Russian education is an excellent illustration of the gap between state and people. By 1914 education had undoubtedly progressed, but this was more a result of public energy than government action, even though the education budget was increasing much faster than total government expenditure.

The most influential sector was the elementary education provided by schools founded by the *zemstva*. At the turn of the century, four-fifths of the funds of elementary education came from *zemstva* and town councils, yet the ministry of education controlled these schools, repressing initiatives uncovered by its inspectors, standardizing approved textbooks, controlling the smallest details of their teachers' working and private lives. The church schools, declining in quality and importance, were also supervised by the ministry.

Apart from the local councils, various enterprising bodies or individuals established schools, but all (except those established by other ministries) felt the mortifying hand of the ministry. By 1914 the *zemstva* were in theory not allowed to communicate with the teachers of the *zemstva* schools or to interfere in the education they provided, while the school buildings built out of *zemstva* funds were declared to be state property. When quota systems had denied most Jewish children an education, they began to go to private schools, but within a few years the quotas were applied to the latter too. Adult schools, another interest of the *zemstva*, soon felt the supervision of the ministry. Even private schools were not allowed to choose their own teachers. All teachers were underpaid, few had meaningful qualifications, most had lost enthusiasm, were subject to frequent transfers, and obliged to follow to the letter the prescribed programmes and procedures. They could be dismissed for subscribing to journals of 'advanced' views. In 1913 a meeting of teachers in Yaroslavl to discuss two papers (on new tendencies in grammar and on self-expression in primary schools) was banned because it threatened 'to disturb public tranquillity'.

Many of the most damaging educational restrictions had been introduced under Alexander III, including one ironically referred to as 'the Regulation Concerning Children of Cooks'. Part of the latter (1887) was as follows:

The gymnasiums and pro-gymnasiums, therefore, shall be freed from the attendance of children of drivers, footmen, cooks, laundrymen, small traders and other persons similarly situated, whose children, with the exception perhaps of exceptionally gifted ones, should not be encouraged to abandon the social environment to which they belong.[12]

In the pre-war decade the Duma, by voting more money for education than the ministry wanted, and by denouncing the ministry's attitude, helped to

---

12. Quoted in P. N. Ignatiev et al., *Russian Schools and Universities in the World War* (1929), 31.

meet popular demand for more and better education. But it was not until the war and a change of minister that the government changed its course. In 1916 the ministry agreed that the post-war schools would not be differentiated according to social classes but would form a unified system with all students able to pass from one grade to the next. Moreover, lower schools would use the local language, and there would be compulsory education provided for all children by 1922.

In the final Romanov decades there was a steady increase in the number of specialized and technical institutions. This was especially marked outside the capital, many technological institutions being established in provincial cities. Also notable was the increase in agricultural colleges and, to a lesser degree, of commercial schools. Women had access to both agricultural and commercial instruction. Schools of art and of music were quite generously financed, and those of St Petersburg and Moscow enjoyed international repute. Various ministries still had their own higher educational establishments; the ministries of war and commerce were pre-eminent in this respect but were not alone. Even the department of posts and telegraphs of the ministry of the interior had its very modern Emperor Alexander III Electrotechnical Institute.

In 1899 there were still nine universities, but their enrolment had risen to 16,500 degree students of whom one-quarter were at Moscow University. The typical university had four faculties, of which the largest was Law and the smallest History/Philology; the other two were Medicine and Physics/Mathematics. Certain superior colleges, such as the three lycées, also existed and gave university-style courses in a limited range of subjects. University autonomy had been restricted by the statute of 1884. In particular, rectors, deans, and professors were no longer appointed by the university councils. The university rector was appointed for four years by the minister of education and was subordinate to the curator of his educational district. Vacant chairs were advertised, and candidates investigated by the university council, but the latter could only make recommendations to the minister. The minister also appointed the university inspectors, who were charged with supervising discipline. Under Alexander III many professors were dismissed for alleged disloyalty, often after they had protested against the expulsion of dissident students.

For women there was a limited opportunity for higher education before 1905. The St Petersburg university-style courses for women continued, and had about 1,000 students, but similar courses in Moscow were banned in 1888 and reinstated only in 1900. Some provincial universities were also giving special courses for women. The pioneer medical school for women at St Petersburg, which opened in 1872, had been closed ten years later, but reopened in 1897. Financed largely by *zemstva* contributions, it gave a five-year course and its graduates, idealists, tended to enter *zemstvo* service, devoting their lives to the rural medical services. But most ambitious girls if they had the means went to foreign, especially German, universities. No doubt they were inspired by the example of Sofia Kovalevskaya, the mathematician. This talented woman, born in 1850, had shown signs of mathematical talent at the age of 16 but, unable to enter the all-male Russian universities, graduated abroad. She was later appointed to a chair at Stockholm, thereby becoming, apparently, the world's first female professor.

The Russian student at the turn of the century was very different from his western contemporaries. He was young but not youthful. He did not seek outlets for boisterousness in sports because he was not boisterous. Rather was he gloomy and tense. All too often the future before him was a choice of becoming a cog in the bureaucratic machine or following his own inclinations and risking exile. It is true that the universities contained many students from the rich nobility, who resembled in some ways (and tried hard to resemble) the students of Oxford and Cambridge. But the Russian institutions were not the preserve of the well-to-do; most of their students were poor. These less wealthy students had entered university via the gymnasiums, where they had learned the classics by rote and practically nothing else. Until the reforms of the twentieth century the gymnasiums did not provide real education; they provided a valuable diploma. Even the classics were not taught with a view to understanding, but only with a view to repetition. Thus in the gymnasiums only the dull were content. The majority learned to despise school authorities, and at university it was a short step from this to despising all authority.

Although a greater proportion of students received financial assistance than in most other countries, the sums received were very small. The student without his own financial resources lived a cold and hungry life. He would probably share a room (and books) with four or five others, and on the coldest days would not attend lectures because he had no adequate clothes or footwear. He would talk endlessly about academic freedom, about Russia, and would probably learn more from reading and discussing the newspapers and journals than from his teachers. Student meetings were forbidden; porters and lodging-house keepers were required to inform the police of any student gatherings (which would then be broken up) and of students' habits, reading, friends, and movements. The university inspectors were hated by all. They could expel students at will. They could cancel or grant government financial assistance. They could forbid a student giving private lessons (an essential source of income for many). They could impose penalties for lateness, improper hairstyles, or untidiness. They spied on professors. Whereas under Alexander II the number of expulsions rarely exceeded 100 in any one year, under Alexander III they sometimes reached four figures. In general, the student unrest which intensified each year was the result of increasing repression and not vice versa, although the more revolutionary students and the more reactionary officials drew strength from each others' extremism; each needed the other to attract support from the moderate majority caught in the middle.

Student unrest, which had originally centred around university conditions, under Nicholas became more concerned with general social and political issues. A student council was organized at Moscow University in the late 1890s, and this petitioned for the abolition of inspectors and the admission of women. Its leaders were promptly arrested but a new council was formed. There were affrays with the police and 660 students were expelled. At St Petersburg in 1899 the police for the first time used whips to disperse students; thereupon, 13,000 students throughout Russia, enraged that they should be treated like peasants, went on strike. The universities had to close, and the government responded by allowing the organization of student clubs and by making an effort to improve student housing. But at the same time the number of inspectors was increased to an average of one per 150 students, students were requested to attend the university of their home district, and student eating and reading cooperatives were banned. More teachers were expelled, and about one-third of the striking students were refused readmission. Following a brainwave that afflicted Witte, a new law allowed hundreds of students considered dissident to be drafted into the army. The war minister, Kuropatkin, thereupon took it upon himself to share a piece of his mind with Nicholas; he thought it dishonourable to treat the army as a penal colony and moreover, he darkly commented, the students were spreading bad ideas in the army. This last argument was compelling, and in 1901 Nicholas ordered the army to discharge the students.

Cossack whips were increasingly called upon to break up student demonstrations. Some students were killed. One expelled student murdered the minister of education in 1901; the minister had just drafted 200 students into the army. Literate public opinion, already shocked by police attacks on students, approved the assassination. In 1903 Warsaw students protested against Russification. In 1904 the minister of the interior (Plehve) ordered the breaking-up of a meeting of professors from all over Russia, and some of its participants were exiled.

The 1905 crisis, in which university students played a leading role, resulted in certain concessions. Student organizations were again permitted, and university councils and their rectors were given back their responsibility for university discipline and other matters. The emergence of open political parties in Russia led to open political associations in the universities. Hitherto the semi-legal or illegal left wing had been predominant. But with the formation of moderate and right-wing associations this predominance diminished, although it did not disappear.

One of the gains of 1905 was women's access to the previously men-only courses at university. Although they did not have all the rights of male students, the government did eventually allow them to take the state university examinations. By 1909 there were 640 of them. Diehard officials tried sporadically, with varying success, to re-exclude female students, and it was not until

1915 that the latter could feel secure. Male students, including those who previously had preached sexual equality, did not at first take kindly to female intrusion. One girl wrote:

At first there was embarrassment when we were working on a corpse; the male students regarded us negatively, not having matured sufficiently in a spiritual sense to the point where they could accept working alongside them women who retained feminine spirit and beauty. In time both we and they got used to it and the awkwardness disappeared.[13]

Another female student wrote:

I think our presence in the universities has softened the male students. Fewer resort to drunkenness . . . there is no bad language . . . competition forces the male students to work harder out of vanity, for fear that the women will do better in the examinations than them.[14]

By 1910, mutually catalysing dissidence and right-wing pressures led Stolypin to new repressions in the universities, which he regarded as the main source of unrest. Not for the first or last time, a non-Russian was chosen to chastise respected Russian institutions; Kasso, a Bessarabian, was appointed minister of education. Using as a pretext student demonstrations (held to mark the death of Tolstoy), Kasso forbade all non-academic meetings in universities, and the police were empowered to enter universities to enforce this regulation without consulting the rector. There was a student strike in protest. The professors, who had mostly opposed the strike, were enraged by the often brutal activities of the police; some resigned, while others who merely protested were dismissed. Disturbances of one sort or another continued until 1914, and at least 6,000 students were expelled for various periods, some being exiled. Yet in 1914 the universities responded loyally to the Empire's danger. Students and professors ceased their protests and engaged in voluntary work until defeats and official mismanagement (and perhaps the extension of the call-up to students in 1916) turned this enthusiasm into something else.

Not all was black during the pre-war years. State education was beginning to mean public education. Foreign observers were favourably impressed with the teaching and research in Russian universities and higher institutions. In 1914 there were thirty-nine institutions classified as higher, including ten[15] universities (Saratov University had been founded in 1909; Perm University would be opened in 1916). In the universities between 50 and 60 per cent of the students were of middle-class or noble origin, which suggests that in 1914 access to a university was by no means impossible for a talented youth of the

13. *Vestnik Evropy*, 9 (1912), 376.
14. Ibid. 375.
15. This does not include the Shanyavski 'people's university' in Moscow, founded by a private benefactor in 1905 to provide low-cost, co-educational instruction, with no diploma required for entry. Nor does it include Helsinki University.

lower classes (although in comparison with the population the number of places was small). Many poor families of the middle class, of the bankrupt nobility, of the skilled working class, and especially of the priesthood impoverished themselves to support a son at university, hoping thus to raise themselves from their low estate. For some, the result of this sacrifice was a disappointment, because government offices and many commercial firms were becoming hesitant in employing former students from the poorer classes, who were increasingly regarded as being revolutionary or, if not revolutionary, bloody-minded.

Science and technology

Russian science by 1914 had enhanced its international reputation earned in the previous century. Pure mathematics and its applications in engineering and other fields had always been a strongpoint of Russian scholarship. Although no Russian mathematician quite attained the fame of Lobachevsky, there was a host of brilliant men, including Markov (theory of numbers and probability) and Bernstein (theory of functions). In biology Mechnikov was a leading figure, having earned his reputation in the study of infection and immunization; he worked mainly in France, directing the Pasteur Institute from 1895 and receiving a Nobel Prize in 1908. The physiologist Pavlov was popularly regarded as Russia's greatest scientist. The son of a priest, he spent much of his life at the Institute of Scientific Medicine at St Petersburg, receiving a Nobel Prize for his work on digestive enzymes. His study of the conditioned reflex, using bells and salivating dogs, brought him renown among the general public. Mendeleyev, a Siberian who died in 1907, made a brilliant career in chemistry, evolving his Periodic Table and describing several new elements. Michurin was producing an enormous range of new hybrid fruit trees with his grafting technique, and an enormous range of controversial conclusions. Russians were recognized as pre-eminent in soil science and petroleum chemistry.

During the Stalin period of Russian history, many claims would be made that Russians had been the first to invent almost all the innovations of the previous century. Although these claims were unbalanced, and attracted thereby some ridicule, they were not always baseless. Russians had indeed invented or researched new machines and techniques, but all too often their experiments were abandoned because obtaining financial support from the government was a long, uncertain, and bureaucratic process. Moreover, the bureaucracy was usually unwilling to grant patents, which it regarded as exceptional privileges rather than a device to prevent the theft of inventors' hard work. It refused to sign the Paris Convention of 1883 and it refused to set up an independent patent office (the Soviet government would maintain this obstructionism).

Among the technologies in which Russians had a claim to leadership was hydrodynamics, in which the work of Krylov is still basic; Krylov lived long enough to modify in 1904 the hulls of the battleships sent to Tsushima, and to receive a Stalin Prize in 1941. Popov had at least as good a claim as Marconi to distinction in the field of radio. Yablochkov, as early as 1875, invented and patented the world's first successful electric lamp, using the arc. The same year Lodygin's electric lamps were illuminating a St Petersburg shop and he went on to patent the wolfram filament lamp. The use of oil fuel in locomotives and ships was pioneered in Russia, where residues from the Caucasian refineries were cheaply available.

Russian technology was particularly distinguished in aviation. Even before the internal combustion engine became available, a steam aeroplane was built by a Russian army officer; its aerodynamics were very advanced but had little chance to display themselves because it was too heavy to leave the ground. Zhukovsky and Chaplygin at the Institute of Aerodynamics worked out such essential airflow problems as those of lift and wing loading, wing and propeller shape. At about the same time Tsiolkovsky, more visionary but rightly regarded as one of the fathers of space flight, was working on large rockets. He built a wind tunnel in 1897 and six years later produced his theoretical book *The Investigation of Space by Rocket Devices*. In the Soviet period he would make further contributions to aviation and space flight; he forecast multi-stage rockets and space stations. In the actual design and production of aircraft Sikorsky was already distinguished. Thanks to him, Russia in 1914 had four-engined 400 h.p. aircraft capable of carrying sixteen passengers. Aviation aroused great interest in Russia, and a number of universities and technical institutes founded aero-clubs. The latter, being 'unofficial' organizations, soon aroused official suspicion:

Bearing in mind that the student milieu is a particularly fertile soil for the development of extreme revolutionary ideas and that in these circumstances the activity of student aero-clubs could easily take an undesirable direction, the Deputy Minister of the Interior, commanding the special gendarme section, has graciously noted the necessity, in towns having institutions of higher learning, of establishing the closest surveillance over the persons and activities of student aero-clubs.[16]

During the final Romanov decades scientific and exploratory expeditions were mounted more and more frequently. These went to Central Asia, Siberia, the far north, and the Arctic, as well as to more familiar parts to search for minerals. In 1915 two icebreakers completed the first voyage by the Northern Sea Route from the Pacific westwards across the top of Russia.

But compared to other countries, scientific research was not well provided for. A handful of ministries, notably those of war and transport, set up

16. From a confidential circular sent in 1911 to local police and Okhrana authorities, published in *Istoricheskii arkhiv*, 3 (1961), 286.

their own research institutes, but such institutes were few. Higher education establishments, whose main function was teaching, provided few facilities. Much inventiveness was self-financed, or at the mercy of grants administered by the state-financed Imperial Academy of Sciences. Nevertheless, there was a flourishing of scholarly societies and journals. The non-academic public was encouraged to take an interest in scientific life by popular scientific societies, by new observatories, botanical gardens, museums, and public lectures. Meanwhile the growing educated class meant a growing demand for books and journals. Hitherto, Russian publications had small circulations and rather high prices, but from about the 1870s this changed. In 1874 a French novel by Zola was printed in 7,000 copies, and this was considered the best-seller of that year (after the new *Conscription Regulations*, published in an edition of 50,000 copies, but exceptional). In the 1880s, however, one publisher introduced cheap editions of Russian classics, printing at least 100,000 copies of each volume. Similarly, the 'thick' journals were being supplemented by the 'thin'. Most popular of the latter was the illustrated weekly *Niva*, which flourished from 1870 to 1917. Vaguely liberal in tone and designed for 'family reading', in 1900 it had a circulation of 235,000. Its readers liked its presentation of Russian realistic painting, and of modern authors like Chekhov. With a circulation like that it could pay quite generously and it could be a lifeline for promising but unestablished writers. There was also *Ogonyok* ('Flamelet'), whose circulation approached a quarter-million in 1914; it belonged to a stable of publications owned by an Austrian entrepreneur. Women's magazines had also appeared by 1914, including the mass-circulation *Zhenshchina* ('Woman') but also more modest publications like the Bolsheviks' *Rabotnitsa* ('Woman Worker'). The Bolsheviks also moved with the times by introducing a woman's section to their *Pravda* newspaper.

The arts

By 1914 the writers of the great age of Russian literature were dead, and there were already harbingers, like Gorki, of a later generation of proletarian writers. Chekhov had been a link between the generations; influenced by his friend Tolstoy (whom he predeceased in 1904), he in turn influenced Gorki. The grandson of a serf, Chekhov qualified as a doctor after working his way through university, but soon devoted himself entirely to writing. He had grown up in a penurious middle-class family, and it was the middle class and the official world which predominated in his sketches, stories, and plays. He claimed that comedy was the essence of all his works, but his 'superfluous man' tended to become the melancholy man, leading an empty and repetitive life, dreaming of a more stimulating life but lacking the incentive to transform dream into reality. Chekhov's plays (*The Cherry Orchard, Three Sisters*, and others) became standard repertory offerings both inside Russia and abroad.

They were staged by the innovative Moscow Art Theatre, which had been founded in 1898 by Stanislavsky and Nemirovich-Danchenko. The performances were made memorable by the direction of the former; what became known as the Stanislavsky System was admirably suited to Chekhov's subdued style. There were no conventional histrionics, each actor was made aware of the importance of pauses, slight changes of tone, and complete naturalness. The stage success of Chekhov and Stanislavsky led to a brief popularity for Russian dramatists (including Gorki), but by 1914 it was foreign playwrights such as Bernard Shaw and Ibsen who were most fashionable. By that time Stanislavsky had been joined by younger inventive directors, of whom Meyerhold was the most notable.[17]

Maksim Gorki, who as a young orphan had wandered from place to place and job to job, achieved success with his short stories about lowly characters like those he had met in his wanderings. Outside Russia he became well known after the translation and staging of his play *Lower Depths*. This was set in a cheap boarding house inhabited by a collection of semi-human misfits, degenerates, and murderers, who were what they were because poverty had made them so. Gorki gave financial help to the Bolsheviks, but from 1906 was anti-Leninist. He criticized the Bolsheviks' seizure of power in 1917 but was later reconciled with the regime. Of the writers influenced by Gorki, Bunin was perhaps the most notable, although he had not yet published *The Gentleman from San Francisco* (1915), with its portrayal of cigar-smoking shapers of men's lives. In 1933, in emigration, he would become the first Russian to win a Nobel Prize for literature.

By the turn of the century critical realism was under attack by newer movements. The most concerted attack took the form of a symposium called *Vekhi* (1909), in which non-radical philosophers, critics, and politicians presented a new assessment of values. Some of the contributors, like Berdyaev and Struve, were former marxists (Berdyaev would soon become a well-known Orthodox philosopher). Others were simply admirers of Dostoevsky, or of the Christian idealist philosopher Vladimir Soloviev. Their ideas, vulgarized, tended to inspire and reinforce that obsession with the occult and the mystical which became noticeable in St Petersburg society. By 1914 the Belinsky tradition was in a retreat which would continue until its resurrection in the 1930s as the basis of Socialist Realism. In 1914, of the foremost writers only Gorki and perhaps Bunin and Kuprin represented this tradition. In poetry, N. Nekrasov's *Who Can Live Well in Russia?* (1866) had probably approached the peak of critical realism with its exquisite portrayal of the seamy side of Russian life. In following decades there was a reaction leading to the emergence of Symbolists like Merezhkovsky and Blok, who in their turn were

---

17. Meyerhold continued to direct after 1917, but he and his wife disappeared one night in 1939, a few days after he had publicly described Socialist Realism as a 'pitiful and sterile something'.

challenged by the Futurists (notably Mayakovsky) and other hopeful trend-setters. In prose, Belyi and Andreyev were prominent Symbolists, but were themselves challenged by the Neo-Realists like Aleksei Tolstoy. All these movements influenced Soviet literature of the 1920s.

The novel was also attracting a popular readership. Aleksei Suvorin, publisher of the right-wing newspaper *Novoye Vremiya*, also produced cheap editions of novels, many of which were sold by his chain of railway-station bookstores. He patronized new authors (and painters) and paid them well. The popular woman's novel was also emerging, the first notable offering being Anastasia Verbitskaya's *Keys of Happiness*, which despite (or because of) its alleged lack of refinement and depth managed to sell 30,000 copies in four months. Eudoxia Nagrodskaya's *Dionysius' Wrath* did even better, although that may have been the result of erotic rather than literary merit.

In painting, the second half of the nineteenth century had been marked by a conflict between different schools. In 1863 St Petersburg art students refused to paint the subject chosen for their annual competition; they wanted to paint a real contemporary scene, not 'The Banquet of the Gods in Valhalla'. This preference accorded with the precepts of critical realism, emphasizing content rather than style. The students, helped by the industrialist and collector Tretyakov, formed their own 'Society of Circulating Exhibitions', which enjoyed great success, although the movement later ossified. These artists (the *Peredvizhniki*, or 'Wanderers') valued the realistic presentation of ideas and tended to minimize technique and artistic truth. They soon became over-didactic, but when more attention was paid to form and colour, as it was by Repin, realism was reinvigorated. Like other Peredvizhniki, Repin was addicted to the storytelling picture, which he accomplished very well and thereby created paintings which are often used to illustrate history textbooks (Ivan the Terrible after murdering his son etc.). But he was versatile; he had worked with the traditional icon-painters in his youth and later produced some religious compositions, as well as portraits of notable Russians.

Although by the turn of the century realists like Repin were being over-shadowed, in the eyes of the fashionable, by Russian impressionism, realism as such never disappeared from Russian art; it coexisted. Of the new impression-istic school Vrubel and the portraitist Serov were the most notable early examples. In 1898 the periodical *Mir iskusstva* ('World of Art') was founded, and this name was attached to the movement of artists and critics who opposed utilitarian and realist art, and who advocated art-for-art's-sake. *Mir iskusstva* in its articles brought together modern west European trends and the traditions of old Russian art, especially of icon-painting. It also organi-zed exhibitions for its members. Although the periodical ceased publication in 1904 the ideas of the movement lived on, influencing, among others, the Futurists. By 1914 St Petersburg was considered the capital of the world of progressive art. The experimentalist Kandinsky was regarded as the first really abstract painter, and Expressionism was joined by Rayonnism, Suprematism, and Constructivism. The new styles were not to the taste of traditionalists and frequently invited ridicule, but a public certainly existed for advanced art.

In the nineteenth century ballet had flourished in Russia, but it was hardly specifically Russian, being strongly influenced by the French and Italians. However, in the 1890s Russian music was increasingly being used, and in 1909 the Ballets Russes was launched by the impresario Diaghilev. The success of this company abroad was based on previous performances of Russian music and opera which had attracted growing appreciation, aided by star attractions such as Chaliapin singing the title role in Musorgsky's *Boris Godunov*. The Ballets Russes, which from 1911 to its disbandment in 1952 was permanently abroad, owed its success also to the masterful combination of several arts: choreography by Fokin, sets by new and original Russian artists, and star dancers like Nijinsky and Pavlova. Music was contributed by the innovative Stravinsky, whose pre-war *Firebird*, *Petrushka*, and *Rite of Spring* established the foundation of his subsequent reputation as perhaps the most important composer of the twentieth century.

St Petersburg by 1914 was an exciting city of advanced culture. In the arts Russia was no longer backward, no longer so many decades or centuries behind the west. In the theatre, poetry, music, and painting she was in front, even if many of her innovations had their roots in the west. Perhaps this was why the once-compelling question of Russia's place in the world seemed to lose its significance. It had become easier to accept that Russia was Russian; whether Russia was of the west or of the east or of neither seemed no longer a burning issue. A more compelling question in this last decade of Romanov rule was whether Russia was destined for a renaissance or for a revolution. For the alert and intelligent citizen of that time there were abundant signs of both.

Stability or instability?

Historians disagree on whether revolution was inevitable by mid-1914. Many regard 1905–14 as a period of stabilization and progress brought to a premature end at Sarajevo; in short, if there had been no 1914 there might not have been a 1917. Others regard the Revolution as historically logical, as inevitable, and discern a revolutionary upsurge in the industrial unrest that began in 1912. Soviet historians claimed that by August 1914 Russia was ripe for an imminent revolution, for which the Bolsheviks had begun to plan in 1913, and that the war in reality delayed this revolution until 1917.

Certainly, the first five years after 1905 were years of reaction and repression (that is, of stabilization). Many intellectuals, depressed by the defeat of 1905, or not relishing their memory of armed workers and peasants, abandoned radical causes. The working class relapsed into apathy, chastened by the failure after the first heady days of the rebellion. The urban middle classes seemed willing to work for reform within the limits set by the government; they too had been alarmed at what they considered to be the excesses of the workers and peasants in 1905, and had abandoned the struggle when the October Manifesto seemed to offer them a way out.

But after 1910 it seemed that the situation was changing in the towns.[18] There was a return to industrial growth, more spontaneous than that of the 1890s. The industrial labour force in 1914 was about 2.5 million strong, almost a third more than in 1910. This labour force included a new generation whose resentments were not tempered by any memories of 1905, and an influx of peasants squeezed off the land by agrarian reforms. When strikers at the Lena goldfields were shot down in 1912, sympathy strikes were called throughout the Empire, and from then until 1914 strikes became ever more frequent, bitter, and confused in their objectives. The climax came in July 1914, when the St Petersburg Bolsheviks instigated a strike in protest against police repression of another local strike. In the working-class districts, barricade-building and violence recalled the events of 1905, but there was little sympathetic response from other sections of society, as there had been in 1905. The strike was finally suppressed less than a week before the outbreak of war.

This 1914 experience, added to memories of the 'desertion' by the middle class after October 1905, persuaded many politically conscious workers that a 1905-style cooperation between the workers and educated society was no longer feasible, and this would have its repercussions in 1917. At the time, what seemed more important than the gulf between the workers and 'public opinion' was the stalemated hostility between the latter and the bureaucracy, official Russia. Whereas 'unofficial' educated Russians had been striving to make the most of the concessions won in 1905, the regime was trying with some success to whittle away those concessions (for example, by tampering with the Duma, arresting leaders of 'legal' organizations, confiscating 'legal' publications). By 1914 former reformists were beginning to regard violence as the only means left to loosen a regime which seemed more and more intolerant, intolerable, and, worse, untalented. This trend meant that the political parties were splitting at all possible seams. The Octobrists' left wing split away, the Kadets were uneasily divided into left, right, and centre, while the businessmen's new Progressist party actually made overtures (neither accepted nor rejected) to the Bolsheviks. Had there been no war it seems possible that a realignment of parties would have occurred, with the emergence of a strong and respectable movement prepared to support violent change.

The Beilis Case and the rise of Rasputin seemed symptoms of the increasing rottenness and incapacity of the state administration at a time when modernization of Russian society made the educated and professional classes all the

---

18. Peasant disturbances had declined drastically in 1908–9, but by 1914 they, too, seemed to be on the upswing, although numbered in the hundreds rather than the thousands of 1905–7.

more essential to the state. The autocratic Empire was desperately trying through modernization to remain a great power. Indeed, with Germany to the west and Japan to the east, the Empire could survive only as a great power. Yet modernization, which few Russians could envisage without an accompanying westernization, could only threaten internal stability in the short term. Modernization meant the rise of new classes, skilled workers and professionals who would use their new importance to demand political rights. Modernization meant squeezing peasants off the land and bringing them to already overcrowded cities where, cramped in their own stink, they formed a dissatisfied class of unskilled and underprivileged workers. Modernization meant westernization and the erosion of stabilizing traditions and values; how much resentment such an erosion created cannot be measured, but Peter the Great, the greatest westernizer of all, had certainly had cause to reckon with it. Modernization, as under Witte, meant a minimal standard of living for the majority, in order to save resources for investment.

Perhaps, if there had been no war, the most painful stages of change would have been passed, and some of the fruits of modernization enjoyed by the people. And perhaps not. But, as 1905 demonstrated, the regime could always win the last trick so long as it could rely on the army. In July 1914 the forces of revolution were in dynamic equilibrium with the forces of stability, and the key stabilizing force was the Russian army. But after Sarajevo another army, the German, upset the balance.

9

The Empire's last war

Tsarist foreign policy

THE first care of the tsars was defence of the frontiers and of the autocratic regime within those frontiers. Under the last Romanovs, the Empire's diplomacy usually compensated for the disparity between Russia's claims as a great power and her actual economic potential. Alliances were made with suitable European powers, to ensure that Russia would have strong friends at times of crisis.

With the end of the Napoleonic wars, the expansion of Muscovy into territories held by weaker neighbours reached a natural conclusion in northern and central Europe. The absorption of Poland meant that there was no longer a buffer state separating Russia from Prussia. Finland had been acquired, and St Petersburg thereby made more defensible. But Russia still had aspirations, although no definite plans, in south-eastern Europe. A Russian presence at the Straits was still strongly desired, while racial and religious obsessions with the Balkans meant that this was an area in which policy might not always be rational. In Asia, expansion could continue at the expense of weak or fragmented neighbours.

Throughout most of the nineteenth century the foundation of Russian foreign policy was friendship with Austria and Prussia. They were ideologically congenial, and their close proximity enhanced the strategic value of their friendship. But after Bismarck's successors neglected to renew the 'Reinsurance Treaty', Russia felt compelled to seek alternative friends; the 1894 alliance with France resulted. Britain, however, was still at the turn of the century regarded as a likely enemy, and this feeling was mutual. But while British newspapers and parliamentarians spoke knowingly of dark Russian designs, the Russian foreign ministry in reality was preoccupied with security, although that did not exclude Russian agents, especially in the Balkans, embarking on all kinds of intrigues to win influence.

When the Russo-Japanese War ended, the French alliance seemed even more needed; attempts by Nicholas and the Kaiser in 1904 and at Björkö in 1905 to initiate a new treaty between their two empires had been frustrated. Britain's support for Japan was no longer an issue, and with French encouragement some of the outstanding issues dividing Russia and Britain were settled in 1907; Persia was to be divided into two spheres of influence, Afghanistan was not to be annexed by Britain, Tibet was to remain Chinese. In 1908 King Edward VII visited the Russian Baltic port of Reval. By 1914 the Anglo-French understanding and the Franco-Russian alliance had merged into the Triple Entente. But although when war began Russia appeared to be on the strongest side, in retrospect it might seem that the Empire would have done better if the old alliances with Berlin and Vienna had, instead, been maintained. Whatever material advantages the Triple Entente offered were outweighed by Germany's and Austria's contiguity; the war presented right from the start the probability of strong hostile armies marching on the Empire's heartland. The French army was weaker than the German, while Britain's celebrated dreadnoughts, as critics said, were of little use to Russia unless they could move on wheels.

Neither the earlier alliance with Berlin and Vienna, nor the later Entente with Paris and London, furnished allies willing to embroil themselves on Russia's side in the Balkans. With the shrinkage of the Turkish Empire, the consequent emergence of independent and sometimes Slavic Balkan states, the simultaneous ambition and instability of the Austro-Hungarian Empire, and continuing Russian interest in the area, conflict was almost inevitable. In the 1908 'Annexation Crisis' Russia was openly humiliated. Her new foreign minister, Izvolsky, unwisely agreed with Vienna to support Austrian annexation of Bosnia-Herzegovina (which Serbia regarded as Serbian) in exchange for Austrian diplomatic support for another Russian attempt to gain free passage through the Straits. The great powers accepted Austria's gain but would not countenance a change for the Straits. Germany threatened to support Austria should a Russo-Austrian war develop from this situation. Conscious of military weakness, St Petersburg was wise enough to refrain from war, despite resentment at Germany's action and emotional links with the fellow-Slavs of Serbia. The Russian government's prestige fell further with the Balkan wars of 1912–13. Russian semi-official agents, hopefully advising the independent Balkan states to join forces against Austria, succeeded only in uniting them against Turkey. Having won Macedonia from the Turks, the coalition quarrelled over the spoils, with the result that Bulgaria, which had done most of the fighting and was in spirit closest to Russia, came out badly.

Once again the Russian government wisely refrained from intervention, but once again Russian public opinion had been angered. In 1908 and 1913 governmental rationality prevailed over public irrationality, but this did not guarantee cool heads in the future. That Russia's 'mission' in the Balkans was not simply a right-wing myth was demonstrated by the emergence of the so-called Neo-Slav movement. Whereas Panslavism implied an eventual Russian-controlled federation of Slavic peoples, the Neo-Slavs envisaged truly independent Slavic nations in a free association. The Neo-Slavs included many prominent Russian liberals; conservatives were usually opposed to the movement because it implied eventual independence for Poland and the Ukraine.

Summer 1914

In July 1914, using the murder of its archduke by Serb nationalists as a pretext, and confident of German support, Vienna determined to crush once and for all troublesome Serbia. On 28 July Austrian troops commenced hostilities. The great European war, that awesome contingency for which military staffs had long been planning, now seemed imminent. The German war plan (the 'Schlieffen Plan') envisaged an initial concentration of forces against France so as to drive the latter out of the war within the first few weeks, and then the transfer of the German troops to the Eastern Front to deal with Russia.

This exploited the well-known fact that, because of long distances and sparse railways, Russia's mobilization would need more time than those of the other powers. The Russian mobilization plans were very complex interlocking schedules, drawn up every few years at secret conferences. Each railway section received the part of the plan relevant to it in the form of a sealed packet, which was placed in an iron box to be hidden until the fateful day. The plan covered the first two weeks, and envisaged the suspension of normal railway services so that the railways would be completely devoted to military movements in those weeks. There were two variants of the plan; Plan G was for a war against Austria and Germany if Germany was the main enemy, Plan A was for a war against Austria and Germany if Austria was the main enemy. In 1914 a new plan to take account of increased line capacity was being worked out, but was not yet in force; thus in 1914 the railways had more capacity than the existing plan called for, which is one reason why the 1914 mobilization went so smoothly. During the initial two weeks it was planned to mobilize and transport about half the infantry, together with supporting arms. The remainder would follow according to circumstances.

Military planners believed firmly (although incorrectly) that because each part of the mobilization plan was interlocked and coordinated with the other parts, once mobilization was started it could not be modified or halted without throwing the country's defences into chaos. Also, it was clear that if Russia mobilized, Germany would be compelled to mobilize too, without delay. For these two reasons, mobilization was almost equivalent to pressing the button in the age of the nuclear deterrent, or to reaching for the personal deterrent in the age of the cowboy. So Russia's decision to mobilize on 30 July made war virtually certain.

The Tsar was well aware of all this. On 25 July, on the advice of his ministers, he consented to the call-up of reservists, the cancellation of soldiers' leaves, and to a partial mobilization, if need be, against Austria. He also suggested that the Austro-Serbian dispute be submitted to the Hague International Tribunal, a suggestion which does not appear to have been passed on by his foreign minister, Sazonov. On 28 July Sazonov announced the partial mobilization against Austria. It was only after this that Sazonov, the Tsar, and the ministers were informed by the chief of staff that partial mobilization was impossible. Both Plan G and Plan A envisaged war against Germany and Austria, not against one of the two. Russia's great deterrent was indivisible and therefore inflexible.[1] But by now, for Russia to retreat would mean a crushing international humiliation. So in the morning of 29 July the Tsar signed the order for general mobilization. That same evening, conscious of what this order meant, Nicholas cancelled it. The next morning, besieged by his military and diplomatic advisers, all urging that without general mobilization Russia would stand unprepared before disaster, Nicholas restored the mobilization order. The rest was ultimatums.

The campaigns

The war minister, Sukhomlinov, was expecting to command the army, but instead it was the Tsar's uncle, Grand Duke Nikolai Nikolaevich, who became C-in-C. He took as his chief of staff Yanushkevich, at 44 the army's youngest general. Although a gifted quartermaster-general partly compensated for Yanushkevich's shortcomings, by late 1915 it was clear that the latter was a disaster. It was Yanushkevich who, imposing harsh regimes in areas occupied by the Russian army, dissolved the sympathy with which local populations regarded Russia's fight against the Teutonic threat. His murderous treatment of the Jews seemed likely to cause intolerable embarrassments abroad.[2] After the defeats of 1915 Nicholas transferred the Grand Duke and Yanushkevich to the Caucasian front and himself went as C-in-C to GHQ, the collection of railway cars sidetracked at a junction near the front. Nicholas's wish to be with his troops was laudable, and he had chosen a very competent chief of staff, but his absence from the capital meant that too much political responsibility would be placed on unreliable informants and advisers. His ministers had been against the move, partly (and plausibly) because they feared that the Emperor would henceforth have to take personal responsibility for defeats. Nicholas may have been partly motivated by a suspicion that his uncle had too close a relationship with certain liberal members of the government and had become too popular for comfort. A Caucasian posting therefore seemed appropriate. As Nikolai Nikolaevich was devoid of military talent and was

1. When the chief of staff, Yanushkevich, was asked why he had not mentioned this disconcerting fact previously, he explained that he had held his post for only five months and had therefore been unacquainted with the mobilization plans. Only five months!

2. In 1915, with the assent of the Council of Ministers, the army broke the Pale of Settlement convention by driving Jews from the frontier areas into the interior.

advised by a chief of staff of comparable incompetence, his replacement by Nicholas was positive from the military point of view.

The Russian plan for the first weeks of war took account of the expected German strategy. The initially small German forces would be held by just one Russian army, and three of the other five armies would attack Austria, hoping to rout the latter's forces before the full strength of the German army could be transferred from France. But, to help the French, this plan was changed; two Russian armies advanced into eastern Prussia and won early successes, before the arrival of fresh German troops and generals led to a damaging defeat at the battle of Tannenberg. The Russians had advanced before they were properly mobilized and this was later criticized, but the fact remains that nine German divisions were transferred to eastern Prussia just as the German thrust towards Paris was failing on the Marne, putting an end to German prospects of a quick victory. Various Russians at various times have argued that in both world wars their country saved the west from defeat. In the case of the First World War there is much to support this argument; both the Marne and Verdun were held with the aid of the Russian army.

Meanwhile, the Russian south-western armies successfully defended Poland against an Austrian offensive and then themselves captured large areas of Austrian Galicia. One fiery commander, disregarding instructions, even rampaged around the Hungarian plains; this was Kornilov, later famous in another connection. He was a real cavalry officer, being described by his contemporaries as 'having the heart of a lion and the brain of a lamb'. German troops were sent to rescue Austria, and by early 1915 the Russian armies were in retreat on both the northern and south-western fronts. By the end of the summer they had been driven out of Galicia and had lost Poland and part of White Russia. The front then became more or less stabilized until 1917, running southwards from near Riga, through the Pripet marshes, to the Romanian frontier.

By 1915 the Russian army was losing its professional sparkle. Losses had been heavy, and replacements were inexperienced and sometimes only semi-trained. The weapon and ammunition shortage was becoming catastrophic, Russian guns were sometimes limited to four shots a day or less. Trainees, and sometimes front-line reinforcements, had to share rifles. There was an almost total lack of barbed wire. Russia, like other belligerents, had not expected a long war and was less successful than others in overcoming production difficulties. Nevertheless the army, although it lost territory, was never destroyed. Not for the first or last time, its deficiencies were compensated by a lavish expenditure of its sturdy soldiers. During the first year of war it lost about 4 million men.[3] By 1915 it was facing poison-gas attacks, but these new

---

3. Russian casualties for the entire war were about 8 million, including 1.7 million dead and 2.4 million captured.

manifestations of German technological superiority neither terrified nor surprised the Russian soldier. After all, there was a well-known Russian saying, 'it must have been a German who invented the monkey'.

War against Turkey began in October 1914, when Odessa was bombarded. Militarily, Turkey presented little threat, but henceforth Russia could receive supplies from the Allies only through Archangel (Murmansk until 1916 lacked a railway) or through Vladivostok. This was one reason why the Allies in 1915 embarked on the Dardanelles campaign. One cause of the failure of the latter was Russia's refusal to approve the participation of the Greek army in the venture. The Russian government had obtained secret Anglo-French assent to a post-war settlement of the Straits question by which Russia would acquire Constantinople. Greek participation seemed a potential threat to this long-sought gain because Greece, too, had her ambitions.

In the winter of 1915–16 the Russian army began to recover from its mauling. There was time to train the conscripts properly and to build up ammunition stocks. Machine and field guns were more plentiful and rifles were being produced at the improved, though still insufficient, rate of 10,000 monthly. The Red Cross detachments organized by the Union of *Zemstva* found time to attend to the soldiers' recreational and morale needs as well as to medical matters. In February 1916, in response to French requests following the first German attacks on Verdun, the Russian western armies began advances which developed into a costly retreat, but what was a setback for the Russians was a gain for the French. After further urgent requests from Britain and France, GHQ adopted a plan for an offensive against Austria on the south-western front, to be followed by an even stronger thrust against the Germans by the western armies in Lithuania. This plan was submitted by the commander of the south-western armies, Brusilov, who then worked out its execution in meticulous detail and with an understanding of Russian logistic difficulties. As he himself wrote later, 'Knowing the limitation of our railway transport . . . I knew that while we were entraining and transporting one army corps, the Germans would manage to transport three or four.'[4] This meant that a Russian breakthrough might be blocked by fresh enemy troops before Russian reinforcements could be brought up to exploit the situation. For this reason Brusilov ordered each of the four armies of his front to prepare their own attacks; there would be four breakthroughs and no reserves.

On 4 June, as the siege of Verdun reached a climax and as the Italian army was reeling from Austrian attacks, the Brusilov Offensive[5] was launched. It was a crushing success. Great areas of territory were occupied. Hordes of prisoners were taken. The Austrian commander, Archduke Josef Ferdinand, was shelled in the middle of his birthday party. But what might have been a war-winning

---

4. A. Brusilov, *A Soldier's Notebook* (1930), 239.
5. It was the only victory of the war to be named after its commander.

triumph remained only a great victory, because GHQ did precisely what Brusilov had warned against. Instead of starting the planned follow-up attack by its western armies just as the enemy was off-balance, it sent western troops to reinforce Brusilov. This left the German commanders free to send their own reinforcements to aid the Austrians, and to arrive there first. Nevertheless, the offensive, apart from being a great boost to Russian and foreign morale, forced the withdrawal of thirty-five German divisions from France. Verdun did not fall. Russian losses had been heavy, about half a million casualties. There was little possibility of another offensive on such a scale being launched before many months of recuperation. There was also the question of morale after the offensive became a retreat. It seemed unlikely that the army and the public could accept many more hundreds of thousands of killings, maimings, gassings, and mental derangements.

There was another side effect of the Brusilov Offensive which seemed at first a great success but later proved catastrophic. Throughout the war the belligerents' diplomacy had concentrated on persuading, by threat or bribe, the remaining neutrals to join in on their side. The western Allies had lost this game in Turkey, and even in Slavic Bulgaria. But Romania, always an expert fence-sitter, was still waiting to make absolutely sure which side would win before throwing in her lot with the victor. The Brusilov Offensive, coupled with some diplomatic action by the admiral commanding Russia's Danubian flotilla (who distributed 2 million roubles' worth of trinkets to the wives of influential Romanians), finally won the day for the Allies. The almost immediate result was the rout of the Romanian army by the Central Powers, the occupation of much of that nation by enemy forces (facilitating communication with Turkey), and the hasty dispatch of Russian units to help the Romanians. In effect, Romania's accession meant the extension of Russia's war front down to the Black Sea, a dilution of troops she could ill afford.

Protection of St Petersburg by a mine barrier across the Gulf of Finland was the first priority of the Baltic Fleet, and was finished before war was declared; this quiet mining in peacetime of international waters was achieved without any accidents or diplomatic embarrassments. Eight lines of mines, 3,000 mines in total, were laid. Later in the year Russian minelayers went out at night to lay mines in enemy waters, especially in the approaches of Danzig, and these caused some serious losses. The German battlefleet, preoccupied with the British navy, never made any deep offensive sweeps into the Baltic. But smaller ships did, and also appeared as escorts to the ships supplying the German army as it advanced along the southern shore of the Baltic. Of the several German cruisers and destroyers lost in the Baltic the most significant was the cruiser *Magdeburg*, which ran aground in 1914 and was located by Russian radio-direction stations. Russian cruisers discovered that the *Magdeburg* had been abandoned, and succeeded in finding the German naval code book, which was sent to the British Admiralty. On the Black Sea, initial

Russian naval superiority was challenged by the entry of the ex-German battlecruiser *Goeben* and its accompanying cruiser *Breslau*. This pair, though vulnerable to the newer Russian battleships (which on one occasion did damage *Goeben*), could make damaging raids and escape by virtue of their higher speed. The situation was further complicated by the appearance of U-boats in the Black Sea. These, despite defensive net- and minelaying, sank about one-quarter of the supply ships on which the Russian armies depended. When Admiral Kolchak took over the Black Sea command in 1916 the position improved. Kolchak abandoned defensive minelaying in favour of offensive. Night minelaying expeditions were made to block the Bosporus and Varna, and shallow-draught minelayers were sent in to lay additional mines in already existing fields in case the enemy had already cleared the latter. In three months 2,000 mines were laid. From November 1916 few, if any, enemy ships could leave the Bosporus, and Turkey was in the throes of a coal famine, for she depended on coastal shipping to connect her coalfields with her towns and industry. Thus by 1917 Russia had regained control of the Black Sea. The Russian army, which was performing well against the Turks in the Caucasus, could be supplied by sea. A combined operation to capture the Dardanelles (and Constantinople) was being studied.

When the Allies began to ship supplies to Archangel, the White Sea acquired strategic importance. Warships from the Pacific Squadron were therefore sent to this new theatre. Japan, now an ally, sold back some of the ships which she had captured or salvaged in the Russo-Japanese War. These were also dispatched to the White Sea. One of them, a battleship which had been scuttled at Port Arthur, went down for a second and last time in the Mediterranean, after striking a mine while on her way home.

Russia as an ally

There was a certain pro-German sentiment in Russia among some right-wing groups, but it was never as strong as the Allies feared. There was also a tradition of anti-British feeling, dating back to the mid-nineteenth century and fed by Britain's determination to keep Russia out of the eastern Mediterranean. In general, there was an underlying friendliness towards France and the USA, and equally towards Frenchmen and Americans. In the Russian army the officers of the old school (in effect, the senior officers) had more respect and understanding for their German counterparts than they had for the Allies, although the reserve officers, being younger, less militaristic, and more liberal, were just the opposite.

At the beginning of the war many prominent Britons and Russians openly wondered whether they had chosen the right allies. British liberals did not relish the idea of fighting alongside the most reactionary of the Great Powers, whose Cossack troops were already killing Russian Jews in the border areas, while Russian conservatives regretted that Russia should be fighting against the two empires which represented traditional monarchy. As the war became more arduous these feelings became muted; nevertheless the question of a 'separate peace' was a basic issue in the diplomacy of this period. France and England feared that Russia, because of the influence of the pro-German element or because of the heavy losses she was sustaining, would make peace with Germany and enable the latter to exert all her strength against the west. Germany did make peace offers to Petrograd. The first appears to have been conveyed by one of the Empress's maids of honour, who lost her job in consequence. Nicholas had no intention of breaking his promises, but rumours spread that Russian officials were in touch with the Germans, thereby aggravating suspicions that part of the government was in league with the enemy.

The apparently successful, if secret, solution of the centuries-old Straits problem was not matched by a corresponding decision on Poland. Sazonov, the foreign minister, urged his government to promise an autonomous Poland and a united Poland (that is, the reunification of Russian, Austrian, and Prussian Poland) in the post-war settlement. However, the suggestion was rejected; an autonomous Poland, even under the Russian crown, was too much for influential right-wing figures in Petrograd. The Polish independence movement concentrated its propaganda work in Paris; since the French were traditional friends of the Poles this agitation caused the Russian government the maximum of embarrassment. Less damaging, although more spectacular, was the anti-Russian Polish legion led by Pilsudski, sponsored by Austria and fighting on Austria's side. All the belligerents intrigued to exploit their enemies' weak points, especially national minorities whose nationalism might be turned, by skilful propaganda, against their governments. In addition, the Germans sought to foment industrial unrest in Russia. Funds were sent, via Scandinavia, to Russian revolutionaries organizing propaganda and strikes. During 1916 the strike movement in war industries became quite serious, but real privation rather than German money was the spur.

By 1916 the Russian need for material assistance and the Allied need for a staunch partner in the east led to the exchange of several delegations. As the Russian government became weaker and obviously more ineffective the western Allies began to apply, in a gentlemanly way, real pressure. Just three months before the February Revolution, during an inter-allied conference in Petrograd, Lord Milner indicated that further British munitions would not be forthcoming unless British officers were allowed to supervise their use by the Russian army. Furthermore, he hinted that the British government did not approve Nicholas's choice of ministers, and he praised the work of the *zemstva* voluntary organizations.

The French had already asked for 400,000 Russian troops, and by 1917 about 50,000 had arrived, divided between the Western Front and Salonika.

Their departure was semi-secret, because many Russians were against the idea. These soldiers learned of the February Revolution (from French newspapers rather than from their officers) and some demanded return to Russia. In April 1917 General Pétain refused to permit Russian units to go to the front until their soldiers' committees (allowed by the new Russian government) were disbanded. He complained that 'the introduction of committees into your army has encouraged several cases of indiscipline in our own, which is now demanding similar committees'.[6] Semi-mutinous Russian troops were attacked by French infantry and arrested. Some were shipped to forced labour in Africa, but others formed a legion to continue the fight against Germany.

The home front

When war was declared, the St Petersburg students, who recently had been protesting against the government, once again broke the ban on demonstrations and marched on the German embassy. This, a new and barracks-like building, was sacked and its mass of external copper statuary toppled into the street. Some days later students toured the city with pots of paint, obliterating German street and shop names. Somebody wrote to one of the capital's most Panslavic and anti-German newspapers, complaining that its title was set in Gothic type.[7] Not since 1812, it seemed, had the people seemed so united with their tsar. The war was seen as an attack by Germany on Holy Russia, rather than as simply a quarrel with Austria over Serbia. The Duma only needed one day to approve the war credits, the Social Democrats and the Trudoviki abstaining. Although both main factions of the Social Democrats opposed the war verbally, only the Bolsheviks urged Russians to fight their own government rather than the Germans (which was why, in November, the five remaining Bolshevik Duma members were arrested and exiled). Newspaper correspondents described how young and old were volunteering for the army. The German-sounding Sankt-Peterburg became Petrograd. There were declarations and street demonstrations by workers and others in support of their tsar and country. And yet, impressive and frequent though the demonstrations were, they did not prove very much. As with all demonstrations, the majority who stayed at home were not noticed. There were some observers who quietly wondered how far the bureaucracy's traditional skill in organizing spontaneous demonstrations had been brought into play. Even the French ambassador wrote in his diary about groups of 'poor devils at each corner shouting hoorah! under the eyes of a policeman'. Certainly public opinion, the collective expressed view of journalists, officials, gentry, politicians, and other influential figures, was strongly for the war, and would

---

6. *Krasnyi arkhiv*, 44: 155.
7. The editor defended his paper by claiming that the London *Morning Post* used the same style.

probably never have forgiven Nicholas if he had not made a stand. But in Russia public opinion is not necessarily the opinion of the public. If those newspaper correspondents reporting the demonstrations and the flow of volunteers in the cities had ventured to the villages where the reservists were making ready, they would have found no demonstrations to report. If they had listened hard, they would have heard the sound of weeping.

There were over 2 million German-speaking people in the Empire, including many German and Austrian subjects. In Petrograd it was quite normal to hear German spoken in the streets, for the capital had its own German community with its own shops and newspapers. The loyalty of citizens of German descent was not questioned by the government, but towards the end of 1914 German and Austrian subjects were expelled.[8] This was not enough for the extreme Panslavists. The popular and illiberal Petrograd newspaper *Novoye Vremiya* conducted a vicious campaign against the Baltic Germans, dredging up supposedly damaging facts (e.g. that von Zeppelin's wife was a Baltic German) to imply that they were disloyal. The government was carefully watching for pro-German sentiments in the Baltic provinces but did nothing drastic, although in some cities of the Empire the assembly of more than two German speakers was forbidden, and public use of the German language was banned. But after the defeats of 1915 there were lethal pogroms against 'German elements' in which, in Moscow at least, the governor and local priests participated.

Coinciding with the 1914 mobilization, the often-recommended prohibition of the sale and consumption of vodka and similar spirits was decreed. Astonished eyewitnesses reported that drunkenness suddenly disappeared (except in Archangel, where the crews of British freighters soon organized a black market in Scotch whisky). This prohibition, together with the relative prosperity which war brought to the villages, was one explanation for the wartime decline in the rural death rate. In the towns there was a reduced crime rate, and higher productivity. That the Empire began the greatest war in its history by sacrificing its most valuable source of revenue was considered highly eccentric, but not without merit. An embarrassing consequence was that Russians were left with more money to spend on food and goods, which were in short supply, thus exacerbating wartime inflation.[9] Although small-scale illegal distillation of spirits became popular in the villages, in general sobriety prevailed until the Revolution.

In 1914 many of the outstanding members of the Duma and of the *zemstva* went to the front and organized hospital services, for the war ministry had

---

8. In one Moscow district the police mixed up their lists, rounding up all the British residents and not interfering with the Germans until a detained Englishman politely suggested that a mistake might have been made.

9. In 1941, when Hitler attacked, the gesture was not repeated; instead, the price of vodka was quintupled.

made few preparations for the enormous influx of wounded. In August 1914 the Tsar had given his approval for a union of *zemstva* so that the various local *zemstva* could pool their resources and their experience in order to make a really worthwhile contribution on a national scale. Soon after, the city councils formed a similar union with the same purpose. The *zemstva* not only fitted out hospitals and hospital trains, but they organized in their various localities new industries to provide army boots, tents, hospital supplies, and other items which were in quite inadequate supply. The government also set up relief organizations, while the Empress and her daughters enrolled as nurses and did not shirk the most gruesome of nurses' duties.

Another non-governmental organization was the War Industries Committee, established in 1915 to stimulate the production of munitions, its members including representatives from ministries, industry, and the *zemstva* and cities unions. Guchkov, the prominent Duma member, was its chairman. It was notable also in including ten workers' representatives. It did much to bypass cumbersome bureaucratic channels, which is one reason it and similar organizations were disliked and often obstructed by officials but welcomed by the generals. Moscow industrialists also welcomed and supported it, because it gave government orders to their smallish enterprises, hitherto neglected in favour of the big Petrograd companies. Also important in 1915 was the formation, with the Tsar's approval but with the misgivings of many of his ministers, of the National Defence Council, which included nominees from the more important ministries, from the War Industries Committee, and one each from the unions of *zemstva* and cities. Its associated councils for food, fuel, transport, and refugees included many nominees of the non-official organizations, and seemed to be bodies which would give the public representatives a real influence. The minister of the interior did not like this dilution of the autocratic principle but was soon replaced by a man who had attracted notice by his skill in breeding horses for the army. In June 1915 the war minister, Sukhomlinov, generally blamed for the munition shortages, was replaced by Polivanov. With the exception of just one or two ministers and of the prime minister, Goremykin, the Council of Ministers now consisted of reasonably capable men who were willing to cooperate with the Duma leaders.

The mood of the Duma was unfavourable to the government, but not irrevocably. The Kadet, Progressist, and Octobrist liberal parties combined to form the nucleus of a new grouping, the Progressive Bloc, which demanded a 'government of public confidence'. This would not have been too difficult to achieve at that time, only a few ministerial changes being necessary to achieve a government consisting of men having the trust of the Duma rather than being merely the Tsar's nominees. Some demands of the Duma were already being met. For example, the stream of Jewish refugees fleeing from the German and Russian armies made nonsense of the much-resented laws of

Jewish settlement, and the government was opening other parts of Russia to them (but not Moscow and Petrograd).

The problem of the military zones was not solved. Under war conditions the military were given complete control not only of the frontier area, but of the areas behind the frontiers, including Petrograd. In these areas they exercised civil control, did not allow entry to non-military persons without permission, and in various ways antagonized the inhabitants. The *zemstva*-organized medical services were among those with restricted entry, which was an obvious handicap in their work. Conflicts between civil and military authority were frequent and damaging to the war effort, and were usually the result of obstinate ignorance on the part of army officers. At one stage of the war, for example, there was a coal famine because empty railway cars being sent to the Donets mining area were held 'in case of need' by the military authorities through whose zone the railway passed; no empty cars south meant no loaded cars north, no loaded cars north meant no fuel, no fuel meant no factories operating, no factories meant no munitions.

The morale of the war-fighting classes, despite ecstatic claims to the contrary, could not be relied upon. There had been draft riots in 1914, that at Barnaul being the most serious. Horse requisitioning committees aroused anger. Many men applied for deferment, although there were others who were keen to go and fight, and yet others who eagerly denounced shirkers and evaders. After 1915, when many more men were needed, exemptions became a big issue. The three big exemption categories were only sons, non-Slavic ethnic groups, and reserved occupations. Reserved occupations failed to include many categories of skilled worker required for the war effort, but it did include a blanket exemption for policemen, which was much resented. However, the interior ministry staunchly protected its policemen from any change in this regard. Ethnicity ceased to be a bar, and few problems were experienced in recruiting Muslim nationalities from the Caucasus. However, the nomads of Central Asia were not considered good material, so they were recruited for non-combatant duties. Those families who resented the call-up were joined by those resenting this slur on their military competence, and scheduling the call-up during Ramadan was not a bright idea. The whole region rose in rebellion, with thousands of deaths and atrocities. This rising, hardly reported, was still in progress in 1917.

Peasant soldiers for the most part did not feel they were defending the Russian state, although they did believe they were fighting for Holy Russia and its tsar. Being torn from their villages and thrown into the external world, they did widen their views. In their home villages there was also a mental change. The *zemstva* introduced adult classes in the villages, teaching about the external world in order to boost patriotism. Soldiers' letters and printed news about the war also encouraged people, and especially soldiers' wives, to crowd into the literacy classes that the *zemstva* had been organizing for some years.

Military reverses led to increasing dissatisfaction with the government. In particular, it seemed that the 'public organizations', like the War Industries Committee and the *zemstva* bodies, were much more capable of administering the war effort than the ministries. In other words, an alternative government was being born—and this process was reflected in the various requests of the Duma leaders, industrialists, city councils, and *zemstva* for more authority. Liberals predominated in the 'public organizations' and sought to exploit their indispensability in the war effort as a lever to obtain a government 'responsible to public opinion'. By this they meant a government whose members would need to retain the approval of the Duma. For most liberals (and Nicholas) it was a case of now-or-never; if the liberals did not gain their objective during the war, they would be very vulnerable after it. In mid-1915 there was a majority of ministers who favoured the formation of a responsible government, but the Tsar and the prime minister (Goremykin) were unreceptive. When in September 1915 Nicholas left to take command at GHQ, against the advice of most of his ministers, it seemed that any hope of a responsible government, or of a united government, had disappeared. Following the Tsar's decision, the more capable ministers resigned or were dismissed. Even Goremykin was replaced in early 1916. Henceforth, and until 1917, a dreary succession of nonentities would play musical chairs around the cabinet table, with the Empress and Rasputin hovering in the background.

The Empress and Rasputin

Alexandra was in many respects a superb woman, even though she was fated to bring into public gaze her failings rather than her virtues. Nominally a German princess, by education and upbringing she had been essentially a part of the British royal family. She brought to Russia not only the haemophilic gene of her grandmother Queen Victoria, but a sincere prudery, a deeply religious mind, and a repugnance for the rituals and empty pomp of court life. Being required by her marriage to adopt the Orthodox faith, she became more fervent than the born Orthodox. For someone like Alexandra, whose marriage was also a choice of profession, the Orthodox Church seemed to offer, apart from spiritual nourishment, the soundest way to understand the soul of the ordinary Russian. The Empress, and Nicholas, really did imagine they could share the lives of the people, of the peasants. But the people never really accepted her, especially after 1914. Moreover, when she and Nicholas after about 1905 limited their expected but vapid participation in court life, preferring to spend their spare time with each other, the Empress became unpopular with St Petersburg society.

Rasputin became a political influence in about 1911, but it was not until later that this was generally realized. Prior to 1911 he had been an intimate of the royal family, but little more. When, in 1903, he arrived in St Petersburg from his native Siberia, he was in his thirties, and already enjoyed the reputation of a holy man. His acquaintance with Nicholas and Alexandra began in 1905, a bad year for the imperial couple. There were the defeats of the Russo-Japanese War, the internal upheavals, and above all the cruel shock of discovering that the long-awaited, long-prayed-for, and long-despaired-of male heir, who had finally appeared in 1904 to the accompaniment of a 300-gun salute, was haemophilic. The young Alexis was permitted to lead as normal a life as possible; some risks were taken and some serious crises thereby created. In 1907 the Tsarevich seemed to be dying a prolonged and agonizing death after a minor fall, but he began to recover after Rasputin had been called in. Previously, miraculous cures of other sick or injured people by Rasputin had been reported. Only the most hostile of Rasputin's detractors have found it possible to find conventional explanations for each and every manifestation of these so-called miracles. In the case of Alexis, it has been plausibly suggested that Rasputin kept away the official doctors, whose repeated prying and prodding of the patient were precisely what a haemophiliac must be spared. In the other cases, it is possible that the confidence inspired by Rasputin's presence was a saving factor. Rasputin did have some hypnotic power, but this was not exceptionally strong.

Nicholas's faith in Rasputin was somewhat less uncritical than that of his wife, and he realized that not all the tales of the holy man's drinking and womanizing achievements were the product of jealous or envious rumour-mongers. Nevertheless, by 1914 Rasputin was firmly installed as the imperial family's confidant, and through the Empress he could influence policy, although it is not true that Nicholas blindly followed Rasputin's advice; more often than not he ignored it. But when in 1915 Nicholas went to the front, Rasputin's influence was strengthened simply because the Empress had such magnified authority. The first major change, engineered by ambitious men who took great trouble to gain Rasputin's favour, was the appointment of Khvostov to the key office of minister of the interior. Khvostov's ambition and cunning far outstripped his talent, but the Empress found him a charming genius. *Khvost* means 'tail' in Russian, so it was not long before she began to refer to him as 'my tail' just as she referred to Rasputin as 'our friend'. This virtual personification of her anatomy became known, and doubtless there were those who soon found even more homely words for Khvostov.

Once Khvostov and Rasputin were firmly in place as the Empress's advisers, the better ministers one by one were dismissed or resigned, being replaced by what the triumvirate liked to call 'our men'. 'Our men' all too often were those who knew how to flatter, how to propose actions they anticipated would be pleasing to the Empress, Rasputin, and Khvostov. A climax came in February 1916 with the replacement of Goremykin as prime minister by the even more incapable Sturmer. Some indication of the inner life, the network of intrigues (with each ambitious participant contriving to endear himself to Rasputin in private but to have no connection with him in public), the corruption, the hosts of worthy and unworthy petitioners beating on Rasputin's door, the mismanagement of the inner life of the country and of the defence of the nation, can be gleaned from the pages of the official post-revolutionary investigation, which includes Russian-style soul-baring confessions by several of those most deeply involved. Rasputin was finally murdered in 1916 by a group of conspirators of whom the young and rich Prince Yusupov (related to the Tsar by marriage), the Tsar's young cousin Dmitri Pavlovich, and the right-wing Duma member Purishkevich were the most important. The plot was successful, although almost every move was bungled. The assassins were regarded by the public as heroes who had rid the country of an evil influence and probable German spy. They were unobtrusively defended by some members of the royal family, including Grand Duke Nikolai Nikolaevich, and the government merely exiled them to their country estates. Although they had acted to save the monarch's reputation, they probably damaged the government; the prime minister who had been appointed to replace Sturmer a few weeks earlier was more capable than the latter, but was dismissed in the aftermath of the murder.

The facts and rumours of Rasputin's influence aroused great popular resentment against the regime. Yet Rasputin may well have been a man of goodwill, who failed to make Russia a better place only because he lacked the education and experience to see through those who, protesting friendship, were merely using him. There seems little doubt that Rasputin had a horror of war, a real understanding that the Christian phrases about the brotherhood of man are inconsistent with sending millions of men to their deaths for the sake of national honour. It was said, quite plausibly, that he helped to dissuade Nicholas from war in 1909 and 1912, and he did his best to avoid the 1914 war, foreseeing its results for the Romanovs and for Russia. During the war, when hatred of the Germans was whipped up to a peak and when talk of a separate peace was regarded as treason, Rasputin nevertheless urged an end to hostilities. War to the Russian royal family had never been a big thrill, and Rasputin made it impossible to forget that war had nothing in common with those stirring peacetime parades. In 1916, apparently, Rasputin urged that the Duma should be reconvened, against the advice of Khvostov. He also suggested that Nicholas should break precedents and address the Duma; this was done, and the Tsar made a good impression, even referring to the members as 'representatives of the people'. It was Rasputin who, realizing that standing from wintry dawn to dusk outside a breadless bakery could turn the meekest housewife into a flaming revolutionary, urged that priority be given to food trains.

The last months of the Empire witnessed the Empress, aided by incompetent and intriguing denizens of the court and ministries, attempting to guide affairs in Petrograd and telegraphing all kinds of admonitions and advice to Nicholas at the front. 'Be an Emperor. Be an Ivan the Terrible . . . Send Milyukov, Guchkov, and Polivanov to Siberia.' She may have been right, but to the population at large, 'that German woman' seemed to be the source of all Nicholas's troubles. The peasants' proverb summed up many people's feelings: 'It's a sad home where the cow instructs the bull.'

10

1917

The February Revolution[1]

IT was only to be expected that after two years of war and sacrifice, with no apparent result, Russians would be beginning to ask themselves whether their country was being properly led. This question had been asked by men of knowledge or influence ever since the war started, but during 1916 lack of confidence in the government spread to the people as a whole. 'That German woman', the Empress, was suspected of sympathy towards the enemy, and when it was realized that she was, in effect, at the helm in Petrograd while her husband was at GHQ, popular alarm grew. The influence of Rasputin, which was common knowledge, was equally resented. The feeling that there were many in the government who wanted the Germans to win, or who were in German pay, gained sustenance from memories of the alleged chaos in the ministry of war in 1914, blamed on the war minister, Sukhomlinov. The campaign seemed to be going so wrong that it was easy to believe rumours that he was a German agent; in fact, Sukhomlinov was one of the more far-sighted tsarist generals, which is probably why he became a target of other military men. His protégé Colonel Myasoyedov was executed as a spy in 1915, arousing further public misgivings, even though the trial and conviction resulted more from personal animosities and paranoia than from any real evidence of treason. Sukhomlinov was subsequently imprisoned as a traitor.

In February 1916 the appointment of Sturmer as prime minister in place of Goremykin aroused fresh suspicion; not only was he dishonest and incompetent, but he had a German name. There were occasions when Russian attacks at the front had been met by withering resistance, and it seemed not only to the uninformed soldiers but also to their officers that Russian plans had been betrayed to the enemy. In fact, careless talk and unciphered communications gave considerable help to German intelligence.

1. Russia changed from the Julian to the Gregorian (western) calendar on 14 February 1918, which became 1 February of the new style. This is why the February Revolution may also be described as the March Revolution, and why the revolution occurring in November was celebrated as the October Revolution.

The main source of the rumours of treason in high places was liberal politicians, many of whom beneath their veneer of western parliamentarianism were just as dishonest, ambitious, wishful-thinking, and uncompromising as their political rivals. Desperately anxious to so weaken the monarchy that Nicholas would feel forced to grant them greater influence through some kind of responsible government, before the end of the war ruined their chances, the liberals appear to have changed their tactics after 1915; hitherto they had merely spread doubts about the government's competence to win the war, not about its willingness. Of all the influences which, in turning public opinion against Nicholas, prepared the ground for the Revolution, the liberals were the most effective. At the same time, thanks to their contacts, through the 'public organizations', with the front line, they strove to influence the generals who, in the last resort, would regard military victory as more important than the survival of autocracy. But they operated cautiously, remembering 1905 and the dangers of a revolution that might run out of their control.

Although workers were beginning to heed anti-war agitators, the strikes in key industries were largely a result of the superior bargaining position of workers that resulted from growing labour shortages. Most Russians did not condemn the war as such, only the way it was being prosecuted. Partly influenced by anti-German propaganda, but mainly impelled by the belief that this war had not been sought by St Petersburg but had been imposed by the Central Powers, Russians intended to continue the war until the defeat of Germany. But by the end of 1916 almost all the feasible age groups had been conscripted, and a stream of gassed or maimed soldiers was returning to the towns and villages, not to speak of the long lists of dead which were posted in public places to be scanned by those with relatives at the front.

The drafting of more and more peasants was not the cause of the food shortages which developed in 1916 and 1917. The Russian countryside was still overpopulated and in most regions could afford to shed young men, and even horses. The process could not continue indefinitely, and there was some fall in output as women, old men, and war-wounded came to dominate agricultural work. But the cessation of grain exports and vodka distillation compensated for the production loss. Overall there was enough food for everybody. The urban food shortages which triggered the February Revolution were not the result of insufficient supplies, but of inefficient wholesale and retail distribution.

Distribution troubles were partly caused by the failure of the railway system to meet the demands of war. This failure was not so much the failure of the railways themselves, but of the way they were administered. In fact, during the war railway construction proceeded at a rapid pace.[2] However, rolling stock

2. Among the many new lines was the Murmansk Railway, finished in 1916, which together with the widening of the narrow-gauge Archangel line promised to reduce the enormous dumps of strategic imports which had accumulated at those two ports.

was lacking, because railway works had been transferred to munitions production or had lost skilled workers to the army. A crucial factor in the transport failure was the division of the railway network into two administrations; about one-third of the mileage, the railways of the western region, was placed under military administration, and the civilian administration of the remaining lines was expected to cooperate with the former. This it did, and in a short time the western railways had accumulated masses of rolling stock which they were unwilling to relinquish but unable to utilize efficiently. In these circumstances it was hardly surprising that the railways were unable to cope with the change of traffic flows caused by the war. Food trains for the cities, which had a low priority, became fewer and fewer, resulting in reduced stocks. It was the bread shortages in Petrograd which, justifiably, caused the political police the most worry. Their agents could feel the strength of the indignation of those women who queued all night at the bakeries only to be told that because of a flour or fuel shortfall there would be no bread after all.

On 23 February 1917, against a background of continuing strikes, women workers in the Vyborg district of Petrograd became so frustrated with their unrewarded queuing that they became an indignant and unruly mob that grew into a crowd big enough to frighten the police into violent action. Within hours their protest had the support of demonstrations by the more militant Petrograd factory workers. Cossacks, intended to disperse the crowds, had by oversight been dispatched without whips and therefore lacked their customary zest. As the days passed, the crisis deepened. There were reports that officers were joining with students in singing revolutionary songs on the streets.

Although Nicholas, from GHQ, ordered the general commanding the Petrograd garrison to put down the disturbance, he seemed unaware of its seriousness. This was unsurprising, since he was not told very much. For example, on Sunday, 26 February, that same general, just as he was issuing orders for troops to open fire on demonstrators if they refused to disperse, was cabling Nicholas that blue skies and freshly fallen snow were creating a holiday atmosphere in the capital.

In the Duma, Kerensky, the leader of the Trudovik socialist group, was unsuccessfully urging the assembly to take the lead. He even went as far as asserting that only the removal of Nicholas, by force if necessary, could save the Empire. Kerensky already had a high reputation among socialists. His Trudoviks were a kind of upmarket fraction of the Socialist Revolutionaries, and later he would transfer his allegiance to the latter party, whose central committee never seemed quite sure of what to make of him. A lawyer, he had made a reputation defending or advising left-wing activists facing trial on political charges, and himself had had several brushes with the Okhrana. In June 1914 he was sentenced to six months' imprisonment (never served) for his part in protests against the Beilis Case; this made him even more popular at a time when the only other left-winger capable of matching his oratory in the

Duma, the Bolshevik Malinovsky, had disappeared in the wake of the revelation that he was a police spy. In 1915, Kerensky's support of strikers and his obvious belief in revolution caused the Okhrana to regard him as the 'chief ringleader' of the revolutionary movement. For seven months in 1917 he would be the key political figure in Russia and at times was wildly popular. This popularity would fade as it became clear that he could deliver no miracles, and his post-1917 reputation was not improved by the memoirs in which he sought to excuse his failures. But it is doubtful whether anyone could have done better in the circumstances of 1917. In 1917 he was clearly the right man at the right time, but he was not right enough.

What made February 1917 different from previous protests was that many of the soldiers, and some of the officers, were refusing to shoot down their fellow-countrymen. The whole basis of the autocratic system was the ability of the autocrat, as a last resort, to set his army against those who challenged his authority; Nicholas was losing that ability in Petrograd, where the soldiers were largely resentful elderly reservists, recuperating war-wounded, and new conscripts. Rodzianko, president of the Duma, wired Nicholas that Petrograd was descending into chaos; there was a food and fuel crisis, and shooting on the streets. He asked Nicholas to form a new and responsible government. The Tsar responded by proroguing the Duma. Duma members, however, remained in the capital and met informally on 27 February. On this day the streets were crowded with strikers, demonstrators, and students, with soldiers openly consorting with the protesters.

On the first day, workers may not have predominated in the protests, while women workers, soldiers' wives, and middle-class protesters were more numerous than on subsequent days. After the soldiers' mutinies that began on 27 February, and the opening-up of prisons, the more moderate demonstrators tended to retire to their households as the crowds became more violent. There were some deaths on the streets, which was hardly surprising with the new easy access to alcohol and weapons. There were always looters, seeking to exploit the situation. Attempts at strong law enforcement were rare and unsuccessful; even the dreaded Cossacks seemed to show signs of sympathy towards demonstrators. As the days passed the 'Give us Bread' slogans began to give way to 'Down with the War!' and 'Down with the Tsar!'

A Petrograd Soviet of Workers' Deputies, modelled on that of 1905, was set up by socialist intellectuals on 27 February; its first chairman was the Georgian Chkheidze, leader of the Duma Mensheviks, and its vice-chairman was Kerensky. Soldiers and workers invaded the prisons and released political prisoners as the various factories elected delegates to the Soviet. When representatives began to arrive from the regiments of the capital, announcing that their units had decided to join the revolution, it seemed clear that the regime would be unable to call on immediate military support. This feeling was reinforced when even the crack Semeonov Guards mutinied. To accommodate the regiments' delegates, the Soviet was renamed Soviet of Workers' and Soldiers' Deputies. A proclamation drawn up by the Soviet was published the next morning in the first issue of its own newspaper, *Izvestiya*. This proclamation announced the formation of the Soviet, appealed for the maintenance of order, and demanded the election of a constituent assembly which would decide how the new democratic Russia would be governed.

In this first Soviet, soldiers vastly outnumbered workers. Most soldiers were peasants in uniform, and the Soviet's chaotic proceeedings were not unlike those of the village assembly. This general chaos meant that the Soviet's executive committee, mainly of intellectuals, was where most decisions were made. Here, there was a general assumption that the revolution would follow western models.

The Soviet had great power, even though it did not demand responsibility. In the Petrograd area it could determine which industrial work should continue and which should be strike-bound. Its soldier-members could to a large extent approve or veto the use of armed force. Without the approval of the Soviet the trains might not run, electricity and other services could not continue. Yet it did not pretend to be the government. It was the Duma leaders who began to fulfil that function; they at least had been elected, and represented the whole country, and included men well known for their organizing ability.

As the politicians in Petrograd hurried to and from urgent meetings, trying to agree on what to do, special trains began to move, necessarily passing through junctions that might be controlled by garrisons of changeable disposition. Train movements were organized by the transport ministry in Petrograd, headed by managers who were mainly in favour of the revolution. With its own telegraph system, this ministry was in a good position not only to control movements but also to question its officials about the state of affairs in the country outside the capital:

'How are things in Gatchina?'
'Twenty thousand loyal troops here.'
'What do you mean by loyal?'
'Not revolutionary.'
'Get it, once and for all, that they are rioters. Loyal means those on the people's side. So, Gatchina is in the hands of rioters? Continue.'[3]

The railways' key role continued as Nicholas decided to return to his palace at Tsarskoye Selo, outside Petrograd. Hitherto, at GHQ, he had not received a true account of what was happening and, when told of the army mutinies, merely ordered fresh troops under General Ivanov to go to the capital to restore order. The approach of the imperial train put new pressure on Rodzianko and his associates. When it was reported on the main line 100 miles south of Petrograd, Rodzianko ordered that it be stopped, without specifying

---

3. Yu. V. Lomonosov, *Vospomininiya o Martovskoi Revolyutsii* (1921), 42.

how. The joint efforts of local railwaymen, who put one of the royal engines out of action, of the local railway manager who helped send the train off, and of the imperial staff who could not think of any better idea, resulted in its going back the way it had come. When next reported, the imperial train was proceeding west, towards Pskov, where it was feared it might join with friendly troops. It was slowed down by various expedients, like placing stationary freight trains in front of it, but meanwhile another railborne threat appeared in the form of General Ivanov who, under the pretext of an exhibition of captured trophies being staged at Tsarkoye Selo, had managed to secure clear passage for three trainloads of reliable troops to that town. From there he could join with more troops at Gatchina, and advance on Petrograd.

Railwaymen on the spot (some of whom he executed), and managers in the ministry, together kept Ivanov under control. His advance north was delayed by the removal of those vital track components, switch frogs, and his excursion ended when his train was dispatched with only enough water to allow the locomotive to get halfway to the next watering point.

Meanwhile another railway drama was played with a succession of special trains ordered by Rodzianko to take him to meet the Tsar. Holding these trains ready and cancelling other train services to give them a clear run took longer than expected, because Rodzianko kept delaying his departure and the imperial train's movements were unpredictable. Eventually, after three main lines from Petrograd had been successively paralysed by this situation, a train carrying not Rodzianko but Guchkov was guided down the line to Pskov, where Nicholas's train had finally arrived. Guchkov and another Duma member formed a delegation charged with bringing Nicholas's abdication document back to Petrograd.

The Tsar had already been persuaded by his generals to abdicate, but had decided not to transfer the burden to his son Alexis. He named his brother Mikhail as his successor, but Mikhail, on learning from the Duma leaders that the Soviet opposed the continuation of the Romanov dynasty, refused the succession.

The Provisional Government and the Soviet

Before the abdication, the leaders of the Duma, accepting the Tsar's order for dissolution but unwilling to disperse, had formed a temporary committee of members drawn from all the parties except the Bolsheviks (whose deputies were in exile) and the extreme right. It soon appointed commissars to replace the Tsar's ministers and arrested most of the latter; only the trusted navy minister Grigorovich remained in office. Members of the police were also arrested, some at their own request to save themselves from a worse fate. Meanwhile the Moscow garrison mutinied, leaving that city in the hands of the revolutionaries. Outside Petrograd the Revolution spread almost bloodlessly; whereas in the capital there had been more than a thousand casualties in the disturbances, elsewhere the transfer of power took place almost by mutual consent. A major exception was the Baltic Fleet, where mutineers murdered many officers.

The Petrograd Soviet agreed, on certain conditions, to support a provisional government which the Duma's Temporary Committee was endeavouring to establish. The new cabinet was headed by Prince Lvov, who had made a good impression on public opinion as head of the Union of *Zemstva*. The most energetic minister was Milyukov, leader of the Kadets, who was entrusted with foreign affairs. The Octobrist Guchkov became minister of war, and Kerensky minister of justice. Kerensky, whose acceptance of the post was against the wishes of many of the leaders of the Soviet, was the only minister to be also a member of the Soviet.[4]

With successive reshuffles that gave moderate socialists more influence, the Provisional Government lasted more than seven months. This in itself was quite an achievement, for it had little power and faced enormous problems. The Soviet's Order No. 1 (see p. 229) threatened to deprive the government of an effective army. The old police had by general consent been disbanded, but the militia which was to replace them never became an effective force. The Soviet, because it controlled the workers' organizations, could deny vital services if it so chose; thus the measures taken by the Provisional Government needed the acquiescence of the Soviet leaders if they were to be effective. The Provisional Government, co-opted from members of a Duma elected on a narrow franchise and consisting of gentlemen favouring a western-style parliamentary democracy, could hardly claim to be a popular government, even though it was popularly accepted for the time being.

Meanwhile, Russia's problems did not disappear with the abdication. Rather did their solution become more urgent as public expectations rose and were transformed into spontaneous and unsanctioned actions. The central problem was, of course, the war, about which public opinion gradually became less enthusiastic. The Kadet leaders, who, because the old conservative parties had disappeared, were now regarded as right-wing, wished to continue the war until victory, so as to qualify for the anticipated territorial gains (notably Constantinople and Galicia) and because they believed that the people had overthrown the Tsar primarily because he was failing to win the war. Most of the socialists, including the bulk of the Soviet leaders, accepted that Russia must fight on, but simply in order to protect the Revolution; peace

4. For the masonic links that may have helped Kerensky as he dealt with other party leaders in the Provisional Government, see R. Abraham's *Alexander Kerensky* (1987). Evidence (not conclusive) that the self-appointed Provisional Government consisted largely of men who, well before February 1917, were linked in a conspiratorial semi-masonic secret society aimed against the autocracy, and that a *coup d'état* had been planned for spring 1917 by Guchkov and others, is presented in G. Katkov's *Russia 1917* (1967).

should be made as soon as possible on the basis of no annexations and no war indemnities. Most of the Bolshevik leaders regarded the war as an imperialist phenomenon and believed it could be ended by calling on the working class of the belligerent nations to force their governments to make peace. It was Milyukov's promise to the Allies to maintain the existing understandings on the prosecution of the war which finally impelled the Soviet to oppose the Provisional Government in May, a collision which resulted in the first reshuffle of the cabinet (Milyukov and Guchkov resigned, Kerensky became minister of war, and five other socialists joined the government in a bid to associate the Soviet more closely with the administration). In July Kerensky became prime minister.

The war made almost inevitable the end of the Provisional Government. To keep the Revolution under control would have been near-impossible in any case, with the sudden release of the enormous social pressures accumulated by centuries of autocracy. To fight the war and conduct the Revolution simultaneously was a hopeless endeavour. Yet if the government had decided to end the war on unfavourable terms at this time it would probably have been overthrown, because too many Russians would have rejected such a defeat. Pride, patriotism, and the lure of territorial gain still had their effect, while most socialists believed that surrender to the Germans would mean the Kaiser would triumph over the Allies and then be free to send his armies to suppress the Revolution.

The pressures of the Revolution followed four main channels. There was the disintegration of the army. Then there was the nascent disintegration of the Empire as those claiming to speak for non-Russian nationalities demanded autonomy and usually received a sympathetic hearing. The peasantry was preoccupied with taking for itself the fields of the gentry, while the workers were striving to protect their jobs and their wages, and above all to assert their self-respect.

The first decree of the Provisional Government, drawn up just before the abdication, set the tone for the new regime. It was composed with the participation of the Soviet leaders; both the cabinet and the Soviet agreed that political and personal freedom should have first priority. The decree introduced an amnesty for political, military, and religious prisoners. It completely abolished the death penalty. It established freedom of the press (although hardly for the reactionary press), freedom of speech, the right to strike and to organize trade unions. Social or religious or national discrimination was declared illegal, a measure which benefited mainly but not exclusively the Jews. It abolished the existing police organization. It accorded to soldiers the same rights as civilians except in the front line. In response to pressure from soldier-members of the Soviet, it agreed that the Petrograd regiments which had participated in the Revolution would not be sent to the front. And it promised to arrange for elections, by universal suffrage, of a Constituent

Assembly, whose members would determine Russia's future form of government. There was thus some justification for Lenin's remark that in the summer of 1917 Russia was the freest country in the world.

However, one result of these upheavals was that the Provisional Government was disarmed. The disappearance of the old governors and their experienced administrators (a disappearance resulting more from spontaneous local actions than from government policy) and the disintegration of the police meant that a government intent on establishing a rule of law to replace tsarist arbitrariness had no means of enforcing its laws.

Although differences of nationality were not the dominant issue of the Revolution (except perhaps in Latvia where a native Latvian working class and peasantry confronted a mainly Germanic middle class), it was only natural that the various nationalisms uneasily contained in the Empire would make their own contribution to the instabilities of revolution. Probably it would have been best to make concessions to local demands for autonomy but, as in so many other fields, the moderate socialists and a section of the liberal parties that would have favoured such a compromise were checked by the Kadet leadership. The latter's reluctance to grant independence was partly emotional but also partly based on reluctance to offend the army officers, who were still thought capable of overthrowing the Revolution. As it was, granting independence to Poland, which was under German occupation, seemed no great loss and the Kadets agreed to this. The case of Finland was postponed until after the Constituent Assembly had been elected, although many Finns were not satisfied with this and demanded immediate independence and the evacuation of Russian troops. In the Ukraine, where national sentiment had been released by the Revolution, agreement might have been reached if the Kadets had not carried their objections as far as precipitating the first of the cabinet reorganizations.

In the early months after the Revolution different sections of society went through a short honeymoon period which was particularly evident in industry, where managers and factory-owners, quite pleased with the end of tsarist mismanagement, were willing to satisfy the requests of their workforces. However, unpopular foremen, and sometimes unpopular managers, did not always benefit from this relaxation. Some were physically expelled from the workplace, and others suffered more grisly fates, like being dumped down the nearest sewer. Wages rose, an eight-hour working day was agreed, and, above all, workers' committees were formed in the factories. These committees, which the Provisional Government approved, gave workers' representatives an increasing say in the conduct of work, but originally their main concern was to keep the factories going at a time when shortage of materials and, sometimes, lack of demand were threatening closures. Later in the year, when it appeared that factory-owners were ceasing production simply to avoid losses at a time of inflation and economic crisis, the committees became more interventionist, giving rise to the phenomenon known as workers' control, with the workers' committees closely supervising the management.

Although the government did establish a state monopoly in the grain trade and took power to requisition grain at fixed prices, its agents hardly made use of their powers, partly because most of them were opposed to coercive measures. Later, when peasants were refusing to market their grain until prices improved and more goods were made available to them, the government did send troops into the countryside to requisition grain but this, like a bread rationing scheme, did little to ease governmental and popular anxieties about food supply. Raising grain prices to encourage peasants to market their grain was found to infuriate the poorer peasants, who had no surplus to market and needed to buy seed grain.

The long-awaited share-out of the large estates among peasants was postponed until the Constituent Assembly was in being. The Kadets were sincere in their belief that this was too important a matter to be hurried but it placed them, and the government they dominated, in the situation of delaying a transformation that was impatiently awaited. Spontaneous takeovers of estates by local peasants, usually acting on the principle of fair shares for all, became ever more widespread.

In its first days the Petrograd Soviet was a very informal body, with a membership fluctuating between 2,000 and 3,000 as new delegates dropped in and old delegates dropped out.[5] In the beginning the regiments had a disproportionate number of seats but soon equality was imposed, with one delegate per 2,000 workers or soldiers. Most of the Soviet's decisions were taken by its executive committee, which itself had a smaller nucleus of twenty-four key members who met separately to discuss basic issues. All the socialist parties were allocated seats in the executive committee, although at first the Mensheviks and Bolsheviks were represented by secondary figures because their leaders had not yet returned from exile. It was a Menshevik exile, the Georgian Tseretelli, who on his return became the most dominant personality of the Soviet and succeeded through logic and oratory in imposing some kind of order and direction to its discussions. It was largely Tseretelli's persuasion which in May coaxed an unwilling Soviet to allow six of its members to become ministers in the Provisional Government.

Soviets were established more or less spontaneously in the provinces in the month following the Revolution. Like the Petrograd Soviet, they could limit both economic and military activity in their locality; any attempt to defeat the Revolution could be neutralized by a cessation of railway and telegraphic services, and perhaps demonstrations by the local garrisons. In the ensuing

5. Most regarded their delegates as 'elders', for the election of elders was one of the village customs which had been brought to the factories from the countryside. The dual leadership of Soviet and government might also be regarded as traditional, in the sense that both before and after 1917 there were executive bodies or persons supervised by 'watchdog' bodies or persons.

months neither the government nor the Soviet had great power in the provinces, which tended to enjoy their freedom from the capital, and witnessed more cooperation between the political parties, with local Bolsheviks more willing than their Petrograd colleagues to compromise with other left-wing parties. Many towns had 'committees of public safety' preceding or paralleling the soviets, and numerous interest groups were founded.

In April there was an All-Russia Conference of Soviets in Petrograd, and henceforth the Petrograd and the provincial soviets maintained a closer coordination. Moreover, by admitting representatives from the provincial soviets into the Petrograd Soviet, the latter became almost a national organization.

That real power lay more with the Soviet than with the Provisional Government became increasingly obvious. This implies that the causes of the 'failure' of the February Revolution should be sought in the Soviet rather than in the Provisional Government. In the Soviet, the Socialist Revolutionaries had a strong majority and in addition enjoyed the cooperation of the Mensheviks. They had massive popular support and their leader Chernov was trusted even by his opponents. But Chernov never emerged as a strong leader, perhaps because the different factions in his party were too unwilling to compromise. Moreover, in the early months of the Revolution the Socialist Revolutionary-Menshevik bloc failed to obtain what it, the people, and the Revolution needed; that is, an end to the war. It did dispatch delegations and appeals abroad, seeking a 'just peace without annexations or indemnities', but not only were these frustrated by the belligerent governments, but even the socialist leaders of France, Germany, and Britain were only lukewarm in their support. The hatreds of war defeated the Russian appeals to humanity and common sense. Having failed to obtain peace, the non-Bolshevik socialist leaders seemed to lose their bearings; in May they had forced the resignation of Milyukov because he advocated an energetic war effort for the sake, it seemed, of territorial gains, but in June they accepted the desirability of another offensive at the front. Another factor inhibiting the Soviet leaders was that the disastrous falling away of middle-class support towards the end of the 1905 Rebellion had convinced them that the 1917 Revolution should not in any circumstances become too radical. Whereas Lenin had concluded that revolutionaries should be prepared to act without middle-class support, the Mensheviks and Socialist Revolutionaries in 1917 were reluctant to arouse the enmity of the Kadets. Moreover, for marxists the February Revolution was the bourgeois revolution which Marx had said would be followed by a bourgeois government. Thus the existence of the 'bourgeois' Provisional Government, even though it lacked the power to govern, was necessary for the ideological peace of mind of many revolutionaries. For these reasons, when in July the Provisional Government seemed at the mercy of street demonstrations, and the demonstrators urged the Soviet to take power in accordance with the anarchist-inspired and Bolshevik-sponsored slogan 'All Power to the Soviets', the Soviet refused.

The army in 1917

Accounts differ about the spirit of the Russian soldiers in 1917, although all agree that the morale of the front-line troops remained much steadier than that of the rear garrisons. Similarly, the navy's small ships, frequently operating in dangerous waters, had steadier crews than the battleships, which had remained month after month in harbour. But front-line servicemen were depressed by the rumours of treason in the capital, of ministries dominated by the Empress and Rasputin. In March 1917 censorship ensured that only incomplete accounts reached the troops about the end of the Romanov dynasty; not for the last time, many Russians learned of great events through foreign broadcasts, in this case placards hoisted above German trenches, announcing the abdication of Nicholas. The abdication seemed to raise the question of whether the war might soon end, and whether the landowners' land would be redistributed. Natural reluctance to become the final casualty of the war, and rumours that back home the peasants were already taking over the land, caused many a soldier to desert. However, it was not until the summer that the desertion rate became alarmingly high.

The desperate world war which had made possible the Revolution also provided the worst possible conditions in which to carry it through. The Soviet and the Provisional Government feared that officers would use the army to restore the monarchy. This fear was largely a result of their being convinced by their own propaganda, for the army officers with few exceptions had lost their faith in the monarchy months earlier. Even in 1914 a large proportion of the officers had been liberal to the extent of preferring a constitutional form of government. Moreover, the revolutionaries' fear of the army as a counter-revolutionary threat fitted awkwardly with the reality that this same army was the only barrier between them and the German Empire, which if it broke into Russia would assuredly reassert the monarchical principle.

The chosen remedy was to subordinate the officers to the men, and to instil political vigilance in the latter. Manifestations of this policy included the famous Order No. 1, the soldiers' councils, the commissars, and visits from agitators and speechmakers. The Petrograd Soviet's Order No. 1, and its subsequent amplifications, removed the traditional authority of officers over men. It ordered units to elect their own soldier-representatives to form councils (soviets), and it was these soviets which would approve orders. Officers would be retained for the sake of their technical and leadership training, but would be responsible to their soviet. The Declaration of the Rights of Soldiers soon followed. This removed some of the humiliations to which the private soldier had hitherto been subjected, and went somewhat further by forbidding

the employment by officers of orderlies, and outlawing disciplinary punishments imposed by officers. Meanwhile, in accordance with the new freedom of
speech introduced in the country, speechmakers and agitators of varied points
of view were allowed to visit the front and address the soldiers. Those who
opposed the war advocated fraternization between the German and Russian
front-line troops. This did take place, but it was usually in the form of implicit
'if you don't bother us we won't bother you' understandings. The German
troops were still the Kaiser's troops, subject to strict military discipline, and
seemed disappointingly uninterested in revolutionary propaganda.

The dissolution of the officers' authority could not fail to break the army
eventually, but it was not a fast process. At the front the situation differed from
unit to unit. Many officers were insulted and some were barbarically slaughtered, usually because they had made themselves unpopular or, more rarely,
because the soldiers, inflamed by a visiting orator or a resident revolutionary,
were carried away by a sudden and short-lived bloodlust. But most unpopular
officers were merely asked to leave, and in many units, especially those in
which there had been good relations between officers and men, there was no
violence. The soldiers' councils, although they might spend hours arguing,
made administrative decisions which were wise and well thought out. Frequently, too, the officers would be respectfully consulted. However, many
officers could not face the breakdown of all the accustomed forms, and tended
to find new postings in rear administrations. Drill and field training were
neglected, and it was obvious to the front-line officers that, though their men
would resist attacks by the enemy, not all would agree to themselves attack.
But patriotism among soldiers was still strong.

In the capital, especially in the newspapers, there was great talk of the
wonderful fighting spirit of the army under the new regime, and the anti-
German fervour which had been deliberately fostered during the war was still
at a high pitch. To this aggressive spirit on the part of those Russians who were
safely in the rear were added French appeals for a new Russian offensive, and
the belief of the new war minister, Kerensky, that a successful offensive would
act like a tonic on morale at home, and thus strengthen the government. To
boost the morale of the front-line troops and counteract the influence of
anti-war and anti-government propagandists, Kerensky sent out to the units
his ministry's own propagandists, called commissars. These men were also
intended to mediate between the soldiers' councils and the remaining officers.
The war ministry at the same time was having moderate success in regular-
izing and controlling the proliferating mass of soldiers' soviets and committees. Kerensky made tours of the front, making those fiery speeches in which
he excelled and inspiring his listeners with a temporary thirst for offensive
action against the German Empire. Old-school officers contemptuously
referred to their war minister as the 'Persuader-in-Chief', but others respected
his energy and devotion.

In the middle of June, just as the Petrograd garrison was demonstrating against the continuation of the war, the Russian troops at the front began their offensive. The ground had been well prepared by an intense artillery barrage and the Austrians were soon in flight. General Kornilov, in particular, made a wide and dangerous breakthrough. Yet even at this stage many units refused to go into battle. The death penalty had been abolished in the army; no longer was it possible to drive soldiers into an attack at gunpoint. The most effective troops were the Czechs, those former soldiers of the piebald Austro-Hungarian army who had amicably allowed themselves to be taken prisoner by their fellow-Slavs, and then volunteered to fight against Austria for an expected independent Czech state after the war. Also distinguished were the so-called shock units, consisting of officers only.

The initial successes did provoke some enthusiasm at home. Streets which on one day were thronged by anti-war demonstrators were the next day filled with enthusiastic warmongers parading icon-style portraits of Kerensky. But as soon as German troops were sent to help Austria, the Russian offensive collapsed and turned into a rout. Henceforth the Russian army was incapable of offensive action, unwilling to exert itself, but still able to put up some resistance to an enemy advance. Soldiers who had hitherto elected Mensheviks or Social Revolutionaries to their committees did not forget that these two parties had agreed to the unwanted and unrewarded offensive.

The Bolsheviks

That the Bolsheviks played so minor a role in the early weeks of the Revolution was partly because their leaders were dispersed in exile, and partly because they had little support outside the working-class districts of the big cities. The years since 1905 had not been prosperous for any of the Social Democrat factions, even though on the eve of the war there had been signs of a recovery. Membership had fallen drastically, especially among older supporters. Intellectuals, in particular, had deserted the Social Democrats. This meant that, while there was a higher proportion of proletarians, there were fewer competent agitators, polemicists, and writers. The average member was now in his mid-twenties, and deplored the factional struggles which seemed to him a result of irrelevant émigré wranglings. In 1914 there were no fewer than six recognizable Social Democrat factions.

In the repressions following 1905, the Bolshevik underground was demoralized by defeat and ideological wrangling. It was the Mensheviks who seemed to recover from defeat most readily. In the relatively peaceful labour situation which existed up to 1912, the Mensheviks fostered the development of legal workers' organizations: trade unions, insurance societies, night schools, cooperatives. From these, it was hoped, would grow an experienced workers' intelligentsia; leadership would thus grow out of the labour movement itself, rather than be supplied by middle-class intellectuals. Some progress was made despite governmental harassment of even legal workers' organizations,[6] but after 1912 it was Bolsheviks, not Mensheviks, who tended to be elected to leading positions in these organizations. Mensheviks and Bolsheviks co-operated in the elections to the Fourth Duma in 1912; the Bolsheviks won six seats, only one fewer than the Mensheviks.

Meanwhile, the economic revival brought more workers into the labour force, especially into areas where the Bolsheviks were strong, including notably the engineering industry and the factories of St Petersburg. On the other hand, the Bolsheviks faced serious problems. By 1914 most of their best-known intellectuals had quarrelled with Lenin's tactics and deserted the party. The violent bank robberies and other 'expropriations' made by the Bolsheviks to raise funds not available from an unsympathetic public also damaged their reputation. In 1914 it was quite clear to everyone except Lenin that the leader of the Bolsheviks in the Duma, Malinovsky, had long been a police informer; it took Lenin several years to accept this bitter truth.

Also, while simple uncompromising Bolshevik slogans attracted the younger or most reckless workers, it was not certain that the Bolshevik leadership could control these new adherents; when the St Petersburg Bolshevik Party Committee called off the strike of July 1914, the Bolshevik rank-and-file disregarded the instruction. The outbreak of war further damaged the Bolshevik cause, at least in the first year. Most of the Bolshevik leaders, like most of the Menshevik and Socialist Revolutionary leaders, opposed what they regarded as an imperialist war, but they were probably more extreme in their anti-war pronouncements at a time when most of the population was gripped by excited patriotism.

When in 1917 the new freedom of the press allowed *Pravda* to recommence publication, it was Molotov[7] who became editor. This was a key position, because *Pravda* was the most important link between the Bolshevik leaders and the ordinary members. It was *Pravda* which indicated what the correct attitude on current problems should be (that is, the 'party line'). Molotov was in his twenties, had been a Bolshevik since 1906, and was the most senior member still at liberty of the Russian Bureau of the Central Committee. Under his editorship *Pravda*, contrary to popular feeling at the time, advocated resistance to the Provisional Government, termination of the war, and immediate distribution of the landowners' estates to the peasants. But it was

6. The Okhrana, still regarding the Bolsheviks as useful splitters of the revolutionary movement, preferred the arrest of Mensheviks.

7. His real name was Skryabin. Bolshevik and Menshevik leaders often adopted pseudonyms. Usually these were intended to conceal their identities from the authorities, but after the Revolution the pseudonyms were retained, partly because they were more familiar to the public, partly out of pride, and sometimes because they sounded Russian although their owners were non-Russians. Other pseudonyms included Stalin (Dzhugashvili), Zinoviev (Radomyslsky), Kamenev (Rosenfeldt), Trotsky (Bronstein), Kirov (Kostrikov), Martov (Tsederbaum), Kaganovich (Kagan).

not long before Molotov was replaced by a trio, including Stalin and Kamenev, of more senior Bolsheviks recently released from Siberia. Under this new direction the party line was reversed. The new editors, believing that the Provisional Government was the bourgeois government which, in Marx's forecast, would rule after the bourgeois revolution, advocated support of the government. Like the other socialists, they believed that it was in danger of overthrow by a counter-revolution of reactionaries, with the latter including the generals; it was not yet realized that the generals had diminishing command of their men.

Pravda's line infuriated Lenin. During the war he had lived in Switzerland, occupying himself by organizing international anti-war meetings of left-wing socialists. He had broken with many of his former associates and his closest colleague was Zinoviev. He now strove to find a way to return to Russia to take personal command of his party. This was not easy, because to reach Russia from Switzerland he had either to pass through Germany or Austria, which were at war with Russia, or through one of the Allied powers which, aware that he opposed Russia's continued participation in the war, would be unlikely to facilitate his passage. (Trotsky, returning to Russia from New York, was arrested by the Allies in Halifax for this reason, and was only released after the Provisional Government had applied pressure in London.)

Until he could leave Switzerland, Lenin attempted to direct the party *in absentia*. The first of his 'Letters from Afar' was printed in *Pravda* in mid-March. In this he attributed the February Revolution to the machinations of Britain and France, which had heard that Nicholas intended to make a separate peace with Germany and therefore determined to overthrow him. Rather less wild was his assertion that the Provisional Government was continuing the war so that the Allied powers, Russia included, could enjoy territorial gains at the expense of the Central Powers. But although his letter was discussed it did not change the policies of the Bolshevik leadership inside Russia. Despite Lenin's condemnation, Stalin and his colleagues still advocated support of the Provisional Government, the continuance of the war, and the merging of the Bolsheviks with the Mensheviks' left wing.

By this stage of the war the direction of German policy was in the hands of generals such as Hindenburg and Ludendorff. Intent at all costs on preserving their professional reputations (that is, to avoid obvious military defeat), they received sympathetically the suggestion that Germany should facilitate the return of émigré revolutionaries. The German Chief of Staff (Hoffmann) wrote later that Germany had just as much right to attack Russia with Lenin as with poison gas. Thus the expedient of sending Lenin and other émigrés to a Baltic port in a sealed (that is, extra-territorial) railway car was quickly approved.

On the train crossing Germany, when not complaining about the noisy behaviour of his fellow-returnees, Lenin devoted himself to composing what would later be known as *The April Theses*. In this, he abandoned the two-stage revolution theory and announced his programme for exploiting the existing situation in Russia to create an immediate socialist revolution. There would be simply a second stage of the existing Revolution, which would place power in the hands of the workers and the poorest peasants. The power would be transferred to the workers' soviets, which Lenin described as the only possible form of revolutionary government. The ten theses were briefly expressed, with little theory in support; they were a programme of action which, as things turned out, would determine Russia's fate.

Like other returning exiles, Lenin was met at the Finland Station in Petrograd by a welcoming delegation led on this occasion by the Menshevik Chkheidze. He responded coldly to the latter's speech of welcome and made it clear that he had no intention of cooperating with the other socialists. Then he met his Bolshevik colleagues and assailed them for their timidity. Not all were convinced, and Lenin was himself strongly criticized by several of them. On the following day, when Lenin at a meeting of all Social Democrats refused to countenance a merging of the different factions into one party, he was again attacked by fellow-Bolsheviks, who accused him of fomenting a civil war with his allegations that the other socialists were in fact betrayers of socialism. At the same time Lenin's reputation among the urban masses was deteriorating, especially when it became public knowledge that he had returned to Russia with the assistance of the hated Germans. On the other hand, Lenin acquired a valuable ally when Trotsky joined the Bolsheviks.

The Mensheviks and Socialist Revolutionaries had agreed to join the government at a time when there was a honeymoon between potentially con-flicting forces. Moreover, they regarded their coalition partners, the Kadets, as essential propitiators of the officer corps. But almost as soon as the coalition government was formed the economy took a further turn for the worse. Rapid inflation prompted workers to demand wage increases that the industrialists were unwilling and sometimes unable to grant. The honeymoon was over. The government's efforts to create a civil society in which concepts of contract, private property, and trespass would be a major part, about which decisions would be taken deliberately and at great length, had coincided with a period in which the population was demanding fast action on major issues: the war, the land, the economy. With the prospect of a Constituent Assembly receding (for the Kadets were now holding back the organization of an election, allegedly because they feared its result but also because they wanted the procedures to be perfect; lawyers were well represented in that party) and with the new-found confidence of the various workers', soldiers', and peasants' committees, it seemed increasingly clear that the Soviet was quite capable of taking over the government and doing what needed to be done. The Provisional Government seemed to have become merely the protector of a status quo that was acceptable to only part of the population.

This change of mood was reflected in elections to committees. The Bolsheviks, whose arguments began to match most closely the actual situation and who had consistently opposed the government, were the main beneficiaries. The Socialist Revolutionary party split, with the Left Socialist Revolutionaries, indignant at the failure to settle the land question, taking their own independent path. In the various local committees, where Bolsheviks (often contrary to the instructions of their leadership) did cooperate with other parties, they tended to find common cause with the Left Socialist Revolutionaries.

Gradually the Bolsheviks' influence increased, although they lacked an agreed policy. At the top, Lenin was frequently opposed by his colleagues, while at the bottom the party members active in committees tended to act according to their own appreciation of the local situation, of which they had a more accurate understanding than the Central Committee. The popular demonstrations of June and July emphasized these differences. Lenin, who feared that a successful coup in Petrograd would be suppressed by forces outside the capital, preferred to wait until the government and other socialists had lost more support, while lesser Bolsheviks, in closer contact with the mood of the streets, favoured conversion of the protests into riots leading to the overthrow of the government. Lenin's *April Theses*, published after his return and advocating that the Soviet (in which he hoped sooner or later to have a majority) should take power, was gradually winning acceptance within the party, but some members felt the party might lose some of its support to the anarchists, who were less restrained than the Bolsheviks.

At the All-Russia Congress of Soviets held in June, Kerensky was able to ridicule Lenin's assertion that the country's problems could be solved by arresting a hundred capitalists and by the Soviet overthrowing the government. Yet the audience, largely workers and soldiers and sailors, evidently found Lenin's ideas more to its taste.

In June the Bolsheviks called for street demonstrations in favour of their programme, which by this time included such slogans as 'All Power to the Soviets' and 'Bread, Peace, and Freedom'. Apparently it was intended that pro-Bolshevik army units would take part, carrying arms. Chkheidze warned the All-Russia Congress of Soviets that the Bolsheviks were planning an insurrection, and many delegates spent the night visiting factories and barracks to dissuade intending participants. This caused the party to cancel the demonstration at the last minute. Stalin was among those who opposed cancellation, but he was outvoted in the Central Committee. Despite the widespread belief that the Bolsheviks had only narrowly failed to take power by force, they were not arrested. They merely lost prestige for a few weeks.

After the chastening experience of June, the news which Bolshevik leaders received in July of an impending uprising was probably unwelcome. The unrest was caused by the Kerensky military offensive in June, which had aroused great resentment among the Petrograd soldiers and the Kronstadt sailors after its initial successes against the Austrians degenerated into a rout. If the Bolsheviks failed to lead this uprising they would inevitably lose much support among the soldiers and sailors. Yet an uprising still seemed premature; it might be aimed at persuading the Soviet to take power, but the other socialist parties would be opposed to a coup, as in June, and after all it was the Socialist Revolutionaries who had most support in the country and in the soviets. The Provisional Government, apparently, could command loyal troops from outside the capital. Lenin was resting in Finland and could not be consulted conveniently by the Bolshevik leaders. Moreover, when the time came to make a final decision, Kamenev and Zinoviev were absent. So it was Stalin who, consulted by the Kronstadt leaders, obliquely approved the dispatch of 20,000 armed sailors to the capital. However, when it became clear that the Provisional Government was making careful preparations to squash the rising, the party's Central Committee decided that, after all, it would not take command of the demonstrators. As in June, *Pravda* appeared on the day with a blank space where the proclamation announcing the party's sponsorship of the demonstration had been hastily removed. The sailors marched in, listened to a fierily non-committal harangue by a hastily summoned Lenin, who told them they were beautiful, and then marched off to the Tauride Palace, seat of the Soviet and of the old Duma. As they marched they became more disorderly, the capital's population became excited, and shots were fired. There was looting, and well-dressed individuals were beaten up, killed, or taken into custody. Chernov, the Socialist Revolutionary leader who came out to address the sailors, was attacked and seized, to be rescued by Trotsky, whose never-failing oratory convinced even the unruly sailors that they were helping nobody by arresting stray individuals. After this, the sailors reacted to the anticlimax by disappearing. They were replaced at the Tauride Palace by a pro-Bolshevik regiment which had been marching to their aid. The soldiers did not seem to have a clear idea of what they were supposed to do and there were no Bolsheviks around to guide them. They were thus easily persuaded by a Menshevik leader (who himself did not know quite what was happening) that they had been summoned to guard the palace. And thus it was that the 176th Regiment, which in the morning had left its barracks to overthrow the government, in the afternoon vigilantly stood on guard outside the Tauride Palace, symbol and seat of the status quo. Here it blocked the third wave of pro-Bolshevik assailants, this time the armed workers of the Putilov factory. Only a few of these could penetrate into the palace; one worker made a short speech, urging the unenthusiastic Soviet to take power, before sheepishly picking up his rifle and following his comrades home.

Although Bolsheviks and their historians later wrote nostalgically of the heroic 'July Days', the truth is that the party's activity at this juncture produced a shambles. It would have been better if the Bolsheviks had not at first encouraged the rising, but this was not Lenin's doing. Nevertheless, the

Provisional Government took advantage of the failure of the rising to issue warrants for the arrest of the leading Bolsheviks. It also released what was claimed to be evidence that Lenin was a German agent. Although the more sophisticated realized that this evidence was at least partly fabricated, to the ordinary revolutionary masses it appeared convincing, especially as they remembered how the Germans had helped Lenin to return to Russia. He became highly unpopular as a result.

After the July fiasco Lenin, against much resistance, persuaded his colleagues to drop the 'All Power to the Soviets!' slogan, on the ground that the Soviet, under Socialist Revolutionary and Menshevik leadership, had supported what he termed the 'counter-revolution'. This was one of those occasions when the refusal of lower Bolsheviks to obey instructions saved the party from the consequences of its ill judgement, and some weeks later this powerful slogan, which local Bolsheviks had continued to use, would be reinstated.

At this low point in his fortunes Lenin sought refuge from the arrest which he believed was threatening him. For two weeks a rural hut was his shelter and then, disguised as a locomotive fireman, he rode over the Russo-Finnish border on a locomotive. He then took up residence in the home of the Helsinki chief of police, a Bolshevik sympathizer, waiting for better days.

The Kornilov affair

The Bolsheviks, in the aftermath of the July 'rising', strove to increase their weight in the factory committees, which were increasingly important. By August they were considerably more influential in the Petrograd factories than the Mensheviks, but the latter were strong in the provinces, while the Socialist Revolutionaries still had the allegiance of the bulk of the politically conscious peasants. At the end of July Kerensky, seen as a bridge between right and left, succeeded Lvov as prime minister, and his government, though it contained more socialists than non-socialists, was moderate in its approach.

Kerensky moved into the tsars' Winter Palace; this gratified his vanity at the expense of his reputation but might, possibly, have enhanced the authority of his office. He tried to reduce the influence of soldiers' committees. Some Bolsheviks were arrested, including Trotsky and Kamenev. The death penalty was restored at the front in response to General Kornilov's demand for measures to halt the alarming desertion rate, as soldiers left their posts to participate in the share-out of land in their native villages. In August the Germans captured Riga. There was a railway strike. Bands of deserting soldiers alarmed the population.

Citizens were forbidden to keep weapons, and some of the most trouble-some regiments were disbanded. Many conservatives and moderates began to look for a new leader, someone who would restore order and legality, by dictatorial means if necessary. Brusilov, considered too moderate by many of his generals, and additionally handicapped by his reluctance to pander to Kerensky's vanities, was dismissed and replaced as C-in-C by Kornilov, a man admired by many as the strong disciplinarian that the country needed.

Kerensky appointed Kornilov on the advice of the former Socialist Revolutionary terrorist Savinkov who, reputedly the murderer of Plehve, was now the trusted administrator of the war ministry. Kornilov and Kerensky agreed that the Bolsheviks should be quelled and public order restored, and each sought to use the other to this end. Kornilov seems to have had little political sense and in 1917 was influenced by his adjutant and other officers. His directness, combined with his unsophisticated mind, meant that his hesitancies could give an impression of unreliability, even untrustworthiness. Like other generals, he regarded Kerensky as a windbag who, unless he was pushed, would never take the decisive action that Russia needed. Kerensky, for his part, saw Kornilov as the man able to deliver the military strength needed to restore order.

Exchanges between the two men centred on the possibility of establishing some kind of dictatorial government to meet the challenging circumstances. Whether Kornilov or Kerensky would be the strong man of such a government seems to have been left open. Soon there came a rift between the two, largely due to a failure of communication, the latter consisting of the stuttering teletype of that period and untrustworthy go-betweens. What became known, rather grandiosely, as the Kornilov Revolt began when Kerensky, in the capital, suspected that Kornilov, at GHQ, was planning to eliminate him, while Kornilov simultaneously became convinced that Kerensky needed military support. Kerensky dismissed Kornilov and the latter, probably believing that the prime minister was acting under duress, ordered General Krymov's cavalry corps to advance on Petrograd to rescue the government.

Kerensky, having lost left-wing support when he had complied with Kornilov's request to restore the death penalty at the front, was already seeking a way to recover his credentials. Probably seeing the course of events as his opportunity, he denounced Kornilov as a counter-revolutionary bent on overthrowing the government. Kornilov meanwhile issued a proclamation saying that he was acting to save the Russian people from becoming slaves of the Germans, that he was himself the son of a Cossack peasant with no political ambitions, and that he would support the decisions of the forthcoming Constituent Assembly. However, Krymov's advance fizzled out when his already unenthusiastic troops were further demoralized by agitators sent out from Petrograd, and when the railway workers, on the instructions of the Soviet, refused to transport his supplies and reinforcements. General Krymov, in despair, shot himself.

Meanwhile, the non-Bolshevik socialists rallied to the support of the Provisional Government, while the Bolsheviks used the crisis to extract their arrested leaders from gaol and to obtain the approval by the Soviet's Committee against Counter-revolution of an armed workers' militia to defend the Revolution. In this way the already existing armed Bolshevik supporters (the 'Red Guard'), who helped to defend Petrograd against Kornilov, received the Soviet's recognition.

The Kornilov thrust was suppressed with little bloodshed. Kornilov and generals thought to be implicated were arrested and put under guard in a monastary. They were well looked-after and took the opportunity to hatch their plans for what later became the anti-Bolshevik Volunteer Army. But meanwhile soldiers and sailors, infuriated by what they were convinced was essentially an officers' plot, began to turn on officers who were still serving with their units. Hundreds of army and naval officers were murdered, often in brutal circumstances. Yet the Kornilov affair had demonstrated that the once-feared generals had no real power to move against the revolution, or even to defend themselves. The 'loyal' units, quite impressive on paper, were composed of soldiers who would not fight.

The Bolshevik Revolution

After the Kornilov affair, Kerensky and his government began to lose their grip, and society seemed about to break up. In many localities it became clear that the deprived were also the depraved. There was a renewed assault against the landowners, this time more violent and organized by the more revolution-ary peasants (typically army deserters) of a locality; by this time village soviets were being formed, seeing their role as righting the ancient injustices of land ownership, organizing village life, and keeping the government at a distance. Landowners and their families were ejected, sometimes assaulted, and felt lucky to escape with a few belongings. Many were killed. Their manor houses, some of great architectural merit, were burned down. Also burned down were libraries and art galleries in provincial towns. In the towns, popular street justice, which had appeared earlier, also flourished. Vigilante action, lynch law, and getting onlookers to vote whether apprehended thieves should be executed were features of 1917 that could be repellent but yet explicable in the absence of an effective police force.

Partly because so many people did not vote, the city council elections of summer 1917 registered a swing toward the Bolsheviks. Indeed, in Moscow they won 51 per cent of the votes. So it is unlikely that the Kornilov affair caused that recovery of the Bolsheviks' strength and prestige which became marked in September and October, except in so far as its failure demoralized right-wing forces. The Bolsheviks' popularity was already increasing before the July disturbances brought them into temporary disrepute. With workers and soldiers becoming ever more assertive and frustrated in their expect-ations, that party which was closest to their bitterness was bound to attract favour. Anarchists, gratified by the Bolsheviks' regard for workers' factory committees, which they themselves advocated, supported Lenin's party until after October, when it became clear that the Bolsheviks believed in strong government. How far anarchist support helped Lenin is difficult to judge because, being an attitude more than an organization, the strength of anarchism in 1917 seems indeterminable. In mid-September two events showed how far the Bolsheviks had progressed. For the first time, the Petrograd Soviet passed a resolution proposed by its Bolshevik faction. In re-elections to the soldiers' section of the Soviet, hitherto dominated by the Socialist Revolutionaries, the Bolsheviks gained nearly half of the votes.

A coalition government of all socialist parties was increasingly favoured, and it was hoped that the Democratic Conference of left-wing parties organized in September would result in this. But the parties could not agree; the Bolsheviks were hostile, and the parties simply did not understand how agreements are reached in the setting of an open debate. Kerensky did not perform well, and henceforth survived only because there was no obvious alternative.

The government in the meantime fixed elections to the long-awaited and long-postponed Constituent Assembly for 25 November. To bridge the gap until its convening, Kerensky organized a 'Pre-Parliament' to fulfil the temporary role of popular assembly. Lenin, still in Finland, sent a furious letter to the Bolshevik leaders in Petrograd when he learned that they were participating in these arrangements. The Central Committee, surprised but not submissive, quietly agreed to burn this letter. The Pre-Parliament was an obvious failure and Lenin continued to bombard his lieutenants with demands for a forcible seizure of power. This represented a change of programme, and it was not easy to persuade the party to accept it. The arguments which he used may be summarized: the party was now capable of obtaining majorities in the Petrograd and Moscow soviets (in early October, Trotsky was elected chairman of the Petrograd Soviet), thus the early Bolshevik slogan of 'All power to the soviets' was paying off; Kerensky, whom Lenin described as a 'Kornilovite, Stolypinite, and Bonapartist', might well surrender Petrograd to the advancing Germans simply because the Bolsheviks' strength lay in the capital; to wait for the Constituent Assembly or for the next All-Russia Congress of Soviets (scheduled for October) would be purposeless and indeed harmful, for the Bolsheviks would be outnumbered in these bodies; the Bolsheviks had at their disposal more armed strength than any of their opponents and the few army units which remained loyal to the government could be neutralized by skilful agitators; once having acquired power, the Bolsheviks could retain it because their first acts would be to legalize the seizure of private land by the peasants and to promise an end to the war; these two policies would automatically assure the allegiance of the soldiers, but the promise of peace would lose its effectiveness if the Allies and Germany made peace first, or if Kerensky, out of spite against the Bolsheviks, himself negotiated peace.

The Central Committee of the party in Petrograd forbade Lenin to return from Finland. He tendered his resignation, and under this threat the Bolsheviks did walk out of the Pre-Parliament, Trotsky alleging that the bourgeois parties were determined to block the election of the Constituent Assembly. In the villages the Bolsheviks were seeking an alliance with the dissatisfied left wing of the Socialist Revolutionaries. This would soon be in formal alliance with the Bolsheviks, broadening the appeal of the latter because in the countryside, where Bolshevism had not been strong, the Bolsheviks could now claim connections with the Socialist Revolutionaries. Lenin meanwhile returned in disguise to Petrograd, and at a crucial meeting of the party Central Committee on 10 October urged his colleagues to seize power before the election of the Constituent Assembly.

Most of the Central Committee opposed Lenin's demand. Kamenev was probably the strongest opponent, for he had always believed that the Bolsheviks should work closely with the Soviet. He was supported by Zinoviev, who had cold feet, and others. But eventually, in a Central Committee meeting attended by just over half its members, and after hours of wearying argument, Lenin won a majority.

Lenin wanted an immediate seizure of power, but Trotsky and others insisted that it should coincide with the forthcoming All-Russia Congress of Soviets, thereby enabling the Bolshevik coup to be presented as a transfer of power to the Soviets. It would also mean that the resulting Soviet government would be a coalition of the parties in the Congress, because the Bolsheviks were unlikely to have a majority in it. Lenin found this concept intolerable, for it would entail compromising with Mensheviks and Socialist Revolutionaries. An immediate seizure of power, on the other hand, would enable the Bolsheviks to offer the already-won power to the Soviets, but on Bolshevik terms.

Most Bolsheviks assumed that the rising would take place, but at an unspecified date in the future. Not only Kamenev and his supporters in the Central Committee, but Bolshevik leaders on the streets and in the factories, warned that workers and soldiers would not fight for a Bolshevik seizure of power, although they would almost certainly take up their arms again should the government or counter-revolutionaries threaten the Soviet. Lenin argued that a coup would not need great force; it could be a neat military operation in the prevailing state of the capital. Such was the power of his uncompromising, bullying argumentation that he finally won a majority in the Central Committee for a resolution to initiate preparations for an immediate (though undated) rising.

Kamenev thereupon published an indignant article in Gorki's *Novaya zhizn'* newspaper; in this way the Bolshevik intentions became a matter of public argument. The Menshevik and SR leaders, remembering the Bolsheviks as comrades of the past, were unwilling to take action against them and

Kerensky, confident that they lacked public support, took no immediate measures to protect the government. The one significant step he did take, announcing his intention to dispatch the Petrograd garrison to the front, played into Lenin's hands. The furious soldiers threw off their allegiance to the general staff, and placed themselves at the disposal of the Military Revolutionary Committee. (The MRC had recently been set up to coordinate the armed forces available for defending the Petrograd Soviet. It was essentially controlled by Trotsky, although a compliant Left SR had been installed as its chairman, giving it the appearance of a Soviet organization.)

The MRC on 21 October announced that henceforth it was in charge of the garrison and dispatched its own commissars to displace the units' commanding officers. On 23 October it even took over the Peter-Paul Fortress, symbol of Russian state power and, moreover, overlooking the Winter Palace.

Thus Trotsky, who in the absence of Lenin was in control of Bolshevik activity in the capital, found that although he had not fixed the date for the uprising he already had local military control.

On 24 October Lenin wrote to his Central Committee, explaining why it was necessary to act that same evening rather than await the uncertain votes of the All-Russia Congress of Soviets which was to begin its meetings on the morrow. He added that 'the people' had the right to make historical decisions by force rather than by vote.

On the same day Kerensky revealed to the Pre-Parliament that he had evidence of a planned Bolshevik insurrection, and asked for members' support of strong action against the party. However, the Mensheviks argued that the majority of Bolshevik rank-and-file were opposed to an armed seizure of power, but would become more militant in reaction to the strong measures which Kerensky proposed. After a long discussion the Pre-Parliament voted for the Menshevik resolution and against Kerensky. As things turned out, at this point the Bolshevik conspiracy could have been nipped in the bud by a few companies of reliable troops. In the Petrograd Soviet, opposition to the Bolsheviks grew as their intentions became clearer, and *Izvestiya*, the newspaper of the All-Russia Central Committee of the Soviets, declared that if the Bolsheviks did succeed in seizing power against the will of the other socialist parties the result could only be civil war.

In the evening of 24 October the MRC commissars, more or less on their own initiative, moved small bodies of troops and Red Guards to key objectives like railway stations and post and telegraph offices. The police stations were also covered. Lenin, around midnight and in disguise, managed to reach the Bolshevik headquarters in the Smolny Institute (a former nobles' girls' school). Here he persuaded his colleagues to finish the job before the morrow's opening of the Congress of Soviets. Having taken this decision, they nominated each other for posts in the forthcoming government and decided that their new ministers would be called 'people's commissars' to emphasize that a real revolution had taken place.

So, on 25 October, the seizure of power continued as the normal daily life of the capital proceeded. Homeward-bound theatre-goers did not pay much attention to odd shots and scuffles; they could recall noisier nights. The Winter Palace, where the Provisional Government was in emergency session, was still uncaptured but was threatened by the guns of the cruiser *Avrora* and of the Peter-Paul Fortress across the river. Red Guards, Bolshevik soldiers, and Baltic Fleet sailors had surrounded it and, to Lenin's irritation, preferred to negotiate rather than shed blood. It would not be until the small hours of 26 October that, with some sporadic shooting and scuffling, that part of the government's guard which had not melted away in the darkness was overcome. The ministers were led off to the Peter-Paul Fortress.

Meanwhile, the Congress of Soviets was getting into its first sitting. Bolshevik seizure of power, Lenin had insisted, needed to precede the Congress; in the event, it was a dead heat, which was good enough for Lenin. Just as Martov seemed to be persuading the Congress delegates to form a united Soviet government, the majority of his party and the moderate SR delegates committed the grossest of tactical errors by walking out in protest at the Bolshevik resort to violence. The Congress of Soviets was now in the hands of the Bolshevik delegates and their Left SR allies. Martov lingered, enabling Trotsky to pour scorn on his proposal for a coalition government, and to cast a final 'Go to the garbage bin of history!' taunt.

The Bolshevik victory

Early on 26 October Kamenev told the still-sitting Congress that the Provisional Government had been arrested. Then a manifesto prepared by Lenin, proclaiming Soviet power and promising land, liberty, and peace, was read out and accepted. The Leninist faction, of the Bolshevik faction, of the Social Democratic faction, of the Russian revolutionary movement was in power, ostensibly on behalf of the Soviet.

On the streets, Bacchus was in power. The extensive wine cellars of the captured Winter Palace had been broached, facilitating a mass inebriation which continued for many days in spite of the martial law imposed to quell it. Bullets were fired by drunken soldiers as they roamed the streets looking for plunder and trouble, and by temporarily sober soldiers sent, in vain, to enforce order.

Meanwhile, Kerensky was still at large, for he had left earlier to seek loyal troops outside the capital. But his quest was forlorn, not only because few soldiers were willing to fight for his government, but because those that were willing were led by officers who themselves were not. Not only the more reactionary officers, but many others, had been so incensed by what they considered to be Kerensky's betrayal of Kornilov that they refused to lift a finger to help him. He did, however, find some support among the Cossacks of General Krasnov, and these troops succeeded in capturing Tsarskoye Selo. But here they stopped, and there were discussions between revolutionary envoys and the Cossacks. Kerensky was placed under guard by Krasnov for his own protection, while revolutionary sailors also took up their own guard duty. Much of this mutual escorting and guarding took place in the same building, with the local revolutionary leaders and Krasnov's staff occupying different floors; it was not quite clear who had captured whom and who was protecting whom. When it appeared that the Cossacks were about to accept the sailors' offer to capture and surrender Lenin to them in exchange for Kerensky, Krasnov evidently decided that Kerensky should be allowed to escape; the prime minister slipped out dressed as a Baltic Fleet sailor. He passed along the streets just as revolutionary and Cossack search parties were rushing out in search of him. He subsequently appeared in western capitals and toward the end of his life began an academic career in the USA, where he died in 1970.

The Revolution followed different courses in different places. In Moscow, where sectional animosities were more moderate than in Petrograd, the Bolsheviks had won a small majority in city elections and were well placed to seize power. Neither they nor their opponents, on hearing the news from Petrograd, showed much enthusiasm for armed conflict, but small groups of extremists on both sides managed to give an impression of heavy fighting, until a truce was followed by the Bolshevik assumption of power. In the army, most divisions did not welcome the Bolsheviks' coup. The soldiers' soviets were in general not pro-Bolshevik, and while the soldiers were not prepared to fight for the Provisional Government, they were not willing to exert themselves for the Bolsheviks either. The general staff, led by the chief of staff Dukhonin, refused to obey Lenin's order to negotiate a ceasefire at the front. Red Guards were thereupon dispatched to GHQ, and Dukhonin was murdered.

It may be easy to list reasons why it was the Bolsheviks who succeeded in taking power, but it is harder to list them in order of importance. The insuperable problems faced by their rivals were certainly factors. Each party had its own quite valid reasons for its policies, but circumstances developed in such a way as to make the Bolsheviks' concepts seem most relevant. The Socialist Revolutionaries, who had enormous electoral support, were handicapped at first by what they saw as the need to conciliate their coalition partners the Kadets, and they were unable to get the prompt land redistribution that had been the centrepiece of their programme. The Mensheviks believed that government intervention was necessary to solve the economic crisis, but could not persuade their partners. They, too, saw a need to keep the Kadets on the side of the Revolution. The Kadets had a strong left wing, but on the whole they were devoted to that kind of civil society sometimes termed 'bourgeois', in which property rights were seen as an essential part of freedom. They, too, had good reasons for what they did (and for what they stopped others doing) and it was not irrational to suppose that the presence of their party in the Provisional Government would placate the property-owning classes and make a counter-revolution less likely.

But the coalition of Kadets and moderate socialists could not achieve what ordinary people saw as urgent tasks: ending the war, redistributing the land, providing a decent living standard for the workers.

It was the Bolsheviks who hammered away at these failures. It was the Bolsheviks who (unlike the Mensheviks) asserted that the working classes were quite capable of running the country and should do so through their Soviet. It was the Bolsheviks whose doctrine of the class struggle seemed to be validated by the increasing 'them-and-us' split between the government and most of the population.

Additionally, the Bolsheviks had the advantage that their membership was strongest in Petrograd; that is, in the centre of a very centralized state. Some of them, although not Lenin himself, may have been more understanding of the people on the streets.

After their successful coup the Bolsheviks were regarded by their fellow socialists, and even by some of their own membership, as dishonest power-seekers. But that was not the full story: in staging the October coup the Bolshevik leadership had pushed Mother Russia in at the deep end, in the sublime expectation that she could be made to swim.

11

The Civil War

The Bolsheviks in power

IN the days and months following October the Bolsheviks abandoned many of the aims which had been professed by generations of Russian revolutionaries, including themselves, and they reintroduced, often in a more repressive form, long-reviled tsarist practices which had been abolished after the February Revolution. The period following October 1917 was a period when the Bolsheviks were driven to pile contradictions on top of paradoxes, and all too often temporary expedients became basic and seemingly eternal principles.

Some Bolsheviks were quicker than others to accept the necessities of power (which was why there were splits and disagreements) and some had fewer illusions to begin with, but the communist party[1] which emerged from the Civil War was morally very different from the party which had taken power in 1917. In this period few, if any, had a clear idea of what was happening, although some thought they had. It was a period of continual jumping from a greater evil to a lesser, as measures to solve one problem raised new problems elsewhere. Lenin's first priority throughout was retention of power, although in the early days even he had his doubts about whether his regime could survive more than a week or two. Retention of power at any price meant that when Lenin died he bequeathed overwhelming problems to his successors; he did live long enough to persuade his party in 1921 to make the change of course known as the New Economic Policy, but there remained other dangerous tendencies.

The main issues and events of 1917–21 are dealt with in the following sections. It should be remembered, however, that the Bolsheviks could not lay out their difficulties in this neat way. For them, it was not possible to deal with one set of problems while leaving aside the others. Problems assailed them from all sides and were interconnected.

---

1. At Lenin's urging, in 1918 the Bolshevik party was renamed the Communist party.

The first steps

With a majority assured in the Soviet, the Bolsheviks could obtain a favourable vote and thus 'legitimacy' for their new government and its policies. The soviets stood high in the estimate of the workers, soldiers, and Bolshevik rank and file, who looked forward to a *Soviet*, rather than a Bolshevik, regime. Lenin obtained the Congress's approval for his first two decrees, which were designed to capture mass support (especially from the peasantry, who so far did not favour the Bolsheviks) by promising what the masses wanted, land and peace. The Decree on Peace called for an immediate truce and a just peace, and could be interpreted as an appeal to foreign peoples over the heads of governments. The Decree on Land sanctioned what was already happening, the takeover by peasants of private land, but specified that the distribution should be arranged by village soviets.

The Decree on Peace had no influence on the other warring nations, as might have been expected. The Decree on Land was contrary to the Bolsheviks' agricultural theories, as it split the land into smaller average allotments and strengthened the 'petty bourgeois' proprietary instincts of the peasantry. But in order to retain power the Bolsheviks in this and other cases were obliged to sidetrack their theories. As it happened, this land policy was virtually the Socialist Revolutionaries' policy and helped to propitiate the Left Socialist Revolutionaries.

The Congress of Soviets also approved the new government ('Council of People's Commissars' or *Sovnarkom*) and, having thus conferred a degree of legitimacy on the new regime, was disbanded, still in the belief that the government was its own Soviet government.[2] Perhaps to maintain this supposition, many of the new ministers ('people's commissars') were not leading lights, but secondary figures, of the Bolshevik party. Lenin was prime minister ('chairman of the Council of People's Commissars'), Trotsky had foreign affairs, Stalin the nationalities, but Lunacharsky, who had only recently rejoined the Bolsheviks, was entrusted with education, while the key commissariat of the interior fell to Rykov, who in 1910 had broken with Lenin and returned to the party only to become an advocate of conciliating the Mensheviks. Initially the Left Socialist Revolutionaries were also represented in the government.

Over subsequent decades, the Bolshevik takeover was portrayed as the October Revolution, achieved by the working masses and soldiers. In fact

2. The Council of People's Commissars was nominally answerable to the Congress's Central Executive Committee, which remained in being. The latter now had a Bolshevik majority and Sverdlov as its chairman. In summer 1918 Menshevik and SR members of the Central Executive Committee were expelled, another big step towards the one-party state. The Central Executive Committee and Soviet Congresses continued to meet until the introduction of the Supreme Soviet in 1936.

the Petrograd working class had taken only a small part in events; it had been more concerned with its jobs and wages and hoped that the future would lie with socialists cooperating in the Soviet. When, just three days after the Bolshevik coup, the railwaymen's trade union (capable of calling a crippling strike) issued an ultimatum demanding that the Bolsheviks set up an all-Soviet government, it received a good deal of support from workers. Because at this time the railwaymen's cooperation was urgently needed in the anticipated struggle against Kerensky's forces, and the Bolsheviks were being hard pressed in Moscow, the Central Committee agreed to negotiate. But as soon as Kerensky was thrown back and the situation in Moscow improved, the Bolshevik leaders withdrew their proposed concessions and Lenin even talked of arresting the railwaymen's leaders as 'counter-revolutionaries'.

Many, probably a majority, of Bolsheviks had long believed that a coalition with other socialist parties was the correct course. In the Central Committee, Kamenev, Zinoviev, and Rykov were especially opposed to Lenin on this issue. Lenin did renew the alliance with the Left Socialist Revolutionaries and the latter finally broke with the moderate wing of their party. Lenin always intended to do things his way, and that meant refusal to compromise. With the collapse of the railwaymen's initiative, Bolshevik dominance seemed assured, and Lenin could turn to his Central Committee and assert his dominance there. This he did by browbeating his colleagues, one by one, into agreeing to the abandonment of the talks with the other parties. Some members of the Central Committee resigned on this issue. Zinoviev returned, tail between legs, four days later, but Kamenev and Rykov did not return to the fold for three weeks. Lenin was clearly in command of the Bolsheviks, and the Bolsheviks were in command of Russia, but few people thought this could last.

Some Bolsheviks also resigned when in November a decree was passed abolishing press freedom, one of the most cherished gains of the February Revolution. This meant the suppression of many socialist as well as right-wing papers. Lenin described all parties that had opposed the Bolsheviks' October coup as counter-revolutionary, and therefore depriving them of their press was quite justified. The printers' trade union threatened a strike, but the MRC sent in gangs to smash the presses and arrest the editors of unfriendly newspapers.

The most dramatic reversal in practice of policies the Bolsheviks had earlier advocated was the treatment of the Constituent Assembly. Before October they had repeatedly embarrassed the Provisional Government by accusing it of postponing the election of the Assembly, which was intended to decide the nature of the future Russian democracy. At the time of taking power, elections had already been arranged for the Assembly and Trotsky advised Lenin that to annul the arrangements would arouse a dangerous reaction. Thus the election was allowed to take place with little interference.

Because of shifting allegiances and coercive tactics the results have never been precisely agreed, but a plausible tally gives the Socialist Revolutionaries 370 out of 707 seats, with 175 seats for the Bolsheviks, 40 for the Left Socialist Revolutionaries, 16 for the Mensheviks, and for the Kadets (who were never allowed to take their seats) 17. The SRs did not really have a working majority since some of their ostensible members came from non-Russian branches of the party; in any case, with Bolsheviks holding majorities in key urban soviets, an SR government would have faced crippling resistance.

When the results became known, the Bolshevik Central Committee ordered the arrest of the electoral commission; Stalin claimed that the commission had forged the results. This was a bad beginning for what was claimed to be Russia's first freely elected popular assembly. Worse was to come. The Bolsheviks launched a propaganda campaign to discredit the Assembly, but this failed to shake the faith of soldiers and workers in it. For Lenin, the Assembly was a dire threat to his concept of the Bolsheviks directing the course of the Revolution, so it had to be neutralized. He transferred politically reliable Latvian infantry to the capital.

Despite interference, the Assembly duly met. Street demonstrations staged to welcome it were lethally dispersed by troops shooting down from the rooftops. The Bolshevik delegates walked out after failing to get their resolutions passed, and on the second day Bolshevik troops barred entry and the government ordered its dissolution. At the same time bands of sailors and hooligans murdered two Kadet leaders in hospital.

A new constitution, confirming the supremacy of the Soviet, formalized the end of the Constituent Assembly. Members of the other parties were described as counter-revolutionary. There was little outcry in the country as a whole but, although Lenin's uncompromising firmness had won the day, it helped to make civil war inevitable. The Socialist Revolutionaries could claim that it was they, not the Bolsheviks, who had popular support. Of the eighteen anti-Bolshevik governments which developed in 1918 in Russia proper, several, including the Samara and the North Russian governments, were headed by Socialist Revolutionaries who had been elected to the Assembly.

The CHEKA

For many, the most chilling evidence of Lenin's ruthless and uncompromising rejection of calm and conciliation was the CHEKA. Influenced by his interpretation of French history, Lenin had well before 1917 envisaged the use of terror in the post-revolutionary period. Thus in December 1917 the All-Russian Extraordinary Commission for Fighting Counter-revolution and Sabotage (whose abbreviation was CHEKA) was set up. Its head was Dzerzhinski, a Polish communist who had been released from Siberian exile by the February Revolution. Lenin often complained that Russians were 'too soft', and it may well have been this which influenced him in this appointment. Dzerzhinski additionally was reputed to be incorruptible and devoted to the cause.

The CHEKA established its permanent headquarters in the offices of an erstwhile insurance company in Lubyanka Street, Moscow. In subsequent decades 'the Lubyanka' would be the end of the road for thousands of victims, executions being carried out in its basement or courtyard. But it was not simply a prison and place of execution, it was a complex system of offices and departments administering the ever-widening bureaucratic empire of state security. In 1918 there were CHEKA detachments in all localities under Bolshevik control. The CHEKA was instructed to act according to its 'revolutionary conscience' in protecting the Revolution. In practice, it arrested and sometimes shot arbitrarily those whom its operatives considered dangerous. Anybody who looked like, or was denounced as, a 'bourgeois element' was in danger:

Do not demand incriminating evidence to prove that the prisoner has opposed the Soviet government by force or by words. Your first duty is to ask him to which class he belongs, what are his origins, his education, his occupation. These questions should decide the fate of the prisoner.[3]

In the summer of 1918 the CHEKA's arrests changed from a retail to a wholesale operation. Instead of individuals, whole sectors of the community were dealt with. The stimulus for this launching of mass terror was the activities of the Left Socialist Revolutionaries. As the Bolsheviks' grip became firmer, Lenin had been less inclined to compromise with his allies, and the latter had been particularly incensed by the re-establishment of the death penalty and by the peace treaty with Germany. (This, the Brest-Litovsk Treaty, had also aroused intense anger elsewhere in society.) The Left SR representatives in the Council of People's Commissars resigned, leaving an all-Bolshevik government. However, their members continued to occupy posts in the CHEKA.

In July two Left SR members of the CHEKA applied to see the newly appointed German ambassador, on CHEKA business. In the presence of the German military attaché, one of these CHEKA officials fired five shots almost point-blank at the ambassador. All the bullets missed, whereupon the second assassin threw a bomb, whose blast felled the military attaché who was just rising after throwing himself flat on the floor. A lucky shot from the second assassin finally killed the ambassador as the latter ran off. Concurrently, the Left Socialist Revolutionaries organized anti-Bolshevik risings in many towns; in Yaroslavl the rebels succeeded in gaining control for several days, and in Moscow the rebels, led by a veteran female terrorist, captured the telephone exchange. Not for the last time, Dzerzhinski displayed a lack of brilliance; he

3. Pravda, 25 Dec. 1918, printing the advice of a leading CHEKA official.

found himself taken hostage by the rebels, but was released unharmed. The revolts were mastered and the period of mass executions began. Not only Left Socialist Revolutionaries, but former officers, prosperous farmers, some workers, priests, lawyers, doctors, and members of pre-revolutionary governments were among those shot. Others were sent to prisons or prison camps.

There was still sporadic resistance, however. On one August morning the head of the Petrograd CHEKA was murdered[4] and in the afternoon Lenin was badly injured by well-aimed revolver shots. The alleged attacker here was a half-blind woman with a revolutionary past. She was promptly executed without trial; Sverdlov, who had taken command, wanted to show his decisiveness. Both this attempt and the Petrograd murder were ascribed to the Socialist Revolutionaries, and provided a pretext for an intensified Red Terror. Members of the non-Bolshevik parties, past, present, or suspected, were prime targets but the process spread so fast, with both the CHEKA and Bolshevik leadership saying it was better to kill ten innocents if only to catch one guilty 'counter-revolutionary', that few were safe from arbitrary arrest followed by imprisonment or execution, and torture if the victim had extra bad luck. For Lenin, this mass slaughter was part of the class war, and necessary to maintain power.

It was at this time that the CHEKA, aware that British diplomats were engaged in anti-Bolshevik plots, scorned diplomatic immunity and dispatched an armed detachment to invade the British embassy. In the resulting shoot-out a British naval officer defending the grand staircase (probably to win time in which documents could be burned) was killed, resulting in an Anglo-Russian diplomatic commotion that was eventually settled by an exchange of Britons arrested in Russia for Bolsheviks arrested in Britain.

The CHEKA was distasteful to many, probably most, Bolsheviks, and came into frequent conflict with local soviets. There was an attempt (repeated in later decades) to present the CHEKA as a glorious and virtuous institution; Lenin referred to it in terms reminiscent of Benckendorff's praise of the rather more innocuous Third Section. In fact the CHEKA was deplorable in so far as it accepted the principle of killing people, not because of what they had done, but because of what they were (or even because of what their parents were).

CHEKA operatives saw things differently. In an article celebrating the tenth anniversary of the founding of the CHEKA, the former head of its Moscow branch reminisced:

There were centres of counter-revolutionary organizations all over Russia, and all counter-revolutionary conspiratorial threads came together in Moscow . . . at the same time there was a marked development in Moscow of activity by speculators and

4. In due course, direction of the Petrograd CHEKA fell into the hands of one of the Latvians who had killed three policemen in the 1911 London drama known as the Sidney Street Siege. This is indicative of the ragbag composition of the CHEKA. Typically enough, this man later rose high in the OGPU but met a sticky end in Stalin's purge.

criminal bandits . . . the fact that we discovered the secret conspiratorial threads, and the counter-revolutionary bandit and speculation organizations was not thanks to some Sherlock Holmes sitting in the CHEKA, but was due to the fact that the CHEKA was a revolutionary organ of struggle for the defence of the revolution and was closely coupled to the party and the working class.

The writer went on to discuss the highlight of his career, the investigation of an explosion in late 1919 at the headquarters of the Moscow party committee, which had at first been blamed on White agents:

workers and Red Army travellers on the train were talking about the explosion and expressing their indignation at this work of the Whites, those betrayers of the revolution. A young woman travelling in the same car broke into the conversation and said that maybe the explosion had been carried out not by Whites, but by genuine revolutionaries and defenders of the people. This seemed suspicious, and the passengers detained her and handed her over to the CHEKA at the next station. It turned out that this girl belonged to the anarchist group *Nabat* . . . a letter was found on her from a leader of the group in which he vaguely wrote to a friend of similar views that the explosion at the Moscow committee was carried out by a group of 'underground anarchists' . . . the Moscow CHEKA in consequence was able to quickly uncover and liquidate the entire band.[5]

When in 1921 it was decided to replace 'War Communism' by a new, more moderate, economic policy, Lenin felt that a more relaxed Civil Code was desirable. This, at his insistence, still allowed for state terrorism, but judgements and sentencing were to be taken out of the hands of the CHEKA and entrusted more formally to the existing revolutionary tribunals. The CHEKA itself, largely at the prompting of Kamenev, was disbanded in 1922 and replaced by the Main Political Administration (GPU, later OGPU. The GPU was part of the interior ministry). What in fact happened was that leading CHEKA operatives, with Lenin's encouragement, took charge of the GPU. However, these changes did mean that citizens could sleep more peacefully. Provided they did not get up to mischief, they were safe.

Or so they thought. It was not to be quite like that. Lenin did not believe in universal civic rights, he did not believe in impartial courts (that is, courts that would treat all classes equally), and he did not believe that potential opponents should breathe freely. Towards the end of the Civil War the Socialist Revolutionaries, because they were mainly fighting on the Red side, enjoyed an amnesty but when hostilities ended, and the Bolsheviks were attempting to placate the peasantry (the SR's traditional friends), Lenin decided to stage what he called a 'model trial' of leading SRs. This took place in 1922, and was a precursor of the show trials of the following decades. The charges were fabricated and heavily publicized, and typically accused the defendants of working for the Whites or for foreign powers. Lenin's last

5. *Izvestiya*, 18 Dec. 1927.

illness, and pressure from foreign socialist parties, meant that the death sentences were commuted. But as a propaganda exercise, and as a threat to all dissidents, the trials served their political purpose.

The end of Nicholas

The Provisional Government had at first intended to send the royal family to Britain, but the British invitation was withdrawn. For their own safety the royal couple and their children were then sent to Tobolsk in Siberia, but when the Bolsheviks took power they were transferred to Ekaterinburg, in the Urals. Here they lived, under guard, in the house of a merchant. Other members of the royal family were kept near Perm, also in the Urals.

Trotsky, it seems, had visions of putting Nicholas on trial, with himself winning renown in the role of public prosecutor. But evidently others in the party had different ideas. The continued existence of the new regime was threatened by the survival, not only of Nicholas, but of any possible heir; an anti-Bolshevik movement with a royal heir as its figurehead would have a strong claim to legitimacy. In the summer of 1918 the Civil War was not going well, and it seemed that Czech troops would soon capture Ekaterinburg and Perm. The decision was taken to kill the royal family, using the Czech advance as an explanation.

The eleven victims at Ekaterinburg were the Tsar and his family, together with their doctor, cook, valet, and housemaid. Elsewhere, at the same time, the other detained grand dukes and their families were killed. The official announcement of the execution of Nicholas declared that the Empress and the children had been 'sent to a safe place'. This euphemism was used to avoid admitting that women and children had been killed. Moreover, the government at the time believed that it was on the brink of war with Germany; to announce the execution of the Empress (a German princess) would only have increased this danger.

The execution was a macabre and bungled affair, with several of the victims requiring extra shots to finish them off. The disposal of the bodies presented two irreconcilable problems. From their knowledge of Russian history it must have seemed inevitable to the Bolshevik leaders that, following the death of Nicholas and his heirs, there would appear pretenders claiming to be Nicholas or Alexis or a daughter or a grand duke, miraculously escaped from execution. But to prove that they were really dead by exhibiting the bodies would have risked the creation of a whole new set of holy relics, with the backward masses revering real or faked bones of 'Nicholas the Martyr' and his family.

It was decided that the remains should be unfindable and unrecognizable, and this was more or less achieved. The Whites did disinter some oddments, but these did not make satisfactory relics. Pretenders did appear, and continued to appear for decades afterwards. But they embarrassed mainly the

Whites and, later, the émigrés. The first pretender appears to have been an 18-year-old telegraphist in a remote village in Kolchak territory. He dressed himself in a sailor's uniform and claimed to be the Tsarevich Alexis. He sent a telegram to Kolchak's forces asking for a bodyguard to protect him from the Bolsheviks, and meanwhile enjoyed the favours and feasts offered him by the villagers. The bodyguard arrived, but took him to gaol.

The Red, White, Green, and other Armies

Before the Civil War really started, Lenin was convinced that it was over; he did not anticipate the strength of the gathering anti-Bolshevik forces and after a few skirmishes in late 1917 concluded that the Bolsheviks were not endangered. His decision to create a new, Red, army had more to do with his hopes of protecting and expanding his revolution outside Russia. Disillusionment was prompt, as the Whites' Volunteer Army assembled in the south and foreign powers prepared to help it.

The old army, on the verge of complete disintegration, formed the basis of the 'Workers' and Peasants' Red Army', founded in early 1918. That discipline and some degree of professionalism were restored was largely due to the energy and persuasive oratory of Trotsky, who at critical periods could usually rely on Lenin's support (Lenin concentrated on economic and political problems, leaving Trotsky to handle the Civil War). As commissar for war from 1918, Trotsky visited the fronts in his special train, ordering executions for failures and promotions for successes, arranging supplies, haranguing the troops, encouraging the faint-hearted, and carrying through against opposition a number of radical measures which determined the subsequent form of the Red Army.

Conscription, abolished in 1917, was reintroduced, bringing back into service thousands of men of the old army, but also making the peasantry the dominant social class in it, which was not to the taste of most Bolsheviks, who regarded themselves as a workers' movement. Since only the village communes or their Soviet successors knew which residents were eligible for military service, evasion of call-up was widespread. 'Bourgeois elements' could not be trusted with weapons, so conscripts of this description were organized into unarmed rear-service battalions. Trotsky offered commissions to former NCOs of the tsarist army, and opened schools to train promising young soldiers as 'commanders' ('officer', like 'minister', was by now a derogatory term). More significantly, since the Bolsheviks could not supply from their own adherents sufficient qualified men to direct their forces, Trotsky, against bitter opposition from party members, re-established experienced tsarist officers as 'military specialists'. Since numerous officers had joined the Whites, while others had White sympathies, many party members doubted the reliability of those who joined the Reds. For this reason, each 'military specialist' was supervised by a political commissar, which meant that units were managed by the dual leadership of commander and commissar. By the end of the Civil War about four-fifths of the Red Army's commanders were former officers. While it is true that most signed up because they badly needed a job, and that some deserted (partly because they were often treated with hostility by Bolshevik colleagues), their collective contribution to the Red victory was great, and probably decisive.

The Red Army's political commissars were officially established in April 1918, although they had been preceded by the commissars sent to the front by Kerensky in 1917. They were reliable party members whose task was to encourage (and watch) the loyalty of officers and men, to boost morale and efficiency, and to explain the policies of the party and government. The 1918 decree emphasized that a prime function of the commissar was to ensure that the Red Army did not become independent of the Soviet government (that is, hatch any military conspiracies). To enhance the commissar's power, only orders with his countersignature could be considered as valid (this seems to have been rigorously applied; one of the causes of the Red Army's debacle in Poland in 1920 was the refusal of one Red commander, Budyenny, to obey an order signed by Tukhachevsky, a former tsarist lieutenant, but not by Tukhachevsky's commissar). The best of the commissars did much to raise the fighting efficiency of the units to which they were attached, while the worst did much to lower the effectiveness of the commanders whom they were supposed to supervise. Some commissars fancied themselves as tacticians, tried to supplant the nominal commanders, and developed 'revolutionary' theories of warfare. One of the important roles of the former tsarist generals was to discourage such theories at the higher levels. When necessary, Trotsky supported them in this, which was one reason why many Bolshevik military leaders detested him.

A Red Army unit's fighting efficiency could usually be gauged by the proportion of party members and of workers in it. Units with more than one-fifth of workers were regarded as crack troops, while those with more than 95 per cent peasants were of little use. The Red sailors and the Red Cossacks had the most fighting spirit, but this was devalued by their volatility, disobedience, and general unruliness. Supplies were usually short, and sometimes non-existent. Some battles were fought barefoot, some petered out because of weapon shortages. Supplies and weapons that did arrive were often looted. There was an enormous desertion rate, especially of peasants who had gone home in 1917, only to be reconscripted in 1918. Trotsky reduced, but did not eliminate, this drain by his prompt reintroduction of the death penalty for desertion. The most reliable Red troops, especially in the early and less brutal stages, were Latvians and Central Asians, who had no compunction about killing Russians.

After the end of the Civil War several writers who had served with the Red Army began to record their impressions, in fictional or documentary form. It is these writings which show the ordinary men and women fighting for the Bolsheviks as they really were; not as clean-cut heroes with the correct political ideas, but as a heterogeneous collection of characters, each with his own blemishes. An illuminating example of the documentary approach in Civil War literature is Serafimovich's *The Iron Flood*. It is based on a real incident, a Red army making an epic march out of encirclement. Its hero, Kozhukh, is a thinly disguised version of the celebrated real-life commander Kovtiukh, who was a Bolshevik hero in the 1920s, although purged in the 1930s. The hero's past, as described in the novel, is not untypical of those once-alienated young men who distinguished themselves in the world war. Kozhukh had been a non-Cossack settler in the Cossack lands, and therefore has a background of poverty and humiliation. In the Great War his bravery earns him a place in an officer training school, but he is so mocked and despised by the socially superior instructors and fellow-cadets that he fails his examinations. Eventually, after two more attempts, he gains his officer's epaulettes, but his fellow-officers look down on him while the soldiers, who previously had admired him, no longer quite trust him. When the Revolution comes the ordinary people, to whom Kozhukh feels he belongs, begin to kill the officers and his hard-won epaulettes become dangerous. For his own safety he tears them off and returns home disguised as an ordinary soldier. But soon

the powerful hate of officers with which he had been filled now seemed trivial beside his feelings for the unlimited class struggle. The officers were simply pathetic lackeys of the landlords and bourgeoisie.

He determines to prove himself by work and sacrifice for the party. The story of *The Iron Flood* is how he imposes through strength of character some kind of order and battle-worthiness on the wild and unruly Red army which is entrusted to him. Kozhukh's warriors consist of three elements. There are the infantry and artillery, who are an undisciplined mob of peasant soldiers demobilized from the Tsar's army, plus a few who have joined the Reds after the Revolution. They are from the surrounding local Cossack territory and are mainly former hired peasant labourers who have been long trodden down by their Cossack landowning superiors. For them the Revolution has opened up the chance of overthrowing their social superiors and overcoming their poverty. The second element is the Cossack cavalry. Like most Cossacks who fought for the Reds, they tend to be of the poorer families, but nevertheless are smart and full of pride. Thirdly there are the Red sailors; these fight savagely, but far from being 'the pride and joy of the Revolution' (as Trotsky described the Red sailors) they are little better than land-going pirates. They tease and provoke the unruly peasant soldiers, they start rumours against the commander, they consider themselves an elite and will not submit to orders unless the latter are backed up by a machine gun. The turbulence of the foot soldiers is recorded early in the book. Democratically assembled to discuss their tactics, they curse and shout down their commanders, killing one. Later, they fight fierce battles against each other as each tries to reach a vital bridge first. They have a weakness for strong drink. They are cruel, but although they shoot their prisoners—men, women, and children—they do not mutilate them as do the Whites. After a battle they insist that a priest be summoned to give their fallen comrades a proper funeral with all the trimmings: crosses, incense, and fervent intonations. And it is these men, dishevelled, bedraggled, hungry, and despairing, who beat the Whites and thereby make history.

Babel's sketches published under the title *Red Cavalry* are also illuminating, with each story telling of an episode in the life of Budyenny's celebrated cavalry corps in the Polish campaign. The author's Jewish background and his own unpleasant experiences when serving in this unit probably explain why his stories emphasize the unnecessary savagery practised by both sides, and the discrepancy between the communism as promised and the communism as practised. Taken alone, these stories perhaps reveal only one side of the truth, but as such they are useful as correctives of the later glamorized versions. With his unflattering allusions to artificial legendary heroes like Budyenny and Voroshilov, it is hardly surprising that Babel perished in the purges of the 1930s. Among the memorable characters of *Red Cavalry* there is the former swineherd who returns to his village as a high Red commander. Encountering his hated former master he does not shoot him, but stamps and tramples him to death because 'shooting only kills a man . . . you never get at the soul'. There is the unlucky soldier who escapes after five years in a German prisoner-of-war camp, crosses Germany and Lithuania, and, when almost within sight of his home and wife, is conscripted into the Red Army. There is the ignorant and savage warrior who, though not really understanding what the Revolution is about, uses the new terminology and practices to justify his own conduct. Describing his murder of a woman, he reports, 'I took my loyal rifle down from the wall and washed away that stain from the surface of the Workers' Land'. Then there is the regimental washerwoman, the mistress of the *Red Trooper*'s correspondent, whose boring revolutionary monologues drive her into the bed of the regimental cook. Finally there is the narrator himself, the unhappy Jewish intellectual whose heart is in the cause but not in the fighting. Accused by his fellow-soldiers of being a 'milk-drinker' and 'God-worshipper', he soldiers on, 'begging fate to grant me the simplest of abilities, the ability to kill my fellow-men'.

Other themes, like the contradiction between peasant leaders' desires for farming freedom and the reality of the Bolsheviks' intentions for the peasantry, occur over and over again in the fiction about this period. Another theme is the effect of the war on those who fought it, how young idealistic men from the towns became of necessity hardened killers, how a commander of 20 after a few months would look as though he were 40. There was a recognition, too, that the Revolution had not put an end to the scoundrels of tsarist times. The latter might skilfully adopt Red language, fight for the Reds, and yet remain scoundrels. Several writers highlighted the dull stupidity of the 'liberated' peasants, the farce of local elections, and the unprincipled demagogy of many Bolsheviks. The devoted revolutionary is another familiar character. One such is the heroine of Lavrenev's highly praised *The Forty-First*, who falls in love with a captured White lieutenant whom she is escorting. When White forces approach she shoots him to prevent his escape.

The Red Army was frequently troubled by peasant rebellions in its rear, but the White Army suffered even more from these, as well as from urban disturbances fostered by underground communists and Socialist Revolutionaries. The Whites were led by generals who were quite unable to adapt to the new circumstances. When fighting and assembling in non-Russian parts of the old Empire, they only caused trouble for themselves by making reassertion of Russian rule in the old Empire one of their priorities. Their General Denikin made a point of referring to Ukrainians as 'Little Russians'. Driving into the huge rural expanses of Russia and the Ukraine, they returned land to the former landowners and thereby added an intense grievance to the list of other resentments that they built up among the peasants; conscription, executions, seizure of horses. These last three injuries were inflicted on the peasantry by the Red forces too, and the Bolshevik grain requisitions, which sometimes left the peasants without seed corn, were also hated. But the Bolsheviks, at least, did not seek to overturn the peasants' appropriation of noble land. (What the peasants really wanted, having achieved their sacred goal of land seizure, was to be left alone by all sides. In this they often succeeded; some villages and districts even declared independence for a time, and had their own border guards.)

The White Army was much smaller than the Red and no better supplied, but it had a surplus of officers, many of whom agreed to serve as ordinary soldiers in the Volunteer Army which was formed in the south in early 1918. Later the Whites resorted to conscription, when reliance on Cossacks to provide the rank and file proved mistaken, due to the propensity of Cossacks to change sides according to where they considered their immediate interests lay. However, White conscripts, like Red, were prone to desert. Until Wrangel took over the southern Whites, their army was even more chaotic than the Red Army, and many of their officers set bad examples of drunkenness, intrigue, looting, and violence, which were usually unchecked.

In most periods, both sides killed more civilians than enemy soldiers, and both sides multiplied their atrocities to a level of routine. Death by staged dismemberment could be inflicted when time permitted. Pushing prisoners into furnaces or locomotive fireboxes saved both time and ammunition. Some unfortunates had their ears, noses, or eyes cut away and were then released, as a lesson to others. When the Reds or Whites talked of terror tactics, they meant just that. As well as known or suspected Bolshevik sympathizers, the Whites tended to kill any Jews they could find as they advanced. They were even more savage when they retreated. Many of their Cossacks, in particular, enjoyed pogroms, and were egged on by some of the White generals. Within the overall theme of rape, mutilation, and murder, preferably in front of the victims' families, agonizing variations would be invented. Although many Red Army commissars were Jewish, Jews did not find much comfort in Red-occupied zones either, partly because they were apt to be lumped with the 'bourgeoisie', to be humiliated, looted, and perhaps killed.

In the east, events were determined by the Czechoslovak Legion. This had been formed mainly of disaffected Czech and Slovak soldiers of the Austrian army who had allowed themselves to be taken prisoner by the tsarist army. The intention had been to deploy them back against Germany and Austria, but the Revolution intervened and in 1918, at the request of the western powers, they were to be shipped to France's Western Front via Vladivostok and the Trans-Siberian Railway. Some were already distributed along a length of that railway. They were distrusted by local Soviets and what started as a routine drunken brawl was magnified, with the help of Trotsky's savage reaction, into a revolt by the whole Legion. Blocking the railway and forming the most effective body of troops in the country, the Czechs and Slovaks soon made themselves felt.

At Samara, they helped install an anti-Bolshevik government based on moderate Socialist Revolutionaries, and a few others, who presented themselves as the true descendants of the Constituent Assembly. But although the Assembly had been regarded with high expectations in 1917, once it had been dispersed the mass of the population had abandoned it as an ideal. The peasantry, on whom the Socialist Revolutionaries relied, proved a disappointment. Having got what it wanted, it was not going to risk it all by supporting one political party against another. The Samara government, ruling a population with a strong anti-socialist element, needed to make compromises, which included giving some land back to the landowners. It was unable to conscript a strong army and when the Czech Legion lost its enthusiasm the Samara government came to an end. For a time it negotiated a junior partnership with the right-wing Omsk government, but the latter soon suppressed it.[6]

The White regime at Omsk had also been rescued by the Czechs. At one time commanding a vast area and threatening to advance towards Moscow, it was a reactionary government over which Admiral Kolchak was installed in late 1918 as 'Supreme Ruler'. He had been a popular and efficient tsarist admiral, but lacked political gifts. Largely in the hands of right-wing officers,

---

6. In the later stages of the Civil War the surviving Socialist Revolutionaries and Mensheviks tended to support the Bolsheviks, as the lesser of two evils.

but supported by many native Siberians dreaming of an independent Siberia, the Omsk regime relied on repression rather than conciliation of its local population.

In the Far East, in Kolchak's rear, there was Semeonov's Japanese-supported regime. Nominally a White, Semeonov was little better than a terrorist, but his savage little empire lasted until the Japanese withdrawal.

In the far north there were anti-Bolshevik forces around Archangel, coexisting with British, French, and US forces there, while in the Baltic lands west of Petrograd there was the White army of General Yudenich. The Allied troops at Archangel and Murmansk had been sent there to protect munitions shipments which had accumulated at those ports in 1916 and 1917; a German thrust towards Murmansk seemed quite possible. In March 1918 further British troops were sent to Archangel (with Trotsky's acquiescence) and the same year the British entered the Caucasus to protect the oil region from possible Turkish occupation. When the World War ended in November 1918 several influential voices favoured the transformation of these precautionary troop movements into an active intervention to suppress the Bolsheviks. In Britain, Churchill and Milner were the main advocates of this, but Lloyd George, fearing disaffection among war-weary troops and workers, was opposed. The French, mindful of the thousands of small investors who seemed to have lost their savings in Russia, were more anti-Bolshevik than the British. Foch proposed a plan for a multinational crusade against Bolshevism, but this plan was rejected by the Supreme Allied Council in March 1919. President Wilson was for mediation, and in general US troops were committed to Russia more to keep an eye on the other interventionists than to suppress the Bolsheviks. Churchill and Foch could argue that Bolshevism was threatening to spread through Europe; the 1918–19 revolution in Germany, which before it was suppressed established soviet governments in Bavaria and several cities, was plainly aided by the Russians (notably by Lenin's representative, the Bolshevik propagandist Radek). Moreover, in early 1919 Bela Kun engineered his short-lived Red revolution in Hungary, helped by money supplied by Moscow. Lenin would have liked the Red Army to advance so as to permit a rail link between Soviet Russia and 'Soviet Hungary', but the threat of Kolchak in the east made the opening of a new front too risky, and Kun's republic collapsed.

For Churchill and Foch the idea of quarantining Bolshevik Russia behind a 'cordon sanitaire' of nations like Poland and Romania seemed insufficient. But after the rejection of Foch's plan the half-hearted build-up of foreign forces in Russia halted. At the end of 1918 there were only about 15,000 Allied troops in north Russia, probably 17,000 Japanese troops around Vladivostok (accompanied by several thousand US troops sent to forestall a permanent Japanese annexation), French and British warships in the Black Sea, substantial French forces at Odessa, British warships in the Baltic ostensibly protecting Latvia, Lithuania, and Estonia from Bolsheviks and German 'volunteers', and small British detachments in the Caucasus and Turkestan.

Thus the western intervention was feeble and unenthusiastic. Allied soldiers were war-weary, and repelled by the cruelties of their Russian allies and enemies. In north Russia the British troops, including Royal Marines, even went as far as mutiny.

I came back from the patrol thinking that this so-called war was a fantastic charade, far removed from real soldiering. My illusion was rudely shattered by a talk I had with a young officer who had been serving with the partisans.

'I commanded the partisans who retook Tivdia,' he said.

'That must have been exciting.'

'Exciting hell—it was ghastly. You see, when the Bolos took Tivdia they killed everyone they could find—all the old people, women and children. I had a number of men from Tivdia with me—they told the others. So when we retook the village, they began to kill all the Reds. I did my damnedest to stop them—quite useless. They nearly killed me too. So I went away into the forest for about half an hour. When I came back it was all over. I couldn't really blame my men—they thought they were exacting justice for the murder of their parents, wives, and children.'

'. . . I was with a Marine officer when he was selecting men for a patrol. The men fell in in a half-hearted manner. They were badly dressed, and some were unshaven and dirty. To my astonishment they began to answer the officer back. 'I can't go sir, I've got a sore toe!' I can't go sir—me stummick's bad!' And so on.[7]

In early 1918 the Allies would have helped the Bolshevik government if the latter had been willing to continue the war against Germany (and at one stage the Bolsheviks were indicating that they might indeed accept help), but the encouragement of communist revolution in Europe, the murder of the Tsar (a cousin of the British King and the object of much sympathy after his abdication), the nationalization without compensation of foreign-owned enterprises, the Red Terror, and various hostile acts and speeches discouraged those who advocated acceptance of the Bolsheviks and encouraged the interventionists.

The French contingents left in 1919, the British in 1919 and 1920. The Japanese stayed until 1922, when British and US pressure persuaded them to leave. The direct military contribution of the intervention was negligible; a few skirmishes were fought against the Reds, and a few communists executed. Western governments (and the Poles and the Finns) were especially reluctant to give full military support to the Whites after the latter had refused to recognize the new states (like Poland and Finland) created from the nations of the old Russian Empire. However, western military supplies were a great help to the Whites (and often to the Reds, who at times relied on arms captured from the Whites). Some British tanks and aircraft were used by the Whites.

---

7. From an unpublished memoir by Lt. W. G. Irvine-Fortescue, Royal Engineers, describing experiences in north Russia in the late summer of 1919.

But much western aid never reached the front line, being sold for private profit en route. This was one reason why the British halted supplies in 1919, when the Denikin offensive failed. This decision, just as much as the retreat itself, took the spirit out of the White armies.

Apart from the armies of the Reds, Whites, and interventionists there was a great variety of lesser armed forces fighting at certain times and places. Among these were the Greens, consisting mainly of deserters from other armies and fighting both the Reds and Whites according to circumstances. Then there were the semi-independent peasant armies, which usually fought on the side of the Bolsheviks and owed their military efficiency, if any, to their chosen leaders, several of whom were remarkable men. Chapayev became the best known of the pro-Bolsheviks, being subsequently portrayed as a simple man capable of inspiring his unruly and illiterate soldiers to heights of endurance and heroism. There were also bands of anarchists, the most important of which was Makhno's army, which successfully fought Reds, Whites, and Germans. After the Civil War the Bolsheviks quelled these peasant and anarchist forces, but not before, in 1920–1, Green uprisings around Tambov and the Volga gathered sizeable support. Makhno escaped with his life across the frontier, but Antonov, leader of the Tambov revolt, died fighting.

The Civil War campaigns

The Civil War was fought mainly in the east and south, although at one stage the north-western front became critical. The Bolsheviks managed to hold the central region (including Moscow and Petrograd) but their constantly expanding or contracting territory was smaller in area than that of their opponents (which was one reason why foreign governments were unwilling to recognize the Bolshevik government). Campaigns tended to be fought along railway routes, which sometimes made the armoured train decisive. Because Russian railways mainly radiated from Moscow and Petrograd, the Bolsheviks enjoyed interior and centralized lines of communication, enabling them to shift troops from one front to another at short notice.

Although in the Don Cossack country the Civil War dates from late 1917, it was not until the summer of 1918 that the Whites assembled major forces in the south and east. In the south, under General Denikin, they gained control in the Don and Kuban regions and advanced towards the Volga, with the eventual aim of linking up with Kolchak's Siberian forces. By the summer of 1918 they were besieging Tsaritsyn, through which passed grain supplies for the Bolshevik cities. The Reds determined to hold Tsaritsyn at all costs, and Stalin was sent there as the party's supreme representative. Among the defenders of the city who collaborated with Stalin were Voroshilov, son of a railwayman and a former party secretary, who commanded the defending army, and Ordzhonikidze, a Georgian who was political commissar of

Voroshilov's army. Both these had previously worked with Stalin, and their close relationship with him was cemented by this siege. Also at Tsaritsyn, and working with Stalin, was Budyenny, commanding what was later to be the most celebrated of the Red cavalry units. These four combined against several of Trotsky's initiatives, and intrigued against the former tsarist officers admitted to the Red Army by Trotsky. But their energy and decisiveness helped to defeat the White siege. In 1925, to commemorate Stalin's role, Tsaritsyn was renamed Stalingrad, the first major manifestation of what would later be called Stalin's 'cult of the individual'.

Despite the failure at Tsaritsyn, Denikin's army staged another offensive in 1919. This was loosely coordinated with attacks mounted from other anti-Bolshevik fronts: there was to be a joint Franco-Ukrainian offensive in the southern Ukraine, Kolchak was to advance towards the north-west, to link with White forces around Archangel, and General Yudenich's White army in the Baltic states was to advance on Petrograd. But while Denikin's offensive was spectacularly successful, coming to within 200 miles of Moscow, the other sectors were disappointing. Yudenich was easily defeated by the determined Red Guard of Petrograd. Kolchak's advance was crippled by internal quarrels, by the apathy of the Czechs, by partisans in the rear aroused by the reactionary policies of the White Omsk government, by revolts staged by Socialist Revolutionaries, and by strong Red counter-attacks led by Frunze, Kuibyshev, and Tukhachevsky. All these factors turned Kolchak's advance into a long and hopeless retreat, Kolchak being captured and shot in 1920. In the Ukraine, the planned Franco-Ukrainian offensive came to naught when Paris, alarmed by communist-inspired mutinies in its warships off Sevastopol, ordered its forces home, leaving the way open for the declaration of a Soviet Ukrainian Republic.

The defeat of Denikin was delayed because Trotsky's plan was opposed by Stalin and others. Eventually, after Lenin had backed Trotsky, the plan was put into effect with a startling sweep by Budyenny's cavalry through Denikin's rear. Henceforth the White Army was in retreat, finally evacuating the Crimea (and Russia) at the end of 1920. By that time Denikin had been succeeded by Wrangel, whose better political sense came too late to save the White cause. Meanwhile, since 1919, the Bolsheviks had been fighting a new enemy, the Poles. Dissatisfied with their eastern frontier (the Curzon Line) as proposed by the western Allies, the Poles hoped to take advantage of Russia's disarray to annex territory which had once been part of the Polish Empire. At first their troops, led by Pilsudski, were victorious, capturing Kiev in May 1920. Kiev was the capital of the Ukraine but also regarded by Russians as the cradle of their nation; there could have been nothing more effective than this Polish invasion in arousing Russian patriotism and nationalism.

The strength of Russian nationalism surprised the Bolsheviks, and they soon took advantage of it. A short-lived movement known as National

Bolshevism emerged, including non-Bolsheviks who believed the Bolsheviks were at least standing up for Russia's interests. Thousands of deserters returned to the army, although it is possible that this phenomenon was related less to love of Russia than to dislike of Poles. Many retired officers, including the popular General Brusilov, changed their allegiance and rallied round the government. The Poles were forced back to the Curzon Line and Lenin, against Trotsky's advice, decided to push on to Warsaw, hoping to establish a Soviet government in Poland and thus make physical contact with Germany, whose masses were still believed to be on the verge of revolution.[8] This, the first clear attempt to spread the Revolution by force, failed when the Red Army was defeated by Polish troops advised by the French General Weygand. The Red defeat might have been avoided if Tukhachevsky's advanced army had been properly supported by the forces under Egorov, Budyenny, and Stalin. The dilatoriness of this trio was later ascribed to jealousy, but was probably a result of confusion. The result of the defeat was that in 1921 the Treaty of Riga, ending this war, allotted to Poland considerable Byelorussian and Ukrainian territory which the USSR did not regain until 1939.

The Russian emigration

Before 1917 Russian émigrés consisted of disaffected intellectuals, working for (or at least hoping for) a revolution, and concentrated in such cities as Geneva, Paris, and London, and of peasants and Jews who had settled in the west, especially in the Americas, and who had no intention of returning. Ten years later the picture had changed completely. The pre-1917 intellectuals had gone home (although many of them, alarmed or disappointed, soon returned), and there had been a new flow of refugees after the defeat of the White armies.

In 1917 life in Russia became horrifying for families that were regarded as class enemies. Conditions varied from place to place and from time to time, and there were many cases of middle- and even upper-class people surviving and doing well. But the bulk of them, regarded by Lenin's regime as 'looters', were looted in their turn. They had no protection against the violence that was directed at them. Frequently they were forced to work in humiliating jobs. When rationing was introduced, they received entitlements at a reduced level, or not at all. At this period the once-prosperous would go down to the markets with their surviving paintings, china, clothing, and even the occasional grand piano, which they would exchange for a sack of flour or basket of eggs. In the early 1920s about one-tenth of city prostitutes were from noble families.

Unsurprisingly, those who could leave did leave, making their perilous way to White-held territory or to foreign countries. When Wrangel abandoned the

---

8. 'Feeling out with bayonets' was Lenin's term for this, in a speech at a party conference which was heavily censored in the Soviet press.

Crimea he was accompanied by about 150,000 refugees. These were settled in temporary camps in Turkey. About 60,000 of them were soldiers and, expecting a Bolshevik collapse, an effort was made to keep this army in being. However, it soon dispersed, although the Russian Imperial Navy continued to exist for some years, anchored off Bizerta and training annual intakes of cadets. Several of the Slavic states of eastern Europe aided the refugees, while many Russians settled in Paris, Berlin, and the western hemisphere. In addition, there were sizeable Russian communities in Manchuria, composed largely of refugees who had arrived after the defeat of Kolchak: many of these moved to Australia and elsewhere when the communists attained power in China in 1949. During the 1920s many dissidents, intellectuals in particular, were allowed or compelled by the Soviet government to emigrate legally.[9] Refugees continued to arrive in the 1930s, and during and after the Second World War there was a new wave, of a rather different type.

Although much émigré publishing was done in Berlin, Paris was the political centre of the refugees. Here, in various organizations, members of the old political parties continued their previous and often sterile disputes. The Grand Duke Cyril Vladimirovich was proclaimed Tsar Cyril I by émigré monarchists. Of more concern to the Bolsheviks was the émigrés' Union of Servicemen, a White veterans' association which could conceivably re-form into a new anti-Soviet army. In the Russian tradition it was soon infiltrated by agents of the Soviet government; some of the most vociferously anti-Bolshevik officials of this and other émigré organizations were in contact with Moscow. Two chiefs of the Union of Servicemen were kidnapped and removed to the USSR in 1930 and 1937. The émigré scene was both enlivened and distorted by the activities of various fringe organizations. Not the least eccentric of these was the Young Russia Movement, whose slogan was 'For Tsar and Soviets', and whose leadership included Soviet agents.

The bulk of the émigrés settled down quietly throughout the world, often in their own communities. These communities began with a few families, which would contrive to build a church, then a school, and then a meeting hall. In France in the late 1930s there were nearly seventy Russian schools. In Paris there were several thousand Russian taxi drivers, and Russian was almost an official language at the Renault works.

The emigration was a great, though unmeasurable, loss to the USSR, because it contained a disproportionate number of professionals and intellectuals. Emigration and Red Terror were partly responsible for that chronic problem of the Soviet economy, shortage of managerial talent. Many of Russia's most useful scholars and scientists were among the émigrés, and later

9. The number of Russians who emigrated as a consequence of the Revolution is unknown; certainly there were several hundred thousand and one estimate, apparently well based, goes as high as 1 million.

occupied prominent positions in western universities and western industry. They included, to mention only a few: Sikorsky, who had developed four-engined airliners for Russia and would develop the helicopter for the USA; Struve, who made revolutionary discoveries in astronomy; Zvorykin, celebrated for having the last entry in the New York telephone directory but also regarded as the inventor of modern television with his iconoscope; and Vinogradsky, the world-famous microbiologist. With this elite there were hundreds of other eminent names, of professors, engineers, researchers. At the Pasteur Institute, much frequented by Russian scientists before 1917, a virtual colony of émigré biologists developed. At times Russian émigré biology seemed more productive and creative than Soviet biology.

In the arts there was a similar picture, although several men and women of talent, unable to create when cut off from their native soil, returned to Russia and were generously received by the Soviet government. Among the repatriates were the proletarian writer Gorki and the composer Prokoviev. While Lenin was alive it was possible for distinguished figures to obtain permission to reside abroad legally, and many took advantage of this. Others, including the future Nobel Prize winner Bunin and the philosopher Berdyaev, were deported in 1922. In music Russia lost S. Rachmaninov and Stravinsky, as well as Chaliapin. Among artists Chagall was perhaps the most prominent loss; he had been appointed director of an important art academy in the euphoric days following October, but had caused some consternation among party critics by celebrating the first anniversary of the Revolution with a portrayal of green cows and horses capering in the sky. He had then lost his job because, it was said, he was unrevolutionary. As for Repin, he went to Finland to paint icons.

Muscovy and the outside world

For much of the Civil War period the Bolshevik state was reduced to little more than the old Muscovy, as former subject nations broke away and hostile armies invaded peripheral territory. After October 1917 there were three basic problems in external policy. These were Russia's still continuing war against the Central Powers, the urge towards independence of non-Russian nations of the former Russian Empire, and the unconscionable slowness of the expected world revolution to develop in Europe. These three issues, like all issues which faced the Bolsheviks, were interconnected, but will be treated separately here.

Lenin had wanted Trotsky to become people's commissar of the interior, but Trotsky had declined on the grounds that placing this office in the hands of a Jew would, in many Russians, arouse hostile emotions. So, instead, he was entrusted with foreign affairs. The early Decree on Peace was widely disseminated at home and abroad, but its proposals of a just peace without annexations raised little enthusiasm in belligerent capitals. The western Allies tried without success to persuade the new Russian government to remain in the war. Lenin at this time expected, and preferred, a German victory; he believed Germany was on the point of revolution and a strong revolutionary Germany was better than a weak revolutionary Germany. The publication by the Bolsheviks of the secret treaties of the tsarist government, including a 1915 agreement between the Allies concerning the partition of a defeated Turkey, caused embarrassment and further resentment in London and Paris.

In early December a one-month truce was negotiated on the Eastern Front, followed by peace negotiations at Brest-Litovsk. The Central Powers demanded as their prize Poland and the southern Baltic provinces, but when an anti-Bolshevik Ukrainian delegation appeared at Brest-Litovsk to demand independence for its nation, it became clear that the Ukraine would also be lost to Russia; and the Ukraine was the source of grain as well as four-fifths of Russia's coal and metal production.

Although the Bolsheviks' declared policy was to allow non-Russian nationalities to secede if they wished, few Russians and few Bolsheviks could face the prospect of accepting the terms offered. But the Russian army by this time was, as Lenin said, not even capable of making a retreat. Although Lenin clearly realized that for the sake of peace any German demand, except a demand to change the government, would be acceptable, his colleagues insisted on rejecting the peace terms. Finally Trotsky was allowed to return to Brest and carry out his own plan, but Lenin extracted a promise from him that if he failed he would support Lenin's proposal to accept the peace terms. Trotsky's plan proved to be one of his more notable fatuities. He declared to the astounded German and Austrian delegations that their conditions were unacceptable and that his government had adopted a policy of 'neither peace nor war'. This idea of neither fighting nor surrendering made a fine theatrical stir, and Trotsky had the satisfaction of hearing the German negotiator, General Hoffmann, exclaim 'Unheard of!' But that was the full extent of his satisfaction because the Germans and Austrians thereupon set their troops in motion.

By the end of February German forces were occupying the Baltic provinces, much of the Ukraine, parts of the north Caucasus and the Crimea. Petrograd was in danger. A socialist and nationalist government was established in the Ukraine under German auspices. Yet Lenin was still unable to convince a majority of his Politburo colleagues that peace with Germany was worthwhile at any price. Some suggested accepting western assistance, others like Bukharin proposed a picturesque 'fight to the last man'. Eventually Lenin was able to get his own way, but by this time the Central Powers' demands had stiffened: all the Baltic provinces, the Ukraine, Finland, and certain territory on the Russo-Turkish border were to be abandoned, and an unfavourable trade treaty to be signed with Germany. The resulting Treaty of Brest-Litovsk was signed in March 1918, the Bolshevik signatory being Sokolnikov because other more prominent Bolshevik leaders refused to attach their names to it.

Lenin intended to denounce the treaty at the first opportune moment. He believed that the Germans might still renew hostilities, which was why Russia's capital was moved from Petrograd to the less vulnerable Moscow in March. When Germany was defeated in November the Bolsheviks declared the Treaty of Brest-Litovsk null and void.

The magnitude of the problem posed by the different nationalities of the former Empire was little realized at first. When the Bolsheviks took power they were confident that their intention to allow the non-Russian nations to secede if they wished would not raise great difficulties. There had been various independence movements afoot since the February Revolution, but the Provisional Government had done little to satisfy them. When Stalin, who some years previously had made a study of the nationalities problem and was himself a non-Russian, was appointed commissar of nationalities, one of his early acts was to grant independence to Finland (November 1917). The independence of Poland was also accepted by the Bolsheviks, but they had optimistic expectations that the seceded nations, most of which had significant Bolshevik parties, would eventually return to the Russian fold in one way or another. In Finland the local Bolsheviks, supported initially by Russian troops who were stationed there, staged a rising in January 1918 which developed into a civil war in which the anti-Reds, led by a former tsarist general, Mannerheim, and with German support, emerged victorious, subsequently inflicting various cruelties on their defeated enemies. In Poland Pilsudski, once an unwilling resident of Siberia and no friend of Russia, became head of state. The Ukraine, which during 1917 had established a quasi-autonomous status for itself, after the Bolshevik Revolution declared itself to be the Ukrainian People's Republic. It demanded that Ukrainians in the Russian army be released to form the Ukrainian army.[10] The Bolsheviks responded by creating their own Ukrainian government, whose forces threatened to conquer the entire territory.

During the Civil War the Bolsheviks invaded the Ukraine three times, finally re-establishing Russian rule. The Ukrainian nationalists had held power in two periods but were unable to engender much national feeling, despite the arrogant behaviour of Russian Bolsheviks (who, however, were less arrogant than Ukrainian Bolsheviks). At one point the 'legitimate' national government appealed to the Germans. It was thus clear that the Bolshevik acceptance of secession for the nationalities could, in the case of the Ukraine at least, create a threat to the Russian government. So in early 1918 Stalin qualified the earlier declaration; he reserved the right of secession for the 'working masses' of a given nation. In effect this meant that if the Bolshevik leadership considered secession was not conceived by and for the working-class cause, it would not be granted. But during 1918, sometimes under direct

10. Such a release could only cause chaos in the Russian army, and seemed a threat to Bolshevik power.

or indirect foreign protection, nationalities of the Russian Empire in Europe began to create their own states. However, with the exception of Finland, Poland, and the so-called 'pygmy states' of Estonia, Lithuania, and Latvia, the new republics were short-lived. As early as 1919 new Bolshevik regimes were imposed in White Russia and the Ukraine. In 1920 the independence of Azerbaizhan was brought to an end by a Bolshevik rising, and Armenia was forcibly dismembered by Turkey and Russia. But Georgia was recognized by the Bolsheviks as independent in that same year. It had a Menshevik government which enjoyed considerable support both at home and among socialists abroad. However, on Stalin's initiative, the Red Army invaded and conquered Georgia in 1921.

Perhaps the biggest disappointment endured by the Bolsheviks in their early years was the failure of the 'world revolution' to materialize. According to marxist theory, the initial triumph of communism in Russia was premature in so far as the theory prescribed that the proletariat would rise first in the most advanced capitalist countries, not in the most backward. Moreover, socialist society could be built only in prosperous conditions. Trotsky, among others, solved this theoretical problem by regarding the Bolshevik Revolution as a trigger which would detonate 'the permanent revolution', a series of revolutions in the more advanced countries; the victorious proletarians of the latter would then provide communist Russia with the economic aid which she needed. In October 1917 the Bolsheviks expected an immediate spread of their revolution, in the first place to Germany, which was economically advanced and whose armed forces were under great strain. In the first year of the Bolshevik regime hopes were maintained, but gradually the Bolsheviks resigned themselves to the possibility of a long wait. But it was not until the 1920s that the theory of permanent revolution was finally discredited.

To catalyse the world revolution, the Third International (Comintern) was established in Moscow in 1919, with Zinoviev as its chairman. The Comintern was to link and coordinate the efforts of all communist parties in their efforts to spread the revolution. It was not long, however, before it became a means of putting the interests of 'the first socialist state' before the interests of the individual parties. This was not unfair or illogical, since the survival of Bolshevik Russia was evidently crucial to the communist cause in general, but it was applied rigidly and selfishly in later years. The Comintern through its agents and other resources did its mediocre best to stimulate revolution in those early years. The year 1919 had been disappointing. Spontaneous risings had had initial success in Bavaria and Hungary but had been soon suppressed (although the Bavarian Soviet Republic lasted two months). In 1923 the Comintern attempted another rising in Germany. This achieved an enormous failure; the thousands of armed proletarians whom Zinoviev believed to be on the march in Germany simply did not exist, and the German communists did not even produce a general strike. The ultimate beneficiary of this attempt was

Hitler, who would owe his rise to power very largely to his promises to fight the Bolsheviks. Zinoviev's prestige was damaged even further when he instigated a similarly abysmal attempt at revolution in Estonia, to be started by Red Army men in plain clothes.

The Comintern did little good for the Red cause. It failed to make revolutions, and its machinations gained support for right-wing governments and fascist movements abroad. In Italy, Bulgaria, and Germany its directives to the local communists to struggle against the other socialists, sometimes in alliance with fascism, were a crucial factor enabling the extreme right to defeat the left in those countries. It embarrassed the commissariat of foreign affairs because foreigners would not accept that it had no connection with Soviet foreign policy; in the 1930s the distrust which it had sown was one of the factors discouraging a common front of the west and Russia against fascism. And it discouraged the initiatives of foreign communist parties, while making them vulnerable to accusations of putting the interests of Moscow before those of their own peoples.

The party

Both in the centre and in the provinces the Bolsheviks were deeply unpopular in the Civil War years, yet stayed in power. This was because they dominated the soviets and the latters' executive councils. They excelled at winning elections to these bodies; sometimes they used blatant fraud, but the practice of open election by show of hands was easily exploited; with a few CHEKA operatives present to record the names of people brave enough to vote against the Bolsheviks, opponents could easily be eliminated or brought to heel (but not, usually, in village soviets, where Bolsheviks were given a hard time). When town soviet elections produced a Menshevik majority, which did happen sometimes, the central government declared the result invalid. Becoming the only legal party also gave the Bolsheviks a crushing advantage.

Service in the Civil War, both at and behind the fronts, encouraged party members to adopt a military style; this persisted for years, until it was imitated by the fascist parties of western Europe. It was partly terminological, partly sartorial. Communists liked to use military-sounding terms; nationalization of industry was 'seizing the commanding heights', dissidents were 'traitors', putting policies into practice was a matter of 'launching offensives'. Until 1935 party members were allowed to carry small arms. With junior party officials fond of dressing in machoistic black leather, a meeting could resemble a cockroaches' tea-party.

For many, party membership was the road to riches. Given heavy responsibilities for the distribution of much-needed items, which could sometimes include the right to live, they had great opportunities for theft and bribe-taking. Even without abusing their privileges, they could still benefit from the rights granted to party members, like extra rations (the restricted stores where party officials could obtain items not available to the general public date from this period and would later become a feature of Soviet society). At this period, too, party members were not subject to execution (Trotsky's violation of this convention at the front caused some alarm). Many Bolsheviks of this period were indeed like those of subsequent Soviet novels: brave, devoted to an ideal, and ready to sacrifice themselves for it, even doing horrible things for the good of the cause. But many others were of low character and small competence, eager to use party membership as a way of climbing over others. The party soon was regarded as a powerful and privileged minority, rather like the old nobility had been. Party leaders lived in fine country residences.

At the end of the Civil War an effort was made to take the party in hand, and the party organization began to take the forms which would prevail over the following decades. By 1921 there were about 730,000 members.[11] Although at times of intensified recruitment in the Civil War and in the 1920s and 1930s entry standards were lowered, in general members were carefully selected. It was not a mass party, but an elite which was rooted in the masses and would lead the masses. Membership was a privilege and could be withdrawn; thousands of members were expelled for drunkenness, apathy, and other faults. The quality most sought by the party was obedience; the leadership's decisions were only valid so long as the membership could be relied on to carry them out without questioning or foot-dragging. Democratic centralism, which was the concept on which the party was based, implied this, but also offered ordinary members the chance to influence the policies which would be handed down to them. Such influence was exercised by the party organizations, in which every member had a voice, which sent delegates and resolutions to the higher organizations. The lowest party organization was the cell, which could be formed wherever a minimum of three members was located in a given unit of production or institution (for example, a workshop or a warship). The cell members would be represented in the next highest organization (a town or district committee). The latter would be represented in the next highest organization in the same way. The top of the pyramid was the Party Congress, which at this period met annually. To carry on the day-to-day work of the party, the Congress selected a tenth of its members to form the Central Committee. In the critical post-revolutionary years the Central Committee proved too large for making quick decisions and this meant greater influence for its political bureau (*Politburo*). The latter, for most of the Civil War period, consisted of only five members (of whom two were always Lenin and Trotsky). Since the Central Committee rarely objected to the decisions of its Politburo, the latter (or its majority) was the effective ruling body.

11. On the eve of the February Revolution membership had probably been around 20,000. This grew to between 100,000 and 400,000 (according to whose estimates are believed) by October.

With party members dominating administrative bodies, which included the people's commissariats (ministries) at the top, those bodies functioned as executors of party policy. Policies hammered out in party committees would be handed down to the Soviet (that is, government) departments for execution. Thus there developed a system of rule in which party organizations and government organizations were nominally separate but worked in parallel. The central government came to consist of the Council of People's Commissars headed by its chairman (prime minister). The governmental administration, like the party, had its subordinate provincial, district, and village organizations. Both local and central administrations were answerable to elected soviets, the lowliest (and often illusory) body being the village soviet. The party's control of the governmental administration was secured by the dual membership of individuals in party and governmental institutions. In the higher government organs there was 100 per cent party membership: key administrators would be members of key party organs at the same level (for example, the 'prime minister', Lenin, was a member of the Politburo).

One of the main functions of the party was therefore the provision of reliable administrators ('leading cadres') for governmental and non-governmental bodies at all levels, ranging from people's commissars to newspaper editors to factory managers. The new administrators would take their instructions from the party, would be responsible to the party, and would conduct affairs in conformity with the party's priorities and aspirations. Administrators and specialists on the party-approved list formed what would become known as the *Nomenklatura*. Top Bolsheviks, naturally enough, appointed their own friends and relatives; Lenin's brother-in-law became commissar for railways, while Stalin placed his friends on a wholesale basis.

Other members, primarily the rank-and-file, were supposed to verify the fulfilment of the party's directives in their own locality, and to 'mobilize' the non-party masses by means of example, exhortation, persuasion, and propaganda. As time passed, the differing functions and the differing capabilities of members were expressed in the informal division of the party into several categories. First there were the full-time paid party organizers, who collectively made up the *apparat* and became known as *apparatchiki*. The secretaries of the various party organizations were the most prominent among these. These were the men who selected members for various posts and tasks and who were responsible to the superior party bodies for the carrying out of the party's wishes in their own area. Whether they were the party's general secretary in Moscow, or local party secretaries in the districts, they were the key figures in their particular spheres. A man who was appointed party secretary had moved a long way up the ladder; later he might find he had a long way to fall.

This party bureaucracy amounted to about 8 per cent of the party in the 1930s. Well before then, the bureaucracy had become a world of its own, of multiplying offices enthusiastically filled by applicants eager for a job title that required little from them but was the key to a privileged existence. Efforts to control the bureaucracy, like establishing the Workers' and Peasants' Inspectorate (*Rabkrin*), simply created thousands more of such jobs. In the factories, it was typical for bureaucrats to outnumber production workers. Many of these non-producers had little idea of what they were supposed to do, but reassured themselves with the circulation of documents that would be progressively obliterated by rubber stamps.

The next most influential group were those members who occupied administrative and governmental posts. Much of the 'white-collar' element of the party was included in this group. Finally there was the rank and file, in which the working class and peasant membership seemed to concentrate (partly because, when workers and peasants were promoted to administrative posts, they became classified as 'white-collar' in the statistics). In proportion to its numbers in society, the white-collar category was over-represented in the party; it was about 30 per cent of the total in 1917, 70 per cent in 1941. This was partly because such people had most need to join the party (to hold or obtain administrative jobs), knew people who would sponsor their admission, had the time to devote to party work, were less liable to resign from the party, and possessed the skills the party needed in its effort to run the country.

From time to time there were purges of the membership. These were started during the Civil War to rid the party of 'radishes' (red outside but white inside) who had joined not from conviction but for personal advantage. In the early purges (which involved calling in party cards and reissuing them only after due appraisal), shameful personal behaviour (notably drunkenness), indiscipline, and non-participation in party activities were the most frequent causes of expulsion. Many members also left voluntarily, either because they were disillusioned, or found the party's demands on their time too burdensome. The first of the really major purges was in 1921–2, when no less than a third of the membership was eliminated, bringing the total down to below half a million.

The role of party members in the Civil War was as stiffeners of morale, leaders of detachments, organizers, and administrators; members were mobilized and sent to whichever sector of the front or link of the economy seemed to be critical. As always, war with its succession of crises and urgent requirements necessitated authoritarian central direction; reasoning why was a luxury in wartime, doing and dying was the role of the communist. Thus it became accepted practice for the party *apparat* to direct particular members to particular tasks, to appoint and dismiss, without discussion or appeal. The working of the party became less democratic and more bureaucratic, while certain questionable practices, like sending contrarious members to distant posts, developed unchecked.

War Communism

The period of the Civil War coincided very closely with the period of 'War Communism', a term used to describe the economic and social climate produced by the interaction of rigorous government policies with the confusion, chaos, and anarchy of post-revolutionary Russia. Frequently, the policies of the Bolsheviks bore little resemblance to their earlier intentions; it was a case of riding on the tide or perishing. However, most Bolsheviks believed, or persuaded themselves with varying degrees of willingness, that the policies adopted out of necessity were in fact truly communist. Party members varied in their economic views, and the same members might at different times hold diametrically opposite opinions. Lenin himself changed course frequently and succeeded not only in retaining power but also, in 1921, in persuading the party to accept a radical change of economic course.

The Decree on Land, which broke up private landholdings and distributed them to the peasants, was followed (still in November 1917) by the Decree on Workers' Control. The latter gave additional powers to the already-existing workers' committees, which before October had been established in the factories. At this time the trade unions (where Bolshevik influence was still weak) were not considered a suitable medium of industrial control, which is why the workers' committees (which were independent of the unions) were favoured. However, the committees were by no means subordinate to the party and tended to run their factories for their own benefit. They made life difficult for the factory managements, no doubt they protected the enterprises from possible sabotage by disaffected managers and owners, and they probably had an educational value for those who participated in them, but that was all. The committees were later merged into the trade unions, after the latter had been taken under firmer control by the party.

The problem of the trade unions was not finally resolved until the 1920s. Essentially, the unions in 1917 wanted to run their own industries in co-operation with the government, whereas the party (or at least Lenin and Trotsky) felt that the unions' role should be merely the application of the party's policy. Until March 1918 the railwaymen's union succeeded in running the railway network independently, but with its subjugation by the Bolsheviks in that month the first stage of union opposition to the party was over. Trotsky later introduced martial law on the railways, and proposed the similar militarization of other industries, but the 'labour armies' he began to create in 1920 from demobilized Red Army men had Lenin's only lukewarm support, and did not develop very far, even though Stalin became head of the short-lived 1st Labour Army.

Lenin had initially expected to proceed very cautiously in the takeover of industry and commerce, cooperating at first with the capitalists and their managers. But, as in agriculture, events forced his hand. After the October coup few managers or bureaucrats expected the Bolsheviks to survive long, so they saw no need to cooperate with them. When the new people's commissars arrived to take over their ministries the permanent civil servants all too often treated them, at best, patronizingly and, at worst, with a total lack of cooperation. An early crisis occurred when officials of the State Bank refused to make money available to the new government; this led to an immediate physical takeover of this bank and the nationalization of all others. In December 1917 the Supreme Economic Council was established to supervise the economy and to operate nationalized enterprises. It was still hoped that nationalization would be initially limited to a few key industries (the 'commanding heights' on which other industries were dependent: fuel, transport, banking, foreign trade, etc.), but local soviets all over Russia were already 'nationalizing' on their own initiative the enterprises in their areas. In February foreign debts were cancelled.

To retain the expertise of hostile managers and bureaucrats, it became the custom to send trusted party men to supervise them. Younger employees who could pass themselves off as Bolshevik sympathizers found themselves promoted over the heads of others, soon becoming managers irrespective of their experience or competence. This was one of the roots of the long-term Soviet problem of incompetent, insensitive, dishonest management; when the wrong people reach top positions, they tend to breed their own kind.

War Communism is reckoned to have begun in mid-1918 with the Decree on Nationalization, making all large-scale enterprises liable to nationalization without compensation. In the following three years there was wholesale nationalization, grain requisitioning, extreme inflation and the virtual disappearance of a money economy, a chaotic decline of industry, rationing, hunger, and disease, a decline of urban population, a gradual subordination of the unions to the government, and a Civil War which demanded the dispatch of all available human and material assets to the fronts.

Of these features grain requisitioning was perhaps the most important. Even without the Decree on Land there would have been a food shortage, but in 1918 the Bolsheviks made things worse with their State Grain Monopoly. Deliveries to the towns fell as peasants waited for the state to offer fairer prices for their grain. The government responded by sending armed detachments of workers or of the CHEKA to the villages, with instructions to confiscate grain stocks beyond the personal needs of peasant families. At the same time the opportunity was taken to 'fan the class war' in the villages by establishing 'committees of the village poor', whose task was to spy out the hidden grain stocks of the richer peasants. This naturally led to animosity and violence; since it was a crime to 'speculate', and the holding of grain stocks was considered evidence of speculation, any peasant holding grain stocks was vulnerable.

Bolshevik-led detachments would take peasants' personal grain stocks and often their seed corn, leaving families facing death by starvation. Many peasants were hanged, either to encourage the others or because the requisitioners were convinced that they had hidden their grain (sometimes they had but more often they had not). Many participants were horrified by what they were doing; some acted for fear of punishment if they failed while others genuinely believed that it was 'for the good of the cause'. It was not simply a case of finding food. It was also a conflict of worker against peasant launched by the Bolshevik leaders in their self-proclaimed role as vanguard of the proletariat. The peasantry with its individualistic, superstitious, and backward mentality comprised four-fifths of the population and produced the workers' food, so it had the power to frustrate the Bolsheviks. Somehow it had to be neutralized.

But 'fanning the class war' in the countryside produced more smoke than fire; most of the alleged 'kulaks' or rich peasants were not rich and more often than not were relatives of the poor peasants who were intended to savage them. In the villages, some peasants were certainly richer than others; usually they were the most productive and when their surpluses were thus confiscated they naturally reduced their sowing areas so as to produce less. The peasantry realized the Bolsheviks were intent on creating social strife in the villages, and hatred of the village poor committees became so intense that they were disbanded in December 1918.

In the towns there was a rationing system for food and other necessities. Rationing was discriminatory; workers and soldiers received most, the bourgeoisie least. At times the ration, even for workers, was well below starvation level but could be supplemented by the black market. The latter was illegal, but usually tolerated. Whether a black marketeer was shot or made a handsome profit depended on luck and the time and place of his operations. Private trade in necessities was forbidden, but since most state trading organizations and cooperatives were chaotic and seemed incapable of feeding the citizens it was the black marketeer, the 'speculator', who kept people alive. The 'bagmen' who would bring to the towns grain they had purchased from the peasants made a big profit on resale, but were liable to be shot if caught by a CHEKA man in a bad mood.

The constant movement of lousy troops, the absence of soap and hot water and medical supplies, combined with malnutrition, meant that millions of Russians died in the Civil War from diseases, of which typhus was the most lethal. Disease, battle, rebellion, and repression caused about 10 million deaths, of which only a tenth were military. Townspeople fled to the countryside, where they believed starvation was less likely; the number of workers fell from 2.5 to 1.25 million. In 1921 the gross output of industry was one-fifth of the 1913 production, and in some key sectors the decline was even more catastrophic; while coal production had fallen only from 29 million to

9 million tons, sugar had dropped from 1,300,000 tons to 50,000 and steel from 4,300,000 tons to 200,000. Small wonder that from 1917 to 1921 the prevalent attitude towards the Bolshevik government changed from apathy to resentment. And yet there were many party members who relished the almost total breakdown of Russian society. For them, this was communism.

Among these enthusiasts were those who saw in inflation a welcome 'inevitable dying-out of money', an institution which they considered 'bourgeois'. The economist Preobrazhenski described the money-printing press as a 'machine gun which has attacked the bourgeois structure in the rear, through its monetary system'. By October 1920 the rouble stood at 1 per cent of its 1917 value and would decline even faster in subsequent months; in May 1922, for example, railway fares were 1 million times higher than in June 1917, and in the following November 4 million times higher. In industry, money ceased to be a meaningful medium of exchange because inter-enterprise transactions became merely bookkeeping transactions and labour and materials were more and more paid for in kind, either with an enterprise's own products or by items such as food or clothing made available by the government. In early 1921 more than nine-tenths of wages were paid in kind. In addition, services, like transport, were made free services. In many towns the trams (streetcars) had ceased running, but they were free. In the spring of 1919 another decision on nationalization specified that all enterprises employing more than ten workers were to be nationalized (even 'left communists' like Bukharin rejected the idea of nationalizing the smallest enterprises). But again the process followed its own localized courses, irrespective of what Lenin or Trotsky or Bukharin intended. According to one source over 30,000 enterprises were nationalized by 1920, including many (like windmills) which employed only one worker. How the Supreme Economic Council could find able and reliable communists to supervise these enterprises was apparently not considered by the more ardent nationalizers, for whom the nationalization process was simply taking a few armed men and declaring a given enterprise or workshop or mill to be the property of 'the people'.

In 1920, with the critical period of the Civil War over, there was a continuation of the same ruthless and rigorous atmosphere. Lenin, unusually late in recognizing the inevitable, discouraged those who recommended moderation in economic life. Proliferating peasant revolts he blamed on the Socialist Revolutionaries. Declining sowing areas he proposed to counter with a plan for each peasant, specifying how much land should be planted. The overloading and confusion of the Supreme Economic Council was met by making it subordinate to the Council of Labour and Defence, of which Lenin was chairman. 'Communist Saturdays', the voluntary labour of workers on their day off, were spoken of as the way to tackle post-war restoration. But in the countryside peasant revolts were becoming widespread and threatening. There was no longer the need to support the Reds simply because they were a lesser evil than the Whites, so the savage resentment aroused by grain requisitioning was no longer constrained. By the end of 1920 the Civil War had merged into a peasant rebellion.

Lenin seems to have decided to reverse course in early February 1921, accepting the need to replace grain requisitioning with a system which would increase food production and mitigate the animosity of the peasant masses. To persuade his party of the need for this 'New Economic Policy' was a formidable prospect; that Lenin achieved it so quickly was due to peasant risings, strikes, and especially the Kronstadt Revolt of late February, which shook the party more than the Whites had ever done.

By 1920 most peasants realized that the freedom to be themselves, which they thought had been won in 1917, was under attack by the Bolsheviks. Bad weather added to savage grain requisition was causing famine. Increasing numbers of desperate villages were taking up arms and thousands of grain requisitioners were killed. CHEKA and Red Army units sent to suppress the peasant rebels were sometimes worsted, sometimes victorious (sometimes it was pitchforks versus machine guns). In many regions Bolsheviks were safe only in the towns. The Tambov Revolt was the most threatening of the peasant revolts, but there were hundreds of lesser outbreaks. The general aim of these rebels was expressed in the slogan 'Up with the Soviets. Down with the Communists!' Meanwhile, similar slogans were being displayed by the growing number of worker-protesters. In Moscow in early 1921 troops refused to fire on strikers, so special communist detachments were sent to spill the required blood. A few days later, massive strikes and violent repression began in Petrograd. The Petrograd workers were demonstrating against the Bolsheviks on several grounds; economic privations, Trotsky's so-called Labour Army (in reality, organized strike-breakers sent to discontented factories), the fixing in the Bolsheviks' favour of elections to soviets and trade union organizations, the presence of armed communist detachments in the factories, and the arrests and executions carried out by the CHEKA (which did not spare the workers). These complaints were distorted by the press. A communist later wrote:

The truth seeped through little by little, past the smokescreen put out by the Press, which was positively berserk with lies. And this was our Press, the Press of our revolution, the first Socialist Press, and hence the first incorruptible and unbiased Press in the world! Before now it had employed a certain amount of demagogy, which was, however, passionately sincere, and some violent tactics towards its adversaries. That might be fair enough and at any rate was understandable. Now it lied systematically.[12]

The Baltic Fleet sailors of Kronstadt, still regarded as the heroes of the Revolution, noticed glaring differences between what the newspapers said about the Petrograd disturbances and what their sailors' representatives

---

12. V. Serge, *Memoirs of a Revolutionary* (1963), 126.

reported from the capital. They noticed that the party and the press were misrepresenting the workers' demands and concealing the repressive actions which were being taken. The Kronstadt sailors in a succession of meetings thereupon made demands on the Bolsheviks in the form of resolutions. They demanded new elections to the soviets with a secret ballot and other measures to prevent the Bolsheviks rigging the vote. They demanded freedom of speech and of the press for all of the left wing, freedom of assembly, liberation of left-wing political prisoners and a re-examination of the cases against other political prisoners, freedom to bring food into the towns from the countryside, abolition of extra rations for privileged persons, withdrawal of armed guards from the factories, and other lesser liberties.

Party spokesmen were shouted down, since they refused to concede these demands. Trotsky delivered a menacing ultimatum, which was rejected. Tukhachevsky was summoned to capture the island of Kronstadt. The first assault across the ice failed, largely because the attacking troops sympathized with the rebels, and two weeks elapsed before more reliable troops, stiffened with communists from the concurrent Party Congress, could be launched for a second attempt. This eventually succeeded after heavy losses. Some sailors escaped to Finland but thousands were executed or sent to a slow death in the first of the Soviet concentration camps, on a White Sea island.[13]

The revolt was passed off, and sixty years later was still passed off, as a White conspiracy aimed at the restoration of the monarchy. In fact, as Lenin said, 'it illuminated reality like a flash of lightning'. Whether or not Lenin realized its full implication is not clear. If the demands of the rebels are examined it is evident that what they were demanding, and what the Bolsheviks would not concede, was virtually what most Bolsheviks and their supporters had believed they were struggling for in 1917. Nothing could have been more revealing of the gap between the aspirations of the Bolsheviks in 1917 and their intentions in 1921. In the intervening four years the Bolsheviks had given the retention of power overriding priority in their struggle against all kinds of perils. In their own terms they had emerged victorious, but in terms of ideals, of ambitions, of compassion, of all the things which make a revolution worth while, they were no longer the same people. The communist party of 1921 was not the Bolshevik party of 1917.

When Lenin spoke of Kronstadt as 'illuminating reality' the reality to which he referred was ostensibly the reality of economic policy. But there was another reality: the Bolsheviks had won the Civil War, but had lost themselves.

---

13. This was the subsequently notorious Solovki camp. Other camps soon followed, partly to house those peasant hostages, largely women and children, who had been taken in the effort to suppress peasant risings. With the aid of hostage-taking, executions, village-burnings, Red Army campaigns, and even poison gas, the peasant revolts were slowly suppressed during 1921; the concessions of the New Economic Policy helped to pacify the peasantry.

Famine

For Russians, hunger was not a new experience. There had been especially serious famines in 1833, 1840, 1867, 1873, 1891, and 1911. That of 1891 had been the most lethal, and had left long-lasting resentment because although the government could not be blamed for the crop failure, it could be blamed for the high taxation that had robbed peasants of the chance to build up reserves. But the 1891 famine was exceeded by the famine of 1921–2. With the area under oats and summer wheat at less than three-fifths, and under winter rye at four-fifths, the 1917 extent, it could hardly have been otherwise. Signs of an impending crisis were evident in 1918; deaths from hunger were rare, but deaths from malnutrition were rising. Some figures for Petrograd are indicative.[14]

	City population (million)	Births per thousand of population	Deaths per thousand of population
1914	2.2	25.0	21.0
1917	2.5	18.0	25.0
1918	1.5	15.0	44.0
1919	0.8	15.5	81.5
1920	0.6	12.0	[a]

[a] Uncertain, between 90 and 120.

There was widespread drought in 1920 and 1921. As food became short the older and weaker began to die. There was an increase of orphans and of physically defective infants. Crime grew, new criminal careers typically beginning with theft of food. Such thefts might progress to armed attacks by groups on such life-or-death objectives as granaries or potato fields. The towns emptied as their populations left to seek food in the countryside, while at the same time starving countryfolk thronged the railway stations as they sought to reach some rumoured area of plenty. The railways were already barely functioning; the few passenger trains which were running were crammed with the starving, the weak being pushed off to make room for the strong at each station. Those without strength or hope huddled for days and weeks on the station platforms, quite silent, occasionally picking off each other's lice as they starved to death.

In such times there could be no morality. Party officials entrusted with food distribution sometimes gave short rations for their own profit. Cannibalism appeared, and so did body-snatching:

14. L. A. and L. M. Vasilievskii, *Kniga o golode* (1922), 64–5.

Sometimes insensate mothers and fathers feed their children human meat as a last resort. Sometimes a starving family eats the body of one of its junior members. Sometimes a father, seeing no other way, cuts the throat of a neighbour's child and brings it to his children as 'mutton' (his own poignant term). Sometimes parents at night seize part of a body from the cemetery and feed it to their children.[15]

These observations were written by two doctors working in one of the worst famine areas, the Ufa region. They mentioned another case:

A Tartar killed a thirteen-year old girl, a relative, who had come to visit him, by hitting her over the head with a log. He not only ate her, but also cut off from her several pounds of fat, which he sold at the market.[16]

There was a definite preference for child-meat. Among the starving, eating the dead was not considered sinful, because the souls had already left the bodies; killing for food was different, and could trouble the conscience.

In the villages, where there was no grain and no seed, where the emaciated horses and bone-dry cows were being eaten, there seemed to be no hope unless the promises of government help on the way, made by the local party men, were miraculously kept. But few by this stage had much faith in party promises. As a young noble in the 1891 famine, Lenin had criticized charity-aid, which he regarded as sentimentalism. Echoes of this attitude were perhaps present in the Soviet government's pretence that there was no famine until, largely at the urgings of Gorki, public appeals for international help were made in summer 1921. Many charitable organizations responded, and others were set up for the purpose. The work of Herbert Hoover's American aid project, of the Quakers and other religious groups, and of Nansen's organization, together with exertions by the government, partially coped with the disaster. At first there were difficulties because the authorities did not wish potentially subversive westerners to be at large in the countryside, while the foreign organizations, fearful that their supplies might be distributed only to known supporters of the regime, insisted on keeping distribution in their own hands. Eventually a compromise was reached, but throughout the crisis there were arrests of relief workers in Russia, especially of those Russians employed by the various agencies. In 1922 prominent members of the Russian famine committee were arrested by the CHEKA and exiled.

This famine probably took about 5 million lives.

---

15. L. A. and L. M. Vasilievskii, *Kniga o golode* (1922), 81–2.
16. Ibid. 178.

12

Disputes and decisions

The New Economic Policy (NEP)

AN indication that Lenin was willing to abandon the economic practices of War Communism had come in February 1921, when he accepted the idea of a tax-in-kind to replace grain requisitions. With a tax-in-kind fixed in advance, peasants would know that they could dispose of any surplus over the tax in their own most profitable way, and would therefore increase production and sown area. Such a change was long overdue. If it had occurred a year earlier both the peasant revolts and the famines would have been moderated.

The Party Congress, shaken by the Kronstadt Revolt, did agree to this change, which became even more radical when the tax-in-kind for the various food products was fixed well below the previous requisitioning targets. This meant that the peasantry would certainly produce a marketable surplus and, since the state was not in a position to organize a marketing and distribution system, the return of private trade had to be accepted. Once the private trader (soon known as the *nepman*) was admitted in one sector, it was not long before he began to dominate all retail trade; the peasant with money in his boot wanted somewhere to spend it, and neither the state nor the cooperative movement could organize adequate retail distribution.

In the changed atmosphere, and with the critical industrial situation, the readmission of private enterprise into industry was also accepted, although Lenin needed all his powers of persuasion to convince his party of this. While taking care to retain in state ownership the 'commanding heights' of the economy, small-scale manufacturing was largely returned to private management. By 1924, while the state still owned and managed 98 per cent of large-scale industry, small-scale factories were about four-fifths privately run, and one-fifth cooperative. Since the state and party lacked enough talented administrators to run all enterprises efficiently, placing the majority under private management was a wise move from the economic point of view, though distasteful to the party. This distaste was sharpened when it became clear that the private managers were producing more efficiently than the state-managed industries; they were paying higher wages, too, and were attracting the better workers.

The year 1921 was one of great industrial crisis. There were mutually exacerbating fuel, food, and railway crises, causing many enterprises to close. Radical measures in that year to increase industrial productivity created additional short-term chaos. Hitherto, enterprises had been subordinate to one or other of the departments of the Supreme Economic Council, and their task was to produce rather than to cover their costs. Money hardly entered their calculations; they received allocations of raw materials from the Supreme Economic Council, which in turn allocated their output. Wages were paid in food rations, clothing, and services. In 1921 this high-cost, low-output, and bureaucratic system was changed. Enterprises were reorganized and grouped into trusts, which had some autonomy, and were expected to observe conventional accounting procedures. Materials were to be paid for out of income, and so were wages; free rations, and rationing, were to be eliminated. The State Bank was to provide credit, and in 1922 a new rouble was introduced to create a stable currency. To improve standards of management further, and to acquire advanced plant, foreign entrepreneurs were invited to participate in Russian industry. Few were willing, but foreign trade increased, and a commercial agreement was made with Britain in 1921. But the big state industries tended to rely on state subsidies to fill the financial gap left by their continuing poor management. Wages were lower than in 1914 and were habitually paid late.

The 'scissors crisis' of 1923, so called because two divergent trends resembled scissors when plotted on a graph, was less serious than it seemed at the time. It was essentially a marked disharmony between food prices (that is, the peasants' income), and the prices of industrial products (the peasants' expenditure). At its worst, industrial prices were nearly three times higher than pre-war, whereas food prices were slightly lower. This problem caused further discontent among the peasantry, and a diminution of the market for manufactured goods, before it was overcome.

The private entrepreneur, both in trade and industry, performed essential tasks which official organizations were unable to handle. He made a handsome profit in doing so, and the conspicuous luxury in which some *nepmany* indulged was one of several features of NEP which irritated the more sensitive party members as well as much of the public. By 1923 *nepmany* handled three-quarters of all retail trade. Not only were they able to get goods from producer to consumer faster than state or cooperative organizations, they were able to do so more cheaply because their operations were less bureaucratic. Cooperatives, for example, marked up their prices for commodities like sugar or cloth by about 100 per cent over the ex-factory price; the *nepmany*, who dealt with state-produced goods as well as private, could operate profitably on much narrower margins.

Various types of marketing, retailing and production cooperatives also flourished in this period. Production cooperatives included several forms of farm which were voluntary and quite productive. Cooperatives had become popular in tsarist times, and by the end of NEP about half the peasant house-holds belonged to them. They seemed to appeal to the peasantry especially, and were a way of reducing costs and improving supply without recourse to coercion.

Until 1926 the trade of the *nepmany* rose absolutely, although it fell proportionately after 1923 as the state, through the newly formed people's commissariat of trade, made efforts to compete. In general, the first three or four years of NEP were the heyday of the *nepman,* but also a period in which the government and party succeeded in extricating themselves from the self-defeating economic policies of War Communism. By 1926 in most products the economy had regained the 1913 output level, although this meant that the economy was still thirteen years behind. Much of the advance had been obtained simply by putting disused assets back into service.

The moulding of minds

Freedom to describe things as they really were became increasingly limited during the 1920s, making it possible to construct a false, yet undeniable, image of life in communist Russia. The image was of a bright new society making its optimistic way towards socialism, led by the only party which knew the way to get there; a society in which things were getting better and better but which was nevertheless threatened externally by the capitalist world and internally by traitors, enemies of the people, and survivals of the 'bourgeois' mentality. Within a decade no other view could be voiced in public, and it was increasingly inadvisable to do so in private. Statements of the obvious would become impermissible.

As the Civil War drew to a close the party established its Agitation and Propaganda Department (*Agitprop*) which, with its local offices, ensured that the approved picture of Soviet society should prevail. It had a multitude of specialized sub-departments (for schools, publishers, cinemas, radio, theatres, literature, and so on) which closely monitored what was being offered. All books and periodicals published by non-Bolshevik presses were read and registered. Libraries were purged of undesirable books. Sundry films and plays were banned.

Yet, in various nooks and crannies, truth did survive, hoping for better days. One nook was inside people's minds, accommodating alternative narratives based on the individual's own experience. An important cranny was to be found inside the state security service, GPU. In their role of sniffing out all dissident views GPU operatives were watching and listening everywhere. Their reports were collected and sifted in the localities, resifted in the centre, and put into documents labelled 'Completely Secret'. At regular intervals compilations of these reports were supplied by the GPU to a few dozen top people in party and government.

The GPU reports were very different from those sent in by party organizations. They were not afraid of calling a spade a spade, or a strike a strike, and detailing or summarizing people's opinions as heard on the streets or in various meetings. Thus a handful of party leaders, while sticking to the accepted, largely false, image of the new society in all their public appearances, in fact had a very different picture at the back of their minds. GPU operatives had no interest in minimizing bad news and although in later decades their reports might not be so accurate as in the 1920s (partly because people were learning to keep their mouths shut, even in private, and partly because interior ministry officials sometimes placed their own filters on this information), the secret reports of the security organization would remain an important source for a few privileged decision-makers for the remainder of the Soviet period, and beyond.

Myth is an ingredient of most societies, but the achievement of the Russian communist party was to construct a new society whose foundation as well as framework was held together with falsehood, as the Soviet state became the most total of twentieth-century totalitarian regimes. The period of NEP was later regarded, both by Russians and by outside historians, as an abbreviated golden age in which the future really did seem to promise great things. This nostalgia was not misplaced, but nevertheless this was a period in which things went badly wrong.

Meanwhile, in the 1920s new and idealistic standards were being set for people's behaviour. There was to be a New Soviet Man embodying these new standards, and at his side would be the New Soviet Woman.

By 1928, of the approximately 1 million party members, less than 70,000 were women. This does not imply that the party was indifferent to women, but it may reflect indifference of women towards the party. Revolutionary women had usually regarded themselves as revolutionaries first and women second, believing that revolution would itself bring an end to gender inequalities. Veteran women Bolsheviks for the most part stayed with this concept after 1917, although a few of them, and young female entrants to the party, took a more assertive stance. For these women, the 'Old Bolshevik' Aleksandra Kollontai was the inspiration. A member of the party's Central Committee in 1917, she was commissar for social security for a few months. She believed that in the new socialist society individuals could have relationships with the opposite sex for a variety of purposes and durations. She also believed in practising what she preached. Lenin, for whom sex was one of those subjects on which he preferred not to hold forth, distrusted her views on free love but appreciated her qualities, and it was only after his death that she was shunted off as Soviet ambassador to Norway. In the meantime she had persuaded the party to establish its central women's department, with branches throughout the country.

The main task of the women's departments was to recruit women for the party (and younger women for the communist youth organization, the

Komsomol). The main mechanism for this was addressing women at their place of work, persuading them to elect delegates, and then holding delegate conferences where lectures and discussions could proceed, during which the more outstanding delegates could be discerned and persuaded to join the party. But delegates were bored by the lectures, and it soon became hard to find women who wanted to participate. Those who did get enrolled frequently opted for truancy; there were even cases of women being dragged to conferences by the police. Party recruitment fell far short of the targets.

Unfortunately the party had restricted the fields of activity of the women's departments, limiting their freedom to act in matters where women would have found them most useful. Women's low pay was a big issue, especially when state industry in 1926–7 sought to improve its balance sheet by increasing workloads while decreasing wage rates. This particularly affected women workers, who tended to occupy the poorer-paid and less-secure jobs (but who nevertheless were more likely than males to down tools or vociferate their grievances).

Factory women were concerned above all with sexual abuse practised at the workplace by their male overseers ('Come to me after work or you'll lose your job'). Although a few officials of the women's departments did overstep their responsibilities by helping women with divorce and child maintenance problems, women in general received little help from party or state offices. Both state and party had long decried 'bourgeois morals' but had done nothing to moderate the consequences of their new morals. Divorce on demand, introduced in December 1917, could be seen as a fine liberalizing advance but it tended to liberate men more than women.

The women's departments were not helped by the image of the New Soviet Woman that the party and its publicists were creating. The concept of the 'strong woman', exerting an attraction over men not so much by physical allure as by inner strength, competence, and intellectual quality, was well known to readers of classical Russian novels, and the intellectual male seemed to fancy such women so long as they remained safely on the printed page. Thus it was not a long step to the short-haired, leather-jacketed, nicotine-stained woman with a party card in her pocket and a revolver in her belt. This product of the Civil War years lived on as an image on which the new Soviet woman was invited to model herself. But it was not an image to which women aspired in the relaxed years of the mid-1920s. At one end of the social spectrum were the wives and girlfriends of rising party officials, who adopted the styles of previous elites (their ostentatious display aroused such antipathy that the party at one point instructed its women not to wear their diamonds in public). Far more numerous were working women, who preferred to spend their leisure hours at the cinema or dance-hall. These were women who would spend their meagre wages on a good dress, cosmetics, and a hairdo, who would model themselves on what they picked up from Hollywood films, and were interested in finding or keeping a good man.

So great was the influence of Hollywood that the party sought ways of banning foreign films, only to discover that without them the cinemas would be empty. Not only did Hollywood encourage women to use cosmetics (that is, choose the wrong image) but it also introduced to society such vices as the fox-trot, a dance which kept the eyebrows of the censorious in a permanent state of uplift. It was not so much that the fox-trot brought the sexes into a fairly close physical proximity. Its danger lay in that it was un-Soviet, un-Russian, and was performed by two partners who had chosen each other in a blatantly un-collective way. Worse, it was widely popular. To ban it was considered unwise. Instead, Komsomol and other organizations put on rival evenings of folk dances, which were undeniably collective in form and socialist in content. These did not become a great attraction. Some of the more percep-tive officials arranged combined evenings, in which a political lecture was followed by ballroom dancing, and in this way they had a chance of reaching their all-important participation targets by exploiting the fox-trot.

The Komsomol, like the party, remained unattractive to women. Many fathers forbade their daughters frequenting Komsomol clubrooms; this was less a manifestation of outmoded patriarchal authority than of plain common sense, for such premises could be the scene of alcoholic and sexual orgies. The Komsomol therefore remained primarily an organization for young men. It was meant to be a first step toward full party membership, but its political activities in most localities were confined to the superficial, exciting, and unchallenging. Throwing stones at priests could sometimes be one such activ-ity, perhaps because it satisfied all three of these criteria. Over the decades the Komsomol would become more respectable, and more young women would join. It would come in some ways to resemble, say, the Young Conservatives in Britain, offering the ambience of a dating club and bringing young people into contact with politicians, and into forms of activism like electioneering. It would differ from the YCs, however, in that membership would be almost essential for anybody wishing to get ahead.

Literature and the arts

The arts did not flourish during the years of revolution and civil war. In literature, there was a shortage of paper and of writers. Only poetry made headway, for it could express the spirit of the times while requiring a min-imum of paper. Two celebrated poets of the Revolution, with little in common except their premature deaths, were Blok and Mayakovsky.

Once called 'the last of the penitent nobles', Blok had already established his poetic reputation by 1917. He had long felt the coming of the Revolution, which he knew would be distasteful to him but which he acknowledged to be justified historically and spiritually. His verse, though highly innovative, had its roots in classical Russian poetry. After 1917 his everyday themes, and his acceptance of the Revolution, meant that Blok more than any other poet was able to interest and even enthuse the proletarian masses.

Mayakovsky was revolutionary from his childhood, and had joined the Bolsheviks while still an adolescent. The most celebrated of the pre-war Futurists, by temperament and style he felt absolutely at home in revolutionary Russia. Devoting himself to its cause, he expressed the feelings of the people in revolt, without lowering himself or his talent as did some other poets. His poetry was novel in both form and content. Of his several poetic tributes to the Revolution, *150,000,000* became best known. The 150 million are the Soviet people, the hero of the poem. This people is opposed by one person, President Wilson. The poem is a partisan portrayal of the conflict between capitalism and socialism, an essay in anti-Americanism, and an affirmation of polarization (there are two extremes, red and white, and nothing in between). Later, particularly after the end of War Communism, Mayakovsky seemed to grow disenchanted with the Bolsheviks, resenting in particular their philistinism and their reincarnation of the old bureaucracy. In *The Bathhouse* (1930) he bitterly and satirically portrayed a government department headed by a communist official named Pobedonosikov, 'a living piece of socialism' who spends his virtuous and ideologically pure life composing speeches on revolution, signing documents, and applying rubber stamps. Although Mayakovsky earned the active dislike of officials, there remained many old Bolsheviks who regarded him as their own poet; his suicide in 1930 was a great shock for the party. After his death he was enshrined as the poet of the Revolution, but editions of his works omitted his later, stinging, poems.

In the early 1920s the spirit of new freedom, which pervaded many sectors of Russian life, encouraged writers to experiment with lively new ideas. Provided writers were not blatantly anti-revolutionary they were free to write what they wished; they were not forced to follow any dictates from the party, as they would be in the following years, although they might be subjected to humiliating criticism. Not many of the pre-war giants of Russian literature were still writing in the 1920s and this, together with a growing literacy and the government's encouragement of literature, provided a healthy demand for the work of new writers. Starting in about 1922, new novels began to appear as young writers returned from their service with the Red Army or with the partisans, ready to give their experience a fictional form. The Civil War phase of the young Soviet literature culminated in 1929 with *And Quiet Flows the Don*, a long novel worthy of comparison with the great Russian novels of the nineteenth century. Basically it is a novel about the impact of the Great War, the Revolution, and the Civil War on the life of the Don Cossacks. The main character joins the Red Army for a while, before his distaste for the cruelty of the Whites is joined by an equally strong distaste for the cruelty of the Reds (he finally joins the Greens). The action takes place over a wide range of time and place, and the plot contains secondary characters and themes, together with real-life personalities undisguised by fictitious names. In all this it resembles, although hardly rivals, *War and Peace*. The author portrays the Whites and Reds with commendable impartiality, but some changes were made in the later editions. It was with this book that Sholokhov established a reputation which his subsequent productions hardly maintained.

Not all writers during the 1920s occupied themselves with Civil War subjects, and there was much experimentation as new, revolutionary, writers were encouraged to show what they could do. Although writers directly opposed to the regime were not published, not all of the new generation were committed to communism. Those who were thus committed were classified by the critics as 'proletarian writers' while those who merely accepted the Revolution were called 'fellow-travellers'. Some of the 'fellow-travellers' were influenced by Zamyatin. The latter, already established as a writer before the Revolution, in the 1920s began to imply that communism had an inhumane side; his novel *We*, which foreshadowed Orwell's *Nineteen Eighty-Four*, was one of the first Soviet novels to achieve world renown while being banned at home. But while the regime refused to publish *We*, it tolerated the satirical works of Il'f and Petrov, who poked fun at the New Soviet Man. Especially popular among Russians were this pair's *The Twelve Chairs* and *The Golden Calf*, which portrayed the conventionalized eccentricities of the 1920s as people habituated themselves to the new revolutionary standards: the compulsive slogan-eering ('Brass Bands: The Path to Collective Creativity'), the street renaming ('Lena Massacre Street'), the compromises between tradition and revolution ('Cooperative Saviour Square'),[1] the boring formal speeches by party men and officials on all possible occasions, the former noblemen quietly working as bureaucrats in government offices, the 'Moscow Bun Artel' which baked no buns but speculated in clothing.

Among the émigré writers who reconciled themselves to the new regime and returned were Aleksei Tolstoy and Gorki. Tolstoy in the 1930s turned to adulation of Stalin in his *Bread*, but he also wrote a notable trilogy describing the agonies of the intelligentsia between 1914 and 1921 (*Road to Calvary*). Gorki, who had been appalled by the Bolsheviks' actions, yet respected them and Lenin as possible saviours of Russia, emigrated in 1921 but returned in 1928. He became a Soviet icon, praised the regime, and used his influence to protect the arts and artists.

In the late 1920s, Russian writers came under severe pressure. The 'fellow-travellers' fell out of favour, and the proletarian writers were elevated to a position in which they could dictate literary policy through their Association

---

1. But life could still be stranger than fiction; St Petersburg's Maternity Centre became the Rosa Luxemburg Milk Drops Centre.

of Proletarian Writers ('RAPP'). But this and other associations were abolished in 1932, and replaced by the Writers' Union. This became the sole professional organization of writers and contained within itself a party organization to ensure, among other things, that writers either conformed or remained unpublished.

The party

During the Civil War the most valued party members had been those who best fulfilled urgent tasks, if necessary by holding a bayonet at their fellow-countrymen's throats. But under NEP many of the more hardened Bolsheviks found that their rough-and-ready methods were no longer appreciated by party organizers who now worked in neat offices with neat typists and neat rows of rubber stamps. At the same time, the authority which party organizers had acquired over members did not disappear, even though the practice of party bureaux directing unquestioning members was incompatible with the pre-revolutionary concept of the party; 'democratic centralism' had become all centre with no democracy. Meanwhile, those appointed to administrative posts tended to lose contact with ordinary party members and ordinary people. When there was a conflict, administrative convenience usually prevailed. When Lenin in his final years railed against 'inner-party bureaucracy' it was these tendencies that he had in mind.

Nevertheless Lenin attacked groups which criticized what they regarded as the deterioration of their party. Prominent among these were the so-called Left Communists, who had regarded such decisions as the peace with Germany and the employment of ex-tsarist officers as threats to the party's purity. There was also the Workers' Opposition, which grouped members who believed that the workers were not receiving their just reward from the revolution they had made, and that non-worker elements were too influential inside the party. Then there was the group for democratic centralism, which demanded more genuine democracy in the party. Spurred by his antipathy toward the Workers' Opposition, Lenin persuaded the Party Congress, at the time of the Kronstadt Revolt, to approve a 'ban against factions'. This meant that, although a member might oppose a proposal, joining with other members in opposing it after it had been adopted as policy could lead to expulsion. This ban effectively ended real discussion of many critical issues, but was justified by the leadership on the grounds that the party was still in danger and could not risk splits. Since the other left-wing, non-Bolshevik, parties were about to be finally eliminated[2] this meant there was no longer a tolerated source of organized

2. This would be achieved by the 1922 show trial of surviving Socialist Revolutionary leaders. Many SRs and Mensheviks had already joined the Bolsheviks. Among the ex-Mensheviks were Lenin's commissar for foreign affairs Chicherin (an aristocrat of ancient lineage), and Vyshinsky, who would lower himself into high office in the 1930s.

criticism of current policies. The ban on factions (in effect a ban on one member joining with one or more others to express dissent) helped to ensure that ideological intolerance would steadily impregnate the communist party. It would later help Stalin to overcome his critics piecemeal.

Another, more basic, threat to the party was the disappearance of its ostensible *raison d'être*, the proletariat it was supposed to lead. Not only had the Revolution occurred in a country lacking the developed capitalistic society which Marx had envisaged, but the small proletariat had almost disappeared during the Civil War. True, there were urban workers, but few of them were the experienced and politically conscious men of 1917. The latter had been killed while fighting for or against the Bolsheviks in the Civil War, or had become Bolshevik officials and army officers, or had left the factories in favour of the countryside. The factory workers of the early 1920s were largely ex-peasants, ill-educated, ill-disciplined, and not particularly interested in the party. Thus the Bolsheviks, who claimed to be 'the vanguard of the proletariat', found themselves in the van with nothing to guard. This is what Lenin implied when he surprised his followers by saying that the workers were uncultured in terms of education and behaviour, and that the first task was to raise them to at least the level of bourgeois culture. This is what he meant when he opposed the admission of too many additional workers into the party.

Typically enough, after Lenin's death the leadership did precisely what he would have deplored by starting a mass party recruitment drive which, again typically enough, came to be known as the 'Lenin Enrolment'. Recruiting targets were set for the various party districts, which they had great difficulty in filling. This difficulty came partly from a general reluctance to join a party that was so much distrusted, and partly from selection processes that tended to exclude the mentally or psychologically unfit. Various sticks and carrots were proffered, but the most useful remedy was a lowering of selection standards.

After this drive the party could roughly be divided into three components: the small and diminishing number of members who had struggled and suffered under the tsars, the members who had joined in the Civil War, and the large number recruited in the Lenin Enrolment. The 'Old Bolsheviks', which included most of the party's intelligentsia, was a diminishing band although it was well represented in the senior reaches of the party. To some extent it liked to regard itself as the conscience of the party, which meant that at times it had the aspect of an embattled minority. Members enrolled in the Civil War were mainly addicted to wartime standards of behaviour, placing great faith in the effectiveness of violence. This cohort had difficulty settling down in the more pacific atmosphere of the New Economic Policy. Some of its members gave up their ideals and simply exploited the opportunities that party membership gave them. Some were expelled from the party in periodic purges. Others, notably in Siberia, cherished their violent traditions and, joining together, indulged in 'Red banditry', burning the property of the newly rich, operating protection rackets against the private entrepreneurs they so much deplored, and generally escaping justice because they were, after all, party members. Members of the Lenin and subsequent enrolments tended to be poorly educated, and many were illiterate. Special schools were organized for them, where they learned to cope with words and figures and emerged with the ability to understand and carry out party directives, but not much else. Together with some remnants of the Civil War recruitments, it was these new men and women who would be pushed upwards to take over the positions of the senior administrators and managers destined to be purged in the oncoming years. These rapidly rising people were called *vydvizhentsy*, one of those words whose meaning depended on the tone in which it was voiced ('high-flyers' as against 'upstarts'). Some of the *vydvizhentsy* became genuine successes, but the majority were mediocrities, or worse, who needed, and would be needed by, the Stalinist way of life.

For those not destined to fly high, party membership nevertheless gave a social uplift that increased opportunities for inebriation and womanizing. Many found ways of enriching themselves, parading themselves in their own vehicles and parading their wives in smart clothes, who in turn paraded their poodles or other treasures. In these manifestations they were no different from the most ostentatious of the new private traders, and sometimes they indeed were the new private traders. In the countryside, where party members were very few, some tried to follow party instructions and found their lives were made uncomfortable, while others tended to sympathize with their neighbours and disdain the instructions they received from their district secretaries. Here too, but more so, party membership gave a social boost; the poor peasant who signed up in the Lenin Enrolment might set about marrying the daughter of a rich peasant, or even of the village priest. This was not quite what communism was about, and serious party activists saw it as another example of how the new relaxation was threatening to make a mockery of the Revolution. The frequent failure of village party members to gain election to village soviets emphasized their disquiet (these local elections were relatively free and open in the mid-1920s).

The end of Lenin

From late 1921 to his death in January 1924, Lenin suffered a series of major and minor strokes. Some deprived him temporarily of the ability to write or speak, while that of March 1923 virtually ended his life in politics. Far from withdrawing into inactivity during this painful period in which haemorrhage succeeded haemorrhage, Lenin, so far as he was able, devoted himself to combating dangerous tendencies in the party. In early 1922 it appears that he was not as greatly alarmed as later. He had approved the ban on factions and the appointment of Stalin to the new position of general secretary (that is, chief secretary) of the party. It was perhaps these two moves more than any others which laid the foundations for the misfortunes which were to befall the party in later decades.

A serious difference, which deepened Lenin's misgivings about Stalin, arose over Georgia. The Georgian communists did not relish Moscow's suggestion that Georgia, Armenia, and Azerbaizhan should be amalgamated. But the Politburo's representative in Georgia, Ordzhonikidze, and his fellow-Georgian Stalin (still commissar for nationalities) nevertheless tried to impose amalgamation. Also, Stalin's proposal for a Russian Federation in which nations like Georgia and the Ukraine would be constituent 'autonomous republics' was unwelcome both to the national communist parties and to Lenin. In the Politburo, Stalin condemned Lenin's counter-proposals, accusing his absent leader of 'national liberalism'. But when it became evident that the Politburo majority supported Lenin, Stalin backed down.

In Lenin's scheme, the Russian Federation was not governed by the Russian Republic's government, but by a union (i.e. federal) government, making the Russian Republic the equal of the other national republics. Because Georgia, while welcoming this, still opposed the amalgamation of Georgia, Armenia, and Azerbaizhan, Stalin and Ordzhonikidze conducted a Georgian-style vendetta against the leaders of the Georgian communist party. What was probably the turning point in Lenin's attitude came when he heard that Ordzhonikidze had struck a Georgian communist leader; Lenin's own appointee, in other words, had behaved like one of the very worst tsarist governors. Henceforth Lenin was determined to solve the nationalities problem without recourse to 'Muscovite chauvinism', and to cleanse the party leadership of its high-handed and bureaucratic characters. In December 1922 he asked Trotsky to form a 'counter-bureaucratic' bloc.

Despite his stroke of 13 December, Lenin began a thorough examination of the Georgian affair. He worked through his wife and secretaries, writing and telephoning when he was able; he no longer trusted the information supplied by Stalin. The latter was disquieted by the increasingly intimate correspondence passing between Lenin and Trotsky, and telephoned Krupskaya to arrange a meeting between himself and the invalid. Krupskaya refused to allow such a visit, and Stalin showered her with threats and vintage adjectives.

After another stroke on 23 December, Lenin was allowed to dictate only for a few minutes each day, and that is how in that last week of December the various notes known as Lenin's 'testament' were written. Lenin wished, before it was too late, to moderate the party's bureaucratism and authoritarianism. Although he appeared close to death, he refrained from suggesting who should succeed him, but he did offer some guiding comments. Most quoted is his comment on Stalin: 'Comrade Stalin, having become General Secretary, has concentrated unlimited authority in his hands, and I am not sure whether he will always be capable of using that authority with sufficient caution.'[3] Then followed an appreciation of Trotsky's pre-eminence in terms of sheer ability, coupled with a warning of his excessive self-confidence and high-handedness. After this there was an ambiguous reference to Kamenev and Zinoviev, simply mentioning that they had opposed the October uprising but should not be condemned for this. Lastly, Lenin envisaged a bright future for the young pair Bukharin and Pyatakov. The comment on Stalin was not as damaging as it might seem, because by mentioning Stalin before Trotsky it acknowledged that Stalin was now pre-eminent. Zinoviev and Kamenev, who fancied themselves as Lenin's immediate colleagues, were relegated to a passing mention. Lenin probably had reached the conclusion that there was no one person fit to succeed him; until younger aspirants matured, the best hope lay in an unlikely cooperation of Trotsky and Stalin, with the party keeping a stern eye on both. Lenin must have realized that as general secretary Stalin had amassed so much personal leverage that, irrespective of ability, he had much greater power than the other leaders. Presumably he also feared that Stalin's great and growing power would prevent a dual Trotsky–Stalin leadership on equal terms after his death.

This problem, the imbalance caused by Stalin's power, Lenin tackled two weeks later in a postscript to his 'testament'. In the meantime he had been investigating the Georgian affair; the more he learned of this the more he distrusted Stalin. Hence the hardened attitude expressed in this postscript. He now proposed the dismissal of Stalin from the general secretaryship, replacing him by a man 'more patient, more loyal, more courteous, and more considerate of his comrades, less capricious'. Lenin also dictated five newspaper articles which, among other things, castigated Stalin's management of the Workers' and Peasants' Inspectorate.

In early March Lenin's secretaries presented him with their conclusions on the Georgian affair, confirming his earlier misgivings. As part of his 'testament' he had in December written that Ordzhonikidze and Stalin had acted like bullies, aided by Dzerzhinski, showing that intense Russian chauvinism so typical of Russianized non-Russians, and that all three should be condemned by the party. Now, conscious that his days were numbered, he asked Trotsky to defend the Georgians before the Central Committee against the persecutions of Stalin and others. About the same time he wrote to Stalin demanding an apology for the insults which the latter had directed at Krupskaya. The next day he had a severe stroke. By 10 March he was half-paralysed and speechless; his political activity was finished. In his last active days he had done what he could to reduce Stalin, to overcome party bureaucracy, and to fight 'Great

---

3. Lenin, *Sochineniya*, 4th edn., xxxvi. 544.

Russian chauvinism'. As things turned out, he failed. Lenin was only 54 when he died. Stalin would live another three decades, to the age of 73.

Stalin

Born in Georgia in 1879, Iosif Vissarionovich Djugashvili later adopted the name Stalin as a revolutionary pseudonym. His father was violent, and his mother pious. He attended a local church school and then went to train for the priesthood at the Orthodox Seminary in Tbilisi. At school he impressed his teachers, and threw his weight around among his fellow-pupils. His record at the Seminary was also good, at first. As his later career demonstrated, he had all the makings of a successful Orthodox churchman and would no doubt have gone far if his mother's pious intentions had not been frustrated. While at the Seminary Stalin became interested in revolutionaries and their ideas. His sympathy towards them became known to his teachers. His academic work deteriorated. He failed to attend the penultimate examinations and this, almost automatically, led to his expulsion. He emerged as a mixed-up teenager, seeking a job and closer contact with the revolutionaries. By this time his basic characteristics were entrenched. He remained a Georgian even though he had received a Russian education. His priestly education later seemed to be reflected in his outward humility, and in the style of his writings and argumentation, which suggested that he might well have become a convincing preacher.

By his early twenties he was well known among local Social Democrats. He took some part in the strike movement in the Caucasus and attended party conferences abroad, including the 1907 London conference. He was also one of the organizers of armed 'expropriations' (including the notorious 1907 Tbilisi banknote robbery) which simultaneously financed and discredited the Bolshevik faction. During the pre-war decade he was arrested and exiled from time to time, but except in the final case escaped. In 1913 he was in Vienna, writing a theoretical treatise, at the request of Lenin, about the nationalities problem. He then returned to Russia, was arrested, and sent to Siberia, where he stayed until liberated by the February Revolution. Until Lenin's return he supported Kamenev's policy of cooperation with the other socialist parties, but then became a loyal adherent of Lenin's policies. After October he was appointed people's commissar for nationalities; being himself a member of one of the national groups of the former Russian Empire he was a natural choice for this post. During the Civil War he was also a military commissar and clashed with Trotsky on several matters. From 1919 he was additionally in charge of the Workers' and Peasants' Inspectorate, which gave him a right to interfere in the operations of all government departments. He was closely associated with the party's organization bureau (*Orgburo*), which allocated and recalled members to and from key posts. Then, in 1922, the Politburo appointed him to the new position of party general secretary.

Party leaders, well versed in European history, had always been vigilantly on guard against a Bonaparte emerging from their ranks. But while watching for Corsicans they overlooked the Georgian in the woodpile. They were pleased by Stalin's assumption of the drudgery which his new office implied; while he was labouring over his files they could devote themselves to higher things. The new duties inevitably led, however, to great influence inside the party. With two associates, Molotov and Kuibyshev, as assistant secretaries, Stalin appointed and dismissed party organizers (enabling him gradually to place congenial men in key posts), and prepared the agenda and supplied information for Politburo meetings. Power devolved onto what Trotsky disgustedly described as the 'secretarial bureaucracy'.

In the disputes which split the Politburo after Lenin's departure, the rival factions discovered that Stalin was a required ally because, among other things, he had by this time been able to install many of his protégés in the Central Committee; in other words, he could deliver the votes. Trotsky may have called him 'the most eminent mediocrity in the party', but in the 1920s it was votes, not intellects, which counted. And in any case Stalin may not have been all that mediocre. Despite their refined intellects, men like Zinoviev and Bukharin habitually backed the wrong horses. Surrounded as he was by highly developed minds which clouded and distorted every problem with all kinds of complexities, Stalin's outward simplicity must sometimes have seemed like genius.

Stalin and the succession

Trotsky was the man whose intelligence matched that of Lenin, but he lacked the ability to lower himself into the drudgery of politics and moreover from time to time could act with fascinating idiocy. He did not have Lenin's prestige in the party, and hence had less power of persuasion. He excelled as the commentator, the critic, the orator, the executor of policies, and as such had been an ideal complement to Lenin. With Lenin gone, Trotsky lost his most important role.

After Lenin died in 1924, the body was brought to Moscow. Like a saint of the Russian Orthodox Church, it was embalmed and glass-cased, and later put on permanent exhibition in a red marble mausoleum.[4] Subsequently, the locomotive of the funeral train was laid to rest in a temple-like structure in Moscow, to be revered by guided tourists.[5] Thus sanctification of Lenin, and all things (but not persons) connected with Lenin, had begun almost before the body was cold. Trotsky was not at the funeral (he was taking a health

---

4. For those who might be interested, there is a very detailed account of Lenin's embalming, by one of the embalming team: I. Zbarsky, *Lenin's Embalmers* (2001).

5. In the 1990s this 'temple-like structure' became a showroom for German-made automobiles.

cure and later claimed that Stalin misled him about the date). In the funeral rituals Stalin stood out as the first disciple of the late leader, and soon began to use the term 'Leninism' to support his own arguments. 'Leninism' began to denote orthodoxy, the 'correct' party line as laid down in the words of Lenin.

The term 'struggle for power' is misleading when applied to the party disputes of the 1920s. Issues of policy were deeply felt and could transcend personal discords. For the most part, the intrigues and manoeuvres of the contestants were motivated not so much by desire to get to the top as by the desire to keep others away from the top. Although Stalin seemed to win every trick, he did not follow a long-term plan. He did not need to, he could stand back and watch his rivals dig their own graves, occasionally offering his spade to one or other of them.

Trotsky lost an opportunity when, contrary to Lenin's wishes, he did not attack Stalin on the Georgian question. This was the penultimate occasion when he could have opposed the general secretary with Lenin's prestige behind him; his failure to do so is perhaps explicable by his awareness that over previous months several party leaders had been chafing at Lenin's authoritarianism and had had some doubts about his judgements. The last chance was Lenin's 'testament', but this was neutralized with Trotsky's acquiescence; when in May 1924 the Central Committee was acquainted with Lenin's criticism of Stalin, it was proposed that since Stalin had since improved, there was no need to carry out Lenin's wishes in this matter. This was agreed, and it was also decided to keep the 'testament' secret.[6] Thus another damaging weapon against Stalin had been voluntarily sheathed, and could not be bared again without defying the decision of the Central Committee.

While Lenin was dying a triumvirate of Stalin, Zinoviev, and Kamenev had provided the party's leadership, and had already fired the opening salvos against Trotsky. The alliance of these three was essentially a means to prevent Trotsky gaining a majority in the Politburo, and thereby becoming *de facto* leader of the party. Trotsky's arrogance and conceit made him very unpopular in certain sections of the party: the *apparat* tended to dislike him, partly because he was an upstart ex-Menshevik, but largely because he attacked the bureaucratization of the party and because the intellectuals of his own generation could not forgive him his arrogant brilliance. Nor did the new generation of workers favour Trotsky. On the other hand, students and recent students, government workers, and much of the Red Army respected him. The expansion of the party brought in a mass of ignorant and docile characters, willing to vote the way the local party organizers wished (and the local party

6. It was published by the *New York Times* in 1926, but was not revealed in the USSR until after Stalin's death.

organizers were more and more Stalin's men). Meanwhile, purges of the existing membership tended to discriminate against members known to be supporters of Trotsky.

By 1925 party membership was just over 1 million. The new members were easily controlled by the party organizers; many workers were glad to be admitted because unemployment was rising and party membership helped to obtain, or retain, a job. Others found themselves on committees or taken into full-time party work. Contrary to the party's rules, the new members were allowed to vote in the selection of resolutions and delegates to be sent to the 13th Party Congress in 1924. When that Congress opened in Moscow, it was largely composed of delegates who would turn a deaf, if not uncomprehending, ear to Trotsky's oratory.

The policy issue on which Trotsky and the triumvirate were opposed at the Congress was the contradiction between NEP and the 'permanent revolution' as propounded by Trotsky. But there was little genuine debate as at previous congresses; instead, there was mass applause, mass condemnation, and predetermined votes as the well-instructed Stalinist delegates went into action. Trotsky's arguments were defeated by non-argumentative means and he was unwilling to split the party by forming an oppositional bloc. Nor did he seek to take belated advantage of Lenin's 'testament'. Later, Trotsky was to declare that 'a man can be right only with the party'. This reluctance to split the party was one of the basic reasons for his fall. After his defeat at this Congress his hands were tied; in 1921 he had warmly approved the ban on factions and now this ban could be used against him if he sought to organize opposition. However, he did not accept Zinoviev's demand to recant publicly his past errors. And in October he published *Lessons of October*, a pamphlet on party democracy which bitterly criticized Kamenev and Zinoviev.

With Trotsky weakened, Stalin began to diverge from Zinoviev and Kamenev. In the preceding controversies he had remained in the background, allowing his two allies a free field in their disputes with Trotsky: the wrangles thus tended to lower the public reputation of Zinoviev, Kamenev, and Trotsky, but not of Stalin. At this time NEP and 'socialism in one country' were complementary. Bukharin was a proponent of NEP, and Stalin was a champion of 'socialism in one country' (the concept[7] directly opposed to Trotsky's 'permanent revolution'). Hence there was emerging a new alliance between Bukharin and Stalin, both of whom advocated peasant prosperity and, following from this, more peasants in the party. But in Leningrad and the north-west, the local party organizers were still largely Zinoviev's protégés, and ignored the summons to foster peasant recruitment. Meanwhile the Zinovievites prepared to argue for a reversal of the party's pro-peasant

7. The theory of 'socialism in one country' held that it was indeed possible for Russia to build a socialist society without waiting for more advanced countries' revolutions to take place.

recruitment drive at the forthcoming 14th Congress in late 1925. But by this time the press was largely a controlled press, and one feature of a controlled press is the ease with which it can promote the uncorrectable smear. For example, one of Zinoviev's supporters had advocated that 90 per cent of the party should be workers and *Pravda* chose to interpret this as a ludicrous suggestion that 90 per cent of the workers should be party members. In ways similar to this, the other arguments of the Zinovievites were distorted, and at the 14th Congress Zinoviev and Kamenev were defeated when they proposed a vote of no-confidence in Stalin. Many of Zinoviev's and Kamenev's supporters did not dare to vote for their patrons.[8]

Consolidating his victory, Stalin sent Kirov to undermine Zinoviev's position as Leningrad party secretary. Kirov succeeded so well that in 1927 he was himself elected in Zinoviev's place. Kamenev and Zinoviev were already seeking an alliance with their old enemy Trotsky, and in 1926 all three had unfruitfully criticized party policy before the Central Committee, pointing to the soft line towards the richer peasants, the growing bureaucracy, and failures abroad. Following this, Zinoviev was excluded from the Politburo.[9] Kamenev lost his position as commissar for foreign trade, being replaced by the Armenian Mikoyan. Trotsky had already been deprived of his key (and potent) position of commissar for war in January 1925. Nevertheless the opposition continued to oppose, sometimes even visiting party cells to agitate among the grass roots. The *apparat* responded with 'spontaneous' interruptions of speeches, and other short-term measures. In October 1926, Trotsky and Kamenev were expelled from the Politburo, and Zinoviev lost his chairmanship of the Comintern. But the leadership's failures abroad during 1927, especially the massacre of the Chinese communists, again aroused the opposition. Trotsky even hinted that if, as seemed likely, Russia was again attacked by foreign powers, he would ask for dictatorial powers and direct the war effort.

Trotsky and Zinoviev were expelled from the Central Committee and, after some of their supporters had attempted to organize street demonstrations, they were expelled from the party as well. Other pressures later resulted in the expulsion of about seventy-five of their leading supporters, and the suicide of others. At the 15th Party Congress in late 1927, appeals by both 'left' and 'right' spokesmen to give the accused a hearing were shouted down by the majority, Stalin's 'centre'. Complete confession and recantation were demanded. Eventually Kamenev and Zinoviev did recant, enabling them to be readmitted to party activity for a few more pathetic years. Trotsky refused to recant. In 1928 he was bundled by the GPU into a train for Central Asia. At first his exile was

8. By this time the GPU was intervening, at the lower levels, in party quarrels.

9. Until 1925 this top decision-making party body consisted of Stalin, Trotsky, Bukharin, Kamenev, Rykov, Tomsky, and Zinoviev, but in that year Stalin had added three of his adherents, Kalinin, Molotov, and Voroshilov.

fairly comfortable, and he maintained contact with some of his supporters. However, when Stalin adopted an industrialization programme very similar to his own, many of his adherents transferred their loyalties to Stalin. Perhaps because of this, Stalin felt strong enough in 1929 to expel Trotsky from the USSR.

With most countries refusing to receive him, and with both Stalin's agents and bitter White emigrants threatening his life, Trotsky finally made his home in Mexico. Assisted by other left-wing emigrants, he published a succession of damaging anti-Stalinist books and articles which Stalin appears to have taken very seriously, if not fearfully. Stalin's secret agents kept Trotsky under very effective surveillance and, in individual swoops and in the purges, Trotsky's family and former colleagues were obsessively hunted down. Trotsky himself was finally assassinated in 1940.

A man of great literary and expositional talent, at the peak of his career Trotsky had been admired by many though liked by few. His air of intellectual superiority seemed threatening to some, and unlikeable to others. He had shaped the Bolshevik Revolution so much that even after years of vilification much of what he had done still stood. This included many of his lies (his explanation of the Kronstadt Revolt, for example, remained the standard Soviet version). The oath sworn by Red Army recruits continued to use his formulation of words, and so on. More fundamentally, Lenin and Trotsky were co-inventors of the twentieth-century violent one-party state, a concept which they brought to fruition in and after 1917. They both rejected the warnings of other socialists about what the replacement of democracy and legality by coercion could lead to. But those socialists, so decisively routed in 1917 and 1918, were proved right in the end. Trotsky's triumph in consigning Martov to 'the garbage bin of history' was premature indeed; better the garbage bin than the chamber of horrors.

Agriculture under NEP

After thus defeating the 'left' opposition with the aid of the 'right', Stalin was ready to turn against his former allies. A conflict impended as soon as Stalin decided that a hard line should be taken with the peasantry.

The expropriations of 1917–20 meant that average landholdings grew smaller as the larger holdings were divided up.[10] Among those who lost their land were many of those who had taken advantage of the Stolypin reforms

---

10. By 1919, 97% of the arable land was held by individual peasants, with the remainder farmed by communes, *artels*, state, or collective organizations. While the proportion of landless peasants had fallen from 11% in 1917 to 6% by late 1919, and the proportion of horseless peasants from 29 to 18%, the proportion of landholdings larger than 22 acres had dropped from 8 to 3%. About four-fifths of peasant households had land areas of less than 11 acres. The proportion of households with more than one horse fell from 16% in 1917 to 8% in 1920 (Yu. Polyakov, *Perekhod k Nepu i sovietskoye krestyanstvo* (1967), 98, 103, 120).

and launched themselves as independent private farmers; most of them rejoined the commune so as to qualify for a share of the redistributed land. The *mir* and the unproductive strip system and three-field rotation prevailed. While the strengthening of the *mir* had a negative effect on productivity, more serious was the decline in marketability caused by the shrinkage of the average landholding. The poorest peasants produced no marketable food, consuming not only all they grew but often using income from other sources to buy additional food, whereas the pre-revolutionary rich peasants and landowners had marketed almost all their grain.

Thus after 1917 not only did production fall, but the food which was produced tended to be eaten by the peasants rather than sold. Demobilization of soldiers and the exodus from the towns meant more mouths in the villages to be fed from the same total land area. Savage requisitioning, sometimes of the seed itself, killed not only people, but incentive too. It was largely to remedy this situation, virtually an industrial revolution in reverse, that NEP was introduced. As such it was very successful. The financial inducements permitted by NEP not only encouraged peasants to sow more but, gradually, persuaded them to use more efficient methods (yields improved greatly during NEP). Thus surpluses were harvested that could be marketed (that is, used to feed the towns or gain foreign currency).

The party still lacked total control in the villages. The rural soviets were largely composed of peasants who gave priority to the interests of their own community. Peasant party members were few, partly because peasants saw party membership as a way of escaping from the villages. The younger generation of peasants also tended to move out, although enough stayed to dilute the conservative influence of the elders; this had been a factor in the spread of better farming techniques but had not made the villagers any more willing to be controlled by outsiders.

Once the famine of 1921–2 was over, it seemed that there would be enough food for all and for export too. This would permit reurbanization and reindustrialization. The party's dilemma in this situation was that the more the peasants prospered, the greater the ideological threat they seemed to present. The peasantry still represented 'petty bourgeois' attitudes, mixed with a dark, primitive, superstitious conservatism. And it vastly outnumbered the proletariat which, led by the party, was supposed to form the dictatorship of Russia. To many it seemed that any step to encourage the peasantry to produce more was a step which weakened socialism. The more the peasant exerted himself in response to the government's plea for more production, the more he prospered and developed bourgeois attitudes. Hence the disputes within the party on the correct attitude towards the peasants. Hence, too, the contradictory nature of the party's pronouncements, with exhortations to the peasants to prosper mixed with warnings of the fate awaiting rich peasants.

The great debate which, intertwined with the struggle between factions of the leadership, dominated the party for the half-dozen years following the death of Lenin was concerned above all with the problem of how to have productive agriculture without a prosperous 'bourgeois' peasantry. For without productive agriculture industrialization was impossible, and without industrialization there could be no socialism, it was thought.

But this 'great debate,' valid though it was, told only half the story. Stalin and a handful of other leaders would have been aware, from the secret GPU reports, that the government and party was in danger of losing control of the countryside. A nightmare that had its roots in the peasant revolts of tsarist times, and in memories of the 'Green' peasant armies in the Civil War, seemed to be once more threatening the regime. Food production had been increasing largely because the richer and middle peasants had been doing well. At the beginning of NEP there was more tolerance of the richer peasants; in fact for a time the term *kulak*, or 'tight-fist', had been dropped in favour of the more complimentary if equally absurd 'more cultured peasant'. Middle peasants who had the will and intelligence to increase their output also did well, which in the definitions of the party meant that they came to swell the number of richer peasants. This aroused the anxiety of party theorists who may, or may not, have been comforted by the statistical sleight of hand that raised the barrier leading to rich status; for example, in 1928 possession of six cows was enough to place a peasant in the category of kulak, with its attendant increased taxation, disenfranchisement, and expulsion of children from school, whereas in 1925 the barrier had been set at only three cows.

Thus there was a new and growing class of successful peasants. They were shrewd, too. They could outwit hostile party people or, worse, knew how to enlist their support. In fact the local party members for the most part saw clearly that the quasi-market economy of the villages was leading to greatly increased food production, and they had the choice of supporting this new class of forward-looking peasants or of opposing this new class of rich bourgeois elements. Those who supported the new class might quietly look the other way when a prospering peasant divided his assets among friends so as to avoid passing into the 'rich' category, or might even join a comradely combination of rich peasants to give respectability to a larger and more efficient production unit that could qualify for one of those tractors the government was selectively allocating to the villages.

Richer peasants tended to get elected to their village soviets and were frequently summoned to district conferences where they were compelled to listen to lectures by party functionaries. But they were not afraid to express their opinions, and there was a widespread demand for a peasant trade union to protect peasant rights (in particular, to protect, or reinstate, the peasant's right to a fair price for produce). A peasant trade union was the last thing the party wanted, but despite efforts to repress the idea the demand persisted.

The enlarging class of richer peasants also had the power that money can give. They had the kind of confidence that is built by success in the face of obstacles imposed by those of little understanding. They had the intelligence to exploit all possible loopholes. Above all, they seemed to exemplify a way of life vastly more promising than the variety of socialism pursued by the communist party.

To label this unwelcome class as kulaks, and then to set about 'destroying the kulaks as a class', therefore seemed to Stalin, and others, the best if not the only way to preserve themselves and the concept they called Leninism.

The industrialization debate

NEP had been accepted by the party as only a temporary retreat from its principles and intentions; following this breathing space there would be another economic offensive and further social reconstruction. The question of how long NEP would continue had never been settled, and from about 1925 a growing number of members favoured an early termination of the policy. This was partly because the question of 'where do we go from here?' became more acute at that time: pre-war industrial production was almost regained by 1926 and further increases could no longer be obtained merely by restoring existing plant.

Nor was it only a question of when. The most bitter dispute in the party was over the question of how. What came to be known as the Left Opposition (Trotsky and his supporters, joined after 1925 by Kamenev and Zinoviev) believed that NEP was a rotten compromise and was too soft towards the rich peasants. What was needed was rapid industrialization, for only thus would Russia become proletarianized and be ready for socialism. In order to raise capital for industrialization, the Left Opposition recommended a squeeze on the peasants, who would be required to sell their products cheaply while buying manufactured goods dearly. Trotsky's theory of permanent revolution was quite reconcilable with this industrialization, for the latter would be much more rapid after Germany and other industrial nations had undergone their own revolutions, enabling the proletariat of these more advanced nations to give economic aid to Russia. The so-called moderates (Bukharin, Rykov, Tomsky, and, at first, Stalin) ridiculed the high rates of industrialization advocated by the left. They considered that there should be a slow but steady industrialization. Industry would concentrate on consumer goods, and the availability of the latter would encourage the peasants to produce more; more grain meant more industrialization because it would permit growth of urban labour and of export earnings.

The conflict between these two views concerned means more than ends. Certain basic premisses were accepted by all: the party's retention of power; the need to industrialize; the need to prevent *nepmany* profiting from the shortages and confusion which industrialization would entail; the need to absorb the increasing unemployment caused by efficiency drives in industry; the desirability of exploiting the stronger position which the party and government had won over the previous four or five years. By 1927 there were additional reasons for industrialization; there was a genuine fear of war following setbacks in foreign policy, and the policy of maintaining low prices with goods in short supply was simply encouraging *nepmany* to buy cheap and sell dear. In general, therefore, the various anti-*nepmany* and industrial measures adopted between 1925 and 1928 had the approval of the whole party. These measures included railway tariff surcharges on 'private' freight, increased taxation of private activities, and the more stringent application of penalties for so-called speculation and hoarding.

The few leaders privy to the secret reports of the security service additionally knew that workers were drawing their own conclusions from the contrast between the low-productivity state industries and the efficient and prospering private industries, and moreover were staging strikes in favour of higher and punctual wages. The sad record of state industry was attributed by workers to party bosses, Jews, and the bourgeois technicians; show trials of technicians on charges of 'wrecking' would absorb some of this proletarian wrath.

Despite the shortage of funds, industrial investment was doubled in the year 1926–7. In that year were started some of the projects which later became famous as examples of economic achievement: the Dnieper hydroelectric scheme, the Stalingrad Tractor Plant, and the last link of the Turkestan–Siberia Railway. Then, in 1927, the Council of People's Commissars called for a national plan of industrialization: the planned economy was about to emerge.

The State Planning Commission (*Gosplan*) had existed since 1921, and some experience of nationwide planning had been gained in *Goelro*, a 1920 ten-year plan for electricity generation. Gosplan, staffed mainly by non-communist economists and statisticians, had at first merely produced sets of control figures. These were forecasts of what the various branches of industry could be expected to produce in a given period. They served as guidelines for economic decisions but were not targets; except for one or two key products, the trusts planned their own outputs and inputs. Later, as statistical services improved, Gosplan pioneered the formulation of 'national economic balances'. The latter were quantified analyses of the interconnections between different branches of industry so that, for example, a statistical forecast could be made of the changes in the forestry industry which would be required for a doubling of newspaper circulations. Such balances (on which the five-year plans would be based) could only be imperfect, because accurate statistics were not always available, and they could only be incomplete, because only the key branches of the economy could be covered by the limited number of clerks and statisticians available. Nevertheless, they were a great step forward in non-capitalist enterprise.

Such were the difficulties encountered in collating and formulating the First Five-Year Plan, a book-size document, that it was presented to the 16th Party Conference only in spring 1929, even though it covered the period October 1928 to September 1933. It was presented in two variants, a standard version and an optimum version with somewhat higher targets. The latter was chosen. Here are the rounded-off figures for three key industries:

	Coal (million tonnes)	Oil (million tonnes)	Pig iron (million tonnes)
Actual annual output 1927/8	35	12	3
Planned annual output 1932/3	75	22	10
Actual annual output 1932	64	21	6

In reality, both variants were overoptimistic. In existing circumstances the target of doubling industrial production over five years seemed impossible; there was simply not enough investment capital available. There was an emphasis on the output of means of production (that is, products which would be used to produce additional output): fuel, cement, machine tools, metals, timber. Grain was to be exported in exchange for modern machine tools. These salient aspects made the plan irreconcilable with the views of the moderates. However, Stalin had already politically routed the Trotskyites and could now make final his break with the Bukharinites. As for experts who condemned the plan as too optimistic, these were intimidated by the Shakhty show trial, which convicted several 'bourgeois' technicians of 'sabotaging' a mining enterprise. The road now seemed clear for Stalin's own revolution. This, which Stalin correctly termed 'the intensification of the class struggle', would be first felt in the villages.

Collectivization

There was a plausible economic argument for collectivization. Investment capital had to be squeezed out of the peasantry, and collectivization would make it easier to achieve this by procuring grain at rock-bottom prices. It would also release labour for the new factories, and by permitting large-scale operations would increase grain production. There was also the ideological argument. The alliance between workers and the not-so-rich peasants for which Lenin had hoped seemed unlikely to materialize. The peasantry were supplying the grain needed by the workers only on the basis of an un-socialist, if not downright bourgeois, way of life and work. From the ranks of the allegedly dull and superstitious rural masses a new and dangerous class of prosperous farmers was developing. The patience of Stalin and his supporters was wearing thin, and it is in terms of their desperate grasp for a final solution that the cruel fatuities of the collectivization drive are best understood, if understood at all.

Ever since 1917 there had been a tense expectation each autumn as Moscow received from the provinces accounts of how much grain had been marketed or procured. Fear of famine had perhaps receded during NEP, but the availability of grain for the towns and export was crucial. Under NEP food production had made a rapid recovery, exceeding the pre-war level in 1925. There was plenty of scope for further increase; for example, locusts, rats, and other pests were destroying, according to one Soviet economist, about one-third of the potential grain supply, and in 1927 there were 5 million hopelessly inefficient wooden ploughs still in use.

From the mid-1920s the private grain trader, who often paid the peasant double the state's price for grain, was increasingly restricted. Thus state and cooperative grain-purchasing organizations were in a stronger position, and could progressively lower their procurement prices. In 1924 the peasants' tax-in-kind had been replaced by a money tax, so in order to pay his taxes, as grain prices fell, the peasant would sell increasing amounts of grain. Or at least that was the expectation. In practice, this situation might initially have increased the grain marketed by the peasants, but in time economic reality and human nature triumphed; with grain prices falling and meat prices rising, peasants fed their grain to livestock, and those peasants who could afford to wait kept their surplus grain in the expectation of an increase in the state's purchasing price. At the end of 1927 incoming statistics showed that the grain procurements might be only three-quarters of those of the previous year.

Bukharin and others did advocate an increase in grain prices. For them, War Communism had shown the impossibility of coercing the peasantry. For others, however, War Communism was more an example to be exceeded. Many party members regarded long-standing economic realities simply as remnants of bourgeois thinking; the party which had stormed the Winter Palace was surely capable of overthrowing old economic concepts. So instead of substantially raising grain prices, Stalin went to western Siberia with a retinue which included police officials. Some of Stalin's trusted colleagues went to other grain areas. Using the Criminal Code's article on hoarding and speculation, and backed by police, it was possible to assert that any peasant with stocks of grain had broken the law, and that his grain was therefore liable to confiscation. Despite the soul-searching of local party members and officials, a thorough and sometimes violent programme of grain confiscation was carried out on these lines. These tactics, virtually a return to the forced requisitioning of War Communism, did bring forth needed grain, but reinforced old antagonisms.

Conciliation of the peasantry, as advocated by Bukharin, was no longer practical. However, in early 1928 the 'moderates' had not been eliminated from the party and their criticisms induced Stalin to promise that his extraordinary measures would not be repeated. But the promise was not kept; the 'Siberian method' would provide guidance for the future.

Partly because of the weather and partly because peasants reduced their sown area, the 1928 harvest was poor. Bread rationing was reintroduced. The 1929 harvest was good, yet by August 1929 grain procurements were causing anxiety. The several government and cooperative procuring agencies were uncoordinated, and there was corruption as well as bad management among their officials. The latter were not as adept at handling grain consignments as had been the private traders (who were finally eliminated in 1929). Peasants saw, or heard, how the grain which had been forced from them was left to rot in unprotected storage. The few state and collective farms were as reluctant as the independent peasants to deliver their grain; in 1929 some farms were even 'decollectivized' as a punishment for this recalcitrance. Some local party officials complained that after requisitioning no grain was left for local consumption or even for seed. By October there was extensive though unorganized peasant violence which might conceivably, given leadership, have been transformed into a new Pugachov Rebellion. At this point *Pravda* began to hint about mass collectivization.

Hitherto the party had accepted only a gradual increase of *kolkhozy* (collective, cooperative, or communal farms) and of *sovkhozy* (state farms with wage-earning peasants). In 1928 about 3 per cent of the acreage was farmed by these organizations. The Five-Year Plan envisaged that up to 20 per cent of agricultural output would come from *kolkhozy* or *sovkhozy* by 1933. Collectivization was to be voluntary but the supply of tractors and combines to collectives was expected to prove a great inducement to join. The party, including Stalin, had accepted that a faster rate of collectivization was out of the question. Agricultural experts and rural party administrators were too few, and so were tractors and machines.

Thus massive-scale collectivization was regarded as impractical for the time being. Yet early in November 1929, just as Bukharin lost his seat in the Politburo, Stalin announced the decision to begin mass collectivization immediately. In December he declared the intention 'to liquidate the kulaks as a class'. In reality there was no such thing as a kulak class. In tsarist times kulak had referred to those rich peasants who lent money or services at extortionate rates to their poorer neighbours. When Stalin spoke of kulaks in 1929 he meant the richer peasants. These kulaks were hardly a class; they were an integral part of the villages, having family ties with poorer neighbours. They often set an example of good agricultural technique, they often owned machinery (including tractors) which they hired out at reasonable rates, they were usually respected by their neighbours, and more than others they responded to official encouragements to grow and sell more grain. During the forced procurements of 1928 and 1929 they had been hard pressed. Evidently seeing which way the wind was blowing, many had reduced their operations so as to merge into the mass of 'middle peasants' (the press hinted that this 'self-dekulakization' was some kind of conspiracy). In many localities, their land and implements had been confiscated because of alleged speculation, but in autumn 1929 the most serious action which the party Central Committee was prepared to take against them 'as a class' was to exclude them from collective farms.

What happened in the three months between Stalin's December announcement and his statement in March 1930 that 58 per cent of peasant households had been collectivized was ghastly. Party officials and members, often unwillingly, obeyed the instruction to 'fan the class war' in the villages. Poor peasants were invited to rob the richer. Of the so-called kulaks, some were sent to concentration camps and their families deported, others were merely deported to inhospitable regions. Some, lucky or regarded as innocuous, were allowed to stay in their district and were allocated land considered too poor to be worth collectivizing. This last group was subsequently eliminated by the imposition of impossible grain-delivery quotas, followed by deportation for failure to deliver. Peasants who resisted collectivization were classed as kulaks, or 'ideological kulaks', or 'sub-kulaks', and treated in the same way. One estimate was that at least a million families, or about 6 million people, were transported or expelled from their home villages as kulaks (a later, 1988, estimate went as high as one-eighth of the 25 million peasant families). Calculation is hampered by the circumstance that the number of those who set out was considerably more than those who arrived. The conditions of the transportation were not, as was later said, an anticipation of Hitler's Final Solution; they set a standard of depravity that Hitler never quite attained:

The old party member E. M. Landau in 1930 met one of these batches in Siberia. In the depth of winter a big group of kulaks with their families were being taken on carts 300 kilometres into the backwoods of the region. The children were shouting and crying from hunger. One of the peasants, who could no longer stand the cries of a baby sucking the dry breast of its mother, seized the infant from his wife's arms and smashed its head against a tree.[11]

The fundamental idiocy of the campaign is indicated by the 58 per cent collectivization claimed in March. To explain how such a massive rural reconstruction could be carried out in a few weeks at the height of the Russian winter must surely have strained the wits of the most flexible propagandist. What typically happened was that party or government activists, with police or military support, would persuade or force peasants to sign a register signifying their demand for collectivization. Then the party organization would duly report another village collectivized. Stock, implements, and buildings taken from the 'kulaks' usually formed the basis of the new collective farms.

11. *Novyi mir*, 3 (1988), 18, quoting the historian R. Medvedev.

By March in many localities the peasants were in a state of rebellion, and so were some party members. Since the spring sowing could not be postponed, the breakneck speed of collectivization was slackened. Stalin blamed local officials for so-called excesses. Making them look like fools, he accused them of being 'giddy with success':

by 20 February 1930 we had over-fulfilled the five-year plan for collectivization by more than 100 per cent . . . but successes have their dark side, especially when they are achieved with relative 'ease'—'unexpectedly' as it were. Such successes sometimes induce a spirit of conceit and vanity . . . people not infrequently become intoxicated by this kind of success . . . Can we assert that the voluntary principle and the principle of taking local peculiarities into account are not violated in some areas? No, unfortunately we cannot say that . . . Is it not clear that the authors of these distortions, imagining themselves to be 'Lefts', are really serving Right opportunism? . . . One such over-zealous 'socializer' even goes so far as to issue an order to an *artel* including the following instructions: 'all poultry of all households are to be registered within three days' . . . to say nothing of those revolutionaries (pardon the expression!) who begin the work of organizing artels by removing the church bells. Just think, removing church bells—how very revolutionary![12]

Thus, just as in tsarist times, the peasants were led to believe that their misery was due to the officials interposed between them and their 'little father' at the top. When Stalin announced that those peasants who so wished could quit the collectives, there was an immediate exodus. By June 1930 only 24 per cent of peasants were collectivized. However, a new drive, coercive but less hasty, brought 98 per cent of agricultural land into collective or state farms by 1941. The village commune, which in the 1920s tended to be much more influential than the village soviet, was abolished by decree in 1930.

A natural consequence of the upheaval was the deaths of millions of peasants in the rural famine of 1932–3. This famine, which may have equalled that of 1921–2, was not admitted and there was therefore no appeal for foreign aid, despite the agricultural glut which the capitalist world was enduring at that time. Not only the peasants' winter supply, but also sometimes seed grain, was requisitioned. The resultant famine was very much man-made, and affected the Ukraine in particular. Starving peasants were discouraged from stealing their own grain, intended for the towns or for export, by the extension of the death penalty to 'pilfering' state property.

At the height of the collectivization campaign many peasants slaughtered their cattle, rather than see them taken and collectivized. For those cattle which were collectivized, fate was often crueller: they froze to death because there were no large barns for them. Slaughter of horses meant that the shortage of farm tractive power became even more acute. By 1932 the cattle and pig population was half that of 1928, and the sheep population two-thirds.

12. *Pravda*, 2 Mar. 1930.

Urban communists sent to supervise the new collectives were ignorant of agriculture. Food production dropped abruptly and recovered very slowly; on the eve of the Second World War production may have even been lower than on the eve of the First World War.[13]

According to Churchill, Stalin privately admitted that the years of forced collectivization and famine had been the most frightening of his life. And well they might have been; many party members, as well as Stalin's wife Allilueva, committed suicide in this period. Paradoxically, the uproar in the countryside strengthened Stalin's position in the party. Even those who suspected the truth realized that Stalin was the leader most capable of mastering a peasant uprising.

Despite the elimination of the most productive peasant farmers, collectivization was regarded as having at least enabled agriculture to supply the capital and labour required for industrialization. But even this is not certain. It is true that procuring grain from collectives was relatively easy, but the total grain available was reduced. It is true that peasants left the farms to work in industry, but this was simply because industrialization and rural poverty made it advantageous for them to do so.[14] Collectivization did not raise labour productivity. It did eliminate rural unemployment since the unemployed were absorbed into the collectives, but collectivized peasants did not work so well. It seems likely, therefore, that collective farms were able to stand the initial loss of workers to the towns, not because they economized on labour, but because there had been a labour surplus before collectivization. Until tractors and machinery were plentiful, collective farming could not benefit from the larger-scale production units. And despite crash programmes and much talk of 'tractorization', there would remain an insufficiency of farm tractive power for several decades. Perhaps, to a revolutionary party, tractors and big fields had greater emotional appeal than fertilizers and mousetraps, but the 1930s would not have been so hungry if investment had been made less in tractors and more in fertilizers and pest control, and if the shift from small-scale to large-scale farming had been postponed.

The collective farm

Collective farms, varying from simple cooperatives to establishments of 100 per cent communal ownership, had been set up on a small and experimental scale well before 1929. As confirmed by the Model Collective Farm Charter of

---

13. Changing frontiers and statistical inadequacies mean that this is more a supposition than an assertion.

14. In some years they left in such embarrassingly large numbers that measures were taken to restrict their movement. When, in 1932, tsarist-style internal passports were revived, they were issued only to urban-dwellers. The peasant had to apply for official documentary permission to move from his village.

1935, the post-collectivization form of *kolkhoz* was the so-called *artel*. This was not regarded as a completely socialist form of production, but at least it was not capitalistic. Members of a *kolkhoz* pooled their implements and livestock in order to make production a communal task. They were granted the use of the land, though not its ultimate ownership. Their main task was the cultivation of the collective land, but each household was allowed to keep its own private plot of up to 1 acre, and could keep privately a cow, a pig, four sheep, and unlimited fowl. Moreover, the private animals could be pastured on collective land.

A typical *kolkhoz* consisted of from 50 to 100 households, and was generally rather decrepit-looking with few, if any, new or even painted buildings. Its chairman was unlikely to know much about farming, and was usually newly appointed, for this office had a high turnover, as each incumbent was dismissed by the local party secretary for failure to reach one or other of the production targets. The latter were frequently fixed at an impossible level so as to squeeze the maximum effort from the peasants. Although nominally organized democratically, with the members meeting in an assembly, in reality decisions were made by the farm chairman. Additional supervision was exercised by the management of the local machine and tractor station (MTS). The MTS were established to make the best use of the scarce tractors and farm machinery. They kept, manned, and maintained these machines, hiring them out to the surrounding collective farms.

Collective farmers were credited with 'workdays' in exchange for their labour on the collective fields. The workday value varied according to the quality of the particular kind of work,[15] so that it was possible to earn more or less than one workday in a working day. Peasants received no wage, but at the end of the agricultural year the profits of the farm were divided among the peasants in proportion to the workdays credited. Payments were also made in produce (usually grain) according to the same principle. In Stalin's lifetime the cash received by the peasant was negligible or non-existent; agricultural prices were deliberately kept low, so that very few farms made any profit. At the same time, prices of products bought by the peasants were allowed to rise steeply (cloth by up to ten times, sugar by six times).

The first priority of the collective farm was to meet its procurement quota of grain or other products. This delivery to the state was at very low prices; the state sold it in the towns at higher, but still low, prices (thus providing cheap food). If the state quotas were met peasants could sell the surplus on the free market. The latter, in its legal and typical form, was a few stalls in a nearby town where peasant women purveyed food to urban-dwellers. The main significance of this market, which was a bastion of free enterprise in a socialized

---

15. In the 19th century the French observer Le Play had noticed a similar workday scheme applied by landowners in southern Russia.

economy, was that peasants could sell there the products from their own private plot and livestock. Food was short, and products like meat, eggs, butter, honey, fruit, and vegetables could fetch a good price. Thus it was more profitable for the peasant to work his own private economy than to work on the collective fields. Even though from 1939 all able-bodied peasants were obliged to contribute a minimum number of workdays to the collective, they still worked more enthusiastically on their own plot.

13

Stalinism in action

Industrialization

HISTORIANS differ as to whether the 1930s constituted the final stage of the Russian Revolution, or whether this was a revolution in itself, or even the 'real' revolution. Few Soviet citizens had the time or inclination to ponder this question; they were in the thick of things, involved in an industrialization drive that brought hardship for most and tragedy for many.

The unprecedentedly high demands of the First Five-Year Plan were met in some quarters with enthusiasm, in others with pessimism, and in yet others with apathy. Among the apathetic were many of those peasants who, to escape the miseries of collectivized agriculture, went to the towns to work in the new industries. Thanks to their influx the industrial labour force doubled during the plan, as against an expected increase of about one-quarter. Among the pessimists were some economists, as well as managers faced with targets that they believed to be unfulfillable. Those who voiced their doubts too strongly were soon removed from the scene by accusations of 'sabotage' or 'wrecking'. The party's enthusiasm was, for the most part, genuine; the planned transformation of the USSR into a great industrial power was indeed something to get excited about. Many workers, and especially the young, were similarly inspired by the great task, really believing in the worth of what they were doing and prepared to make sacrifices for its achievement.

But high-pressure optimism was taken too far. If some of the voices urging moderation had been heeded, the industrialization drive might have been accompanied by less inefficiency, fewer failures, and less muddle. But over-enthusiasm prevailed; by the end of 1929 it was already decided to complete the First Five-Year Plan in four years.

At the end of 1932 Stalin declared that the plan had been fulfilled or over-fulfilled in its main sectors. In reality, most branches of industry had under-fulfilled their targets, but nevertheless almost all had achieved remarkably large increases of production, mainly by developing existing plant. Electric power production, for example, had almost trebled, but its target had been much higher. Similarly, coal and iron ore both doubled their output. Steel production achieved only a one-third increase, compared with a planned increase of two and a half times. The chemical industry did badly, which implied a shortage of artificial fertilizers (but by this time Stalin was persuaded that fertilizers were overrated—see p. 392). The railways had been deliberately starved of resources; a few lines had been built or doubletracked, but main reliance had been placed on the utilization of unused capacity. It was in consumer goods that the shortfalls were most marked. Targets for these had been comparatively low from the start, and even these were not reached. Woollen textiles actually declined during the Plan, instead of trebling as intended. Small-scale handicraft industry, once important for supplying consumer goods, largely disappeared. The urban housing situation, which had been bad in 1928, was abysmal by 1932.

In the coal and metallurgical industries the bulk of the investment was in the old region of the Don Basin, but a decision was made to create a second iron and steel base east of the Urals. This was the Urals-Kuznetsk Basin Combine. The ores of Magnitogorsk in the Urals and the coal of the Kuzbas (1,250 miles to the east) were to be exploited by new furnaces in both locations, with trains conveying coal westwards and ore eastwards. Artificially low rail tariffs disguised the fundamental inefficiency of this scheme. Even so, it was probably justified, because the need for vastly increased steel capacity, and the strategic desirability of locating such an industry far from the frontiers, outweighed conventional profit-and-loss considerations.

In general, efficiency took second place. There was much investment in high-cost projects, and so much emphasis was laid on target fulfilment in terms of gross output that efficiency of production was mainly ignored. A manager was more likely to lose his job (and much else) for non-fulfilment of plan than for compelling his workers to work more than the legal hours, or relaxing safety precautions, or even for poor quality of output. Managers acquired greater responsibility in this period. On the one hand the individual enterprise was made the basic unit of management (the former functions of the trusts and the Supreme Economic Council were largely taken over in 1932 by four ministries: the people's commissariats of heavy industry, light industry, timber, and food). At the same time 'one-man management' was re-established; the enterprise party organization and the trade union branch lost their power over the manager. (But local party secretaries, or party troubleshooters sent from Moscow, could and did intervene.)

The waste, chaos, confusion, and mismanagement of these years of breakneck industrialization were enormous. There were many instances of expensive plant being ruined by untrained workers. To a large extent the blame for such breakdowns was laid on 'wreckers' and 'saboteurs' who were taken to court and usually convicted. Also taken to court were 'bourgeois specialists', those technically educated men of the pre-1917 generation who had continued their professions under the new regime and proved to be ideal scapegoats for production failures. At the Metrovick Trial, British specialists were involved.[1] It was at these show trials that men like Vyshinsky gained the experience in stage-management which they would utilize in the political trials of the late 1930s.

The 1931 annual plan and 'the Five-Year Plan in four years!' slogan represented the height of blind overconfidence. Far too many big projects had been started that would take years to finish. The enormous Dnieper hydroelectric station was indeed finished promptly, only to find that its clients were not yet built. The Gorki automobile plant, when it opened, was hampered by inadequate power supply. Both the Gorki and Dnieper projects relied heavily on American equipment and so did the Chicago-style meat-processing plants (so efficient, boasted trade commissar Mikoyan, that they 'use every part of the animal except its last breath'); the latter opened for business just after Soviet farm animals had been virtually wiped out by collectivization.

Central planning had not imposed the expected rationality. There was upheaval in the countryside and a consequent food shortage. Rationing had been reintroduced in the towns in 1929, but possession of a ration card did not guarantee that rations would be available at the state outlets at state prices:

Customer: Is this the meat shop?
Shop assistant: No, young lady. This is the shop that has no fish. The shop that has no meat is just down the road there.

Recourse to the unrationed 'commercial' outlets was possible, but they averaged a sixteen-fold price increase during the First Plan.

Economic depression in the west had turned the trade balance against the USSR. The Japanese, having invaded Manchuria in 1931, were openly discussing the best time to invade Siberia. In spring 1932 reports reached the Politburo of serious worker protests in the textile industry at Ivanovo, not far from Moscow. Also in spring, and no doubt connected with the protests, came the decision to give peasants the right to sell their surplus products at market prices, even though that seemed a step back towards NEP. There was also a decision to ease the plan for 1933. Molotov, prompted by the finance minister (who did not have a Politburo seat), urged a reduction of investment and Stalin agreed. There was a realization that things could not go on in the same way, with targets repeatedly raised in a spirit of inflexible ecstasy. A limit had been reached in what the economy could do and what the people could take. Real wages had been halved since 1928. Living conditions were by this time horrifying, initial enthusiasms of the First Plan had worn off, and the population had become too apathetic to respond to any further coercion. There was a feeling in the party that Stalin had again overdone things.

---

1. Many foreign specialists were employed in Soviet industry at this period, some as consultants and others as employees of foreign companies supplying equipment or building factories for the USSR. The Metrovick Trial took place just as the USSR was becoming less dependent on such foreign help. The British subjects found guilty were later released.

So the ambitious Second Five-Year Plan (1933–7) was rewritten in its first year of operation. The great leap forward had been leapt and henceforth consolidation, the improvement of efficiency and technique, and better living standards had more emphasis. For three years things did get better for people. Together with increases in most fields of production there was a perceptible improvement in living standards. Projects uncompleted in the First Plan began to contribute to the economy, new mining projects were opened in Central Asia, and a start made in developing a second oil area in the Urals/Volga region.

But from 1937 growth rates slackened. In the high-priority iron and steel industry, output actually declined in 1938. A main cause was the purges which were then taking place. Not only were thousands of key technicians and managers removed to labour camps, where there was little scope for their talents, but those who inherited their jobs took care to avoid making decisions whenever possible. The Third Five-Year Plan (1938–42) was curtailed by the war. It envisaged a doubling of production and, like the Second, promised an increase in consumer goods production which did not materialize in full. It also witnessed an abrupt shift to military production; by 1940 armaments approached one-third of total industrial production. During the first years of this plan there were signs of strain; there was a fuel crisis, caused largely by the failure of the oil industry to meet its not especially high goals, and there was a severe labour shortage. However, the total productive capacity of the USSR was strengthened by the territorial acquisitions of 1939–40.

Interestingly, the planned economy as it expanded did not eliminate booms and troughs. There were two periods of very fast growth (1928–30 and 1934–6) and two of slow growth. Over-investment in the first three years of the First Plan contributed to the hesitant growth of the following period (in 1930 there was an absolute decline of production and productivity for some months). However, the effects of collectivization and purges, as well as the destabilizing shift to war production in the late 1930s, were more influential. The rising output achieved during the five-year plans is tabulated on p. 614.

Statistics of this period are very unreliable and would be misleading even if they were not. The copious publication of statistics, a habit handed down from tsarist Russia, largely ceased in 1930 and figures tended to be regarded as state secrets that could be released only selectively. One difficulty is that output figures did not reflect quality of product: in these years quality in terms of design or specification usually improved, but quality of production often declined. For example, Soviet steel output began to include higher-quality steels that previously had not been produced, but which were very necessary for new engineering products, yet at the same time rails produced by the same steel industry had an increasingly high breakage rate.

Modern technology was acquired by inviting western companies to design and build plants for the USSR, or by acquiring examples of western products which would form the basis of new Soviet designs. In the case of locomotives, Russian engineers were dispatched to study and purchase US designs and then, on their return to the USSR, were arrested and in confinement produced their own new designs that were very close to the American originals. This happened in some other industries, too. In the case of tanks, after importing Vickers tanks from Britain and Christie tanks from the USA, the USSR founded its own tank industry whose T34 medium tank was the world's best when the war began. Synthetic rubber and long-distance electricity transmission were two other fields in which Soviet technology advanced to the front. A rocket technology institute was founded as early as 1933. But these were exceptions. Because of reluctance to interrupt production flows by design changes, imported models frequently remained in production while foreign industries advanced to new improvements. For example, when the automobile factory at Gorki was organized by Ford engineers, the existing American motor truck design was used and this remained in production after Ford had produced far better designs in the USA and elsewhere. Moreover, the very superior Ford V-8 engine was introduced in the USA just as the Gorki plant was getting into its stride, and it was not adopted for Soviet production. Also, new technology was concentrated on a few favoured sectors. Some industries, like construction and the railways, had a very small slice of this particular cake; the railways' dieselization programme, which was in advance of the rest of the world, was ended by Kaganovich in the mid-1930s.

Thus the Soviet lag in technology that attracted so much comment in the 1980s had its roots in the 1930s. All the same, despite the failures, despite (or because of) the savage drop in real wages since 1928, and despite the decline of food consumption per head over the same period, by 1941 the main aim of Stalin's policy of rapid industrialization had been achieved. The USSR, though politically demoralized, was one of the world's great industrial powers.

The planned economy

Fundamentally, the system of economic planning which evolved during the 1920s and 1930s was designed to do two things; to coordinate the activities of the various branches of production, and to make optimal choices between alternative methods, techniques, investments, and other economic strategies. In the classical capitalist economy these goals were attained, more or less, by the adjustment of supply and demand through the price medium. In the USSR the aim was to replace the price mechanism by a supposedly more rational system of economic administration which would itself decide how resources should be allocated, what should be produced, and how, where, and when.

The Stalinist concept of five-year plans lasted from the late 1920s to the late 1980s, but it was greatly modified in the difficult period covering the end of the First Plan and the start of the Second (1931–3). This was when Stalin and his colleagues were cornered by reality, and saw that economic heights are not necessarily captured by absurd overconfidence. After 1933 the targets were more realistic, the use of incentives was accepted as a supplement to exhortation and coercion, and there was even a faint softening of the ideological distrust of market relationships. In 1932 individual craftspeople, a diminishing breed, were allowed to sell their products at market prices instead of state-fixed prices. The assumption by many officials that money would be abolished, giving way to a kind of barter economy using 'labour tokens', was dropped, as was the assumption that the state would plan absolutely everything in the economic sphere. Equally important, the notion that the state would plan and direct labour to where it was needed was replaced by an acceptance that wage differentials had their uses. However, the emphasis on the production of means of production and of armaments was retained, and there was no intention of allowing these objectives to be compromised by excessive concern about hunger and want.

By the end of the 1930s almost all state enterprises were subordinated to a people's commissariat (ministry) specializing in one or another branch of industry.[2] Plans were evolved for various periods. The five-year plans, which received the most publicity, were perspective plans for the national economy which could be modified during their term; they laid down the general direction, using numerical targets. There were also one-year and quarterly plans which had a more operational nature, and were more detailed. The five-year plans were legislative acts, so that failure to meet a plan's target could be treated as a criminal offence. Bonuses were payable to those enterprises which overfulfilled the plan. In theory enterprises had a say in the formulation of the plan, for draft plans were submitted to scrutiny by the enterprises and by workers' meetings before being formally promulgated. This gave an opportunity for alterations suggested 'from below', although in the Stalin period such suggestions took the form of 'spontaneous' demands that the enterprise in question be set even higher targets. Detailed plans were worked out by each commissariat for its own enterprises on the basis of the general targets set by Gosplan for that industry. Gosplan was the coordinator of the plans, and the intermediary between the industries and the party. It was the party which decided the general economic strategy with its key targets, and it was the

---

2. By 1941 the Council of People's Commissars had expanded to 27 industrial and 9 'traditional' ministries, and 6 chairmen of key committees. The industrial commissariats ranged from heavy industry to fisheries. By 1947 new industrial ministries brought the total to 60. Under Khrushchev there was a short-lived but drastic pruning. In the late 1980s an amalgamation of ministries reduced them from 55 to 37.

party's representatives who checked the fulfilment of the plans and who could intervene in critical sectors and override local management. (A high-level example of this was Politburo member Kaganovich becoming railways minister in 1935, when industrialization seemed to be threatened by a new transport crisis.) A disadvantage of the system was its demand for paperwork. In practice, much of the feverish activity in planning organs was nothing but paperwork; as always in Russia, there was a wide divergence between what was intended to occur, what was said to occur, and what did occur.

The economy and its problems were less complex than they would be twenty years later. Thus the system worked reasonably well in the 1930s, was admirably suited to wartime with its ruthless fixing of priorities, but was unsuitable in later years.

The planned economy might have been unbearable but for the existence of the illegal, 'black', economy. This on both large and small scales filled vital gaps left by the planning system. Factory managers faced with high targets and short supplies would use 'pushers' to root out 'unofficial' supplies from murky sources. The favoured position of Leningrad and Moscow retail stores meant that countless individuals could make money by utilizing cheap train fares, travelling to the two capitals, buying as much as they could carry of scarce items, and returning home to resell at mark-ups of tenfold or more. The 'closed' stores, open only to the privileged, with their low prices and good supply, were also a source for black economy trading; they tended to do most business in the small hours, people said. Manipulators in these trades faced heavy penalties as 'speculators' but were often tolerated because officials could see that they were easing people's lives.

Regional party leaders saw that local prosperity depended very much on how much investment the centre could be persuaded to make in their regions. To compete for funds against other regions, they were inclined to make promises they could not keep. For example, seeking a new industrial project, they might exaggerate the quantity of raw materials they could supply from local sources. Any expert or local party official who queried these promises might well be denounced as a wrecker or Trotskyist or Japanese spy, and that would be the end of him.

When the centre was compiling its plans, regional leaders, to gain extra investment, might demand higher targets. When in due course the region could be seen as failing to meet its promises, blame would be placed on a new wave of wreckers. The individuals chosen for sacrifice would not necessarily be connected with the failure, but typically were people whom the local party leadership wanted to eliminate. Thus a high proportion of those who knew what they were talking about, and were not afraid to say what they thought, were incarcerated or executed. Meanwhile local leaderships, in order to conceal their shortcomings, did what they could to prevent accurate information reaching Moscow. Among managers and officials accused of giving information to foreign intelligence agencies were those who had simply given accurate information to Gosplan or a people's commissariat.

Meawhile tensions within industry built up as heads fell. Management of blame became a necessary skill. Underfulfilment of plans was blamed on supplier industries. Supplier industries blamed their clients' muddles. Denunciations flew in all directions, being largely a form of self-protection against potential criticisms that could swiftly develop into accusations of counter-revolutionary activity. By the end of 1937, most regional leaderships had been arrested and carried off.

Expectation of life in Gosplan had diminished likewise. So much so that it was impossible to compile a proper one-year plan for 1938. The purge of Gosplan and the industrial commisariats placed more responsibility on the regions. The regions had been wanting this for some years, being painfully aware of how Moscow sent detailed instructions that were impossible to fulfil and took little account of local circumstances. However, the regions' experienced administrators had largely been purged and it took time for new leaderships to establish themselves, even though the pace of arrests slackened. The Second World War would, of necessity, carry on this process of regionalization, but after the war the central commissariats began to win back their old power. It was only when Khrushchev, against fierce opposition from the ministries, replaced industrial ministries with regional economic councils that the regional cliques triumphed over the centre. But not for long.

Regions reporting to Moscow, and industrial enterprises reporting to their commissariats, tended to conceal both over- and underfulfilment of plans, correctly judging that smoothing out the good and bad periods would lead to less trouble; known overfulfilment could result in the next period's targets bring raised while underfulfilment, in the worst cases, could result in accusations of wrecking or anti-revolutionary sabotage, and then the dreary passage through denunciation, arrest, trial, and sentence.

Personal predilections of Stalin sometimes occasioned serious errors. He eliminated pessimistic statisticians and economists, replacing them with those who would present the figures he wanted. In the absence of voices pointing out errors in good time, there was a tendency for mistakes to be big mistakes. Relative neglect of the oil industry and over-reliance on coal was one mistake. So was the investment in inland waterways at a time when the railways could have made more productive use of capital. Two contradictory policies sometimes coexisted, as with machine tools, where the policy of concentrating on the mass production of a few basic types (mainly designed in tsarist days) conflicted with another policy of producing small runs of highly specialized tools. There was serious over-investment in the mechanical engineering industries, which meant that new plant was underutilized. But at least Stalin's regime got things done, and in Russia this is always a rather special achievement.

Labour

There had never been a deep-rooted trade union tradition in tsarist Russia, so the subordination of the Soviet labour unions to the needs of the government (as opposed to the needs of the workers) was not perhaps surprising. During the 1930s Stalin actually accused trade union leaders of 'trade-unionism', but long before then it was clear that workers' organizations would not be allowed to obstruct the government.

After the Revolution, Bolshevik trade unionists tended to put workers before party, and Lenin in 1920 was still trying to persuade them it was not the role of workers to provide management. At that time many enterprises had a workers' representative at the top, with specialists (that is, members of the old managerial or technical staff) to guide him. Others had a specialist manager, supervised by one or more commissars representing the workers. During the NEP the *troika* system became common, with management consisting of a specialist (usually 'bourgeois'), a trade unionist, and a party representative. All these models attempted to combine the experience of the old managers with the political vigilance of the new class, but they all led to confusion, or at least inefficiency, and Stalin was right to reintroduce one-man management.

Trotsky in 1920 advocated the militarization of labour to meet the crisis of that time. Such a subjection of workers to martial law did occur, notably on the railways, but was not generally accepted. In the 1920s, trade unionist Bolsheviks like Tomsky were in a difficult situation; they felt the privations of the workers deeply, yet could not allow labour movements to hinder the party's policies. Thus although there were occasional strikes in protest against low wages and poor conditions, these did not usually have union backing. For the union leaders, production was already the priority, although they were consulted on matters of welfare, and although workers did participate in factory consultative councils (where they did little, but gained experience of managerial problems). In the 1930s the trade unions became completely docile. Many of their officials suffered in the purges, and there was a shameless neglect of industrial safety and working conditions.

During the 1920s there was considerable unemployment, amounting to 1.5 million in 1929. But this was fully absorbed by the demands of the First Five-Year Plan. The number of workers doubled to 23 million by 1932. The eight-hour day for industrial workers had been introduced in 1917, and in 1939 there was a short-lived and partial seven-hour day. But in 1940 a reduction of wage rates was accompanied by a reinstatement of the eight-hour day. Compulsory overtime was significant, and by 1940 national holidays had been reduced to seven.[3] The working week was also changed; many industries

3. These holidays were New Year's Day (which served as a substitute for Christmas), 1 and 2 May, plus Lenin Day (22 January), October Revolution Anniversary (7 and 8 November), and Constitution Day (5 December).

worked non-stop and individual workers had different rest days (making it difficult for couples to have the same day off). Abolition of Sunday as a day of rest gave additional scope, and had the additional advantage of disorganizing church attendance. In 1939 workers were allowed to rest every sixth day. But in 1940 there was a reversion to a rest every seventh day, and Sunday was re-established as the general rest-day.

In 1914 women comprised about 30 per cent of the workers in large-scale industry, and about 40 per cent by 1917, but the subsequent decline of industry meant that only in the mid-1930s did the proportion regain the 1917 level. But then it rose rapidly; women were valued because many were already urban-dwellers so did not require housing, and married women tended to change jobs less frequently than men. Educated females took over much of general medicine and school teaching, while the less educated became labourers or factory workers. They began to enter industries formerly considered unsuitable. While continuing to predominate in textiles, for example, by 1935 they also accounted for almost a quarter of the coal industry's labour force.

Most of the new workers recruited in the 1930s were peasants. There was an enormous influx in the First Plan and this raised many problems. Despite emergency measures it was impossible to train them properly, so that much inefficiency, as well as accidents to people and machinery, resulted. The peasant was unused to factory discipline. He was used to working hard and long at certain seasons and taking things easy at other times, and this attitude, far from being eradicated, was transferred to industry; as late as the 1980s the party would be condemning *shturmovik* methods (slack work in the first part of a planning period followed by a feverish effort to reach the production target at the eleventh hour). The new worker did not always realize that punctuality was essential, or that a recalcitrant machine could not be cured by a hammer or a smear of grease. In these years it was quite typical for workers to change their jobs four or five times a year, making it even more difficult to train them.[4]

In 1929 rationing had been reintroduced in the towns to permit low prices for scarce necessities. Wages were usually piece-rate, to provide incentive. In the 1930s the difference between the highest and the lowest rates of pay was very much widened to provide yet more incentive. In 1935 bread rationing was abolished and all rationing had ended by 1936. To maintain a limit on consumption, de-rationing had to be accompanied by price rises, so it was

---

4. It was for such reasons, and because of managerial inexperience, that the early projects were so inefficient. The Stalingrad tractor plant, for example, was finished several months ahead of schedule by its American constructors but it needed another three years to reach its planned output. The American-built Gorki automobile works, approved in 1929, began production in 1932 but then stopped because of component shortages. Up to the Second World War it never reached its planned output. See *Slavic Review*, 2 (1990), 200–12.

resented by the lower-paid part of the population. Women protested more than men against the abolition of rationing; they knew the system and its interactions. In 1932 an item could be bought at four different prices: the normal (low, state-fixed) ration price in the towns, the rural price, the higher 'commercial' unrationed price in state shops and cooperatives, and the *kolkhoz* market price which really was a market price. Prices and trade were the province of the trade commissariat which in 1930, when rationing and state monopoly were still regarded as the shape of the future, was temporarily renamed the supply commissariat.

There were also psychological incentives, such as the award of honours to outstanding workers or teams. In the Second Plan labour productivity improved, partly because training programmes were taking effect. There was also the Stakhanovite Movement. Stakhanov was a Donbas miner who produced several times the normal tonnage of coal per manshift, using more intelligent work organization. His example was widely publicized and others were invited to emulate him. Thus there appeared in all branches of the economy workers who vastly exceeded the norm and were duly rewarded with red carpets, cash prizes, trips to Moscow, and medals. Once these men had proved it could be done, their exceptional output was treated as the norm for all. That is, the base piece-work rate was fixed at the new output. Since there was often a good deal of chicanery in the making of a Stakhanovite (he might be given the best tools and assistants and materials), the Stakhanovite Movement soon attracted intense unpopularity, but it was not until the 1950s that its shortcomings were acknowledged. Meanwhile, resentment was mollified by extending the honour, so that a quarter or so of workers in an enterprise could qualify as Stakhanovites. Despite its injustice and its blatant exploitation of man by man, it did emphasize that existing plant was capable of greater output, and it was used to demonstrate the alleged conservatism of managements. Many managers, who realized that Stakhanovism produced greater wear and tear, were unenthusiastic but were soon purged. Indeed, the chastisement of management was an essential part of the Stakhanovite Movement.

During the Second and Third plans there was increasing control of the workforce. At the same time, extra financial incentive was provided by workers' need to pay for 'voluntary' purchase of state bonds which amounted, on average, to two weeks' pay per year. In 1940 new restraints were placed on workers. Absenteeism, which previously was punishable merely by dismissal, became a crime: second offences brought a heavy sentence, and twenty minutes' lateness was counted as absence. The courts were inundated with cases of workers who had broken the new regulations, and there was a procession of skilled and other workers to labour camps. Many workers, lacking the cynicism required for those times, were deeply hurt when a late train or bus delivered them to work a few minutes late and thereby converted them into criminals. The year 1940 was one of last straws, and there were frequent suicides by workers. Nobody was allowed to change jobs except in exceptional circumstances. Some workers, to leave a hated job, committed a small theft to obtain expulsion from the workplace. The state's answer to this strategem was to increase the minimum penalty for any theft of state property; in practice this meant that stealing a turkey from a canteen could be punished more severely than murder. School-leavers were drafted to certain key jobs where there was a labour shortage (those who were drafted to the railways were trained on short narrow-gauge 'children's railways' set up in public parks). Earlier, labour books had been issued, to be carried by all workers; these listed an individual's jobs, misdemeanours, and qualifications. Like a report card, unfavourable entries could have serious repercussions. Most of these measures remained in force until the 1950s.

The party purged

In 1928 the differences between Stalin and the 'moderates', especially Bukharin, Tomsky, and Rykov, came to a head. Although the dispute was not publicized, it is apparent that Bukharin concluded not only that Stalin was no longer in sympathy with his ideas, but that he was totally unscrupulous. Unwisely, Bukharin turned to his former opponent Kamenev for support. This not only gave Stalin a new accusation to level at him, but also disconcerted Bukharin's fellow-moderates, who had long been struggling against Kamenev's 'left'. By this time Bukharin and Stalin differed not only on economic policy, but also on foreign policy. Stalin insisted that the Communist International (of which Bukharin was chairman) should mobilize the communist parties of Europe against the non-communist left, whereas Bukharin believed that European communists should be fighting the emergent fascist movement in alliance with the other socialist parties. In January 1929, Bukharin published an article in *Pravda* in which he recalled Lenin's exhortation to the party to move from the political struggle, which had been won, to a policy of non-violent persuasion and cooperation between worker and peasant. Since Stalin was at this time already suggesting the 'rekindling of the class struggle' it was clear against whom the article was directed.

In April 1929 Stalin attacked the moderates before the Central Committee, accusing them of aiding the counter-revolution by defending the kulaks, and of consorting with the already condemned 'leftists' of the Kamenev group. The moderate leaders were duly reprimanded. In summer 1929, as soon as his industrialization policy had been approved by the 16th Party Conference, Stalin felt strong enough to pursue his former allies further; Tomsky was replaced by the Stalinist Shvernik as head of the trade union organization, and in November that year Bukharin was obliged to relinquish his membership of the Politburo. Rykov, the most innocuous of the trio, was not ejected until the following year from his premiership (which he had held ever since he had succeeded Lenin in the post). In late 1929 the three attempted to restore their position in the party by accepting the condemnation of the Central Committee. However, the latter found this acceptance to be insufficiently humble, because the trio had not completely admitted the error of their ways. The three thereupon presented an amended version in which they fully acknowledged their sins and promised to fight against future deviations from the party's line. Thus there was no opposition a month later when Stalin announced his intention 'to liquidate the kulaks as a class'.

As for the dispersed leftists, many made their peace when they realized that Stalin in his new industrialization policy was in fact adopting their own proposals. Even Trotsky, in exile, could not condemn Stalin unreservedly. Meanwhile, a new purge of the party took place in 1929 and 1930. This was especially severe in the rural areas, where many party members had shrunk from their collectivizing tasks. Moderates were again badly affected by this series of expulsions, which removed a tenth of the membership. Moreover, fear of being branded as a 'rightist' discouraged members from criticizing the new policies of the party.

In mid-1931, Stalin began to transform the party into a primarily white-collar organization. Hitherto white-collar workers, although by this time regarded as part of the intelligentsia, had not enjoyed great prestige, for it was the working class which the party claimed to lead. But with the five-year plans the manager and the administrator became key figures, and it was desirable to associate them more closely with the party. Managers who were members would be more likely to understand and apply the wishes of the party. Moreover, Stalin argued, the old dependence on bourgeois specialists was becoming a thing of the past as more and more workers or sons of workers were taking over managerial positions. Hence there was a recruiting drive among the intelligentsia, the eventual aim being to ensure that most managers, and all top managers and administrators, should be party members. This aim was in the main achieved, although it meant that over succeeding decades more and more white-collar employees joined the party to further their own promotion prospects, rather than for reasons of deep political conviction.

In early 1933 party recruitment was stopped for three years while the party underwent the first stages of its most serious purge. Throughout the half-century after 1917 there was a tendency for the party to increase its membership at times of crisis. The Civil War was one such crisis, the upheaval of 1929–32 was another. When a crisis was over, the need for broad support was diminished and the party reduced its ranks, striving by means of the purge technique to dispense with its least valuable members: the drunkards, the moral degenerates, the self-seekers, the unenthusiastic. The purge of 1933–5 can partly be explained in this light, especially as a disproportionate number of the expellees were those who had been recruited in preceding mass-membership campaigns (during which admission standards had been lowered). However, there was a definite attempt to use this purge as a means of expelling members suspected of critical views towards the party line as laid down by Stalin. The exhortation to purge 'enemies and deceivers' as well as other degenerates indicated that the party leadership was determined to weed out of the lower ranks those members who might one day turn against Stalin. Including those members who voluntarily withdrew from the party, this purge reduced membership by no less than one-third. Before it was completed, it was overtaken by a new and bloody purge which followed the murder of Kirov in 1934.

The party's unpopularity in 1933 even exceeded its unpopularity of a decade earlier. The violence, death, destruction, and officially sanctioned robbery of collectivization had turned the peasantry into such enemies of the regime that the murder of rural communists was quite common. Possibly, by 1933 the party was equally disliked by the town workers; the enthusiasms of 1929 had been dissipated by hunger, privation, overcrowding, and regimentation by party bosses. Stalin, and those of his type, flourished in such times just as they had flourished during War Communism; at times of confusion and peril such people were needed for the party to survive.

For some time, a few respected party members had been discussing the possibility of moderating the breakneck pace of industrialization, giving the masses more food and clothing and living space, and replacing Stalin by a less unbalanced leader. Led by M. Ryutin, they drew up a 200-page, alternative party programme which, among other things, criticized Stalin's power-hunger. Not many party members read this, but Stalin did, for informers were active. The miscreants were sent into exile for fifteen years. Stalin wanted to execute these dissidents (hitherto, disgraced members suffered a more-or-less comfortable exile, living in distant parts under police supervision, as in tsarist times), but this wish to treat party opponents in the way non-party opponents had been treated in the past, that is, to unleash terror tactics against former comrades, was resisted by his colleagues. Of the nine full members of the Politburo, only Molotov and Kaganovich were sufficiently devoted to Stalin to support him on this. The others, willing to support Stalin in most things, were either reluctant (Voroshilov and Kalinin) or entirely opposed (Kirov, Kossior, Ordzhonikidze, Kuibyshev, and Rudzutak). None of the five last named would survive the upheavals of the next few years. Nor would Ryutin. He was secretly tried in 1937 and shot. Of his immediate family, all but one daughter were subsequently killed.

Kirov, one of the most moderate of the Politburo members at this time, was regarded by many as a suitable replacement for Stalin. He was popular, he was handsome, and above all he was a Russian. At the 17th Party Congress of 1934 he appears to have received as much applause as Stalin himself, an ominous distinction. At this Congress there were signs that Stalin had read the portents and was prepared to hasten more slowly. The targets for the Second Five-Year

Plan were indeed more modest than those of the First; so-called former oppositionists (including Bukharin, Zinoviev, Kamenev) were allowed to address the Congress, and the new Central Committee elected by the Congress included men who had opposed Stalin in the past. Even Bukharin, Tomsky, and Rykov were elected as candidate members. The new Central Committee elected a new Politburo whose nine members included only two totally loyal Stalinists (Molotov and Kaganovich), and three who might well oppose Stalin (Ordzhonikidze, Kirov, Kossior). The new Party Secretariat had three assistant secretaries under the general secretary (Stalin). They were the two Stalinists Kaganovich and Zhdanov, and Kirov.

In December 1934 Kirov was shot in his Leningrad party headquarters by a young communist. There are a number of circumstances, including the death of a key witness in a faked car accident, that suggest that the investigation may have been a cover-up. There was an allegation by Khrushchev in 1956 that suggests Stalin himself was behind this crime (although allegations by Khrushchev should not be confused with evidence). The murder certainly offered Stalin a way out of a difficult situation, and he had the recent example of Hitler's killing of Brownshirt leaders to inspire him. The crime, which shocked and alarmed the party, was at first blamed on foreign powers, then on the Zinovievites, then on the Trotskyites. It was followed immediately by that campaign of terror for which Stalin had been hankering. A decree was issued which specified that persons accused of 'preparing terroristic acts' should be investigated immediately and that execution should follow directly after conviction; there would be no appeal and no rights of defence. This was in effect a *carte blanche* for mass judicial murder (or, as Khrushchev expressed it more delicately in 1956, 'it became the basis for mass acts which abused socialist legality').

In the arrests which followed in Leningrad non-communists seemed to suffer as much as communists. But former party members, and members who had once supported certain opposition factions, were among the first to be arrested and deported or executed. The net spread outwards from Leningrad. In 1935 the deputy prosecutor Vyshinsky, an unscrupulous lawyer and devoted Stalinist, announced the forthcoming trial of Kamenev, Zinoviev, and some of their supporters on charges of organizing a secret conspiracy. The trial was in secret and the accused were imprisoned. This, the first imprisonment as criminals of party figures, seems to have aroused protests inside the party. Meanwhile, reliable Stalinists took control of the key organizations; Yezhov became head of the party's Control Commission,[5] Zhdanov succeeded Kirov as head of the Leningrad party organization, while Khrushchev moved from the Ukraine to lead the Moscow party organization. Poskrebyshev, of whom little was known but who became influential, was head of Stalin's personal

5. This, one of the Central Committee's most important organs, supervised party discipline.

secretariat. Vyshinsky was soon to become chief prosecutor. Beria, a Georgian who was the ostensible author of a history of the Caucasian Bolsheviks which grotesquely exaggerated the role of Stalin in the pre-revolutionary years, became the leading party figure in Georgia.

A new purge was launched in the party in 1935, before the previous purge had run its course. Local organizations were ordered to 'unmask' Trotskyites and other enemies of the people. But in 1935 Malenkov (another Stalinist, who with Yezhov was entrusted with the party purge) complained that there were 'liberals' in the party organizations who were 'unmasking too few criminals'. In 1936 the reissue of party cards was made the occasion for yet another purge.

In mid-1936 began the so-called 'Great Purge'. Party organizations received a letter from the Central Committee saying that there were still at large too many 'Trotskyite-Zinovievite monsters ... enemies of the people ... spies, provocators, diversionists, whiteguards, kulaks', and ordering their unmasking, no matter how well they were camouflaged. This was the signal for a mass orgy of accusations, denunciations, confessions, and deportations. The records of all members were scrutinized for dangerous tendencies. One comrade might have given a testimonial ten years previously to a member since convicted of Trotskyism. Another might have failed to denounce a suspect colleague. Another's wife's aunt might have emigrated from Russia in 1918. Another might have approved concessions to the peasants in 1925. Their fate was the same; they were 'unmasked' by one or another of their colleagues, invited to confess before a mass meeting, were only sometimes found to be innocent, lost their jobs, were usually deported to work camps of low survivability, and their families and associates were next to be 'unmasked'. Not only were party members treated thus, but others also, varying from former party members (a very vulnerable group) to confused simple people like the peasant woman mentioned in the Smolensk Archives,[6] who was discovered to have a portrait of Trotsky hanging among her icons.

In August 1936 sixteen former 'Left Oppositionists', including Zinoviev and Kamenev, were tried in public, accused of organizing a terroristic centre which had murdered Kirov and prepared to murder Stalin and others. All but one confessed the accuracy of these charges, were accordingly found guilty, and were shot. During the trial, dominated by Vyshinsky as chief prosecutor, confessions and questions implicated other former 'leftists', as well as Bukharin, Tomsky, and Rykov of the so-called right. Vyshinsky ordered an investigation of the latter three, and newspapers published resolutions said to have been

---

6. In 1941 the German army captured the records of the Smolensk party organization, covering the years 1917–38. They were later acquired by the US army and a selection, with commentary, was published: M. Fainsod, *Smolensk under Soviet Rule* (1958). Usually referred to as the Smolensk Archives, these provided Cold War era historians with a wealth of information about inter-war Russia.

passed at mass meetings of workers, demanding death sentences. Tomsky committed suicide.

Evidently the spectacle of 'Old Bolshevik' leaders like Zinoviev dying from the executioner's bullet aroused some misgivings among Stalin's associates. Ordzhonikidze led the opposition to similar reprisals against Bukharin and Rykov. The investigation ordered by Vyshinsky was cut short and Bukharin and Rykov were declared clear of the charges. Nevertheless, in early 1937 a new batch of former 'leftists' faced charges at a second big show trial. In the meantime Yezhov had replaced Yagoda as head of the people's commissariat of the Interior (NKVD), which by this time had absorbed the functions of the former OGPU. Yagoda had apparently been too scrupulous; his dismissal was followed by that of his subordinates.

The second show trial included Radek and Pyatakov among the accused. There were seventeen in all, accused of conspiring with Germany and Japan to divide the USSR between those two powers. Pyatakov (who had been a deputy commissar of heavy industry) was also accused of wrecking and sabotage; he was a convenient scapegoat for the current shortcomings of the industrialization programme. From the official transcript[7] of the trial, it would seem that Vyshinsky was his usual self:

This trial has uncovered and demonstrated the stupid obstinacy, the reptilian cold-bloodedness, the cold calculation of professional criminals, shown by the Trotskyist bandits in their struggle against the USSR ... Beginning by forming an anti-party faction, they moved to ever-sharper methods of struggle against the party and became, after expulsion from the party, the main mouthpiece of all anti-soviet groups and trends, transforming themselves into a fascist vanguard operating directly on the directives of foreign intelligence services. The liaisons the Trotskyists had established with the Gestapo and the fascists were exposed at the trial of the Trotskyist-Zinovievist centre last year. The present trial has gone even further.

The confessions of the accused again implicated Bukharin and the moderates as well as Tukhachevsky, the Red Army C-in-C. Thirteen of the accused were executed, and four were deported to camps which they did not survive. Radek was one of these latter four, and probably received this charitable sentence in recompense for the artistic confession he produced:

The question has been raised whether we were tortured while being investigated. I have to say that it was not I who was tortured, but it was I who tortured the investigators and made them do a lot of useless work ... I have to make one more confession. Having confessed my guilt and revealed the organization, I obstinately refused to testify about Bukharin. I knew that Bukharin was in just as hopeless a situation as I was because we were guilty of the same thing, essentially if not legally. But we are close friends ...

7. Lengthy extracts from this transcript are included in T. Riha, *Readings in Russian Civilisation*, vol. iii (1964).

By this time there seemed little hope of resisting Stalin's forcefulness. The judiciary was safely in the hands of Vyshinsky and the NKVD in those of Yezhov. There were arrests of thousands of lesser members, including 70 per cent of the Central Committee and more than half (1,108 members) of the 17th Party Congress, few of whom survived.

The leadership of the Young Communist League (Komsomol) was next to be purged, and this movement was reorganized. Then, in March 1938, came the third of the big show trials, with Bukharin, Rykov, and Yagoda among the twenty-one accused. Sabotage, anti-Stalin conspiracy, espionage for Germany and Japan were the main charges. In addition, Yagoda was accused of poisoning Gorki and Kuibyshev, when he had been in charge of the NKVD.[8] Bukharin was also charged with plotting to murder Lenin in 1918. All but one of the accused confessed. The exception was Krestinsky, who in court revoked his confession, which he claimed had been obtained through torture. But, after a night with the NKVD interrogators, he revoked his revocation the next day, and was executed along with Bukharin, Rykov, Yagoda, and most of the others.

At the time, many commentators outside Russia believed that the show trials were genuine, even when they simultaneously felt there was something not quite right. Thus the US ambassador, who attended the trial of the 'Anti-Soviet Trotskyite Centre', believed that there was indeed a plot but could yet record:

I noted particularly that after Serebryakov, who was an old railroad man, was called to his feet to corroborate the fact of a peculiarly horrible crime (which he did laconically), he sat down quite unconcerned and yawned . . . In the case of one defendant the prosecutor had even to admonish him to get down to the case and not embroider his testimony with additional crimes.[9]

Among party people, the practice of patronage, once so essential for advancement with upward-moving figures carrying on their coat-tails trusted assistants and friends, changed from a ladder to a snake. Once a party leader was denounced, his associates, even from decades back, were next on the list, and then the associates and friends of that second batch. And so it went on. A purpose can be discerned here, because there were cliques in the party leaderships, especially in the regions, and they did sometimes seem slow to respond to directives. So thoroughly was the old party liquidated that, of the 1939 membership, four-fifths had joined since 1930. A new recruitment drive was begun, directed mainly towards the white-collar intelligentsia. By 1941 the party had about 4 million members.

8. This accusation gave some plausibility to the rumour that Gorki and Kuibyshev had been poisoned on Stalin's orders after they had protested against the first wave of executions.

9. J. E. Davies, *Mission to Moscow* (1942), 35, 37.

The repellent truth about the purges tended to be voiced abroad mainly by conservatives and anti-Soviet observers. However, in 1956 Khrushchev indicated that the allegations of the anti-Soviet commentators were indeed true and many more details were revealed after 1985. Millions of innocents had been condemned. Physical and mental torture had been used to obtain confessions. Many signed confessions because they believed it was for the good of the party, or because their families were threatened, or because they were isolated for months, beaten up, promised merciful treatment if they cooperated. Some went to their deaths believing that 'an unliquidated counter-revolutionary centre', unknown to Stalin, was at large in the NKVD and extracting false confessions. Many who did not confess were quietly shot.

Some of those sentenced, including some who had publicly confessed, wrote to party leaders asking for a reinvestigation or reprieve. They did not receive a reply but their letters were filed away, to be unearthed by later generations. In 1953 the recipient of many of these despairing letters, Beria, would be writing to Khrushchev with the same plea, and with the same result.

The people purged

The word purge means simply a thorough cleansing, and was used quite naturally to describe the periodic weeding out from party membership of those characters deemed unfit. From this small beginning the word came to describe a monstrous process of arbitrary arrests, fake trials, mass executions, and forced labour camps which the weak and unlucky could not survive. The treatment of the so-called kulaks during collectivization belongs to this story (some million families were exiled and about 30,000 kulaks shot). By the time Stalin died there were few families that had been untouched by the process. Children of the victims frequently went through life concealing the disgrace of having 'enemies of the people' as parents, always knowing that among their friends and colleagues there were those who would eagerly 'unmask' them at the slightest suspicion. It was only after 1985 that some of these middle-aged collateral martyrs decided they could reveal their pasts. They were allowed access to security service archives, and there were those born in the 1930s whose first and only glimpse of their father was the yellowed photograph accompanying his death warrant.

The great purge of 1937–8 is best understood (and it is not yet completely understood) if it is regarded not so much as an event but as a state of mind. Purging had come to be accepted as a way of getting rid of unwanted people and it was a technique that could come into play for a whole series of real or imagined crises. The arrest, trial, and punishment of top leaders was only the most spectacular of these occasions. For many Russians it was virtually the icing on an otherwise drab cake, for there was a strong them-versus-us climate of opinion, and the casting-down of the top party bosses brought great satisfaction. The same treatment accorded to local bosses and managers was also enjoyed by many.

The subsequent army purge can hardly be detached from the threatening international situation, a feeling that the officers might not know their jobs, and the mistaken belief that generals were consorting with dangerous foreigners. Purges of managers and responsible workers were used, especially by local party officials, to provide scapegoats for failure to fulfil production plans. In the background, and happening both before and after 1937–8, was the purging of ordinary people.

This purging of the inconspicuous could be described as administrative, as it was designed to get rid of undesirables, mainly from the cities. Such undesirables included the long-term unemployed, who were regarded as parasites, and people who had been deprived of rights. The latter included former nobles and their children, quietly hiding their origins and trying to make a living, so-called kulaks who had anticipated the collectivizers and fled to the towns in good time, and families (including distant cousins) of former members of anti-Bolshevik parties. Some of these people, and others too, had been driven by necessity into activities like 'speculation' and prostitution. Keeping track of all these 'socially harmful' people had been made easier by the reintroduction of identity papers (internal passports). Ostensibly to help control the flood of peasants to the towns (peasants were not issued with them except on request, which was not necessarily granted), they helped local police to file away the names of those who did not have them, who had been refused them, or 'were known to the police' for other reasons. A growing number of cities were declared to be restricted to passport holders, which was a way for city authorities to rid themselves of these undesirables. But these people had to go somewhere; often they infiltrated back to where they had come from, or they settled in towns that were not yet restricted. The regime regarded them, logically enough, as potential enemies; after all, they were resentful people who had nothing to lose. So the idea of shooting them or sending them to labour camps was quite attractive, and this is what happened. Some were arrested and taken through the courts, but a growing number were gradually dealt with by NKVD boards. In due course, arrest targets were set for the localities, which is when the index-files at police stations came in useful. Contrary to impressions at the time, arrests were not random, but based on police records. Denunciations, although important, played a smaller role than was thought.

Meanwhile, as undesirable individuals were pinpointed from the police lists, other lists were produced to cover not so much individuals as whole categories. In 1937 there was a succession of instructions emanating from the NKVD to its operatives, listing groups to be dealt with. Among the first listed groups were recently naturalized foreigners, and army officers who had been at any time expelled from the party for political reasons; these were most likely regarded as possible spies and traitors.[10] A directive to institute a purge of people engaged in water supply and in microbiological research also had a hint of rationality for a fearful regime. But once started, this process of elimination took on a momentum of its own. Next to fall victim, joining managers and administrators of enterprises failing to meet targets, were army officers, Civil War veterans, former Stalinists, foreign communists (the entire leadership of the Polish communist party, living in exile in Russia, and the Hungarian communist Bela Kun, died), Russians who had returned from service in the Spanish Civil War, ex-Mensheviks and ex-Socialist Revolutionaries, former members of Gosplan, and associates of Kirov.

By the end of 1937 the NKVD was pursuing broad social groups rather than special sectors. Many denunciations were defensive; there was a feeling that one had to be quick on the draw to survive. There was also awareness that many were arrested for 'lack of vigilance'. The NKVD found ways to persuade those arrested to denounce their friends or colleagues. Some persons denounced to settle old scores, some to prove their vigilance and virtue, a few in the hope that they would inherit the apartment or job or lover of the victim, and some because they were 'invited'. Once a denunciation was made there was little the victim could do, and his family and friends automatically became suspect. In the party purge even Ordzhonikidze (who committed suicide soon after) was unable to save his subordinate Pyatakov. Successful defence was unlikely:

Polish rabbit: Why have you fled to Poland?
Russian rabbit: Stalin is preparing a bear hunt.
Polish rabbit: But you're not a bear.
Russian rabbit: No, but I can't prove it!

In a category of their own were whole national groups deported to inhospitable regions. Tension with Japan caused the deportation of thousands of Koreans living in the Soviet Far East; they were sent to Central Asia. Other waves followed, especially during the Second World War when Chechens, Tatars, and other nationalities were deported from their territories in the Caucasus and Crimea. The centuries-old German settlements also fell victim.

Workers were in no way spared. On the railways, for example, locomotive men were shot both for driving their trains at less than the maximum possible speed ('sabotage' of the plan) and for attaining maximum possible speeds ('wrecking', because it caused extra wear and fuel consumption). A plant

10. The Spanish Civil War sharpened several of Stalin's nightmare scenarios. It brought into being the term 'fifth column' for residents waiting to betray their country, and its International Brigade showed that there were still Trotskyists ready to take up arms.

foreman who removed a component from an inactive machine in order to replace a failed part of an active machine could be accused of 'wrecking' and dealt with after due process ('spontaneous' meeting of 'outraged' fellow workers demanding maximum punishment, trial before an NKVD board, bullet in the back of the neck). The harsh tightening of labour discipline in the 1940s brought a new influx of workers to the labour camps.

The Red Army purge was something special. In 1937, Tukhachevsky and several other Red Army generals were arrested and shot. They were accused of spying for Japan and Germany and of planning to establish a right-wing Trotskyite counter-revolutionary whiteguardist regime in Moscow. Confessions were extracted by torture. The execution of Tukhachevsky, whose Civil War reputation far outshone the manufactured military reputations of Stalin and Voroshilov, must have brought personal as well as political satisfaction to the latter pair. Among other charges, Budyenny accused the generals of 'wrecking' by advocating the replacement of cavalry by tanks. At least one faked letter, purporting to be a wife's renunciation of an accused general, was published in the press. Tukhachevsky's brothers and sisters were arrested, and most of them killed. His younger daughter attempted suicide after being mocked by her schoolmates. Wives and children of the other generals were incarcerated, and most were shot in 1941 in the orgy of preventive executions after the German invasion. These arrests were followed by others, and by the end of 1938 about 35,000 Red Army officers had been arrested. About one-third were reinstated, so about 11 per cent of the total officers became victims. That the army purge resulted from Stalin's suspicion that the high command was plotting against him, or might soon plot against him,[11] was reflected in the rank of the victims, who comprised all the deputy commissars for war, nine-tenths of the generals, four-fifths of the colonels, and smaller proportions of the lower ranks. This brought better promotion prospects for the survivors, but for the more thoughtful officers this was not necessarily a blessing. Marshal Zhukov, in a part of his memoirs which was withheld from publication until 1991, wrote of 1937:

Frankly, in a way I was glad I was not promoted, because at the time there was a particularly active hunt going on at the higher levels on the part of the state security organs. No sooner did you succeed in getting a high appointment than you were taken under arrest as an 'enemy of the people'.[12]

If the purge had continued accelerating past 1938, it would eventually have made every Russian a prisoner. It was not unknown for a prisoner to encounter his recent interrogator or accuser in the same camp. Some intended victims living at remote addresses were saved because the officials charged

11. Forged evidence, probably concocted by Russian émigrés and incriminating the generals in an international conspiracy, found its way to Moscow via the well-meaning Czechoslovak president.
12. *Gudok*, 5 July 1991, 4.

with their arrest were themselves arrested before they could find them. To speed up the legal process special three-man NKVD boards (*Troikas*) were set up for fast high-volume sentencing. Outside big cities, new, covert, cemeteries were opened to receive the bodies of the executed; sometimes the executions themselves would be carried out there, usually at night. Families of those executed were told that the accused had been sentenced to 'prison without right of correspondence'. Close relatives would spend days waiting outside prisons and offices for news or to hand over food parcels, and for the most part were ignored or insulted. The much-respected poet Anna Akhmatova composed a very moving poem, *Requiem*, about these vigils, which was breathed around until, three decades later, it could be published.

As 1938 passed, with administration and industry disorganized, with nervous breakdowns and heart attacks becoming a mass phenomenon, as citizens listened apprehensively in the small hours for the dreaded knock on the door which would mean immediate and probably eternal separation from their families, Stalin called a halt. Aware, no doubt, that anti-purge leaflets had begun to appear, he blamed Yezhov and Yezhov's subordinates for the excesses. Beria replaced Yezhov, and promptly arranged executions for him and his subordinates. The pace of arrests slackened (but did not cease until after 1953), and a few inmates of camps were released.

The NKVD itself lost about 20,000 operatives in the purge, of whom some were punished for reluctance to carry out orders. It grew vastly in this period, not only because it operated the purge mechanisms but because it also organized the labour camps, which in certain sectors of the economy were very vital. By 1941 the NKVD economic units were responsible for about a quarter of the construction projects, including mines, railways, roads, and some factories. Because forced labour could be made to work in inhospitable regions, the NKVD became responsible for gold and diamond production, as well as for much of tin and nickel output. It is not proven, however, that it was demand for labour that caused the expansion of the purge in the late 1930s and after the Second World War, even though a point was reached when targets were set for the volume of arrests in a given period. Industrial managers in remote locations welcomed labour allocations from the NKVD's special settlements; such workers would stay on the job, unlike free workers who tended to leave after a month or two.

Historians are still arguing about the total number of victims, and the exact figure is unlikely to emerge, ever. Archives opened since 1985 suggest that by 1941 the forced labour system (which included a proportion of ordinary criminals) held about 3,350,000 prisoners, of whom a third were in labour camps and about a million in 'special settlements' (less rigorous, perhaps, and the usual habitation of families of kulaks and of the families of purge victims). In 1953, when Stalin died, the overall figure had risen to around 5,500,000. Survivabiity in the camps depended largely on the period. In the war the camps' average annual death-rate was 170 per thousand, compared to 91 per thousand in 1938. Most deaths in the purge, therefore, were not the result of death sentences. Executions also varied from year to year; in the purge peak years of 1937 and 1938 about 780,000 executions were recorded. The aggregate death toll ('excess deaths') in the 1930s, including deaths from famine as well as purge victims, was probably around 10 million.

The dismantling of the NKVD penal system began after Stalin's death, and by 1959 there were only about 11,000 'counter-revolutionaries' still held. In the twenty-first century it is still possible to meet former purge victims. Many prefer to remain silent, but there is a surprising number who still believe (or need to believe) that the arrests were fully justified; it is just their own particular case that was a dreadful mistake.

The 1936 Constitution

From the early days of Russian marxism, Marx's doctrines had been adjusted from time to time to suit Russian realities. Lenin's innovations, which produced what would be known as Marxism-Leninism, related more to the struggle for power than to the post-revolutionary society. He had asserted (and in 1917 proven) that a proletarian revolution could occur in a primarily peasant society, if the peasantry was regarded as an ally. He had adopted the Populist Lavrov's concept of the small professionalized party, and had proposed that such a party could capture the state bureaucratic apparatus and, through that apparatus, carry out a social revolution. Lenin had also made democratic centralism the basis of party organization, thus combining the democratic discussion traditional in radical circles with the centralized authoritarian system traditional in bureaucratic circles.

After 1917 there had been other modifications in Russian marxist doctrines, some of them introduced by Stalin; hence until 1953 the term Marxism-Leninism-Stalinism was in frequent use. Among ideas sponsored in Stalin's time were those that propounded that socialism could be 'built in one country'; that the 'Law of Industrialization' meant that economic planning would create the industrial base on which socialism could be built; that class conflict intensified after the Revolution (which explained the violence of the 1930s); and that the state would not automatically wither away, but would be needed to supervise the economy and to deal with internal enemies and 'capitalist encirclement'. Stalin also reiterated that before proceeding to Marx's final stage of communism, where the ruling principle would be 'From each according to his capacity, to each according to his needs', the preliminary stage of socialism had to be attained ('From each according to his capacity, to each according to his work'). In 1936 Stalin declared that the USSR, hitherto 'on the road to socialism', had duly reached socialism. The Stalin Constitution was to mark this achievement.[13]

Stalin by the late 1930s was intent on stabilizing Russian life; in fact the purges, among other things, took out of the party those who were revolutionaries at heart. The model charter for the collective farms which confirmed the status of private plots, the reintroduction of Russian history as a school subject, concessions to the Church, social changes such as limitations on divorce and fewer limitations on inheritance, and a partial return to a genuine rule of law, were other signs of stabilization, and so was the new Constitution.

The first Soviet Constitution had been that of 1918, which was acknowledged to be a temporary document, and was adopted because some formal statement was required and because a constitution was what revolutionaries had been demanding during the preceding century. The 1924 Constitution was more significant, for it formalized the creation of the federal Union of Soviet Socialist Republics, in which the national republics were subordinated in important matters to the central commissariats in Moscow. The 1936 Constitution was largely drafted by Bukharin and Radek; this was their last important service to the party before their arrest. It became known as the Stalin Constitution and as such was propagandized throughout the world. In its provisions it seemed to be the most progressive constitution ever devised, but in reality the articles guaranteeing various rights and freedoms were quite meaningless, because the Politburo or the NKVD could override any legal obstacle.

Lenin had always been passionately protective of the nationalities, genuinely deploring the Great Russian arrogance and exploitation that they had suffered. Stalin, belonging to one of those nationalities, had taken a great interest in the subject and had been a natural choice as commissar of nationalities under Lenin. That these two quarrelled over nationalities policy is unsurprising, because both cared very much about it and it was a highly complex matter. It can be said for both of them that they understood the crucial importance of the nationalities problem, unlike their predecessors and successors, and that their eventual solution was not bad.

According to the 1936 Constitution the USSR was a federation of Soviet republics.[14] The union (that is, federal) government in Moscow monopolized

---

13. Two decades later Stalin's successor Khrushchev would announce that the growing strength of the 'socialist camp' had put an end to capitalist encirclement, and that the necessary industrial base had been created. Hence the USSR had entered 'the road to communism'.

14. At the time these were Russia, Ukraine, Byelorussia (White Russia), Georgia, Armenia, Azerbaizhan, Kazakhstan, Kirgizia, Uzbekistan, Turkmenistan, Tadzhikistan. In 1939–40 they were joined by Latvia, Estonia, Lithuania, Moldavia, and Karelo-Finland. (The last named was absorbed by the Russian Republic in 1956.)

such matters as defence and foreign policy, but in other cases the commissariats were not 'all-union', but 'union-republican'; that is, the federal commissariats acted through similarly titled commissariats of the republic governments. In a few fields the republics had complete jurisdiction (primary education was one such field). Conflict between the union government and the republics was muted because party leaders controlled both. Moreover, the union government had control over the republican budgets, and all-union laws could override republican laws. According to the Constitution, a union republic had the right to secede from the Soviet Union (although in 1951 party leaders in Georgia were executed on the grounds that they were planning to do just that).

Inside some republics there were autonomous republics, and the smaller autonomous regions and areas, to accommodate nationalities either too small to justify a union republic or not located on the periphery of the USSR (a condition for union republic status). The Russian Republic (Russian Soviet Federative Socialist Republic, or RSFSR) had as many as fourteen autonomous republics and several autonomous regions and territories, including vast areas of the north and pockets of Tatars and other peoples left high and dry by successive advances of the Russian Empire. In the four categories of national division, local cultures were to be 'national in form' but 'socialist in content'.

This administrative redrawing of the old Russian Empire was largely Stalin's work adapted from the 1924 constitution, and was one way of preserving that empire and both maintaining and restraining feelings of nationality. Frontiers delineating the Central Asian republics sometimes had little correspondence with the ethnic boundaries, because defining nations was both difficult and delicate; however, the priority given to language was sensible. Inevitably there were frictions. Just as the nationalist intelligentsia of tsarist times had created almost artificial nations by dint of rescuing or developing a dying language or cultural tradition, in the USSR it could be said that there were nations that did not really want to exist. There were said to be 192 languages in the USSR and the ideal, never achieved, was to impose 192 cultures and publish newspapers and books in 192 languages. Local leaderships and administrators everywhere were expected to work in the local language, which implied a lesser role for Russians outside the Russian Republic. In due course people's nationality was registered in their passport, but some people were given a nationality they did not want. Worse, they might be required to learn a language that was not their own (but others objected to their children being required to learn their national tongue, realizing that to get on in the world Russian was the key language). The Chechen and Ingush people were lumped together as one nation, which neither relished, and there had to be other cases where the frontier of one nation might divide, or engulf, another. But in the circumstances it was the best that could be done. The ultimate, very ultimate, aim was to bring the nations to the same level of political, social, and economic development, at which point their merging into one big state would be possible. Russia, in the meantime, comprised the territory left over when the other union republics had been divided off. It lacked many institutions that the others had (it did not even have its own communist party), but it was the location of all-union (Soviet Union) institutions and Russians played the dominant role in them.

The exclusive right to make all-union laws was vested in the Supreme Soviet of the USSR. One of the several ways in which the 1936 Constitution resembled that of the USA was the structure of this body; it had two houses, the Soviet of the Union with members elected by electoral districts (one member per 300,000 people), and the Soviet of Nationalities (twenty-five members per union republic, eleven per autonomous republic, five per autonomous region, one per national area). The Supreme Soviet was to meet twice each year; the meetings lasted only a few days, during which the elected members were acquainted with the government's policies and gave their approval to whatever measures they were summoned to approve. It was thus not really a legislative body in the western sense, but it gave its members, and those who elected them and heard their reports, some sense of participation. Also, members did not need to give up their regular employment since sessions were so short. The quadrennial elections were not competitive, only one candidate being nominated for each electoral district. In practice, the aim at elections was to obtain for each candidate as near 100 per cent of the votes as was physically possible, thus demonstrating the mass support of the electorate. From the Supreme Soviet was elected the Presidium, the chairman of which fulfilled the functions of president of the USSR but had little real power. Also from the Supreme Soviet was elected the more important Council of People's Commissars, the chairman of which continued to be the equivalent of a western prime minister. In the union republics, government was similarly organized, but the supreme soviets had only one house.

Article 126 implied that the party was the real ruling force, that is, it 'forms the nucleus of all the public and state organizations of the working people'. That 125 other articles preceded this declaration hardly concealed that this was indeed the basic and distinguishing fact of the Soviet system of government.

There were several resemblances, perhaps interesting more than significant, between the Soviet and tsarist systems of government. For example, just as under the tsars there were, apart from the formal channels, many other ways of introducing laws (by decrees or manifestos, preceded perhaps by the tsar scrawling 'So Be It' on the proposal of a minister), so in the USSR people's commissariats and other bodies could issue their own orders, which were not laws but had the force of law. Again, people's commissars, like tsarist ministers, were heads of departments and belonged more to the bureaucracy than to politics. In some cases a minister might occupy his position for decades.

Just as Kankrin served as tsarist minister of finance for twenty-one years, so did the Soviet minister for railways, Beshchev, serve from 1948 to 1977.

Chapter 1 of the Constitution laid down the fundamental concepts on which the Union of Soviet Socialist Republics was based. Among the more important were: the USSR 'is a socialist state of workers and peasants'; 'The political foundation of the USSR is the Soviet of Working Peoples' Deputies, which grew and became strong as a result of the overthrow of the power of the landlords and capitalists and the conquest of the dictatorship of the proletariat'; 'All power in the USSR belongs to the working people of town and country as represented by the Soviets of Working Peoples' Deputies'; 'The economic foundation of the USSR is the socialist system of economy and the socialist ownership of the instruments and means of production, firmly established as a result of the liquidation of the capitalist system of economy, the abolition of private ownership of the instruments and means of production, and the elimination of the exploitation of man by man'; 'Work in the USSR is a duty and a matter of honour for every able-bodied citizen, in accordance with the principle: "He who does not work, neither shall he eat."'

Some of these declarations seemed somewhat optimistic; formally or theoretically the working people may have held all state power through the soviets, but in reality this proposition could hardly be sustained. If 'exploitation of man by man' was defined as a consequence of some men privately owning the means of production while others owned only their own labour, it was true that exploitation had ceased, but in fact there were many other possible forms of exploitation.

When the population discovered that in the 1937 election there would be one candidate for each seat, its interest in the new democracy promised by the Constitution diminished somewhat. But there were many citizens who did not want full democracy. They believed in the dictatorship of the proletariat, which the new Constitution seemed to dilute.

The USSR was not claimed to be a classless society. Stalin, introducing the Constitution, said only that the old conflicting classes had been abolished, leaving the workers and the peasants. The latter formed two mutually amicable classes and therefore, said Stalin, there was no need for a multi-party system, because political parties represented conflicting classes. As for the intelligentsia, Stalin described this as a stratum, not a class, and as a working-class intelligentsia rather than the old bourgeois intelligentsia. This explanation of the new class structure contained elements of self-deception, although undoubtedly the situation in 1936 was different from that in 1916 (see table, p. 611). In reality there was an upper class in Stalin's Russia but, true to marxist analysis, it did not regard itself as such because it did not own property. It was a privilege-using class, regarding itself as culturally superior, and enjoying state-provided luxuries like dachas, cars, servants, and educational advantages for its children.

In the last decade of the tsarist regime the class structure had been in a confused state of change. There were the old official 'estates' (nobles, priests, peasants, and others) which, even with the addition of distinctions like 'honoured citizens', could hardly accommodate the ever-growing number of those who did not fit into the old categories. Cutting across the official and mainly hereditary divisions were the new unofficial but very real differences of economic status. Moreover, noble status was becoming ever less exclusive; the universities and officer-training schools provided a ladder enabling men of peasant or petty bourgeois origin to climb into the nobility. Establishing one's category was a required preliminary for any official dealings (as it continued to be, in its own way, in Soviet times; 'Your documents, please!' was one of the most pervasive and familiar requests of both tsarist and Soviet Russia, symbolizing and enforcing the citizen's subordination to the state). In the nineteenth century Anton Rubinstein found he had to describe himself not as a musician, for which there was no category, but as 'son of a 2nd-Guild merchant', and that was simply to get himself registered for confession in the Orthodox Church.

In 1917 the existing class system had been abolished, but this did not mean the end of class distinctions. Except during War Communism and the first two years of the five-year plans, egalitarianism was rejected. In 1931 Stalin came out against equality; industrialization demanded wide differentiation of incomes, in order to provide incentives. In the USSR the gap between the highest and lowest incomes became very wide indeed. The new intelligentsia which Stalin fostered in the 1930s tended to enjoy high salaries, although these were matched by a few of the very best industrial workers. In time the well-paid and influential stratum of 'leading cadres' came to resemble a privileged class.

Around 1929 and 1930, when the social upheaval and re-evaluation of so many principles amounted to a cultural revolution, there was a campaign to 'unmask' those so-called 'former' people like nobles or oppositionists who had sought to disappear from sight. Many lost their jobs and became unemployable. But after this, in the mid-1930s, these and other 'deprived ones' became less of a target because the regime felt strong enough to accept, for example, that because a young person had a priest or noble or a Social Revolutionary for a father, that did not mean higher education should automatically be barred and the vote withheld. 'A son should not answer for his father!' declared Stalin, wisely if belatedly. But although the 1936 Constitution would mark this change, in practice the former deprived ones could still find themselves purged, or at best quietly disadvantaged, and most attempted to cover up their past.

Justice

The quest for stability reflected in the Constitution was also a feature of the judicial changes of the late 1930s. The new general theory of Soviet law was laid down by Vyshinsky in his *Law of the Soviet State*,[15] a turgid work whose crudities camouflaged its underlying conservative principles. While describing other countries' laws as 'inhuman and bestial', Vyshinsky rejected the 'putrid, vaporous' theories of revolutionary Soviet legal theorists of the 1920s. His book prescribed a law that was depoliticized except in those cases where political factors were considered important; the concept that all law and all cases are inherently political was condemned. Perhaps central to the Vyshinsky theory was the resulting proposition that there should be a genuine due process of law in all cases, except where violence was considered necessary. However obscure and unconvincing the theory, in practice it meant some real changes. There was stricter adherence to the law and to the correct procedures. The Soviet 'doctrine of analogy' was severely limited: this doctrine had meant that acts which were not crimes according to the laws could often be punished as crimes if a court considered them nefarious. Personal guilt in a crime became necessary for punishment; in other words, close relatives or friends of convicted criminals could no longer be punished with them. These improvements did not apply to cases defined as political, and at this period the NKVD investigators usually succeeded in fabricating a political crime for anyone whom they decided should be eliminated. Moreover, judges were expected to follow their 'Bolshevik consciousness'.

The courts of law were headed by the Supreme Court of the USSR, whose chairman was a top party official rather than a top lawyer. The republics also had their own supreme courts. Then there were *oblast'* courts[16] and the People's Courts (courts of first instance). The 'bourgeois' jury system had long been abolished, and cases were decided and sentences handed down by a judge, assisted by two lay assessors. Judges and lay assessors were elected (by the corresponding soviet, or, in the case of People's Courts, by the local population, but in reality the appropriate party organization was most influential in their selection). Judges could be recalled before the expiry of their term if they were considered unsatisfactory. They were not required to have legal training. The procuracy (abolished in 1918 but reinstated in 1922) became highly centralized, with the prosecutor-general (Vyshinsky) appointing and supervising republic and district prosecutors. The procuracy was mainly

15. The English edition was published in 1948. The original Russian edition (1938) was titled *Soviet State Law*.

16. The *oblast'* was the Soviet equivalent of the tsarist province. The district (*raion*) was a subdivision of an *oblast'* or of a city.

concerned with its role as state prosecutor, its role as supervisor of the judicial system being largely taken over by the commissariat of justice, which existed from 1938 to 1956.

The Church

Lenin's pre-1917 attitude towards the Church included a belief that the state should permit each citizen to follow his professed faith, but should not allocate public funds to any religious activity. At the same time the Bolshevik party should wage a propaganda struggle for people's minds, to convince them that religion was indeed an opium. For the Church, the October Revolution was a disaster, because during the Provisional Government it had been preparing to reassert itself. In people's minds the Church had sunk even lower during the final tsarist years when, it was believed, the Synod was dominated by Rasputin. After the February Revolution the Church saw an opportunity to break away from state control without sacrificing the privileges which cooperation with the state had obtained. Among other activities, it finally triumphed over Peter the Great by re-establishing the office of patriarch. The first incumbent was Tikhon, after an election in which he did not receive the most votes. On the other hand, the Provisional Government did end legal discrimination against the minor religions and weakened the hold of the Church on education.

The Bolshevik Revolution meant that a small atheistic party would attempt to rule a devoutly Christian republic. This contradiction was at first as great an embarrassment for the party as for the Church, and the contradiction was transformed into conflict within weeks. Lenin foresaw that the Orthodox Church, if left alone, would sooner or later become an inspirational centre of anti-Bolshevik movements. The first priority was therefore the destruction of the Church as an organization, but not the destruction of Russian Christianity (which in the short term was out of the question). A decree issued in February 1918 disestablished the Church and confirmed the equality of all religious faiths before the law. Disestablishment was accompanied by such measures as elimination of references to a citizen's beliefs in official documents. 'Religious associations' (of which the Orthodox Church was one) had the right to conduct their ceremonies but henceforth could not punish, or extract fees from, their adherents. What really hurt was the depriving of all religious associations of the status of a juridical person. This meant they could not own property, and the decree provided for the expropriation of church land and buildings: believers would lease back their churches from the state. Later, believers were organized into local religious associations (consisting of at least twenty members), and it was these which arranged the lease-back and hired 'servants of the cult' (that is, priests). Religious instruction of children was banned, and conferences of clergy could be held only with official permission. The 1918

Constitution introduced further restrictions; the clergy were disenfranchised and classified among the 'non-toiling' (which entailed high taxation).

Strictly speaking, the conflict between party and Church had been started by the latter for, in January 1918, Tikhon publicly laid his patriarchal curse on the government: 'Come to your senses, ye madmen, and cease your bloody doings!' But the anti-Church measures of 1918 and 1919, the Red Terror being applied against the Church, and the failure of the Whites persuaded Tikhon in 1919 to call on his clergy to accept the regime.

The next crisis came with the 1921–2 famine. The Church was prepared to sell some of its possessions in aid of famine relief but the government (in effect, Lenin) demanded that the Church hand over its consecrated valuables in addition. This, in the eyes of the Church, would be sacrilege. Tikhon's instruction to his priests to resist premature demands for their valuables was easily presented as proof that the Church still thought more of wealth than welfare. When émigré Orthodox priests appealed to foreigners not to contribute to Russian famine relief because this would help the Bolsheviks, the impression of clerical selfishness was strengthened. In early 1922 a decree ordered local soviets to organize the removal of all precious church items. In some places the detachments sent to do this work met no resistance, but at a few others there was a violent reaction from local inhabitants. Machine guns were used against the protesters in some instances, and in this period several thousand priests and nuns were killed. Some, including the metropolitan of Petrograd, were executed on charges of counter-revolutionary activity. Lenin, who had no intention of devoting to famine relief the money raised, expressed a preference for exterminating the entire priesthood which, he alleged, was linked with the notorious Black Hundred of tsarist times.

At this point a group of priests less unsympathetic to the Bolsheviks took over the leadership, calling themselves the Living (or Renovationist) Church. They were more cooperative, and replaced bishops who were openly hostile to them or to the regime. The latter helped by arresting priests who opposed them. Patriarch Tikhon was deposed by the Living Church and his state trial was fixed for the spring of 1923. However, he signed a confession, and publicly repented his anti-Bolshevik past. This earned his release and he immediately reasserted himself as head of the Church. He was unsuccessful, however, in imposing the new 'Bolshevik' calendar; believers threatened to drown as heretics those few priests who tried to make this change, so the Church kept its old calendar, and still does. Many who had adhered to the Living Church transferred their support back to Tikhon. Some priests had liked the Living Church reforms, especially its permission for second marriages of priests, and there had been fears in the party that it might try to become a kind of Soviet Orthodox Church. The Living Church continued to exist, much weakened, and occasionally the Soviet government played off one church against the other. When Tikhon died in 1925 his testament recommended believers to support the Bolsheviks. Nevertheless, his successor did not take office until 1927, because all candidates were arrested. Metropolitan Sergius was finally released from gaol, after promising good conduct, and permitted to head the Church, although his installation as patriarch did not take place until 1943.

Although there was frequently a difference between practice and theory, throughout the Soviet period the official attitude towards the Church had much to recommend it; the individual was allowed to find what comfort he could in the religion of his choice, but the Church as an organization was denied temporal power. Lenin, while despising the religions, nevertheless felt that freedom of belief should not be attacked. In fact religious belief was not necessarily a bar to party membership: in the 1920s it was not unknown for members in Central Asia to take their prayer mats to party meetings. Individuals might in effect be denied the full practice of their faith because their church might be closed, or their local priest might be imprisoned, but such actions did not restrict their freedom of belief, and of private observance. The Church as an organization was not treated so tolerantly as its individual adherents: it lost legal title to its property, many monasteries were converted to barracks or hospitals, its priests were sometimes persecuted, and the 1936 Constitution, while restoring civil rights to priests, confirmed the illegality of religious propaganda, while permitting anti-religious propaganda.

The party, while allowing the state to tolerate religious belief, was determined eventually to eliminate such 'harmful superstitions' by means of propaganda. One of the most successful propaganda onslaughts took place soon after the Revolution, when the silver-and-glass cases containing the relics of saints were publicly opened in the presence of Church, press, party, and believers' representatives. In some cases the long-revered bones were found to be fabrications of wax or plaster: films of the disinterments were shown throughout the republic and were a persuasive anti-religious weapon. In 1925 the Godless League was founded: at first this was a crude and farcical organization, whose young militants smashed church windows and vandalized cemeteries more to satisfy their own psychological needs than for the anti-religious enlightenment on whose behalf they claimed to be acting. The Godless League organized meetings in the villages but the audiences consisted largely of devout believers (sometimes including the village priest) who came because they wanted to show how obliging they were. Anti-religious lectures were given, and anti-religious books and journals published. One of the latter, *Science and Life*, survived as a popular magazine for decades. Like many others, it sought to show how science was making nonsense of traditional religious beliefs, and its popular-style scientific articles were good. If its atheistic articles were somewhat primitive, illustrated with caricatures of black spiky-tailed devils, this was only a reflection of the primitive nature of the Church's own teaching, which played on ignorance and superstition rather than its earlier spirituality. Over the years the Godless League abandoned its cruder and more violent activities, concentrating on pure propaganda work. One of its enterprises was trips above the clouds for village folk, using the big passenger aircraft which Tupolev and others had designed. The object was to demonstrate that there was no God and no heaven up there, but the frequency of plane crashes in the late 1930s allowed another conclusion to be drawn.

Godless propaganda was primarily directed at the peasants, and a great effort was made to associate the priests with reaction: it was the priests who liked to see the peasants get drunk in the village *traktir*, it was the priests who opposed modern science and who opposed collectivization because it threatened their hold on the peasants. In a handbook for Godless agitators,[17] riddles were recommended as one effective form of propaganda:

With an 'i' it drinks up people's money
With an 'o' it helps work the land
And this machine is so strong
That it destroys the power of the priest
(Answer: *traktir/ traktor*)

Quizzes were also useful:

Q. How do you reply to a priest who says 'your communism is just another religion'?
A. All religions involve belief in the supernatural. Communism does not.
Q. How did Karl Marx describe christianity?
A. As the Executive Committee of the bourgeoisie.
Q. Who said 'the best religion is the stupidest'?
A. Pope Alexander VI.
Q. In which country is the church separated from the state only on paper but in reality is in union with state power?
A. America.
Q. Which well-known imperialists are sectarians?
A. Lloyd George, Rockefeller, Coolidge.

The influence of the Church in the countryside was obviously of great relevance in the government's struggle with the peasantry. In the circumstances, the Church escaped relatively lightly from the turmoil of 1930–3. However, in the early 1930s there was a spate of church closures, and the Godless League appeared to flourish (its peak was probably in 1932, when it had about 5 million members), but it had little money and its members were highly transient. After the collectivization drive had been brought to a triumphal conclusion, Church and state coexisted more peacefully, even though anti-religious propaganda continued. This set the stage for the wartime reconciliation. The Godless League was finally disbanded during the war.

17. S. Glyazer and N Kopievskii, *Dosug bezbozhnika* (1930).

A new culture

During the shortages of the First World War a few people developed the habit
of lining up in any queue they saw, without even asking what product was
being sold or was expected. This became a mass phenomenon in the 1930s.
The idea was that whatever scarce item was obtained, it could be bartered off
to somebody who actually wanted it. This habit persisted at least up to the
1990s. There were funny stories, naturally, about the fate of people who joined
a queue near the city divorce office. The piquancy of such jokes lay in the
suspicion that at some time and place, inevitably, the funny event would have
happened in reality.

When Stalin welcomed the Stakhanovite Movement his upbeat 'Life is
getting better, comrades! Life is getting better!' implied that with greater
productivity there would be greater consumption. From 1932 there was a real
effort to put more consumer goods in the stores, and parallel with this the
concept of 'culturedness' was put forward as part of a policy, long needed, of
softening the harshness of social life. It was a campaign that was to last for half
a century and despite recurrent absurdities would do much to enhance the
lives of ordinary people. The social upheavals and conflicts, the end of tsarist-
style deference, and in particular the flow of peasants into the towns had
meant that in public people were uncongenial and at home led narrow lives.
The aim henceforth was that people should be shown how to be 'cultured'.
Often this meant the reintroduction, or imposition, of ways that hitherto had
been derided as 'bourgeois', like changing one's underwear punctually. The
quest for hygiene was one of the first cares of this campaign, and this was
linked with a sub-campaign to clean up the shops. Shop assistants in food
stores were required to wash their hands with soap, and shelves had to be
cleaned regularly. Spitting was discouraged, although with slow result.

A new kind of Soviet man and woman was publicized, people who cared
about possessions and strove to improve their standard of living. In the mid-
1930s it was expected that production of consumer goods would increase and
people could look forward to buying nice things. Magazines began to show
their public how to be discriminating in both taste and quality. At the same
time new stores were opened, modelled on what was thought to be American
practice (a Soviet delegation had also visited British stores, but decided that
there was not much worth imitating in that country). In the bigger cities
department stores appeared, offering advice as well as products. With the end
of bread rationing new bakeries were established and consumers were offered
a wide range of loaves and were bidden to be choosy. All this, in a condition of
general scarcity, gave rise to some bitter comments. How is a shop assistant to
wash her hands if soap has been unobtainable for weeks? How do you change
your bed-linen if you have only one set and there is none in the shops?

The enchanting range of new items shown in the magazines was well out of reach of the ordinary citizen. But there was a new class of people whose affluence enabled them to pay the high prices of the most select stores, and this was targeted as a class that might serve as a role model over subsequent years. To this class belonged the wives of the new highly paid men, typically the 'senior cadres' and 'responsible workers' of government and party institutions. It was these, in the first instance, who would be encouraged to install lampshades and lace curtains and white tablecloths in their homes. In fact, as the years passed, more and more people did adopt these ways, the time-lag being very variable. Part of 'culturedness' was self-improvement and there was a drive to encourage reading, with books published in huge print-runs. This was quickly taken up by almost everybody who was literate, to the benefit of all.

The new, relatively well-off, class of women was encouraged to spread the new gospel of culture. Being the wives of influential males they could often pull strings, or impose their wills, to obtain what they wanted. They were organized into local associations to get things done. Workers' dormitories were a first priority. The women made sure they were cleaned up, perhaps painted, and that no beds touched each other. More remarkably, they might install curtains to act as partitions. The Russian language had no word exactly corresponding to the English 'privacy', but at this time the concept of privacy was certainly in people's minds. In small ways (like installing shower cubicles in place of a common unpartitioned bathroom) it was accepted that there was a public life and a private life.

Much of the effort, in common with other campaigns, was wasted, unappreciated, and taken to absurd and unpopular lengths, but much lived on and developed. This was a case when Stalinism seemed genuinely to add something good to people's lives. It took decades, and indeed in the twenty-first century there remained much to be done, but the objective in making 'culturedness' the norm was achieved, making Russia a more congenial place.

14

The Great Patriotic War

A Japanese hors d'oeuvre

In its expansion from grand duchy to empire, Russia created for herself long frontiers that needed more military support than the economy could provide. One way of making this burden manageable was a good intelligence service, which might at least predict from which direction the next blow would fall. Over the centuries the Russians did develop great skills in maintaining intelligence networks abroad, initially as part of Russian diplomacy.

The Russian espionage tradition was carried further by the Soviet government, which by 1939 had informants all over the world, often in respectable government positions. It was largely due to its agents in Japan that it was able to defeat Japan's Manchurian Army in 1938 and 1939. The Japanese military government's ambition to invade the Russian Far East had been clear for some years, and there was an incursion in force in mid-1938, resulting in the Lake Khasan battle which stopped but did not defeat the Japanese. General Blyukher, who had successfully commanded the Red Army in this operation, was then arrested, tortured, and shot as part of the Red Army purge, so it was a new Russian commander, Zhukov, who faced a second Japanese assault in mid-1939. Well informed by an agent inside the Japanese army command, Zhukov launched an offensive just when the Japanese were in the process of preparing their own attack, and routed them at the battle of Khalkin Gol. This misled the Japanese high command into the belief that the Red Army was strong, despite the purges, and that aggressive expansion would therefore be best directed not against Russia but towards the south.

Foreign policy between the wars

The New Economic Policy had been accompanied by a realization that improved relations with other powers were desirable, in order to preserve the peace which Russia so badly needed, and to attract foreign economic and technical assistance. Diplomatic recognition of the new Russia was a first step, because foreign businessmen were reluctant to trade with, or extend credit to, a state which their own government did not recognize. (American businessmen were an exception; they made private commercial agreements with the USSR long before the USA belatedly recognized the latter in 1933.) Western governments were hesitant to recognize the USSR. All, and especially the USA, were periodically affected by 'red scares' agitating public opinion. The British government was additionally alienated by communist anti-colonial propaganda which was disseminated by Comintern agents in Britain and its empire, while French governments were never allowed to forget the thousands of French investors who had lost their capital after 1917.

A trade agreement with Britain in 1921 implied *de facto* recognition, and about the same time Moscow began to cultivate good relations with Germany. At this time Germany and Russia were the black sheep of the European community, so a rapprochement between them seemed only natural. Because arms limitations had been imposed on Germany, her general staff was glad to take advantage of a secret arrangement for military cooperation (see p. 354). On the diplomatic level, Britain and France were disagreeably surprised in 1922 when Russia and Germany signed the Treaty of Rapallo, which re-established relations, renounced financial claims, and envisaged economic cooperation. For Russia, this was the first *de jure* recognition by a European power. Relations with Germany were good following this agreement, but later became uneasy. Partly the deterioration was caused by the dissonance between the people's commissariat of foreign affairs and the activities of the Communist International. The former, like its tsarist predecessor, was doing its best to promote Russia's interests within an existing world order, whereas the latter stood for the destruction of that order.

In 1924 the new Labour government in Britain recognized the USSR *de jure* and a new trade treaty was drafted. The principal obstacle to the latter, the payment of compensation for British property nationalized by the Bolsheviks, seemed about to be bypassed (in 1922 the Soviet government had agreed in principle to negotiate the settlement of such foreign debts). However, in October 1924, the Conservatives won a British general election which had largely been fought on the issue of the Labour government's alleged softness towards Russia. Just before polling, Conservative newspapers published a letter signed by Zinoviev, apparently sent by the Comintern to the British communist party, in which revolutionary activity inside the British army and in Ireland was suggested. Fears of communism, exacerbated by this so-called 'Zinoviev letter', helped the Conservatives to win, and they refused ratification of the Anglo-Russian trade treaty. Subsequent anti-Soviet actions of the Conservative government were partly provoked by the Comintern's encouragement of British workers in the 1926 General Strike. The British government's rupture of diplomatic relations in 1927, however, was hardly warranted. When in 1929 a Labour government restored relations it was in a sense too late, for the actions of the Conservatives had been taken just in time for Stalin to use them as arguments against the conciliatory foreign policy recommended by Bukharin and Rykov.

In Asia, despite treaties with Turkey, Iran, and Afghanistan, the picture was clouded by events in China. Because the Soviet government believed that it was worthwhile supporting 'national-bourgeois' revolutions in countries seeking to free themselves from foreign domination, aid had been given to the Kuomintang revolutionaries of southern China. Among the Kuomintang officers sent to Moscow for training had been Chiang Kai-shek, who by 1925 was leading the Kuomintang. Although Trotsky and others opposed support of the Kuomintang, preferring to channel Russian aid to the Chinese communists, Stalin insisted that the latter should ally themselves with Chiang Kai-shek. But after the communists had helped Chiang Kai-shek to win his 1926 victories over the Chinese government, they were attacked by the Kuomintang and, for the most part, killed. Only a remnant eventually reached safety in western China and were re-formed into a viable force by Mao Zedong and others.

Soviet foreign policy of the 1930s, because it culminated in the Nazi–Soviet Pact of 1939, has not been favourably regarded. But the Soviet government was far from being the most blameworthy in the events leading to war, even though it is true that Soviet policy helped the rise of Hitler. The succession of Comintern-inspired and abortive revolutions in Germany after the First World War did much to inspire that fear of communism which Hitler exploited. Furthermore, the instructions (originating from Stalin) to the strong German communist party, demanding that it struggle not against the Nazis but the Social Democrats, fatally split the left in Germany during those critical years in which Hitler finally reached the chancellorship. After Hitler came to power the Russo-German military arrangements were finally terminated. Stalin, learning from his mistakes, instructed the Comintern to ensure that the French communist party allied with other left-wing parties in a 'Popular Front' to struggle against emergent fascism in France. In 1934 the USSR joined the League of Nations and her foreign minister, Litvinov, was active among those seeking 'collective security' against fascism. Unfortunately, the events of 1936–8 suggested that with France and Britain pursuing policies of weakness, the League of Nations would remain ineffective.

The Spanish Civil War was an embarrassment to Moscow. A fascist victory might have led to a fascist coup in France, but a victory of the Republicans, with their strong communist element, might have driven the French to seek an anti-communist alliance with Hitler. But if the USSR was to intervene, it could only have supported the left, and this is what happened after a long delay. First the Comintern arranged arms supplies to the Republicans, then organized the International Brigades. Moscow persuaded the Spanish left not to be too radical in its aspirations (that is, to respect foreign investments, and private property). The USSR sent arms and advisers to Spain, but could not match the scale of German and Italian intervention. Although Russian support was appreciated by the Spanish Republicans and their international supporters, the USSR lost prestige, not because the Nationalists won but because of the activities of the NKVD elements which accompanied Soviet aid to Spain. Partly because of a wish to dominate the Republican cause, and partly in order to damage the non-Stalinist left (such as the émigré Trotskyists and anarchists) who were participating in the International Brigade, all kinds of intrigues, secret trials, murders, and arrests were perpetrated by the Soviet security services, and not all could be kept secret.

With Hitler rebuilding the German forces and openly talking of his intention of annexing the Ukraine, and the Anti-Comintern Pact signed by Germany and Japan in 1936, the USSR was faced with the prospect of a war on two fronts without effective allies. While the USSR was coping with the Japanese incursions in the Far East, Hitler annexed Austria and made demands on Czechoslovakia. Among the several treaties which the USSR had made in previous years was a 1935 tripartite pact in which Moscow promised to assist Czechoslovakia if the latter was attacked, provided that France did likewise. Despite Polish non-cooperation, which meant that to help Czechoslovakia the Red Army would have needed to force a passage across Poland, the USSR might well have been willing to meet her obligations under this agreement, but France (with Britain) shrank from a war against Germany. Reasons for this reluctance were lack of confidence in the Red Army following the purges, a disinclination to go to war for a small, distant country, and perhaps a feeling among some conservative politicians that German expansion eastwards was not a bad thing. (Soviet historians gave precedence to the latter reason.) Thus the Munich agreement of 1938 was not only a betrayal of Czechoslovakia, but in a sense of Russia too.

In March 1939 Hitler breached the Munich agreement by occupying the remainder of Czechoslovakia. Most observers expected that a German attack on Poland would follow, sooner or later. Stalin replaced the Jewish Anglophile foreign affairs commissar Litvinov by Molotov, soon to be nicknamed 'Auntie Mol' by British diplomats. In June Germany signed pacts with Latvia and Estonia. The situation was obviously perilous for the Soviet Union, which might soon face German troops on its western frontiers. In the early summer of 1939 negotiations were in progress between France, Britain, and the USSR with a view to an alliance. The British were evidently in no hurry to reach an agreement; their prime minister, Chamberlain, remembered that Britain had been dragged into the tragedy of the First World War by a treaty link with Russia. When, after weeks of procrastination, the British agreed to enter into talks designed to work out a military agreement to set alongside the hoped-for political agreement, their military mission consisted of second-rank officers conveyed in a second-rate steamer.[1] By the time they sat down to business the Russians were already negotiating with the Germans, having given up hope of an alliance with Britain and France, and doubting whether the Anglo-French guarantee of the Polish frontiers in the event of a German attack could be taken seriously.

For the Soviet Union, after losing the hope of an alliance with Britain and France, the best way of securing a few more peaceful years seemed to be an alliance with Hitler. The ten-year Non-aggression Pact which resulted from Nazi foreign minister Ribbentrop's visit to Moscow came as a great shock to western public opinion and especially to the communist parties of the west, which had to support the Soviet alliance with their most dangerous enemy, the Nazis. It came as a surprise to the Russian people too, who for years had been drilled about the evils of fascism. The shocked might have been shattered had they known of the secret protocol of the Pact. This divided Poland into Russian and German sectors, and allowed the USSR to regard Finland, Estonia, Latvia, and Bessarabia as her own sphere (Lithuania was later added).

Two and a half weeks after Hitler's invasion of Poland, the Red Army invaded eastern Poland and advanced to a line previously agreed between Germany and Russia. When Ribbentrop revisited Moscow in the same month, September 1939, it was agreed that Poland would be partitioned between the two victors, and cease to exist as a state. Having done what he could to secure his western approaches, Stalin turned to the defence of Leningrad. He induced the governments of Latvia, Estonia, and Lithuania to permit Russian bases on their territory and then in 1940, with this military leverage, coerced them into requesting absorption as republics of the USSR. Their leaders were deported to prison camps by the NKVD together with thousands of others suspected of being anti-Soviet or potentially anti-Soviet.

Another independent state, Finland, was within shelling distances of Leningrad. Stalin tried at first to safeguard his military position here by negotiation. In exchange for a withdrawal of the Finnish frontier back from the existing line near Leningrad, the grant of bases on Finnish territory at the entrance to the Gulf of Finland and at Petsamo, and some minor concessions, the USSR offered Finland an area of Russian territory in a less valuable region but of double the size. After agonized negotiations the Finnish government refused, largely because it feared that agreement would lead only to further Soviet demands. In November 1939 the Red Air Force bombed Helsinki and the Red Army crossed into Finland. A new People's Government for Finland had already been collected from Finnish communists resident in Russia; it was

---

1. The British military mission travelled in a passenger-carrying freighter badly in need of overhaul. Train travel was ruled out because it would mean passage through Germany, deemed too embarrassing. In contrast, at the height of the Russo-German conflict in 1942, Molotov would travel to London in a Soviet bomber, actually overflying German territory, though at a great height. He survived, despite the Red Army's anti-aircraft gunfire that greeted his return.

never installed in Helsinki as intended but was stabled in a small town on the Finnish side of the frontier. The Red Army in the first month of the campaign was tactically defeated time and again by the much smaller but more versatile Finnish forces. It was only after Finland had exhausted her reserves that she was obliged to negotiate a treaty by which she lost rather more than the territory originally requested by the Soviet Union, including the city of Vyborg. In this campaign the USSR lost enormous prestige, almost provoked hostilities with Britain and France, convinced Hitler that the Red Army was worthless, and ensured that when Germany did attack, Finland would be Hitler's ally. In the meantime the USSR was expelled from the League of Nations.

In 1940, while Hitler was occupied with the conquest of France, the USSR annexed Bessarabia and adjoining northern Bukovina. The latter had not been allotted to the Russian sphere of influence, and Stalin's action annoyed Hitler. For this and other reasons Russo-German relations became uneasy. In December 1940, Hitler ordered preparations to be made for invading Russia in May 1941. In the nick of time, it seemed, Stalin achieved the signature of the Japanese–Soviet Neutrality Pact in April 1941.

Western memoirists, especially in the Cold War years, tended to deplore Stalin's machinations in 1939 and 1940 but, given the circumstances, he achieved the best that could be done, which is more than can be claimed for the British and French governments.

The Soviet armed forces

After Trotsky's departure from the war commissariat in 1925, the army was reduced to under 600,000 men, with a strong cavalry element. Discipline was tightened. Smart drill, well-kept uniforms, and a general staff were three reversions to old army practices. The new soldiers were conscripts from the cities, and the poorer peasants. Rich peasants and 'bourgeois elements' were conscripted into non-military and arduous labour battalions.

In the late 1920s, after Stalin's old crony Voroshilov became war commissar, Russo-German military cooperation reached its peak. Among the achievements of this concealed activity were the joint Russo-German tank training school at Kazan, a poison-gas training centre, a joint pilots' school, and a reorganization of the Soviet armaments industry. Russian officers attended German war colleges and German officers participated in Soviet military manoeuvres (incidentally familiarizing themselves with the border regions, where Russian manoeuvres were traditionally held). The termination of this cooperation in 1933 was regretted by both armies.

By that time the five-year plans were ensuring that the USSR would soon be well supplied with armaments. The new tractor plants at Stalingrad and Kharkov would be easily adapted for tank production should the need arise to supplement the existing works. The tension caused by the rise of Hitler, together with uneasiness in the Far East, prompted an expansion of the Red Army, which exceeded 1.25 million men by 1935. However, there was much that was still imperfect. The peasants who provided most of the infantry were alienated from the regime (and from the officers, who were almost entirely from the towns), and were difficult to train. The exclusion of men of 'bourgeois' origin from the army meant that there was a shortage of young men capable of mastering the theories of military engineering and artillery; all too often officers were men whose main claim to preferment was their proletarian background. This situation was remedied by making all classes of young men liable to conscription into the Red Army.

In 1934 the higher direction of defence was entrusted to the commissar of defence and his eleven specialist deputies. In 1935 officers' ranks were re-established, including the rank of marshal for the top five commanders. This was the start of a process which would culminate in the restoration of officers' epaulettes, the old symbol of tsarist militarism. In effect, a truly professional officer corps was being re-established. The revolutionary Red Army's tradition of badges of rank being worn only in operations, of commanders eating with the men, of the absence of saluting, would be replaced by conventional officer status and authority so that by the mid-1940s a harsh officer was regarded as a good officer and friendliness between officers and men was condemned.

In the late 1930s most officers were mediocre. The old military specialists were disappearing, like their civilian counterparts, the 'bourgeois' specialists, in industry. The majority of the top officers were Civil War veterans, many of whom could not see why the next war should not be fought in the same way as the last, or were men who had been appointed for reasons of political rather than military merit. Nevertheless, there was a nucleus of far-sighted high and intermediate officers whose anticipations of the next war were very close to reality. Tukhachevsky was the best known of these. It was he who largely wrote the new Field Regulations, which foresaw the use of massed tank formations, a high degree of cooperation between infantry, armour, artillery, and air power, and the use of motorized rather than foot-slogging infantry. There was also an emphasis on the use of parachute troops. The world's first parachute troops, it was claimed, were Russian; in 1931 exercises Russian infantry, wearing American parachutes, clung to the wings of German planes and dropped off one by one.

The Red Army purge of 1937–8 had a number of bad consequences. General Vasilicvsky, one of the generals who emerged from the Second World War with a high reputation, had this to say after the war:

You say that without 1937 there would have been no defeat in 1941. But I would go further. Without 1937 there might not have been any war at all in 1941. That Hitler decided to start the war in 1941 was largely thanks to the degree of destruction that our military cadres had gone through. In 1939 I was at the transfer of command of the

Leningrad military region ... there was a whole series of divisions that were commanded by captains, because half the higher officers had been arrested.[2]

Of the higher officers, those spared by the purge were mainly Stalin's old associates of the south-western front during the Civil War. For the most part, they were unfitted to apply the advanced theories adopted by their predecessors. In 1939, just as Hitler was about to demonstrate his panzers to the world, the new Soviet military leadership abandoned Tukhachevsky's concept of massed tank operations and reverted to the more familiar deployment of tanks in small numbers as infantry support.

The main reasons for the poor showing in the war against Finland were the lack of winter training, the mediocrity of the officers, and the disappearance of that close inter-arm coordination which the Tukhachevsky school had so valued. Time and again in this campaign masses of Russian infantry were sent against strong points which the artillery had failed to damage in the preparatory barrage. Repeatedly the artillery missed its targets, because there was no spotting service provided by the air force. Sometimes Russian tanks supporting the infantry would be picked off in turn by just one Finnish anti-tank gun. Almost invariably officers refused to depart from the regulations, or from their orders, to meet an unexpected situation; officers did not dare to be daring.

In addition to their fear of chastisement from above, the officers had difficult relationships with their men following the purges. Soldiers only with some reluctance obeyed orders from superiors who, even if they had escaped the purges yesterday, might tomorrow be declared enemies of the people. This mistrust, as well as resentment aroused by the technical incompetence of many officers, was probably aggravated rather than moderated by the free and easy (or, in some opinions, slovenly) relationships between officers and men.

The performance of the Red Army against the already-shattered Polish army in 1939 was generally pathetic. While officers stumbled around, unable to read a map correctly, soldiers were most interested in piling into Polish shops and acquiring the undreamed-of products to be found there. NKVD men found the cramming of alarm clocks and womens's fashions into soldiers' knapsacks ideologically dangerous. The poor performance of the Red Army in the Finnish campaign, when added to the confidential reports sent in by NKVD and army political commissars during the Polish campaign, aroused great anxiety in the party's Central Committee and the defence commissariat. Timoshenko was put in place of Voroshilov as defence commissar and was charged with putting things right. A number of old officer privileges were restored and officers were required to re-establish a proper hierarchical gap between themselves and their men. Harsher discipline was introduced. Among other things, this allowed officers to shoot soldiers for refusing to obey

---

2. Marshal Vasilievsky, as quoted in K. Simonov, *Glazami cheloveka moego pokoleniya* (1990), 357.

an order in peacetime as well as in war. The inability of troops in the early stages of the Finnish war to carry out simple routine functions, like digging a trench or crossing a stream, was noted, and the performance of proper training programmes became a priority. Some changes were pushed to absurd lengths; for example, the Red Army's deficiencies in snow warfare were reflected in the institution of new winter training procedures so harsh that many soldiers died. And however hard Timoshenko might labour to put things right, much was irremediable because so many of the shortcomings reflected the realities of Soviet society. Timoshenko and his colleagues could not put an end to the NKVD's activity in the army, so destructive of morale, nor could they create a society that every soldier would fight for. The panics that so often overcame Soviet front-line units were not caused by character defects but resulted largely from the cult of secrecy so treasured by the NKVD. The habit of treating any item of information as a state secret meant that units were not told what to expect. Quite often, neither the soldiers nor their officers were told where the enemy was, or in what strength; such information was restricted to the higher officers who issued the orders to the unit. In such conditions panic and an inability to react to circumstances were quite understandable. But this was not unwelcome to senior officers, who did not like their juniors to show initiative, a quality that can can easily merge into insubordination.

Successful field officers of the Finnish war were brought to the defence commissariat. The new chief of the general staff was Zhukov, the victor of Khalkin Gol. Not least, the concept of mass tank formations was restored. Despite these measures, the year's breathing space before Germany attacked was largely misused, because Stalin rejected the possibility of a German attack so soon. The navy commissar later wrote:

In my opinion the great authority of I. V. Stalin played a dual role in military matters. On the one hand everybody believed firmly that Stalin had better knowledge and, when the time came, would take necessary measures. Secondly, this belief discouraged those close to him from having their own opinion, and expressing it directly and decisively.[3]

There was much confusion in the defence commissariat, with urgent decisions being repeatedly postponed. Sometimes the generals could not agree about priorities, sometimes there was time-wasting interference by Stalin's protégés or representatives. It was apparently for resisting such interference that in June 1941 the commissar of the armaments industry was arrested.[4]

Several generals were purged on the eve of the war. In some cases this may have been to encourage the others but at least one of the victims, the air force commander, paid for an indiscretion; reproachfully, he had told Stalin that he

---

3. *Oktryabr*, 11 (1965), 148.
4. He was one of the lucky ones who were released and reinstated when the war started.

was losing too many pilots because they were forced to fly in unsafe aircraft. Many other generals were executed after the invasion, in some cases because they had obeyed orders and not made adequate preparations to meet an attack. Yet others were executed after the war for allowing themselves to be captured. On the whole, with a few glorified exceptions, it was not a good war for generals.

A continuing problem, unique to the Red Army, was the role of the political commissar. In the late 1920s, because so many commanders were party members, the commissars were no longer required to countersign orders of the commanders except in the case of major orders or decisions. In 1934 one-man leadership was further strengthened when commanders were given complete authority in both military and political matters. The commissars were renamed 'political guides' and henceforth were merely to assist commanders in the political education of their men, and advise them on questions of morale and discipline. The army purge did not spare the political directorate of the Red Army. The head of this directorate, Gamarnik, was one of the first victims (like many others, he committed suicide when faced with arrest). At the same time political commissars were restored to their former authority; probably Stalin wished to forestall the resentment aroused in the army by the activities of the NKVD. The dual command of units which was thus re-established was one of the causes of the poor leadership demonstrated in the Finnish campaign. So in 1940 the pre-1937 system was restored, with the commissar again named 'political guide' and subordinated to the unit commander. During and after the war there would be more changes; there was no system which could at once guarantee the party *apparat*'s control over commanders yet at the same time allow commanders the freedom of command which they needed to perform their tasks.

The air force and navy were considered primarily as adjuncts to the army. When the war started in 1941, most Soviet aircraft were of old design. The standard fighter was slower than the German bombers. As with tanks and guns, the changeover to advanced designs, with its inevitable short-term disruption of production, had been too long delayed. The Soviet aircraft industry was capable of doing more than had hitherto been demanded of it, even though some of its best designers, including Tupolev, had been arrested.[5]

The reconstruction of the navy had been slow. The defeat of the Kronstadt rebels had not rid the fleet of its indiscipline and resentment. Moreover, the surviving ships had been in poor condition. Until the late 1930s, when Kuznetsov was appointed people's commissar of the navy, a purely coast defence role was envisaged. The Russo-German cooperation before 1933 had brought blueprints and advice on submarine-building, and by the mid-1930s a

---

5. Individuals with especially valuable talents were sometimes allowed to continue their work as members of incarcerated design teams.

substantial underwater fleet had been created, intended for the coastal waters of the Baltic and Black seas. Then, in 1938, a new navy was planned. Most admirals would have liked aircraft carriers, especially for the new Far Eastern Fleet, but Stalin preferred the more traditional battleships and cruisers:

In their interventions, members of the government often emphasized that the project for one ship or another had been approved by I. V. Stalin personally. This was to imply that such a project was not open to discussion.[6]

The navy remained without aircraft carriers. Some of the cruisers were completed, but the battleships were destined to be destroyed in the shipyards to avoid capture. The Red Navy played a modest role in the war, never quite recovering from the loss of ships and bases in 1941.

June 1941

The Nazi–Soviet Pact could hardly have been regarded by the Soviet leadership as anything but a precaution which would remain effective only so long as Hitler was engaged in western Europe. The USSR loyally fulfilled its obligations under this agreement. Strategic materials were shipped to Germany. Arctic anchorages were made available to German ships. Communist parties were persuaded to hinder the war efforts of those governments at war with Germany. Even German communists, sheltering in Russia from Nazi persecution, called on German workers to support Hitler's war effort. At first, Germany also carried out her obligations; Soviet missions visited German military establishments and industries, and a half-finished German cruiser was transferred to the USSR.

According to some accounts, Hitler's decision in late 1940 to invade Russia in 1941 was known to Soviet intelligence within a week or two. In any case, indications were not long lacking. At the new Russo-German frontier in what was once Poland, the German guards who had previously saluted the appearance of Russian officers no longer did so, confining themselves to derogatory gestures. In February, a sympathetic German printer brought to the Soviet embassy in Berlin a new Russian phrase-book which he had been ordered to print in large numbers; the book included phrases like 'Are you a communist?' and 'Hands up or I'll shoot!' German reconnaissance aircraft made ever-more frequent appearances over Soviet territory. Not all this information was presented directly to Stalin. Since the Nazi–Soviet Pact was concurrently being praised as one of Stalin's great achievements, and since Stalin openly rejected the possibility of German treachery, the reports he saw discreetly minimized what was happening. In a private letter Hitler assured Stalin 'in confidence' that the German troops concentrated in Poland were there to preserve them

---

6. Admiral Kuznetsov, in *Oktyabr*, 9 (1965), 175.

from British bombing raids, and Stalin believed him. Zhdanov, the party leader entrusted with naval and military affairs, was not suited by character or ability for his role as Stalin's military adviser. He did not question Stalin's conviction that Germany would never fight on two fronts and that the English Channel was already one such front. Stalin believed, rationally enough, that Hitler would turn east only after the defeat of Britain, unless there were successful 'provocations'. It was this fear of provocations, of anti-Russian German officers on their own initiative beginning hostilities which would be impossible to stop, that was largely responsible for the lack of preparations behind the frontier. Individual officers who, aware of the danger, might have tried to take precautions, would have done so at their own great risk, for they would have been opposing the official line; their political officers, or the NKVD operatives, would hardly ignore such 'alarmist' moves. While this equation of vigilance with 'alarmism' handicapped the military, the constant reiteration of how right Stalin had been in signing the Nazi–Soviet Pact prevented any psychological preparation of the population against a possible German attack.

In early summer there were more signs of danger. Warnings by western governments could be plausibly dismissed as efforts to embroil the USSR in war against Hitler. But German troop concentrations were not so easily explained, nor were increasing incursions into Soviet airspace by German aircraft. Stalin responded by placatory measures. Delivery to Germany of raw materials was speeded up, Soviet diplomats assured Berlin of Russian loyalty, and on 14 June TASS[7] issued its notorious communiqué on Russo-German relations. This message, given the widest possible publicity, stated that the recent dispatch of German troops 'to the eastern and northeastern regions of Germany must be presumed to be in connection with motives quite independent of Soviet–German relations', and that 'in Soviet opinion, rumours of Germany's intention to break the pact and attack the USSR are baseless'. This communiqué has been described as the 'final tranquillizer' administered to the Red Army; after this authoritative statement it was virtually impossible for any Soviet commander to do anything to meet the threat. Thus, years after other world leaders had realized the futility of appeasement, Stalin had emerged as the biggest appeaser of them all. Yet he was acutely aware of danger; the invasion found him both unsurprised and unprepared.

The abrupt departure of all German ships from Soviet ports, the arrival on the Soviet side of the frontier of sympathetic German deserters (most of whom were categorized as spies and shot sooner or later), and bolder German preparations, persuaded Stalin to call an emergency meeting of defence officials on the afternoon of 21 June. Telegrams were then sent to units near the frontier, warning of a growing threat but urging restraint in the face of

7. Telegraphic Agency of the Soviet Union, founded 1925 as the sole Soviet news agency.

provocations. Many units did not receive these telegrams until it was too late. Others replied by asking whether they should fire, if fired upon; to this they received no satisfactory answer.

Operation Barbarossa, which had been postponed for one month following Hitler's difficulties in Yugoslavia, began at 4 a.m. on 22 June, preceded by air attacks on certain towns. Radio announcements that the USSR was at war came only at noon. From the memoirs of those who were there, it would appear that as dawn broke on 22 June the same scene, with variations, took place wherever officers met: against a background of flame and smoke from Soviet airfields, fuel and ammunition dumps, amid bodies and shattered buildings, Soviet officers with voices raised over the din of German dive-bombers and exploding shells turned to each other and asked, 'Are we at war?'

General Pavlov, commanding the western front, waited three hours before receiving permission to fight back. He was the most prominent of the generals executed in the following weeks for alleged failure to carry out their duties.

The frontier guards of the NKVD also seemed to be unprepared. One detachment later sent in a report which may profitably be read between the lines:

Exactly 0400 Moscow Time 22 6 41 the Germans began to bombard the town of Taurog . . . the first shells destroyed the fuel stock, all autotransport, and food supplies . . . the documents of the detachment were loaded on to two vehicles and sent to Shanlyai. The Battalion Commander in person took away, by car, party documents, registration cards, blank forms, party cards.[8]

The course of the war

Because Soviet military theory was still based on the doctrine of the immediate offensive, many Red Army units and supply dumps were within easy range of German artillery, and were destroyed in the first hours. The Red Air Force was shattered, most of its losses being aircraft destroyed on the ground. Against the advice of his general staff, Stalin had placed the main weight of the Red Army to cover the Ukraine rather than the centre, and this proved mistaken. The German offensive was three pronged: towards Leningrad, towards Moscow, and towards the Ukraine and south-west. Although the objective of destroying the entire Red Army was not achieved (because German intelligence was weak, and had not realized that a Russian redeployment had started in 1941), the Soviet forces were soon in disarray, suffering enormous losses. Several Red Army generals were shot for retreating, and others committed suicide to avoid a similar fate. Unlike the Metropolitan Sergius, who immediately issued a patriotic proclamation, Stalin was silent and shocked in the first few days, but in early July finally made a broadcast in which his appeal for a

8. *Istoricheskii arkhiv*, 3 (1961), 78–9.

total war effort was based more on patriotic than ideological themes; he even addressed his listeners as 'brothers and sisters, dear fellow-countrymen'.

Meanwhile the traditional *stavka* (GHQ) was reinstated. This was located in Moscow and consisted at first of four generals (Voroshilov, Budyenny, Shaposhnikov, and Zhukov) and two party leaders (Stalin and Molotov). Despite the general collapse and at times headlong retreat, Hitler did not succeed in his object of capturing Moscow and Leningrad. The drive on Moscow was delayed by Hitler's order to his armour to halt awhile outside the capital. When an assault was launched it was too late, although some German units reached the suburbs. On 15 October Stalin ordered the evacuation of party and state institutions from Moscow that same day, and demolition charges were laid. He himself was to leave the following morning. Workers were to be given two weeks' pay, and also evacuated from 17 October. But because the military situation improved, the movements planned for 17 October did not take place and their proclamation was not published. In Moscow there had been a short panic, accompanied by looting. Crowds besieged the railway stations and there was some anti-Semitic activity by optimistic Nazi sympathizers. The NKVD execution squads, ordered by Beria to deal with political prisoners, worked overtime (that is, they killed during daylight as well as in the customary night-time hours).

One night, in strictest secrecy, the body of V. I. Lenin was taken out from the Mausoleum and sent under strong guard in a special railway car to Kuibyshev.

There was one point in this proclamation that Stalin wanted nobody to hear about, especially when it became clear that Moscow was holding. It said that Comrade Stalin was to go into evacuation as soon as the proclamation was published.[9]

When it became clear that Moscow was holding out, and that Stalin was still there, the Muscovites settled down to the struggle. Meanwhile, in the north, Leningrad was soon besieged; Voroshilov's handling of the northern forces had not been in keeping with his inflated reputation and he was preparing to abandon Leningrad when Zhukov arrived to take things in hand. However, despite a gruesome siege of twenty-eight months, during which about 700,000 of the population starved or froze to death, Leningrad, like Moscow, never fell into German hands. The German south-western offensive was spectacularly successful. In just two pincer movements, a million prisoners were taken; Odessa was captured and also much of the Crimea. By the end of 1941 the western part of European Russia was occupied.

Although one of the stated reasons for creating the Urals-Kuznetsk steel combine had been the desirability of shifting industry away from vulnerable regions, little had been done to relocate arms industries before the war. Almost all the aircraft industry, for example, was in areas that would be

---

9. V. Karpov in *Gudok*, 19 July 1991, 3.

overrun by the Germans. A relocation would have conflicted with the ruling military doctrine that a future war would be short and offensive. This doctrine meant not only that preparations for the air defence of industry had not been made, but also that plans for evacuating industry were not developed. However, in the short time available the railways and industry worked wonders in evacuating whole factories to the east. Some were taken into Siberia and Central Asia, but most were set down, usually on unprepared sites, in the Urals and Volga regions. Over 1,500 large-scale enterprises were said to have been moved in this way. Once set down, it took months to get them into production, because the necessary components, raw materials, and workers had to be obtained. Despite a cataclysmic cut in civilian production it took time for the war industries to get going. The year 1942 was the worst, with arms and munitions production falling far short of requirements.

However, the German situation in late 1941 was not easy. The Wehrmacht was facing ever-stronger counter-attacks as the Red Army received fresh troops, and it was ill-equipped for winter; its tank engine cylinders cracked in the cold, its army boots, tight and steel nailed, proved disastrously successful heat conductors (at one stage it suffered a thousand frostbite casualties daily), and its supply routes were long, slow, and subject to partisan attack.

Despite his generals' caution, Hitler decided to mount new offensives in the summer of 1942. The main target was to be the Caucasian oilfields, but it was also intended finally to capture Leningrad. Moscow was not considered a prime target. The Wehrmacht did advance through Rostov, capture Sevastopol, and occupy the north Caucasus. The loss of the Crimea and the debacle of the Kerch peninsula were disgraceful episodes that subsequent histories glossed over. The Red Army collapse here was partly because of interference by the feared army commissar who was monitoring proceedings, but displayed other symptoms of deep-rooted incompetence, including a cavalry charge against tanks. General Mekhlis did not allow his troops to dig trenches for fear that they might become defensive minded.

But the German army did not capture the main Caucasian oil region. It might have been more successful if Hitler had not diverted 300,000 men to capture Stalingrad. This city, though of strategic significance, was not all-important, but both Hitler and Stalin chose to regard it as such (it was, after all, 'Stalin's City'). An impressive array of Soviet political and military talent was sent to the city: Vasilievsky, the new chief of the general staff; Zhukov, just appointed a deputy defence commissar in recognition of recently won distinction; Chuikov, commander of the city's garrison; Malenkov, Stalin's personal representative; and Khrushchev, now a senior military commissar, who had retreated with the Red Army from the Ukraine. While a deliberately small holding force defended the city, street by street, house by house, and room by room, big Russian reserves were assembled. As the winter started, these reserves, commanded by Rokossovsky, Yeremenko, and Vatutin, routed Italian and Romanian forces covering the German rear. Hitler refused to allow his commander, Paulus, to withdraw. Goering was unable to keep his promise of a supply airlift. Relief forces failed to break through. Winter became bitter. In February 1943 Paulus and his army surrendered. It was a great Russian victory, especially psychologically. Coming soon after Alamein, it confirmed that the Germans could be beaten; henceforth the Russians were sure that they would win the war. To regard Stalingrad as the turning point of the war in Europe is justified.

The year 1943 was one in which both sides had successes and failures, but the German army was well back from its late-1941 positions. The battle of the Kursk Salient was the first time a German offensive had been stopped on its own start line. Hitler still insisted on rigid defence lines; the German army would have suffered less if he had sanctioned an elastic and mobile defence. In 1944 the big Soviet offensives began, and the Germans thereafter never regained the initiative. In this year (The Year of the Ten Victories) Leningrad was relieved, Sevastopol and the Crimea were regained, the Finns were pushed back in Karelia, the Vistula was reached in Poland, German divisions were cut off in the Baltic states, and the Red Army entered Hungary and Yugoslavia. Finland and Romania ceased hostilities, and Bulgaria (which had declared war against Britain but not against the USSR) was invaded. In January 1945 began the drive towards Berlin, which was captured in May, thereby bringing the war in Europe to a close. By previous agreement, three months later the Red Army attacked Japanese forces in Manchuria, capturing a large part of the region before (and after) Japan's surrender.

The Red Army at war

By 1941, in terms of quantity of men, weapons, and reserves, the Red Army was the world's biggest. Qualitatively it was not so outstanding. Hitler, expecting the Soviet railways to fail in wartime, and influenced by the poor showing of the Red Army in Finland, was not deterred by the numerical disparity. He could even have allocated more forces to the invasion if he had so chosen. As it was, he committed only 182 divisions against about 200 Russian divisions, and about 3,000 tanks against the Russians' 20,000. After 1941 this disparity grew as the USSR's enormous manpower reserves were mobilized and new production lines were opened; in its final offensive against Germany in 1945, the Red Army disposed of more than 5 million men, and could mass 480 guns per mile of front in key offensive sectors.

As in previous Russian wars, defects of leadership were compensated by the sacrifice of masses of infantrymen. Some German eyewitnesses reported how formations of Red soldiers, primed with vodka, would march shoulder to shoulder against strong points, cheering and singing until they were cut down by machine guns. Right up to the end of the war the casualty rate remained very high. During the war, Red Army men killed or missing amounted to between 7 and 10 million, compared to German Eastern Front losses of about half that number (precise figures are not available for either side). Hints as to why Soviet casualties were unnecessarily high are provided by several Russian war novels. In two prizewinning novels about Stalingrad, Simonov's *Days and Nights* (1944), and Nekrasov's *In the Trenches of Stalingrad* (1948) there appear, as subsidiary characters, officers who order one suicidal attack after another (both receiving their due reward, lethal shrapnel in one case, posting to a lethal penal battalion in the other). In a post-Stalin novel, *Men Are Not Born Soldiers* (1963), Simonov portrays mediocre life-squandering officers who owe their positions to generals who themselves are mediocre and owe their appointments to Stalin, who prefers mediocrities. There is also an incident where a commander is removed because his plan of attack, although likely to gain a bloodless victory, would not capture a key objective in time for the Red Army Day celebrations. Kazakevich's short story *By Light of Day*, published in the same period, likewise deplored the haste and coercion:

'Listen, Colonel. You see Height 61.5? You will capture it tomorrow morning. If you take it you will be . . . a Hero of the Soviet Union. If you don't you'll be shot.'

The rule that only written orders were valid caused many costly delays until 1942, when oral orders were allowed for units at battalion level and below. The purges had not been forgotten, even though some of the surviving victims (including the subsequently distinguished General Rokossovsky) had been released. Thus there was usually a strict adherence to orders. Many a key bridge, requiring just the push of a button to demolish it, was captured intact by the Germans because the officer in charge had not received orders to destroy it (often because the next superior officer was awaiting permission from his own superior officer). In 1942 there was another attempt to solve the political commissar problem; since effective command was now all-important, the commissars were reduced to 'deputy commanders for political affairs'. As in the Civil War, these men varied in character; some did resemble the near-perfect heroes of war novels, but others were interfering, paranoid, and sometimes cowardly.

Many wartime novels sought to instil confidence in the military commissars. For example, Grossman's *The People Immortal* (1943) seemed designed to counter two tendencies, that of military men to distrust or belittle their commissars, and the apathy with which many Russians seemed to regard the Germans in the early part of the war. The hero of this novel, Bogarev, is a military commissar and one of those faultless characters so often encountered in Russian literature of the period of Socialist Realism. He is a teacher, critic, and father to his men. When demoralized stragglers are addressed by him their shoulders become squarer, their faces calmer, and their eyes wiser. They decide to collect their precious scraps of tobacco and present them to Bogarev, who refuses twice but accepts the third time with tears in his eyes and a lump in his throat. Later, Bogarev incisively criticizes the unit's commander, a 'front-line man' who (it is implied) has little respect for commissars. Bogarev's comments turn out to be justified when the commander's attack fails. Bogarev reduces to the ranks an officer who openly admires German efficiency, and threatens to have him shot. His motivating force is love for his fellow-countrymen and hatred of the Germans: 'I shall devote all the power of brain and spirit to arousing hatred and vengeance! . . . We must learn to hate, or we shall not win.' In a subsequent novel Grossman again has a commissar hero, this time a stirring character who goes into the attack waving an automatic in one hand and his party card in the other.

The common soldier tended to be of great endurance and stolidity. Individuals at times of isolation often demonstrated a certain cunning and initiative but on the whole the soldiers fought bravely and intelligently only when well led. In the final stages of the war, when the Red Army advanced into Germany, tales were spread of how Russian soldiers relieved the local population of their watches, and how no female between 8 and 80 was safe. Something of the same might have been said about other victorious armies, but the Red Army, after four years of barbarous war, was in a class of its own.

When the war started the Soviet arms industry had only just changed over to new models, but the new weapons, though few, were often exceptionally good; the T34 was probably the most successful tank of the Second World War. But the Tukhachevsky principle of using tanks as a separate arm, en masse, and using tanks to fight tanks, had not really been grasped by the generation of officers which rose to high positions during the purge. The tsarist tradition of high-quality artillery had been continued in the Red Army, but arrests had deprived this arm of many skilled officers. There was also a shortage of good gunners. This was perhaps why during the war there was a great reliance on mortars of various sizes, and why indirect artillery fire was less used than in other armies. In the latter part of the war, large numbers of caterpillar-tracked, armoured, self-propelled guns appeared, and gave the Red Army much-needed mobile artillery support. Also, there was the 'Katyusha', a multiple rocket projector mounted on a truck, which could saturate the enemy positions with its pattern of missiles. It was very effective and, being simple, was ideal for mass production. Mass production was essential, for Soviet strategy and tactics were based on a prodigious expenditure of lives and machines. The average expectation of life of a newly built tank or aircraft was about three months. A somewhat longer life was enjoyed by horses, which, because of the absence of motor trucks, were allocated to infantry divisions on the scale of one horse for every five men.

When Hitler invaded Russia, Britain assured the latter of full support, but this could not be immediately translated into action (however, it was gratefully received, because Britain's attitude might have been different). When in December 1941 the USA entered the war, this not only relieved the apprehension that Japan might turn against the USSR, but also secured preferential access to US industry. But transport difficulties limited this latter advantage, even though there was an Anglo-Russian occupation of Iran to provide at least one route for supplies (the perilous Arctic sea route was also used). At first deliveries were almost negligible, but in 1943–4 a peak was reached, and in those years Allied deliveries were probably equivalent to the output of 7 million Soviet workers. Over the war as a whole about one-sixth of Soviet aircraft were imported. Supplies of some commodities, including aviation fuel, telephone wire, and quality metals, were at times crucial. The Red Army's sweep into Nazi-occupied Europe was accomplished by soldiers wearing American boots, riding in American trucks, and feeding on American Spam. The British contribution was much smaller than the American, although Britain was expensively involved in the transportation of the Allied supplies.

The Red Army was not the only Soviet army. There were also the ground forces of the NKVD. At the beginning of the war these may have approached 200,000 troops, with their own armoured formations. The regular army was irritated by the NKVD's poaching of the best recruits at the conscription centres. The NKVD was by this time a great industrial/military complex. It ran its own industrial enterprises with its forced labour army, and it maintained security with its own military army. Among the sections of the latter were the frontier guards, who formed Russia's first line of defence; it was the NKVD, not the Red Army, which watched the frontiers. Inside the Red Army there were both open and covert NKVD elements. The covert element was made up of informers in the guise of officers and men whose task it was to report any signs of disaffection (often imagined rather than real). Among the overt detachments was SMERSH (a Russian acronym meaning 'death to spies'), one of whose main activities in the war was the shooting of Soviet troops as part of the NKVD's 'special detachments'. It was such detachments, standing with sub-machine guns behind Red Army units, which made it safer to advance than to retreat. In general, Red Army officers and men regarded the NKVD with impotent resentment and fear, but it was not until after 1953 that they would be able to reveal their feelings. It was the NKVD which regarded troops straggling back out of German encirclement as traitors. It was the NKVD which arrested the gifted artillery officer and future writer Solzhenitsyn, who had made some ironic references to 'the man with a moustache'. It was the NKVD which, later, applied Stalin's 1942 instruction that any Red Army man who allowed himself to be taken prisoner was to be considered a traitor (which also meant that his immediate family could be deprived of their ration cards).

Another incentive was the penal battalions, which were made up of officers and men who had behaved badly, or who were regarded by the NKVD as suspect. The penal battalions were used for sacrificial enterprises; it was not unknown for them to be marched through minefields to clear a way for assault troops. Later in the war, the tsarist distinction of Guards units was re-established. Divisions which had distinguished themselves and were of high quality were granted this elite status. They received double pay, better equipment, and were rarely squandered in hopeless attacks.

Russians at war

The war began on a Sunday. Horrified citizens, beset by rumours and hearing little from official sources, gathered together to discuss the news or proceeded to their place of work to ask their bosses or party secretaries what was happening. This spontaneous move to the factory or collective for information and instruction implied much about Soviet society, but what was worrying to the authorities was the messages being received via local party and NKVD sources about the state of public morale in those first hours of war. Sharp criticisms were being voiced by ordinary people, it seemed. These ordinary people were broadly of two types. There were the straightforward, unsophisticated characters who believed that people arrested for anti-state activities in the past really had been guilty, and they therefore did not realize the peril into which they put themselves by saying openly that the party, the government, and Stalin himself had made a mess of things. Then there were those who for years had been seething with impotent fury, who hated the communist party and its works, and at this time of peril and confusion felt they could express themselves openly. The common theme of critics was that the pro-German shift of the recent past had been stupid, and that Stalin was responsible for it. There was a feeling that the party had brought the country to this pass and it could not expect ordinary people to risk their lives to save the situation. There was also the feeling, frequently expressed, that the oncoming Nazis would make short shrift of Jews and communists, which would be no bad thing. The previous widespread faith in the Red Army's ability to crush the Germans had been replaced by pessimism after Germany's defeat of France in 1940. There were queues at the banks as people withdrew their savings, but the government soon placed a limit on the amounts that could be withdrawn.

Several measures were taken to counter this unpatriotic wave. In the first days there were arrests, and genuinely spontaneous meetings of workers were gradually replaced by organized spontaneous meetings at which only the proper sentiments were expressed. There were practice air-raid alarms (in the first of these, people rushing to the bomb shelters typically found them locked up). Passing on information that was contrary to that offered by the official channels became a capital offence. Nevertheless, it took some months for the Soviet population to place itself full-heartedly behind the leadership. Most people supported the government, but public opinion was mixed, if not mixed up. There were great scenes of despair and drunkenness at reservists' assembly points, but on the other hand thousands of citizens clamoured to volunteer for service, anxious to join up in time for the imminent storming of Berlin.

It was the German failure to capture Moscow in late 1941 that solidified public opinion. Even though right from the first week the authorities had wisely described the conflict as a patriotic war, the patriotic response had not been total. But at Moscow the Red Army finally demonstrated that it might after all be able to stop the Germans. Equally important, the Red Army at this time actually recaptured lost territory. Such territory was small, but was large enough to reveal that it was not just communists and Jews who faced extinction by the Nazis. For the first time, what Nazi occupation might mean could be seen and publicized. When the Germans had first approached Moscow there had been disorder in the streets; some citizens fled and others took the opportunity to loot, and attack Jews. But that was the trough of public morale. Henceforth the Russian response to invasion was tough and solid. In the face of Nazi barbarity even the most resentful Russians could forget the past and give their support to Stalin and the party.

In the non-Russian borderlands there was a different situation. In lands occupied by the Red Army in 1939 or 1940 there was naturally little support for Moscow. In the Ukraine, where the memory of the imposed collectivization and famine was still strong, and to a lesser extent in White Russia, feelings were potent enough to impel inhabitants onto the streets to welcome the German invaders. Perhaps if Hitler had promised to abolish collectivization the peasants of the Ukraine, and of Russia too, might have risen in a final and triumphant rebellion against the state. Hitler, however, chose to regard the Slavs as an inferior race, to be exploited until hard labour and hunger caused them to disappear; collective farms seemed an excellent system for this exploitation, and it was not until the tide turned against the Nazis that a few experiments in decollectivization were started.

In the unoccupied zones life was extremely hard. There was a bread rationing system which, as previously, was discriminatory. However, the discrimination was no longer on a class basis, but varied according to employment. Bread became sacred, enormous care being taken to see that people got their daily ration, ranging (in 1943) from 4,418 calories for coal miners to 780 calories for non-working adults. Other foods, rationed according to local schemes, were often unobtainable and never enough. People had to rely on unofficial sources: factory allotments, private gardens, collective farm markets, and barter; but slow starvation was the fate of millions. The only sections of the ordinary population that were guaranteed adequate food supply were front-line troops and some manual workers in vital heavy industries. Labour was completely mobilized, including pensioners and adolescents. Workers could be sent anywhere, and holidays were abolished. Deaths from cold, malnutrition, and overstrain were common. Characteristic of the time were workers who quietly died at the workbench after weeks of malnutrition.

At Leningrad, besieged for more than two years, public hardship was taken to an extreme not seen elsewhere. Food stocks were plainly inadequate, there was daily bombing and shelling, and a breakdown of services such as electric power, heating, and sanitation. The first winter of the war, which was a very cold winter, saw the death of more than half a million people, leaving about 2 million either to live or die in the succeeding months of the siege. Unburied corpses were everywhere, as the funeral service could not cope. At the cemeteries, piles of bodies were an invitation to cannibalism. Even wallpaper was stripped so its paste could be eaten. All available animals were eaten. But rats managed to survive. They swarmed around the one surviving flour mill and an attempt to crush them with tanks failed. When, towards the end of the siege, a rail connection was re-established, one of the first moves of the city soviet was to bring in four freightcars loaded with cats.[10] But even in heroic, suffering, Leningrad, when things went wrong officials could still be arrested for 'counter-revolutionary sabotage'.

Including deaths from enemy action, probably about 15 million Soviet civilians died because of the war. With military killed-and-missing at between 7 and 10 million, this suggests that more than one in ten of the population died during those four years. Millions of the 5 million or so who returned alive from German captivity were sentenced to labour camps.

Thus Soviet press reports of the physical sacrifices made by ordinary Russians were not exaggerated. Some press campaigns, though, were unconvincing, as in the case of the drive ostensibly designed to raise funds for weapons but actually intended to absorb the public's spending power. Letters to Stalin like the following began to be printed in the papers:

Dear Iosif Vissarionovich,
In response to your historic report and order of the day, I am subscribing all my savings—155,000 roubles—to buy a tank . . . May the tracks of this tank mercilessly crush the German Fascist invaders.

LOKTYEV, Evgenii Ivanovich
Kolkhoz beekeeper[11]

---

10. See *Gudok*, 8 Feb. 1997, 4. Even at this dire time, the Russian bureaucratic tradition prevailed. Not only was the volume of cats specified, but also the origin (Yaroslavl) and the breed (Russian Grey, because administrative omniscience defined those as the best ratters).

11. *Izvestiya*, 26 Dec. 1942. This tank would carry a plate: 'Donated to the Red Army by Beekeeper Loktyev'. Public voluntary subscription for weapons was not new to Russia. After the Russo-Japanese War several patriotic citizens had bought ships for the navy. Prince Sheremetiev, for example, gave £201,000 and was rewarded, not entirely tactfully, when one of the 'Fish' class submarines was named *Sheremetiev*. The Sheremetievs were reputed to be tsarist Russia's biggest landowners; perhaps Loktyev was the USSR's biggest beekeeper.

Of real significance was the reconciliation with the Church. There had been signs of this before the war, but after June 1941 the Church's influence as a patriotic force was of vital importance, especially as in some occupied areas local priests were encouraging their flocks to take a pro-Nazi and anti-Soviet attitude. By 1942 there was a tacit understanding between Church and state that their differences were to be forgotten in the common struggle against the foreigner. This alliance seemed to be cemented when Sergius (who had been allowed promotion from metropolitan to patriarch) published a message to Stalin in *Pravda*, 'I cordially and devoutly greet in your person the God-chosen leader of our military and cultural forces'. Additional spiritual reinforcements were dispatched by the Mufti of the Muslims: 'May Allah help you to bring to a victorious end your work of freeing the oppressed peoples. Amen.' Then, after a discreet interval, the president of the Moscow Jewish community sent his own fiery encouragement to Stalin: 'the Almighty has prepared for the Fascist horde the inglorious and shameful destruction suffered by all the Pharaohs, Amalekites and Ammonites.' The support which these messages symbolized was a real asset in sustaining the morale of the Soviet people.[12]

The role of the partisans, small in the beginning of the war, grew later. They flourished especially in the woodlands of White Russia and the Ukraine, where huge tracts of country remained in their control. They were composed largely of Red Army men cut off in the retreat, party members who had been deliberately left behind or parachuted in later, and local inhabitants who joined to avoid deportation or as a reaction to German reprisals in areas subject to partisan activity. Local inhabitants resented the partisans as much as the Germans did, because it is the aim of such guerrillas to prevent any compromise between locals and occupiers. On the whole, Russian inhabitants of German-occupied territory wanted to get on with their lives, and were prepared to cooperate with the Germans who, at least at first, treated them correctly. In occupied areas, local Russian administrators tended to stay in office, as did the police and other local personnel. Burgomasters were appointed from the local population to head districts, and headmen to administer villages; sometimes the headman was the former *kolkhoz* chairman. Ex-communists were sometimes placed in responsible positions; it was possible to find a former Soviet judge working for the Gestapo. Although collective farms were not broken up, peasants were usually allowed to enlarge their private plots. Locals were permitted to start (or repossess) small businesses. Inside the occupied zone about fifteen battalions of the 'Kaminski Brigade' were formed from anti-Soviet inhabitants. They were mainly used against partisans but also took part in suppressing the Warsaw rising of 1944. These brigades had their origin in the People's Socialist Party of Russia, formed with German connivance and publishing its own newspaper. This party, standing for socialism without communists (and without Jews), aroused some alarm in Moscow, and partisans were organized to wipe out its leaders, which they did in 1942. However, its brigades lived on.

Among some non-Russian nationalities there was a certain sympathy with the Germans. In Lithuania there was an anti-Russian rebellion on the eve of the German invasion. A Cossack unit was formed by the German army and, in the Ukraine, General Vatutin was one of many killed by anti-Soviet partisans in a late stage of the war. Nevertheless, the deportation en masse, under lethal conditions, of the Volga Germans, Crimean Tatars, Chechens, and other small nationalities was hardly justified, although it is true that the Germans had formed unenthusiastic Crimean Tatar and Volga Tatar units from prisoners of war. As so often in Russian history, people suffered not for what they had done but for what the security organs suspected they might conceivably be thinking of doing.

Nazi ideology ruined the prospects of the anti-Soviet Russian army which was formed from prisoners of war. This army could have been a million or more strong and, if well armed, might have proved decisive on the Eastern Front. The leader of this army was one of the most popular and successful of the Red Army generals, Vlasov, who decided to make common cause with the Germans after he and his troops were captured thanks to Stalin's refusal to grant permission for a timely withdrawal. But Hitler could not relish the prospect of a Russian army winning successes over Stalin which the racially superior Wehrmacht had failed to win, so the majority of Vlasov's units were employed in non-combatant roles. In 1945 the Allies, in their cynically named 'Operation Keelhaul', rounded up and handed back to the USSR those 'Vlasovites' who fell into their hands. Vlasov was publicly hanged on Red Square.

One of the reasons why so many Russian prisoners of war volunteered for Vlasov's army was that the alternatives were less attractive. Branded as traitors at home because they had allowed themselves to be taken prisoner, they had poor prospects should the USSR win the war. On the other hand, being 'racially inferior', they were not granted the conditions enjoyed by other Allied soldiers in German captivity (Hitler claimed that this was justified because Russia had never signed the Geneva Convention). Over 2 million Red Army men died in captivity. In addition, about 3 million Russian civilians were deported to German labour camps, where they toiled until they dropped. Jews and communists suffered disproportionately, since it was the German practice to execute them immediately. Some communist prisoners survived by concealing their party membership, but usually there was somebody who would denounce them. Similarly, massacres of the Jews were not always unwelcome in the Ukraine and White Russia, where the old anti-Semitism lingered on. The worst massacres were at Babi Yar, outside Kiev, where many thousands of Jews were shot.

Russia and the Allies

Wartime cooperation between the USSR and her Allies was marred by friction. In particular, Stalin in 1942 and 1943 railed against the absence of a Second Front. The Soviet press waged a campaign against idle British generals, and the half-truth was spread that the Americans were willing but the British were not. But Stalin did not see the enormous risks involved in a seaborne invasion. Moreover, Allied forces in Africa already held down significant German forces, and the mere threat of a Normandy landing prevented Hitler concentrating his troops against Russia. Also, Allied bombing of Germany obliged the Luftwaffe to allocate most of its fighters to home defence, enabling the Red Air Force to gain supremacy for the Soviet offensives of 1944–5. Nevertheless, although Stalin did not understand that the west could not wage war like he did, could not sacrifice masses of men simply to gain quick victories, it is also true that the western Allies failed to understand the underlying causes of Russian resentment. There were memories of the First World War, when costly Russian offensives had been launched to take the pressure off the Western Front, and there was an enormous difference between the war being fought in Russia and the war in western Europe. Whereas the latter was national and political, fought with a certain restraint, the Russo-German war was a quasi-racial war, fought with extreme savagery. The sacrifices of the Soviet Union were enormously and horribly greater than those of her Allies. Hitler made a deliberate distinction between his plans for the Russians, and his intentions towards the Anglo-Saxons.

A particularly contentious issue was the fate of Poland. Some Polish prisoners of war from the 1939 campaign, released from Soviet camps, were organized in a new Polish army under General Anders to fight against the Germans on the Eastern Front. However, most of them, including Anders, were anti-Russian, so after some strained discussion between London and Moscow they were allowed to join the Polish forces in Britain. About 15,000 Polish officers and men captured by the Russians had disappeared, and in 1943 German propaganda broadcasts reported the discovery of mass graves of Polish officers in the Katyn forest. Despite a subsequent denial by a Soviet commission of inquiry, it was widely believed that they had been executed by the Russians. That the Soviet investigators were headed by Vyshinsky, well known for falsehood, tended to throw doubt on their published findings; the German investigating commission had included neutral experts. However, until the war was over most western newspapers supported the Soviet view; Allied unity was all-important. It was only four decades later, under the Gorbachev regime, that Soviet responsibility for this crime was confirmed. Apart from the Katyn victims thousands of other Poles, civilians and soldiers, perished in Russian-held territory at the same period.

The Katyn affair led to a breach between the Polish government-in-exile (in London) and the Soviet government. The latter assembled from Polish communists a rival government, which, despite British objections, was installed by the Red Army when it advanced into Poland. The London Poles lost strength when the Warsaw Resistance, which they supported, launched an ill-advised rising as the Red Army approached the city. The Red Army did not attack Warsaw when expected, and the Germans had time to suppress the Resistance. Contrary to its earlier intentions, the British government acquiesced in the new Polish frontiers demanded by Russia; eastern Poland (annexed in 1939) was to remain in the USSR but Poland's western frontier would be moved westwards to the line of the Oder and Neisse rivers. Although this latter demarcation was regarded by the western Allies as provisional, the deportation of the Upper Silesian Germans from the area, and post-war circumstances, made it permanent. Thus the Second World War, which had started on behalf of Poland, ended with Poland's relocation and subjection to a pro-Soviet government. But in view of traditional Polish dislike of Russia, and Poland's own inter-war record, there was something to be said for Stalin's solution of the Polish problem. At that time the peace of Europe was perhaps best safeguarded by a government in Warsaw responsive to Soviet requirements, though this was not appreciated by the long-suffering Poles.

Soviet relations with her western Allies improved after 1943. The Comintern, which the war had made largely irrelevant, was dissolved in 1943 as a placatory gesture. More important, foreign communist parties after June 1941 were instructed to back the war effort of the Allies. When France and Italy were liberated the local communist parties made no attempt to seize power, even though they had great political strength, a fine record in the Resistance, and a stock of arms. Stalin, Roosevelt, and Churchill conferred at Tehran in 1943 and Yalta in 1945. At these meetings Stalin was able sometimes to play off the Americans against the British. This, plus his frequent intransigence, meant that more concessions were made to the USSR than by the USSR. At Yalta, however, Stalin's demand for a seat at the proposed United Nations Assembly for each of the constituent Soviet republics was turned down, although seats were allocated to the Ukraine and White Russia as well as to the USSR; the latter was thus the only state to have three UN votes. Stalin did not welcome Roosevelt's conception of the UN; he would have preferred a world run by Britain, the USA, and the USSR. This was why he ensured that the veto powers of the 'Big Five' would be extensive.

Together with the 1945 Potsdam meeting, these conferences outlined the post-war territorial changes. For Russia, the main gains were confirmation of her acquisitions of 1939–40, together with part of east Prussia (Königsberg becoming Kaliningrad) and, in the Far East, the Kurile Islands and the former Japanese parts of Sakhalin.

15

Consolidation and ossification

Post-war reaction

DESPITE the suffering, the war years were in one sense easier years because, as in 1812, the state and the people grew closer. At the end of the war there was a more relaxed atmosphere, which Russians hoped would continue. Instead, there was a return to the old ways. Unlike most of the other ex-belligerents, the USSR turned its back on change and returned to the 1930s. The western influences that had penetrated during the war were one of the prime objects of attack. 'Soviet patriotism', which resembled Russian chauvinism, was propagandized at the same time as western books, films, music (especially jazz), and technical or social achievements were vilified. In a 1947 admonition to Soviet writers, Zhdanov expressed himself in terms worthy of Nicholas I's publicists:

Is it appropriate for Soviet patriots like us, representatives of progressive Soviet culture, to take the role of admirers or disciples of bourgeois culture? Our literature reflects a society which is on a higher level than any bourgeois-democratic society, a culture which is obviously superior to bourgeois culture and therefore, it need hardly be said, has a right to teach to others the new, universal, morals. Where can one find another people like ours, or a country like ours? Where can one find such wonderful human qualities . . . ?

Information about the outside world, restricted in the 1930s, was even more distorted after 1946, and domestic information was only marginally better.[1] Censorship was more intolerant and more rigorously applied than in tsarist times, and this persisted after Stalin. There had never been any mention of the 1932 famine in the Soviet press.[2] Post-war encyclopedias contained no entry for Trotsky and in 1954, after Beria had been shot, subscribers to the *Great Soviet Encyclopedia* received neatly tailored pages about the Bering Strait to be pasted over the text of Beria's entry. Musicians still needed a special pass to

---

1. People who had dutifully handed in their radios on the outbreak of war got them back when that was possible. But standard Soviet radios did not receive foreign transmissions. The latter were jammed as an additional precaution.

2. Even under Khrushchev, Russian calamities (for example, air crashes) were not mentioned unless foreigners were involved. Foreign disasters received good coverage, however.

listen to recordings of Stravinsky. The censorship, whose existence was not publicized, effectively blocked the publication not only of heretical views but also of any facts which might possibly cast doubt on official ideology or official information. Newspaper editors had regular meetings with officials, in order to plan future news. Newspapers were censored twice, before printing and before distribution. The exhaustive pre-print scrutiny explains why Soviet newspapers were so admirably free of misprints.

The kind of propaganda which was inflicted on the Russian people was also inflicted on the outside world, through local communist parties or associations set up and financed either by Soviet agencies or by communist sympathizers. However, in conditions where there were several competing sources of information this propaganda probably made more enemies than friends. There was something ludicrous, for example, in the claim that Britain was planning war against the USSR at the very time when the British government was permitting the export to Russia of jet aero engines, of which the USSR had little experience. The 'Stockholm Peace Appeal', launched to obtain millions of signatures to a petition directed against war, seemed similarly inept, especially as it originated in the nation with the world's largest standing army.

Stalin was 66 in 1945, and he retained the two key posts of head of government (which he had assumed in place of Molotov in May 1941) and party secretary. His desire to run the USSR in the old ways was expressed in the post-war composition of the Politburo, which was basically the same as in 1939 (both the 1939 and 1948 Politburos contained Stalin, Molotov, Voroshilov, Kaganovich, Mikoyan, Andreyev, and Khrushchev. Two 1939 members, Kalinin and Zhdanov, died in 1946 and 1948, while Malenkov, Beria, Voznesensky, and Bulganin joined after 1939). In the early 1940s, Zhdanov and Malenkov seemed to be Stalin's favourites. Zhdanov was the guardian of ideological and cultural purity. He had been in charge of Leningrad during the siege, although true leadership had been provided by Kuznetsov, Zhdanov preferring to spend his time in a bomb shelter. Malenkov had risen rapidly since his first appointment to the *apparat* in 1925. There was personal jealousy between Malenkov and Zhdanov, and Stalin was aware of it.

When Zhdanov died in 1948 there was a purge of his associates. About 200 were purged and the affair became known as the 'Leningrad affair' because the victims were current or past officials of the Leningrad party organization. Among the executed was Voznesensky, whose demise removed a figure whose economic views were too rational for comfort, and Kuznetsov. The latter was first secretary of the Leningrad party organization, and was said to be somewhat restrained in his public praise of Stalin. Nevertheless Stalin had appointed him to supervise the MVD[3] and security organizations, and this

---

3. In 1946 the people's commissariats were renamed ministries. Hence the NKVD became MVD.

could hardly have failed to arouse the jealousy of Beria who, with Malenkov, engineered the Leningrad affair. A few of Zhdanov's Leningrad protégés, including Kosygin, were spared.

It was in the wake of the Leningrad affair that Khrushchev was recalled to Moscow; possibly Stalin felt a new counterweight to Malenkov was needed. At the 19th Party Congress in 1952 a nice balance of power was implied in the choice of Malenkov to present the Central Committee's main report, and of Khrushchev to present the new party Rules. This congress was the first for thirteen years; the party had lost its pre-eminence in the 1930s, having become simply a tool of Stalin. It had grown enormously during the war because large numbers of servicemen had been enrolled with little check on their qualifications; the 1940 membership had been around 4 million, but this had grown to 6 million in 1945, even though wartime losses had been very heavy. At the time of the 19th congress three-quarters of the membership were under 45 years of age.

After the war the party continued to be an instrument of administration. Party professionals in a locality were responsible for coordinating economic activity, helping managers do their job. But it was quite common for them to interfere in management, which in principle was deprecated. During the war the party had become more directed, and continued to be an auxiliary of the government rather than an independent force. Because of its huge wartime intake, many of its officials were inexperienced and lacked confidence; the blind imposition of central directives came naturally to them. Most had little feeling for the old revolutionary traditions, little knowledge of the outside world, but a great regard for the regime which had educated them and found white-collar jobs for them. In the post-war years there was a curtailment of recruitment, with stricter entry tests, and many party organizations which had become cliques during the war were purged. In these years some real headway was at last made in strengthening the party in the collective farms, while at the same time there was a drastic and intended fall in army membership.

The 1952 Congress was followed by the initial stages of what seemed to be a new massive purge. Possibly Stalin realized that his principal lieutenants were ageing men, out of touch with the new generation of the administrative and technical elite. He had begun to treat his former friends Molotov and Mikoyan with a brusqueness that could only throw doubt on their longevity. Khrushchev's memoirs suggest that a new purge, once started, would have spread to all ranks of the party organization. In January 1953 it was announced that nine doctors (of whom seven were Jewish) had been accused of working for a US Jewish organization and of killing Zhdanov and other high Soviet leaders whom they had treated. The minister of state security, Ignatiev, was told (according to Khrushchev) that he would be shortened by a head if he did not obtain confessions from the doctors. The confessions were duly obtained.

(although two of the doctors died in the process) but Stalin died before executions could take place. The surviving doctors were then released, the 'Doctors' 'Plot' was declared a fabrication, certain MVD officials were executed, and the doctor (a part-time MVD informer) who had been awarded the Order of Lenin for her vigilance in first denouncing the doctors handed back her decoration.

Post-war reconstruction

Even allowing for the fact that, when the rubble was cleared away, many 'completely destroyed' structures were revealed as partly intact, the physical damage caused by the Germans was enormous. Apart from the normal destruction of war, there was the Russian 'scorched earth' policy of 1941, and the systematic destruction by the retreating Germans after 1943. When the war ended, at least 25 million Russians were homeless. Long lengths of railway track had been torn up. Dams, bridges, and factories had been wrecked and livestock destroyed.

The Fourth Five-Year Plan (1946–50) was designed to restore the Soviet economy to the pre-war level; Stalin promised at least two more hard five-year plans to follow. In fact the economy recovered very rapidly, pre-war standards in industry (but not agriculture) being largely reached after three years. The main credit for this belonged to the unbelievably hard work and unbelievably harsh privations of the Soviet people. The labour of at least 2 million prisoners of war, reparations from Germany, Finland, Romania, Hungary, and Manchuria, one-sided trade agreements with the people's democracies, deliveries of some key items by UN agencies, Britain, and Sweden, and the advantages, in situations of scarcity, of strong central planning also made substantial contributions.

This achievement was marred somewhat, especially in the Fifth Plan, by the resources devoted to the 'grandiose Stalin construction projects'. Among these was the expensive Volga–Don Canal, which had very little traffic but many statues of Stalin. The enormous hydroelectric schemes, which converted long lengths of the Volga into artificial lakes, were also unwise in so far as they tied up great quantities of labour and material in projects which would take years to become productive.

The wartime relaxation of control over the farms had, among other things, meant that much collective land, implements, and stock had found its way into the private economy of the peasants. The party was very weak in the countryside. Many farm chairmen abused their positions. There was a shortage of tractors and horses, which meant that women were sometimes harnessed to the ploughs. The more able-bodied men had tended to move to the towns before the war, and many of those who had stayed had been later killed at the front. It was possible to find villages entirely populated by widows and children. The poor harvest of 1946 resulted in a partial famine in 1947, accompanied by rioting in some localities.

Khrushchev, who after the dismissal of Andreyev fancied himself as the party's agricultural expert, proposed the amalgamation of adjacent farms to form units which would be more easily controlled and which would be big enough to maintain party cells. This (which was the reverse of what needed to be done) meant that by the end of 1952 the previous quarter-million collectives had been merged into about 100,000 larger units. However, Khrushchev's advocacy of even bigger concentrations, 'agrotowns', was rejected. During this period peasant income was negligible. Strong measures were taken against misappropriation of farm property in 1946. Stalin tried to impose the 'Travopolye' rotation (see p. 392) and an additional burden was another of Stalin's grandiose transformations: the planting of extensive belts of trees in semi-arid regions, in order to improve the climate of the USSR. This scheme failed because most of the trees died from lack of moisture.

Russia and the world

When the war ended the Red Army was the world's most powerful, and it occupied most of central and eastern Europe. Although Stalin publicly belittled the significance of the atomic bomb, its possession by the USA did dominate the strategic balance. Outside the Soviet orbit Russia had earned great respect and popularity during the war. In Britain a Labour government was anxious to fulfil its election promise that 'left can speak to left'. But in the USA the sympathetic Roosevelt died in 1945 and was replaced by Truman, whose experience as a Missouri politician had not predisposed him towards favouring the communists; one of his first acts was to suspend Lend-Lease to Russia. Nevertheless, it seems doubtful that the so-called Cold War would have been avoided by a different US president; Stalin was already too distrustful. The Cold War resulted from a mixture of mutual distrust and genuine differences.

The gradual establishment of Stalinist people's democracies in central and eastern Europe was one cause of dissension between the former allies. The process which had started with Poland during the war was repeated in the cases of Hungary, Albania, Bulgaria, Yugoslavia, and Romania. Finland and Czechoslovakia were spared. Indeed, Finland was treated in the way which the west had envisaged for all of Russia's neighbours; there was an independent and freely elected government which regarded friendly relations with the USSR as a first priority. In Czechoslovakia the communist party was able to establish itself as an important partner in the government by virtue of its genuine electoral support; in 1946 it received more than one-third of the votes. One people's democracy which failed was that of the Soviet zone of Iran. Northern Iran, occupied by the USSR at the same time as southern Iran was occupied by the British, was due to be evacuated after the war. The USSR was at first reluctant to abandon this outpost in the Middle East, in which a 'people's government' had been installed. But the Red Army was finally withdrawn in 1946, and the 'people's government' abandoned its people and retired to the USSR.

The Soviet Union was determined to transfer to the USSR German plant (and some key personnel) located in the Soviet zone of occupation. It also demanded a share of the industry of the Ruhr, as well as a share in the administration of that region. This Ruhr claim was rejected by the western Allies. Moscow retaliated by refusing to sign an Austrian peace treaty. In Manchuria, the Red Army succeeded in stripping much of the local industry before that region was handed back to the Chinese.

The western press was beginning to talk of Soviet espionage, but its readers were unaware that western intelligence services were themselves engaged in anti-Soviet activities. The CIA was busy supporting the armed nationalists in the Ukraine, while British intelligence was shipping anti-Soviet emigrants back into the Baltic republics where, it was imagined, they would form the nucleus of an anti-Soviet rising. Neither the Americans nor the British were a match for the Soviet security organizations, and hundreds of Ukrainians and Lithuanians were sacrificed. But other Ukrainians carried on a guerrilla war into the 1950s. In 1946 came Churchill's Fulton speech, warning America of dark Soviet intentions, and the first steps towards the long-term division of Germany; the British and American occupation zones were amalgamated and, together with the French zone, later became the West German Republic. At the same time the Soviet zone of Germany was becoming the German Democratic Republic. Over the years there were attempts to reach agreement on the reunification of Germany, although it is doubtful whether any government, apart from the US and West German, genuinely wanted reunification. Stalin's unsuccessful attempt to blockade the western sector of Berlin in 1948 was an incautious endeavour to force Britain, France, and the USA out of Berlin.

The USSR delegation to the initial talks on the Marshall Plan staged a walk-out, led by Molotov, and Soviet pressure prevented Czechoslovakia's participation in this 1947 US aid project for war-torn Europe; it was seen as a device for opening up Europe for American capitalism. In the same year a new uncompromising Soviet line in foreign policy was presented by Zhdanov, who stated that the world was irrevocably split into two camps. To replace the Comintern, the Communist Information Bureau (Cominform) was established to coordinate the policies of the main European communist parties. In France and Italy the strong local parties were instructed to begin a campaign of strikes, demonstrations, and sabotage. When the latter caused casualties the communists lost much of their popularity in those two countries, and their electoral position worsened.

The year 1948, with its deepening of the German crisis, also saw a transformation of the 'socialist camp'. The Soviet treatment of the people's democracies had not been as sympathetic as their communist governments had expected. Commercial agreements were imposed in which Soviet exports were priced high and Soviet imports priced low. This reduction of the people's democracies to a colonial status was accompanied by close political and MVD supervision. Their governments were compelled to introduce socialism strictly on the Russian model: 'there is only one road to socialism, the Soviet road.' In this way friendly post-war governments and often sympathetic people were replaced by fawning governments and resentful people. Soviet security personnel orchestrated periodic purges inside the east European communist parties. East Germans, as well as some Red Army men, deserted to the west.

In February 1948 a coup placed the Czech communists in absolute power, but in 1951–2 many agents of the coup, stalwart communists like Slansky and Clementis, were tried on charges of spying for Britain and Israel, and were executed. These and other arrests and executions in the people's democracies were occasioned by the defection of Tito's Yugoslavia in 1948; potential 'Titoists' elsewhere were liquidated as a precaution. Unlike other people's democracies, Yugoslavia was isolated from the Red Army, had a popular leader who had not depended on Soviet support to gain or maintain power, and was thus able and willing to resist Soviet interference. After the parties and governments of Russia and Yugoslavia had exchanged accusations of spying on each other, the Cominform expelled the Yugoslav party. Tito, in the vituperative language which for years had been favoured by Soviet propagandists, was called 'a capitalist hyena' and his government 'terroristic, shameful, and quite Turkish'. With strong support from his own people and party, and some help from the west, Tito, to Stalin's disgust, survived and purveyed the dangerous suggestion that the Soviet road to socialism was a cul-de-sac.

In 1948 the USSR was the first country to recognize the new state of Israel *de jure*. It provided arms to help fight the Arabs and apparently believed that the Israeli Mapam party was pro-Soviet. Stalin soon changed his mind. There was an anti-Jewish campaign inside the USSR. The wartime anti-fascist Jewish committee was closed; its leader was killed in a staged car crash and then given a state funeral.

In the Far East the communists finally overcame the Kuomintang and set up the Chinese People's Republic in 1949. Stalin had neither expected nor hoped for this success and had done little to help the Chinese communists. However, after 1949 Soviet economic and technical help was given to the new Chinese government, although the Soviet technicians included the usual complement of security men.

At the United Nations Vyshinsky (who was foreign minister up to 1953) specialized in negative vituperation. His conduct earned the resentment of smaller nations which had placed great hope in the UN. Goodwill was also lost elsewhere. The west formed an armed anti-Soviet alliance, NATO, two of whose member-nations (Norway and Turkey) bordered the USSR and thus outflanked the line of people's democracies which formed a buffer between the USSR and the west. In the west, the USSR rather than the North Korean government was portrayed as instigator of the Korean War.

Population

According to the 1926 census, the population of the USSR was 147 million, and growing at the rate of 3 million annually. The 1937 census result was suppressed, and its compilers purged. A new and less reliable census in 1939 produced a figure of 171 million. The growth rate had fallen partly because of several million unnatural deaths but largely because of a fall in the birth rate. The rural population had fallen from 82 to 67 per cent of the total and urban families had a birth rate even lower than usual because of the housing shortage. Nevertheless, in 1939 the population was a young population, which was a great advantage in the war years. The war brought great losses, and also the acquisition of new peoples in the annexed territories. There was a good deal of what euphemistically was called relocation but in practical terms was the uprooting of whole communities. From the new, formerly Polish, territories many supposedly unreliable Ukrainians and Byelorussians were moved out, while new Russian and Ukrainian settlers were brought in, some from as far away as Siberia. Some of the nationalities moved during the war were allowed home, but not the Crimean Tatars, who were still regarded as traitors and many of whom were settled in the ostensibly Jewish autonomous region of Birobidzhan. In order to Russify the Baltic republics, the heavy loss of natives by war and deportation was made up by the settlement of Russians; in the late 1940s Estonia received 180,000 Russians, an influential number because its pre-war population had been little more than 1 million. In Latvia, Russians accounted for a quarter of the population by 1959, compared to about 12 per cent in the 1930s. Most of the Russian intake to the Baltic republics came willingly, but this was not always the case with the half-million peasants drafted to the former German territory of Kaliningrad (Königsberg), to eastern Siberia, and to Sakhalin, although the settlers were chosen from the more overcrowded lands of European Russia and, in the end, were probably better off for the change. In newly acquired territories, 'sovietization' was also undertaken, culminating in collectivization and deportation of so-called kulaks. In the case of the Baltic states, the western Ukraine, and western Byelorussia, as well as most of Moldavia, this collectivization was imposed in 1949.[4]

4. Collectivization was also imposed in the people's democracies. Whether it should be regarded as a seal of approval, a *pièce de résistance*, or a *coup de grâce* is perhaps a matter of taste. But there was something obsessive about the importance Moscow attached to this change; almost as though, by repeating the process of 1930, collectivization could be proved right. The Poles managed to avoid large-scale collectivization.

After the war the population soon recovered; those who had died from the privations of war were largely the old and weak and there was therefore a drastic decline in the death rate in the immediate post-war years. Thus, although the birth rate continued to fall, the population reached about 209 million in 1959, and 242 million in 1970. After 1963 the urban population outnumbered the rural (for fuller population statistics, see p. 606).

The introduction of civil marriage after the Revolution had made both marriage and divorce cheap and easy, but these advantages were seriously offset by the number of hastily contracted marriages which broke up, leaving children more or less abandoned (between 1920 and 1927, which admittedly includes the famine years, about 2 million children were abandoned by their parents, and many died from cold and hunger). In 1926 abortion was legalized to reduce the number of unwanted children, and this caused a fall in the birth rate. In 1936, to halt a further and unwanted fall in the birth rate, measures were taken to 'strengthen the family'. Divorce became expensive and difficult. Abortion was forbidden except where the mother's health was in serious danger. Financial allowances were granted for large families. The war resulted in a further fall in the birth rate, a shortage of marriageable men, and a distressing number of young widows. In 1944 a new decree was issued; distinctions were introduced for fertile mothers (those who reached ten children became 'mother-heroines'), allowances were improved for large families, special financial and other help was granted to unmarried mothers, and extra taxes were levied on bachelors, spinsters, and childless couples. The birth rate did rise, and in the 1950s averaged twenty-five per thousand, but began to fall noticeably in the 1960s. In 1955 abortion on request was relegalized with negligible effect on the birth rate, although in the 1960s abortions outnumbered births. In the towns, housing problems affected family size; even the housing achievements of the Khrushchev era were largely in terms of small-size apartments. Policy on birth control seemed indecisive; the right of a woman to choose the size of her family was unquestioned, yet incentives continued for large families. In the late 1960s the Supreme Soviet on average conferred 9,000 'mother-heroine' titles each year. Special allowances for unmarried mothers continued. In the 1970s the contraceptive pill was virtually unobtainable.

According to the 1959 census, two-thirds of females over 14 years old were gainfully employed, ranging from one-tenth of the 14–15 age group to four-fifths of the 20–39 group. Although the official retiring age for women was 55 (for men it was 60), one-third of the women over 60 were still at work, although half of these were peasant women working on their household plots. Partly because about 55 per cent of agricultural workers were female, about four-fifths of Soviet female workers were unskilled and therefore low-paid.

By 1948 over 8 million soldiers had been demobilized, yet labour still remained short. In 1945 Russian prisoners of war and other displaced persons were returned home, typically being met at the frontier by brass bands before appearing before NKVD commissions that allowed some to go home but sent others, including most of the officers, to labour camps as 'unreliable elements'. There were also German prisoners, the majority of whom were made to work in harsh conditions until they died. Enemy prisoners, former Russian POWs, civilian repatriates, and the civilian criminal and political prisoners collectively made up the convict labour force of several million souls. To recruit free workers for unskilled work in arduous locations the recruitment organization *Orgnabor*, which had been useful in the 1930s for signing up peasants, offered contracts and found many takers among demobilized soldiers in the collective farms. There was also conscript labour, a continuation of the compulsory labour service introduced during the war.

One problem in the post-Stalin period was the uneven distribution of population. Whereas the cities of European Russia were overpopulated[5] the continuing priority placed on development of Asiatic Russia demanded an influx of new settlers. Yet in the 1950s and subsequent decades more people emigrated from, than immigrated to, Siberia; not only involuntary inhabitants in labour camps, freed by the death of Stalin, but also recent immigrants tended to return to European Russia, which they considered a more attractive place to live in.

Living standards

During the NEP period living standards had risen slowly, but after 1928 they fell, and remained low, with troughs of privation in 1933, the war, and 1947. Various means were adopted for extracting the maximum effort from the people with the minimum satisfaction of their needs. In the First Five-Year Plan there was inflation, and in 1931 the Turnover Tax was introduced. This, a value-added tax, was a device for absorbing spending power, and became the main source of taxation revenue; as in tsarist Russia, personal income tax was negligible in Soviet Russia.

Retail trade, like the industrial system as a whole, did not have goods seeking a buyer, but always the reverse; this is one reason why the professional salesman was absent from the scene, although not the tolerated but sometimes shady character known as a 'fixer' or procurer. Shortages meant that the consumer had to 'take it or leave it' (a situation later described as the 'imposition of compulsory products'). Factory managers often found that the best or only way of fulfilling their plan was to supply poor-quality products. From 1938 to 1941 there seems to have been little or no improvement in living standards over 1937, and the effect of the war was cataclysmic. There were some Russians who did quite well (peasants who were able to get astronomical

5. By 1979 Moscow had 8 million inhabitants and Leningrad 4.6. Eight other cities had more than 1 million. Permission to settle in the bigger cities was not easily obtained, and could be withdrawn.

prices for those products which they could market in the towns, and many factory workers). But since there was little to buy, those who enjoyed high money incomes could only save and hope.[6] In terms of what wage-earners could actually buy with their money, 1945 standards were around 40 per cent of 1940, which had been a barely tolerable year. The years 1946 and 1947 witnessed a repetition of the conditions of the First Five-Year Plan, but in 1947 there began a slow improvement. Wartime rationing was abolished. By 1952, the 1940 standard of living had been reached by average workers, although they were working more hours (ten to twelve hours and six days a week) than in 1940.

The inadequate urban infrastructure was probably felt as much as shortages of goods. Poor public transport meant that for many workers the day included hours of uncomfortable travel to and from work. The deliberate neglect of 'unproductive' services like retail stores meant that everyday necessities like bread or vegetables were acquired by long queuing. Since, in order to make both ends meet, it was usual for both husband and wife to work, there was an important role for the grandmother: *Babushka* would look after the children, queue for food, and keep the household going while the married couple would earn the family income. The really black spot in Stalinist social policy was housing. Little provision was made for the vastly increased urban population. In the mid-1930s, only about 6 per cent of households in Moscow had more than one room, one-quarter shared a room with one or more other households, one-quarter of the households (mainly one-person) lived in dormitories, and about 5 per cent had neither room nor dormitory, living in a bathroom, kitchen, corridor, or hallway. The war made this situation considerably worse, and it was only after Stalin's death that a housing drive was started. What sometimes shocked even sympathetic western observers was that while Russians were abysmally and miserably housed, great prestige projects pre-empted valuable building resources. Before the war there was the Moscow Metro, in which every station was an underground palace. After the war there were great skyscraper buildings, usually containing state institutions. But housing was cheap, few families spending more than about 8 per cent of their income on rent. Also, the Soviet equivalent of Cubs and Brownies, the Pioneers, with their daily programmes and holiday camps, took pressure off big families living in cramped quarters.

While strikes were almost unthinkable, and trade union economic demands non-existent, the unions did perform a role in their administration of various welfare services. The local trade union branch would, in the biggest enterprises at least, provide sports facilities, meeting halls, film shows, and other cultural services. In addition, it might negotiate with management over questions of factory amenities. It maintained its own cooperative store and

---

6. The hope was misplaced; in 1947 a revaluation of the rouble wiped out most of those savings.

sometimes its own hospital. Also, it might operate in one of the resorts its own sanatorium and holiday centre (often a confiscated pre-1917 palace). Every worker was entitled to two weeks' holiday with pay, although when labour discipline was tightened this became dependent on good behaviour. Some workers went on cheap holidays subsidized by their union. However, such accommodation covered only a fraction of those who would have liked to make use of it, and the selection process of applicants was yet another incentive for workers to become 'deserving'. Sick pay was also administered by the union.[7] Expulsion from a trade union could therefore be a serious matter; with union membership went the right to work in that particular industry (and therefore the right to live in factory housing), and a host of welfare services.

As in education, Soviet medical services had a pre-revolutionary foundation on which to work, but this does not detract from the achievement, especially as the number of doctors lost between 1914 and 1920 was disproportionately great. Just as education was designed to be available to all, so were medical services planned to benefit the entire population. Compulsory vaccination programmes were carried out, and in 1921 and 1970 cholera outbreaks were contained by ruthless quarantine and mass vaccination. From 1928 to 1940 the number of doctors increased from about 70,000 to 155,000; there had been 23,000 in 1913. By 1958 there were 362,000 and in 1967 this rose to one doctor for every 450 people, a better rate than in the USA. In terms of hospital beds, facilities rose from about 207,000 in 1912 to 247,000 in 1928, 791,000 in 1939, 1,533,000 in 1958, and 2,567,000 in 1969. These figures do not include sanatoria, which provided about 300,000 beds by 1958. The numbers flatter, because most hospitals were very badly equipped and maintained. The health service emphasized preventive medicine; all sanitary inspectors were doctors. The service was and remained authoritarian. Patients had little choice of treatment; they did what the doctor told them, even if this meant accepting vaccinations or operations they did not want, and they waited hours and even days for attention. In some ways this was the best way to run a health service, the wastage of frivolous demands and hypochondria being largely eliminated. On the other hand, there was a disdainful neglect of psychological and nervous complaints. Expansion of health services was made possible by the intake of women training to become doctors or *feldshers* (trained medical assistants), encouraged by the Bolshevik resolution to give equal professional opportunities to females. In 1970 about 70 per cent of doctors were female (compared with 10 per cent in 1913). Training of Soviet doctors (six years) was perhaps less thorough than in other countries, and the pharmaceutical industry was backward. Apart from a few special clinics reserved for top people, there was

7. Unemployment pay was abolished when unemployment was officially declared non-existent in 1930.

also a small private practice; although doctors were attached to hospitals and clinics they were allowed to treat private patients, their fees being rather highly taxed. After the 1920s, all patients, private or otherwise, paid for their medicines. The last year of Stalin's life was especially difficult for the medical profession, overworked in any case. The 'Doctors' Plot' meant that vicious allegations about 'assassins in white coats' were repeatedly purveyed by the press and propagandists, so that medicine became a high-risk profession, especially for Jews. The MVD was eager to arrest doctors, who knew that they might be denounced by any patient dissatisfied with his treatment.

Education

Before 1917, the Duma had made plans for universal education by 1922, but this programme had doubtful prospects. After the Bolshevik victory a reconstruction of education was regarded as essential. Lunacharsky was appointed commissar for education in 1917, and supervised all schools and institutes except those operated by other ministries. In 1918 the church schools were taken over by local soviets. From 1917 to about 1931 educational policy was ostensibly revolutionary; old principles were overthrown and new theories applied. In 1919 the 8th Party Congress laid down the principles on which communist education should be based. These included free and compulsory education up to the age of 17 (this was not achieved because of teacher and building shortages, although from 1927 it was applied up to the age of 12). The basic type of school was the 'polytechnic' (a form of comprehensive school which would eliminate class divisions in education). Although both Lunacharsky and Krupskaya (who took a great interest in education) strongly favoured the polytechnic principle, others were reluctant to jettison the high-quality nine-year schools which had been developed from the tsarist schools. This disagreement continued until, in the 1930s, separate technical schools came back into favour.

One important measure was the establishment of 'workers' faculties' (*Rabfaks*). These were intended to bring workers up to the level at which they could enter higher education. Many workers volunteered for these courses which, though they were of variable quality and had a high wastage, did limit the lowering of academic standards caused by the policy of making higher education especially accessible to workers and peasants. Many party and government leaders of later decades, including Khrushchev, were *Rabfak* products. The *Rabfaks* survived until the 1940s, by which time they had been largely superseded by correspondence schools.

Another important side of educational policy was the energetic campaign against illiteracy. Although rather more success was claimed for this than was actually justified, and although the foundations for universal literacy had been laid in tsarist times, the effort and the achievement were great. The Red Army was perhaps the most effective force in the campaign, all illiterate recruits attending classes as part of their service. There was also a Literacy League, with its periodical *Down with Illiteracy!* By 1939 illiteracy was increasingly confined to the elderly. According to the census of that year, of those aged between 9 and 49, 94 per cent in the towns and 86 per cent in the villages were literate (by 1959 these had increased to 99 and 98 per cent respectively).

In the 1920s there was a great interest in foreign educational theory, and much was applied in Soviet schools; especially John Dewey's 'progressive' education with pupils engaging in projects rather than formal learning, teachers less authoritarian, and examinations discontinued. There was also a stronger trend towards polytechnics where students could mix labour experience with formal learning. The universities remained partly proletarianized as workers and peasants gained admission at the expense of children of 'bourgeois' parents.

Much of this was reversed from about 1931, as the five-year plans and collectivization reached their climax. Lunacharsky was dismissed, and several educational theorists and psychologists were purged. Foreign educational theorists were condemned. Secondary education almost came to a standstill in 1931–2, and when it recovered there was a partial reversion to tsarist practices. Teachers were enjoined to discipline their pupils. The old examinations and marking systems were re-established. New standardized textbooks were introduced, so that pupils could learn, among other things, that Stalin was a genius. The influence of Zhdanov, who fancied himself as the party's cultural expert after the departure of Lunacharsky, was responsible for the more reactionary of the new measures. Nevertheless, while school education became less lively, pre-school education took the opposite course; in the nurseries and kindergartens, fairy stories and dolls once more became popular.

Because of the social upheavals, there was an alarming increase of juvenile delinquency in the 1930s, with violence and vandalism especially noticeable in the cities. In 1935 the age of criminal responsibility was therefore lowered to 12 (10 in some cases) so that troublesome children could be treated as criminals. This not only made possible the imposition of savage sentences on children, but also provided an additional means of getting at their parents.

In 1932 the official requirement (often circumvented) that universities should take two-thirds of their students from the working class and peasantry was dropped. This meant that the children of administrators had a better chance of entry, and also that academic standards rose.[8] Working-class education also suffered in 1940, when fees were introduced for higher education and for the final three years of secondary education (after 1934 education was compulsory for the four primary years and the first three secondary years offered by 'seven-year schools'; the final three years provided by 'ten-year

8. After the mid-1930s children of the former bourgeoisie were no longer formally denied entry.

schools' were voluntary. Fees meant that these final three years were attended largely by children of the white-collar workers). But there were extensive opportunities for part-time, adult, and correspondence study, and many took advantage of these.

Efforts made during the war to preserve education could only be partly successful, due to the heavy toll of teachers and buildings. Among the measures taken during the war was the extension of military training from the peacetime 6 per cent to 11 per cent of the total secondary course. Partly because of this (girls were taught more nursing and less warfare than boys) single-sex education was re-established, although never fully applied. For educating the sons of servicemen killed in action, many 'Suvorov' and 'Nakhimov' boarding schools were founded, their pupils being themselves trained for service careers. In 1943 there was a whole series of reforms. Educational theory was again in favour, and the Academy of Pedagogical Sciences was founded. The lower age for compulsory schooling was lowered from 8 to 7. New evening schools were established for young workers and peasants whose education had been cut short by the war. Twenty rules were evolved for pupils' behaviour, and these had to be learned by heart.[9] The old school-leaving certificate ('attestation of maturity') was restored.

Recovery was fast in the post-war years. There remained a great shortage of school space, and many schools worked a two- or three-shift system. In time, the low wartime birth rate helped to mitigate this problem. Teachers, usually female in secondary and elementary schools,[10] varied in quality, but few could be lazy. In the non-Russian parts, the official requirement that Russians should learn the local language and the locals learn Russian was circumvented by the Russians. In any case, even with formal equality of languages, the local language tended to be displaced, since Russian was virtually essential for those aspiring towards higher education or wider job opportunities.

Compulsory ten-year education, instead of seven-year, for all urban children was planned for 1955. But this did not happen.

Science and technology

By the end of the Civil War, much of Russia's intellectual and scientific talent had died or emigrated. A new Soviet science had to be created from the remnants of the old. The tsarist government, distrusting the universities, had favoured the Imperial Academy of Sciences as the main centre

9. The first rule was: 'It is the duty of each school child to acquire knowledge persistently so as to become an educated and cultured citizen and to be of the most possible service to his country.' Others bade pupils to respect their teachers, 'greeting them with a polite bow', and obeying their instructions without question.

10. By the early 1970s more than two-thirds of the schoolteachers (and one-quarter of secondary-school heads) were women.

for research, and the Soviet governments, with their preference for a centralized system, also followed this course. In 1925 the old Academy was transformed into the Academy of Sciences of the USSR, and placed in direct touch with the government. The Academy of Sciences, with the academies of science of the separate republics, was largely responsible for the organization of scientific research in the USSR. It defined tasks (with a view to the government's requirements), and allocated tasks and funds to selected research institutions or research teams. Membership of the Academy was highly prized; there were only a hundred or so full members, and membership brought great prestige and reward. Until about 1935 Soviet scientists enjoyed an increasing reputation in the outside world, and there was considerable scientific interchange. Foreign scientists visited the USSR to lecture or to share in research, and Soviet scientists visited the west. Some Russian scientific journals were printed in English or German to facilitate this interchange. In 1935, Kapitsa, a Soviet physicist working at Cambridge, did not return from a visit to the USSR, and this coincided with the end of the close ties between Russian and foreign scientists. Science in the USSR, like other fields of intellectual life, was feeling the tightening control of men like Zhdanov.

Soviet science suffered badly in the purges. For example, the world-famous Pulkovo Observatory was crippled by the arrest in 1937 of most of its astronomers, of whom several died in captivity.[11] The Kharkov Physical-Technical Institute, founded in Soviet times and already the home of the country's first linear accelerator, was devastated with the execution, imprisonment, and deportation of its most outstanding scientists; possibly its success in attracting outstanding scientists from other countries led to its downfall. At a more technical level, the device of arresting complete design teams (as happened in the aircraft and locomotive industries, and others) preserved skills and inflated the self-importance of the NKVD (which administered the captive design offices).

The five-year plans would have been unrealizable but for the flow of new technologists from the institutes of higher education. On the other hand, the international reputation, as well as the contribution, of Soviet science was undermined by some of the more eccentric of Stalin's scientific notions. The most notorious instance was the case of Lysenko. Lysenko, of Ukrainian peasant origin, was a biologist and agronomist who propounded a new revolutionary theory of genetics which was greatly to the liking of a party which still claimed to be revolutionary. Building on Michurin's achievements in the breeding of new strains of plants, he rejected 'conventional' theories of heredity. For Lysenko, chromosomes were not necessarily relevant; heritable

---

11. Like other such instances, this process seems to have entailed a blend of NKVD arbitrariness and professional jealousies among the scientists. See *Slavic Review*, 1 (1990), 100–17.

changes could be achieved by subjecting plants to changes of environment. His experiments, in which wheat subjected to low temperatures allegedly produced seed grain which could be planted in the colder zones of the USSR, were of great interest to a party committed to the transformation both of nature and of the Soviet Union. In 1938 he was appointed head of the Academy of Agricultural Sciences. Those who disagreed with his theories were execrated and removed from their posts, sometimes with the help of the NKVD. Among Lysenko's victims was the founder of the Academy, Vavilov. Vavilov was a world-renowned geneticist who, despite Lysenko, upheld the relevance of the chromosome. Because of this, and because of the 'western' nature of his views, he was one of those arrested; he died in captivity. In 1948 the Lysenko controversy, muted during the war, was resurrected. Zhdanov's son (Stalin's son-in-law), who was the Central Committee's man in charge of science, criticized Lysenko's work and behaviour. Lysenko wrote a letter of complaint to Stalin and Zhdanov. Some weeks later he met Stalin, proposed that his supposedly revolutionary wheat strain should be called 'Stalin Branched Wheat', and claimed that it would multiply yields by four or five times (this it did not do; it was a spindly plant derived from ancient times, very frail and with low protein content although high-yielding by weight). Shortly afterwards the Central Committee of the party solemnly pronounced that Lysenko's theory of heredity was marxist and therefore true. Such a declaration invited foreign ridicule, but was the signal for the end of normal genetics in the USSR and the emergence of Lysenkos in other branches of Soviet science. In line with Zhdanov's cultural and intellectual offensive, scientists who believed in the validity of 'western bourgeois' theories were hounded, while scientists claiming to have developed revolutionary Soviet theories were elevated into high positions. Einstein's theory of relativity was ostracized by many scientists in the cause of self-preservation, while quantum mechanics and cybernetics were virtually banned. It was not until the death of Stalin that Soviet scientists were free to pursue openly their former fruitful courses. Lysenko was then denounced by Khrushchev; he was accused of falsifying his experimental results, and also of giving diplomas to worthless students whom he happened to like. In 1958 he made a partial and temporary return to favour, several of his scientific enemies losing their jobs. But Khrushchev's demise, and knowledge that the derided conventional genetics in the west was producing truly revolutionary improvements in yield, finally brought his career to an end.

Another scientist who appeared to gratify Stalin, the Russified Celtic American Vilyams (ancestral name Williams), also had a deleterious effect on agriculture, though probably not a great effect on Soviet science. A party member since 1928, Vilyams developed the system of *Travopolye*: the use of grasses in a system of crop rotation. This system could, it was claimed, be applied in any soil conditions. Reliance on this theory, which was not baseless but was taken to extremes, was one of the reasons why artificial fertilizers received such a low priority in the five-year plans.

When the atom's potential was realized, physicists and nuclear engineers became a kind of protected species. They were protected from too much interference, and sometimes they could offer protection to other scientists; for example, they set up a project involving radiation of seeds, enabling them to give employment to biologists ousted by Lysenko. But scientists' technological arrogance was a worldwide phenomenon and could easily get out of hand in the USSR. Hence there was a neglect of safety and environmental issues, leading to subsequent ecological disasters like the dumping of nuclear reactors in coastal waters. Physicists like Igor Kurchatov (who led the Soviet development of nuclear bombs) and Andrei Sakharov (who helped) were able to exploit their indispensibility to get what they wanted, But it was these two, with some colleagues, who were sufficiently secure in 1954 to send a paper to Malenkov and thence to the Politburo explaining how the use of hydrogen bombs would mean the end of civilization (and how, by implication, the triumph of socialism over capitalism in a possible future war was no longer inevitable).

Until 1945 nuclear research had not received great priority. It is true that this field was pursued from about 1930 in Leningrad at the Radium Institute and the Physical-Technical Institute, that there was a cyclotron in action by 1937, and that by 1941 prominent Soviet nuclear physicists such as Kapitsa and Kurchatov were well aware of the potentialities of nuclear fission. But when the extensive Soviet espionage organization in North America obtained information about the Anglo-Canadian-American atomic programmes, its significance does not seem to have been recognized. After the atomic bombs had been exploded over Japan, Stalin publicly minimized the significance of the new weapon, just as a decade later Mao Zedong would do. However, there was a crash programme, supervised by Beria and the MVD, to make a Soviet atomic device. The latter was first detonated in 1949, to the consternation of the western press, which had been misled by its own stories of Soviet technical incompetence. The contribution of German scientists acquired in 1945, and of Soviet espionage, to this achievement was quite important. Much more a product of Russian scientists was the thermonuclear device exploded in 1953, and the first hydrogen bomb, successfully dropped in 1955, came a year before the first American one. A dubious distinction perhaps, but proving that when sufficient resources were allocated Soviet scientists could deliver the goods.

Literature and the arts

The writer, said Stalin, was 'the engineer of men's souls'. His task was to produce fictional examples of the New Soviet Man which the party was creating, and thus give his readers a guide to correct behaviour. In practice, over the decades, the Writers' Union served to repress all talent which was not submissive (expulsion from the Union could mean that the victim would no longer be published). At its first conference in 1934, the Union was addressed by Zhdanov, who introduced the doctrine of Socialist Realism as the only pattern to which writers could work. Socialist Realism was a term whose meaning varied over the years but, officially, it was defined as the depiction of revolutionary reality, with a view to the re-education of the population in the spirit of socialism. In conforming to these dictates, the quality of literature fell. There was a flourishing of mediocre writers, while the genuinely creative tended to be repressed or, sometimes, suppressed. The low quality of much contemporary literature, combined with growing literacy, was partly responsible for the enormous demand by readers for the old classics of Russian literature, which were reprinted in millions of copies.

The so-called five-year-plan novel became prominent in the 1930s. The style of this had been set in 1925 by Gladkov's *Cement*; the object was to show how a certain sector of the economy fulfilled or overfulfilled its plan, despite wreckers, saboteurs, pessimists, and other perils. The new literary hero was the peasant who, by intelligent use of manure, doubled the potato crop despite the machinations of the local priest, the bus driver who by careful driving reduced his fuel consumption, or the factory worker who overcame all kinds of obstacles and produced rounder and shinier ball bearings. None of these novels was outstanding, but they were read by millions.

About a thousand members of the Writers' Union served at the front during the Second World War and about one-fifth of them were killed. Most were newspaper correspondents and many took advantage of their situation to collect material for novels which would be written in calmer years. During the war, Soviet writers benefited from the relaxed ideological atmosphere and from the renewal of cultural contacts with other countries. This relaxation came to an abrupt end in 1946, when Zhdanov opened a new campaign against 'cosmopolitanism' (interest in things foreign) and 'apoliticism' and 'objectivism' (failure to commit work absolutely to the current party line). Zhdanov singled out especially the humorist Zoshchenko and the veteran poetess Akhmatova. Akhmatova, who persisted in writing lyrical poetry rather than political poetry, was described as poisonous, halfway between a prostitute and a nun. As for Zoshchenko, Zhdanov said,

If you bother to read his *The Adventures of a Monkey* closely you will discover that . . . the monkey can make the filthy, poisonous, and anti-Soviet judgment that life in the zoo is better than life outside, that you can breathe more freely in a cage than among Soviet people. Morally and politically, how much lower can you get?

These denunciations were followed by a period of repression which lasted until 1953 in all the arts and intellectual pursuits. Mediocrities flourished; their works elevated all things Russian, denounced all things western, and included admiring references to Stalin. Features of this period were the condemnation as putrid and lecherous of almost all foreign contemporary novelists, and the reissue of Soviet novels with new excisions and, sometimes, additional paragraphs elevating Stalin's role in the events portrayed. Among the books treated in this way was Fadayev's *The Young Guard* (1945), which was printed in millions of copies and received a Stalin Prize before the party critics had second thoughts. This novel, based on fact, told how teenage boys and girls formed a partisan unit in Krasnodon and, after many brave exploits, were arrested and shot. The very spontaneity of this group implied that the local party organization had made no preparations for the city's occupation by the Germans. Moreover, the author's depiction of the loss of Krasnodon gave a poor impression of the Red Army. In 1947 the author prepared a revised edition in which the Red Army did better, but the critics were still not satisfied. Eventually a revised revised edition appeared, in which the Krasnodon party played a much bigger role and in which new passages in praise of the Red Army and of Stalin were incorporated.

One writer who fell foul of Zhdanov's call for vigilance was Kazakevich, who restored himself to favour with two novels (*Spring on the Oder, House on the Square*) which even the most paranoid party hack could hardly find wanting. These novels have the same hero, Lubentsov, who is broad-shouldered with friendly, intelligent, and humorous blue eyes which seem to say 'I love you all because we are all from the Soviet Union and doing the same thing'. He is a professional soldier and party member with impeccable social origin; his father was a lumberjack and his mother a peasant (and, as if this were not enough, he has never worn a tie in his life). He is brave, loved by his subordinates, and respected by his superiors. He turns down a safe HQ posting because he wants to share the common dangers of the front line. The only characters who criticize him are plainly bad characters. One of the latter, however, seems to utter a perfect description of the Stalinist literary hero. 'Lubentsov', says this low type, 'walks around as though he is an icon.'

Administrators of the Writers' Union, as well as of the corresponding artists' and musicians' unions, were part of the state elite, well provided with luxuries and privileges. It is not surprising that such officials, decades later, would resist the reforms of Gorbachev. These cultural officials and favoured writers were not shy in making requests, even writing to Stalin or Molotov with a request—usually granted—for a private automobile or a decent dacha. Deputy prime minister Kosygin satisfied a request by an actors' group for enamelled bathtubs.

The party's long-standing ambition to offer everyone access to the printed word meant that books were cheap and that by 1959 there were about 135,000 libraries holding 800 million volumes (both these figures are about ten times greater than in 1913). The biggest reference library was the Lenin Library in Moscow (19 million titles), developed from an 1862 foundation. In Leningrad there was the Saltykov-Shchedrin Library (12 million titles), based on the former Imperial Library, and the Library of the Academy of Sciences, founded in 1775 and possessing 12 million titles. At 64,000 the 1958 total of book titles published was more than double the 1913 figure. There were over 10,000 newspapers published in 1958; most of these were very minor, but they had a combined circulation of 59 million. The four main newspapers, edited in Moscow but circulating throughout the USSR, were *Pravda* (still the party's paper), *Izvestiya* (the organ of the government), *Komsomolskaya Pravda* (organ of the Communist Youth League), and *Trud* (published by the Central Council of Trade Unions).[12] Newspaper editors whose presentation and ideological interpretation of the news could be relied on were carefully chosen. Under Stalin, and after, Soviet newspapers tended to exhort rather than inform, but perceptive readers could read between the lines. News was as far as possible planned in advance; for example, news of Khrushchev's death in 1971 was delayed, to avert a demonstrative funeral. A sure sign of unexpected big news was the delayed appearance, or even non-appearance, of newspapers, while editors sought official guidance.

Stalin took a great interest in film-making, making suggestions and approving or disapproving new films. Lenin had said that the film was the most important art for purposes of propaganda. As in literature, the blending of party requirements with art was not always successful. But film-making and film-showing were generously aided by the government.

Russian film-making on a regular basis had started in 1907. By 1917 there were about 1,000 cinemas; despite illiteracy, which limited the value of subtitles, large audiences were found. Many notable feature films were made, usually taking the form of dramatizations of one or other of the classics of Russian literature. The first feature cartoon film, *The Grasshopper and the Ant*, appeared in 1913.

Before the revolution almost all films had been made in Moscow, but in the 1920s Leningrad took the lead, Lenfilm beginning with imitations of American and German films. *Counterplan* was the first major film to propagandize the five-year plans, and duly included a traitorous 'bourgeois specialist'. Shostakovich produced its music, and one of its pieces later became the anthem of the United Nations. One of the film's two directors was a former NKVD man.

The cinema industry was subordinated to the commissariat of education at first, but in 1929 was made directly subordinate to the Council of People's Commissars. From 1946 to 1953 there was a cinema ministry, but films then became the province of the ministry of culture. As in literature, there was a good deal of experimentation. The exploitation of montage in particular was studied in Soviet studios. The 1930s were difficult for Soviet film-makers

---

12. By 1967 *Izvestiya* had the largest circulation, nearly 9 million.

because the onset of Stalinism coincided with the changeover to sound films. A number of experimenters were removed, although their influence lived on in their pupils, of whom Pudovkin, Dovzhenko, and Eisenstein became best known. These three had already achieved fame with, respectively, *Mother*, *Earth*, and *Battleship Potemkin*, which inspired the Italian realism of the 1940s. From the early 1930s to the death of Stalin, the Soviet film industry was artistically limited by outside pressures. But despite this, good work was done during the Stalin years. Many film-makers who fell into disfavour became teachers in film courses, and the 'diploma' films which their pupils made were a far cry from the turgid studio productions made for public screening. Thus, when there was a cultural relaxation after 1953 the new generation of film-makers was well prepared. Soon, notably sensitive films were appearing; some of these (*The Cranes are Flying, Ballad of a Soldier*) made a great impression abroad. By 1960 there were 59,000 permanent cinemas in the USSR. In 1940 fifty-four feature films and 198 shorts were made, but after the war only tried and trusted directors were allowed to make films, and the latter were in any case often banned. With the 'Leningrad affair', even Lenfilm, Stalin's favourite, virtually ceased production for a while. In 1952 only five feature films were made, rising under Khrushchev to 145 in 1959.

Painting and sculpture went through a similar sequence to the other arts. Experimentation during the 1920s (Kandinsky was even appointed director of the new department of fine arts) was followed by the imposition of Socialist Realism. In painting, the latter term implied a rejection of abstract art; portraiture predominated, being the most convenient genre for combining objective realism with adulation. There was a steady output of photographically detailed pictures, like the enormous painting entitled *Stalin and Voroshilov in the Kremlin*. Other paintings portrayed stirring events in the economy (*The Milkmaids, A Factory in the Urals*, etc.). Many painters, like writers, created original works for their own private satisfaction or for exhibition in better times; after the death of Stalin a number of abstract works emerged from attics and cellars. Under Khrushchev abstract art did not have official approval, but it was allowed to exist. Khrushchev did visit an exhibition of abstract art, but let his opinion be known in a choice sentence referring to what donkeys might do with their tails. Sculpture under Stalin likewise did not flourish. There was a boom in busts, but busts of Stalin, with few exceptions, were production-line rather than artistic creations. An attempt by two leading sculptors in 1950 to establish a monopoly in the making of political busts was rejected by the Council of Ministers which, on this occasion, declared in favour of competition.

'The camera can't lie' is a saying which is unsustainable in any case, but enrolment of photography into the Stalinist propaganda campaign advanced falsified imagery to an art form. Stalin, a fairly short man, was typically shown in photographs towering over his taller colleagues. The air-brushing out of since-disgraced luminaries like Trostky from photographs of great events, and their replacement by bushes or other objects, required great skill and imagination. In the post-Stalin years the air-brush continued in use. The ailing Brezhnev was pictured hale and hearty and even Gorbachev, when a mere Politburo member, had the rather endearing birthmark air-brushed off his forehead.[13]

Russian architecture had experienced a neoclassical revival in the later nineteenth century, which produced many graceless banks and railway stations but also some pleasant country houses. There was also an effort, favoured by Slavophils, to revive old Russian styles; Gothic architecture had never come to Russia, and in place of the Gothic Revival of the west there was the Russian Revival, few of whose structures were aesthetically very pleasing (the redbrick Historical Museum on Red Square is an example). From 1917 until the mid-1930s there was intensive (and sometimes hare-brained) innovation, with Moscow seeming to become the centre of the world's most progressive architecture. Architecture was to be revolutionary and international; past forms were rejected in favour of the forms of the so-called machine age. A theatre was built at Rostov in the shape of a tractor, the glass wall was introduced to a land of climatic extremes, the innovative French architect Corbusier designed a new Moscow ministry. But from the 1930s Socialist Realism was applied to architecture (but not so uncompromisingly or bloodily as in other arts). Neoclassical forms were extolled and imitated, heavy ornamentation, high ceilings, and grandiose monolithic façades became popular. In general, Stalinist architecture was ponderous, ostentatious, inconvenient, and sometimes badly built. On the other hand Soviet urban planning, only to a certain extent building on tsarist foundations, achieved much. It is true that some of the new wide streets of replanned Moscow were dull and uninspiring, but the 'parks of culture and rest', which were laid out as places of relaxation and entertainment in the big cities, were a valued asset for local populations.

Music also suffered from the perversions of the 1930s and 1940s. However, composers and instrumentalists were honoured and rewarded, and the extension of musical opportunity to all sectors of the population meant that talent was discovered which otherwise might have been neglected. Of the Soviet composers, Khachaturyan, Prokoviev, and Shostakovich attained the most fame outside Russia, but there were many others whose talents were only appreciated at home. The Armenian Khachaturyan graduated from the Moscow Conservatoire in 1934 and soon became known by his original rhythms which often incorporated themes from Armenian folklore. Prokoviev, already well established, returned to Russia in 1933, finishing his ballet *Romeo and Juliet* in 1936. Dmitri Shostakovich, son of a St Petersburg chemical engineer,

13. For before-and-after reproductions of such pictures, see D. King, *The Commissar Vanishes* (1997).

wrote his first composition at the age of 11. His opera *Lady Macbeth of Mtsensk* was condemned in lurid terms by *Pravda* in 1936, and he was in disgrace until the war; it was said that he might have met a sad fate had not Aleksei Tolstoy interceded with Stalin on his behalf. After the war he was again banned, but was rehabilitated in 1956. His music was characterized by great individuality, sometimes bordering on the sensational.

Addressing Soviet musicians in 1948, Zhdanov defined what Soviet music should do:

There are two very responsible tasks facing Soviet composers. Firstly to develop and to perfect Soviet music. Secondly to protect Soviet music from infiltration by elements of bourgeois corruption. We should not forget that, as in all other fields, the USSR is the true protector of mankind's musical culture, a wall guarding human civilization and human culture from bourgeois decay.[14]

Fifteen years later Soviet musicians were still facing 'responsible tasks', but somehow Khrushchev seemed less ominous than Zhdanov:

In the spiritual life of our nation, in ideological work, music has a great and important role. It therefore seems necessary to make some judgments about the trend in music . . . In brief, we are for melodious music that has meaning, stirs people's spirits and inspires powerful sensations . . . Who is there who does not know the *Internationale*? For how many years have we been singing this song? It has become the working class international anthem. How it inspires revolutionary thoughts and feelings, elevating people and mobilizing them against the foes of the workers! When I listen to the music of Glinka rapturous tears invariably come into my eyes . . . But there is some music that gives one a bellyache.[15]

The nationalities

After the mid-1930s Stalin's policy was to Russify the political institutions of the nationalities. The purge trials of 1938 made victims of many so-called 'bourgeois nationalists' among the leaders of the national communist parties. There was a diffusion of Russian bureaucrats into the key posts of the national republics, although this was frequently disguised by having a native in the ostensibly senior position, and a Russian in the actually more powerful position of deputy. But by the time Stalin died there had been created young national elites, Russianized, qualified, and loyal enough to occupy important posts. In time it was hoped that the lower strata of the national populations would themselves become Russianized, adopting Russian language and attitudes for their own advantage. In this transition the question of language was vital. In one of his last theoretical works (1950), Stalin condemned the

14. Zhdanov's various pronouncements on the arts are available in English in A. Zhdanov, *Literature, Philosophy and Music* (1950).
15. *Pravda*, 10 Mar. 1963.

'revolutionary' theories of the linguist Marr. Marr in the 1930s had propounded that a revolutionary new socialist system would develop a revolutionary new language. In rejecting this, Stalin suggested that the new socialist system would use the language of its strongest member, Russia. The compulsory study of Russian at school in the people's democracies was justified by this; compulsory Russian was already taught in the various national republics of the USSR.

According to the 1959 census, there were 114 million Russians in the USSR, many of whom lived in the non-Russian republics. The second largest nationality, the Ukrainians, amounted to 37 million, although the population of the Ukraine was only three-quarters Ukrainian (17 per cent was Russian). The third nationality, Byelorussian, numbered 8 million. Altogether, by 1959 there were twenty-two nationalities with populations of 1 million or more, plus a host of smaller groups. Three of these twenty-two (Jews, Tadzhiks, Mordvinians) had decreased since 1939. Kazakhstan by 1959 was the most diluted of the national republics, with the natives in a minority (they constituted 30 per cent, with Russians 43 and Ukrainians 8 per cent). The Kirgizians also were a minority in their own republic. Russians were widespread; only in Byelorussia, Armenia, and Lithuania did they amount to less than a tenth of the population. This Russian presence greatly facilitated the process of Russianization. Intermarriage also tended to be a strong Russianizing factor.

Of the major nationalities, the Jews were exceptional although it was true that three others (Poles, Germans, Moldavians) also might look to 'home' states outside the USSR. Unlike these three, however, the Jews were widely distributed throughout the Union. In the 1930s the difficult task of creating a national republic for the Soviet Jews had been tackled, an area near Khabarovsk in the Far East being delineated as the Jewish Autonomous Oblast, with its capital at Birobidzhan. This did not attract many Jewish migrants because of its remoteness and the arduous life which it offered to the first settlers. During the war there were enormous Jewish losses in the occupied zones. In the post-war period, soon after the creation of Israel, there was a campaign against 'Zionism'. Some Jewish leaders were executed, and cultural freedoms which had previously been allowed ceased to exist; Yiddish publishing, theatres, and schools were abolished. After Stalin's death there was a slight relaxation, although it would seem that Khrushchev was not without a streak of anti-Semitism. The press gave considerable publicity to certain Jewish 'speculators' who were tried and executed in the 1960s. However, taking the Soviet period as a whole, there was no definite intention to encourage anti-Semitism. The Nazi occupation of regions which under the tsar had been endemically anti-Semitic caused a reactivation, and post-war circumstances permitted this to linger. Post-war policy was usually to distinguish between 'Zionism', which was attacked, and the Jew, who was not. The 'Doctors' Plot' of Stalin, and some of the acts of Khrushchev and his successors, could be considered as temporary aberrations of this policy. The situation of the Jews was exacerbated by Middle East conflicts; although the USSR had approved the creation of Israel, by the mid-1950s it had close relationships with Egypt and other Arab states. But in the 1970s, largely as a gesture to the outside world, the authorities eased (without making easy) the emigration procedures for Jews. This was followed by a quite substantial flow of emigrants. Similar concessions were made to citizens of German origin.

16

The Khrushchev Revival

The end of Stalin

RUMOURS that Beria had arranged Stalin's death seem highly improbable, even though he had the means and may have feared he was next on Stalin's shopping list. That both Khrushchev and Stalin's daughter later wrote that Beria drove off from the death scene with a wicked smile on his lips raises the question 'He would, wouldn't he?' as well as 'They would, wouldn't they?' Stalin certainly did not get prompt attention after suffering a stroke at his country dacha after a late night spent bingeing with his colleagues. When first seen lying on the floor, he was assumed to be in a state of hangover. But the security men had second thoughts and notified the party leaders. The latter came, sniffed the air, and went home. But they came back some hours later, when it seemed there was indeed cause for alarm. Doctors were summoned and the leading specialist, according to Khrushchev, was clearly disinclined to touch Stalin, no doubt wondering if this was to be a new chapter of the 'Doctors' Plot'. Stalin was partly paralysed, and speechless, and within a few days he was dead. An autopsy revealed long-standing cerebral sclerosis.

His unnerved successors discussed funeral arrangements, and divided offices among themselves. Some discussion was devoted to the question of precisely how and when the news should be broken; evidently there were fears that some kind of popular explosion might ensue and the communiqué, when it appeared, included some unusual appeals to the population to resist panic and confusion. Internal security troops were placed at strategic points in the cities, but the absence of obvious upheaval is explicable less by the presence of troops than by the shattering effect the news had on a people long habituated to living under the one true god. The most dramatic occurrence was the loss of control over crowds pouring into the centre of Moscow to pay their last respects. In a small-scale re-enactment of the catastrophe which had accompanied Nicholas II's coronation, lack of imagination on the part of the police resulted in loyal citizens being crushed to death.

To Stalin's successors fell the task of finding a new course, directed away from the cruel absurdities of the Stalinist years, without discrediting themselves in the process. But although the Politburo[1] leaders agreed that things could not go on as before, their unity did not extend much further than that. Not for the first time in Russian history, a relaxation of pent-up tension was seen to be both perilous and urgent, and there were conflicting views as to the speed and manner of this transformation. Added to this were conflicts between personalities. Stalin had not selected his closest subordinates with a view to their forming a closely knit band of brothers, and this meant that the contest for power would not be purely a matter of conflicting policies.

Khrushchev

The year 1894, in which Russia's last tsar came to the throne, was also the year in which, with somewhat less ceremony, Nikita Khrushchev was born to an impoverished peasant family in a thatched hut at Kalinovka, in the Ukraine. At the age of 15 he abandoned rural life and went to the mining town of Yuzovka to seek a better fortune. By 1914 he was responsible for the operation of a pithead elevator, which gained him exemption from military service. He joined the Bolshevik party in 1918, served as a Red Army commissar during the Civil War, and then returned to Yuzovka as an assistant manager. In the early 1920s, his first wife having died during the famine, he studied at a technical institute, where he became a party representative. Soon he was a district party secretary and stayed with the Ukrainian party *apparat* until his appointment in 1931 as party secretary of two Moscow districts. Within four years he was party secretary for Moscow and a candidate member of the Politburo. During the next three years he was largely responsible for the purging of the Moscow region and in 1938, having won Stalin's confidence, was transferred to the Ukraine to scourge the party there. In 1939 he became a full member of the Politburo, and during the Second World War played a worthy role as an army political officer. At the end of the war he was both party secretary and chairman of the Council of Ministers of the Ukraine. His was an especially important responsibility, because Ukrainian nationalists, separatists, and anti-Soviet partisans had thrived during the German occupation. Like every other public figure who wished to survive, he was ever eager to praise his leader:

All our successes we owe to the great Bolshevik party, to the experienced guidance of our beloved leader and teacher Comrade Stalin (stormy applause). Millions of workers in all countries of the world see how the Soviet Union is successfully carrying out the great socialist ideas, the ideas of Marx-Engels-Lenin-Stalin.[2]

---

1. From 1952 to 1965 what was essentially the Politburo was called the Presidium of the party's Central Committee. This was one of Stalin's last ideas; the Presidium would have been expanded with younger members and may have been a device to simplify the elimination of the older, ex-Politburo, members. For simplicity, the term Politburo has been retained for these years.

2. From a report of proceedings at the congress of the Ukrainian communist party, in *Bolshevik*, 3 (1949), 7.

Khrushchev was a man of great vitality, and under him the Ukrainian party flourished; unlike the All-Union Central Committee, the Ukrainian Central Committee met often and regularly. He was soon recalled to Moscow where agriculture became his main interest.

The leadership after Stalin

After Stalin died Malenkov became chairman of the Council of Ministers, a post which he expected to hold concurrently with his party secretaryship. This elevation of Malenkov was attained with the support of Beria, who became the minister of a new ministry of the interior (MVD) which was to absorb the previous ministry of state security (this was a kind of promotion, for although under Stalin Beria had been in charge of security services, he had not been their minister). Voroshilov replaced the dull protégé of Stalin, Shvernik, as 'president' of the USSR. Molotov, Kaganovich, Bulganin, and Beria became deputy chairmen of the council of ministers, while Khrushchev received no ministerial appointment but wielded great power inside the party secretariat and in the Politburo.

It seemed that Malenkov and Beria were working hand in hand, but the situation was fluid. Beria not only controlled the MVD with its industries, troops, and informers, but he had developed self-confidence during Stalin's time. He had long had the habit of disparaging Stalin in private (being in charge of security and its informers, he was presumably the only citizen who could do this with impunity). He had been closer to Stalin than other leaders. Khrushchev remarked that when Beria and Stalin clashed, it was not an execution affair, just a lovers' quarrel; Georgians quarrelled to amuse themselves and would make up in the end.

Beria seemed not only all-powerful, but sinister too. His colleagues, in view of his unsavoury past, regarded him not only as a menace to the USSR but as a threat to their own lives. The demotion of Malenkov, achieved just two weeks after Stalin's death, was the result of a concentrated effort to weaken the Malenkov–Beria ascendancy. Malenkov kept his chairmanship of the Council of Ministers but his party secretaryship was transferred to Khrushchev. Since under Stalin it had been the council of ministers which had wielded the most influence, with the role of the party downgraded, this change at the time was probably not seen as giving Khrushchev much new power. But since others besides Khrushchev realized that one of the first tasks of the post-Stalin leadership was to restore the party to its previous eminence, the post did have great potential, of which Khrushchev made full use. The concept of 'collective leadership', introduced to describe a regime which would no longer be dominated by one man and in which the party and government would work hand in hand, was taken very seriously by Khrushchev. Malenkov's prime-ministerial decisions would need the approval of his colleagues, and

Khrushchev's opinion was increasingly first among equals, for his was the voice of the party.

The new leadership was evidently inclined towards a relaxation in all fields of Soviet life. Malenkov was especially forthright in this; he even went so far as to admit that atomic war would be catastrophic for all mankind (but he was soon persuaded by his colleagues to backtrack. He then said that atomic war would be catastrophic for the capitalist world, a prophecy which raised fewer awkward questions). Khrushchev at this stage was noticeably less 'liberal' than Malenkov, and was not conspicuous in his support for the production of more consumer goods and for measures to improve the lot of the peasantry. Meanwhile, a start was made in releasing political prisoners. Some of the labour camps were closed and their inmates freed. It was not long before those who feared that a release of tension could be catastrophic began to receive apparent confirmation. At a particularly arduous Arctic labour camp, at Vorkuta, the prisoners actually went on strike for better conditions. This outbreak was led by a Pole, and was overcome when the MVD troops opened fire on the protesters during negotiations. When the expectations of relaxations in East Germany and Poland were disappointed there were strikes and demonstrations in those two people's democracies.

It is often assumed that in these early weeks Beria represented the forces wishing to maintain a tyrannous atmosphere. One source of this belief is Khrushchev's subsequent reminiscences. Beria did not have a chance to compile his own memoirs,[3] for he was shot in 1953, and his execution was cleverly used in the delicate manoeuvres aimed at what was later to be known as 'destalinization'. In fact, as the head of an organization which had great opportunities for evaluating public opinion not only in the USSR but also in the people's democracies, Beria was more aware than his colleagues of the urgent need for a retreat from repression and rigidity.

According to Khrushchev, Malenkov was the hardest to persuade to join a united front against Beria. Kaganovich agreed as soon as he realized that the conspirators had a majority, while Voroshilov welcomed measures against Beria but was slow to reveal his hatred of the latter, fearing betrayal. Molotov was the first conspirator to advocate 'extreme measures' against Beria, rather than mere dismissal. Beria was denounced by his colleagues at a Kremlin meeting and was then arrested at pistol-point by army generals who had been secreted in an adjoining room.

In July 1953, a week after Beria's arrest, a plenary session of the party's Central Committee took place. The content of Malenkov's report, and the debate and resolution that followed, was not released, although the resolution that was passed was revealed to selected party officials throughout the USSR

---

3. But his son later made a good job of this: S. Beria, *Beria: My Father inside Stalin's Kremlin* (2001). This at least gives an excellent insider's view of life at the top.

and to the highest officials of foreign communist parties (it was through the latter that details later leaked to the west). The substance of the resolution was that there was much that was wrong in the USSR. Industry was backward. Agriculture was pitiful, with entire rural districts abandoned. The party had unjustifiably been put into the background, had been unable to participate in decision-making because of the emergence of a 'personality cult' in the party. But instead of directly accusing Stalin for all this, the resolution heaped all the denunciations on Beria, whose MVD had dominated, it was said, both the party and government, and enabled Beria to damage the party, ruin the collective farms policy, distort Soviet policy in eastern Europe, and pervert relationships with the non-Russian nationalities of the Soviet Union.

There was a five-day secret trial of Beria and six of his colleagues, resulting in executions and fifty volumes of testimony. The press began to print editorials that were obviously inspired by the change of outlook contained in the plenum's resolution. In December there was a brief announcement that Beria had been executed, together with some of his closest associates in the security services.

However, there was still an eminent skeleton in the Kremlin cupboard: open repudiation of Stalin had not been attempted. Such a repudiation would have threatened disarray, uproar, and even perhaps revolt. Not only had the population at large been taught to worship Stalin and all his works, but the party and government officials (that is, the entire administration of the USSR) owed their positions to adherence to Stalin's policies and concepts. A premature attempt to wrench Stalin from people's hearts and minds would have seemed to be an attack on their souls, and an attack which might well have generated desperate resistance. It was not until 1956 that a big move could be made against the Stalin myths. By that year Khrushchev had established himself as leader of both party and government.

From the start, Khrushchev as party secretary began to place his own nominees in key positions; many of them were former colleagues from the Moscow and Ukrainian party organizations. At the same time he was reasserting the influence of the party over the administration. At this period there seemed to be a marked division of the party into those who regarded themselves as administrators who happened to be party members, and those who saw themselves primarily as party members having the duty of participating in administration. In general the latter tended to support Khrushchev, and the former Malenkov, in the various policy disputes of 1953 and 1954. Among the most important disagreements were the government's intention of shifting resources from heavy to light industry (which Khrushchev opposed at this time), and the policy of ploughing up the 'Virgin Lands' to solve the food problem. Malenkov was unenthusiastic about the latter policy, which was Khrushchev's own scheme and which was executed by party and, especially, Komsomol volunteers, rather than directly by the government.

By early 1955 Khrushchev and his followers were able to compel Malenkov to resign. The latter's position was weak because many of those who favoured him in general had been antagonized by particular policies; Molotov and Kaganovich resented the diversion of resources from heavy to light industry, and other relaxations. Molotov favoured a continuation of the hard line in foreign policy, especially towards Tito. Reasons given for Malenkov's relegation from prime minister to minister for power stations included his alleged mismanagement of industry and agriculture, but in private he was blamed for his part in the Leningrad affair.

The new prime minister was Bulganin, a man whom Khrushchev could usually dominate. However, the latter's position was by no means secure, especially after his 1956 denunciation of Stalin, and his over-energetic innovations elsewhere, had made new enemies. In 1957, while he and Bulganin were making one of their frequent foreign visits, colleagues conspired to demand his resignation. When the two tourists arrived back by train from Finland they were greeted by their fellow-leaders with the usual bouquets, but at the following meeting of the Politburo Khrushchev was attacked and found himself in a minority. However, he insisted that the eleven-member Politburo did not have the right to decide his future; that was the right of the much bigger Central Committee. Assisted by an airlift arranged by defence minister Zhukov, Khrushchev was able to assemble a majority in this latter body. His opponents (Malenkov, Molotov, and Kaganovich) were outvoted and labelled the 'anti-party group'. They were expelled from the Central Committee and rusticated to minor and remote jobs. Soon after, Khrushchev felt strong enough to dismiss Zhukov.

Zhukov was popularly regarded as the outstanding Soviet war leader, and enjoyed great and uncontrived prestige. His US equivalent, Eisenhower, had shown that such a man was in a good position to achieve the greatest political triumphs. Zhukov's demotion was therefore more than a matter of putting the army back in its place. Still, the army undoubtedly had been deprived of its most powerful spokesman, and with the 'anti-party group' shattered, and the MVD firmly under the control of the party, it was not difficult for Khrushchev to make the final move. In March 1958 Bulganin, accused of supporting the 'anti-party group' in 1957, was dismissed. Khrushchev took over his office, thus combining once more the party secretary and the prime minister in one person. Apart from the elimination of Beria, which had been a collective move, Khrushchev in his rise to power had not killed any of his competitors. This, and subsequent events, seemed to confirm that there was an implicit understanding among Soviet leaders that Stalinist bloodbaths should not be repeated.

Khrushchev transformed Soviet society, even though many of his innovations failed and he was dismissed in 1964. His successful destruction of the Stalin myths just three years after the dictator's death resembled Alexander's abolition of serfdom, in that it opened the way to a whole series of long-needed changes. Stalin's brand of totalitarianism had been much more total than others, but Khrushchev was able to bring about an almost bloodless relaxation, although he made many enemies in the process. Unlike so many of his opponents in the administration, he was a man who was willing to respond to a new idea with 'why not?' rather than 'whose idea is it?'

Khrushchev's 1956 'secret' speech

Even before 1956 the worst features of Stalinism were being checked. The MVD had been brought under party control and there had been a new insistence on 'socialist legality', consumer-goods industries had been helped, the ponderosities of Stalinist architecture had been condemned, relations with Yugoslavia had been restored, the Kremlin was opened to the public, many labour-camp inmates had returned to normal life, a few foreign tourists were allowed into the USSR, some critical novels had been published, and leaders (especially Khrushchev) had begun to visit foreign parts and actually to talk with ordinary people in various parts of the Union.

In 1955, at Mikoyan's suggestion, a committee had been set up to examine Stalin's repressions, and this committee's material was used for Khrushchev's anti-Stalin speech to the delegates of the 20th Party Conference in 1956. His speech was preceded by contributions from Mikoyan and others, in which the late-lamented dictator was not shown the customary respect. In particular, liquidated Bolsheviks, whose names had hitherto been unmentionable, were spoken of in respectful tones. The tendentious party history was condemned. The bloody dissolution of the Polish communist party in 1938, the post-war imprisonment of its leader Gomulka, and the execution of the Hungarian revolutionary leader Bela Kun were among many acts which were now held against Stalin.

Khrushchev went further. Lenin's 'testament' was read to the delegates together with Lenin's last letters condemning Stalin ('commotion in the hall' was noted at this point). Then Khrushchev, while condemning Trotsky, Zinoviev, and Bukharin, expressed doubts on whether their executions had been necessary. He pointed out that anybody who disagreed with Stalin 'was doomed to ... moral and physical annihilation'. Using material taken from the MVD archives, Khrushchev read out some of the last appeals sent by condemned Bolsheviks to Stalin and never delivered; well-known revolutionaries had written that false confessions had been tortured out of them, or that they believed that an anti-party group was at work in the NKVD, and that they were the victims of it. Stalin's role in the war was then condemned; the catastrophes of 1941, which earlier had been referred to as masterful tactical retreats, were directly blamed on Stalin's refusal to heed warnings and to make strategic retreats at the right time. The 'personality cult' was Khrushchev's term for describing the unquestioning adulation which Stalin had invited. The Stalin Prizes, which were intended to rival Nobel Prizes, and the naming of innumerable towns, institutions, collective farms, and streets after Stalin, were among the practices condemned.[4]

For anyone who had not lived under Stalinism the devastating psychological impact of Khrushchev's revelations was difficult to grasp. For a quarter-century the party and the population had been taught to regard Stalin almost as a god. On any question, whether it was scientific or political or cultural, Stalin's opinion was the correct opinion; unquestioned omnipotence easily imposed unquestionable omniscience. Right from childhood the Soviet citizen had learned to associate Stalin with all that was right and correct, and to regard his defeated critics as one or other of the zoological hybrids mentioned in party histories; fascist hyenas, capitalist running-dogs, white-guard reptiles. All kinds of sacrifices had been demanded, and obtained, of the people in the name of Stalin; many had sacrificed the urgings of their better nature and committed shameful deeds for Stalin. The 'personality cult' had meant that portraits and busts of Stalin were to be seen everywhere; not only on walls and in parks but at street corners, on railway locomotives and buses, on barn doors. Books, articles, and radio programmes on any kind of subject were prefaced with some kind of obeisance to the great man in the Kremlin. 'Long live Stalin!' and 'Glory to Stalin!' had been favourite slogans decorating all possible sites. And now the successor and former comrade of Stalin, in the presence of other former comrades, had catalogued the lies and tragedies of the Stalin era.

Khrushchev had carefully constructed his speech so as to hint at the complicity of old Stalinists like Molotov, Kaganovich, and Malenkov in the crimes of the Stalin era while keeping clear of any insalubrious incidents in his own career. Among the lesser party members, there were, no doubt, many who feared that their activities in the purges might be investigated, while others, equally shattered, realized that they had closed their eyes or sacrificed their principles for no real end. There were suicides, while in Georgia, Stalin's homeland, students rioted against his dethronement.

The contents of Khrushchev's speech were not published, but were gradually made known to party organizations both at home and overseas, so that all communists could be acquainted with them.

Intelligent non-party citizens realized what had happened, and even the unintelligent could note the consequences. In the west, leaked copies were published in the press, which tended to accept Khrushchev's strictures about Stalin as the whole truth and nothing but the truth. In reality, his speech was

---

4. Stalingrad was promptly renamed Volgograd. It became a rule that leaders' names could not be used for such purposes during their lifetimes; Voroshilovgrad once more became Lugansk, Molotov once more became Perm, and so on.

well lubricated with exaggerations (like the claim that Stalin used a globe to plan the Red Army's campaigns). It was only in 1961 that an openly published wave of anti-Stalinism was unleashed by Khrushchev, at the 22nd Party Congress. His speech acknowledged that ordinary Russians, not just the party, had suffered, and for symbolic emphasis Stalin's embalmed body, which had hitherto lain in a glass case beside Lenin's, was removed and buried beneath the Kremlin wall alongside Dzerzhinski. Khrushchev's successors later allowed the grave to be marked by a bust.

Agriculture

Khrushchev rather fancied himself as an agricultural expert, and throughout his ascendancy intervened in most aspects of agricultural policy, readily replacing his ministers of agriculture and reducing the ministry of agriculture to little more than a research establishment. Agriculture, and especially the circumstances of the collective farms, was perhaps the sector of Soviet life in which glowing description diverged most markedly from grim reality. Although Khrushchev, when it suited him, did not hesitate to call a spade a spade, much of the new criticism of life down on the farm came not from him, but from Soviet fiction. In fact it seems to have been the writer Ovechkin who first drew public attention to a few home truths about Soviet farming.

Although Ovechkin adhered to the convention that criticism of officials was permissible, but criticism of the system never permissible, he was certainly bold, for his first critical sketch appeared in Stalin's time, in 1952. This, *Day-by-Day in the District*, was followed during Khrushchev's time by a series of similar documentary sketches in which the role in agriculture of the district party secretary was critically examined. One of the most memorable of Ovechkin's characters is Borzov, a first secretary of a district party committee and an archetype of the bullying careerist who knows how to give an outward impression of devotion and efficiency while actually engaged in a life of mindless imposition of central directives, composition of window-dressing reports about invented successes of farms under his supervision, and harrying of peasants who, in the end, always seem to find ways of achieving failure. Ovechkin's hero is another party district official who realizes that the peasants must be treated more generously and given material incentives, if they are to put their energies into the collective farm.

Khrushchev's stormy entry into the agricultural scene encouraged other writers to follow Ovechkin's example. Perhaps the best informed was Troepolski, a professional agronomist. His *Notes of an Agronomist*, structured like Turgenev's *Sportsman's Sketches*, in which the narrator travels around not so much villages as collective farms, attacks by heavy implication the party hacks of the district committees who hinder the work of the farms by issuing directive after directive, directives based on the directives which the committees themselves receive from Moscow, and which all too often are in conflict with local circumstances or the weather. The way in which the district secretaries, themselves subject to dismissal if the farms under their supervision fail to meet their targets, appoint and dismiss collective farm chairmen on the same principle is mocked in the character of one Prokhor, who is nicknamed Prokhor XVII because he is his farm's seventeenth chairman. Prokhor has had a succession of responsible jobs; he has made a mess of all of them but survives because of the patronage of a higher party official, the chairman of the regional party executive committee. In addition, Prokhor owes his survival to his aptitude at playing safe, and to his obsequiousness towards those who might make or break his career.

As writers complained from below, Khrushchev acted from above. During his regime, and especially in the first half, he had many successes, but nevertheless shortcomings on the farms were a major reason for his dismissal. He had a good appreciation of what was wrong, but his reforms were all too often taken to extremes, or had adverse side effects. Towards the end of his career, when the earlier agricultural successes were overtaken by new misfortunes, he made so many changes and reorganizations that agricultural administrators became hopelessly confused.

Some of the twists and turns were forced upon Khrushchev by the need to placate or outmanoeuvre his critics. Just as Stalin had exaggerated the supporting opinion of a section of party activists to justify his collectivization drive, so Khrushchev relied heavily on a few voluntary or semi-voluntary supporters among the local party committees. A bizarre sequence occurred when Khrushchev introduced impossibly high growth rates for meat production. Opposed by almost all who were familiar with the condition of agriculture, he could point to the success of the party secretary of the Ryazan region, who was putting on the market vastly increased supplies of meat. In the first year of this great Ryazan campaign, almost every available animal on the Ryazan farms was butchered to produce impressive statistics. In the following year, to avoid a scandal, Ryazan quietly bought up the required numbers of cattle outside the region. But the whole fiasco was soon uncovered, to the embarrassment of Khrushchev and of the Ryazan party committee, whose secretary committed suicide.

Khrushchev's main changes involved organization, incentives, and choice of foodstuffs for production. The ministry of agriculture was gradually reduced from a centralized authority over the farms to a mere consultative and advisory body. In its place, local party organizations were given greater opportunity to supervise, although many of their members, being reliable urban party administrators transferred to the countryside, were not really ideal for the purpose. There was also a continuing trend towards farm mergers, making the collectives fewer but larger; by 1967 the number of collective farms had declined to 36,187, with each on average comprising 418 households, while state farms, which on average were more than double the size of the collectives, had risen to 12,773 (this process continued after Khrushchev, so that by 1978 the corresponding figures were 26,700, 495, and 20,484). State farms increased partly because new ones were used to develop the 'Virgin Lands', and partly because some collectives were converted to state farms (to the dismay of their peasants, who found that state farmers' private plots and livestock were minimal). Also noteworthy was the disbanding of the machine and tractor stations. There had always been a conflict between these and the farms because while farms wanted to use the MTS service as little as possible to save expense, the MTS wanted to provide as much service as possible and hence extract higher payment-in-kind. In 1958 the MTS were abolished, and their equipment purchased by the farms they used to serve. The standards of maintenance, never very high, deteriorated. Even though tractors were worked rather intensively, this did not fully account for their short life. In 1969, according to official statistics, tractor production rose to 441,700, but the number of tractors possessed by state and collective farms was only 1,704,000, or four years' production at the current rate. (In 1978 the ratio had hardly improved, the corresponding figures being 576,000 and 2,297,000.)

In a speech to the Central Committee in 1953 Khrushchev admitted that agricultural production under Stalin had been inferior to that of the last tsarist years in many respects; this had been concealed by statistical sleight of hand. Incentives for peasants to work and for farms to invest was a first priority. So the prices paid for state procurements were increased, and some procurement quotas were reduced (leaving farms more surplus produce, which they could sell at higher prices). Other moves were promised to connect more farms with the electricity grid (most farms were without electricity, although some had their own diesel generators), and to reduce (and later abolish) taxes and state delivery quotas which had been imposed on the peasants' private plots. A 1953 concession which reveals how far exploitation of the peasantry had been carried in Stalin's time was that those peasants who did not possess animals were no longer required to deliver a quota of meat to the state. On the other hand, measures were taken to increase the time spent by peasants on collective work, and delinquents could be punished by a reduction of their private plot. Over the years, as party secretaries and farm chairmen endeavoured to win praise by squeezing the last ounce of effort from their peasants, this meant that despite higher state procurement prices (and hence higher incomes from collective labour) the peasants felt that they were worse off because they could no longer spend so much time on their much more profitable private production. Also, after the first few years, Khrushchev seemed to become alarmed at the size of the private agricultural sector. In particular he staged a campaign against private cows, and local parties responded by persuading many peasants 'voluntarily' to transfer their cows to the collective farms. This resulted in discontented peasants and, judging from milk production figures, discontented cows.

Khrushchev did not spare himself. He spent much of his time in the countryside, conferring with party secretaries, cajoling farm chairmen, making promises to the peasants in the kind of earthy language they could understand. This in itself was a great advance; for the first time since Peter the Great there was a genuine interchange between tsar and people. But the results in agriculture were disappointing. The basic difficulty was that what Khrushchev said to the peasants in order to shake them from apathy was taken by local party organizations as justification for excesses. Thus when Khrushchev condemned the *Travopolye* crop rotation system, party secretaries urged the local farms to plough up their grassland, even though grass might have been the best crop at particular times and places. The year after Khrushchev had said a few words in favour of legumes, there were extensive areas of Russia where grain had been displaced by beans and clover. Khrushchev was especially passionate in his advocacy of maize cultivation; with the Virgin Lands under wheat, the old ploughlands of European Russia could profitably turn from wheat to maize, with its high tonnage per hectare and its suitability as fodder. But again the intention was carried to excess, many farms unsuitable for maize being persuaded or coerced into transferring to this crop. After Khrushchev's visit to the USA a new use for maize was urged: the cornflake was introduced to Russia, and a people long habituated to buckwheat porridge discovered shop windows laden with cornflake boxes. At first, unwilling to squander this luxury of the western world, citizens contented themselves with breakfasting on a few flakes sprinkled over a bowl of milk.

Khrushchev's failure to remedy many of the long-standing ills of the countryside found literary expression in Abramov's short story 'The New Life', published in 1963 by the 'thick' journal *Neva*. The between-the-lines implication of this tale was that woes persisted not despite Khrushchev, but sometimes because of him. The hero of this story is Mysovski, an ageing party official and collective farm chairman who finds himself in the characteristic no-win situation in which peasants refuse to work enthusiastically, or at all, to fulfil the inept directives received from the local district committee. The story revolves around one particular directive, that preparation of fodder should proceed parallel with haymaking. The farm assembly had decided that in view of the dry weather all hands should be used for haymaking, as fodder preparation was less dependent on the weather. In other words, the farm's decision to make hay while the sun shone conflicted with the instructions from above, and the district committee was not going to ignore this disobedience. Mysovski receives the first warning over the telephone: 'Perhaps the district committee will make an exception, but you really should be aware of the political line in this matter.' The second warning is less gentle: 'How do you expect me to interpret your obstinacy? Sabotage? Or uncomprehending pigheadedness about the basic economic problem?' Then comes the district committee's resolution:

For his political underrating of fodder as the foundation of collective farm cattle-raising, it is resolved to severely reprimand A. E. Mysovski, chairman of the 'New Life' collective farm ... Comrade Mysovski is obliged within five days to liquidate the intolerable delay by the 'New Life' collective farm in the storage of green fodder.

Mysovski's ambulations about the collective, trying to persuade reluctant peasants to turn out for some real work, form the bulk of the story and provide the opportunity for the author to relate a series of case studies which are only superficially fictional. There are, for example, the women who prefer to brave the chilling dampness of the woods to gather mushrooms rather than spend their days in the collective fields. After all, said one, they could sell the mushrooms to the local cooperative and thereby have a few kopeks in their hands, whereas the whole summer she had toiled in the fields and had so far received no remuneration. And with so much hay about, it was disgraceful that however hard they worked they couldn't afford to buy their own cow. The cow question gets several airings in this tale, as possession of a cow made all the difference to a peasant family. One peasant, asked if he will turn out for the special 'Working Sunday' fixed by Mysovski to catch up with the haymaking, replies that he probably will not; if he had a cow to feed he might have thought the effort worth while. Mysovski reflects:

The cow problem again! And in a farm virtually smothered with pasture ... at least a half of the peasants did not have their own cow. Fantastic! But there was a very simple explanation. For his work-day a peasant would get ten per cent of the collective hay he gathered ... So a peasant had to gather enough hay for at least eight or nine cows in order to look after his own ... Each farm chairman in one way or another tried to find ways around this system, but at that point a district prosecutor or the district commit-tee secretary would intervene with threats, 'How dare you! Anti-government practice! Encouragement of private enterprise!'

The Virgin Lands in Kazakhstan, on which Khrushchev had staked his reputation, turned out to be an achievement concealed within a failure. The achievement was that land under wheat increased to 165 million acres, com-pared with 96 million in 1950. For the first years the production of these lands justified the investment (of machinery, buildings, roads, railways, and labour). But Khrushchev, as usual, was not content to leave success alone. The pro-gramme was expanded, the land was worked intensively, and wheat was not alternated with other crops. It was not long before the warnings, by Soviet as well as western specialists, of future land erosion and infertility were shown to be justified. Erosion and exhaustion, combined with bad weather, suggested that the Virgin Lands had been merely yet another exercise in futility. But this was not so; farmed intelligently the lands were capable in an average year of making a great contribution to food supplies. But bad weather in both old and new agricultural regions led to a very bad harvest in 1963. There was a food shortage, and the USSR, which at the time was also supplying Cuba with grain, was forced to import grain from other countries, notably from the USA and Canada. The spectacle of four decades of Soviet agriculture culminating in food shortages and imports from the capitalist world was a sad blow to the prestige of the USSR and of Khrushchev himself. It accelerated the move to oust him; the good harvest of 1964 came too late to save him. As might be expected, the first result of grain shortage was a reduction of fodder available for livestock, which led to renewed meat shortages. The pig population, as always, was the most vulnerable, and fell sharply from 70 million to 40 million, a loss which was only made good after ten years.

The economy

The death of Stalin opened the way for a whole series of reforms in all aspects of Soviet life. Many of the reforms which took place under Khrushchev were minor, and did not originate from him. But the more important changes were usually carried out through his initiative and energy. Some were fundamental and long-lasting, but others were merely the product of his passion for changing everything (or meddling, as his critics subsequently called it).

One of Khrushchev's major reforms was the 1957 elimination of most of the central industrial ministries, as part of a scheme to bring planning into line with local conditions. He divided the USSR into 105 economic regions, each with its own economic council (*sovnarkhoz*) to plan and supervise its affairs. Administrators in the ministries naturally resented this change while local party organizations, which gained importance through the change, did not show much gratitude toward Khrushchev. These resentments meant that the *sovnarkhoz* idea never got beyond its teething problems and was jettisoned as soon as Khrushchev lost office.

There was a renewed emphasis on consumer goods; evidently Khrushchev's earlier opposition to Malenkov's wish to make more goods available in the stores had been prompted by tactical considerations. In time, not only larger quantities, but also a greater range of items became available to the Soviet citizen. After he returned from his travels in America, Khrushchev also encouraged the development of advertising, despite the absence of commercial competition. Aeroflot, the state airline monopoly, showed how it could be done, erecting a huge neon sign in the centre of Moscow flashing the words FLY BY PLANE.

Although the wage increases initiated by Khrushchev benefited mainly the lowest-paid, there were also price reductions which benefited all. Pensions became more meaningful, and for the first time small pensions were granted to peasants. In 1958 compulsory voluntary subscriptions to state loans were abolished, although interest and redemption for existing loans also ceased (in 1971, at the 24th Party Conference, Brezhnev promised amid prolonged applause that all such loans would be repaid by 1990). The worker's lot was also improved by the gradual introduction of the seven-hour day (with six hours on Saturdays; but by the early 1970s the transition to a five-day week was well under way). Factory trade union committees were given more responsibilities. The 'bachelors' tax was restricted to males, and the tax on childless couples removed. Small quantities of imported goods found their way into Soviet shops and usually were sold within minutes. However, living standards remained abysmal, especially in the lesser industrial cities. In 1962 workers at Novocherkassk rioted in protest against shortages and increased food prices. Twenty were killed during the suppression, and a few more executed later. News of this bloody event, and of others at different times and places, was successfully concealed by a censorship and suppressive apparatus that had lost little of its effectiveness.

The targets of the Sixth Five-Year Plan (1956–60) being over-optimistic, this plan was abandoned after two years and replaced by a seven-year plan (1959–65) which was itself subsequently replaced by the Seventh Five-Year Plan (1961–5). Khrushchev's insistence on shifting priorities from the traditional favourites of the planners (such as coal and steel) to modern industries which had been neglected in Stalin's time (in particular the chemical industry, especially its plastics and fertilizer sectors) brought benefits to the consumer, to agriculture, and to the economy in general. But Khrushchev's exuberant slogan 'Catch up and overtake the USA in per capita output by 1970', although widely publicized in the early 1960s, was rash indeed. By 1970 the gap between the USA and the USSR had certainly narrowed, but the Soviet growth rate, hitherto very fast, was declining. The year 1963, with its poor harvest, produced a growth rate lower than that of the USA. In the 1960s, heavy spending on advanced armaments and on the space programme held back other sectors of the economy. In particular, the bold housing programme which had earned Khrushchev the gratitude of millions of urban Russians had lost momentum by 1964.

In Khrushchev's early years there was new confidence in Soviet technological progress. There was large-scale railway electrification and dieselization; one of the accusations levelled by Khrushchev against Kaganovich in 1957 was that he was too fond of reactionary steam locomotives. In the air, the Aeroflot corporation was expanded in order progressively to relieve the railways of their role as the major long-distance passenger carrier. As early as 1956 it was flying the Tupolev-104 jet aircraft, and its fares were being lowered, in some cases to a level below those of the railways. In 1959 the world's first civil nuclear-powered ship, the icebreaker *Lenin*, was completed. Many of the products of advanced Soviet technology were proudly exhibited to the world;

the USSR mounted impressive displays at both the Brussels and Montreal world fairs in 1958 and 1967, among others.

However, the most effective demonstration of Soviet technical competence was the launching of the earth's first artificial satellite (*Sputnik*) in 1957. Although there had been several announcements of the intention to achieve this feat, when it happened the western world, misled by its own press, was startled. The alarm stemmed from the prickly question of how a nation previously depicted as technically backward, oppressed, and crude, could have achieved such sophistication. Fortunately, though not quite accurately, western opinion concluded that the answer lay in the great attention paid to education in the USSR. Thus *Sputnik* not only resulted in great technological prestige for the USSR, but a more generous provision for education in the budgets of most western nations. Educationalists, following in the path of generals and industrialists, discovered that the best way to obtain funds was to relate their needs to what Russia was doing.

In 1961 Gagarin became the first human to fly in space. Khrushchev had a sharp appreciation of the publicity value of Soviet cosmonautics, and his urge to follow each success with another meant that for a time steady progress was sacrificed for showy exploits. A two-man flight was readily achieved by cramming two cosmonauts into a capsule really only big enough for one. In 1963 Tereshkova became the first woman cosmonaut.

'Socialist legality'

The retreat from Stalinist terror and arbitrariness towards what was called socialist legality began with the early release of those accused in the 'Doctors' Plot'. Almost all the surviving inhabitants of the work camps were steadily rehabilitated and sent home, including even surviving members of Vlasov's anti-Soviet army. A few highly placed victims who had died in captivity or had been executed were posthumously rehabilitated; this allowed a pension and a return to respectability for their families. Political terror disappeared; although there was no cast-iron guarantee that it would not be reintroduced, there could be little doubt that the party was determined to prevent a recurrence of the excesses of Stalin's day. The three-man special boards of the MVD, which since 1934 had had the power to dispatch suspects to camps without trial, were abolished. The security service was removed from the MVD and placed under a Committee of State Security (KGB) which was headed by Shelepin, a young man who had risen in the party as leader of the Komsomol organization. The Procuracy, the foundation of the judicial system, was reformed; among other things it was empowered to supervise all criminal investigations made by the KGB, and its officials could be punished if they closed their eyes to malpractices in prisons and camps. Anti-state crimes (this term replaced 'counter-revolutionary crimes') could no longer be tried in secret, and the military courts, hitherto widely used in political cases, were limited to espionage and crimes committed by servicemen. Relatives of those servicemen who deserted to the west could no longer be punished for the desertion. Vyshinsky's doctrine that confessions were sufficient evidence for a conviction was repudiated, and so was his doctrine that in counter-revolutionary cases the accused is guilty unless he proves himself innocent. 'Terrorist acts' no longer included such misdemeanours as punching a party secretary's nose, but were confined to grave bodily injury to state or party officials, with a political motive. The doctrine of analogy was finally eliminated. After an acquittal the accused was no longer subject to a review of his case at any time; such a review had to be initiated within one year of the first trial. Penalties were reduced for many crimes. The labour camps were officially abolished, being replaced by labour colonies; these were usually the same institutions but with better conditions. Some criminal offences were abolished (abortion, absence from work, leaving a job without permission). Another step forward was the progressive declarations of invalidity extended to certain laws, decrees, and edicts issued in Stalin's time. Also noteworthy was the higher status assumed by jurists, who since 1917 had not been held in high esteem. They never attained their pre-revolutionary influence, but they were consulted when judicial changes were contemplated.

Moderation of the rigours of the law was followed by an increase in crime. This in turn led to a partial return to harsher measures in 1961. The death penalty, which had been reinstated in 1950, was extended from serious cases of espionage, treason, 'wrecking', aggravated murder, terrorist acts, and banditry to large-scale theft or embezzlement of state or social property, counterfeiting, 'speculation in foreign currency', aggravated rape, murder of police or auxiliaries on duty, and serious and repeated bribe-taking.[5] For some of these crimes the new penalty was applied retroactively, past offenders already serving their sentences being shot (a special decree of the Presidium of the Supreme Soviet in July 1961 authorized this unusual step). Bribery was widespread in the USSR and its classification as a grave crime did not mean that a minor bribe would result in a death sentence or even imprisonment. Executions for black market offences were quite rare and selective, although an ingenious Ukrainian who in the 1970s laid a pipeline from a distillery to his own premises and sold the alcohol on the black market received a death sentence. He had done two dangerous things, stealing state property on a large scale, and dealing in a socially sensitive commodity, as well as making an enormous profit for himself.

A retrograde step was the 'Law against Parasites'. This was directed against

---

5. The death penalty was abolished in Russia in 1754, 1917, 1918, 1919, 1947, and 1996 but only the short-lived 1917 abolition was totally effective (it did not exclude sentences passed by military courts). From 1932 the death penalty (known as 'the highest form of social defence') was applied to theft of state property and political crimes.

persons 'evading socially useful work' and could be applied without the usual guarantees of the criminal law; in fact general meetings of a social organization (the workers of a factory, inhabitants of an apartment block) could impose the penalty of two to five years' internal exile (with possible confiscation of property) on one of their number, provided the decision was confirmed by the town soviet. In the first year of its operation, 2,000 'parasites' were exiled from Moscow alone. This law, and the stiffer penalties against hooligans, were largely directed at the growing number of dissatisfied young people who indulged in various kinds of delinquencies. In some cases the advantage of popular participation in justice was counterbalanced by the citizens' willingness, sometimes prompted, to hit out at nonconformists. There was a case of a young very nonconformist poet, who was exiled as a 'parasite', it being adjudged that he could not be a 'real' poet because he had no document to prove it. The 'Parasites' Law', which had antecedents in communal custom of tsarist times, was soon withdrawn in many of the republics.

The trial of Daniel and Synyavsky in 1966 marked a step backward, in that they were denied certain rights officially granted to the accused, and in the abuse (not for the first or last time) of the law against 'agitation and propaganda directed against the Soviet system'. Daniel and Sinyavsky had published abroad, under pseudonyms, works which because of alleged anti-Sovietism were not allowed publication at home. There was no law against this, so they were accused of anti-Soviet propaganda. The trial was preceded by newspaper articles in which the accused were regarded as unquestionably guilty. Their right of defence was curtailed by interruptions from the judge and the apparently hand-picked audience of hostile spectators. Thus the prosecution was able to present anti-Soviet statements by fictional characters in the novels as words actually voiced by the accused. The latter were sent to labour colonies.

But despite the occasional step backward, in the 1960s and 1970s there seemed little reason to doubt that the post-1953 law reforms had been a sincere and definite step forward. Certainly there were complaints, not unfounded, of police repression. But repression, like freedom, is a relative term and, as Alexander II discovered, it is when freedom is extended at the expense of repression that complaints of repression become loudest. Under Stalin, political intercourse, even between consenting adults in private, was perilous. Under Khrushchev and his successors individual Russians could safely criticize their government, provided they did not seek a large audience, or join together to form anything which might be described as an 'organization'.

The arts

After Stalin died, one of the most popular 'thick' literary journals[6] published an article suggesting that the true test of a literary work was sincerity, not conformity to officially imposed stereotypes. There was much opposition to this from those for whom 'party-mindedness' remained the key index of a work's value. They argued that if a writer is 'ideologically incorrect', or has 'alien attitudes', his sincerity only increases the harmful effect he has on his readers; sincerity is therefore dangerous and harmful. The struggle between liberals and conservatives was clearly evident in literary circles throughout the late 1950s and 1960s. During that period there was an initial move towards greater freedom, especially after Khrushchev's destalinization speech, then a few scandals, followed by the reimposition of stricter controls. The latter, distasteful though they were, tended to set limits to the new freedom rather than reimpose the old restrictions.

By 1954 novels were appearing which quietly drew attention to the evils of the Stalinist way of life. For example, V. Nekrasov's *Home Town* showed how returning servicemen were disappointed at what they found back home. Ehrenburg's *Thaw* gave its name to the initial period of post-Stalin relaxation; in Russian, 'thaw' suggests not simply a melting of ice but the spontaneous renewal of life as the grip of winter breaks up. *Thaw* referred casually, though unexpectedly to the Soviet reader, to such things as the talented artists who either starve or paint murals of collectivized cows or shock-workers, and the local Jewish doctor terrified by press accounts of the 'Doctors' Plot'. It portrayed a rank-and-file Stalinist, Ivan Vasilievich Zhuravlev, a factory manager who cares more about plan fulfilment than the health of his workers:

the factory was in excellent order. There had not been one breakdown for six years. True, the Deputy Minister had told Ivan Vasilievich that he had spent illegally the funds intended for building living quarters, but Zhuravlev had decided that this was just for form's sake: 'the Ministry, like me, is interested above all in output'. Naturally, he had hastened to assure the Deputy Minister that all the workers had accommodation and that there was nothing catastrophically bad . . . In town people were saying, 'Zhuravlev's going up in the world'. It was not surprising that Zhuravlev was now having his portrait painted.

From the mid-1950s some condemned authors were rehabilitated post-humously and their works republished. Anna Akhmatova, whose poems had been condemned by Zhdanov, was once again praised. A wider range of foreign authors were published in Russian editions. There was some resistance from officials of the Writers' Union, and the head of the latter, Fadayev,

6. *Novyi mir*, 12 (1953). *Novyi mir* after Stalin's death was the most adventurous of the literary journals; *One Day in the Life of Ivan Denisovich* and *Not by Bread Alone* were first published in it. Its editor was the poet A. Tvardovski. After the departure of Khrushchev this journal's output was progressively restricted and its editor and board replaced by more conservative people.

committed suicide in 1956 (rather unchivalrously, his death was ascribed to alcoholism).

Poetry, which under Stalin had been little more than rhymed information, also reasserted itself. The nature of Stalinism itself, and why people had tolerated it, was one of its concerns. P. Antokolski ended one 1956 poem with

> He who has died we hate
> Less than our silence.

while Tvardovski treated the same theme with

> And who was there who did not praise him in his presence,
> Did not glorify him – just find such a one!

and in his '1945' Boris Slutskii referred to the Stalinist practice of rebuilding people's homes last:

> From all the stones crunching underfoot
> Were built first palaces, and then homes.

It was the young poet Yevtushenko who attracted most popular enthusiasm, both by his printed poems and by his public appearances at poetry-reading performances. With his anti-Stalinist approach he became almost an official poet for Khrushchev, although it was an uneasy relationship and he was sometimes in semi-disgrace. Yevtushenko, and a very few other poets, made frequent poetry-reading visits to the west, where they were well received.

One of the first writers to dispense with Stalinist literary conventions and thereby create a best-seller was Dudintsev, whose *Not by Bread Alone* (1956) showed how a talented, honest, and potentially valuable individual was held back by an entrenched clique of bureaucrats who opposed innovation as a threat to their vested interests, and even managed to get the hero sentenced to prison camp. Solzhenitsyn's *One Day in the Life of Ivan Denisovich* (1962), apparently published on Khrushchev's instructions after the censors had rejected it, was a short novel bringing home with powerful understatement the miseries of daily life in a labour camp (of which the author had several years' first-hand knowledge). A best-seller, it helped Khrushchev's campaign against the spirit of Stalinism; it was novels like Solzhenitsyn's which made Russians realize the enormity of the abuses perpetrated by Stalin and the MVD. Yet the work which caused most embarrassment was not particularly dangerous, until it had been made so by the antics of the censors. Pasternak's *Doctor Zhivago* (published abroad in 1957), while certainly presenting an un-Soviet though not especially anti-Soviet view of the Russian Revolution, would never have attracted such widespread attention had not the censors belatedly cancelled its publication in the USSR after the author had already arranged publication of an Italian edition. The Italian publisher refused to abandon the contract, which means that what was possibly the greatest

Russian novel of the twentieth century was a best-seller abroad while banned in its country of origin. It was well known that Pasternak was a man of great literary sensibility who had refused to lower his standards during the Stalinist years. Thus when, a sick man, he was forced to refuse the Nobel Prize and was condemned by the Writers' Union, foreign communist intellectuals were among those who protested. Yet Khrushchev had not, apparently, been consulted about the ban.

Education

Khrushchev, himself a self-made man with little formal education, was not well disposed to those who wished to escape physical work through academic success. Moreover, a shortage of skilled and semi-skilled workers seemed to be approaching. Educated young people who had failed to get into university were unfitted by their education and aspirations to enter industry. The universities themselves were turning out similar misfits (described by one critic as like stuffed fish: you could not tell what kind of stuffing they had, but you knew they could not swim).

Khrushchev therefore favoured the 'polytechnic' principle, which meant inserting substantial periods of industrial or agricultural work into the curriculum to provide vocational training. The intention of providing compulsory ten-year education for all was abandoned, but those wishing to proceed to higher education could stay at school for additional years; Khrushchev had earlier abolished the school fees imposed by Stalin. This move to end 'the divorce from life and work' of students was carried out too hurriedly and was neither popular nor especially effective.

Another innovation was the secondary co-educational boarding schools. They were a failure, and were progressively closed. They had tried to accomplish two inconsistent aims: to provide a good educative environment for socially unfortunate children (typically children of one-parent families), and at the same time to constitute an example-setting academic enterprise. Many parents saw them as an attack on the family, and preferred the 'extended day' offered by some schools, where pupils stayed into the evening, pursuing informal activities. Single-sex education had been finally ended in 1954.

A basic tradition of Soviet education was that schools were to be comprehensive; children were not to be divided between schools on the basis of ability. Even within schools there was no 'streaming'. There were a few exceptions, like the Kirov School of Ballet in Leningrad, but these were obviously special. Under Khrushchev, however, special schools for children exceptionally gifted in mathematics and languages were created and in general were a success.

Under Khrushchev's successors the new 1977 Constitution promised full secondary education for all, and in 1984 there was an educational reform.

Labour training and 'socially productive' work hours were doubled in the general schools. School starting age was reduced from 7 to 6 (giving some relief to working mothers and also bringing children's upbringing into the state's influence at an earlier age). Perhaps the most progressive step of this reform was the introduction of senior compulsory classes in information technology.

However, the 1984 reform came just before Gorbachev's total reconstruction of the USSR and was therefore subjected to prolonged criticism and tampering. Henceforth, more initiative and openness was expected. There was a long debate between conservatives and innovators. The Academy of Pedagogical Sciences represented the old, authoritarian, approach and was a quite useful body which had a monopoly of educational research, which it performed through subsidiary institutes like the Institute of Pre-school Education and its establishment for studying handicapped pupils, the elegantly named Institute of Defectology. It had relieved teachers of the need to concern themselves with studying methods, but at the same time had also prevented teachers from interesting themselves in innovation. Under Gorbachev the Academy did lose its monopoly. A new teachers' union was set up (the 'Creative Union of Teachers') to unite educationalists, teachers, and parents with a view to innovation. There was also a 'Eureka' programme to promote innovation in given districts. Meanwhile lycée- and gymnasium-type schools were being set up, often by devoted individuals, the usual aim being a wider curriculum and the encouragement of pupils to think for themselves.

Ambitious or caring parents supported these new schools. Such parents were both a positive and negative influence. The comfortably placed, string-pulling family was a familiar and generally unloved segment of Soviet society, but it did sometimes get done things which needed to be done. On the other hand, from Stalin's time to Yeltsin's time, there was a good deal of bribery, corruption, string-pulling, and pressurizing as influential parents strove to ensure that their own children would receive favourable attention from teachers, examiners, and entrance boards.

Khrushchev's campaign to bring the educated into closer touch with life also brought expansion of part-time and correspondence courses. By 1964 there were about 1,708,000 correspondence and 569,000 evening students in higher education, compared with 1,584,000 in full-time regular courses (although the full-timers usually completed their courses faster). Correspondence students were treated more generously than their counterparts in the west, being given time off work in order to follow short courses or consult their tutors. By 1969 there were 794 institutes of higher learning with nearly 4,500,000 students. The forty universities were outnumbered by other institutions, which included technical institutes, agricultural institutes, more than eighty medical schools, teacher-training institutes, and others. In 1965 the management school appeared in the USSR. As in the secondary schools, the higher education teaching process was largely the ingestion of facts and their successful evacuation at examination time. Unlike western universities there was little emphasis on problem-solving. It was held, perhaps rightly, that it was better to learn how to solve problems later, on the job. University students were required to devote a tenth or more of their lecture hours (which averaged 1,000 hours annually for five years) to political knowledge (Marxism-Leninism, Dialectical Materialism, etc.). Although this subject was examined it appeared to arouse no great enthusiasm among students, partly because of natural cynicism and partly because of unimaginative presentation (e.g. 'It is vital for all Soviet citizens to understand the class struggle . . . In the Soviet Union there is no class struggle'). Cynicism was unsurprising in a generation which noticed the difficulties of their history teachers, who could not foresee what, tomorrow, would happen to yesterday. In 1956, throughout the Soviet Union's secondary-school system, the examinations in final-year history (History of the Soviet Union) were abruptly cancelled because Khrushchev had made obsolete what was being taught.

Except for a few students with rich parents, all were eligible for grants. The average grant was meagre but could be varied upwards or downwards according to the student's academic performance. Poor performance could entail loss of grant until an improvement was recorded. Graduates were required to spend the first few years of work in a job and place to which they were directed in accordance with national needs. Many pulled strings to escape this obligation and, just as the best tsarist cadets were allowed to choose their regiment, so the top graduates were allowed to choose their place of work. It was the mediocre graduates with uninfluential parents who would find themselves directed to their first job in some arduous region; to make sure they arrived their diploma was dispatched to their future place of work. In the 1960s, few Soviet students were interested in drugs, but many listened to foreign broadcasts, which was a cheaper way of obtaining nonconformity and an expansion of mental horizons. On occasion, Soviet students openly disputed with lecturers purveying official truths, and this was quite shocking for traditionalists.

The armed forces

After the death of Stalin the generals had great public prestige, and seemed relatively untainted by Stalinism. Even though Zhukov, like other successful generals, had been given a secondary and remote posting after the war, he was rightly regarded by Russians as the architect of victory. It would be several decades before his reputation could be impartially evaluated; in his own lifetime the history of his battles was rewritten more than once to fit political requirements.

In the mid-1950s the generals were in a strong position and their acquiescence, at least, was required by the new leaders. Zhukov became minister of defence. But after the defeat of the 'anti-party conspiracy', Khrushchev could dispense with active army support. In October 1957 *Pravda* appeared with a front-page article celebrating Zhukov's return from a successful visit to the Balkans, while the back page of the same newspaper carried a small notice of his dismissal as minister of defence.

In the four years preceding Zhukov's dismissal the army officers had firmly reasserted themselves. The war's history had been revised so that Stalin was no longer portrayed as the great strategist and tactician, with the generals merely his executives. More important, although the long-suppressed desire of officers to avenge the purge of the 1930s was not gratified, their wish to reduce the role of the army's political officers was partly satisfied. Among other reliefs, professional army officers were no longer obliged to attend political lectures. After Zhukov's fall from grace, he was accused of hindering the party's work in the army and the political commissars regained some of their lost authority. Zhukov was also accused of 'Bonapartism', and new war histories ascribed to him much of the responsibility for the disasters of 1941. Khrushchev gradually appointed to the higher defence positions men whom he had known in the Stalingrad campaign, men whom he felt he could trust. However, these officers sometimes refrained from public approval of certain of Khrushchev's moves, an unmistakable sign of disagreement. This disagreement seems to have centred on Khrushchev's reductions of defence expenditure.

In Stalin's later years, military technology had stagnated. Stalin even seemed reluctant to acknowledge that the atomic bomb had changed the military situation. In the mid-1950s Khrushchev was able to win the acceptance by the more influential generals of a reduction of the army, in exchange for investment in new military technology; rockets would be substituted for regiments and submarines for cruisers. However, in 1960 Khrushchev embarked on a new reduction of the armed forces, from the existing 3.6 million men to 2.4 million, the last figure being approximately half the 1953 strength. This attempt to demonstrate the sincerity of the policy of 'peaceful coexistence' with the west, and to divert military spending to civilian, did not go smoothly. Although demobilized soldiers found places in the economy, thousands of prematurely retired officers were less easy to accommodate. Some found lowly clerical or manual work, but their loss of status and prospects was shattering. It was this, with the humiliation in Cuba in 1962, and hints of further cuts, which ensured that there would be no military support for Khrushchev when his own retirement was demanded in 1964.

The people's democracies

Khrushchev's denunciation of Stalin weakened communist leaders in other countries and was one of the factors in the 1956 revolts in Poland and Hungary. Other factors were the dissolution of the Cominform, and the joint declaration by the Soviet and Yugoslav communist parties that the 'road to socialism' could be different for different countries. After the workers of Poznań rebelled, the Polish communist party ejected the most prominent Stalinists from its central committee and appointed Gomulka as its first secretary. The Red Army and Baltic Fleet staged ominous movements, but Gomulka was able to obtain a compromise agreement by which internal policy would be relaxed, Moscow's 'viceroy' in Warsaw, Marshal Rokossovsky,[7] would be withdrawn, but Poland would maintain the unquestioned supremacy of the communist party and would stay in the Warsaw Pact. The latter, Moscow's answer to NATO, coordinated the armed forces of the Soviet bloc in Europe.

Hardly was the Polish crisis eased when a far more serious situation arose in Hungary. When Stalin was denounced in 1956, and when the news came of Poland's successful assertiveness, the Hungarian workers and intellectuals who had been criticizing the regime demanded not only concessions, but a radical change. In October the moderate, formerly imprisoned, communist Nagy became leader, and for a time the demands of the dissidents were met: more contacts with the west, release of political prisoners, a freer press and radio. But when Nagy agreed to take Hungary out of the Warsaw Pact Moscow took action. During the next few, confused, days, there was considerable street fighting as both the Hungarian army and civilians resisted the Russians. Some Red Army men, shocked to find themselves fighting not capitalists, but workers, refused to open fire. Hungarian resistance, which cost about 20,000 lives, came to an end after the Red Army arrested the leading Hungarian generals, having invited them into its lines on the pretext of opening negotiations. About 200,000 Hungarians fled to the west. Nagy was executed in 1958.

The spectacle of the Red Army suppressing a genuine people's revolt against oppression caused yet another shock to the communist world. Inside the USSR, most of the population seemed satisfied with the explanation that some Hungarian workers and party members had allowed themselves to be used by capitalist or West German counter-revolutionary conspirators, but even in conditions of strict censorship there were other Russians who worked out what had happened and were uneasy.

---

7. Red Army General Rokossovsky had been appointed Poland's minister of defence, deputy prime minister, and member of the Polish Politburo in 1949 in order to keep an eye on the government and party. Although Rokossovsky was the son of a Polish locomotive driver, he became to the Poles a symbol of Russian domination. Hence the popular demand for his dismissal.

The suppression of the Hungarian revolt showed that the people's democracies would not be allowed to move much further in the direction of greater political freedom than the Soviet Union itself, and they would not be allowed to endanger the system of communist buffer states which were thought to facilitate Russia's defence. More fundamentally, the Hungarian crisis brought into the open the forty-year-old dilemma of the USSR's two roles: the role of a nation building socialism and the role of a leader of world revolution.

China asserted itself quite vigorously against Moscow, while Romania took the lead in questioning Soviet policy in Comecon. This organization, founded to coordinate the communist economies, took on new life after the death of Stalin. Genuine cooperation to mutual advantage was stressed. However, Comecon's plans ran into difficulties. The idea was that each nation should concentrate on producing for the whole bloc those items which it produced best. But in 1963 the Romanians asserted that they had a right to plan their own economy in their own way, and made commercial agreements with western Europe, China, and Yugoslavia. In addition, Romania was offered and accepted credits from the USA, and even opened diplomatic relations with that *bête noire* of the communist world, Western Germany.

By 1964 almost all communist parties had asserted, mildly or strongly, their right to reach communism by their own path. In effect, they implied that communism did not mean Russianism. Moscow was no longer the Third Rome. The leader of the Italian communist party, Togliatti, summed up the new concept in the term 'polycentrism'; there was no longer a world centre of communism in Moscow, but as many centres as there were parties.

Foreign affairs

In the post-Stalin decade, Lenin's term 'peaceful coexistence' was resurrected to describe the new more relaxed attitude; it did not imply friendship with the capitalist world, but admitted the possibility of compromise and contact until such time as the capitalist countries would turn to socialism. There were several reasons for this relaxation; the barrenness of Stalin's hostile isolationism, a realization, openly acknowledged by Khrushchev, that nuclear war was too horrible to be thinkable, the economic burden of arms spending, and the desirability of learning from the west, either by imitation or by entering into commercial and technical agreements.

The new attitudes were soon transformed into deeds. At Geneva in 1954 the USSR helped to negotiate an end to the Korean and Indo-Chinese wars. In 1955 the USSR agreed to sign the long-delayed peace treaty with Austria, by which the Red Army was finally removed from its occupation zone in return for the guaranteed neutrality of Austria. Russian bases in Finland were closed. Khrushchev visited many parts of the world, including India and Britain, and in 1959 toured the USA. Other contacts were fostered. BBC Russian-language broadcasts were no longer jammed; from 1954 foreign tourists began to visit the USSR. The Cominform was dissolved in 1956. Selected foreign films were shown in Soviet cinemas. More trade agreements were made with capitalist countries, although foreign trade remained small. Student exchanges began.

Sometimes there were setbacks to the détente. After the Hungarian crisis the reconciliation with Tito, which, despite Molotov, had been very much on Tito's terms, was shattered for a few years. Washington was reluctant to respond to Khrushchev's conciliatory policy. In 1960 a summit conference came to an early bad end when Khrushchev stormed out after President Eisenhower had refused to apologize following the shooting down, well inside Russia, of a US U-2 photographic reconnaissance aircraft. Eisenhower's successor Kennedy had little understanding of the Russian situation at first and his repeated assertion, which Moscow knew to be untrue, that the USSR was taking first place in the missile race, seemed to contain a threat.

In 1962 there was the Cuban crisis. Khrushchev had hoped to improve Russia's strategic situation (or at least, bargaining situation) by installing nuclear missiles in Cuba. However, President Kennedy, while leaving room for a dignified Soviet withdrawal, made it clear that the USA would use force to prevent the completion of the installation. Wisely, Khrushchev withdrew his missiles. Although he had clearly met with a setback it was only in high party and government circles that this was realized; the Soviet people, unlike the Cuban, were not told the full story.

The problem of West Berlin, which Khrushchev described as 'a fishbone in the gullet', remained unsolved. Undoubtedly the western presence in this enclave inside communist East Germany was a grave embarrassment to the latter, only partly ameliorated by the erection in 1961 of the Berlin Wall to cut off more thoroughly the east from the west. In general, Khrushchev's foreign policy (which he largely determined himself, merely using his foreign minister, Gromyko, as an aide) was not unsuccessful. The USSR became party to a number of international agreements, ranging from the termination of territorial claims in Antarctica to the Nuclear Test-Ban Treaty. After the Cuban crisis Khrushchev and Kennedy exchanged long and private letters on common problems, and this probably did much to moderate tensions. Also to this period belongs the 'Hot Line', a permanent direct telephone link between the US president and the Soviet leader. This was intended to act as a safety valve at times of mounting international pressure.

With the ex-colonial countries, the difficult choice facing the Soviet government was whether to support indigenous communist parties which had little chance of gaining mass support, or the new nationalist governments which had power but were often suppressing local communists. Khrushchev and his successors tended to support the newly established nationalist governments with economic, technical, and sometimes military aid, so as to gain friends and influence in the new nations. This policy gave an opening for Chinese accusations that Moscow was putting Soviet aspirations as a world power before the needs of world revolution (China, and many Russians too, resented Soviet help to the new nations; they could both have used these resources themselves). Another drawback of the policy was that the expected returns did not always materialize. It is true that in 1956 Soviet aid to Egypt provoked the west into an inept self-induced crisis which culminated in the Anglo-French invasion of the Canal Zone and an accelerated loss of western influence in the Middle East, but there were few comparable successes elsewhere. Cuba's entry into the communist camp proved to be a fresh drain on Soviet economic resources. Carefully cultivated leaders like Nkrumah of Ghana were overthrown by their own people. Russian-built steelworks in India supplied cheap steel as raw material for the capitalist sector of the Indian economy. Credits and armaments were given to Sukarno's Indonesia but Sukarno was then violently replaced by a pro-western government. One of the criticisms voiced against Khrushchev in 1964 was that, on a visit to see the Soviet Aswan Dam project, he had conferred on President Nasser the Order of Lenin at the very time when the Egyptian leader was imprisoning local communists.

The relegation of Khrushchev

Khrushchev's successful attack on the Stalinist myths in 1956, his chastisement of the 'anti-party group' in 1957, and the combination in his own person of party secretary and prime minister in 1958 did not enable him to institute his own dictatorship even if he had wanted to. The top leadership of the party worked on democratic principles in so far as Khrushchev depended on a majority of votes. But it was not until 1964 that Khrushchev's rivals and critics, aided by apparent setbacks to his policies, were able to engineer his downfall.

In October 1964 Khrushchev left Moscow for a Black Sea holiday. Two of his supporters who controlled the key news services (the head of the state radio, and the editor of *Pravda*) were also out of Moscow, although Khrushchev's son-in-law, whom he had appointed editor of *Izvestiya*, remained in the capital. Taking advantage of these circumstances, Khrushchev's critics called a meeting of the Politburo, which decided to initiate a long-desired change of leadership and then summoned Khrushchev to appear before it. At this meeting he was condemned, and on the same day at a Central Committee plenary meeting resolutions were passed whereby Brezhnev became first secretary of the party and Kosygin chairman of the Council of Ministers. It was officially announced that Khrushchev had retired because of declining health. Since *Izvestiya* was suppressed on that particular day, while *Pravda* and the radio were carrying the official statement, Khrushchev had no chance of resistance. He went quietly into retirement with a personal state pension.

Khrushchev had broken with the past, but while he had exposed basic problems, he left to his successors the task of finding lasting solutions. Some contemporaries, especially outside Russia, tended to deride Khrushchev. He was a man who came from a simple non-intellectual environment and was able to mix confidently with ordinary people. He was a sharp-witted polemicist (as his press conferences with western journalists showed), but he used simple language, frequently making his point with references to the Old Testament. His enemies accused him of buffoonery, saying that people were simply laughing at him, but this is an accusation often levelled at those in authority who refuse to take themselves too seriously. His frequent overriding of the bureaucracy, a characteristic of those whose contribution to society is the ability to get things moving, made enemies and cooled friends. Poor agricultural performance, which was vital since so many other improvements depended on it, was probably the most important single factor in emboldening his rivals. On 17 October 1964 *Pravda* hinted at the real reasons for his departure in a long editorial which did not actually mention Khrushchev and pretended to be about the communist concept of leadership:

The Leninist party is the enemy of subjectivism and drifting in communist construction, of harebrained scheme-making, of half-baked conclusions and hasty decisions and actions taken without regard to realities. Bragging and phrasemongering, bossiness, reluctance to take account of scientific achievement and practical experience are alien to it . . . It is only on the Leninist principle of collective leadership that it is possible to direct, and develop, the increasing creative initiative of the party.

Khrushchev had no chance of replying to these aspersions. Or, at least, that is what his successors confidently expected. But the former leader had not lost his craftiness. He confided his own account of his political life to a tape recorder, and the tapes were secreted out of the USSR to the west, where they were translated and published. These, Khrushchev's memoirs, are as fascinating and as slanted as any narrative of a retired statesman.

17

Decrepitude

Political life

THE communist party could justify itself as organizer, planner, and ultimate authority at a time when scarce resources had to be rigorously allocated to the most necessary sectors of the economy. With *Sputnik* and other projects it had demonstrated what it could do as organizer and inspirer. But the world was changing, and traditional party officialdom risked being seen as unnecessary, if not actually harmful, in a world where the spontaneity and diversity that come from absence of imposed control seemed to bring good rewards. Under Brezhnev, the party would encounter such problems of modernity without, however, always recognizing them.

After the departure of Khrushchev, the union in one person of the party secretary and the prime minister was studiously avoided by the 'collective leadership' of Brezhnev and Kosygin. But when in 1971 the 4,963 delegates of the 24th Party Conference (irreverently described by western journalists as the 'world's biggest rubber stamp') met to approve Brezhnev's report on the work of the party, it seemed clear that he had become at least first among equals. In its policies the Brezhnevite leadership was pragmatic rather than sensational, and preferred to let sleeping dogs lie. The regime was characterized in the west as dull and conservative; this was perhaps an unfair judgement, although as the years passed Brezhnev did resemble more and more the ailing headmaster of an authoritarian boarding school.

The virtual end of government by terrorism after the death of Stalin had not only lightened the lives of many citizens, but also entailed a new style of politics. Khrushchev's rise and fall had been a function of his ability to gain and hold the support of his immediate colleagues. The latter had personal ambitions, but also represented certain sectional interests. Despite, therefore, the unique role of the communist party in a one-party state, and the continuation of such characteristics as tight censorship and secrecy, a political life with a genuine interplay of interests did exist. Evidently some interest groups were more powerful than others, and there were occasional moves to cut them down to size. Khrushchev in his early years of power was opposed by the officialdom of both the ministry of foreign affairs and the MVD, and (as he later said in his memoirs) the military interest was capable of bringing extraordinary pressure to bear on the government and party leadership.

The basic preoccupation of the Brezhnev regime was the allocation of scarce economic resources between urgent claimants; a choice had to be made between those claimants and ways found to increase the resources available. More specifically, there was a great need to invest more in agriculture. Increased agricultural production would mean an enhanced standard of living (and, after all, the party's claim to its leading role depended very largely on its promise to raise living standards). It would also reduce the expenditure of foreign exchange on the import of grain; such foreign exchange was required for the purchase of western technology with which to modernize Soviet industry. But the traditional claimant of priority for investment was the defence interest, the interest which Khrushchev had described as the 'steel-eaters'. Under Brezhnev, at least until the late 1970s, there was a limitation of the share of resources devoted to defence and a correspondingly relaxed foreign policy.

Podgorny, who had been appointed 'president' in 1965, was so aware of the need for détente that in a major speech at Riga in 1973 his portrayal of what a third world war would really mean was so disturbing that it was omitted from the newspaper reports. Kosygin, whose background was in light industry and who regarded the party as essentially an organization whose first priority was the public welfare, held similar opinions; in 1974, when western economic difficulties led more ideologically inclined colleagues to speculate about the prospect for revolutionary outbursts in the west, he warned that an immediate weakening of the west was not necessarily to the Soviet Union's advantage. But while Kosygin and others were asserting that increased arms expenditure did nothing to reduce the risk of war, Marshal Grechko and his colleagues were making speeches about the need to prepare strong military forces to forestall the stratagems of the imperialists. However, the party approved Brezhnev's policy of 'peaceful coexistence' at its 1971 and 1976 conferences.

An underlying theme of these years was the question of a possible 'restalinization'. By 1966 official anti-stalinism was plainly ended; the trial of the two writers Daniel and Synyavsky, and the castigation of the historian Nekrich (who had written an account of June 1941 which was critical of Stalin), emphasized this. There were many who thought that the condemnation of Stalin had gone too far. Party officials were among those who hankered for the good old days in which they had risen to the top, and had carried out their organizing duties without needing to take people's feelings into account. The age group old enough to have climbed to responsible positions under Stalin but too young to have experienced the mass purges of the 1930s was especially inclined to view Stalinism with a strong sense of loss. The Brezhnev regime seemed to take the pressure of the 'neo-stalinist' wing of the party more seriously than the 'liberal' wing but, in general, succeeded in avoiding real, as opposed to token, moves back to the old ways. In 1966, rumours of Stalin's imminent official rehabilitation caused not only foreign communists but also leading Soviet intellectuals to make successful protests to the party leaders. In 1969, for the ninetieth anniversary of Stalin's birth it was intended to publish in most newspapers a special celebratory article, but misgivings expressed by, among others, foreign communist leaders persuaded the Politburo to change its mind. Most members of the Politburo regarded the Stalin question as a hot potato which was best left to cool in peace. Shelepin appears to have been the centre of 'neo-stalinism', but he was gradually deprived of his offices, ending with his exit from the Politburo in 1975. In 1976 that reliable barometer of the political atmosphere, the *Great Soviet Encyclopedia*, reduced Stalin's entry to four columns.

Destalinization could never be unambiguous so long as a majority of the senior party officials were products of the Stalinist regime. The Politburo was essentially a group of old men; by 1980 its leading members were septuagenarians, and only Romanov, representing the Leningrad party organization, was under 60. Several were in poor health; Kosygin had spent a period away from work, while Brezhnev on trips abroad was seen to be a very ill and stumbling man who confined his participation in negotiations to the reading of prepared statements. His physical handicaps were concealed at home, but commentators abroad wondered how far he was really in control of Soviet affairs, or even of his own body. Yet in summer 1980, when the Federal German chancellor visited Moscow after a period of extraordinary tension and strain, Brezhnev during the playing of national anthems was shown on television standing erect without any visible means of support, a living testimony to Soviet medical science.

In 1976 there were signs of a 'personality cult' enveloping Brezhnev. His experience in the war, when he was political commissar to one of the armies, was presented as a major factor in the Soviet victory. He was also accorded the rank of Marshal of the Soviet Union. Possibly this assumption of the supreme rank gave him much-needed authority in dealing with the military interest; about the same time the defence minister, the civilian Ustinov, was also given this rank. Meanwhile Brezhnev became Hero of the Soviet Union for the second time and received his fifth Order of Lenin. In the press he began to be described as 'The Leader'. Soon his multi-volume memoirs began to appear, were serialized in several periodicals, and printed as large-edition books; for this effort by his ghost-writers he was duly awarded the top literary prize. In 1977 he took the office of chairman of the Presidium of the Supreme Soviet, and thereby combined the two offices of party leader and head of state, or president. Podgorny, the outgoing head of state, was virtually dismissed; he had been in disagreement with Brezhnev at this time. Brezhnev however, did not take over the prime ministership, as had his two predecessors Stalin and Khrushchev. Since his health was poor, moreover, he appointed a deputy to perform most of the routine presidential duties.

By 1977, party membership was approaching 16 million. Already one-third of those citizens with higher education were members. Growth, however, had slowed down, which meant that the average age of members was increasing. Most party members merely turned up at meetings of the party cell. As before, the minority of members holding *Nomenklatura* posts (party and government posts important enough to be filled under close party supervision) composed an influential and privileged group.

A new constitution was presented and adopted in 1977, no fewer than sixteen years after Khrushchev had first mentioned its imminence. It was based on the old 1936 text, with some significant differences. Thus Article 1 described the USSR as a socialist state of 'the whole people' instead of 'workers and peasants'. Moreover, it recognized the intelligentsia as not a mere 'stratum' but as a group of equal standing with the worker and peasant classes. The USSR was described as a 'developed socialist society', a stage leading to the eventual communist society. Evidently Khrushchev's reckless announcement of impending 'full communism' was not to be taken seriously. In this new constitution the 'leading and guiding role' of the communist party was clearly asserted, and as early as Article 6. However, there was no mention of the party's Politburo, the leading decision-making body. 'Democratic centralism' received constitutional recognition at last. The interval between elections to the Supreme Soviet was increased from four to five years (paralleling a previous change in the party rules which made a similar increase to the interval between party congresses). The constituent union republics were no longer granted the rather meaningless right to maintain their own armed forces, but their right to secede from the USSR was maintained. More important, the eventual 'merging' of the various nationalities into one great Soviet nation was no longer mentioned. New articles guaranteed free health services, cheap housing, and public participation in decision-making. Environmental protection received a mention, strengthening the hands of those who were arguing that this was a very important matter. In line with the policy of détente, an article was added about the peaceful aims of foreign policy. This, however, was balanced by another new article stressing the importance of the 'Defence of the Socialist Fatherland'.

At the end of 1980 Brezhnev was still soldiering on, under great strain. Soviet troops were under fire in Afghanistan. Reagan's election as the next US president promised new anxieties. Kosygin had died (the one-time locomotive fireman Tikhonov was his successor as prime minister). Above all, in Poland the workers and ordinary party members, by strikes and demonstrations, had humiliated the corrupt and incompetent party hierarchy and established really free trade unions. There was a clear possibility that the Polish example might spread, but the consequences which could follow an intervention by the Red Army were almost as unattractive. Meanwhile, the censorship and intensified jamming of foreign radio kept the Soviet population ill-informed about the events in Poland and Brezhnev's decrepitude.

His last public appearance was in Red Square in early November 1982, at the 65th anniversary celebrations of the Revolution. A few days later he was dead. On the whole, his regime had been benevolent, with a perceptible attitude of live-and-let-live. His rule was later characterized as 'the period of stagnation' but this stagnation did at least give the population something it had lacked for four decades: stability. One manifestation of this was his slogan 'Respect for Cadres', which reflected his wish to avoid upheavals in the party and state administration and to allow administrators to remain in office without fears of dismissal. By the end of his reign, this had ensured that he had broad support among elderly administrators, but also that a younger generation of middle-aged officials, denied promotion and opportunity for changing things, was dissatisfied. Added to this latent opposition were sizeable sections of the officer corps, which resented the rewriting of military history so as to accord Brezhnev a decisive part in the war against Germany, and deplored the succession of military decorations which he received. Since the highest orders were conferred by the Presidium of the Supreme Soviet, of which Brezhnev was chairman, he himself was in fact awarding the decorations, which included the rare and coveted Victory Medal, hitherto given only to a handful of outstanding generals in 1945. Military officers did not enjoy the same job security and opportunities for enrichment as the upper bureaucrats, and moreover were aware that these bureaucrats were not achieving much success in providing the forward-looking economic and social base on which military power ultimately depends.

Brezhnev had held on to office far too long. Not only was he a very sick man, but by character neither he nor those he had chosen as aides were fitted to take the radical measures needed to remedy what seemed to be economic stagnation and social decay. As impatience with him and his clique of loyal cronies deepened, ways were found to embarrass him. For example, there was the occasion when, by a heroic physical and mental effort, Brezhnev was visiting Caucasian capitals and found himself reading a speech in one city intended for another. This scene, which was televised live, was evidently contrived to show that he hardly knew what he was doing, and the aide who is believed to have switched the speeches was promoted under Brezhnev's successor.

Even more wounding, the anti-corruption campaign, which the KGB had been pursuing energetically, probably more energetically than Brezhnev would have preferred, began to take in not only some of his supporters in the administration, but also his family. His daughter Galina, in conjunction with male friends of varying degrees of intimacy, and including the director of the celebrated State Circus and another character from the entertainment industry known as 'Boris the Gypsy', was allegedly involved in an illicit large-scale jewellery and valuables operation. This involved diamond-smuggling, collection of bribes, and currency speculation. The high positions of those involved (Galina was, additionally, married to a deputy minister of the interior), and the fact that the alleged crimes were grand enough to warrant the death penalty, made this an extraordinarily sensitive case. Eventually, some of the participants were arrested, but not Galina. Her husband, though, was demoted and posted to faraway and uncomfortable Murmansk, before justice and twelve years' hard labour caught up with him in 1988.

The Andropov phase

As Brezhnev's life-tenure was seen to be drawing to a close, most observers expected the succession to pass to Chernenko, another septuagenarian. Born in Siberia, Chernenko became a party official in 1933 and encountered Brezhnev when the latter led the party in Moldavia. Brought to Moscow in 1960, described by the irreverent as Brezhnev's closest drinking companion, Chernenko henceforth remained the most immediate aide and confidant, and there seems little doubt that the general secretary would have preferred him as his successor. However, Brezhnev had shown an unsurprising lack of enthusiasm for grooming possible heirs, and when he died Chernenko was still not firmly in place as heir apparent.

Meanwhile, Andropov, the head of the KGB, had been cementing his own claims to the top office. By this time, many Russians were beginning to hanker for strong leadership, for Brezhnev's brand of benign neglect had obvious drawbacks as well as obvious comforts. It seemed that only a strong leader could impose the change of direction that seemed more and more necessary in the face of disappointing economic performance. Moreover, Andropov's association with the campaign against corruption must have enhanced his credit with those of his colleagues who felt the same way as he did about the blatant exploitation by party and state functionaries of the many opportunities they had for bribetaking, nepotism, and empire-building. When Suslov, grand old man of the Politburo, relic of Stalin's regime, and party secretary in charge of ideological matters, died in 1982, it was Andropov who was transferred to succeed him in most of his offices. From May 1982, therefore, Andropov was in the party secretariat, and clearly many of his Politburo colleagues favoured him.

Born in the Stavropol region of the north Caucasus, son of a railway official, Andropov had worked on Volga riverboats before making a career in the Komsomol. As first secretary of the Komsomol at a sensitive time and place, Karelia in the 1940s, he had an opportunity to show his usefulness, and by the mid-1950s he was Soviet ambassador in Hungary, where he played the key, deceitful, role in the suppression of the 1956 rebellion. From 1967 to 1982 he was in charge of the KGB, where he pursued very successful offensives against political dissidents and against corruption.

He was clearly a man who could get things done, and it was with this reputation that his colleagues in the Politburo appointed him general secretary of the party. The office of 'president' was left vacant, although Andropov assumed for himself the important office of chairman of the Defence Council.[1] Unlike his predecessors, who needed years to assert their authority, Andropov appeared to be in charge right from the start, although he could not ignore the views of his Politburo. Also noteworthy was that he did not find it necessary to dispraise his predecessor, as both Khrushchev and Brezhnev had done. Instead, it was indicated that the Brezhnev line would be followed, and only as time passed did it become clear, by implication, that the Brezhnev line, as continued by Andropov, had been shifted to a new and faster route. Andropov did not encourage a new personality cult for himself, and there was little attempt to reduce the late general secretary to a more modest place in history. That would come later and slowly; for the time being, there was a spate of commemorative renamings. Whereas there had been little more grandiose than an irrigation canal to take the name of Suslov after the latter's death, Brezhnev's name was attached to all kinds of places and objects, including a new nuclear icebreaker.

Andropov's more relaxed approach was also evident from the magnanimous treatment of dismissed party leaders. When Podgorny, who had been retired in some degree of disgrace by Brezhnev, died in 1983, he was interred with full state honours, and the 'thick' party journal *Kommunist* made uncensorious mention of Khrushchev and Malenkov. This new trend outlasted Andropov, with the 94-year-old Molotov being readmitted to party membership in 1984.

As party secretary, Andropov's main attachment was to his kidney machine. Ill health, which was not only renal but cardiac and diabetic as well, meant that he did not have enough time to carry out the changes that were expected of him. In the spring of 1983 both he and the emphysematic and cirrhotic Chernenko disappeared temporarily into hospitals. He reappeared, but was last seen in public in August 1983, although from his sick-room he seems to have controlled events more or less up to his death in February 1984.

He continued the campaigns against corruption, dissidence, and idle workers, made a start in replacing some of the older or incompetent Brezhnev appointees in the bureaucracy, and took some hesitant steps towards decentralized economic decision-making. For the ordinary Russian, the most noticeable change was that the campaign against what was termed 'labour indiscipline' moved from exhortation under Brezhnev to energetic action

---

1. The 1977 Constitution established that this was a state bureau, but it was closely tied to the party's Politburo.

under Andropov. Although foreign affairs were left largely in the experienced hands of Gromyko, Andropov needed to devote some of his all-too-few working hours to the deteriorating relationship with the USA, the unsettled state of Poland, the war in Afghanistan, and attempts to improve relations with China.

The division of Soviet leaders into so-called Stalinists and so-called liberals was shown, in Andropov's case, to be a misleading simplification. For he often contrived to appear a liberal while following policies and expressing views that were muted echoes from Stalin's time. As head of the KGB, he had been responsible for a sustained and harsh attack on the dissidents. In his measures against the work-shy and corrupt, he favoured vigorous penalties more than an improvement of the situations which gave rise to their vices. On the other hand, in an article under his name in *Kommunist* (March 1983), he acknowledged that Soviet society did not match Marx's idea of the socialist future, even though it was painfully treading in that direction. He doubted that the USSR could even be called a true socialist society, since although the people had won the right to become the owners of the common property, they had not become owners in terms of rights. He refused to accept that democracy and discipline were opposed; the USSR needed both and would get both. He pointed to the way local soviets were beginning to oppose ministries on questions involving town planning as an example of developing democracy. Democracy, he wrote, meant a widened participation in arriving at decisions, but such decisions, once arrived at, needed discipline if they were to be carried out. This, evidently, was a variation on the theme of democratic centralism, but seemed to acknowledge that more democracy and less centralism might be an improvement. With such democratic processes, Andropov wrote, there was certainly a place for critics. He called for a freer atmosphere for those who would criticize while confining their remarks within certain guidelines, but with severe chastisement for those critics who refused to come inside the system; that is, for the dissidents.

Two other attitudes expressed in this article gave further clues to what Andropov's USSR might have been like had he lived longer. He made no attempt to claim that Soviet experience was a model for other countries; indeed, he leaned the other way and suggested that the people's democracies had a lot from which Moscow might learn. Finally, he concluded by affirming that nothing was more important for the party and state than preventing a nuclear war, which would be catastrophic for a humanity that was already facing perils enough. This kind of thought, and his patronage of the rising Gorbachev, entitle Andropov to a share of the credit for the transformation of the USSR after 1985.

Chernenko

On the eve of his retirement to hospital Andropov had prepared a speech to the central committee in which, among other things, he suggested that his protégé Mikhail Gorbachev should chair Politburo meetings in his absence. If this wish had been fulfilled Gorbachev would have had a stronger claim to the succession, but Andropov was too ill to deliver his speech; it was distributed in printed form, and somebody deleted the paragraph about Gorbachev. So it was the wheezy Chernenko who, having been rejected for the same office little more than a year previously, found enough support in the Politburo to ensure his selection as the next general secretary.

Just as it could be said that Andropov continued Brezhnev's policies with selective changes of speed and emphasis, so it might be argued that Chernenko continued Andropov's line, with some slackening of pace. Observers who, rather patronizingly, described Chernenko as a watered-down version of Brezhnev were probably wrong. Despite his illness, it was possible to glimpse in him a man who had some ideas of his own that were based on experience and an understanding of people. He emphasized, for example, the need to discover what ordinary people really wanted. His implied opinion that agriculture would benefit more from a comprehensive land improvement policy than from yet another reorganization was not without merit,[2] and when he discussed the new party programme (replacing that of 1961) he had the wisdom to remark that it was folly to lay down a specific timetable for the transition from socialism to communism, especially as it was clear that capitalism was a long way from being finished (or, as he put it, 'still has substantial reserves').

He died in March 1985. In accordance with Soviet practice, right up to the last moment his critical condition was not publicized. Indeed, in late February, when he was already half-dead, he was shown on television receiving his credentials as a newly re-elected Supreme Soviet member. During the thirteen months of his appointment he was often absent, and business was largely left in the hands of Gromyko (foreign affairs), Gorbachev (economy), and Ustinov (defence). Gorbachev was allowed to act as Politburo chairman during these absences; this was one of several factors that facilitated his succession as general secretary after Chernenko's death.

---

2. Land improvement had also been favoured by Brezhnev. Land exhaustion and erosion had been Russian problems since medieval times, and the 20th-century urge to maximize production at the expense of all else had made things worse. Just as Russian forests were damaged by the drive to obtain as much timber as possible at smallest cost, so the soil had been impoverished by over-exploitation and by the circumstance that nobody was held personally responsible for the state of the land.

Renovation of the KGB

Up to the 1960s, Beria excepted, the heads of the Soviet state security system did not remain long in office and often, Beria included, their careers ended nastily. The KGB was a post-Stalin creation originally designed to bring security under some kind of party control. But its early heads, themselves tainted with past misdeeds, did little to create a new image. Andropov was remarkable not only for his long tenure of the post, but also for the revival of the service that took place under his supervision and initiative. Not only did he survive his office, but he also used it as a path to the top. Moreover, riding on his coat-tails, several professional security officers attained high political rank which they retained under Andropov's successors.

Andropov improved the techniques used by the service. Then he concentrated on dealing with two running sores: corruption in the state and party apparatus, and the activities of the dissidents. In his campaign against corruption he could count on the gratitude of the majority of Soviet citizens, and inside the Politburo honest, ascetic characters like Suslov and Ustinov fully approved, as would some party officials in the middle and lower ranks. In the campaign against dissidents, who continued to be portrayed as anti-Soviet elements in the pay of western intelligence organizations, he could count on the blessing of all his party colleagues, which was far more important than the criticism he could expect from abroad.

The KGB was tutored to act in a more sophisticated, yet more determined, way. Crude reliance on part-time informers diminished, being replaced by greater use of well-instructed and intelligent full-time undercover agents. Subtle means were evolved for going round, instead of crashing through, the legal rights which the accused might enjoy. For example, false information was fed to editors of underground journals who, having published this, could then be charged with spreading false reports; this was better than charging them with anti-Soviet propaganda, for it discredited them while making it impossible for them to plead that they had merely published facts. At the same time selectivity, indeed moderation, was applied in the matter of punishment. Internationally known dissidents were deprived of Soviet citizenship when abroad. Lesser-known dissidents were offered a choice of an exit visa or a trial which would put them in prison. Psychiatric institutes were used to take certain dissidents out of circulation, a policy which finally, in 1984, led to the exclusion (until 1989) of Soviet representatives from the World Psychiatric Association. Those who merely dabbled in dissidence were warned off by such means as threats to promotion prospects or to their children's educational opportunities. Such measures began to wear down the dissident movement, and the KGB closed the mesh of its nets so that those who once felt themselves safe (notably, those who had carefully refrained from contacts with foreigners) also found themselves under threat. Although in the mid-1970s the dissident movement had seemed to stand fast, by the time Andropov left the KGB in 1982 it had diminished to a minor irritant, and Andropov's reputation had been enhanced.

In a society where a small class of administrators controlled the allocation to citizens of scarce resources like residence permits, visas, imported goods, housing, educational opportunities, and many other normal requirements of twentieth-century life, the opportunities for bribe-taking and other forms of corruption were great. Under Stalin, corruption was not blatant, but under Brezhnev it was, and it excited disapproval and envy among those who witnessed it and venom among those who suffered from it. Brezhnev himself, by his easygoing reactions and his tolerance of the misdemeanours of his colleagues and supporters, and also by his taste for high living (shared by his family), did little to reverse this trend. It was left to Andropov, with occasional vocal but unspecific backing from Brezhnev, to tackle this problem, although the campaign against corruption continued into the Gorbachev years.

The campaign seems to have been conducted at all levels. It was not fully reported, but the newspapers did mention a selection of cases ranging from big scandals warranting executions to the minor sins of lesser mortals like head teachers and shop assistants, who were reprimanded, had their pay reduced, or were dismissed. A feature of the big cases was the long intervals between arrest, trial, and execution, and this suggested that the accused, especially if they had party affiliations, had protectors in high places; Brezhnev's death was followed by the execution of several offenders whose death sentences had been held up. The events in Poland, where the ruling regime had collapsed amid revelations of gross corruption and self-enrichment, alerted party leaders to the dangers of widespread corruption in their own ranks, and in 1980 the Central Committee passed a resolution against official corruption which made a point of stressing that corrupt officials should be dealt with 'no matter who they might be'.

The 'great caviare scandal' was one of the bigger cases handled by the KGB in the late 1970s. It came to a head in 1979, but the execution of the convicted deputy minister for fisheries did not take place until 1982. This was a large-scale fraud in which caviare was exported in tins labelled as herring, with the foreign importing agents depositing pay-offs in western banks, to be used for currency speculation or high living when the conspiring Soviet officials made their business trips abroad.

Georgia had long been a centre of corruption, and it was the KGB that was behind the purge of the Georgian party organization which resulted, among other things, in Shevardnadze being appointed first secretary of the Georgian party, charged with the continuation of the clean-up. In nearby Azerbaizhan the local party was similarly dealt with, and a KGB professional, Aliyev, became first secretary.

In 1982 the head of the state visa office, who was accused of demanding fees ten times higher than the official rate for exit visas, was dismissed. After Andropov became party secretary a number of deputy ministers resigned either because they were corrupt or had 'failed to prevent corruption' (usually a euphemism for 'not proven'). Meanwhile, Shevardnadze claimed that he had rooted out corruption and nepotism in Georgia, and turned his attention to drug abuse and alcoholism. A public prosecutor in Kirgizia was among those executed for taking bribes. Under Chernenko the campaign retained its impetus. Some officials were executed, several Ukrainian ministers were dismissed for incompetence or corruption, and the director of the State Circus finally came face to face with his sentence, which turned out to be only imprisonment. There were further dismissals in the Gorbachev years including, in 1985, that of a deputy minister of construction, said to have enriched himself by accepting bribes for new apartments.

The rising status of the KGB was accompanied by a tide of books and articles that praised its work and its traditions. Meanwhile, the cunning of the KGB's foes, the foreign secret services, was always kept in the public view with highly imaginative conspiracy theories and calls for constant vigilance. From Tallinn it was reported that these enemies were smuggling subversive T-shirts into the Soviet Union:

They know that not every fashionable young man wants to don a T-shirt with the Stars and Stripes. So they put on the T-shirts the slogan 'July is better than October'. This might seem quite inoffensive – many people prefer warm summer to chilly autumn . . . But our ideological enemies mean something else. In July the US constitution was adopted, and in October the USSR constitution.[3]

Above all, the KGB triumphed over the ministry of internal affairs (MVD), which had rival claims in security matters. Indeed, the protection of corrupt officials, which so often seemed to thwart or weaken KGB investigators, was sometimes inspired by MVD operatives. The minister of the interior, like so many Brezhnev appointees (including Tikhonov, the premier), had attended the same institute (Dnepropetrovsk Metallurgical Institute) as Brezhnev, and had additionally been vice-chairman of the Moldavian republic government when Brezhnev had been first secretary of the Moldavian party organization. He had no police experience, was himself corrupt, and owed his career to Brezhnev. When Andropov became general secretary he dismissed this man, replacing him with Fedorchuk, a KGB professional who had headed that organization in the months after Andropov's departure. The former interior minister was then put under investigation, one of the matters under study being the mysterious diversion of twenty Mercedes cars ostensibly imported

3. From the newspaper *Vodnyi transport*, 13 Dec. 1984, 4, reporting on the responsible tasks of customs officials.

for the police during his term of office. In late 1984 his sudden death was interpreted as suicide.

After Fedorchuk's promotion to interior minister, Chebrikov, a former Brezhnev protégé, became head of the KGB and the latter, in charge of security policing, and the MVD, responsible for ordinary policing, worked more cooperatively together. The MVD had its own problems, for there had been complaints in 1982 that ordinary street crime was becoming a menace in certain cities, with the police often turning a blind, or bribed, eye to it.

With its men in charge of the KGB and MVD, with five of its professionals in the Politburo of 1986 (Aliyev had been brought to Moscow by Andropov), the KGB was strongly represented in state and party. Further signs of its status were the restrictive laws and decrees that were passed in the early 1980s, inspired by the requirements of the security service. In late 1982, new stricter frontier regulations were introduced to help the work of the KGB's military frontier guards. In 1983, further restrictions were placed on the movements and activities of foreign journalists. International direct dialling, introduced to the Soviet telephone system in time for the Moscow Olympics, was discontinued, as the system provided an unwelcome avenue for unofficial contacts between Soviet citizens and foreigners. It became unlawful to send printed material abroad without a permit. In 1984 a new law provided fines for citizens who without official permission gave excessive help to foreign visitors; even offering a lift could be an offence.

Agriculture

Agriculture in the Brezhnev years made good progress, even though the most obvious ways to exploit 'hidden reserves' had been used up by Khrushchev. Nevertheless, ministers of agriculture fell from office at a rate which was very rapid in Soviet terms. Their fall was associated with their scapegoat role in years of poor harvests, even though grain production was more a matter of the weather than of ministerial competence. On the whole, though, bad harvest years registered outputs which were considerably higher than the bad years of previous decades, while good years tended to be record-breaking years.

Notable ingredients of Brezhnev's success (and it is accurate to personalize this success, because Brezhnev clearly was the leading figure in agricultural policies) included the restoration of the old organizational system with the ministry acting through the state organizations in the rural areas, and with supervision by the local party organizations. The latter were still far from satisfactory; their personnel was largely of urban types whose efforts to get things moving on the farms recalled the Chinese saying about how a dog sets about catching a mouse. But it was better to have a stable though imperfect chain of command than a system constantly in the throes of upheaval. On the same principle, the Khrushchev-style campaigns, which had aimed at rapid results in such matters as maize and meat production and even in the latest brainwaves of Lysenko, were abandoned for a more steady approach. However, although the new leadership promised an end to the constant changes of quotas for compulsory procurements by the state, it soon relapsed in the face of supply shortages.

The peasantry benefited from the new leadership's acceptance that increased food production depended largely on incentives. Procurement prices paid by the state for agricultural products rose markedly. This was especially notable in the case of meat, and as the retail prices were kept low, the state subsidy which made up the difference grew correspondingly (by the early 1970s meat wholesale prices were little more than half the procurement prices; this added up to a state subsidy that was enormous even by West European standards). Higher procurement prices helped to finance the decision that peasants should be better remunerated. Higher incomes benefited both state and collective peasants, but the latter were particularly gratified by the replacement in 1966 of the workday system. Henceforth, instead of waiting to the end of the year, hoping that the farm would earn a surplus to finance the cashing-in of their workday credits, they would receive a small regular wage, to be supplemented by an annual bonus if the farm did well. An unprofitable farm would be obliged to pay at least the wage, borrowing from the bank if necessary. Meanwhile, discouragement of private-plot production ceased, so the private husbandries of the peasants began to make an even greater contribution to the Soviet diet (they provided one-third of egg and meat supplies in 1978). Despite much emotional and ideological resistance within the party, Brezhnev succeeded in enlarging to 1.2 acres the size of the private plot allowed to peasant households. With rural incomes increasing somewhat faster than urban, and with the urban economy contributing investment funds for agriculture, by 1980 it could hardly be said that the Soviet economy relied on the exploitation of the peasantry. The improvement of the peasant's status was symbolized in 1974 by the announcement that peasants would be issued with internal passports. These, required for travelling within the USSR, had previously been issued routinely only to townspeople.

With little scope for increasing the cultivated acreage, and with Khrushchev having reaped the gains to be made by ending the most damaging absurdities of the Stalin years, the Brezhnev leadership had to rely on more intensive cultivation to produce the extra grain so badly needed. Grain production was no longer a matter of famine avoidance, but the average Soviet diet was still low in protein, and meat and milk production needed fodder. Khrushchev had realized the need to make greater use of artificial fertilizers. He had secured a quite remarkable increase of production, but the fertilizers were poorly utilized, either because lack of all-weather roads meant that they were delivered to farms too late in the season, or because the farms lacked the skill and equipment to apply them properly. Fertilizer production increased still further after Khrushchev's departure, with the import of western technology having a great and plainly instructive role. Distribution and use were improved, and it can hardly be doubted that fertilizers were the main factor in the increase of agricultural production in the 1970s. The abysmal state of rural roads was still a handicap, and so was the lack of such essential services as storage and refrigeration, which meant that a high proportion of food output never reached the consumer. Brezhnev's 'Food Programme' sought to remedy some of these defects but in general it was one more attempt to solve a long-standing problem by massive investment that was not always wisely directed. Mikhail Gorbachev was given responsibility for this plan but somehow avoided blame for its relative lack of success. Perhaps profiting from his experience, in 1985 Gorbachev, by then general secretary, would introduce a kind of super-ministry, the State Agroindustrial Committee, which took over, among others, the functions of the former ministry of agriculture.

If investment in industries supplying agriculture is added to investment in the farms themselves, annual agricultural investment by 1980 was in the region of a quarter of the USSR's total investment. This was an enormous proportion compared to other countries (the corresponding US proportion was less than 5 per cent). But there were signs that increasing amounts of capital were required to secure the same rate of growth. Moreover, about a quarter of the Soviet workforce was still employed on the land. Neither the collective farm nor the state farm seemed to provide a framework in which peasants would give of their best. Sometimes it seemed that the farms were too large for efficient management even if efficient managers had been available. Peasants who acquired skills still preferred to move to work in the town, leaving the older and unskilled peasants on the farms. This meant that new equipment was badly utilized and frequently allowed to fall into disrepair. Indeed, it seems likely that much of the bright new modern technology led to increased rather than decreased costs. The improvement-that-worsens is of course not unknown in the west, but was probably more of a menace in Soviet conditions. For example, if milking machines were unreliable a farm's routine could be repeatedly disrupted because cows, unlike peasants, could not be kept waiting.

Despite advances in production, therefore, Soviet agriculture performed poorly in terms of labour productivity and yield per acre. How far the Soviet system could remedy these defects without a radical change in the concept of collective and state farms was one of those questions which seemed to demand solution in the 1980s; a new compromise between ideology and economics (more accurately, between ideology and human nature) was needed. But people who suggested introducing small labour brigades with responsibility (and rewards) for given functions only risked their own dismissal. In 1972 a Politburo member was expelled for recommending precisely this.

Table 17.1 Grain production (million tons)

1953	83	1960	126	1967	148	1974	195
1954	86	1961	131	1968	170	1975	140
1955	104	1962	140	1969	162	1976	224
1956	125	1963	108	1970	187	1977	196
1957	103	1964	152	1971	181	1978	235
1958	135	1965	121	1972	168	1979	179
1959	120	1966	171	1973	222	1980	189

Industry

In 1960–5, on average, the gross national product rose by about 5 per cent annually, and in the next five years there was probably a small improvement, with an average of perhaps 5.25. Then came the decline to about 3.75 per cent in 1970–5, and a little more than 2.5 in 1976–80, with a further deterioration bringing growth close to 2 per cent for the first few years of the 1980s. The Soviet view was that this was a temporary fall below a long-term trend which would turn out to be higher, although probably not as high as in the 1950s and 1960s. Outside the USSR, many observers also held this view, but others suggested that what was happening was a long-term drop which had its origins in the nature of the Soviet system and would, therefore, be difficult to reverse.

Proponents of the first view could point to the role of agriculture; better luck with the weather, and some organizational changes, would improve agricultural performance and this would soon be reflected in higher growth rates for the economy as a whole. Moreover, they said, there were certain other bottlenecks that had limited Soviet economic growth but which, when put right, would allow a new upward and onward surge. At the beginning of the 1980s three areas of the economy, apart from agriculture, were regarded as weak. These were ferrous metallurgy, whose average annual growth rate declined to little more than 1 per cent in 1976–80 and on whose output many other sectors depended; then there was construction, suffering from a labour and steel shortage, and whose difficulties manifested themselves in very long building times for projects such as factories and housing; and finally transport, whose inadequacies affected practically all branches of the economy. Beginning with Andropov's leadership, some ministers and deputy ministers in sectors where performance was bad were replaced, but these were really symbolic acts, having the effect of making new and surviving ministers and managements try harder, rather than actually solving the physical problems that industries faced.

In the case of transport, for example, failures were hardly the fault of the minister and his deputies, but were the consequence of policies handed down from above and usually originating in Gosplan. The bulk of freight transport was handled by the railways; in fact their freight traffic already exceeded the freight traffic of all the rest of the world's railways added together. But Gosplan, right from the 1920s, had always held the view that rather than build new lines, the better policy would be to use existing lines more intensively. Possibly, in the 1920s and 1930s, this was justifiable, especially since other branches of the economy were in great need of all available investment. But Gosplan persisted with this policy far too long. New lines were almost always for the purpose of opening up new sources of raw materials, thereby adding to the railways' traffic rather than relieving existing lines. The result was that on some main lines, and especially the east–west trunk lines through the Urals, traffic density began to approach 100 per cent of what was theoretically possible, which meant, among other things, that a breakdown of one train could tie up traffic over hundreds of miles of track. Yet Gosplan still held to the view that technical innovations could obviate the need for more routes. Such innovations, which often had a 'quick-fix' character, included the introduction of eight-axle instead of four-axle freightcars (Gosplan economists seemed unaware that such vehicles would pose stability problems), longer loops and sidings (even though in the most serious bottlenecks there was no space for these), and a proposal for wider freightcars (which, apparently unperceived by Gosplan, would risk the decapitation of any railwayman unwise enough to stand between two passing trains).

The question of how far bodies like Gosplan, and the Soviet planning system in general, were suited to modern economic conditions was indeed discussed, but debate was limited because an exhaustive discussion could easily enter into the sensitive subject of the party's *raison d'être*. In the ultimate analysis, the all-encompassing, all-powerful party justified its position by its role as organizer and distributor of scarce resources for the general good. This was easy enough when industry was mainly heavy industry, and industrial units were large. It was not so easy when, as the experience of the west showed, it was small units which were beginning to make the most significant and useful advances. The possibility that it was not just the economy, but the party itself, that was in need of new mechanisms was not going to be discussed. In the Ninth Five-Year Plan (1971–5) there was for the first time a faster planned rate of growth of the consumer-goods industries than of the capital-goods industries. There was also a new housing programme (as before, concentrating on apartment blocks) which was to contribute 670 million square yards of new floor-space during the quinquennium. However, not all these good intentions could be realized. In this plan and in the Tenth Five-Year Plan (1976–80) there were renewed manifestations of worrying tendencies. The slowdown in the growth rate continued. In 1979, which was an exceptionally unfavourable year, industrial growth was only 3.4 per cent, compared to the planned 5.7 per cent. By the standards of other countries this was a respectable rate, but 1979 also witnessed absolute declines in some outputs, including coal, steel, and timber as well as certain consumer items.

To secure the same additional output an ever-increasing amount of capital had to be found. Resources were not being used efficiently, largely because the methods of the 1930s were not suited to the 1970s. The task of the 1930s, massive increases in the production of a few bulk commodities, had, except in agriculture, been achieved. But the economy was still using yesterday's methods and yesterday's investment to make yesterday's products, which were being replaced in other advanced economies by new products, more complex and often less suited to centralized planning.

In the Soviet Union the increasing number of new enterprises and of products which they supplied to each other entailed a geometric increase in the interrelationships between enterprises and between industries. So many were these interrelationships that they could not all be taken into consideration by the planners; one academician foresaw that within a decade the entire labour force would need to be employed in planning, if plans were to remain workable. In any case the plans were impossible to fulfil precisely, partly because the industrial ministries in Moscow were out of touch with the real situation in the enterprises they controlled throughout the USSR. In 1965 Khrushchev's *sovnarkhozy*, his attempt to solve that problem, had been abolished and industrial ministries re-established, bringing the total of ministries by 1972 to fifty-nine. In the 1970s the introduction of 'production associations' may have signalled the end of Kosygin's effort to give enterprise managements more freedom, but it was also an attempt to remove some information exchange and specialized decision-making from the centre. Plants making identical or interrelated products were grouped together in these associations, in which were vested many quite important decision-making rights and supply channels.

Not only were there problems of plan formulation, but also of plan execution. Enterprises were judged, and received bonuses, on their performance in relation to the output target which the ministries had set. But managers were reluctant to overfulfil this target for fear that it would be raised the following year. They were equally reluctant to indulge in innovation, because for them there was no real gain to outweigh the trouble and risk. Moreover, they tended to understate, to their respective ministries, the productive capacity of their enterprises. Also, since gross output by weight was the main indicator of success or failure, products were deliberately made heavy and little trouble was taken to fit the product to suit its ultimate user. Producers were interested in production, not in sales.

In the 1960s several Soviet economists suggested that enterprises should be set a reduced number of targets, and that bonuses should be related to profitability, not output, and should be fixed not year by year but over an extended period. The profitability indicator would reflect both productive efficiency and volume of sales. There was discussion, too, directed towards what western economists termed the irrationalities of the Soviet system. Such irrationalities produced notorious phenomena such as Caucasian peasants finding it profitable to commute by normal air service to Moscow, taking as their baggage allowance a sack of lemons, lemons in Moscow being unnaturally expensive and air fares unnaturally cheap.

To many in the party, profitability as an indicator was still too closely associated with capitalism. For both ideological and practical reasons, only some of the other suggested improvements could be accepted. In the late 1960s some consumer-goods enterprises were freed from output targets and their bonuses fixed according to the fulfilment of a sales plan. In other enterprises the number of targets was reduced and the volume of sales emphasized. Managers were given greater freedom in decisions relating to the workforce. Charges for the use of capital were introduced. But the centralized allocation of supplies continued, and prices remained fixed at unnatural levels.

Thus Soviet managements by the early 1970s had more, but not much more, freedom. Nor did the managers themselves, raised in the Stalin years, always want responsibility: as Brezhnev remarked, they feared innovation 'like the Devil fears incense'. Those who did try typically made initial mistakes which immediately were followed by a return of party or central intervention. The ideological opposition to greater managerial freedom had been strengthened in 1968 by the events in Czechoslovakia where 'liberal' economists were prominent in the unwelcome movement to build a socialist society blatantly different from the Soviet prototype.

Possibly, given time, managerial reform would have produced the results for which Kosygin and others had hoped. Managers would have learned to take decisions instead of avoiding them, while local government and party functionaries might, just might, have learned not to interfere with factory management. But stability in managerial arrangements was lacking. It was generally agreed that initiative was discouraged, and that central guidance was too often misguidance, but it was less easy to agree on remedies.

Fifty years of five-year plans had shown that the irrational free-market system could be replaced by the planned economy, but they had not shown that the planned economy was less irrational than the free market. Planners imposed their view of what ought to happen on a future which rarely, if ever, conforms to human prediction.

One impediment was informational. Central planners, in order to replace the regulating function of the free market, needed to obtain and process vast quantities of data. Such data were unreliable in quality and indigestible in quantity. Central decisions were therefore made on a basis of partial ignorance. At one time it was thought that the introduction of computers would transform the scene, but a computer was even less likely than a bureaucrat to change its mind, and its information input was dependent on human competence and integrity; it could not, for example, cope with factory managers who, to be on the safe side, inflated their requirements for raw materials.

Moreover, the centralized system did less than it should for coordination, because the various departments in Moscow were reluctant, or unable, to break down the barriers between them. All too often, for example, the eventual user of a piece of equipment had little say in its specification. Producers preferred to stick with old designs, being unwilling to disturb routines by changing production lines from an undesirable to a desirable product. Even the Soviet Navy had to accept what the shipyards offered. This kind of situation was repeated with daily, ubiquitous, frequency, and in total constituted a considerable economic wastage. Administrators at the centre knew about these cases, but the very system into which they were locked frustrated their efforts to improve things.

As Khrushchev discovered with his *sovnarkhozy*, moves away from a centrally directed economy were likely to encounter resistance, or at least foot-dragging. Too many party and industrial administrators liked centralization. Party officials, whether they worked as *apparatchiki* in party organs or as government administrators, liked the importance they enjoyed as part of the chain of command: any move towards using mechanisms like rational pricing to regulate the economy could only reduce that importance. The military and a few other key sectors liked centralization because it gave them priority access to scarce resources.

Brezhnev himself declared to the 25th Party Conference in 1976:

The Central Committee opposes hurried ill-thought-out reorganizations of the managerial structure and of established ways of running the economy. As the saying goes, one should measure the cloth not seven times, but eight or ten times, before cutting it. But once we have grasped that the existing economic mechanism has become too limiting for a growing economy, then we must resolutely improve it.

Under Andropov there was a large-scale experiment in which hundreds of enterprises belonging to five ministries were transferred to a new system intended to give greater responsibility and greater independence to managers. The experiment included a reduction in the number of index figures used to specify and measure plan fulfilment; growth of output (in real rather than money terms), growth of labour productivity, and the extent to which delivery contracts were fulfilled were emphasized as criteria of performance. Achievement or overachievement of delivery contracts resulted in substantial increases of rewards, in terms of wages and social services. In general, the results of this experiment were deemed satisfactory, even though the ministries were slow to lose their habit of interfering in management.

However, the best route to the new proposed 'intensive' economy was still not clear, and Gorbachev would soon be castigating the economics profession which, he belatedly discovered, was unable to provide clear answers to urgent questions. Bottlenecks in the economy still appeared, but it was not until late 1985 that Gorbachev took a step that, in the opinion of many, was already too long delayed: the chairman of Gosplan was removed. Since the notice of his retirement was published without the usual thanks for services rendered, the Soviet newspaper reader would have realized that this was a virtual dismissal. Gosplan had long been criticized, usually indirectly and by implication, for authoritarian interference in details of economic life and for the obstacles it raised to initiative and ideas originating from industry. With the individual enterprise subject to constant interference (or, equally damaging, delayed consents) from its ministry, and with ministries themselves subject to interference and obstruction from the all-powerful Gosplan, it had become progressively clearer that in the modern world, where industry needed to be agile and innovative, flexible and decisive, the Soviet economy was at a disadvantage. When to all these difficulties was added the circumstance that quite often the cooperation and coordination of several ministries were required to get a project moving, the inertia of much of Soviet industry seemed explicable. It was said that the reason why, in the 1970s, Japanese industrialists moved away from many of their expected cooperative ventures with Soviet industry in the Far East was that they could never get a prompt, clear answer to their questions; the Soviet managers with whom they were dealing had to consult the Moscow ministries about quite minor details. In the end the Japanese showed a preference for doing business with the Chinese, who seemed less handicapped by bureaucratic constraints.

In the 1970s the USSR was beginning to face a possible labour shortage, due to birth rate patterns. This meant that labour productivity assumed an even greater importance, but Soviet workers seemed slow to improve their performance; industries which reported great increases of output per worker were those which had installed more modern equipment, and moreover that equipment was less productive than it might have been with a more spirited labour force. By 1980 it seemed likely that the working population of the Russian Republic would actually fall, and in this republic the level of skill was high, compared to the level in Central Asia, where the growth of the labour force was expected to remain rapid.

At the beginning of the 1980s the main economic problem, therefore, was the achievement of policies or transformations that would lead to more, and better-quality, production, with more economical expenditure of materials and human talent. Such changes would be partly technological, but also managerial and political. Enough resources needed to be allotted to internal consumption to avoid popular unrest, and to defence to maintain the balance of strength with the west. Ideally, too, the growth rate would be high enough to maintain (at least) the relationship of economic strength between the USSR and the USA. The last two requirements would be influenced by western economic performance, and the difficulties of the western economies therefore made Soviet economic problems less serious.

In the longer term, the USSR seemed to have several advantages, not least of which was its possession of great raw material resources. The discovery and exploitation of western Siberian oil was a major project of the 1970s, and the rise of world oil prices came at a fortunate time for, together with a rise in the value of Soviet gold production, it signified valuable exports just when Soviet overseas expenditure was uncomfortably high. In the short term, the inaccessibility of raw materials was a handicap. Four-fifths of the Soviet energy resources lay east of the Urals, whereas four-fifths of energy consumption was west of that line. It was not surprising, then, that in 1976–80 one-third of Soviet investment was allocated to Siberia, and US and Japanese cooperation was sought in developing some of the biggest projects. The Baikal–Amur Railway, linking Siberia with the Pacific, and laid north of the Trans-Siberian Railway through mountainous and seismic terrain, was expected to rank as one of the great railway projects of the century, even though its critics said it was being built at the wrong time and in the wrong place.

Technology

Improved technology seemed the best way of improving the growth rate. In the early 1960s the State Committee for Science and Technology was set up to plan, administer, and direct expenditure on research and development. One of its main tasks was the study and acquisition of western technology. Although the Soviet system was said to be more suited than western systems for the central direction of research, in practice this advantage was outweighed by the cumbersome channels of communication between organizations, by the overload of information which made it difficult for central offices to separate the important from the unimportant, and by various other features of the administrative structure which tended to stifle initiative. The level of Soviet technology was lower than that of advanced western countries, and the rate of technological advance remained slow.

There were exceptions. The defence industry was very much a pacesetter. It enjoyed priorities, it was less subject to administrative interference, and could devote all its energies to obtaining the best possible products. It had first call on scientific talent, and its performance was creditable in so far as despite Soviet backwardness in certain vital techniques (in integrated circuits, for example) it found the resourcefulness to create weapons that matched those built by the technically better-endowed US arms industries. Sometimes there was a spin-off to the civilian economy. When enterprises producing weapons devoted part of their output to civilian products the latter were usually of superior quality.

Although efforts were made to stimulate Soviet invention (and the no less important diffusion throughout the economy of useful innovations), the large-scale acquisition of western technology was well worth while. It did require hard currency, but it avoided the duplication in the USSR of research that had already been done elsewhere, and moreover promised a short-cut to advanced technology. The USSR in 1965 therefore at last accepted international conventions on licensing and patenting, and began to purchase rights to selected inventions and techniques. Western firms were invited to tender for the supply to the USSR of complete plants embodying the latest production technology. Several chemical plants were acquired in this way, as well as a Fiat-built automobile plant. The Kama Automobile Plant, designed to manufacture motor trucks, was similarly dependent on western techniques. When the extraction of west Siberian oil and gas became urgent, western oilfield technology was imported on a large scale. A few consumer industries also benefited; to satisfy, at least in part, the thirst for western-style consumer goods, Soviet Pepsi-Cola and Soviet jeans appeared on the market.

As previously, technical information could sometimes be obtained through murky channels. This, for example, benefited the Soviet supersonic airliner, the Tupolev-144, which resembled the Anglo-French Concorde not only in design but in the circumstance that it had been built largely for the sake of vanity. Its prototype was proudly exhibited at the Paris Air Show of 1973, where it crashed. Still, in 1976 the state airline Aeroflot was able to claim that the TU-144 had made the world's first commercial supersonic flight, having stolen a lead on the Concorde by going into service initially as a freight carrier. It did later go into passenger service between Moscow and Central Asia, but was soon withdrawn.

Although it was Americans who first walked on the moon, it was probably Soviet space science which in the 1960s pursued the broader range of achievement. By the late 1970s about a hundred space vehicles were launched each year. Most of these were modest, being of the *Kosmos* series, intended for studying the near-earth expanses. The *Interkosmos* series, started in 1969, involved cooperation with scientists from the people's democracies and included manned ventures in which one member of the crew was an East European astronaut, trained in the USSR. From 1968 the 6.5-ton *Soyuz* spacecraft were available. In 1970 one of these, *Soyuz-9*, spent eighteen days in space with its two-man crew. In 1971 came the *Salyut* manned long-life research orbital stations, one of which studied the moon in that year. In 1971, too, a *Salyut* vehicle exchanged crews with *Soyuz-10* and *Soyuz-11*, but this landmark was attended by misfortune, when the three men in *Soyuz-11* died during descent. The year 1975 was notable for a joint US–USSR space-docking venture, using *Soyuz-19* and an American *Apollo* craft. This event, a highwater mark of US–USSR détente, was also the first Soviet space mission to be shown live on Soviet television. Meanwhile, beginning in 1967, a series of Soviet unmanned spacecraft investigated Venus, *Venus-9* and *Venus-10* going into orbit around that planet in 1975. The *Mir* space station was launched in 1986 with a planned five-year life and hosted over a hundred Russian, American, and other astronauts before, increasingly decrepit, it was allowed to vaporize in 2001. Henceforth Russia devoted her shrinking resources to collaborating in the International Space Station (*Alpha*). In general, while Soviet rocketry was good, instrumentation was unsophisticated by American standards. This illustrated a continuing factor in the Soviet economy: that although in certain fields the USSR achieved great success, this was the result of giving chosen fields absolute priority. And when some enjoyed priority, the less-favoured branches were kept behind. This was why, in Khrushchev's time, the first Soviet supermarkets had used abacuses and not cash registers.

In another high-technology and priority sector, nuclear energy, the Soviet Union was well advanced. In 1954, near Moscow, the world's first nuclear power station (using a water-graphite reactor) had entered service. Later policy was to build nuclear power stations in European Russia, which had an energy deficit, unlike Siberia. By 1979 nine large stations were in use, but the nuclear generating programme was falling behind schedule. The five-year plan specified that 12 per cent of electricity would be nuclear generated by 1985, but this target had to be reduced to 9 per cent. Then, in 1986, came the Chernobyl disaster, which virtually halted the programme. Meanwhile the nuclear icebreaker *Lenin* had been joined by the larger and improved *Arktika* and *Sibir*; the former broke its way through to the North Pole in 1977. In the 1970s the *Tokamak* model for controlled fusion was being developed by Sakharov and others. This model was later taken up by American researchers. This was not the only technology in which there was a good deal of international cooperation, with the Soviet contribution significant. In some fields (high-power electricity transmission was one) the Soviet Union did occupy a leading place. The flurry of licence and patent exchanges of the 1960s and 1970s was not a one-way flow, because a few Soviet inventions were acquired by western firms.

Advanced theoretical work often failed to make the transition to industrial application, and this was notably the case with semiconductors and microminiaturization. The transistor revolution was slow to reach the USSR. The computer industry was held back by lack of coordination between ministries and by its low order of priority. Although computers had been recognized as important in the 1960s, especially for processing the enormous quantity of paperwork originated by the planned economy, the promises of that decade were not kept. However, in the 1970s the utility of the microprocessor was noticed and clones of western chips were developed. Powerful computers were produced by connecting 'slices' of microprocessors in series, a technique that resulted in machines that were failure prone compared to the complex integrated circuits favoured in the west. To secure a reliable microcomputer a copy of the Apple machine was introduced, but this could not be manufactured in large enough numbers. At this time three ministries were each producing IBM-compatible PC machines and they achieved the feat of producing three designs that were incompatible with each other and with western models as well.[4] Later, in the Gorbachev years, legislation that eased the path of Soviet/ non-Soviet partnerships encouraged several joint ventures in computer manufacturing, usually entailing the assembly in the USSR of imported computer parts.

In pursuing new technologies the Soviet Union, like other countries, sometimes allowed progress to proceed faster than was really safe. One catastrophic result of this haste had occurred in 1958, when there was a nuclear accident in the south Urals, owing to improper storage of nuclear wastes. Despite the large number of casualties and the obligatory depopulation of a huge area, this catastrophe was successfully concealed from the Soviet public at large. From the western public too; in what was probably not a conspiracy of silence but may have been a silence of mutual consent, this event was not reported in the west, although it seems unlikely that government scientists were unaware of it for long. There was much less reticence in 1979, when a large-scale and fatal outbreak of Siberian Ulcer (otherwise known as anthrax) occurred in Sverdlovsk. The Soviet explanation that it was only a small and natural outbreak was ridiculed in the western press, which correctly assumed that the USSR was pursuing experiments in germ warfare that were contrary to international agreements. Another activity that raised anxiety was 'peaceful nuclear explosions'. The first initiatives had the support of Sakharov, and were designed to 'correct nature's mistakes'. It was intended to use more such explosions in the grand scheme to change the course of Siberian rivers, but this project fell by the wayside.

'Every such victory brings its own vengeance'

The abandonment of grandiose schemes for diverting northern rivers into the arid south suggested that environmental issues would be treated more seriously, a trend that would be reinforced by the Chernobyl accident in 1986. The environment had been seriously discussed in scientific journals since the 1960s, and as the years passed this discussion moved also into popular publications. The subject found itself mentioned in such diverse places as school curricula, the 1977 Constitution, and the party journal *Kommunist*; the latter, in September 1979, even had an article acknowledging the environmental cost of the nuclear power programme.

The need of the Soviet regime to exploit natural resources as fast as possible meant that in its early decades wasteful and harmful decisions were made. The trough may have been reached in Khrushchev's time, with the near-conversion of the Virgin Lands into a new dust-bowl. It was at this time, too, that the party asserted in its 1961 Programme that communism 'raises

---

4. The international computer industry was on the inch standard but, perhaps to show how progressive it was, the Soviet industry used the metric system. This meant that an ostensibly IBM-compatible Soviet computer could not plug into western IBM-compatible equipment.

mankind to an enormous level of superiority over nature, enabling a greater and more complete use of its inherent forces'. Such assertions had been made in the past, too, and Marx himself had written in the same key (although Engels with his greater perception remarked that the new socialist era should not flatter itself with its victories over nature because 'every such victory brings its own vengeance'). For long, misuse of the environment was treated in the Soviet Union as something that happens under capitalism but not under socialism.

The first of the big public environmental disputes occurred in the 1960s, when the celebrated purity and scientific pricelessness of Lake Baikal appeared to be threatened by new wood-processing plants. In this instance, the combined weight of several scientific institutions won a partial, but significant, victory. Also in the mid-1960s, the Russian Republic issued a decree intended to protect the environment from wrong-headed or vandalistic industrial projects, but this seems to have been largely ignored; in Soviet conditions, a manager was not likely to pay a heavy penalty should he damage the environment in pursuit of his production target. This unsatisfactory situation continued until at least the mid-1980s, but by that time public opinion, as well as party opinion, was ready for more energetic defensive actions. In the 1970s an effort was made to begin cleaning the heavily polluted rivers of the Volga system. Small and middle managers were increasingly taken to court, although their punishment hardly fitted the crime. Managers did not themselves pay fines, for that came out of their enterprises' budget; indeed, some enterprises maintained a fund from which such fines could be paid, a sure indication that it was cheaper to pay fines than take protective measures.

It would not be until Gorbachev became general secretary that environmental issues received the attention they deserved. A State Committee for Environmental Protection was formed in 1988, and a Green Party was founded. Newly uncovered environmental horrors were well publicized. Among them was the shrinking of the Aral Sea due to so much water being diverted to irrigation, and the consequent unbalancing of the region surrounding it. Citizens became more conscious of bad air, and aware of, for example, the high rate of bronchial disease among children in certain industrial areas. Magnitogorsk, a socialist 'company town' dominated by the Lenin Steel Works, was said to exhale a million tons of solids from its smoke-stacks every year, and downwind there was a 100-mile stretch of grey snow in winter and brown grass in summer. In such towns car headlights were sometimes needed during the day, and children and the aged went to clinics for doses of oxygen.

Scientific institutes and local authorities which sought to widen or enforce laws found themselves handicapped not only by the priority given to industrial output but also by the familiar problem of bureaucratic structures. When a beach disappeared because building enterprises had removed sand and gravel at the same time as the electricity industry had dammed the rivers whose flow would normally have washed replenishing sand and gravel onto the depleted beaches, it was impossible to lay the blame against any one ministry. A horrifying source of atmospheric pollution in Georgia, the Zestafoni Ferro-alloy Works, was provided with a smoke-abating system only after managers, as well as district state and party officials, were dismissed or transferred, and this did not happen until nearly 300 meetings had been held to discuss the problem.

For some new big projects various institutions were invited to make detailed environmental enquiries. The misfortune was that such research followed, rather than preceded, the beginning of construction. But in the case of the big river diversion schemes this sequence took a more intelligent course. It would be wrong to describe this as a triumph of scientists over planners, because not all scientists gave priority to the environment over the economy, and not all planners scorned environmental arguments.

The people's democracies

The 1968 Soviet intervention in fraternal Czechoslovakia, whose communist party had merely been trying to create, it said, 'socialism with a human face', was a greater shock to the communist parties of the world than the Hungarian rebellion of 1956. What prompted the USSR to put an end to the Czechs' policy of intervening in their own internal affairs was that while the Soviet government might tolerate economic changes which seemed to move away from the Soviet model, political changes were another matter. In particular, the concept of a ruling communist party prepared to lose its monopoly of political activity could only be seen as a dangerous example.

The intervention in Czechoslovakia by the Red Army and the armies of other Warsaw Pact countries was justified by the so-called 'Brezhnev Doctrine' that socialist countries had a clear right and duty to intervene in any country of the Soviet bloc to prevent a reversion to 'capitalism'. In the long run, the Soviet leadership sought a closer integration of the people's democracies with the USSR. In the Warsaw Pact this had to a large degree been accomplished in the military field, and the Comecon organization secured a degree of coordination in industrial matters. Soviet economic policy had largely lost its exploitative tendency. In fact, Soviet oil supplied to the people's democracies by the 'Friendship' pipeline was sold at prices below the world market level, and the Cuban economy depended very much on Soviet support. But integration was not helped by, for example, the barbed wire, minefields, and Alsatian dogs that sealed the frontiers between the USSR and its fraternal allies. Applying for Soviet visas was a long and often unsuccessful process.

Flourishing 'Eurocommunism' continued to be a threat to the Soviet leadership of the communist movement. The Spanish and Italian parties, in particular, took up positions which the Soviet party could not accept. Their acknowledgement that a communist party might gain power (and by implication lose it) by electoral process was unpalatable. In 1976 the Soviet Union organized a Moscow 'summit' of European communist leaders, but was unable to persuade them to endorse a declaration reasserting the leading role of the Soviet communist party. Leaders of the latter attacked Eurocommunism, and it was stalwartly defended by the Spanish leader and others. So stalwartly that several important non-Soviet speeches were unreported in the Soviet press

After Mao Zedong's victory in 1949 the USSR gave great economic, military, and technical help to communist China, but Khrushchev's 'destalinization' embarrassed Beijing. Open dispute at first took the form of Beijing condemning Tito, regarded as a Russian protégé, for his 'revisionism', while Moscow berated Albania (China's friend) for 'dogmatism'. Long angry letters followed, and then polemics. In one exchange, Mao described Khrushchev as a laughing-stock, 'a Bible-reading and psalm-singing buffoon'. Khrushchev, never at a loss for homely invective, responded by describing Mao as 'a worn-out rubber boot which one can only put in the corner of a room to be admired'. Khrushchev's retirement meant less entertainment but no reconciliation. Both sides accused each other from time to time of consorting with the USA, thereby betraying their nervousness at this possibility. In early 1967 Chinese students studying in Russia mounted a violent demonstration in Red Square. In 1969 there were serious armed clashes, with fatalities, on disputed parts of the Russo-Chinese border. Photographs of these events were published in Soviet newspapers, together with allegations of Chinese atrocities. By this time communist parties throughout the non-communist world were split into pro-Soviet and pro-Chinese factions. From 1971, to Russian consternation, Washington and Beijing grew closer.

After the death of Mao, China ended its friendship with Albania, and Moscow and Beijing strove from time to time to conduct their hostile relationship in a more civilized manner, this resulting in an agreement on navigation rights on the Ussuri River and other practical matters. On one occasion the USSR even apologized for an incursion of Soviet troops into Chinese territory. Fresh animosity was aroused in 1979 when the USSR's protégé Vietnam went to war with a Chinese protégé, Cambodia. Under Andropov there were Soviet overtures, but little Chinese response. The Soviet presence in Afghanistan did not help.

Unrest in Poland grew during the Brezhnev years from simple meat riots, which proved little except that Poles were carnivorous, to the emergence of the Solidarity movement. The idea of a free trade union movement was disturbing in a Soviet Union which at that very time was experiencing weak, but unmistakable, signs of worker unrest. Indeed, a fleeting shift of Soviet trade union attention from output to welfare, which occurred at this time, may be attributed to a realization that unless the Soviet unions did something more to represent the true interests of the workers, then something like Solidarity might be reproduced within Soviet borders.

In late 1981 the decisive step was taken to master Solidarity and, with Soviet assistance, the Polish military leadership took over the government. Great care was taken to filter news from Poland, and the average Soviet citizen, however curious, would have been unlikely to obtain a clear picture of what was happening. For this and other reasons, domestic public opinion was decidedly hostile to the Polish workers, who were regarded as spoiled children, unable to show gratitude to their true friends. But communist parties outside the Soviet bloc deplored the suppression of Solidarity and further loosened their ties with Moscow. Within the bloc, Romania began to play a maverick role. It sent a team to the 1984 Olympic Games, held in the USA and boycotted by the rest of the Soviet bloc. The brother of its party leader minimized the role of the Red Army in a book he published about the liberation of Romania from the Nazis.

Foreign policy

The early 1970s were years of eased relations with the west, and particularly with the USA. In 1972 President Nixon visited Moscow and the following year Brezhnev visited the USA. Several agreements were signed. Although the agreement to restrict anti-ballistic missiles (the 'ABM Treaty') to a certain extent rechannelled research and funds into other weapons, it certainly simplified the nuclear situation. The nuclear accidents agreement had a peacemaking function, and so did an agreement on preventing 'incidents' on and over the high seas. Other arms agreements followed; these were less likely to reduce the arms race than was claimed, but the discussions which preceded them gave each side a valuable insight into the other's anxieties, capabilities, and preoccupations. As forecast to the 1971 Party Congress by Brezhnev in a speech in favour of his 'peace programme', trade and technology was an important aspect of détente. In a 1972 trade agreement the USA even granted Most Favoured Nation trading rights and offered generous financial credits to the USSR. The latter began to settle the Lend-Lease debts of the Second World War (their non-repayment had always been a useful weapon for anti-Soviet propagandists). However, the US Congress had its own views, insisting that certain concessions should not come into force unless the USSR issued emigration visas to thousands of Soviet Jews, and reducing the credit to be made available. In 1975, Moscow decided to abrogate this agreement.

From then until 1980 relations remained eased, but there was less optimism about the future. In a sense the Soviet concept of 'peaceful coexistence' (which rejected war between the great powers, accepted cooperation for mutual advantage, but did not offer any easing of ideological struggle) made a genuine long-term settlement difficult. President Carter in his first year of office emphasized the shortcomings of the USSR in the matter of human rights. Among other things, he wrote a supportive letter to the distinguished Soviet dissident Sakharov. In this way he too was asserting that coexistence did not mean ideological coexistence, but this acceptance of the Soviet interpretation did not please Moscow, and made more difficult the task of those Soviet leaders favouring continued relaxation.

An achievement of the drive for détente was the Helsinki Agreement of 1975. The two super-powers were not the only signatories; since it largely concerned Europe, other European governments, east and west, also took part. It confirmed Europe's post-1945 frontiers, thereby accepting the USSR's territorial gains of the 1939–45 period and the frontiers of the German Democratic Republic and Poland. For this, it was criticized as a 'sell-out' by many western commentators, but in exchange for agreeing on this territorial matter the west secured various undertakings from the USSR. Among these was the latter's agreement to respect a number of human rights treasured in the west. Pessimists said there was no way of ensuring that the USSR would observe its human-rights undertakings. But the emergence in the USSR of a dissident group devoted to monitoring how far the Soviet authorities were respecting their citizens' rights demonstrated that, to some extent at least, the provisions had made a mark. Moreover, the stipulation of the agreement that there should be periodical reviews by the signatories of how far its provisions were being observed seemed to some observers to provide a regular opportunity for washing the Soviet Union's dirty linen before a worldwide audience.

Détente in Europe had been helped by the *Ostpolitik* of the West German Chancellor Brandt. He initiated a policy designed to mend West German relationships with eastern Europe and the USSR. Germany became an important, almost essential, trading partner of the people's democracies, and also exported advanced-technology products to the USSR. The resignation of Brandt was something of an 'own goal' for the Soviet bloc (he resigned after it was revealed that one of his closest aides was an East German spy).

Khrushchev's interest in the Third World was maintained by his successors (the presence in both regimes of the veteran Gromyko as foreign minister both helped and confirmed the essential continuity of foreign policy). Trade agreements, military assistance, and 'treaties of friendship and cooperation' were the typical stages of Soviet involvement with countries in the developing world. Such involvement was not always quite so conclusive as the west feared, for a nation might still reject the Soviet connection when it felt strong enough to do so. In 1972 President Sadat of Egypt asked Soviet military advisers to leave. The USSR generally supported the Arab cause in the Palestine dispute, but was excluded from the peacemaking processes. A marxist regime defeated other revolutionary movements in Angola with the help of Soviet advice and the arrival of Cuban troops, but subsequent Soviet influence in the new government was not especially strong. In Zimbabwe the new independent regime lost no time in declaring that past help gave the Soviet Union no special rights or privileges. Somalia was the beneficiary of Soviet interest, and the Red Navy at one stage had base facilities both in Somalia and in marxist South Yemen. But when the Soviet Union threw its weight behind the new marxist regime in Ethiopia, which was soon fighting a war against Somalia, the latter rejected its Russian alliance.

It was as characteristic of the USSR as of the USA that idealistic or moral considerations tended to be ignored in the choice of allies. The USSR helped the deplorable Amin regime in Uganda, but withdrew its military advisers two months before Amin's fall, a fall that *Pravda* reported only after two weeks.

The Afghanistan conflict that began in late 1979 was several years in the making. After several bloody episodes, a communist government was in power. When this government of unrefined incompetence aroused violent popular resistance the USSR arranged a coup and brought in a new leader, Karmal. Soviet troops entered Afghanistan at the same time to support the new government, and were soon fighting an arduous, inglorious, and savage guerrilla campaign. The Soviet decision to intervene was contrary to the advice of both the military and the foreign service; reluctance to allow a communist regime to be overthrown by its own people, and a fear that a new Muslim or US-supported regime would infect neighbouring Muslim Soviet republics were the main arguments in favour of this, the first Soviet incursion into a Third World country and a country that the international community did not regard as part of the Soviet sphere. The Soviet Army initially believed that it was being sent solely to maintain order in the towns while the new regime consolidated. But in fact it faced years of struggle, thousands of casualties, and loss of reputation at home.

In the early 1980s, expulsions of Soviet diplomats from foreign capitals became more frequent, almost resembling a mass movement. It was not only from capitals of the western world that alleged spies were returned to the Soviet Union, but from Third World states like Bangladesh and Thailand. Even Ethiopia, a Soviet beneficiary, took this action in 1984. Ultra-neutral Sweden was offended by repeated incursions of Soviet submarines into her territorial waters. A number of countries imposed economic sanctions, notably curtailment of trade, as a reaction to the declaration of martial law in Poland. In general, however, the USA was unsuccessful in persuading her allies to take a strong line on trade. In 1981–2, while still profiting from grain exports to the USSR, the USA attempted but failed to prevent certain west European companies supplying equipment for the pipeline being built to move west Siberian natural gas to eastern and western Europe.

The homeward flow of Soviet diplomats was swollen by the protest expulsions which followed the 1983 shooting down, with heavy civilian casualties, of a South Korean civil airliner that had strayed over Sakhalin and Kamchatka on a flight between Alaska and Tokyo. How, or perhaps why, it had strayed was, and remains, unclear. But the fact remained that the Soviet forces had carried out what was seen as a barbaric act.

The deterioration of relations with the USA resulted in the non-appearance of US and other countries' athletes at the 1980 Olympic Games at Moscow, interruptions in commercial relations, and the end of the US–Soviet cooperation in space ventures. Several attempts to reach agreements on arms limitation failed. Western European governments, alarmed by the location of Soviet intermediate range missiles in eastern Europe, persuaded the US government to place intermediate range (Cruise and Pershing) missiles in Europe. Capable of reaching Soviet cities, the short flight-time of these missiles was a frightening new factor for the Soviet defences, and at one stage Andropov stated that they would compel the Soviet Union to adopt a 'launch on warning' policy; that is, Soviet missiles would be launched at the west as soon as the first (and hence unchecked) reports of oncoming Cruise and Pershing missiles were received. Thus this new stage of the arms race threatened to bring closer the possibility of nuclear war by accident.

Later, President Reagan's enthusiasm for his 'Strategic Defense Initiative', however unbalanced and starry-eyed it might have been, caused the USSR new anguish, and to a large extent poisoned, or repoisoned, the waters; at a personal 'summit' meeting at Geneva in 1985 Gorbachev and Reagan appeared to have created a good relationship on the personal level, but this was a long way from being translated into political agreement. Earlier, the US president's public reference to the Soviet Union as an 'evil empire' could only reinforce Soviet suspicion that Washington had embarked on a really active anti-Soviet policy, the substance of which was that US pressure was to force the Soviet Union to devote increasing resources to armaments, thereby making it impossible to find the means required to cope with increasingly urgent economic and social problems.

Taking advantage of what seemed a favourable 'correlation of forces' (to use a favourite Soviet term), the USSR in the 1970s had succeeded in strengthening its influence among the uncommitted nations of the world and in bringing its strategic forces into a position of parity, or near-parity, with those of the USA. But Soviet assertiveness helped to bring about the decay of the spirit of détente. Together with the emergence of an aggressive US administration in 1981, this meant that tension between the USA and the USSR grew at a time when the Soviet Union, in order to tackle economic and other internal problems, needed relief from the arms race and good trading relations with the west. This deterioration could not be blamed on just one of the parties. Both governments faced a task which was so delicate, so dependent on an intimate understanding of the other side's position, that it may well have been a near-impossible undertaking from the start. Relaxation, in essence, meant dropping one's guard by graduated stages, but in both Washington and Moscow there were powerful interests which opposed guard-dropping, usually from quite genuine fears but occasionally from motives of short-term personal and political advantage. Nevertheless, in those two decades a whole succession of crises were defused in one way or another, even though there were always voices which would describe defusing as appeasement.

The armed forces

By about 1970 the USSR had achieved parity with the USA in numbers of intercontinental ballistic missiles, so meaningful arms limitation talks could begin. The first Strategic Arms Limitations Talks (SALT) agreement between the USA and the USSR was in 1972, and marked the abandonment of proposed anti-missile installations as well as the imposition of certain limits on numbers of offensive missiles. The second SALT agreement was heralded by a meeting of Brezhnev and President Ford in 1974 at Vladivostok; after lengthy and very difficult discussions it had been found possible to fix the number of intercontinental missiles allowed to each of the two powers. For one reason or another the confirmation of this second SALT agreement was delayed year after year, the final stumbling block being the reluctance of the US Senate to approve it. In the interim, the two powers agreed to stick to their agreed limitations in the hope that the agreement would eventually be confirmed. In general, SALT did not restrict the powers building the numbers of missiles they wished to build, but it probably did enable them to avoid building more than they had intended. That is, it did not put an end to the arms race in missiles, but helped to keep it under control.

In 1967 the USSR introduced a new conscription law, to replace the 1939 law and its various modifications. Among its provisions was the shortening of the period of service by one year. Henceforth 18-year-olds would enter the army and air force for two years, or the navy for three, while graduates of higher education would serve just one year as officers (those who during their studies had participated in their institutions' officer-training units became second lieutenants in the reserve and did not serve in the active forces). Thus traces of the 1874 army reform, with its exemptions and discriminations, lingered on. Conscription was selective, with the Council of Ministers deciding each year on the size of the call-up. There were general exemptions for young men with two or more children, or with aged dependent parents, or who worked in certain occupations or were studying certain subjects. Local draft boards were supposed to organize send-off celebrations for departing conscripts.

The Red Navy was rapidly expanded to become the world's second biggest. Its smaller missile-carrying ships, in particular, caused western naval staffs to rethink their priorities. In the 1970s, too, the Red Navy acquired its first aircraft carriers. Apart from long cruises in foreign waters, the Red Navy was able to indulge in very extensive fleet exercises. Meanwhile in 1972 its commander-in-chief, Admiral Gorshkov, published what might be called a new doctrine of

Soviet naval power, with emphasis on the value of a seagoing navy for showing the flag, extending and protecting interests abroad, making discreet and finely graduated threats of force, countering enemy naval movements, and, finally, adding a new and decisive element to the waging of a full-scale war. A Soviet naval squadron was permanently stationed in the Mediterranean, and a smaller one in the Indian Ocean. Missile-carrying submarines continued to play their role as part of the Soviet Union's nuclear warfare strategy.

The arts

Brezhnev and his colleagues held the conventional party opinion that litera-ture, if not closely controlled, could set up dangerous movements of opinion. The bureaucratic petty intelligentsia installed in the offices of the Writers' Union ensured that really outstanding critical fiction was not published; writers who published abroad without permission lost their membership of the Union, and hence the right to call themselves writers. However, there was no official discouragement of the developing school of 'native' writers, many of whose works were well worth reading, even if they did sometimes seem to promote Great Russian chauvinism.

Solzhenitsyn, by the late 1960s, was published abroad but not at home. His *Cancer Ward* was essentially a novel about people's souls in the years between Stalin's death and Khrushchev's 1956 speech. The swinish side of Stalinist Rus-sia received a full but low-key portrayal; the political exiles in Central Asia, the arrest of doctors with no arrangements made for the further treatment of their patients, the endless queueing for rubber stamps which enabled the recipient to queue for another rubber stamp, the appointment of mediocrities to respon-sible positions, the shattered lives not only of political prisoners but also of those who, in order to remain free, turned traitor to themselves and denounced their colleagues or voted at mass meetings for exemplary punishment. There was a sensitive portrayal of a member of the new communist bourgeoisie, the official Rusanov, who had a nice new car and a nice new apartment and a nice family which knew which strings to pull to get what it wanted. Although the author did not imply that all officials were like Rusanov, the type was easily recognizable. Rusanov was a stereotypical Stalinist, a man who loved The People but despised his fellow-humans, a man who knew that on certain ques-tions a definite opinion had been established and therefore discussion was no longer permissible. He was a man who had denounced many in his time and was terrified when the government began to release political prisoners. The non-celebration of the second anniversary of Stalin's death, and the dismissal of the Supreme Court's judges, were to him ominous signs that the world in which he had made himself so much at home was about to break up.

Solzhenitsyn was duly expelled from the Writers' Union in 1969, and then in 1974 was banished from the USSR. His long experience of the Soviet literary establishment and the censorship is recounted in his *The Oak and the Calf* (1980). Other literary figures who either defected, or emigrated voluntarily or not-so-voluntarily, included V. Nekrasov, A. Sinyavsky, and I. Brodsky. The latter, a nonconformist Leningrad poet, had been sentenced to five years' hard labour for 'parasitism', but was then expelled for the sake of his health (he would not have survived his sentence). In emigration, he continued to write poetry and in due course received a Nobel Prize. Solzhenitsyn went west with a good deal of work to finish. His multi-volume *The Gulag Archipelago*, just one of his post-expulsion publications, became a best-seller and a classic; in the USSR it was duly described by prominent members of the Writers' Union as a filthy anti-Soviet perversion, although all it did was to add gruesome detail to the revelations made about Stalinist labour camps by Khrushchev himself. In exile, Solzhenitsyn seemed to set himself up as a latter-day Tolstoy, making didactic moralizing forays not only against the Soviet system but against those in the west who seemed to be too tolerant, or unaware, of the Soviet menace. His ultra-Russian, ultra-Orthodox Christian line sometimes irritated dissident Russians.

A feature of the delicate path between freedom for dissemination of ideas and avoiding dangerous movements of popular opinion was the publication of a few bold literary and other works in very small editions. This meant that, as in the west (but for different reasons), it could be said that the smaller the number of copies printed, the more worth reading was the publication. But when in 1979 a group of writers tried openly to publish a small-circulation literary collection, *Metropol*, without going through the various censorship processes, it was suppressed; soon afterwards two of its contributors were expelled from the Writers' Union on grounds of 'insufficient merit'.

In painting, a noteworthy scandal occurred in 1975, when a group of 'unofficial' artists (that is, of people who painted despite their non-membership of the Artists' Union) decided to stage their own, unapproved, exhibition. An open-air display of their work, which had little connection with Socialist Realism, was arranged. This display, and the artists, came under violent attack from 'an enraged public' (a euphemism, with roots in tsarist times, for officially recruited or officially inspired hooligans). To make quite sure of making their point, the authorities even recruited bulldozers to attack the paintings. All this occurred under the eyes of foreign visitors, some of whom had their cameras smashed, and the affair received worldwide publicity. But soon afterwards the local party secretary was transferred elsewhere, and approval was given to the artists to exhibit those pictures which could be patched up. As so frequently happens in Russian history, centrally propagated policies were subject to all kinds of local aberrations. Elsewhere a Novosibirsk art gallery director who tried to organize an exhibition including works by Chagall and a dissident artist was promptly rewarded with an eight-year sentence: one of the charges was that he had offered help to a Chinese spy.

Soviet society

The population of the USSR reached 263 million in 1979. There was still growth, but on average it was moderate. In urban areas of the Russian Republic (and to a lesser extent in the other European republics) an increasing number of families seemed content to raise just one child, whereas the Asian nationalities still usually measured their worldly and spiritual success by the number of children they could bring into the world. By 1980, Great Russians still accounted for more than half of the USSR population, but only just. Meanwhile, the Muslim population was growing fast.

This exacerbated the apparently growing problem of nationalism within the USSR. Nationalism, which at times could better be defined as chauvinism, was notably on the upsurge among the Great Russians, who sometimes felt the other nationalities were being pampered at their expense and were reproducing too fast. Also, there was open nationalist dissent in the Caucasian and Baltic republics, and in the Ukraine it seemed to be barely contained below the surface. In Estonia, in 1980 and 1981, there were actual demonstrations, consisting largely of students, at which the banned Estonian national flag was exhibited and the official union-republican flag burned. The authorities were uncomfortably aware of the ease with which Estonians picked up Finnish television, from which they learned, among other things, harmful versions of what was happening in Poland. Georgians, although enjoying certain liberties unknown to other Soviet citizens, were quick to make protests. They had staged street demonstrations against Khrushchev's repudiation of their compatriot Stalin, and again in 1978, when the draft of the new Georgian Constitution failed to define the local national language as a state language. This threatened boost for Russian at the expense of Georgian was soon reversed.

As elsewhere in the world, the question of nationalism was interwoven with the question of language, and the languages policy of the USSR inevitably raised hackles among the non-Russian nationalities. In principle, Russian was taught throughout the non-Russian republics' schools as a second language, and it could be claimed that this was necessary so as to provide a common language for the whole of the USSR. But the non-Russian languages were hardly taught outside their own republics. This meant that whereas a Russian family moving to a non-Russian republic would find its own language, and hence culture, awaiting it in the new location, non-Russian emigrants would need to accept a degree of Russianization if they were to be assimilated in the Russian Republic. Thus, apart from the historical circumstance that Muscovite expansion had naturally spread Russians throughout the territory of the USSR, Russian migration was further assisted by the language policies. In some republics (including Estonia at 28 per cent and Latvia at 33 per cent) the Russian proportion of the population was large enough to provoke social resentments on both sides. In 1983 the Politburo was discussing measures to actually intensify the teaching of Russian in the union republics.

Another critical social anxiety which the USSR shared with other countries concerned the way the younger generation was being brought up. Both Chernenko and Aliyev spoke of a generation which thought it could earn respect not by its knowledge and diligence but by the costly objects which its parents' money could buy for it. One element of this anxiety was expressed by criticism of the Komsomol organization. This was supposed to attract young adults to politically and socially useful leisure-time occupations, but apparently was having less and less success in pulling young people away from the unproductive pleasures and pastimes which modern times offered. In the 1960s seamen and tourists had found it profitable to smuggle in Beatles' records. Transcribed to tapes (*magnetizdat*) these led to the Russian rock movement of the 1970s. The Beatles' music, and above all their subversive lyrics, were immensely attractive, and not only to the young; the poet Brodsky translated 'Yellow Submarine' into Russian. Of the early pop groups, Acquarium was the most influential; its lyrics echoed the officially disapproved pre-1914 Acmeist poems, as the official watchdogs were among the first to observe. However, the new movement was virtually unstoppable and was an important component of the unsanctioned, anti-ideological movement that would convulse the Soviet system in the 1980s.

Meanwhile, a quite deep reappraisal of Soviet education resulted in 1984 guidelines for its reform. The educational system was turning out twice as many highly skilled graduates as were needed, at the same time as there was an increasing shortage of workers in the middle-skill categories. Entry to the two senior years of secondary school was, therefore, to be restricted, thereby diverting more pupils to vocational training. At the same time, the school starting age was reduced from 7 to 6, making the full school course eleven instead of ten years. The number of school hours to be devoted to 'labour training' remained controversial; in 1977 they had been doubled to four hours a week for the two senior years, mainly at the expense of foreign-language teaching, and in the new reforms eight hours were proposed even though some critics foresaw a resultant erosion of academic standards. Teachers were to be trained for five instead of four years, a response to criticisms of their quality by, among others, Andropov. 'Percentomania' was to be contained by ending the practice of taking into consideration the pupil's average marks over the year when entry to higher education was sought (this had created enormous pressure by parents on teachers and a consequent practice of bribery, blackmail, and threats in pursuit of inflated marks).

Despite occasional calls for a proper 'population policy', in the late 1970s the Soviet government still did not regard the production of modern contraceptives as very desirable. Small quantities of the contraceptive pill were imported from the people's democracies and they were mainly available in

Central Asia (where they were prescribed to local Russian women because Muslim doctors opposed their distribution to the Asian population). For most Russian women of the European regions abortion was the accepted practice. It was calculated that in the late 1960s, taking the population of the USSR as a whole (and thereby underestimating the average for Russian women), there were six legal abortions per woman-life. Infant death rates were deteriorating; they were highest in Central Asia where legal abortions were fewer. In the mid-1970s, towns in the Baltic republics (regarded as the culturally most advanced parts of the Soviet Union) had infant death rates of seventeen to twenty-two per thousand, whereas in towns of Central Asia the rate was more than double this.

By the mid-1970s Soviet males' life expectancy at birth had dropped to 63 years, compared to 69 for American males. The corresponding female expectancies were 74 and 76. This deterioration at a time of rising living standards was puzzling. The average Russian diet, for example, had improved noticeably; between 1965 and 1978 average annual meat consumption grew from 90 to 101 pounds, while potato consumption fell. On the other hand, improved living standards since 1952 meant increased cigarette consumption. Moreover, alcoholic beverages, in an age of more automobile traffic, more machinery in the factory and on the farm, and faster tempos of work might be expected to raise the number of fatal accidents, especially of young males. Nor did improved living standards, of themselves, help to reduce deaths from prolonged exposure to alcohol, or the still quite high prevalence of suicide.

So far as infant deaths are concerned, the USSR had experienced a notable rise in the number of very young mothers, with their higher infant mortality. With most mothers going to full-time work (and with maternity leave terminating just two months after the birth), the number of infants in day-care centres was high, and such centres were breeding grounds for the influenza and pneumonia outbreaks which caused so many infant deaths. Indeed, the inability of so many mothers, for one reason or another, to give their full care and attention to the newborn was probably the underlying factor in most types of infantile mortality. The lot of the Russian woman, especially if she had no mother or mother-in-law to help her, was more arduous than most. To go to work, to attend to children, to look after the home (which included long hours spent queuing for food) was a heavy workload. Possibly it was this continuing daily burden which kept the Soviet divorce rate at such a high level, but family life continued also to be threatened by poor housing conditions.

In the 1960s great efforts had been made to relieve the abysmal housing situation left by the Stalinist years. Outside the city centres huge expanses were covered with apartment blocks which, though sometimes ill-built and aesthetically unappealing, offered a new life to thousands of families. Under Khrushchev's successors residential building continued, and often made use of better or more pleasing designs. However, from 1969 the rate of construction fell behind the increase in the number of families. As before, accommodation that was in the better districts or was more spacious tended to be allocated to the privileged. The unprivileged had to be content (and they were) with cramped and remote apartments and, in the case of one design that was hurriedly altered to save materials, apartments where access from the kitchen to the living room was through the centrally placed bathroom. Housing, like other social services, was regarded as important, but had to take its place in the queue for resources. Defence, industry, and agriculture came first.

Some western specialists believed that the continuing problem of vandalism, petty crime, and hooliganism was partly a consequence of housing problems. The extent of 'hooliganism' was perhaps magnified by the tendency in the USSR to describe as a hooligan any young person whose tastes were not those generally accepted by society. Nevertheless, it certainly existed; for example, passengers on late evening commuter trains often complained that young people terrorized them while the train staff preferred to look the other way. In 1975, in the perhaps optimistic belief that children broke laws because they did not know what the laws were, a one-year course was introduced in schools on 'Principles of the Soviet State and Law'. Pilfering by workers of all ages was another problem. Armed guards had for decades been placed on freight trains carrying easily stolen freight through populated areas, but thefts in transit continued. New automobiles, as they were processed through successive junctions, might be relieved first of their tool-kits, then of their window-wipers, then of their dials and gauges, and might arrive at their final destination without wheels.

Under Khrushchev, and even more so under his successors, the gap between morality and legality remained obvious. But, as in other countries, those operating the legal system, unlike those drawn into it, believed in its propriety and effectiveness. For Soviet citizens the most obviously repellent feature of their system was the duality of justice. There was one privileged class, party and government officials, that was almost above the law. If one of these office-holders broke the law there might be a reprimand from the party organization, but that would usually be the end of it; there would be no court action except in some very serious cases. Ordinary citizens in court found that the whole system was weighted in favour of the prosecution. At some periods acquittals were so rare that the legal profession regarded them as failures that had to be reinvestigated. This meant that the innocent were frequently punished and, moreover, that it was relatively easy for officials to get rid of troublemakers by concocting a criminal case against them. There was a phenomenon that became known as 'telephone law', in which high officials, by a telephone call to the procuracy or to a judge, could decide the outcome of a case. Judges, even that proportion that had a respect for truth, could not be independent; they came up for reappointment every five years and knew that if they displeased the local party organization they would be jettisoned.

Another social service in need of reform was the medical service. For the ordinary patient, the signs of a monstrously defective service included long waits for emergency ambulances, the occasional need to bribe doctors, nurses, and officials for such luxuries as anaesthetics or a place in a ward where there was some space between the beds, inability actually to find and obtain the drugs specified in doctors' prescriptions, and, for alarmists, the dread possibility that the operating team might be too drunk to work safely but not drunk enough to be sent off duty. Doctors, who were largely female, were paid quite low salaries in comparison with other occupations, and this was said to be one of the reasons for demanding bribes. The existence of what in effect was a separate, superior medical service, with its own hospitals and facilities, for the privileged classes of the *Nomenklatura* and certain top institutions was one reason why the plight of the regular health service had been allowed to continue.

Ambulance services were poor and their staff mostly untrained in first aid. This helped to ensure that about 15 per cent of those who initially survived serious accidents died later, a rate which was about ten times higher than in the USA. This in turn was one reason why the USSR, with about one-tenth the vehicle ownership of the USA, had roughly the same annual total of road deaths. Other reasons were poor roads and abysmal vehicle maintenance and, according to some Russian citizens, the high car-ownership among Georgians, for whom spectacularly dangerous driving was irrefutable proof of manliness.

One aspect of society in which Khrushchev had been the very reverse of a liberator was religion. Indeed, the devout could look back to the Stalin days with a certain nostalgia; after the war there had not been a relapse to the violent anti-religious campaigns of the 1930s, and in many cases a blind eye had been turned on religious communities and priests who broke the strict letter of the anti-religious laws. Under Khrushchev, atheistic activity had returned to an abusive and physically violent course. In the Brezhnev years anti-religious legislation was not relaxed but, Khrushchev's policies having strengthened rather than weakened the hold of religion, official behaviour was more circumspect. In 1966 a revised law mentioned the criminality of 'deceitful actions calculated to arouse religious superstitions' and a new family law in 1968 stipulated that children should be brought up according to communist morals and that parents having a harmful influence over their children could lose their parental rights. Both these pieces of legislation were potentially of great utility in the campaign against religion, but they do not appear to have been widely used for that purpose.

The Orthodox Church remained the 'official' Church, with considerable advantages over other Christian denominations. Since 1946 the Uniate Church had been illegal. The Roman Catholics were a special case; in Lithuania the Catholic Church produced many dissidents and was closely linked with the Lithuanian nationalist movement, which was anti-Russian and remained strong despite frequent arrests. The *Chronicle of the Lithuanian Catholic Church* was one of the first well-known *Samizdat* publications in the USSR. Perhaps because the Lithuanian bishops had strong popular support, the Soviet authorities occasionally adopted a concessionary approach, allowing, for example, 10,000 copies of the New Testament to be published in Lithuania in 1972. Muslims were treated rather carefully, and there was a continuing policy of cultivating an officially approved Muslim leadership, representatives of which were sent as spokesmen on visits to other Muslim countries. Buddhists, on the other hand, were treated badly.

Living standards rose sharply during the post-Stalin years. An effort to raise the lowest wages also resulted in a slight narrowing of the gap between the highest- and lowest-paid workers. However, standards were low, and there remained great inequalities in the size of incomes and, especially, in the distribution of privileges. While average pensions rose faster than average wages, most pensions were insufficient for a comfortable retirement. Moreover, higher wages could not always be translated into higher standards, because the desired goods were not to be found in the stores. In Moscow, Leningrad, and a few big cities (especially those few that were open to foreign tourists) the inhabitants benefited from an unpublicized but very effective priority in supplies. Elsewhere in the Soviet Union, higher wages and unnaturally low prices meant that any allocations of the most wanted commodities were bought up in minutes. This situation was reflected in the growing propensity of Soviet citizens to increase personal savings. A particular victim of the unnatural price-and-supply relationship was meat. This was very cheap, thanks to a subsidy, but could only be obtained intermittently, and by queuing for long periods. This obviously aroused dissatisfaction, but the government felt that it was better that citizens should enjoy the thought of low meat prices, even if meat was very difficult to obtain, than that they should be antagonized by a raising of prices which would have resulted in more meat in the stores. Polish workers had several times shown what unfortunate things might happen to the vanguard of the proletariat if it decided to raise the price of the proletariat's meat. Influential persons (that is, the privileged) could always buy their meat at the cheap official prices in the 'closed' stores which had been established for their exclusive benefit. There were only rare occasions when Soviet workers indulged in disorderly protests; the characteristic occasion for such public disturbances was a realization that treasured items of food were not forthcoming even after hours of queuing. In such cases the immediate government reaction was to release from state reserves a special allocation of supplies to that locality, in order to cool the situation. Investigations and perhaps selective arrests could then proceed unhurriedly.

Although ordinary citizens had many occasions for dissatisfaction, their irritation was usually directed, or channelled, towards lower officials. So long as living standards did not actually decline it could be assumed that the leadership was safe from popular discontent. After all, although the claim that there was no unemployment and no inflation in the USSR was exaggerated, these afflictions were unobtrusive.

But although the Soviet masses had little thought of changing the regime, just as in tsarist times there was a stratum of dissident opinion that was willing to take risks in its self-imposed task of fundamental criticism. There were signs of active dissidence in the 1960s. Many intellectuals and others made known their distaste for such actions as the trial of Sinyavsky and Daniel, for the refusal to return their homeland to the Crimean Tatars even though their wartime deportation had been declared unjustified, and for the 1968 action in Czechoslovakia. Some of the protesters used the medium of the leaflet or of the petition, others actually tried to organize street demonstrations, while others embarrassed the government by voicing to western journalists complaints which they could not publicize in the USSR. Dissidents whose opposition was blatant and attracting public attention were sometimes tried and sent to labour camps. Also, Nicholas I's practice of certifying intellectual critics as insane was repeated; this enabled suitable treatment to be administered in psychiatric institutions operated by the security services.

Also reminiscent of Nicholas's reign was the hand-to-hand circulation of writings which could not be printed because of censorship. With photocopying, these *Samizdat* editions could be circulated in hundreds of copies (which is why photocopying machines were not on open sale). A regular 'underground' periodical, the *Journal of Current Events*, provided information about what was really happening in the USSR and in the world. In Leningrad, two feminist *Samizdat* magazines appeared in the late 1970s, but they were soon dealt with, the editor of *Woman and Russia* being expelled from the USSR. Another *Samizdat* publication which attracted worldwide attention was *Thoughts on Progress, Peaceful Coexistence and Intellectual Freedom*. This studied the desirability, for the peace of the world, of a convergence of a freer USSR with a more socialized USA, a convergence which should be fostered by scientists. The author, Sakharov, was a respected and highly talented physicist.

Sakharov, being a top scientist, was not penalized for this publication. Scientists, especially those attached to closed research establishments, had more intellectual freedom than ordinary citizens, and found all the more irksome those restrictions from which they continued to suffer. They were allowed to read western scientific and academic journals, but not always before censoring bureaucrats had removed those parts considered harmful or 'irrelevant'. They had contacts abroad, but their foreign correspondence was opened and examined. They had opportunities to travel abroad, but only after innumerable appearances and perhaps humiliations before party and state officials (they had to collect, in triplicate, testimonials, then assemble their pedigrees and personal biographies, which were scrutinized by four different party bureaux, the KGB, and the foreign ministry). It was from scientists and academics that the nucleus of a new 'public opinion' seemed to be emerging. As the purges receded further into the past, disturbed personal relationships between intellectuals were re-established and they developed a certain professional solidarity. They did not seek a revolution, but they wanted fair use of existing institutions. For example, they wanted the citizens' rights formally granted by the Constitution to be guaranteed in practice, they wanted the soviets to be genuine forums for discussion rather than gatherings of selected yes-men. They probably had little in common (apart from family connections) with the masses, whose preoccupations were still economic rather than political or moral. They probably did not even want to arouse the masses, whose rebellion might so easily be turned against themselves and their privileges; no doubt the Chinese Cultural Revolution reminded them how vulnerable they were. In a sense these discontented intellectuals resembled their predecessors of Nicholas II's time, talented men needed by the state, who strove to use their indispensability as a lever to extract political freedoms.

In the 1970s repression of the dissident movement seemed to intensify. The KGB scored a notable success in 1973, when after a long period of arrest and interrogation two prominent dissidents, P. Yakir and V. Krasin (both bearers of distinguished Bolshevik names), were persuaded to sign confessions that they were agents of foreign anti-Soviet organizations. Many dissidents were allowed to leave, or forced to leave, on one-way trips to the west. One prominent dissident, Bukovski, a specialist (through experience) in the psychiatric treatment of dissidents, went west in a 'body-swap'; a prominent Chilean communist was released and sent to the USSR by the Chilean government in exchange. In 1978 a new law on citizenship made easier the formal deprivation of Soviet citizenship. Among those deprived of citizenship (that is, the right of residence in the USSR) in the following year were the novelist V. Nekrasov, the philosopher A. Zinoviev (who published in the west a long satirical and subversive novel, *Yawning Heights*), and the chess champion V. Korchnoi.

In the months preceding the 1980 Olympic Games the security services felt it prudent to shift many known dissidents away from Moscow, where they might have found audiences among the expected influx of foreign visitors. Sakharov was among those molested at this time, being sent to long-term house arrest in the city of Gorki. Earlier, there had been several more trials of dissidents. Among these was that of Orlov, one of the leaders of a group of concerned Soviet citizens which had established a committee to observe how far the authorities were observing the agreements on human rights enshrined in the Helsinki Agreement. Orlov was sentenced to seven years' hard labour for 'anti-Soviet agitation' and his trial was so unsatisfactory that several western communist leaders protested against it.

Other members of the intelligentsia, while refraining from activities that would put them in the dissident camp, sometimes succeeded by discreet pressure in achieving important aims. They had, for example, a large part in the discouragement of moves to rehabilitate Stalin; the post-1956 line was retained, that Stalin was 'positive' until 1934 and increasingly 'negative' thereafter. Scientific opinion seems to have been a strong influence in the leadership's acceptance of environmental pollution as a problem deserving of attention.

A rather novel, non-intellectual, protest attracted attention in 1977, when six workers, including a coal miner, gave to western pressmen an account of how they had variously lost their jobs after sending in complaints about how their superiors were misbehaving in various ways. There was really nothing new about these complaints, but their chosen method of protest passed beyond what was acceptable in Soviet conditions. They tried to form a 'Free Trade Union of Soviet Workers'. This was more than individual protest (which was acceptable); it was the forming of an 'organization' (which was certainly unacceptable). In 1978 this Free Trade Union appealed in vain to the International Labour Organization at Geneva for support and recognition. Again, here is a little report published by *Pravda* of 26 September 1979. Efimovski, a worker at a Tashkent engineering factory, had many times complained about the neglect of safety regulations. Finally, not having received any satisfaction, he decided to quit:

Efimovski was called to the director's office. There, already waiting for him, were the party secretary, the trade union chairman, and the head of the workshop. The conversation was begun with a threat:

'Well, you have decided to quit? Fine, we'll release you, but you won't be leaving voluntarily. We are going to dismiss you for absenteeism.'

'But I've not been absent', said the astonished Efimovski.

'If you haven't had any absences yet, you soon will have!' replied Yu. Pelishenko, head of the workshop.

They quickly put together a false document about Efimovski's absences, and similar faked minutes of a supposed meeting of the workshop trade union committee, which had 'demanded' the dismissal of the 'truant'.

Managerial misbehaviour was quite common in the USSR, as the Soviet press indicated from time to time. Neglect of safety precautions in order to help reach production targets, diversion of wages and bonuses from those who actually earned them to administrative and managerial staff, the purloining for private use or profit of state materials or products, were the usual fields of such activity. Those who did protest to their trade union or party officials usually received little sympathy. Sometimes they wrote to the newspapers, and sometimes their letter gained a hearing and their complaint was publicized (although not necessarily with any result). If an enterprise was meeting its production targets it was rare for criticisms of its management to have any effect, but once an enterprise lost favour because of output difficulties its management was likely to be assailed by diverse accusations accumulated during past years.

Outside the mainstream of the dissident movement were the Armenian nationalists whose bomb in the Moscow Metro killed several passengers in 1977, and the lone assassin who shot at a motorcade conveying Soviet leaders in 1969. This assassin had wanted to kill Brezhnev, but he fired at the wrong car, killing a driver.

Russian bureaucratic virtue

Those who criticized the post-Stalin governments did usually accept socialist principles. Nevertheless, there was one common thread linking the oppositional movements of the twentieth and nineteenth centuries: the resentment aroused by the ever-present, ever-suspicious, and ever-interfering Russian bureaucratic mind. In brief, this mind relied on two major concepts: the elevation to a principle of the maxim that there is a proper time and place for everything, and the belief that the proper time and place may be specified only by a person adequately certified as someone-who-knows-best. In this mind, the ideal society is one where everyone acts according to a grand design, and yet within that design (prepared by experts) each individual is free to excel. In real life this ideal may be never quite attainable (although in the arts it is achieved by ballet, which does tend to find its most enthusiastic audience in administrative centres like St Petersburg). When the bureaucrat's idea of perfection is backed by the power to impose it by coercion, well-known and perilous temptations arise.

The survival into Soviet times of an all-powerful and coercive bureaucracy repeatedly undermined the promise of 1917. Six decades after the Revolution the gap between 'official' and 'unofficial' Russia, which nineteenth-century visitors so much liked to point out, was still evident. The Russian communists had succeeded against all odds in proving that there was an attainable alternative to capitalism, but in doing so they had used the existing administrative apparatus, an apparatus which was coercive, repressive, and distrusted the people. They had changed the official ideology, but they had not changed the official arbitrariness and authoritarianism which had been the most disliked features of tsarism. Traditional bureaucratic attitudes weakened the state by arousing discontent and by repressing initiative (that is, by perpetuating inertia); therefore their continuation after 1917 was unfortunate, despite their value in governing and guarding an enormous and incoherent state. Despite a realization of the dangers of bureaucracy, and sporadic efforts to curb its most alarming symptoms, both the party and the government came to rely more and more on the old methods. Inside the party, democratic centralism degenerated into bureaucratic centralization, so that by the 1930s there was a wide gap between party officials and party members. In the administration, the old ministers, governors, and most heads of departments disappeared in 1917, but the majority of middle and lower officials remained in, or subsequently regained, their positions. Party members sent to watch over government departments shared the bureaucratic outlook, or acquired such an outlook from those they were supposed to supervise. The pattern of the Red Army, most of whose commanders by the end of the Civil War were former tsarist officers, was duplicated in other departments of state; the CHEKA made use of former Okhrana operatives. Patterns of bureaucratic thought and behaviour were thereby passed on from tsarist times, and were later absorbed by new generations of officials. Towards the end of his life Lenin seemed to realize what was happening. If he had been able to introduce an effective but less arbitrary and repressive mode of administration it would probably have been the most radical achievement of the Russian Revolution. But it is doubtful whether more than a minority of his supporters would have appreciated this. Too many Bolsheviks, both before and after Lenin's death, did not distinguish what was radical from what was merely excessive. Revolution, taking the form of removing church bells and arresting men wearing ties, was more attractive than radicalism. A result of this negligence was that from the 1930s ordinary Russians were enduring official repression more painful and more widespread than that of a century earlier. Subsequent 'destalinization' made life more bearable but was slow to touch the fundamentals. In the 1960s and 1970s the life of Soviet people visibly improved, and not only in material terms, but when the 1980s began there still seemed to be a discrepancy between what the Revolution had achieved on paper, and what the Revolution had achieved in practice.

This was the underlying situation. Party leaders saw the symptoms but did not recognize the disease. Some thought that Russia's big problem was drink, although this was an argument that practised imbibers like Brezhnev and Chernenko preferred to leave to others.

The lazy and the liquorish

Although the campaign against the work-shy came to a peak under Andropov, it had its beginnings under Brezhnev. There was a decree, in 1980, aimed at workers who changed their jobs too frequently or who infringed labour discipline in other ways, and a strengthened 'Parasites' Law' of January 1983 had actually been prepared during the Brezhnev period. The campaign slackened halfway through Andropov's brief tenure of office, was barely kept in being under Chernenko, and was then revived by Gorbachev, although in his first year the latter directed his fire mainly at drunkenness.

Unemployment officially did not exist, and every worker's right to a job was enshrined in the Constitution. Many workers, it seemed, did not feel any obligation to reciprocate by working hard at their jobs. In any case, for other reasons apart from the sheer difficulty of doing so, managements were reluctant to shed workers. Even when factories were automated, the workforce was rarely reduced. In administrative jobs the situation was similar. When Gorbachev announced his new State Agroindustrial Committee, it was intimated that more than 20,000 functionaries would be 'freed', but in fact they stayed on, albeit with different job titles. Low productivity meant an apparent labour shortage, which strengthened the situation of individual workers; if a management took the step of enforcing stricter workplace discipline, by requiring workers to be at the workplace during working hours and to work properly while there, then a worker had no difficulty, apart from waiting out the statutory two weeks' notice, in quitting and finding a more compliant employer elsewhere.

Andropov's campaign was preceded and accompanied by meetings and letters to the press in which workers complained of the soft attitude taken towards drunkards, slackers, and 'rolling stones'. Favourable references were made to past Stalinist practices like the labour-book and the harsh punishments for lateness at work, which, it was claimed, might well be reinstituted; this was another example of the need felt by many for a 'strong' leader. While comments from the working class tended to favour harsh punishments, those published in the more intellectual papers gave more emphasis to the hard living and working conditions which encouraged labour indiscipline.

In early 1983 it was clear that the new regime favoured the harsh approach. The police, aided by civilian volunteers, began to conduct raids in the cities during working hours. Fishing people out of queues, shops, hairdressers, swimming pools, public baths, buses, and underground trains, they demanded their identification papers and reasons why they were not at work. Those who had left their papers at home were taken to the police stations, as were those who could not explain why they were not at work. These latter were then reported to their managements and to their local party organizations, and could face reprimands and pay deductions.

This campaign may have done the state more harm than good, for it aroused a great deal of resentment, particularly among those who, though innocent, were greatly inconvenienced, if not insulted, by the police tactics. It was not long before the more extreme actions were abandoned, and more attention was paid to finding out precisely why so many workers were not at work. One very useful measure resulting from this was that shop opening hours were altered so that they were no longer closed at the times when workers were best placed to use them. It had been realized, belatedly, that the reason why workers went shopping in working hours was that, for many, this was the only time when queuing and shopping were possible.

Concurrently, a new campaign was mounted against workers having a second, 'black economy' job. This, apparently, was based on the shaky assumption that a worker deprived of his moonlighting opportunities would work harder at his regular job. The immediate result was that the Soviet citizen found it even harder than previously to obtain essential services like appliance repair, roof-mending, shoe repair, and countless others which the official service organizations were so bad at providing.

Gorbachev, once in power, continued the campaign, but placed more emphasis on drunkenness, which for some years had been regarded as a main cause of absenteeism, work accidents, and poor-quality output. In late 1982, for example, *Pravda* was naming drink as the reason why so many building sites were inactive on Mondays and on Friday afternoons. During Gorbachev's first year the massive propaganda campaign directed against alcoholism did at least change the atmosphere enough to embolden some managements actually to dismiss workers who were habitually drunk. But the problem was far from solved. Here again, the railways provided good examples of difficulties found throughout the economy. In the early 1980s railway accidents were increasing to an alarming frequency, and a majority of those attributed to human error involved drink. But existing labour legislation made it impossible to prevent a driver taking out a train merely because his breath smelt of alcohol. Moreover, although it was possible to punish a driver for drunkenness by demoting him, labour legislation provided that at the end of a fixed term he had to be returned to his previous job.

In terms of pure alcohol consumption per head, the USSR was not the world's leader, but it was very close behind the world leaders, France and Italy (and after the failure of Gorbachev's campaign would catch up and overtake the leaders by 1990). A very high proportion of its intake was in spirits, much more damaging than wine and beer. Although statistics for Soviet consumption are hard to construct, it seems likely that at least half the drink consumed was in the form of distilled spirits, mainly vodka, with average alcohol contents of more than 40 per cent. Also, Russians still tended to favour the drinking bout rather than the sipped glass; hence fatalities and hangovers were more common, and the death rate was increased by the use of hangover remedies which were themselves liable to induce death. *Samogon*, illicitly brewed spirits, which may have accounted for a quarter of total consumption, is usually reckoned to be more toxic than the factory-made vodka.

Drunkenness in public was an increasing burden for the police, even though production-line methods were used in the form of sobering-up stations to which drunks could be taken, an idea inherited from Beria's time. At these they were typically given a cold shower and a lecture, fined, and had their documents examined in order that their employers could be informed. Drunks who, by excessive intake or consequent accident, were too ill to follow this regime were parked in special hospital wards. In Moscow, in the 1970s, there were about thirty sobering-up stations. A Soviet source estimated that in 1979 some 16–18 million drunks passed through sobering-up stations.

Presumably these thirsty souls, all lit up and nowhere to go, were only the tip of an alcoholic iceberg, for many others would have enjoyed their hangovers in the privacy of their own homes or under the comradely protection of their workplace. In the mid-1970s a Soviet demographer estimated that the social costs attributable to alcohol actually exceeded the value of the profits and duties derived from its sale.

The man on the street had a difficult time in the mid-1980s:

My classmate, for example, was scared of going home by himself at the end of the month. He quite seriously stated that at that time the police would trap lone passers-by.

'But why?' we asked.

'The sobering-up stations have to fulfil their monthly plan', he explained . . .

There were many corroborating stories. 'We still have a plan,' N. Kirilenko, police captain, told me. 'Each year the Moscow City Executive's financial directorate demands 200,000. It's absurd, of course. How can you plan drunkenness?'

And in fact, looking back at the height of the anti-alcohol campaign, people were grabbed as they left restaurants, were 'taken' from weddings, banquets and funerals! And then the old dreary path of the report sent to the place of work, attendance before the trade union committee, loss of bonuses, going to the back of the queue for housing or for a car.[5]

In terms of ready availability in the stores, vodka had rivalled Brezhnev's memoirs, with few interruptions of supply and little need for queuing. The state deployed the price weapon in 1981, imposing considerable price increases. Gorbachev's campaign included a reduction in vodka supply, which meant long queues that incommoded moderate drinkers as well. Non-drinkers were also inconvenienced by shortages of sugar and jam (popularly used for making *Samogon*). The situation provided fresh opportunities for criminals. The state budget, which had drawn about 13 per cent of its income from alcohol taxes, was critically affected.

Gorbachev finally abandoned his anti-alcohol campaign in 1990. Just as with Nicholas II's prohibition of 1914, it had brought great unpopularity at a period when the regime could not afford to lose support. It had reduced the state's income, and it had limited citizens' opportunities of drowning sorrows in drink. Gorbachev had been over-influenced by the fundamentalists of the temperance movement, who had opposed the alternative path of publicizing the virtues of moderate, 'cultured', drinking.

For the next few years the subject was dropped. Under Yeltsin the drink industry was deregulated. Consumption rose again. In the 1990s, though, drinking was more likely to be viewed as a disease rather than evidence of moral failing, and non-governmental organizations like Alcoholics Anonymous, with their softer but more rewarding approach, were being encouraged.

5. *Gudok*, 21 May 1991, 3.

18

Transformation

Gorbachev

WHEN Mikhail Gorbachev was awarded the Nobel Peace Prize in 1990, Soviet citizens made cynical observations about his greater popularity abroad than at home. But the honour was deserved, even though when he resigned in 1991 the USSR would be in ruins and its people, though free, would be facing an uncertain future. He seemed destined to take his place in history alongside other great transformers. Things did not turn out the way he had hoped, but he switched Russia onto a different and more promising track. His work was more destructive than expected, but it made the world a better place, and he managed without blood and iron. In course of time as memories faded of how it felt to exist, think, and talk in the isolated, threatening, monolithic atmosphere of Soviet Russia with its repressive and baleful ambience and unrelenting watchdogs, the depth of his achievement might become harder to appreciate, but would be no less real.

Mikhail Gorbachev was born in the Stavropol region of the north Caucasus in the period of mass collectivization. His father was a tractor driver and, as a teenager, Mikhail worked as a combine-harvester assistant driver in the summers. He went to Moscow University, where he graduated in law, and subsequently followed a correspondence course in agriculture. He began his political career in 1956 as the Komsomol first secretary in Stavropol city, made an impression on the first secretary of the party's Stavropol regional organization, and in 1970 himself succeeded to that post. He attracted the attention of Suslov (who had Stavropol connections) and of Andropov. His ascent was rapid; having become a member of the Central Committee in 1971, he was a full member of the Politburo in 1980. Charm and ability had made full use of his influential connections.

He took part in parliamentary delegations to Canada and Britain. His 1984 visit to England and Scotland came to a premature end at Holyrood House, when he learned that Ustinov had died. He flew home immediately but not before the British prime minister, Thatcher, had declaimed that Gorbachev was a man with whom 'we can do business together'.

Gorbachev was clearly a leading figure in the Politburo, favoured by those who realized that big changes were needed but distrusted by those who preferred things as they were. The Politburo met to choose a new general secretary with almost unseemly haste after the demise of Chernenko in 1985. Gorbachev, as it happened, was in charge of the arrangements and the haste meant that one likely opponent, Shcherbitskii, who had been visiting the USA, did not arrive in time. The decision was arrived at without him, and Gorbachev became the new general secretary.

Unlike Brezhnev, who in his later years had a resuscitation team in constant attendance, and unlike Andropov and Chernenko, Gorbachev had good health and relative youth on his side. When he assumed power he was only 54.

As general secretary, Gorbachev was outspoken, not seeking to cloak criticism with euphemism. He was willing to show himself among ordinary people and enter into impromptu discussions, frequently demonstrating that he had a good idea of what really went on in Soviet society. He referred to ministers who 'try to squeeze as much capital and materials as possible while proposing production targets as small as possible'. He acknowledged that service industries were so abysmal that when people needed something repaired they had to find a person in the 'black economy' to do it for them, and this moonlighter would depend on materials stolen from some state enterprise. Abroad, Gorbachev presented the Soviet case with more charm and intelligence than had been seen since the days of Litvinov.

His political character had been shaped by his career as an *apparatchik*, and he was never able to throw off many of the assumptions and modes of behaviour of his class. At first he aimed to return to the aspirations and standards of Lenin's time, as he saw them. He proceeded cautiously, knowing that what he intended to do would be unwelcome to the bulk of the party apparatus. His 1987 speech celebrating seventy years of Soviet power was possibly the point at which his intentions became plainer, but even that carefully crafted speech was fairly innocuous compared to what came later. In it, he made plain that Stalin had done bad things to be set against the good things, but even that moderate reminder was only grudgingly tolerated by some of his Politburo colleagues.

By moving slowly, while steadily replacing the more conservative party administrators, Gorbachev hoped to transform the USSR through a transformed communist party. But the party apparatus was very slow to reform itself, and he was faced with the same problem as other Russian reformers, how to make changes without unleashing a torrent of pent-up pressures. In the end he was beaten by Pandora, in whose box was not only the party demon but also the even more intractable economic and nationality devils.

The two catchwords of his policies were *glasnost'*, or frankness, and *perestroika*, or restructuring. Because the communist regime had maintained power largely through suppression of information, the new frankness threatened cataclysm for the party bureaucracy. As for restructuring, Gorbachev's realization that Soviet society needed a thorough rebuilding was sound, but in his six years of *perestroika* he succeeded mainly in the destructive phase of reconstruction. So as not to antagonize too many people at the same time, he had to deal with the big issues not concurrently, but successively, and this helps to explain his postponement of the economic reform he knew was needed, and of tackling the nationalities problem that he saw but whose magnitude surprised him.

In the beginning was the word

From 1985 to 1991 the USSR was weakened to the point where it actually disappeared, the communist party followed the same route, and the international situation relaxed. All this happened because freedom of speech and freedom of publication became real under Gorbachev's policy of *glasnost'*. Control of information, which really meant the suppression of truth and the construction of an all-embracing structure of falsehood, was the indispensable support of communist bureaucracies in the USSR and in the people's democracies of central and eastern Europe. Vigilantly on guard against counter-revolution, they proved helpless against counter-revelation. Gorbachev had hoped to achieve a restructuring of Soviet society and especially of the communist party. But truth, once liberated, was too pugnacious to stop at mere restructuring.

All the same, government departments found it hard to break old habits. There was undoubtedly greater openness, but not everywhere. Long after Gorbachev's retirement there was still a reluctance to release bad news:

If, God forbid, the 'Titanic' disaster had happened to us at the present day, and she was flying the Russian flag, they would still be telling us that the voyage was going well, under full steam.[1]

Glavlit, the state censorship organization, was abolished only in 1990, but by 1988 the old barriers were clearly down. The process had not been instantaneous. At first just one or two publications printed material that previously would have been banned, and a few newspapers criticized what had previously been unimpeachable. When editors saw that such ventures attracted public interest and brought no undesirable consequences, the process spread and there developed a real variety of periodicals, ranging from the conservative to the radical. This change was uneven, with readers in many areas having access only to publications that stuck to the old standards, and this was one of the reasons why television was so important in changing the climate of opinion. With the central programmes receivable in most parts of the Union, and with many such programmes in the hands of reformist programme-makers, the

1. S. Kalashnikov, chairman of the Duma's labour committee, in an interview of 17 May 1997.

viewing public (that is, practically the entire population) was exposed to the release of new ideas and previously suppressed facts. Discovering that their long-suppressed thoughts were shared by others, many ordinary people became bolder in their criticism and demands. But there were others who were unable to cope with the overturning of beliefs instilled since childhood.

Influential historians of the servile school, typically heads of departments or institutions, fought hard against *glasnost'*. The rapid exit, in Khrushchev's time, of the historian Nekrich, after he had published an analysis of June 1941, had discouraged bold re-examinations. Nevertheless, after a slow start, original history began to appear and much new light was shed on the recent past. In some cases surviving participants of the Stalinist period were interviewed, and in others long-suppressed documents were published. For the first time in decades Trotsky's work, and works, were publicly examined. Unsurprisingly, after the first burst of curiosity, the Soviet reading public relegated Trotsky to the garbage bin of history. Bukharin, on the other hand, aroused some sympathy partly because, rightly or wrongly, he was perceived as the best of a bad bunch. Gorbachev had initially believed that a return to Leninism was what the USSR needed, but slowly the archives revealed the full Lenin in all his bloodthirstiness, and Gorbachev, like many others, changed his mind. Meanwhile, as early as 1988 it was decided to destroy existing school textbooks on Soviet history. This meant that examinations in this subject had to be cancelled in 1988, an event that was a history lesson in itself.

A good deal of archival material on the Stalinist purges and terror was unearthed and published, including bloodstained reports penned by torturers in the interrogation cells. Some statistics were located, but Soviet researchers had no more success than their western predecessors in accurately counting the number of victims. In 1989 Soviet responsibility was finally acknowledged for the Katyn (and other) mass killings. Not everything went smoothly for the new historians. As late as 1991 the director of the Military History Institute was denounced by the defence minister and had to resign after producing the first volume of a less tendentious history of the Red Army in the Second World War. Not everything was cleared up. Past manifestations of anti-Semitism were revealed but in a low-key and incomplete way. Who had been behind the murder of Kirov remained unsettled and it was reported that some of the documents seen by the members of Khrushchev's interrupted commission on this subject had since disappeared.

Television coverage of political debate was perhaps the most important means of informing the public, but a number of one-off programmes on sensitive issues, together with a few regular current-affairs programmes, were almost as important. For the first time, political problems could be presented from several points of view. One of the first of such occasions was when the British prime minister, Mrs Thatcher, was interviewed and, among other things, explained why she felt Britain should retain nuclear weapons; that the west might feel imperilled by the huge Red Army was a thought never previously explained to a mass Soviet audience.

An evening magazine programme, *Vzglyad* ('View'), soon attracted a growing audience with its well-informed outspokenness. Leningrad TV had a regular programme called '600 Seconds' with a reputation for unearthing scandals. Its presenter and leading spirit became something of a media hero until he criticized the conduct of the independence movements in the Baltic republics, after which rumours spread that he was really a KGB man. In the 1990–1 winter when, still trying to hold the party together, Gorbachev made his unwise 'shift to the right', there was a move towards tighter control of radio and television. A more restrictive head of Gostelradio (the central state radio and television organization) was appointed, and one of his first moves was to eliminate *Vzglyad*. A parallel evening programme, *Vremiya* ('Time'), was retained but this was blander; when in July 1991 a Russian Republic decree banned party activity in enterprises, *Vremiya* waited two days before commenting, and when it did it gave coverage only to opponents of the decree. Meanwhile Gorbachev had decreed that Leningrad TV should be subordinated to Gostelradio.

Yeltsin, as president of the Russian Republic, managed to get a Russian Republic TV programme into operation, broadcasting three times daily on an existing channel, and its magazine programme *Vesti* ('Tidings') soon became more popular than *Vremiya*. During the attempted coup of August 1991 several radio and television presenters showed reluctance to support the takeover, but the general television line was to conform (although on the first day this conformity simply meant little more than playing 'Swan Lake' over and over again, interspersed with the conspirators' press release). After the coup failed many of the conservative controllers, including the head of Gostelradio, were dismissed and replaced by more progressive figures. For the remainder of 1991 the programmes, like much of the press, reverted to their previous outspokenness, only more so.

Newspapers, and the more popular periodicals, played a part in bringing day-to-day criticism to bear, and also, sometimes, devoted lengthy articles to long-standing evils or distorted history. Even *Pravda*, regarded as one of the conservative newspapers, played a big part in this; being the Central Committee's newspaper, a small shift by this paper was more important than a big shift in the views of another. However, as time passed and a spectrum of newspapers developed, *Pravda* and *Sovietskaya Rossiya* remained on the conservative wing. On the other hand *Komsomlskaya pravda*, the newspaper of the Komsomol youth organization, transformed itself into one of the more crusading of the big newspapers. Some new titles appeared, *Nezavisimaya gazeta* ('Independent Newspaper') proving to be one of the most popular. Meanwhile an energetic editor transformed the popular illustrated magazine *Ogonyok* into an investigative, socially aware magazine with an ever-increasing circulation. Another journal, *Arguments and Facts*, thanks to its well-informed and highly factual articles, also reached a very high print run; it claimed a world-record print run of 35 million in 1990. Another high-print-run period-ical was *Rabotnitsa* ('Woman Worker') claiming 24 million. Such huge print runs soon dropped.

Editors had to provide more of what the public wanted. *Pravda* made some kind of an effort to keep up with the times, but its views lost palatability just as did its owner, the communist party. By 1991 its print run, which had once been about 12 million, had declined to about 1 million. In the August 1991 coup it was one of the nine papers that the plotters did not suspend; unsurprisingly, after the coup failed it was banned for a few days, during which its editorial board was changed. In its new form its title was bereft of the image of Lenin, it no longer called itself the communist party newspaper, but it was still the best printed of the papers. Its future would henceforth depend on its commercial success; in late 1991 an issue even appeared with the top of its front page adorned by a page-wide advertisement offering stock-exchange opportunities.

Moves towards market pricing meant that newsprint, ever scarcer because of the problems of the timber industry, became more expensive. With the disappearance or diminution of subsidies, newspaper prices had to rise, and great efforts were made to maintain circulations, but by the end of 1991 some of the more specialized newspapers were in difficulties. Newspaper manage-ments in search of cheap newsprint reported bitterly that new popular and allegedly sleazy magazines, like those published by monarchists and religious interests and those taking advantage of new sexual freedoms, could afford to pay high prices for newsprint whereas more worthy papers, like their own, could not. Tsars, saints, and naked girls, they complained, was where the money was.

The arts

In the graphic arts, *glasnost'* did not release any great innovation, although it enabled innovators to secure a wider audience. Also, and especially in the 1990s, they would enjoy great commercial opportunities for applying their art in the growing field of publicity and advertising.

The 'thick' journals were liberated by *glasnost'*, and were often the first to present fiction that had previously been unpublishable. *Novyi mir*, which had distinguished itself in Khrushchev's time, was again in the forefront, but was joined by several others, while even the journals that were unenthusiastic about reform showed a little more enterprise in defending the conservative position. Much of the Soviet fiction published in the 1920s but subsequently banned was reprinted, and some foreign literature was published for the first time; that Orwell's *Animal Farm* became available is testimony to the no-holds-barred character of *glasnost'*. The same author's *Nineteen Eighty-Four* was also published (as was the Soviet forerunner of this novel, Zamyatin's *We*).

Readers of these journals soon discovered that many of the apparently turgid Stalinist novelists had written other novels which, far from winning a Stalin Prize, had hitherto been unpublishable. One of these surprises was Grossman's *Life and Fate*. Grossman had written several Stalinist best-sellers but in 1961, when he submitted this manuscript to the 'thick' journal *Znamya*, the KGB was informed and every copy of the manuscript confiscated. Grossman died in the belief that the novel was irretrievably lost, but a copy was found and published in 1988. The novel is truthful about the Second World War (some of its scenes take place in Soviet and German concentration camps, an ambience where the naked truth tends to survive) and there are hints that Soviet Russia was not entirely unlike Nazi Germany, that there might be such a thing as Stalin's national bolshevism to parallel Hitler's national socialism.

Vladimir Dudintsev, who found that he could not get anything published in the aftermath of his *Not by Bread Alone*, reappeared with the novel *White Coats*. This was about the Lysenko affair, and reminded readers how ideology can, and did, make a mockery of science. Another notable writer, comparable to Solzhenitsyn in his portrayals of the horrifying realities of labour-camp life, was Varlam Shalamov, whose *Kolyma Tales* was published in *Novyi mir*. Many other unpublished manuscripts were taken from their hiding places and printed.

Some new novels not only told the truth about the past, but also tried to explain it. In many cases this amounted to speculation about Stalin's real nature and motivation, as in Anatolii Rybakov's celebrated *Children of the Arbat*. The author, who had won a Stalin Prize in 1951, tried to get this book published by *Novyi mir* in the 1960s, but failed. It was finally published in 1987. Set in Moscow at the time of Kirov's murder, it has Stalin as a main character; his thoughts are laid out, to create a psychological study that is not necessarily valid but at least poses pertinent questions. Stray references, like that to Stalin's 'Hitler-like moustache' are not hard to interpret even though they may take artistic licence excessively far.

In 1994 the Russian Booker Prize, which had become the most prestigious award for novelists, went to a novel about a *Nomenklatura* family's sufferings in the 1930s purges. But this was almost the last gasp of the ageing generation of dissident writers. The collapse of the communist system had robbed them of their inspiration and, it seemed, relevance. They were succeeded by a younger generation that took the easier route of attracting attention by breaking through all the old taboos of unorthodox sex, bodily emissions, and grotesque injury. Practitioners of this new literature could claim that they were the first to take Sociaist Realism seriously, in that they put in the reality that the old socialist realists had left out. Their critics contrasted them with

Dostoevsky, who could portray evil powerfully without recourse to shocking detail, whereas these new novelists might know how to show, but did not penetrate, ugliness and dirt.

Plays and films made a great mark, just as in the past (probably more so, since many of them were repeated on television). Mikhail Shatrov, a long-established writer of historical plays, made an impression with his portrayals of dramatic events in the early years of the Soviet regime. He was one of the first to dig beyond the 1930s and raise questions about the real history of 1917 and 1918. In *Onward, Onward, Onward*, Shatrov covers the eve of the October Revolution. Prominent personalities are portrayed and they introduce themselves with autobiographies of their whole life. Thus Trotsky duly reports how he was murdered in Mexico (this was news for most of the first-night audience), but Lenin was still favourably depicted. Soon though, theatre tended to lose its role as breaker of new ground; television took over much of that function.

Perhaps because it was concentrated in a few units, the film industry made an exceptionally prompt jump from constraint to liberty. The Cinema Association, the body controlling the industry, normally found its executive committee by electing an officially nominated list of candidates. However, in 1986 its conference included enough rampant members to reject this list and to propose candidates from the floor of the meeting. The result was a completely transformed Cinema Association, one of whose first acts was to prepare for distribution the many films that in previous decades had been refused public showings. Sometimes underlining, sometimes merely implying, the evils of past decades, this collection of films helped to show why reform was necessary.

The film that made the biggest impression was a Georgian production, *Repentance*. Made in Stalin's homeland in the early 1980s before *glasnost'*, with the encouragement of the Georgian party secretary Shevardnadze, it could be regarded as an allegory of Stalinism. But its broad theme was that there were people with guilty consciences about, people who had behaved horrendously in the Stalin years, and that the best thing such people could do was to confess and hope for forgiveness. There was a secondary theme about Russians' insensitivity to non-Russian cultures.[2] A notable documentary film of 1989, focusing on the powerful nostalgia for Stalin still to be found in Russian society, was *Is Stalin Still with Us?*, which interviewed surviving Stalinists (including an NKVD operative who had once guarded Bukharin).

Other notable film treatments of Stalinism included *Defence Lawyer Sedov*, which won prizes at western film festivals and was a low-key but highly effective exposé of the cruel legalities of the purge era. The same director went on to

---

2. This was a film that needed to be seen two or three times to be fully understood, so although it impressed it was not especially popular among Russian audiences. But it was admired abroad.

make *The Tale of the Unextinguished Moon*, after a long-banned story by Pilnyak that had been inspired by the rumour that war commissar Frunze's fatal surgery in 1925 had been Stalin's way of getting rid of him. But examining the Stalinist past was over-exploited by film-makers. The result was often a kind of upturned Socialist Realism that did not enthuse audiences. One of the last such films was *Burnt in the Sun* of 1994, which showed a photogenic military family of the 1930s suffering under NKVD persecution; by this time it was not the film's theme, but its execution, that won audiences. Its director was Nikita Mikhailov, who at the 1986 Cinema Association upheaval had been barracked for his support of the existing administrators. He won an Oscar for this film, and in 1996 went on to take a guiding role in cinema through a new film foundation set up to organize and help finance the industry.

Despite *Little Vera*, the first film to have a nude scene, the most popular films were not those of the new Soviet wave (which were increasingly shown in the more specialized cinemas), but the old Hollywood films that were imported in large numbers. Even a best-forgotten Hollywood 'B' movie could fill cinemas with audiences intent on draining the cup of western culture down to its lowest sediment. But despite the enormous popularity of films like *Crocodile Dundee*, cinema audiences were falling. The most popular Soviet films in the Gorbachev period managed to reach audiences of rarely more than 10 million, compared to 100 million in the Brezhnev period, although this was partly explicable by the larger annual production of films (about 400, compared to 100–150 in the earlier period).

Gorbachev and the party

Like thousands of others, Gorbachev put his faith in the party that had made him. He realized that a reconstruction of the party was needed, to bring into key positions people who, like himself, believed that the leading role of the party should be used to correct the distortions of society and economy that that same party had created. With charm, patience, and ruthlessness he succeeded in steadily replacing conservatives in the party bureaucracy. But this progress was not fast enough, and finally, at the thirteenth hour, he accepted that the party could not, after all, be the instrument of *perestroika*.

In his first two years Gorbachev achieved a faster rate of personnel changes among influential officials than had been seen since the days of Stalin's purges. In the Politburo, Central Committee, and elsewhere, these changes were facilitated by the large number of geriatric leftovers inherited from the Brezhnev years; time-worn officials, who usually tended to be against change, could be retired with dignity. Tikhonov was replaced as prime minister by Ryzhkov, and Gromyko as foreign minister by Eduard Shevardnadze. Gromyko had been one of Gorbachev's supporters and he was kicked upstairs (a new direction of departure for sacked ministers) to become head of state. His successor, Shevardnadze, was a very capable man who been Georgia's interior minister and then party first secretary, and he had distinguished himself as the scourge of both the corrupt and the Georgian nationalists. A history graduate, he was a man whose thoughts moved in mysterious ways. In Georgia he had anticipated *perestroika* in several ways, founding a centre for public opinion and adopting a more flexible attitude in agriculture.

Two early departures from the Politburo were the chiefs of the Moscow and Leningrad party organizations, elderly men who had regarded themselves as the rightful heirs to Chernenko. The new party chief for Moscow was Boris Yeltsin, a combative *apparatchik* in his previous post as head of the Sverdlovsk party organization, but soon showing himself as an implacable enemy of the deep-seated corruption he found in Moscow. As a somewhat tempestuous and impulsive enemy of corruption and sloth he made many enemies, but Gorbachev initially made him welcome in the Politburo.

In the other centre of power, the secretariat of the party's Central Committee (some of whose members also had Politburo seats), nine of the twelve members were appointed by Gorbachev in his first two years. However, in the party apparatus as a whole the picture was patchy. Many party organizations, using familiar party methods, were able to keep reformers out. When the 27th Party Congress was called fifty weeks after Gorbachev's succession many party organizations contrived to send conservatively inclined representatives, even when local members would have preferred reformers. This was a disappointment for Gorbachev and his advisers, who had hoped to make this Congress a starting point for the transformation of the party and hence of the USSR. Nevertheless, the current was flowing in Gorbachev's favour, for at this Congress only 59 per cent of the existing Central Committee members were re-elected (for comparison, at the previous 1981 Congress about nine-tenths of the Central Committee had been re-elected). Although the new Central Committee members included some who could not be regarded as Gorbachev supporters, he was able to get some of his key advisers elected. Among them was Aleksandr Yakovlev, who was probably more enthusiastic than Gorbachev himself for *glasnost'* and was given responsibility in the secretariat for culture and propaganda.

The party congress was followed in April 1986 by the Chernobyl nuclear disaster which discredited the party, especially Shcherbitskii's Ukrainian communist party, and showed that *glasnost'* had still a long way to go. Meanwhile, conferences between Gorbachev and the US president, and a unilateral Soviet moratorium on nuclear tests (which brought no response from the west), showed that Gorbachev fully realized how damaging the east–west conflict had become, but it also aroused fears that he might 'sell out' to the west. Sakharov was released from internal exile in late 1986, one of several steps that emphasized that *glasnost'* was to be taken seriously. The jamming of the BBC (but not, at this point, of the more critical Radio Liberty or Radio Free

Europe) soon ceased, and in February 1987 a large batch of political prisoners was released. Border talks with China were reopened after a gap of nine years. It became easier for Russians to obtain visas for foreign travel. From time to time Moscow intervened to overturn outrageous acts by local party organizations. Such interventions often resulted in the release of wrongly arrested individuals who had in one way or another displeased local officials, and news of such events, no longer suppressed, was cumulative, encouraging more and more citizens to decide that they were no longer going to be pushed around. This change of atmosphere was echoed in the new edition of the *Great Soviet Encyclopedia*, which replaced a curt, dismissive entry for Khrushchev with a longer, complimentary piece.

However, these first two years were hardly a honeymoon for Gorbachev. Apart from covert resistance to his initiatives there was the occasional overt opposition. This took a dramatic form in Kazakhstan, where the party leader was embroiled in a web of corruption of which leading officials and their families took blatant advantage. When he was forcibly retired it was hard to find a suitable, untainted, Kazakh to succeed him and a Russian was appointed. This led to violent riots in the capital, Alma Ata, and although order was restored the outbreak showed how carefully reformers needed to tread, and how easy it was for the ill-intentioned to play the nationalist card.

A plenary meeting of the Central Committee was due in 1986, but was postponed until 1987 because of behind-the-scenes arguments about what should be done. At this plenum the final, decisive resolution was passed only because Gorbachev had suggested that if he could not do things his way then a new general secretary would have to be found. Many participants were firmly against Gorbachev's policies, but an even greater number, although worried, realized that Gorbachev might be their best hope for protection against something worse. Like Stalin, unintentionally, he was making himself indispensable by instigating crisis.

In his opening speech, in convoluted language that everyone understood, Gorbachev made clear his belief that the party had been twisted by Stalin and needed to be untwisted. He referred to the fossilizing of irrefutable so-called truths which, among other things, had condemned the cooperative movement, prevented individual initiative, and robbed money of its role in measuring true value. He blamed past central committees for this and went on to make his main, devastating proposal, which was no less than the democratization of the party. The party was no longer to put itself above the state. It had to end secrecy in nominations for posts, while introducing secrecy in voting on its decisions. It was to end its urge to dominate, to manage the smallest things, to give orders to every individual. Truly independent courts were needed, and the soviets were to be properly elected and take a more genuine role in government at all levels, while non-party individuals should have the right to hold important offices.

He also proposed to hold in 1988 a party conference (the first since 1941) to review how these decisions, as passed by the plenum resolution, had been put into practice. Despite their unpalatability, most of Gorbachev's proposals were included in the final resolution and a day later, in a move unprecedented in the USSR, Gorbachev's final address to the plenum was televised. This secured him popular support that counterbalanced the opposition still evident in the Central Committee.

Gorbachev's next major policy speech was in celebration of the seventieth anniversary of the Revolution, in November 1987. In the intervening period he worked on economic reforms directed at loosening old structures and permitting individuals greater freedom to become independent businessmen. In the summer, the independence movements in the Baltic republics, led by Lithuania, took advantage of the freedom to demonstrate by assembling crowds to listen to speeches and wave the hitherto banned national flags. An eccentric young German secured himself a niche in history by piloting his light plane across the frontier, over hundreds of miles of Soviet territory, to land triumphantly in Red Square. The failure of the armed forces to notice, let alone stop, this incursion brought them into disrepute and Gorbachev took advantage of the situation to dismiss the defence minister and to appoint a more congenial general, Yazov, in his place.

In his November speech Gorbachev went out of his way to praise Khrushchev, and condemned Stalin's crimes. He also announced an enquiry into the victims of Stalin's purges (Bukharin, Zinoviev, Kamenev, and other old Bolsheviks were rehabilitated in the following months). Another, completely revised, history of the communist party was to be undertaken, he said. This speech brought no joy to the hearts of those who still hankered for the good old days of the 1970s, but their opposition was not the only problem facing the new reformist leadership.

Boris Yeltsin, whose rough-and-ready approach endeared him to a large public, began to press publicly for faster reform, and in June 1988 his indiscretions led to exit from the Politburo and from the Moscow party leadership. Troubles were growing in the non-Russian republics, with unrest in the three Baltic republics, and inter-republican struggles in the Caucasus between Azerbaizhan and Armenia.

Among those most troubled by *glasnost'* and *perestroika* were the teachers, and it was appropriate that Nina Andreeva, whose lengthy, well-publicized letter appeared in the conservative newspaper *Sovietskaya Rossiya*, was a chemistry teacher. Published in March 1988, evidently with the connivance of high party officials including one or two in the Politburo, her piece portrayed Gorbachev's reforms and intentions as alarming and excessive.[3] Reflecting the

---

3. The letter as published was different from the letter as first written. Evidently there had been several hands at work.

misgivings of many, and not without a nostalgic glance at Stalin's time and a hint that Jews were not Russians, the text was reprinted in other newspapers, became a rallying point for the controversy currently taking place, and served to assure other doubters that they were not alone in their fears and resentments.

Inside the Politburo Ligachev, who was regarded as number two in the leadership and had been appointed not by Gorbachev but by Andropov, was the inspiration of this opposition, the expression of which was itself a fruit of *glasnost'*. But Gorbachev, by flexibility and comments of the *après moi, le déluge* type, continued on his way. The Politburo lost old and gained new, pro-Gorbachev, members; Aliyev had left in 1987 and Chebrikov and Shcherbitskii would go in 1989. Some of the members dropped from the Central Committee had previously held positions that Gorbachev had abolished; consistent with his intention of reducing the party's interventions, the departments of the Central Committee had been halved, with all the economic departments except agriculture being abolished. In September 1988 Ligachev himself was shunted to the agricultural department, ensuring a dim future both for himself and for agriculture. He held his place in the Politburo until summer 1990, by which time that body had lost most of its importance. In October 1988 the Supreme Soviet voted unanimously (and, likewise in the old style, without another candidate) to replace Gromyko as its chairman (and USSR president) with Gorbachev.

After the elections of spring 1989 Gorbachev was again elected president by the new parliament, known as the Congress of People's Deputies. This was part of the transformed state structure resulting from the Supreme Soviet's substantial 1988 amendment of the 'Brezhnev Constitution'. The parliament had 2,250 seats, and from its membership was elected the new 542-member Supreme Soviet which, unlike its predecessor, became the scene of lively, well-reported debate. The parliament itself would meet only about twice a year for short periods, but as a fifth of the Supreme Soviet membership was to be renewed each year it was by no means a rubber stamp.

For this first, 1989, election the parliament had three classes of seat. One-third was contested in ordinary constituencies, one-third in large so-called national territorial constituencies, and one-third was reserved for 'public organizations'. This latter category guaranteed an advantage for certain interests, notably the communist party, which had 100 of these reserved seats. The Central Committee duly nominated 100 public figures (including Gorbachev but not Yeltsin) who were thus spared the necessity of descending into undignified vote-winning.[4] The trade unions and cooperatives also had 100

4. Nominees for the reserved seats did have to secure positive votes from 50 per cent of the voters. Some unpopular officials failed to clear this hurdle and new elections, with new nominees, had to be called. In December 1989 it was decided that reserved seats would be eliminated for the next election due in 1994.

reserved seats each. In some public organizations, for example in the Academy of Sciences, fierce nomination struggles took place resulting, quite often, in 'old-guard' candidates falling victim to new reformist candidates. Among members elected by the Academy was Sakharov, most distinguished of the one-time dissidents.

Similar structures were created for republican and other local governments, although reserved seats were not provided in some of the republican elections that also took place in 1989–90. As for Yeltsin, he was elected to the USSR Congress of People's Deputies for the national territorial seat of Moscow city with the record-breaking support of 5 million voters, despite all the efforts made to discredit him.

More than four-fifths of the electorate turned out to vote in the USSR election. Almost nine-tenths of the resulting Congress of People's Deputies were party members, who both inside and outside the new parliament seemed so irrevocably divided between reformers and conservatives that a formal split would have been logical. However, Gorbachev did not encourage this; after all, he was the party's leader. There was therefore no dramatic split, but there were successive dramatic resignations by party reformers who declared that they could no longer remain in an organization so unwilling to correct its faults.

The parliamentary members tended to coalesce in blocs, which were alliances in support of particular philosophies. Soon after the Congress assembled, the *Soyuz* ('Union') bloc formed, devoted to preserving the status quo, while about 400 deputies formed themselves into the so-called Interregional bloc, of which Sakharov was a leading light until his death. This pressed for faster reform and was quick to publicize the arbitrary acts of repression that were still the stock-in-trade of old-type officials. Its supporters began to occupy key positions in the press and broadcasting; the media, too, tended to be divided into conservative and reformist camps, with television increasingly exploiting the new freedoms to expose the rottenness of the old ways and, increasingly, the failures of the new.

In 1989 more and more Soviet citizens lost faith in *perestroika*. Worsening shortages were obvious to all, *glasnost'* or no *glasnost'*, but it was media coverage that brought home the collapse of communist regimes in eastern Europe. This demonstration that communism was not, after all, permanent and irreplaceable gave extra inspiration to the growing number of politically active reformers who were beginning to realize that reform without communists was quite feasible. In other words, the neutralization of the party had become a recognized option. The loss of party authority and repute was demonstrated by a shrinking membership and, even more emphatically, by the millions of members who kept their party cards but failed to pay their subscriptions.[5]

5. Formally ending party membership could be an unpleasant business, requiring explanations before a party committee.

In February 1990 a march on the Kremlin, said to involve 200,000 protesters, demanded an end of the party's monopoly, and a party plenum agreed
that this would be a good idea. In March the Congress of People's Deputies,
after some argument, agreed with Gorbachev that a strong presidency was
needed. The constitution was accordingly amended to provide for a US-style
president, and a presidential council to advise him; the 'leading role' of the
party was at the same time deleted. Gorbachev relinquished his now superfluous presidency (chairmanship of the USSR Supreme Soviet) when the
Congress elected him as the new, executive president. It was agreed that
the next presidential election would be a general election.

The president could be impeached by a two-thirds vote of the Congress,
and his nominations for ministerial positions needed the approval of
the Supreme Soviet. So although Gorbachev could issue decrees he was not
all-powerful and, as time would show, not all his decrees would be obeyed
in the republics. But these changes effectively sidetracked the Politburo and
Central Committee, reflecting Gorbachev's intention of transferring power
away from the party to the soviets.

At the May Day parade in Moscow, a big day in the party's calendar, hostile
placards and jeering resulted in the party's general secretary, Gorbachev,
retreating in disgust. In July 1990 the party's 28th Congress assembled. It put
off the formulation of a new party programme, but Gorbachev made it plain
that he envisaged a tolerant, humane, and socialist party that somehow would
stay with 'democratic centralism' yet maintain total freedom of debate.
The Congress adopted new rules that allowed different 'platforms', if not
'factions', and provided for more information to be passed to lower party
organizations and members.

While the new freedom for public organizations resulted in countless clubs
and forums being established to pursue not only hobbies but also political and
philosophical debate, and while new publications appeared, fell, or flourished,
powerful political parties did not appear. Often it was hard to distinguish
between a movement and a party, although in general it could be said that a
movement was larger and might give its support to several parties that it
found congenial. One important movement was *Pamyatnik* ('Memorial'),
which began by urging the construction of appropriate memorials for the
victims of Stalinism but naturally became a movement for defence against
Stalinism. *Pamyat'* ('Memory') had a similar name but was very different. It
was a strong Russian national movement whose members felt that there was
such a thing as a Russian tradition and that it needed to be defended. But it
had an extremist wing devoted to the pursuit of Jews and other real or
imagined enemies of Russianism. By 1991 members of Pamyat' were
distributing leaflets in which the real name of the Soviet prime minister,
Pavlov, was said to be Goldberg, and that of the Leningrad mayor, Sobchak,
to be Finkelstein. On the whole, Pamyat' would have found Nicholas I's

philosophy of 'Orthodoxy, Autocracy, Nationality' quite congenial. Soyuz remained active in the Supreme Soviet and opposed most of Gorbachev's changes. There were hundreds of small parties, some consisting of just one individual. Among them were the Russian Nationalist Monarchist Party, one of whose aims was the canonization of Nicholas II, and the group calling itself the movement of 'Unity for Leninism and Communist Ideals', of which the leading light was Nina Andreeva. This wanted to put Gorbachev on trial, and to make Kaganovich its honorary president.

In the RSFSR (Russian Republic) parliament conservatives were fewer, and the 'Democratic Russia' movement became a powerful group uniting radicals of various persuasions. Yeltsin, who by this time was offering what could be seen as an alternative to Gorbachev's *perestroika* (sovereignty for the republics, establishment of a free market, a directly elected presidency) soon became the inspiration of this movement, which scored a great electoral success in the municipal elections of March 1990. In these elections the official party organizations did particularly badly in Moscow, Leningrad, and Kiev. The 'Democratic Russia' movement's Sobchak was elected mayor of Leningrad, Popov mayor of Moscow, and Yeltsin won a seat in the Russian parliament.

That summer Yeltsin, by then openly opposed by Gorbachev, succeeded in assembling a majority in the RSFSR parliament to elect him president of its presidium. Strengthened by this status, and by the provocative if ineffective declaration of independence by Lithuania, he succeeded in getting his parliament to declare Russian sovereignty. What precisely sovereignty meant was not clear, but it was plainly stated that Russia would have complete authority in all matters except those which it chose to entrust to the USSR. Other republics also made similar declarations and it was evident that the central, USSR, government was losing authority. In the following months a 'war of laws' took place, as republics insisted that republican laws took precedence over USSR laws.

The end of *perestroika*

Communist power was collapsing in 1989 in the people's democracies of eastern and central Europe. For the USSR itself the collapse was yet to come, but the economy and its managers were failing to respond to treatment and the Union was threatened with break-up. Yeltsin, whose supporters were demanding more radical policies, with great publicity had resigned from the party during its 28th Congress. Taken together, these circumstances represented a definite radical swing, which soon produced a reaction. From the autumn of 1990 Gorbachev seemed to ally himself with the more conservative elements, several of whom he had himself appointed to key posts. His inner contradiction was that to preserve the Soviet Union and a united party he needed to reverse his cherished democratic process.

Signs of this change included Gorbachev's rejection of Shatalin's 500-day plan for a shift to the open market, which he had earlier favoured and which had been approved by Yeltsin's Russian Republic. It was not long before the fairly relaxed Bakatin was replaced as interior minister by the harder Pugo, a Latvian with his roots in the KGB. Shevardnadze, alarmed at the trend, resigned his office and publicly stated that he was doing so because he feared the development of a dictatorship. In January 1991 the Soviet army and KGB took various actions against the independence movements in Latvia and Lithuania, with some deaths resulting, and with some newspapers condemning Gorbachev for this return to the old violent ways. In the same month the prime minister Ryzhkov, who had been ill, was replaced by Valentin Pavlov who, like his predecessor, was an economic administrator, but lacked distinction. A new, considerably less tolerant, head of Gostelradio was appointed, although Gorbachev did not carry out his threat to repeal the laws on press freedom. The institution of joint army/police patrols in the cities aroused mixed feelings; they may have been necessary where crime was large-scale and violent, but they were thought to symbolize a reversion to coercive practices. The grant of automatic rights to the KGB and police to enter premises where economic crimes were suspected was another measure that had sinister overtones, but in early 1991 Gorbachev annulled this measure.

Among Pavlov's initiatives was a much-resented sales tax, and a sudden calling-in of all high-denomination (50- and 100-rouble) banknotes that caused immense inconvenience (reimbursement was promised only to those who could show that their wealth had been honestly obtained, and even then they could claim back only a small amount each month). The ostensible intention behind this return to arbitrary measures was to relieve speculators and other get-rich-quick citizens of their ill-gotten gains. In reality, it was ordinary citizens and not the sharp operators who stored their wealth in banknotes. On later occasions, Pavlov tried to explain himself with reference to western plots to ruin the economy by buying up roubles at low rates of exchange, then creating inflation by injecting billions of roubles into the USSR. Evidently scorning *glasnost'*, he never produced convincing evidence of this gigantic conspiracy.

Faced with what seemed a bit-by-bit return to authoritarianism, most reformers turned to Yeltsin for leadership. Meanwhile, Gorbachev, in an effort to stabilize the Union, held a nationwide referendum in which voters were asked whether they supported the continuation of the USSR as a union of sovereign republics. The question was a classic misuse of the referendum technique, asking several questions but requiring a single yes or no answer: 'Do you think it necessary to preserve the Union of Soviet Socialist Republics as a renovated federation of equal sovereign republics in which human rights and freedom for every nationality will be guaranteed?' Three-quarters of that four-fifths of the electorate which voted agreed with the proposition, although in Leningrad and Moscow there were only bare majorities.

It was possible for republics, or districts, to append their own questions to the main referendum. Yeltsin ensured that there would be a supplementary question for voters in the Russian Republic. This asked whether the RSFSR should have an elected president. Voters agreed to this proposal, and to the distaste of Gorbachev (who had been elected to the presidency of the USSR only by a vote of its parliament) a direct republic-wide presidential election was scheduled in Russia for June. Meanwhile, in Leningrad, 55 per cent of the voters surprised commentators by approving a reversion to the old name of St Petersburg (they were not given the choice of Petrograd); the communist party described this change as, in effect, a German victory.

At this period the hostility between Yeltsin and Gorbachev became more open. An attempt by conservative communists to impeach Yeltsin in the Russian parliament failed. Yeltsin, finally granted a television interview, called for Gorbachev's resignation. In Moscow a rally in favour of Yeltsin attracted thousands of supporters.

Meanwhile, Yeltsin was backing one of the most threatening strikes called in this period. Not for the first time during *perestroika*, the miners quit work. This time it was the Siberian miners, who in addition to their economic demands called for Gorbachev's resignation. For a country so dependent on coal this long strike was crippling. Finally Yeltsin stepped in to what was formally a USSR problem and negotiated a settlement that did not include Gorbachev's resignation but promised the transfer of the mines from the jurisdiction of the USSR to the respective republics.

The April '9 + 1' agreement was also largely engineered by Yeltsin. It was an understanding between the USSR (the '1') and nine of the republics. Gorbachev succeeded in including a passage on the need for work discipline and for limitation of strikes but on the other hand conceded, at least by implication, that the Baltic and Caucasian republics could secede. The transfer of much industrial and economic management to the other republics, and the fixing of 1992 for a new constitution and new free elections, were other features. At about the same time Yeltsin secured the right for a Russian Republic television service and for a substantially independent Russian Republic KGB.

The freer atmosphere had encouraged many strikes throughout the USSR. usually in support of wage claims or better conditions. In 1989 there had been a strike by the Donbas miners, once regarded as a Bolshevik stronghold. In April 1991 the workers of Byelorussia, hitherto one of the most tranquil republics, came out on strike, and also in that month the new Independent Federation of Trade Unions called a one-hour strike involving millions (50 million, it was said) of workers protesting against price rises. By this time, demands for an end to party organizations within workshops had also begun to figure in the workers' demands. One of the showpieces of Soviet industrialization, the Uralmash engineering works with its 32,000 workers, voted overwhelmingly for an end to party organizations within the plant.

In June came the municipal and presidential election in the RSFSR. For the Russian presidency, Yeltsin was the favourite, and his chosen running mate for vice-president, the fighter pilot and Afghanistan veteran Aleksandr Rutskoi, was also popular. The party organizations, anxious above all to defeat Yeltsin, mostly favoured Ryzhkov. There were four other candidates, and Yeltsin's margin might have been smaller if the election had been held less hurriedly; he had already built up his popularity but the other candidates had insufficient time to present their cases. Ryzhkov would have done better if there had been fewer candidates. As it was, he came second with 17 per cent of the votes cast. Yeltsin won 57 per cent and the third-placed received 8 per cent.

The latter was Zhirinovskii, who styled himself as a liberal democrat but advocated views not far removed from those of the right-wing nationalists of the tsarist Fourth Duma. His support may well have grown in the later months of 1991 as he learned from experience the potential of populism; already in August he was suggesting it was time to return Finland to the Russian fold. He was adept at answering simplistic criticism with simplistic retorts:

Interviewer: 'Don't you think it's terrible for you to draw parallels between yourself and Hitler?'
Zhirinovskii: 'But I'm not making any parallels. Adolf was an uneducated corporal, whereas I'm a graduate of two higher institutes and know four languages.'[6]

Yeltsin was sworn in as RSFSR president in the presence of USSR president Gorbachev and the Moscow patriarch Aleksii II. His seat was not to be in the White House, the new Russian government building on the banks of the Moscow River, but in the Kremlin itself.

One of Yeltsin's first moves after the election was to issue a decree banning the activity of all political parties and organizations from factories and institutions. Potentially this could have affected trade unions but in fact was aimed, and seen to be aimed, directly at the communist party in the RSFSR. It was a devastating blow to the party organization in Russia, striking at the base of its pyramid.

Gorbachev at this time was moving away from conservatism back to policies more palatable to the democrats. In March he had given a sign that he was ready to shift his ground, when he made a speech attacking 'dogmatic conservative forces supporting socialism without democracy', and by the summer he was clearly trying once again to put some vigour into *perestroika*. However, life had moved on and many of his old supporters were now

6. From an interview (*Gudok*, 4 Sept. 1991, 1) in which he recommended sending half a million troops into East Germany to restore the status quo.

determined to end the party's power, whereas Gorbachev still preserved his hope that the party would eventually become a vanguard of reform. Yakovlev, his old adviser, was summoned to defend himself before the party's higher officials after he had joined with Shevardnadze in July to publish the manifesto of the new 'Movement for Democratic Reform'. Instead of waiting for expulsion, Yakovlev resigned from the party, a move that was more devastating than Yeltsin's earlier resignation because Yakovlev's membership had persuaded many that the party was not beyond redemption.

To varying degrees other republics were asserting their independence and a break-up of the USSR seemed closer. Quite apart from the political and psychological effects of this, there was a clear threat to the economy, which for a century had been based on a specialized division of labour between the various parts of the Empire. To avoid a catastrophic collapse and in the hope of stabilizing the situation, in July Gorbachev, building on the '9 + 1' agreement, succeeded in drawing up a Union Treaty. With the Baltic and the southern republics intent on going their own way, the nine other republics appeared willing to sign this, which gave them much greater power over their economic and financial affairs.

For many, however, this greater autonomy for the republics was a sure sign that the USSR was on the verge of collapse. For some of Gorbachev's colleagues this was a last straw, added to the current disintegration of the economy, of the party, of the world as they had known it. Desperately trying to avert what they believed to be a catastrophe, some of them had tried by the political means available to them to change things in April, when there had been a move to oust Gorbachev at the party plenum, and in June, when an unsuccessful attempt was made to persuade the Supreme Soviet to transfer some of Gorbachev's powers to Pavlov. Gorbachev had skilfully defeated these moves, but his weakness was demonstrated by Pavlov's remaining in office.

In the days preceding the August crisis Gorbachev went to London to confer with western leaders about possible economic aid, then returned to a meeting of the Central Committee in which, although he had his back to the wall, he did not hesitate to suggest a new party programme that talked of a 'humane' socialism rather than Marxism-Leninism. Then he went with his family to his Crimean dacha to take a short holiday before returning to Moscow to sign the Union Treaty.

The handful of men who had decided to take unconstitutional action were very mixed, and the description of them as 'hardliners' was not helpful. Some had more misgivings than others, but persuaded themselves that in his heart of hearts Gorbachev felt the same as they did. He was invited either to sign a state of emergency or to transfer his powers to the USSR vice-president, and when he refused he was isolated in his dacha. The country was informed that he was ill and that an emergency committee (formed of the leading conspirators) was temporarily to take the helm.

In Moscow and Leningrad the plotters had made some half-hearted preparations, but elsewhere they relied on the army and KGB obeying their orders. In Moscow they failed to arrest key figures who might have been expected to oppose them. These included Shevardnadze, Sobchak, Yakovlev, and, most important, Yeltsin. Sobchak rushed back to Leningrad where by sheer force of word and intellect he frustrated officers and officials who were preparing to support the coup. The other leaders made their way to the White House, where hundreds of other citizens joined them in a courageous show of defiance. Here, too, were the deputies of the Russian parliament, popularly elected just like Yeltsin and therefore with a better claim to legitimacy than the 'emergency committee'. The White House remained in communication with the outside world; in fact both the US president and British prime minister telephoned Yeltsin to convey their best wishes at this critical time.

Inside the USSR, Zhirinovskii and Alksnis (a prominent member of the Soyuz movement) supported the coup in radio and television interviews, while in the Russian Republic two-thirds of the communist party organizations willingly acquiesced and the remainder adopted a wait-and-see stance. As for ordinary people, they seemed to have no strong feelings. Television interviews in which the cameras for long periods were focused on the conspirators' nervous, fidgety, hands did not inspire respect. The emergency committee's instruction to live and work normally was unexceptional, but did not prevent pro-democracy demonstrations. What was significant, and seems to have surprised the plotters, was that not only the Red Army but also the KGB had doubts about the proceedings. When troops were ordered into Moscow to 'preserve order' they obeyed halfheartedly, and some men even took a handful of tanks to defend the White House, where they had a psychological effect out of all proportion to their numbers. There were enough disobedient members of a specialized KGB unit to prevent it accepting the instruction to fight its way into the White House. Having had several years of increasing freedom, having for the most part voted for Yeltsin as their president, having, in short, realized that people no longer had to be pushed around, the men in uniform showed that Gorbachev's *glasnost'* was not just a passing fashion.

However, Yeltsin's call for a general strike was only a partial success, with many workers ignoring it. The Ukrainian communist leader Kravchuk was among those urging workers to stay on the job.

In the end the plot failed, its sponsors for the most part lacking the ruthlessness that might, just might, have overcome the reluctance of soldiers and police to obey orders. On the fourth day some of the conspirators, having decided to plead with Gorbachev, took off for the Crimea, hotly pursued by another jet airliner containing an armed party sent by Yeltsin's Russian government. In the end the main plotters were arrested. The interior minister Pugo and his wife gave much-needed dignity to the conspiracy by committing suicide, and the KGB head Kryuchkov, defence minister Yazov, prime minister

Pavlov, the vice-president, and several others were arrested on charges of treason.

Yeltsin, who had led the continuous defiance outside the White House, and whose supporters managed to print and distribute news-sheets as well as run an anti-coup radio station, was rightly regarded as the hero of the hour. In his public statements he had been careful to centre his demands on the restoration of Gorbachev's presidential powers, but in reality those few days had elevated Yeltsin's stature and done nothing to enhance Gorbachev's. In popular perception, Gorbachev had been betrayed by men he had himself appointed and had been rescued by his political opponent.

In the next few days Yeltsin plainly exceeded his formal powers. Some of the instructions he had issued during the height of the crisis, when, in a sense, he was acting on behalf of the USSR as well as of the Russian Republic, were confirmed; the dismissal of the head of Gostelradio had been an example of Yeltsin's encroachments and was not going to be undone. Although Yeltsin may not have approved the so-called witch-hunts in the party and government organizations, designed to sniff out and dismiss those who had actively or passively sympathized with the coup, much of his behaviour at this time was decidedly illiberal. But this could be explained by his belief that it would have been inexcusable to lose the opportunity of crushing that many-headed hydra, the party, once and for all.

He temporarily suspended the activities of the communist party in the Russian Republic, and some newspapers were banned until they had proved that they intended to mend their ways. Soon Yeltsin also banned party activity in military, KGB, and Tass news-agency units stationed in his republic. The party headquarters buildings in Moscow and Leningrad were sealed. This prevented entry to these buildings by party workers, who had already begun to destroy incriminating party documents. A close study began of surviving documents, special interest being shown in those detailing financial transactions. Efforts of the party to secrete part of its immense wealth into foreign banks were studied, and several of the party's financial administrators died, apparently by suicide, in this period. Among other suicides was that of the former Red Army chief of staff Akhromeev, who apparently had taken no part in the unsuccessful coup but left a note which, in effect, was an explanation for both his own and others' suicides at this time: everything to which he had dedicated his life was being destroyed. At his funeral, relatives accused 'liberal fascists' of hounding him to death. He was buried in full uniform, and shortly afterwards nocturnal operators exhumed him in order to steal it.

The August events meant the end of *perestroika*. Gorbachev himself finally acknowledged that it would not be the party that would carry out the changes. He resigned as general secretary, nationalized party property (an enormous but still-to-be-counted collection of assets), called for the dissolution of the Central Committee, and banned party activity in the Soviet forces, KGB, and police. Meanwhile the USSR Supreme Soviet suspended party activity in the USSR. It also signalled the end of the old USSR by proposing a new, looser union of sovereign states.

The remainder of 1991 was largely spent, or wasted, in coming to terms with the new situation. Transfer of power from Gorbachev's USSR to the republics was remorseless, with Yeltsin setting the pace and Gorbachev fighting a rearguard action to preserve the union. At the end of 1991, with the republics collecting and keeping the taxes and with the Ukraine voting for independence, it became clear that the USSR had run its unique course:

Nobody is in any doubt that the state known for decades as the Union of Soviet Socialist Republics has died and will be impossible to resuscitate, although the official funeral – putting an end to the validity of the present USSR Constitution – is yet to come. The problem which most worries us all now is, what kind of state are we going to live in?[7]

As for the communist party, it was returning to its roots almost literally, being driven to a near-underground existence. Its remnants had split, but each was trying to reorganize. In September 1991 the 'Democratic Party of the Communists of Russia' held its founding conference, and in November the 'Lenin Socialist Party of the Working Class' organized itself at a conference in Siberia. Just as some conservative groups seemed to be resembling more and more the right-wing nationalists of the time of Nicholas II, so did the marxists seem to be reverting to the small, barely tolerated, and divided movement of late tsarist times. Some of them were beginning to interpret the Gorbachev revolution as the bourgeois revolution prescribed by Marx but 'delayed' by the Bolsheviks.

The economy

The decline of Gorbachev's reputation after 1988 was largely due to his inability to improve the economic situation, as seen by the woman in the street. The growing queues and scarcities were just one sign of an economic deterioration that could be traced back to the policies of previous decades, aggravated by new policies that crippled old managerial methods without providing an effective replacement.

The miserable inheritance from previous years was reflected, indeed symbolized, by a series of disasters that punctuated the Gorbachev years. The main reason for this catastrophic spate was the toleration of unsafe practices in the quest for ever-higher production figures; the toxic air breathed by a third of Soviet city-dwellers was itself visible testimony of decades of neglect.

The disaster at the Chernobyl nuclear power station, near Kiev, in spring 1986, was a test of Gorbachev's leadership, a warning of international

7. *Za rubezhom*, 22 Nov. 1991, 1. This is an example of numerous editorials of the time, all saying very much the same thing.

significance, and above all an implied condemnation of the Soviet way of doing things. One of the plant's four reactors suffered a catastrophic explosion followed by a fire lasting, in its critical phase, two weeks, during which considerable radioactive material was released into the atmosphere. The initial hours were marked by a characteristic Russian blend of heroism, improvisation, and muddle. Also characteristic was the reluctance to report bad news; local officials tried hard to conceal the scale of the accident but, out of tune with the times, seemed unaware that one kind of bad news is carried by the wind. Despite *glasnost'*, that part of the Soviet public which did not listen to foreign radio was not promptly informed, nor were proper precautions taken to protect the population from fallout. Indeed, the party organization in Kiev decided to continue with the May Day celebrations so as to emphasize that there was nothing to worry about; this, however, did not prevent some party officials, and others in the know, dispatching their children to more salubrious regions. Parts of the Ukraine, Byelorussia, and the Baltic republics were contaminated to varying degrees, as well as Poland and, less severely, other parts of Europe. In a striking demonstration of professional solidarity transcending ideological frontiers, both Soviet and western government scientists for years afterwards minimized the number of deaths that could be attributed to this accident. Years later, large populations were still living in areas of dangerously high contamination.

The accident occurred in a non-Russian part of the Union and its fall-out affected other non-Russian parts. The communist party, since it claimed credit for all technical successes, could logically be blamed for the failures too. Thus Chernobyl was a blow to the concepts of the leading role of the communist party and of a high-technology future.

A horrifying death toll resulted when a Soviet liner collided with a tanker in the Black Sea. Russia's worst railway accident was a consequence of negligent workmanship, negligent maintenance, and unheeded warnings. It occurred when gas from a leaking trunk pipeline accumulated around a railway line and was ignited by two passing passenger trains; hundreds of passengers were incinerated. Even natural disasters could show up the weaknesses of Soviet society. A high-scale earthquake in Armenia was made all the more lethal by the readiness with which poorly constructed buildings collapsed.

These disasters were only the worst of scores of fatal occurrences in which negligence, incompetence, and often drunkenness were involved. Human and material shoddiness was commonplace. So much so, that when a New Zealand government investigation into the sinking of a Soviet cruise liner blamed New Zealand officials and praised the crew, its report was received with some incredulity in the USSR.

Empty stores and numerous accidents were symptoms of more fundamental ills. Although statistics showed continuing, though declining, economic growth up to the end of the 1980s, the real rate of growth (subtracting such items as environmental protection that should have been provided but was not, new equipment that was needed but not supplied, and so on) was probably zero before *perestroika* began. In 1990 industrial production was already falling, although this was partly accounted for by a drastic drop in defence output, which may have declined by a quarter.

Foodstuffs became scarcer even though harvests in 1989 and 1990 were good.[8] Many local authorities introduced rationing schemes in 1990 and 1991. These were of varying types, many of them being designed not to allocate supplies evenly but to prevent certain people getting anything, the target being outsiders (often a euphemism for village-dwellers) who were alleged to visit localities (often a euphemism for cities) to buy available commodities. Because rationing was locally devised, there was no guarantee that coupons would be honoured. In late 1991 St Petersburg, sausage coupons were being exchanged for butter, sugar could be obtained with flour coupons, and there were innumerable other absurdities and paradoxes:

Staff at the corrective labour colony put forward their own equally strong claims and convincingly showed the commission that they eat worse than their prisoners. In particular, the monthly prisoner's ration in this specialized colony is 4.5 kg of meat, 1.2 kg of butter and 300 g of margarine. The colony staff get ration coupons for 1 kg of meat, 250 g of butter and 100 g of margarine.[9]

Shortage, as always, meant leverage. Those who controlled supply could control much else besides. But this power could sometimes be used positively. In Vorkuta, where work accidents were frequent, the town soviet in late 1991 was offering a kilo (2.2 lb) of meat to blood donors, and those lucky enough to belong to a rare blood group received 100 g (3.5 oz) of chocolate in addition.

For years people had been accumulating savings simply because there was so little to buy. This meant there was an enormous purchasing power at large in the economy that could keep the shops empty even if more goods were produced. This purchasing 'overhang' compromised any plan for economic reform; it provided one of the motives for Pavlov's 1991 calling-in of high-denomination banknotes. Inflation, which in 1991 was bordering on hyper-inflation, and which was a well-tried capitalist instrument of expropriation, could be expected to moderate, if not eliminate, this problem.

A growing proportion of industrial and agricultural output never reached the market. It was used, instead, for barter, with a given factory undertaking to supply its products in exchange for products from another enterprise.

---

8. Grain production (million tons)

| 1985 | 178 | 1987 | 194 | 1989 | 197 |
| 1986 | 194 | 1988 | 180 | 1990 | 218 |

9. *Gudok*, 5 Nov. 1991, 1. This labour camp, near Chita, was for infirm prisoners. Other camps were not fed so well.

As we entered the Moven factory in the suburbs of Moscow the unmistakable smell of fresh-smoked fish filled our nostrils. The trouble was, this wasn't a fish factory. It produces industrial ventilators. Alexander Mironov, president of the company, explained; he had taken delivery that morning of a couple of hundred cases of fish from the Baltic in part payment for ventilators supplied. The fish was sold at cost to the Moven's 490 workers who therefore won't have to join the Soviet Union's omnipresent queues which, according to estimates, waste 86 billion man hours a year.[10]

Individual republics, too, made barter agreements between themselves, and took measures to prevent other scarce products being exported across their borders. With the breakdown of the centralized administration, and with its replacement, the free market, slow to appear, this reversion to primitive modes of trade was unsurprising and indeed necessary at times. An unknown but growing proportion of output was stolen, although this eventually found its way through the black market into consumption. At the local level, environmental movements occasionally forced particularly obnoxious factories to close. In 1990, this resulted in an aspirin famine.

More strikes, ever-decreasing incentives to work hard, and supply problems meant that some vital products became rare. The spare-part problem had long plagued Soviet industry, and now became more acute. The old planning system in many cases had concentrated production of certain items on one factory, so interruption of production in one plant might have an enormous impact. The most obvious case of this phenomenon was when the factory making cigarette filters faltered, resulting in a prolonged cigarette shortage throughout the USSR.

A communist party plenum in 1985 had accepted the need for economic reform, and in the next six years a whole series of measures was passed, and even more discussed, but somehow things did not get better. The planned economy, with central institutions like Gosplan and the industrial ministries in Moscow making decisions and controlling activity, was plainly on the way out, but the free-market system which was to follow it was not clearly visualized. Few had experience of the free, or market, economy and indeed there were some doubts about whether Russians as a whole were psychologically prepared for it. Ideally the free economy should have been given decades to root itself, but this seemed impossible.

In the first years of *perestroika* the aim was a 'socialist market economy' in which central planning would be retained for the big matters like choice of investment but the 'market' (that is, prices) would regulate day-to-day production decisions. But by 1990 there was a growing belief that central planning and direction (that is, the planned economy) needed to be excluded from the big decisions as well. There were varying opinions about the degree of economic freedom and an increasing number of politically active people advocated the complete deregulation which, they imagined, enhanced the economies of such countries as the USA and Britain. In the USSR there were very few people who understood how modern capitalism actually worked. The avidity with which the free-market ideology was grasped recalled Marx's cynical comment about the enthusiasm of Russian intellectuals for any new system of ideas, provided only that it originated in the west.

There was a burst of reform measures in 1987, not all of which were put into force. The most important was the Law on State Enterprises. This gave enterprises independence in their decision-making and financial responsibility. But managers, who could now be elected by their workers, still knew that if their costs exceeded their revenues they could ask for a subsidy (and in 1988 24,000 of the 46,000 state enterprises did make a loss). Moreover, as supplies were increasingly scarce managers preferred the old system of centrally allocated materials rather than the new system in which they were expected to seek out and bargain with suppliers. On the whole, this law weakened the old 'administrative-command' system while not really encouraging the emergence of an effective market to replace it.

A price reform, aimed at securing the novel (for the USSR) advantage of prices actually informing buyers and sellers how valuable (in terms of production cost and scarcity) a product really was, had to be postponed when it was realized that freeing prices would inevitably result in a sudden and enormous price rise, something that Gorbachev was very unwilling to accept for political and social reasons. But enterprises did gain some freedom in price-setting and by calling their products new, or redesigned, or improved, they were able to ask considerably higher prices for what were virtually the same items; in this respect, at least, they showed they were quite ready for the western-style economic system.

In 1988, direct planning of output was in a formal sense abandoned. But central planners gave enterprises 'state orders' instead. These obliged them to deliver certain amounts of specified products (usually a high proportion of their total output), and materials for these were allocated from the centre as before. As time passed, however, enterprises showed decreasing enthusiasm for fulfilling state orders; sometimes they could get better prices by disposing of their products elsewhere, sometimes their own republican governments issued orders conflicting with those of the centre.

The 1988 Law on Cooperatives (tightened up later) should have been a decisive step forward in loosening the economy, given the popularity of cooperatives in pre-Stalin times. It enabled the enterprising to set up as manufacturers or business people, actually employing others. Many badly needed products or services were thereby provided, often quite efficiently. But there were problems. Cooperatives usually depended on the goodwill of local authorities and where this was lacking they were soon in trouble; in one case a thriving new enterprise producing hothouse tomatoes was ruined when the power supply was cut off for a few hours in the winter. Some local authorities took 90 per cent of a cooperative's profits as tax. Successful cooperatives could offer higher pay and thus attract workers from state industries and this caused resentment, one of many examples of how general enthusiasm for a freeing of the economy could coexist with horror at its manifestations.

The cooperatives also suffered from growing public distrust, as they helped to establish successful entrepreneurs whose wealth was hard to accept for an increasingly deprived public, culturally opposed to inequality in any case. What made things worse was that a new breed of entrepreneurs was appearing with apparently easy access to capital, and it was soon realized that many members of the communist party apparatus, seeing the writing on the wall, were making use of their existing power to entrench themselves as a new entrepreneurial class. In many cases it was suspected, rightly as it turned out, that these officials were obtaining capital by the fraudulent conversion of party or state assets. The term 'Mafia' was soon in general circulation to describe the invisible yet obvious underworld that sought to control newly emerging enterprise. Some of the shaky banks that appeared after the 1988 Law on Bank Specialization had dubious, if not illegal, foundations.

New freedoms were extended to agriculture, and thousands of 'family farms' were established, although the new independent peasants depended very much on goodwill from the local collective farm administration. While lease of land by families was permitted, actual transfer of land ownership was a very emotional issue and Gorbachev was one of the many who could not face this departure from the morality on which they had been brought up. Land could be granted in perpetuity to families but they could not sell it or employ non-family workers on it. Gorbachev did eventually relent to the extent of suggesting that referendums on the issue might be staged by the different republics. In industry, too, leasing was quite popular, and in due course workers who had leased their state enterprise were allowed to buy it, with a promise that there would be no expropriation later.

Financing by share issue became legal and so, therefore, did trading in shares. Exchanges for commodity trading appeared. Despite some scandals, and the hostility aroused by so-called non-producers making good money, they provided a useful service and were a step towards the market economy.

From 1989 there was a succession of proposals for more radical changes, and in summer 1990 these debates resulted in two major plans for the transition to a market economy. The Ryzhkov and Shatalin plans had similar goals, but the latter envisaged a shorter (500-day) time-scale, and more devolution of decision-making to republican governments (for example, unlike the Ryzhkov, or government, plan, it envisaged the replacement of Gosbank, the central bank, by a federal reserve system after the American model). Both plans aimed at privatization, and normal economic relations with the outside world (and hence a rouble freely convertible to other currencies). Both had difficulty in finding a non-explosive way to free prices. Even though index-ation of wages and pensions was seen as a way to soften the impact, neither pretended that there could be full indexation.

Gorbachev for the USSR and Yeltsin for the Russian Republic announced that they favoured the Shatalin plan, but the Supreme Soviet would not make a choice and gave Gorbachev the right to decide, by decree. At first a combin-ation of the two plans seemed likely, but by the end of 1990 it seemed that Gorbachev had lost his enthusiasm.

Essentially, nothing was then done for a year, during which the economy continued on its downward course. Inflation was accelerating fast. The budget deficit grew despite the introduction of a progressive income tax in 1990 with a rate of 50 per cent for the higher incomes. Thanks to relaxed controls, including the new right of industries to handle their own foreign-currency transactions, to increased imports, and to falling oil output and oil prices, hard currency reserves disappeared and the USSR was unable to pay its for-eign debts. Finally, as the USSR was breaking up, Yeltsin announced a rapid jump to the market economy for the Russian Republic. Prices were to be freed, and privatization pushed forward with retail stores, among other assets, being offered for sale.

Money and credits, once so freely available for projects approved by the party, became scarce. The party had never overcome its fondness for lavish, premature expenditure on projects that took years to build, and in 1991 funds for completing these disappeared. To soften what seemed likely to be a very difficult winter, western help in the form of grain and financial credits was sought and to some extent obtained. However, the steady transfer of powers from the centre to the republics meant that in 1991 western governments, like western companies, had difficulty in knowing which governments and institu-tions had the authority to make agreements. Equally important was the reluctance of western governments to find the necessary money, even though they were aware that failure to help the former Soviet people might open the way for extremist political movements. The Soviet economy had come to depend on democratic western governments with their 'too little, too late' approach, a far cry from communist planning with its penchant for 'too much, too soon'.

In December 1991 Yeltsin announced that as soon as the Russian Republic became fully independent in January, prices would be freed. The neighbour-ing governments of Ukraine and Byelorussia protested against this unilateral decision, fearing that their own scarce goods, still at the low prices, would drain into Russia. In the end, these two governments had to follow the Russian example, protesting that price deregulation before privatization was absurd.

Society

One of the new freedoms brought by *glasnost'* was the freedom to conduct and publish polls. At first they were amateurish, typically involving telephone calls that might be randomly chosen but inevitably recorded the opinions of that small sector that possessed telephones. But by the late 1980s techniques had improved.

Unsurprisingly, polls confirmed that the main care of people was not political freedom, or democracy, or economic reform, but how to obtain the necessities of life.[11] Shortages and poor services dominated lives and therefore thoughts. Of the non-material issues, lack of social justice, caused by string-pulling and influence, consistently ranked high. After 1987 most people believed that they had not benefited from *perestroika*, and by 1990 a majority thought it had worsened their standard of life, as reflected by the perceived gap between their incomes and rising price levels. Gorbachev's personal popularity fell in parallel; from October 1989 to June 1991 the number who fully trusted him fell from 52 to 10 per cent. Blame for the disappointments of *perestroika* was equally levelled at governmental indecisiveness and the machinations of the old *apparatchiki*.

Shortages and increasing crime meant that people were justified in saying, as they frequently did, that things were better in Brezhnev's time. The new political freedoms and the widened range of permissible activities were undervalued partly because most people did not have the leisure to enjoy them and partly because their advent was patchy. As always, local officials and organizations could find ways of blocking change. But, in course of time, *glasnost'* ensured that many injustices were publicized and put right, and this encouraged others to defy overbearing bureaucrats. That defiance became an alternative to servility was an enormous step forward, but not everybody could appreciate this.

The disappearance of the old prohibitions against forming independent organizations gave birth not only to political parties but to interest groups of all kinds. Boy Scout troops began to compete for members with the Young Pioneers. Railway enthusiasts formed a society, and so did the surviving veterans of the atomic bomb tests of the 1950s, able to organize in pursuit of redress for the damage they had suffered when, as soldiers, they were marched into the detonation zone. Long-persecuted religious groups found relief both in the freedom to organize and in the new official tolerance. The Old Believers once more began to needle the official Church, and in 1991 even the Doukhobors resurfaced for a conference.

---

11. The verb 'to obtain', rather than 'to buy', had long been preferred by Soviet citizens, a semantic shift that perfectly fitted an economy structured on shortage.

Under Gorbachev the Russian Orthodox Church recovered from the shattering experience of Khrushchev's anti-religious campaign and began to reassert its traditional functions. In 1988 Gorbachev implicitly promised a better status for the Church if it put its support behind *perestroika*, and a few weeks later the millennium of the Russian Orthodox Church was celebrated with public splendour. In print, the long-imposed 'god' reverted to the pre-revolutionary 'God'. Gorbachev acknowledged that religion and communism had some common aims, and the Church was allowed to take up the charitable activities that had long been forbidden. This enabled it to fill a yawning gap in Soviet society, helping the poor, the sick, and the neglected, opening homes for orphans and old people who previously had only the excrementitious state institutions to look forward to.

Some confiscated churches were handed back, but the new atmosphere brought its complications. There was a split, more implied than blatant, between churchmen who had returned from the labour camps, and those who had progressed upwards by conformity and servility. There was also renewed friction between the Russian Orthodox Church and other, newly tolerated, religious organizations and sects. Among these were the Uniate Church in the Ukraine, which soon took back its confiscated churches from the Russian Orthodox Church. The Russian Orthodox Church seemed slow to condemn anti-Semitism, but its head, Patriarch Aleksii II, handled the political upheaval of August 1991 quite deftly (he waited until the second day, and then declared that Gorbachev should have the right to state his case; this was just enough to escape accusations of supporting the coup).

From 1990 unemployment was officially recognized in the USSR, and it was no longer illegal to be unemployed. Labour exchanges and employment centres were set up and the way was open for a limited allowance of unemployment pay.

Freedom to organize, among other things, meant the end of old labour unions. First one, then another, of the unions was taken over by real workers, usually by the democratic process of a conference and majority voting. The old subservient officials were ejected and the union renamed, with 'independent' usually incorporated in its new title. Alternatively, a completely new labour union was set up, in competition with the old. The new unions paid more attention to poor and unsafe working conditions and had the power to get things done; although several laws were passed to limit strikes, they had little effect. On the other hand, union power was limited in its ability to achieve better living standards. In key industries like mining a strike could eventually produce substantial wage increases but in conditions of scarcity such increases could not always be spent. Soon, union demands included allocations of scarce products.

In 1991 Moscow there were three writers' unions: the USSR Writers' Union, the Russian Republic's Writers' Union, and, newly formed in opposition to the latter, the Union of Russian Writers. That year, a policewomen's union was formed, notable for being the first union to appear in the security forces and for its single-gender membership; the ordinary policeman, and especially the ordinary policewoman, had long been a very vulnerable worker and needed, especially, the legal support that could be offered by a union.

Women began to organize elsewhere, too. Dissatisfied with the official Soviet Women's Committee, which was party dominated and disinclined to struggle against the prevailing patriarchism of Soviet society, various independent women's groups developed and in April 1991 held a nationwide women's conference to discuss the real issues and to form a permanent all-Union organization. To help and advise women at the workplace, from 1990 the 'Eve' association organized regional centres which helped women to requalify and to set themselves up as businesswomen.

In 1930 the party's women's department had been closed, the government claiming that the 'woman question' had been solved. During the Khrushchev years the government, alarmed perhaps by declining fertility and unsatisfying female labour productivity, had been willing to allow studies of female problems, but little resulted from this. Under Gorbachev there was more official sympathy, but the underlying culture seemed likely to hold back the emergence of any real, pervasive, sex equality. The advent of democracy did not give women any more political power; women were less likely to win elective office, because of prevailing assumptions. In early 1991 women constituted 18 per cent of the USSR Supreme Soviet, whereas in the old days they had approached a third.

Women still composed half the labour force, and as a matter of course would take responsibility for running the home as well; that is, to work a 'double shift'. Although they were not badly represented in middle management, few reached the top. In 1991 the increasing unemployment seemed to hit women workers hardest.

Allegations that wife-beating was a mass phenomenon may have been exaggerated, but the prevalent attitude towards women, combined with poor housing, would have created the conditions for it. Abortion was still considered the normal method of birth control; in 1991 it was said that there were 137 abortions for every 100 live births. As for rape, this was a subject from which the forces of law and order preferred to remain aloof. There were some technical reasons for this, not least the problem of proof, but the characteristic response of a policeman to a woman's desperate plea for help against a predatory male, 'How can I be sure he's not your husband?', implied something more.

In the health sector four-fifths of the workers were women; the high concentration of female workers in non-priority sectors like medicine and education was a legacy of the Stalinist years, as was the low pay in these services. The poor quality of medical services was not always reflected in the statistics. For example, the increasing number of medical centres was publicized, but not the number of such centres where there was no running water and no telephone. Shortages of drugs and supplies, and not only of the rarely used varieties, were a daily fact of life and death.

The possibility that the Aids epidemic, hitherto ignored or treated as a disease of capitalist society, might affect the USSR was taken seriously only after the reuse of syringes (a necessary, and therefore normal, practice) infected a large number of children in one hospital. The disease then attracted some attention. Some posters were exhibited, the earliest of which suggested that avoiding promiscuous women was the best safeguard, but the criminality of homosexual acts hampered effective publicity. The interior minister, Pugo, shortly before his own demise, arranged for special police units to be formed with the aim of uncovering and prosecuting people concealing their Aids affliction. The limited study of this epidemic was hampered from 1990 by the disintegration of the Union, because research data from the republics was no longer sent to the central statistical unit in Moscow. The official, and no doubt underestimated, figure announced in 1991 was about 1,200 HIV-positives in the USSR, of whom a half were foreign residents.

Public health campaigns of a type seen in the west were virtually unknown, although under *glasnost'* they could be expected to develop. The level of smoking was reminiscent of 1940s Britain or America. Doctors were themselves among the heaviest smokers; this was part of the reason for their higher morbidity, but stressful work, poor living standards, exposure to radiation from low-standard equipment, and exposure to patients' infections also played a part. The Soviet public was unaware of the potential danger of asbestos; even if it had been told that Soviet Railways ballasted thousands of miles of track with asbestos waste it would not have cared.

Under Gorbachev, *glasnost'* meant that the defects of the health services could be criticized but the general lack of resources meant there could not be an instant remedy for six decades of underfunding. There was the beginning of a drive to decentralize administration, and an experiment in which doctors played a role similar to the western general practitioner rather than performing impersonal functions within the polyclinic system, with its atmosphere of authoritarianism, bribe-taking, and abuse. Psychiatry was slow to improve; easy solutions, in the form of chemical treatments and arbitrary diagnoses, meant a proliferation of cruelties.

With education, the situation was not so grave. There were abuses and defects, but the system was workable. No great changes were undertaken, but *glasnost'* did its job in exposing disgraceful and often remediable situations. Head teachers were able to make limited modifications to the syllabus. The chaos caused by the rewriting of history was manageable; pupils, after all, had a sense of humour.

However, the teenager, more perhaps than other members of society, found it difficult to adjust in an atmosphere of overturned values. The 1986 law permitting the establishment of amateur clubs was followed by a surge of youth groupings that could generally be termed counter-cultural. Western models were often followed; mods and rockers, skinheads, punks, and hippies all found their Soviet imitators. But there also appeared a counter-counter-culture; groups of teenage males whose object in life was to beat up those they considered to have deviated from proper Soviet (later, proper Russian) stand-ards. Often addicts of bodybuilding and martial arts, these young toughs found late-night suburban trains and deserted town streets to be the best battleground for their kind of terrorism.

The grind of poverty, the overturning of morality, and above all the aware-ness that some undeserving people were doing very well indeed, combined with the weakening of the authoritarian state to produce a situation where crime flourished. The immense gains that could be made by the acquisition of scarce products led to inter-gang warfare that could end in murder. Various kinds of protection racket damaged honest traders. Street and other crime increased. Mugging became common, and although the increase of crime was exaggerated in the popular imagination it was certainly true that it became inadvisable to be alone in certain places at certain times. Nor was home safe:

Endeavouring to safeguard themselves from the debauchery of robbed apartments, many inhabitants of Magnitogorsk have begun to acquire dogs of the bigger breeds like sheepdogs and Alsatians. A group of people describing themselves as members of the 'Alex' detective agency have turned up here and begun a lively trade in 'Hound of the Baskerville' puppies. Not everybody is put off by their outrageous prices, but when the puppies grow up they turn out to be not of pedigree blood, but ordinary Little-Russian mongrels. State officials are now investigating those private detectives.[12]

A special armed service of the interior ministry, the *OMON* or 'black berets', was formed to deal with armed gangs, but considerable imagination was required to find daily tasks for it:

Coastal and other tourist resorts of the Krasnodar region recently witnessed intense activity initiated by the newly formed MVD of the Russian Republic. Police heli-copters, armed militia detachments of the regional OMON force, and the highway inspectorate's patrols all took part. Local residents thought a band of desperadoes was being hunted down, but the reality was that they were conducting a purge of undesirables, drunks and criminal elements in preparation for the summer season.[13]

The police and KGB were themselves weakened by the new political situ-ation, although both tried hard to fit into the new norms of social behaviour. The KGB in 1988 was obliged to transfer its notorious psychiatric institutions to the health ministry, and began to engage in various public-relations endeavours, even showing journalists around its head office at the Lubyanka in Moscow. It proclaimed its readiness to answer all reasonable questions, but

12. *Gudok*, 5 Feb. 1991, 4.   13. *Vodnyi transport*, 27 Apr. 1991, 1 (edited).

was the final judge of what was reasonable. It made successive concessions to public opinion, but when Kryuchkov was appointed as its head it seemed ready to relapse into its old ways. He was arrested for his part in the August coup, and the continuing public distaste for the KGB was symbolized in the aftermath of that coup when the statue of Dzerzhinski, founder of the Soviet security service, was badly injured by aroused Muscovites. The KGB was soon split into three separate functional organizations, and many of its officials were replaced. These personnel changes, however, were determined mainly by how a given official had behaved during the coup rather than on competence.

The concept of a 'civil society', long reviled by marxists as simply a class-based façade, but providing a set of institutions, standards, and laws that would act as a check and balance on the state, seemed to be taking birth. But it would not come easily. People who could group together over a single issue or on an ethnic basis found it difficult to unite around something that still seemed abstract and of which they had no experience. A reworking of legal norms and principles was accepted as desirable, but little was done in the years of *perestroika*. It is true that judges responded to the new climate by adjusting their verdicts to fit, and that had a great effect, but in an ideal civil society judges orient themselves not by what politicians currently describe as right behaviour, but by their interpretation of the law.

All the same, in 1988 a 'socialist legal state' was promised. Ideologically, this was a significant step; Lenin and his successors had considered the legal state as simply a bourgeois absurdity. In practice, the changes were limited to improvements rather than radical restructuring. For example, judges' terms were doubled to ten years and they were henceforth to be appointed by the higher soviets; these two changes made them more independent of local party officials. 'Telephone law' was officially abolished and in practice severely limited by the judges' greater independence. The notorious Article 70 of the criminal code concerning 'anti-soviet agitation and propaganda' was not really abolished; instead, it was replaced by a new, somewhat less threatening article about 'socially dangerous acts'. The death penalty was applied to a narrower range of offences, and sentences of internal exile abolished. In 1987 a new law gave citizens some legal rights of appeal against arbitrary decisions by officials.

Meanwhile, the new breed of liberal, democratic, radical activists seemed sometimes to forget the principles it preached; or, more ominously, persuaded itself, like previous ruling bureaucrats, that bad ways were acceptable so long as they were in good hands. An example of this was when the government of Moscow prevented the conservative secretary of the Russian party organization from taking up residence in Moscow, simply by refusing to grant him a residence permit.[14]

14. Despite Gorbachev's and Yeltsin's distaste, a separate RSFSR communist party was established by diehards in 1990.

Residence permits, the old bureaucratic, unjust, illogical, and corruption-ridden method of selecting those permitted to settle in certain cities, were condemned but not eliminated in late 1991. Earlier that year, in Moscow's first open auction for such permits (which took the form of a house and apartment auction, the permits being attached to the properties), one changed hands for a million roubles. At the same period, a permit could also be obtained by marrying a Moscow resident; residents willing to offer themselves for such marriages of convenience were asking 30,000 roubles.

Housing seemed likely to prove a source of social tension in the 1990s. Although there seemed little ambition directed towards the western-style 'property-owning democracy', and little appreciation that property ownership might be a contribution to personal freedom, the transfer of ownership from state authorities to the tenants was seen as a desirable form of privatization. Policies varied from place to place, and some local authorities were entirely opposed to the idea. From 1988 tenants were allowed to buy, if their local soviets allowed them to, and 1991 RSFSR legislation made the process slightly easier. But relatively few actually wanted to buy (the land on which a property was built could not be bought or sold). In practice it was already possible for a tenant to bequeath his or her apartment, which in a sense implied 'ownership', and the tenant was not responsible for repairs (and, more important, for the backlog of disrepair). Faced with this reluctance (up to the end of 1990 only about 20,000 tenants had bought) some authorities experimented with the gratuitous transfer of apartments to their tenants. But even this was unwelcome. Such a policy was said to be grossly unfair; a tenant who by luck or string-pulling had highly desirable accommodation was much better off than someone who for years had struggled in a cramped and insalubrious hovel. Moreover, such schemes were unfair to members of cooperative associations, who had put their own resources into building their living quarters. Prohibitions against resale reduced this friction, but such prohibitions were progressively relaxed in ensuing years. By late 2001, two-thirds of housing was owned by residents or other private owners.

The armed forces

This was not a good period for the hitherto privileged military. The campaign in Afghanistan had brought thousands of deaths, little glory, and finally, under Gorbachev, a withdrawal. The Warsaw Pact dissolved and the Red Army left Czechoslovakia and Hungary by the end of 1991. Withdrawal from East Germany and from Poland followed. Poor housing and living standards awaited those returning to the USSR, and careers were threatened by successive reductions of strength.

Not many officers saw the implications for them of Gorbachev's virtual abandonment of the old international class struggle concept, although when he began to talk of a 'reasonable sufficiency' as a basis for eventual military restructuring the position became clearer: there would be fewer resources allocated to defence. Even then some officers persuaded themselves that Gorbachev was cunningly trying to deceive the west, although most felt that he was giving up long-held positions without receiving much in return. But although within the forces there was a powerful group of officers who resented the spirit of the time, there was also a growing number in favour of army reform. Relaxation of the old repression meant that the general public began to make its voice heard. Mothers of men killed in Afghanistan spoke up. Mothers of other conscripts began to add their weight to existing misgivings about army life. Bullying and beating of conscripts was shown to be widespread, with ethnic minorities, or young men who in one way or another were different, being especially vulnerable. Eventually the Supreme Soviet set up an inquiry which concluded that every year since 1945 thousands of conscripts had died, with suicides accounting for half the deaths. In the 1990s there was little improvement, however. Despite a reduction in its size, the army seemed unable to provide really habitable accommodation for its men. Pay was late, and units were often unable to pay their electricity bills (under Yeltsin, it was made illegal for electric power companies to cut off supplies to military establishments. Such cut-offs could have been catastrophic for nuclear-weapon establishments). Conscripts could be seen begging on the streets, and some traded in weapons. In 1998 it was discovered that a company was relabelling tinned dog food and selling it to army catering units as stew.

From 1990 there was an increased reluctance of young men to answer the conscription summons. In the schools the emphasis on military training was weakening. The navy reduced its conscription term to two years, matching the other services. In 1991 it was announced that the call-up of students would cease. In that year, however, the break-up of the USSR implied the break-up of the forces. The new independent republics announced the establishment of national guards while the Ukraine made plans for a strong army, to be formed of Ukrainians currently in the Red Army. Like other republics, the Ukraine also laid claim to military equipment and installations located on its territory. In late 1991 Azerbaizhan claimed the Caspian Sea Fleet and Ukraine the Black Sea Fleet.

In the Gulf crisis of 1990–1 the USSR did not support Iraq (whose armed forces were equipped by the Soviet Union). The conclusion had to be drawn that US weapons were far ahead of Soviet and that this would damage the prospects of Soviet arms exports. At the same time, high officers were not slow to point out the need of a new generation of weaponry for the Soviet forces. Electronic devices, and also a large military air transport service such as the Americans had, were seen as first necessities. Meanwhile, those who had long been recommending a shift from conscription to a small but highly professional armed force could point to the example shown by the Americans in this war.

The qualitative inferiority of Soviet weapons was seen to have originated in the Brezhnev period when, to save money, industry became the dominant partner in the so-called military-industrial complex. The forces were no longer allowed to pursue several different designs to fulfil one role, and industry was to decide which designs to build as prototypes. This meant that the forces were unable to ensure that they got the designs they wanted. Under Gorbachev, the military interest accepted the conversion of some defence factories to civilian production, finding some compensation in the new possibility of airing their grievances in public, thanks to *glasnost'*. The loss of the experimental, titanium-hull, nuclear submarine *Komsomolets* in 1989 was promptly exploited as an example of what poor design and construction could lead to, and as a reason for greater military control over defence expenditure. Essentially, what the general staffs wanted was the right to decide which projects should receive financial support. Just as with the Third and Fourth Dumas eighty years previously, the existence of free parliamentary debate, and parliamentary defence committees, enabled the generals and admirals to put their arguments to the test of open discussion. The assumption that professional officers were inevitably opposed to new freedoms was as wrong in the final Soviet years as it had been in the last tsarist years.

Empire's end

The USSR and its European 'satellite' communist republics were both largely the creation of Stalin, the first being the tsarist empire under a new type of management and the latter a gain of the Second World War. This structure came to an end in 1989–91; unlike other great empires, it came to an end rapidly, and almost bloodlessly.

Until the very end Gorbachev resisted the break-up of the USSR, but it was his insistence on *glasnost'* and his reservations about the use of force that made this break-up possible. With the satellites his position was different; he did not regard them as essential. He saw that they could be a burden and he made it clear that the Red Army could no longer be used as the ultimate guarantor of the rule of their communist parties.

The Polish ruling party and the powerful Solidarity dissident movement thereupon reached a compromise which led eventually to a democratic government. In the other former satellites, events took different courses but arrived at the elimination of the former communist leaderships, with reform communists and open popular dissent providing the catalyst. Only in Romania did this process produce substantial casualties. Events in the German Democratic Republic were the most dramatic; the East German government, after some personnel changes, acquiesced unresistingly to the new circumstances; some plain speaking from Gorbachev had its effect here. The Berlin Wall was dismantled, and eventually the East German population, offered some financial carrots by the West German chancellor, voted for a party that signified immediate reunion with the rest of Germany.

Comecon came to an end, and the former people's republics were faced with the prospect of paying both hard currency and world prices for their massive imports of Soviet fuel, while the USSR found itself unable to buy, except at world prices and for hard currency, the products supplied by its satellites (and, worse, spare parts for equipment already received). As both sides preferred to spend their hard currency in the western world, much of this exchange petered out.

Multinational empires always present problems. The Bolshevik solution of a confederation of national territories with small, varying degrees of self-government had proved to be workable so long as the central authoritarian regime kept national feelings under control. Under Gorbachev, *glasnost'*, the preference for political rather than authoritarian solutions, and the election of genuine republican parliaments gave pent-up national feeling an opportunity of expression. Nationalist stirrings in the fifteen union republics, including Russia, were first to be noticed, but it soon became clear that smaller entities, the autonomous republics, the autonomous regions, and in some cases nations with neither territory nor autonomy also had ambitions.[15]

As always, there were those who knew how to fan nationalism, and how to make those immune to it feel guilty. On the other hand, the elections and referenda of this period certainly demonstrated a strong wish to throw off alien influences and alien powers. In the Russian union republic (RSFSR), several of the many autonomous territories displayed their own national consciousness. Russian nationalism was an old phenomenon, containing a touch of Panslavism with a nostalgic regard for old Russian traditions and virtues. But when nostalgia for the old Russian Empire crept in, it became a kind of Great Russian chauvinism.

Those who disdain national feeling often get a nasty surprise, and that is what happened to Gorbachev. He did not foresee the extent to which *perestroika* would be bedevilled by nationalism; he foresaw friction, but not the grinding, unrelenting movement towards independence and away from centralized Soviet power. The first sharp shocks to the concept of the Soviet Union came from the periphery. The three union republics of Lithuania,

---

15. Among the latter were the Crimean Tatars, who were finally allowed to return to the Crimea. The Volga Germans, another nationality expelled by Stalin, were allocated territory near Saratov, thereby igniting local protests. Many of them were encouraged by the German government to resettle in Germany. Around Kazan leaders of the Tatar autonomous republic embarrassed Yeltsin by demanding independence from Russia, in the first place to be achieved by becoming a union republic to be called Tatarstan. In Georgia both the Abkhazian autonomous republic and the South Ossetian autonomous region demanded independence, and prepared to fight for it.

Latvia, and Estonia, as well as the Moldavian union republic, dated from the 1940s and still had memories of old, pre-Soviet times. The first, almost symbolic, move from the Baltic came in 1987, when the Estonian government claimed economic autonomy and in 1988 when it claimed Estonian sovereignty. Sovereignty was less drastic than independence, but nevertheless required that republic law should have precedence over all-Union, Soviet, law; that resources listed in the Soviet Constitution as belonging to the state should be transferred to the republic; and that private ownership of the means of production could be legal in that republic. In 1989 Lithuania and Latvia claimed sovereignty, and Latvia and Estonia began to define citizenship to exclude some Russian immigrants. Gorbachev responded to these moves and other claims by repeating that all republics had the right to secede but only after fulfilling certain conditions, which implied a long waiting period.

Lithuania took the lead in early 1990 by declaring itself independent, but was induced to 'freeze' the declaration by pressure both from Moscow and from the French and German governments. Later in 1990 Estonia and Latvia issued their own, somewhat more moderate declarations of independence. In that year most of the other republics declared their sovereignty.

Pressure from the Baltic states was never relaxed; popular fronts had been formed between nationalists and those communists who supported independence, and fresh stimulus was provided by the acknowledgement by the Soviet parliament that the secret protocols of the Nazi–Soviet Pact did in fact exist. Anniversaries of this 1939 pact, which had secured the Soviet takeover of the three previously independent states, were occasions for impressive demonstrations. In the winter of 1990–1 the situation became critical. In January 1991 OMON troops, and sometimes Soviet Army units, went into action. In shows of force, tanks and security police advanced against citizens surrounding public buildings in the Lithuanian capital and the central television transmitter in Latvia. There were several deaths, but the Soviet authorities were unwilling to convert a bloody confrontation into a massacre. There were subsequent provocations, including the murder of frontier guards, but after the August coup even Gorbachev was prepared for the independence of these three states, which soon followed.

Elsewhere, the Moldova Republic was declared, essentially for the benefit of the majority Romanian population. But the areas inhabited mainly by Russians or Turks each set up their own dissident republic and used various means, including the blockage of strategic rail routes, to draw attention to their demands. In 1992 the Moldovan situation would sharpen bloodily.

In the Caucasus, Gorbachev's hard-pressed central government was faced with the duty of moderating quarrels between nations that hitherto had been held in check by authoritarian means. The autonomous Nagorno-Karabakh region of the Azerbaizhan Republic had a majority of Armenians who demanded union with Armenia. Armed conflicts followed in late 1991; there was a semblance of a ceasefire negotiated with the participation of Yeltsin, but this did not last.

The Red Army took part in a 'pacification' of Baku in these troubled times and was blamed, with some justification, for the high casualty rate. In Georgia, too, the Red Army fell into disgrace when its troops attacked an obviously peaceful, though banned, demonstration in Tbilisi. The demonstration was a rally of nationalists inflamed by the demand of the Abkhazian autonomous republic for independence from Georgia. A high proportion of the dead were women and children, victims apparently of shovel blades. Georgia shortly declared its independence under a nationalist coalition government. Soon it was in conflict with an autonomous republic in its territory, Southern Ossetia, which it wanted to retain. By the end of 1991 the Georgian president, popularly elected and with a brave past as a dissident (persecuted by, among others, Shevardnadze), was under shellfire from rebels alleging that he had become intolerant and authoritarian. In 1992 Shevardnadze, who had returned to lead his native country, was berating Moscow for its support of the South Ossetian independence forces.

The smaller Central Asian republics took different courses. Culturally quite different from the rest of the USSR, they were still very dependent on it. Their communist parties tended to survive, although after the August 1991 upheaval they began to metamorphose into new parties with the old faces.

Gorbachev fought hard for the continuation of some form of central government, but he remarked that without the Ukraine any such grouping would be useless. In December 1991 an election and a referendum showed that the Ukraine was as determined as Russia to go its own way. It was a former communist leader who had embraced the nationalist cause, Kravchuk, who was elected as president; the nationalist party, Rukh, which had kept the cause alive, was relatively unsuccessful in the electoral sense though triumphant morally. The referendum had asked whether voters wanted an independent Ukraine but did not ask what kind of independence they wanted. Unsurprisingly, they voted overwhelmingly for the proposition, with majorities even in the mainly Russian eastern part.

The Ukraine and Byelorussia already had seats at the United Nations and, in theory, their own foreign policies. Also, like Kazakhstan and Russia, they provided the sites for nuclear missiles. This was one of the reasons why western governments did not welcome the break-up of the USSR. Another reason was that over the previous five years successive US administrations had begun to appreciate Gorbachev as a reassuring, reliable performer.

In May 1986 the Soviet aspiration to have a defensive capacity capable of dealing with NATO and China simultaneously was quietly dropped. At the Reykjavik summit meeting of 1986 the US president, unprepared for the Soviet readiness to overturn all the assumptions of the Cold War and scrap all nuclear weapons, almost reciprocated, but was recalled to orthodoxy by his advisers. But as Gorbachev continued on his course regardless, relaxing old tensions, speaking of a 'common European home', and disengaging from old allies, both the USA and other western powers realized the gains that could result from quietly supporting him.

The Red Army was withdrawn in 1989 from Afghanistan. Soviet help to Cuba was reduced. Moscow's ally Vietnam withdrew from Cambodia. In Africa, and elsewhere, regimes that had profited from Soviet support found that they were left to fend for themselves. When in 1990 the former Soviet protégé Iraq invaded Kuwait, the USSR approved the use of countering force while striving for a peaceful solution. In 1991 diplomatic relations with Israel were restored and Moscow participated in the Middle East conferences of that year. Finland was allowed to withdraw from the unique and restricting relationship with the USSR that at one time had been regarded as a possible, 'Finlandization', model for other countries in the Soviet orbit.

During these Gorbachev years progress was made, but only slowly, on reaching agreements for limiting both conventional and nuclear weapons. There were political figures on both sides discouraging such moves, and the US insistence on continuing with its 'Star Wars' programme held back Soviet initiatives. But in August 1991 a new START agreement, reducing nuclear weapons by about 30 per cent, was ready to be ratified by the US Congress and the Supreme Soviet. After August, Gorbachev decided to make further substantial reductions in nuclear forces irrespective of what the USA might do. The USA, for its part, fearing the prospect of Soviet nuclear weapons in the hands of newly formed states that might be involved in all kinds of conflicts, decided to respond in kind.

Despite pressures from their 'Cold War warriors', the western powers refrained from embarrassing Gorbachev by, for example, prematurely recognizing the independence of the Baltic republics. Right up to the August 1991 events, they treated Yeltsin with great caution; when he visited the European Community the offhand treatment he received verged on the insulting. Western powers were willing to promise, and to a lesser degree provide, economic and financial assistance.

With Gorbachev's field of authority diminishing as the USSR's powers were assumed by the republics, and with his dependence on financial support from the Russian budget, it was clear in late 1991 that Yeltsin was dominant. This alarmed some observers; they could point to Yeltsin's dispatch of security troops to suppress a nationalist coup in the Chechen-Ingush autonomous republic,[16] and of how after the August events Yeltsin had reanimated Ukrainian fears of 'Great Russian chauvinism' when he spoke of necessary

---

16. This intervention against Dzhokar Dudaev's Chechnya independence regime was a fiasco, largely because the Russian Republic's Supreme Soviet, mindful of its own independence from Yeltsin, refused to approve the action. The troops that had been airlifted in by Yeltsin were bus-lifted out by Dudaev.

rectifications of the Russian frontier in the event of a break-up of the USSR (although, as was often the case with Yeltsin, in both cases he proved ready to listen to advice and modify his stand without a blush).

In December the presidents of Russia, Ukraine, and Byelorussia held a quiet meeting at which the momentous decision was taken to form a new 'Commonwealth of Independent States' to replace the USSR. Although their main aim was to destroy the old Union, neatly depriving Gorbachev of his power, they were immediately accused of concocting a Pan-Slav conspiracy. But at a meeting in Alma Ata the three original signatories were joined by Kazakhstan, Azerbaizhan, Uzbekistan, Armenia, Kirgiziya, Tadzhikistan, Turkmenistan, and Moldova. This was sufficient for the new Commonwealth to take off.

With the Commonwealth replacing the USSR, there was clearly no place for Gorbachev. He resigned his presidency on 25 December 1991. In his last days he was subjected to petty humiliations by Yeltsin, who evidently had not forgotten the slights he had earlier endured. Nevertheless, apart from being the last leader of the USSR, Gorbachev was also the first to retire with dignity.

At the end of 1991, over official buildings, the red flag and the Soviet republic flags were lowered for the last time, replaced by the various national flags. In the Russian Republic there was a design competition for a modern version of the old tsarist two-headed eagle symbol.

Flags into Skirts

Several score flags of the former USSR union republics have become the latest objects of trade, being offered for sale at a bargain shop in the centre of the Sanchur district in Kirov Region. But they are not being acquired as relics. Housewives have been quick to see that they can make clothes and other things from that silk and crepe-de-chine.[17]

17. *Gudok*, 4 Jan. 1992, 1.

19

Shocks and therapies

The post-Soviet republics

THE 1989 census had indicated that 51 per cent or 147,386,000 of the USSR's population lived in the Russian Republic. The next biggest republic, the Ukrainian, contained 18 per cent, and the other republics had much smaller populations. With the exception of the three Baltic states and Georgia, the former union republics had agreed in late 1991 to form the Commonwealth of Independent States. They had little idea of what this meant, but the British Commonwealth had been vaguely spoken of as a model, which was fair enough since nobody quite understood the British Commonwealth. As the months passed, the emphasis was increasingly on independence and less on commonwealth. Some changes cost nothing and meant much. For example, there was a move away from the Russian-style rendering of place names. Belarus became the preferred rendering of White Russia or Byelorussia, Kyrgyziya was preferred to Kirgiziya. Meanwhile, in the English-speaking world *Ukraina* was no longer the Ukraine, but Ukraine, a change recommended neither by history, etymology, or euphony. But at home, Ukraine's decision to replace the rouble by its own currency was a step of some economic and psychological significance.

In Central Asia the newly independent republics began to go their own separate ways. Former communist party stalwarts in most republics came to terms with the new situation although some were ejected from positions of influence. Culture and geography ensured that ties with Moscow were weakened.

In the Caucasus, Armenia and Azerbaizhan were in a state of conflict over Nagorno-Karabakh (a detached Azerbaizhan territory with a mainly Armenian population). In Georgia, an authoritarian ex-dissident president, soon to be forcibly displaced, was in savage dispute with the national enclaves of Abkhazia and the Ossetias. In these conflicts Russian policy would be a fine balance between promoting what were seen as Russian interests while avoiding hostilities with the new republics. This was not always easy. In Moldova there was conflict between the Russian and Romanian components of the population, which would be settled, more or less, by General Lebed, who commanded the Russian troops in that location.

Most Russians had difficulty in coming to terms with the separation from Ukraine and Belarus. Unlike the other new republics, these were Slavic peoples whose histories were intertwined with Russia's history. Belarus quietly went its own modest way, but things were not so simple for Ukraine, which had a substantial minority of Russians, as well as some Poles.

Ukrainians felt they were entitled to a substantial part of the Red Navy's Black Sea Fleet, which was based in Ukraine, at Sevastopol. But Moscow was not prepared to concede on this issue, and took the precaution, much resented, of evacuating a new aircraft carrier from the Black Sea to the Arctic. The Ukrainian response was to change its demand for the greater part of the Black Sea Fleet to a statement that the whole fleet was Ukrainian property.

An equally emotional issue was the destiny of the Crimea. This, one of the more delectable territories of the USSR, had been transferred to Ukraine from Russia by Khrushchev in a fit of generosity. So long as the USSR existed this transfer was only a formality, but the highly Russified Crimean population did not unanimously welcome its inclusion in the new independent Ukraine.

Inside Russia popular resentment on these issues tended to be channelled against the Ukrainian president, Kravchuk, who seemed to be a blatant and all-too-successful example of the party *apparatchik* who had jumped on the bandwagon of change and nationalism just in time to exploit the successes won by courageous and often martyred dissidents. The thought of losing the Crimea to such a man was painful, and the Russian parliament lost no time in declaring void the 1954 transfer of the Crimea to Ukraine. Like so many other declarations of 1992, this made little difference. But both Yeltsin and Kravchuk were aware that conflict should not go beyond angry words, and by the end of the century neither the Crimea nor the navy was a hot issue.

Kravchuk stuck to the agreement that nuclear weapons stationed on Ukrainian territory, like those in Kazakhstan and Belarus, should slowly be transferred to Russia, which would be responsible for storage or dismantlement. He also resisted the temptation of playing the ultra-nationalist card by stirring up animosity against the non-Ukrainian part of the population (for example, he preferred to talk about the Ukrainian state rather than the Ukrainian nation); this could be dismissed as mere common sense; but common sense at such a time was itself a rare and valuable quality.

With the emerging independent Russian Republic, a main problem would be the creation of a national identity. Russia had not been a real nation-state in modern times, although she had once been an imperial power. Self-recognition would be complicated by the twenty-one ethnic national republics contained within her frontiers. They contributed 15 per cent of Russia's population and occupied 28 per cent of her territory. Some of them, like Tatarstan and Karelia, were already demanding independence. Some, including Karelia, had a majority of Russians.

Yeltsin in power

In his triumph over the attempted coup of August 1991, Yeltsin had been clearly on the side of the democratic, reforming, elements in politics, but after August he had slipped into his preferred mode of behind-the-scene deals, in which he gathered the support of other interests, including much of the military and of the industrial managers. Henceforth he was a little less close to his former supporters. This was a foretaste of his subsequent style, when he ruled Russia not so much through democratic institutions as through his own entourage. He liked to surround himself with people he could trust, preferably people he could play off against each other. He valued loyalty above all, and believed in the efficacy of a strong man at the top. At times of crisis his man-of-action, get-things-done character usually served him well, but between crises he seemed to lack zest, occupying himself with intrigues and crony-shuffling.

In 1992 Russians still seemed more like spectators than participants. So far as they could, they continued to work and to live as they had always done, and discussed political events in the same way as they discussed a film or play. At the start of his presidency of the new Russian Federation, Yeltsin was at the peak of his popularity. But the economic situation, despite desperate meas-ures, remained dire. The move from a state planned economy to a capitalist economy was seen as the first urgent task. The term 'market economy' was preferred to 'capitalism', and consisted of two elements: an end to fixed prices and the conversion of state enterprises into privately owned companies. These both promised to be far-reaching upheavals, and it was decided to accomplish them rapidly ('shock therapy'), relying on the momentum of the process to carry through changes that would certainly be painful. Gaidar, a young economist, became acting prime minister.

The freeing of retail prices in January 1992 did not bring the prompt flow of products into the shops that had been anticipated, except in a few special instances. The government survived the impoverished winter but further moves along the road of market pricing, like increases in oil prices, were resisted fiercely and delayed by the parliamentary opposition. ('Market', rather than 'rational', pricing seems the more appropriate term for a period in which the market was producing all kinds of irrationalities; July 1992, for example, witnessed the phenomenon of fruit and vegetable prices actually rising in the summer.) Enterprises were unwilling to reduce their prices in order to sell their products; they preferred the routine of high prices, low sales, and large workforces, relying on bank credits and state help to keep going.

Foreign financial assistance was regarded as essential. In summer 1992 both Yeltsin and Yeltsin's economic reforms were severely criticized. Among others, Khasbulatov, speaker of the Supreme Soviet, voiced the resentment of many

Russians at growing Russian economic dependence on the west. To some, it seemed that the drastic and hurried economic changes were not simply the product of Yeltsin's young economic advisers but were imposed by potential western lenders. This criticism was part of a president-versus-parliament power struggle, and resulted in neither a move towards a more parliamentary democracy nor a reversal of the economic reforms, although the privatizers were obliged to abandon their intention of immediately halting state subsidies for industries; this lifted a threat from the existing managers and their workers, and was a departure from the policy of 'shock therapy'.

Khasbulatov, together with Yeltsin's vice-president Rutskoi, maintained opposition to the reforms. Opposition persuaded Yeltsin to appoint a new head of the Central Bank who immediately expanded credit at a time when the reformers wanted to reduce it so as to counter growing inflation. Inflation worsened, and the reformers were blamed. At the end of 1992 Yeltsin was induced by the Supreme Soviet to appoint as prime minister the head of one of the biggest state industries, Viktor Chernomyrdin of Gazprom. Chernomyrdin promptly reintroduced state-fixed prices for a few sensitive products.

Earlier, in February, there had been conflict between Yeltsin and the parliament over the former's determination to ensure his control of the ministry of state security (successor to the KGB). Up to late 1991 the old KGB had been shrinking, but in 1992 it was again expanding. Some of its operatives were being turned onto the other republics of the former USSR, and there was evidence that the old KGB internal structure of information-gathering was still functioning, although part-time informers were becoming rare and the information was merely filed away for use in better times.

By the end of 1992 Yeltsin had lost much of his popularity. Wages were not being paid, pensions were late, food production was down, people were lining the streets peddling scarce products in a bid to supplement their wages or pensions. Others simply begged. Superficially, capitalism's main impact seemed to be the encampments of kiosks in public spaces, engaged in selling all kinds of home and foreign items at high prices. More and more, goods and services were exchanged rather than bought. The bartering spirit even spread to the army, where unpaid soldiers bartered away their weapons to ambitious criminals. Officials and policemen were even more active in bribe-taking. The rouble lost its value daily, and huge numbers of dollar bills circulated, almost to the extent of an alternative currency. This produced the phenomenon of 'internal capital flight' as masses of unreliable roubles were exchanged for dollars. 'Dollar shops', where only dollars were accepted, multiplied. More constructive, perhaps, was the flow of citizens at weekends to newly acquired plots on city outskirts, where families laboured to grow their own food. And because the reformers had been unsuccessful in ending state subsidies, relatively few people lost their jobs.

In addition to making himself unpopular with economic reforms, Yeltsin was also criticized for his 'loss' of the Soviet Empire. The right-wing liberal democratic party of Vladimir Zhirinovskii and the new communist party of Gennadii Zyuganov both appealed to the millions pained by Russia's downsizing, the latter seeming almost to move from communism to Slavophilism.[1]

Yeltsin was also reverting to the life pattern of the old-style Soviet boss. He seemed to revel in the perquisites of power; riding around in his limousine or exercising in his very own tennis club, he seemed remote from the people. It was also becoming clear that he was surrounding himself with cronies of dubious background. His bodyguard Korzhakov, who sat in the front seat of the presidential limousine and rushed to open the president's car-door, was also for years the presidential drinking companion and political adviser.

Early in 1993 the always hostile Supreme Soviet began impeachment proceedings against Yeltsin. He immediately staged a referendum in which 59 per cent of the population expressed confidence in him. But the Supreme Soviet, under the guidance of Khasbulatov and Rutskoi, could still resist further reforms and, moreover, could prevent Yeltsin advancing the Supreme Soviet elections in the hope of securing the election of a more friendly assembly.

Both by character, and by his upbringing as a party boss, Yeltsin had few inhibitions against arbitrariness and the use of force. He decided to confound his opponents by locking out the Supreme Soviet members. But the plan leaked out and, instead, the members locked themselves in. The resulting stand-off lasted two weeks, and was essentially a contest for supremacy between president and parliament. Yeltsin ordered the army to surround the White House. Rutskoi declared himself acting president. A general sympathetic to Rutskoi sent armed men to capture the Ostankino TV centre; success here would have enabled the White House parliamentarians to propagandize their cause. However, a few soldiers posted at the centre opened fire and the attack failed, with some fatalities. Finally, tanks were sent against the White House. A few shells lobbed into the building ended the contest. The leaders were arrested and placed in the same gaol where surviving members of that other rebellion, the failed putsch of August 1991, were held.[2]

During and after this crisis Yeltsin retained the support of western leaders, whose faith in the new Russian democracy seemed unaffected by the shelling of elected parliamentarians. The west, and the USA in particular, began the 1990s respected and admired by most Russians, but its role at this juncture disappointed many. Western interests firmly believed that Yeltsin represented

1. In November 1992 the Constitutional Court allowed the communist party to refound itself as the Communist Party of the Russian Federation.

2. After the 1993 Duma election Zhirinovskii's party was strong enough to persuade the Duma to vote for the release not only of Rutskoi and his friends, but also of the still-imprisoned perpetrators of the August 1991 putsch. Some of them resumed political life.

the right way forward, and that his great and growing unpopularity at home had no deep significance: his policies were just what Russia needed.

With this support, and having suppressed parliamentary opposition, Yeltsin sanctioned further steps towards a market economy, with privatization accelerated so that by the end of 1994 almost half the industrial workforce was in private enterprises. The range of consumer goods on offer began to resemble that of tsarist times. But production continued to fall, and conditions in the smaller cities could be desperately bleak. It was at this point, late 1993, that national and local elections took place, together with a referendum on a new constitution.

In this election, Gaidar's 'Russia's Choice' party was the government's favourite but, partly because Gaidar was a hopeless television performer and partly because much of the population had been soured by Yeltsin's violence at the White House, the pro-government slant of the television programmes was not sufficient to obtain the hoped-for result. It was the communists who did best, followed by 'Russia's Choice' and Zhirinovskii's Liberal Democrats. This did not mean that a new prime minister had to be chosen; under the constitution, that was Yeltsin's prerogative.

The electorate voted in favour of the new Constitution. This was designed to put an end to the fight between president and parliament. The new parliament would be the Federal Assembly, with two chambers, the State Duma and the Federation Council. The latter, a second chamber, would consist largely of leading figures (including regional governors) and could be expected to support the president since, in effect, so many of them would be nominated or appointed by him. The president would appoint his prime minister, and it would be quite difficult for the parliament to impeach the president.

Indeed, impeachment might otherwise have been Yeltsin's fate, because a widening range of opinion was beginning to feel he was unfit for the job. His association with the up-and-coming financial/industrial 'oligarchs', and a gradual awareness that he, or at least his family and cronies, were engaged in self-enrichment were largely responsible for this growing revulsion. On the other hand, his alcoholic frolics may well have endeared him to many Russians, even when they involved him crawling mysteriously out of a river. Worldwide, audiences were more amused than shocked when he was too inebriated to show his face to the Irish cabinet when it paid a courtesy visit to his aircraft during a refuelling stop.

The bad showing of the pro-government party in the 1993 election prompted Yeltsin to go slow with further economic reform. All the reformers except Chubais left the government and Chernomyrdin appointed men of his own type to replace them, veterans like him of Soviet-era industry. Wherever possible, Yeltsin ensured that his own men would become regional governors (and hence members of the upper house). However, though he was inclined to use the authoritarian tactics he had learned as a risng *apparatchik*, he was limited in his powers; for example, although he could apply pressure to the TV channels he could not ensure that they would refrain from criticizing him, nor could he do much about hostile newspapers. But in any case he had no wish to reimpose Soviet-style repression; he was for democracy, so long as it was democracy as he saw it. Free, though not necessarily fair, elections had become part of life, and so had freedom of the press.

With the dispatch of the Russian army into Chechnya in late 1994 (see p. 537), another demonstration of Yeltsin's willingness to use force, his reputation was further damaged. State Duma elections came up in late 1995. Chernomyrdin formed his own government party, called 'Our Home—Russia', and learned to smile on television. But it was in vain; his party came a distant second to the communists. He stayed on as prime minister, but the foreign minister was replaced by Primakov, reputed to be less friendly to the west, while Chubais, the last of the reformers, left the government. Privatization, however, continued.

The presidential election was due in summer 1996, and Yeltsin seemed likely to lose it. Creditably, he rejected advice to either postpone the elections or exploit loopholes that would give him another term without the need for re-election. He organized a fund that, he claimed, would pay off the workers' wage arrears. He made well-publicized peace overtures to the Chechen rebels. To gratify those who regretted the loss of empire, he signed a document promising political union between Russia and Belarus.[3] He travelled around the regions, promising more state funds for them after his re-election (these funds, like wage back-payments, would diminish as soon as Yeltsin was securely re-elected). Despite these efforts, his prospects did not seem good. Industrial production was down to about half of that of 1990. Polls suggested that the next president would not be Yeltsin, but the distinctly uncharismatic Gennadii Zyuganov, whose communist party was attracting mass support because it promised a return to the old certainties of punctual wages and pensions, law and order on the streets, and an end to economic experimentation.

His prospects were rescued by the 'oligarchs'. These seven men were now at the peak of their power, having already acquired the bulk of their influence and fortunes. Most of them were former Komsomol members, smart characters with ambition. In the privatization years they had seen opportunities and taken them, using their increasing wealth to buy protection from the law. Some had cornered expanding markets, like automobiles, in which killings of competitors were a feature, and then expanded into other lines of business to form conglomerates. A typical method of expansion was to buy, under cover

---

3. Lukashenko, the Belarus president, was the main enthusiast for this union, which seemed destined to remain pie-in-the-sky for the foreseeable future. Russians liked the idea of a union, but many of them found the dictatorial Lukashenko hard to swallow.

of the conglomerate's bank, a controlling share of an enterprise and find ways to divert its revenue flow into the bank before it actually reached the enterprise. The bank, in order to help the enterprise's consequent cash-flow problem, would then make a loan at a high rate of interest or in exchange for more shares.

Vladimir Potanin, based on his Oneximbank, was reputed to be the wealthiest of the oligarchs, and for a time after Yeltsin's re-election he would become first deputy prime minister. But the real political power of the oligarchs lay in ready access not only to Yeltsin's advisers and cronies (increasingly the same people) but to Yeltsin himself. Additionally, two of them, Berezovsky and Gusinsky, owned major television channels and newspapers. Their characters varied. Some were modest and unassuming, although Berezovsky, a one-time university mathematician, seems to have been the reverse. Gusinsky said of himself:

I always risk everything. A man must regularly, every five or seven years, change his life. If he doesn't do that, he becomes internally boring . . . Even dogs no longer come up and sniff him.[4]

These men, foreseeing their nemesis should Yeltsin lose the election, joined forces to use their power and influence in his campaign. Chubais and the surviving reformers, for their own reasons, joined with them.[5] With the oligarchs' money and media ownership, and the political expertise of Chubais, Yeltsin survived the first round of the election. Before the second round he had a heart attack and retired from electioneering; he would have a successful bypass operation in December but was henceforth in frail health. Meanwhile his personal cronies, notably Korzhakov, who by that time was head of the presidential security services, had fallen out with the election team of oligarchs and liberals. Korzhakov's men at one point arrested two of Chubais's aides found to have half a million dollars in a cardboard box, shady money en route to an electoral destination. After this Korzhakov was finally dismissed from Yeltsin's circle.

Yeltsin won easily in the second round, not because he was popular but because so many who deplored him realized that he was the lesser of two evils.[6]

---

4. Quoted in: Chrystia Freeland, *Sale of the Century: Russia's Wild Ride from Communism to Capitalism* (2000), 139.

5. Chubais supped with these oligarchs using an insufficiently long spoon. Hitherto he had been regarded as a rare honest man, but this reputation would be lost when he was revealed to be receiving what seemed to be a disguised bribe from the oligarchs. Widely publicized by the oligarchs themselves in 1997, it took the form of a generous, though not monstrous, promise of an advance for a book about privatization supposedly to be written by Chubais and his colleagues.

6. Zyuganov was a defender of Stalinism. In the campaign he made a point of excoriating Trotsky.

From Yeltsin to Putin

Yeltsin began his second term with Chubais restored and new moves towards a market economy. Chernomyrdin remained as prime minister and the oligarchs frequently conferred with Yeltsin, evidently conveying something more than their best wishes. A few of them, for a time, entered his government, but in 1998 he would shake them off and restore to influence some of the reformers. In 1997 the economy seemed to be doing better, with inflation slackening and production stabilizing. But then came the Asian financial crisis, one of whose results was a lowering of oil prices. By this time Russia was heavily dependent on oil exports and this, together with the continuing outflow of capital, put the government in difficulties. A mass issue of short-term bills, and the appointment of a new, youthful, prime minister, did not mend matters. In summer 1998 the workers, whose patience in a situation of chronic wage arrears had surprised outside observers (unaware of how deeply Russian workers felt attached to their place of work), abruptly changed their attitude. The 'Rail War' began, with miners settling en masse on railway lines and, among other things, bringing the Trans-Siberian line to a standstill.

Ministers flitted around the country, hurriedly signing agreements with the miners. But confidence was shaken, despite a rescue loan from the International Monetary Fund. In August 1998 the government froze repayments of short-term bills and the rouble was devalued. Many banks failed, many Russians lost out, incomes began to drop. Yeltsin appointed a new prime minister, Primakov, an elderly man with an academic and KGB background. Primakov had been a critic of economic reform and his period of office coincided with a strong public opinion (70 per cent) in favour of state ownership of the bigger industries. Thanks to devaluation and other factors, Primakov's period also coincided with an economic turnround. He administered well, and was seen as a good choice. At a time when Yeltsin's popularity rating had fallen to a new low of 2 per cent, Primakov's was 70 per cent. This, it was said, was why he was suddenly dismissed. Others speculated that Primakov was turning his new broom in the direction of corruption by the richer families, and that would be enough to set influential tongues wagging against him. Yeltsin later wrote that he had been seeking someone to succeed him as president, trying out various candidates as prime minister first, and Primakov 'had too much red in his palette'. After another young man had been tried for a short while, Yeltsin in August 1999 appointed as prime minister a virtual unknown, Vladimir Putin. Evidently Yeltsin soon decided that this was his man.

Putin had been a devoted and successful member of the KGB. He had studied law and as a KGB operative had spent time outside the USSR, in the German Democratic Republic. After the KGB had become the post-Soviet FSB (Federal Security Service) he attracted attention and before long was head of that service. At that time he was a relatively young man, smartly groomed, smartly dressed, with a serious yet friendly manner, very polite and with an aura of quiet self-confidence. In the Anglo-Saxon world he would have been recognizable as the kind of man who rings front-door bells with ten copies of the *Watchtower* under his arm.

A few weeks after his appointment two high-rise Moscow apartment blocks were blown up, with massive fatalities. These atrocities were attributed to Chechen terrorists.[7] Putin and Yeltsin decided to settle the Chechen issue once and for all, by a full military effort, and this time the Russian population was all in favour of an aggressive response. In the December 1999 Duma election the new 'Unity' party, associated with Putin, received only 1 per cent fewer votes than the communists; in effect, this meant the end of communist dominance in the Duma.

Yeltsin unexpectedly and cunningly resigned at the end of 1999, just before his term was up. This enabled Putin to take over as acting president, which gave him a great advantage in the presidential election of March 2000, which he won comfortably.

Yeltsin's period of office may have been a great disappointment to many, but he had at least preserved the new basic freedoms. His so-called super-presidential form of government did have echoes of the old tsarist, or Byzantine, autocracy with its omnipotence, irrationalities, and fatherly irresponsibility. But he took office as an elected president and his successor also arrived via an election that was free even if perhaps not quite fair. Yeltsin's failures were many, but in the circumstances of a weak state and powerful adverse currents he preserved a unified Russia. Russian unity and Russian democracy had a natural tendency to work against each other, but under Yeltsin their cohabitation brought no terminal disasters.

Putin

Very much a man from nowhere, Putin the presidential candidate revealed little of himself in the weeks leading up to his election. He seemed to be all things to all men. Conservative voters (and others, too) were pleased by his aggressive war against Chechen rebels. He talked about the need to rescue the military-industrial complex, even drank a toast to Stalin. He declared himself to be proud of his service in the KGB. But at the same time he reassured other voters that there could be no return to the past, and told FSB operatives that they should not allow any repressive violations of the law. It was expected that after his election he would reveal his true self, but in this respect he was a

---

7. Some weeks later three men were discovered with explosive material beneath another apartment block in a provincial city. They were not Chechens, and they were released. The missing ingredient of this story is still awaited.

disappointment. However, he immediately addressed long-standing weaknesses inherited from the previous regime. He cut regional and republican leaders down to size by ending their privileged appointment to the second house of parliament and by sending his own 'presidential envoys' into the regions to ensure that the centre's policies and laws were properly observed. In doing this he enhanced his own, central power. His tidying of political parties had a similar effect (a party, to exist, henceforth had to have 10,000 members, and branches in half the regions; this made the formation of regional parties very difficult). Again, this was seen to be a sensible move which, at the same time, placed more power in Putin's hands.

Significantly, he began to tackle the oligarchs. One, Berezovsky, had so many charges to answer that he became a permanent resident abroad. Another, Gusinsky, also thought it sensible to live abroad and his Media-MOST empire was in financial trouble. He was joint owner, with Gazprom, of the NTV television channel, the only big channel that was independent of the government. Gazprom, with government encouragement, squeezed Gusinsky out and a number of his editorial staff resigned in protest. Pessimists saw the loss of his television company and of his newspapers as a sign of the government taking over control of the press. In 2002 an oil company owning a share in the remaining, medium-size, independent national TV company performed a similar legal manoeuvre, bringing it, too, into line. Putin had earlier expressed his support of free media, but with the ominous reservation that they should act responsibly.

It was evident that Putin was uncomfortable with press criticism, and there can be little doubt that he obtained satisfaction from the prising of Gusinsky from his media empire. That empire had been particularly scathing over Putin's first major public relations failure, when he appeared to take lightly the loss of the submarine *Kursk* with all hands, a catastrophe that the Russian public took very much to heart. But Putin, like part of the public, may have been misled by the navy high command, which in Soviet-style obfuscation attempted to first deny, then minimize, the tragedy. Coupled to the army's failures in Chechnya, the navy's technical state and its admirals' unreconstructed attitude was a dark reminder, to many, that there were still murky corners in Russia where yesterday seemed more inviting than today. It was still too early to know whether Putin's announced good intentions would survive the temptations that enhancement of his power would offer. But those enhancements had arisen because Putin had done what had long needed to be done. After his first year in office Russians still did not feel that they knew him. The most convincing speculation was that he was a man of the state, in the old Russian sense: for him the state had to be supreme, and unthreatened. He seemed to want authority; whether he could get it without lapsing into authoritarianism was what worried people.

Transition democracy

Just as the uncertain course of the Russian economy was given the academically useful but maybe optimistic term 'transition', the democratic reforms of the 1990s might well have been termed 'transition' democracy, for the processes of that decade were not quite a democratization. The 1993 Constitution gave the president rather wide powers, and the parliament and constitutional court rather limited powers. If a constitution balances democratic and authoritarian requirements, then the Russian Constitution was heavily weighted towards the latter. It had not moved far towards the 'legal state', a state in which the rule of law is paramount. The state still seemed closely tied to the prevailing regime, and whether this was a result or a cause of its weakness was disputed. Indeed, the weakness of the Russian state was itself disputed. Many, including international banks lending money to the Russian state, did not know, or chose not to know, that it was indeed weak. But it was plainly unable to freely impose its will on society. It could neither collect its taxes nor keep its promises.

The weak leadership offered by President Yeltsin and his governments enabled the so-called oligarchs controlling the big financial conglomerates to join with the state (the president and his retinue) to mould the changing economic situation. This was notably the case with the enrichments derived from privatization. This alliance of interests was hardly affected by any form of supervision in the form of parliamentary scrutiny and the law. But by the time Putin became president this relationship was showing signs of decay; cooperation between the oligarchs was changing to distrust, and the state's blood had been almost sucked dry.

In the 1990s the general public was reluctant to identify with public institutions or political parties, even though this was a crucial period in which a new society was being formed. It had already had more than enough of the state in communist times. That state had imposed irrationality (party ideology had almost always taken precedence over common sense), and in the Gorbachev years the state had lacked the authority to take over the country as the communist party declined. What the role of the state should be in post-communist times seemed uncertain. It could not be trusted to assert social justice because all too plainly the citizen remembered how the state in Russian history always seemed to pursue its own aims, the citizens' rights having low priority. It could have been the instigator and supervisor of an economic upswing, as had happened in Japan and seemed to be happening in China. But it had done precisely that in Soviet times and had left painful memories.

In the post-Soviet decade the state and parliament and the constitutional court all had some power. But preponderant power lay elsewhere. On the one hand were the financial-industrial conglomerates, headed by the seven 'oligarchs' and with lesser cliques in the regions, and on the other hand were those international forces that globalization had released. The Russian state, when Putin took over as president, was tending to be more a mediator between competing interests than a sovereign actor in its own right.

In the new federal Russia the party system, if system it was, differed from those of older democracies. There was a multiplicity of parties, often formed to fight just one election. Some small parties were founded to satisfy the vanity of people fancying themselves as party leaders. A registered party could qualify for television time, which was an asset for individuals contesting just a few seats, or only one. In the 1995 election there were 43 parties, although some of these joined together in blocs. The right-wing liberal democrats and the communist party were the only parties with a large membership and a long life. The communists appealed to the under-privileged and the older generation, but also attracted some younger people who believed they were a party strong enough to drag Russia out of its predicament. The liberal democrats had a constituency among traditionalist males in particular, and among those who yearned nostalgically for Russia's past greatness. A smaller but long-lived party was Yabloko, which repre-sented the democratic opposition to the government, while rejecting nation-alism and communism. But on the whole the electorate was highly volatile; in the 1995 election, for example, the communist party lost a third of those who voted for it in 1993 yet at the same time doubled its vote. One reason why voters did not take party loyalty seriously was the knowledge that under the Russian constitution a winning party was unlikely to determine the next government; the electors' verdict was more an expression of opinion than a political decision.

The regions

The Federal Treaty of early 1992 was based on developments in the previous year, and had been controversial in so far as there were several ways to approach the problem of minorities forming part of the Soviet-era union republics. Some former autonomous regions of the old Soviet-era Russia drove hard bargains in establishing how far their sovereignty would extend. As finalized, the Treaty acknowledged 89 separate territorial administrations ('federal subjects') composing Russia. Fifty-five of them were regions, which came to be administered by governors, 21 of them were republics accom-modating non-Russian populations and governed by presidents, 11 were smaller ethnic divisions, and the remaining two were the cities of Moscow and St Petersburg under their mayors. Yeltsin tried to move his chosen men into governorships, but was not always successful as these became elected posi-tions. Governors and presidents, together with their leading officials, were preponderantly former party officials, and they had close links with other former party men who occupied positions in industry and commerce; sometimes they themselves had arrived at their political posts from industry. A handful of them, like the leaders of St Petersburg and Nizhnii Novgorod in the early 1990s, were outstanding proponents of reform, but the majority tended to be unenthusiastic, more interested in exploiting their own niches and therefore suspicious of Moscow.

There were frequent conflicts between federal laws and the federal constitution on the one hand and the local laws and constitutions on the other. The so-called 'parade of sovereignties' repeatedly took place when centre and region disputed whose law had precedence in a given situation. Governors and presidents were jealous of their economic prerogatives. Even in the final years of the USSR there were embryonic trade barriers between regions, notably around Moscow where the mayor introduced ration cards to prevent non-Muscovites buying food in city stores. In the Yeltsin years such barriers continued to appear, usually for short periods when one 'federal subject' or another tried to assert itself at the expense of its neighbours. For example, one might seek to prevent export of its products to others as a means of keeping prices low at home; the price of basic foodstuffs in one region could be a third of those in another.

The struggle between the central government and regional or republican governments concerned conflicting rights and laws and, above all, tax. The 'federal subjects' were reluctant to send tax revenues to Moscow, while at the same time they were clamouring for financial help from the centre. Ideally, in a federal state the centre would receive tax revenues and redistribute them so that poorer regions or republics might gain a little. In practice this may have happened in a disorganized way, but there was no agreed plan, merely a series of disputes that were eventually settled fairly amicably by means of bilateral treaties.

The richer 'federal subjects' tended to be those with raw material resources that could be exported. The poorer were those that were mainly agricultural or contained urban backwaters where industries were old-fashioned and loss-making. The richer, raw-material, entities were among the least enthusiastic for economic reform, calculating that things were going well as they were. A handful of 'federal subjects' maintained quasi-diplomatic relations with foreign powers by means of trade delegations and official exchanges.

The existence of powerful local rulers was an important factor in the weakness of the central government. In the Yeltsin years bilateral treaties were made between the federal government and the republics and regions, usually transferring rights and privileges away from the centre, with 'fiscal appeasement' in the form of promised allocations from the central budget (promised, but not always paid). In 1997 the Russian republics were given the right to produce their own school textbooks; what effect this might have on the loyalties of younger generations remained to be seen.[8] Many of the republic constitutions stipulated that only citizens of those republics could become judges, which was quite contrary to the federal constitution.

One of the first cares of Putin, when he became president in 2000, was to reverse the flow of power from centre to regions. He began by grouping the regions and republics into seven presidential districts and appointing his own 'presidential envoys' to supervise them. Yeltsin had earlier appointed his own representatives to the regions with largely the same aim, but they had failed, either because they lacked sufficient power or because they aligned themselves with the regional interests. Putin also acted to deprive the governors and presidents of their reserved seats in the Federal Council, the second chamber of the Russian parliament. A third move was to introduce legal sanctions that would make it possible to dismiss the occasional governor who repeatedly violated federal law.

In the summer of 2000 the federal procuracy ordered its regional prosecutors not to take their summer holidays until all the unlawful acts of regional and republican governments were challenged, prosecuted, and repealed. By the end of that year Putin could claim that 60 constitutions and 2,000 regional laws had been brought into conformity. This did not mean that Putin had won; that was still in the balance. He had faced strong and persistent resistance already, mainly from the ethnic republics that had earlier signed power-sharing treaties with Moscow. This resistance was subtle, consisting of step-by-step reasoned opposition to each federal advance. Tatarstan was the most stubborn. Its president agreed to resume the payment of tax revenues to Moscow yet at the same time insisted on the right to withhold this money in certain circumstances. While conceding federal objections to Tatarstan's coat of arms, the Tatar president continued to advocate the replacement of the Cyrillic by the Latin alphabet, a really deep statement of cultural independence. In Moscow, Mayor Luzhkov continued to defend the *propiska* system (whereby a permit was required to settle in Moscow), which for years had been seen to be illegal because it violated the constitution's provision that everybody should be free to choose their place of residence. The Bashkortostan president opposed the right of the presidential representatives to appoint officials of the regional federal agencies, and moreover threatened to disconnect the telephones at federal offices if this should happen. But slowly, piece by piece, Putin obtained the changes he wanted. How fast the regional and republican leaders would actually put into action what had been so unwillingly agreed was another matter. All the same, Putin had at least reversed the trend of the 1990s, which at one time had seemed to risk a break-up of the Russian Federation.

8. In 2001 the problem of history textbooks became so acute that the prime minister ordered a special investigation. A deputy education minister commented, 'We cannot live in a country with an unpredictable past!'

Chechnya

The Stalinist delineation of the ethnic map, with its union republics, autonomous republics, and autonomous regions, did preserve the various nationalities while avoiding conflicts both between ethnic groups and between ethnic groups and the state. The break-up of the USSR saw the separation of the union republics, but those new independent republics still had potential problems in the autonomous republics and regions they contained. In Russia, the Federal Treaty early in 1992 was signed amicably; it eschewed separatism, stipulated taxes, but preserved ethnic aspirations within the new republics. The Tatar Republic, centred on Kazan, was one of the largest of these, although smaller than Yakutiya, which renamed itself the Sakha Republic. The existence of entities like these owed something to the presence of tightly knit national cliques of former party administrators who were determined, somehow or other, to preserve their positions, harnessing real or not-so-real national feeling to replace the support previously derived from the party. These new national leaders were in constant dispute with Moscow over matters like taxation and the division of powers, but saw no future in struggling for complete independence.

Chechnya was a different matter. It was a land-locked territory just north of Georgia in the Caucasus, and contained the important oil centre of Grozny. The Chechens had shared the Chechen-Ingush autonomous republic, but when the USSR was in its final year a retired Red Air Force officer, Dzhokar Dudaev, declared himself president of Chechnya and demanded independence. Dudaev had originally enjoyed the tacit support of Yeltsin's colleagues, who believed that he would become their man in Chechnya. But he had no such intention. It was not long before he lost the confidence of his people, as various criminal groups found Chechnya a useful field of operations. After his unsuccessful intervention in 1991, Yeltsin was preoccupied with other matters and it was not until 1994 that attention was paid to the Chechnya situation. The matter could no longer rest; the question of how much independence, or sovereignty, the ethnic 'federal subjects' could enjoy was still being debated, and concessions to the Chechens could be expected to elicit demands for the same treatment elsewhere. After a Russian-backed rising failed to dislodge Dudaev, Yeltsin decided to send in the regular army and air force.

The Russian armed forces were in a state of decline. A reduction of numbers was desired, and there had been talk in the Russian Republic of reducing the armed forces to 1.5 million by 2000 and even perhaps building an all-professional army. There had indeed been some shrinkage, but more housing and more job opportunities were needed for a large-scale reduction, two conditions that seemed unfulfillable in the early 1990s. What was not fully understood at the time was how the quality of the armed forces had fallen. Discipline had dissolved. Soldiers had not been paid. Officers were demoralized. Those conscripts who did not evade service were still 'hazed' by their seniors and went on to bully their own juniors. This process, still sometimes fatal and always brutalizing, created an army that was ill-trained for battle. It was this army that was thrown into Chechnya, where frightened soldiers soon decided that brutality was their best guarantee of survival.

Victory over the Chechen rebels was expected to need a week, but no victory ensued, only massive casualties on both sides, with the civilian population suffering most. More than two-thirds of Russians disapproved of the recourse to arms; they dreaded a replay of the Afghan war. Thousands of young conscripts were among the casualties, and atrocities were committed by both sides. Although Russia's defence minister had recommended military action, most of the generals were against it. In the democratic parties opinion was split. Having approved Yeltsin's use of armed force against the parliamentary opposition, the democrats could hardly condemn the use of force against a breakaway movement that seemed to threaten the unity of the Russian Federation. Nationalists, on the other hand, rather resented Yeltsin's adoption of their own line, and largely out of spite withheld their approval. Outside observers saw the conflict as unnecessary, and imposed by the respective vanities of Yeltsin and Dudaev. Leaders in the ethnic republics of the Federation began to get anxious, fearing that the violence being unleashed on Chechnya presaged a harder line of Moscow towards their own republics. In the west, at first, governments did not disapprove, regarding Yeltsin as worthy of support. But in early 1995 western leaders began to urge moderation.

In summer 1995, with the Russians no nearer to a conclusive victory, and casualties mounting, the Chechen rebels made a sally into the Stavropol region and took a hospital as their hostage. Russian troops were sent in, resulting in the death of some of the thousand-odd hostages. In Yeltsin's absence abroad, Chernomyrdin then negotiated a peace which gave the rebels safe-conduct in return for the freeing of the surviving hostages. The rebels thereby accepted much less than what they had originally demanded, but this did not prevent the condemnation of Chernomyrdin for his alleged sell-out. In the Duma, Chernomyrdin lost a vote of confidence tabled by the communists. Yeltsin then intervened and the Duma changed its mind in exchange for Yeltsin's promise to negotiate an end to the war.

A ceasefire was arranged and two delegations met in Grozny. An agreement in principle was reached in which an eventual status similar to that of Tatarstan was agreed. However, Dudaev refused to accept the terms negotiated by his delegation, and there were many influential Russians who preferred to pursue the war. For a time peace was preserved by the efforts of the local Russian commander and his Chechen opposite number, both of whom did their best to talk to each other. It was not long before assassins forced the Russian general off the scene, putting an end to this uneasy peace. Moscow installed its own head of the Chechen Republic who, however, found it wise to move around his capital in the safety of an armoured car. In January 1996 there was another hospital-hostage raid, this time in the neighbouring republic of Dagestan. An attempt by the Federal Security Service to overcome the rebels with the aid of missiles and fighter planes was a conspicuous and bloody failure.

Seeking to recover some kind of initiative, Moscow allocated a large sum for the rebuilding of Grozny, which had been largely destroyed in the fighting. This expenditure on what were seen as rebels aroused anger, and even generated strikes, among Russian state employees whose wages had not been paid by the government for several months. Some of the money seemed to have been taken from an International Monetary Fund credit and not much of it seems to have reached Chechnya, intermediary banks having taken their cut. Some of the hard currency that did arrive fell into the hands of the rebels, who used it to buy arms from local Russian troops.

With the Russian army showing its incompetence on a daily basis, casualty lists growing, international complaints about Russian atrocities, and with an election coming up, Yeltsin announced his readiness to negotiate with Dudaev and to end hostilities. The Chechens responded with some scepticism, and the war continued, thanks to the determination of hardliners on both sides. In April 1996 a missile was homed in on Dudaev as he made a call on his portable phone. His successor was invited to Moscow and a ceasefire, plus an agreement for Russian troop withdrawal and subsequent elections, was reached.

General Lebed, who had retired from the army and also from the second round of the presidential election, was dispatched to Grozny with full powers to negotiate. An agreement was signed, postponing definition of Chechnya's status for five years. Both Chechens and Russians regarded this as a Russian climb-down, although Lebed was rather pleased with himself, having achieved, he said, the impossible. Yeltsin accepted the agreement at the same time as some of his ministers were condemning it. Various supplementary agreements were signed and, to the disgust of many, peace descended on Chechnya.

Over the ensuing three years the various Chechen leaders, or warlords, were unable to agree among themselves. Some of their forces went on the rampage. Foreign aid workers were atrociously killed, and in 1999 Prime Minister Putin decided on a once-and-for all offensive. In this he was supported by a big majority of Russians, who believed that Chechens were responsible for the increasing number of terrorist acts in Russia; the first major attack had been the 1999 detonation of explosives under a tall apartment building in Dagestan (Chechnya's neighbour), which killed 62 residents. This was followed by similar attacks in Volgodonsk and Moscow, killing hundreds of people in their beds.

This second Chechen war did not go well. There were isolated successes, but casualties were high and Russian troops were not only killing the local populations, but doing so with unnecessary cruelty. Chechen fighters perpetrated their own atrocities. By end-2001 the long-sought total victory had still not been won, but the western media was dealing more sympathetically with Russia's dilemma. This was largely because the embroilment of the USA with international terrorism changed many minds. Russia now became a possible ally against a common enemy. Existing tension points, notably the extension of NATO to former Soviet-bloc countries, and the US intention of flouting the long-standing ABM Treaty, seemed to become less unacceptable to the Russian government. Meanwhile, Putin travelled indefatigably in search of better relationships not only to Texas but also to China and western Europe. Overtures to North Korea had at least one interesting result, the operation of an armoured train over the Trans-Siberian Railway to carry its fearful president on a visit to Moscow.

The new economy

In western countries, when the Cold War ended in 1989 a new world view had emerged that was moulded by ideology rather than reality. In the shallow end of the intellectual pool people talked of 'the end of history', and the line of most opinion-formers was that the Cold War had been 'won' by the west, and the winning weapon had been the arms drive (notably the non-existent but much talked-of 'Star Wars' system). The Russians, it was said, had seen the economic impossibility of keeping up with western arms expenditure and had accordingly thrown in the towel. Certainly the arms race was a big factor, but it would have been more useful to have seen 1989 not as a victory for the west, but as a victory of Russian progressives over Russian reactionaries, or of rationality over fundamentalism. In the following years the rational, progressive, wing of Russian political life was struggling against powerful opposition to rebuild Russia into a relaxed democratic state, and it needed western help. But most of that help, financial and moral, was channelled to what was regarded as the defeated Russian state, of which Yeltsin and his friends were guardians; hence the later regrets about 'money down the drain'. As befitted a defeated beneficiary, money was not loaned without strings, and those strings (like the paring of social service expenditure) could, literally, be lethal for the ordinary Russian. Meanwhile, by what seems to have been spontaneous sleight of hand, the end of the Cold War and the disappearance of the Soviet system was seen as conclusive proof of the failure of socialism. That right-wing publicists succeeded so well in equating Russian communism with European socialism had, perhaps, more importance for the European left than for Russia, but in that atmosphere any suggestion that Russia's immediate future would be best assured by anything other than a leap to capitalism had small chance of discussion. Russia, once again, would adopt an ideology designed by, and for, foreigners.

Establishing the market economy in Russia required some determination, for the old system of state control still had strong support, especially among administrators for whom it had become a way of life that was not easily abandoned. The two essential changes were abandonment of state-fixed prices and transfer of industry from the state to private management and ownership. Yegor Gaidar, who had been economics editor of *Pravda*, was appointed acting prime minister and entrusted with economic policy. He was in his thirties, and surrounded himself with like-minded and similarly young economists to work out the lines of the new reform. The youth of this group was bitterly assailed by those opposed to their liberalizing intentions; Rutskoi's comment about 'boys in pink shorts and yellow bootees' was destined for a long life. But at this juncture youthful self-confidence was what the situation demanded.

Later, it was said that the Russian reformers had followed too eagerly the advice of western economists. Certainly, whereas robust western economies could bear the burden of western economists, the fragile Russian economy lacked such resilience. Additionally, there was the traditional Russian over-receptiveness to ideas emanating in the west. In too many cases western economists saw Russia as virgin territory on which they could try out their latest convictions, or give a second chance to ideas that seemed to have failed at home.[9] Above all, western economists were in evangelical mode, spreading the gospel of the market, and expecting their truths to prevail because they were correct. The model at the back of their minds was an idealized version of their own economy back home; this pushed them in the direction of deregulation and competition, and minimal social welfare expenditure, but no great investment in essential public services. They did not seem to notice that they were planting capitalism in a society where there were no reliable property rights, where business decisions could include the pros and cons of eliminating a competitor by gunfire, and where a money-laundering gang could be registered as a bank. Most western governments were ill-advised, as were the international banks that inserted dollars into what they believed was the Russian economy but was all too often a conduit to private bank accounts outside Russia.

'Shock therapy' rather than a gradual transition to the market was adopted, on the grounds that maximum momentum would be required to complete a transformation that would be quite painful. Brushing aside the Russian saying 'the slower you go the further you'll get', the government promised that the gains of the reform would begin to be felt after about a year. As a start, foreign trade was deregulated and retail prices freed from state control in January

9. In 2001, just as the British railways were near-paralysed by a defective privatization scheme, there were British consultants advising the Russian government to follow the British model in the restructuring of Russian railways.

1992.[10] The consequences were very much as the reformers had predicted. To reach their natural 'market' levels (where they make supply and demand of products more or less equal), most prices immediately doubled or trebled, but products that were hitherto much wanted but unavailable in the stores did, for a time, become more available. Because so much money had been saved by citizens in Soviet times, the new prices were at first paid without much protest, but the change did set off high and prolonged inflation, as critics had prophesied. Attempts at limiting the money supply resulted in a cash crisis and the government in mid-1992 was pressurized into printing more money, which made inflation worse.[11]

Because raw material prices were still state controlled, but foreign trade deregulated, it became possible to make fortunes by buying up raw materials at internal prices and exporting them at world prices. This flow of new money encouraged the formation not only of trading companies, but also of new private banks. Domestic industry requiring those materials suffered. Converting internal materials to exports was illegal, but simple, drawing the hitherto blameless into criminality (in ensuing years, the customs service would become notorious for its corruption).

Because of the cash shortage, enterprises were increasingly unable to pay their bills. Payment in kind became common, resulting in all kinds of strange transactions.[12] An enterprise could become technically insolvent even when its creditors amounted to less than its debtors. Meanwhile, the government was failing to gather its taxes, a situation that persisted into the next century. The Soviet system of automatic deduction of taxes fell by the wayside as more and more enterprises left the state system. New federal and local taxes were introduced as replacement, with the local and federal authorities in competition, resulting in overlapping taxes and a tax burden so heavy that an enterprise might only survive by dint of tax evasion. Unpaid taxes meant that the state had insufficient revenue to carry out its obligations, which was why, for example, pensions and soldiers' pay fell into bad arrears. Another effect was increased borrowing by the state, both at home and abroad. It could happen that the state borrowed money that, rightfully, was its own.

State industries could still obtain subsidies, compensating for their lack of initiative and efficiency. Privatization was seen as the necesary remedy for this

---

10. Not quite all retail prices were freed immediately. Bread prices had long been an emotional issue, and they were among the last to be freed.

11. The consumer price index (1990=100) was 260 in 1991, 6,786 in 1992, 63,788 in 1993, before decelerating to 200,934 in 1994. It would surpass 1,000,000 in 1998. These are cumulative indices, not annual rises. Thus 1993 saw a less than ten times increase over 1992, which was devastating enough for anyone with non-dollar savings, despite rising interest rates. Wages rose more slowly, so the real average income in 1998 was about 60 per cent of the 1990 level.

12. For providing transportation service to one agricultural enterprise, the October Railway was regularly paid in chickens. Cases were publicized of workers receiving their wages in the form of toothpaste and sanitary towels. Such transactions made life interesting for the tax authorities.

state of affairs. The privatization process began in late 1992, after all citizens had become entitled to a voucher that could be exchanged for shares in the new private companies. Less than a fifth of the vouchers, which had a nominal value of about six weeks' average wage, were actually used by their recipients to purchase shares. Most voucher-owners invested their vouchers in mutual funds, or sold them, or gave them away. Of this majority, some were swindled and most lost out.

What confounded the reformers was that the existing state managers, former members for the most part of the communist party's *Nomenklatura*, managed to stay in control. There were several approved privatization patterns, and general meetings of enterprises were called to make the choice. In the end, and on average, workforces emerged as the bigger shareholders, with managers holding a sizable proportion as well. In practice, because managers were managers, having background information, access to a firm's bank account, and connections with powerful local figures and groups, it was they who retained control of most firms. They could additionally obtain bank loans to buy additional shares, often under the cover of intermediaries, and such shares might even be purchased with a company's own money. Meanwhile, a new breed of speculative investors was buying up vouchers and investing them in companies that seemed undervalued. New quasi-criminal networks developed, involving banks and other institutions that held accumulations of vouchers in the one hand and privatization officials and managers in the other. This new, ambitious class was interested not in increasing profits, but in the wealth to be gained by acquiring more and more businesses at negligible cost. Because the workforce held a proportion of shares, it was in any case difficult to increase profits by shedding surplus staff.

The reformers held back privatization of the biggest state companies. Some kind of financial stabilization was achieved in 1995 by means of state intervention to keep movements of the exchange rate below the inflation rate and by budget cuts which resulted in renewed paring of subsidies to the defence industry and a reduction of social service spending; the latter economy may be presumed to have contributed to the drastic fall in Russian expectation of life. The issue of short-term state bills was accelerated.

With most medium-sized firms in private hands, and the state in financial difficulties stemming largely from the subsidies it still paid and its inability to extract the taxes that were due to it, it was decided to privatize most of the remaining big state enterprises. By this time, building on profits made from the earlier privatizations, the big banking/industrial conglomerates had emerged, and these had lent money to the hard-pressed government. It was decided that these loans should be paid back in the form of shares in the big state companies. In this way state industries were transferred to private hands at a fraction of their value. For example, a controlling interest in the world's biggest nickel producer at Norilsk was sold to a group for about one-eighth of its true value, and that in a big oil company for about one-thirty-fifth of its value. In some cases the bank entrusted with allocating the assets to the conglomerate offering the best bargain was a bank belonging to one of the conglomerates; the latter would be awarded the shares even though its bid was not the highest.

It was in this way that the seven 'oligarchs' emerged in all their glory, each controlling his own conglomerate. A conglomerate was centred on its own bank, and had one or more influential politicians on its leash. Its wealth was such that it was powerful enough to avoid taxation without making a secret of it. Its armed security force could be relied upon to keep away the taxation police. Conglomerates soon invested in the media, gaining virtual control of television companies and some major newspapers. But much of their gain, instead of being invested at home, was put safely into foreign banks. Scaled-down oligarchs also operated on more local levels, and their money, too, went abroad and bought West Indian villas for them and private education for their children. When their money needed to be 'laundered', western banks could always be found which would cooperate. Russian investigators in pursuit of illicit transfers were not always helped by foreign officialdom. The Swiss, in particular, seemed reluctant to cooperate with the Russian authorities.

Privatization was slowed down by a new law of 1997, which prevented the government staging closed auctions of state property and required it to submit its annual privatization plans to parliamentary scrutiny. That parliament was able to impose its wishes at this time was due to additional discredit accumulated by the conglomerates. They no longer acted together, and their rivalries consisted not only in shady deals, and slanging matches conducted through their respective media organizations, but also occasional confrontations between their so-called security forces.

According to the interior ministry's Economic Crime Administration, at the end of 1996 the capital accumulated by criminal groups amounted to 40 per cent of all money in circulation. There were 500 commercial banks controlled by criminals, as well as about 4,000 joint-stock companies. In 1997 219,000 economic crimes were uncovered, of which half were in the field of foreign trade. Meanwhile the government's statistical service believed that two-thirds of foreign trade transactions were not reported to the authorities.[13]

One big industry seemed to stand aside from the surrounding upheaval. This was Russian Railways, whose head (the railways minister) was customarily a railwayman. The reformers acknowledged that railways were a 'natural monopoly', needing special treatment, and a succession of railway ministers held at bay the more avid privatizers, usually by skilled foot-dragging,

---

13. But then, nor was half the agricultural production. A lot of foreign trade consisted of individuals using passenger trains to cross and recross the frontiers, surrounded by their mounds of unpaid excess baggage which consisted of items bought cheap in one country to to be sold dear in another.

although one minister publicly announced he would resign if the government agreed to a western banker's suggestion that, in exchange for a much-needed loan, the government should privatize the railways. Restructuring the railways was thereby delayed by at least a decade, and was to be achieved largely on the railwaymen's terms. In the meantime the railways provided the service that the country required and at times they seemed to be the only Russian industry that could be described as stable. Sticking out like a healthy thumb, they demonstrated an alternative path that the economy might have taken, not one of quick transformations of routines and structures, but of adaptation to a market economy while preserving all the existing routines and structures that seemed to work. Russian railway personnel at the beginning of the twenty-first century were still wearing their old Soviet hammer-and-sickle cap badges, and the trains were still running to time.

Privatization created huge fortunes for those who were well placed at the start of the programme, or were sufficiently smart and unscrupulous to take advantage of changing conditions. Meanwhile the economy continued to decline, as did the standard of living of most people. Critics were saying that the blanket privatization and enrichment of a few put Russia into the category of Latin American economies, whereas a mixed public and private economy, like the Chinese, would have been better. Much of the money made by the state from the sale of the bigger industries was not used for the investment that was so badly needed, but for propping up companies that were making losses. In 1997 about half the large and medium enterprises were making a loss. Because the state had held on to some profit-making enterprises, in that year the state sector did better than the private, a reversal of what the economic theorists had forecast. Privatization and liberalization became highly unpopular and their proponents had begun to lose political influence.

Reformers argued that despite its faults the privatization programme had been successful, because in a short space of time the economy had been freed from state control, and initiative liberated, and any price was worth paying for that. But despite a minority of forward-looking managers, initiative tended to be not liberated, but blocked, in that majority of firms that remained under their old managers. Such managers often mounted rearguard actions against the infusion of new capital that their run-down companies needed so badly; to acquire capital from outside investors would mean outside influence on their management, and this was the last thing they wanted. To make ends meet, in the absence of production that could be easily and profitably sold, they allowed wages to rise more slowly than inflation.

Soviet-style trade unions, unused to protecting their workers' interests, could not help, and in a few industries new, more aggressive unions were established. But in a declining economy in which workers feared above all loss of their jobs, even these new unions could not achieve much. In general, workers' protests rather resembled outbreaks by peasants in tsarist times; a localized uproar with a concrete incident setting off long-standing grievances, with a quick settlement by the authorities, fearful that the trouble might spread.

While in 1990–8 the gross industrial output attributable to the private sector grew from one-tenth to nine-tenths, in the same period total output halved, so privatization had really made no obvious contribution to growth. The federal bankruptcy service was meant to play a big part in reinvigorating industry. There were many companies that were effectively insolvent but pretended otherwise, meantime benefiting from government subsidy. The intention was that an inefficiently run enterprise, denied subsidy, would become insolvent, be declared bankrupt, and offered for sale to a more enterprising organization. In this way the bankruptcy service weeded out costly loss-makers, but sometimes it seemed to operate as though it had a plan to fulfil, with basically healthy enterprises forced into bankruptcy. Also, forced bankruptcy could put respectable businesses into the hands of big conglomerates. A conglomerate wishing to acquire an enterprise could instruct one of its affiliated companies to place a large order with the target company, and then not pay up. This would cause a liquidity crisis in that company, which would then be declared bankrupt and offered for auction, at which point the conglomerate would purchase it.

The oligarchs liked to compare themselves to the US railroad barons, whose shady operations might have ruined many but at least provided railroads for later generations. The answer to this was that the oligarchs had produced nothing for Russia, not invented a better mousetrap, but had simply cashed in. But not everything is as clear as it might seem. One small example of the difficulties of evaluating the fruits of stolen money is presented by the Russian film industry. The industry was enjoying a notable artistic renaissance in the 1990s, largely financed by what might be described as constructive money-laundering. Investing 'dirty money' in film production and then withdrawing clean money in the form of box-office receipts was a strategem used by several major and minor oligarchs.

In 1998, as western optimism about Russia's economic transformation declined, and world oil prices fell, there was a financial crisis that drastically devalued the rouble. This was ruinous for those who had borrowed money abroad, but the higher import prices gave Russian-made products a better market. The Russian products were sometimes better in any case. It was fashion rather than the palate that had been gratified by Dutch tomatoes and British chocolate; the price of good taste could sometimes be tastelessness.[14]

It was not always a matter of fashion, however, as the 'Chicken-leg War' of 1996 demonstrated. This conflict reached a point where Prime Minister

14. But by 2000 both the Coca-Cola and Pepsi-Cola production lines in Russia were diversifying into Russian-style drinks like *kvas*, as Russian palates recovered their balance.

Chernomyrdin and US Vice-President Gore were exchanging strong notes about the finer points of chicken-leg production. US producers had found a growing market in Russia for chicken legs, and for most urban Russians these became the cheapest and sometimes the only source of meat. Russian inspectors visiting the USA complained that US chickens contained unacceptable levels of artificial hormones and pesticides. With the US authorities seeming to accept these criticisms, the Russian government decided to halt US chicken-leg imports, at which point the war of words erupted. Americans believed that the ban was a form of protectionism, because Russian chicken producers were losing their home market. Eventually Russian officialdom accepted that, in terms of healthy eating, impure US chicken legs were better than no meat at all.

Growing Russian imports could be financed largely by growing exports, which were largely raw materials, notably but not exclusively oil and gas. Russia had returned to her historic and, for some, degrading role of exporter of raw materials and importer of more sophisticated goods. Less historic but equally disturbing was the growing import of foodstuffs, which accompanied a drastic decline in agricultural performance. Soviet agriculture had been hopelessly inefficient, and depended on various open and hidden subsidies. The post-Soviet situation witnessed not only a determination to end state subsidies, but also the opening of the market to external competitors. Producers, typically in the form of state or collective farm chairmen, were against change, and the result was a 40 per cent drop in farm production between 1990 and 1996. The picture, however, may have been over-black, because food grown by citizens on their allotments and consumed by themselves was hard to quantify. The weekend flow of trains from cities into the countryside, heavily loaded with families and their spades and hoes, was convincing testimony to the increase of small-scale food production. It was not only people who had their country dacha, but countless others who had bought or leased or otherwise appropriated plots of land outside the towns. Simple-to-grow crops like cabbages and potatoes were the favourites, so much so that Russian potato output actually grew between 1990 and 1998 whereas in that same period grain production fell by 60 per cent and milk by 40 per cent.

The creation of private farms by former collective or state farmers was encouraged, and by 1996 there were about 280,000 such farms. But they only produced about 5 per cent of grain output and had a negligible effect on agricultural production. Neither these private farmers nor the big collective and state farms could afford to pay the new higher prices for fertilizer and machinery at a time when food prices had to fall in order to keep their markets.

Free sale of land was long sought by the reformers, and long denied by the legislature. Land ownership had for centuries aroused emotions, the common feeling being that land was not given by God, but merely made available by

God. The communist collective farms had never been given their land, but simply had had the use of it. Yeltsin and his reformers included the right to buy and sell land in the 1993 Constitution, but there was no land code to guarantee the rights of buyers and sellers. The missing land code was finally passed in 2001, but only after fisticuffs had broken out during a Duma debate on the subject. So strong was the opposition that agricultural land was excluded.

By the end of the century there were signs of an economic revival. By that time there were growing hopes that the deadweight of the 'insider managers', who had so deftly converted allegiance to the party to allegiance to themselves as owner-managers, would be diluted as more and more were forced by the market to adapt or perish. But this was likely to be a slow process, as indeed were so many of the processes that liberalization was intended to bring about. Most important of all was the continued absence of a 'civil society', in which transactions could take place on a basis of good faith.

Society

'Civil society' is a term of pliable meaning. Perhaps the diary of a government official under Tsar Alexander III comes as close as possible to a useful interpretation:

We still do not have those essential elements without which there may be only civic co-habitation, without civic virtue: that is, public-spiritedness, a feeling for legality, and honourableness . . . Morals above all, morals and lawfulness.[15]

What was true under Alexander was even more true in the USSR, where the existence of any organization without state approval was not permitted, and any handful of citizens meeting regularly might find themselves defined as an illegal organization. Mutual suspicion, rather than mutual trust, was too often the norm. A strong civil society implies that the normal relationship between citizens is trust, that people endeavour to keep their promises and refrain from cheating each other, that they do not give or expect bribes. It is in this kind of atmosphere that the market economy can flourish, and transactions are not seen as agreements in which there must be a winner and a loser, but as an arrangement from which both parties benefit.

In the last decade of communist rule the concept of a civil society was quietly regarded as a hope for the future. But in the Yeltsin years the concept was marginalized in a society where the state was increasingly under the influence of oligarchs and presidential cronies. Nevertheless, at the beginning of the new century there were signs that at least the need for legal reform was recognized; investors, for example, were increasingly wary of a situation

---

15. A. V. Nikitenko, *Dnevnik* (1955), i. 411.

in which they could purchase a share of a Russian company, only to find themselves dispossessed by rivals with the right contacts.

The legal situation was such that it could help neither society nor business. Obsolete Soviet legislation remained in force for the most part, and the legislative process was very slow. Conflicts between federal Russian law and regional laws could be exploited by those with time and money. When Putin became president there was still an urgent need for new land and labour codes, while procedures in both civil and criminal cases badly needed streamlining.

The market economy tended to break up that social solidarity of small groups that had long been a saving feature of Russian society. This was one of the reasons it was unpopular. To fill the gap, and to some extent substitute for the slow-to-develop civil society, features of what was known as the 'third sector' emerged. In the Yeltsin years this grew, and comprised a network of non-governmental organizations that lay between the state and the population in general. Among others, the western foundations that directed funds to Russia made increasing use of such organizations. Funds granted, for instance, to the women's movement could go for distribution not to state institutions, but to non-state organizations set up for the purpose. But useful though it was, the third sector was a professionalized territory of organizations rather than the collective state of mind represented by the long-awaited civil society.

In a sector of their own were the criminal organizations. Whether they were a factor in the degradation of the market economy, or whether they owed their existence to the conditions created by that market economy, is an interesting question from which academics seem destined to derive a good deal of entertainment. The rise in criminality preceded the Yeltsin regime, and could in part be seen as a consequence of the disintegration of the communist system. With Yeltsin's economic reforms, and the weakness of the state, opportunities were presented for any brainy and acquisitive person with less than average scruples. What became known as the Russian Mafia emerged, although it was not really a mafia but rather a collection of hundreds of tiny mafias, each with their own territory or specialization. At the end of the century it was estimated that there were over 9,000 criminal organizations, employing about 100,000 operatives. Not far removed from the mafias were the security organizations operated by the big industrial and financial conglomerates, which were involved in industrial espionage, strong-arm coercion, and production of *kompromat* (compromising material, to be used in blackening the reputation of enemies or, better, getting them imprisoned).[16]

Meanwhile the taxation police was established. This was not a criminal organization, but behaved like one. It was designed to use violence to achieve a

16. The most spectacular *kompromat* was footage, shown on television, of the justice minister enjoying the company of naked women in a sauna. He was soon dismissed and a few years later, incidentally or not so incidentally, was convicted of embezzlement. The origin and indeed the authenticity of the tape was not clear.

most important state mission, collection of taxes. Dressed in camouflage outfits, masked, these armed detachments would descend on businesses that would not, or could not, pay their taxes, and would level their automatics at managers and clerical staff, raid the safe and petty cash, and make off with whatever money they could find. If disappointed in terms of hard cash, they could confiscate equipment, typically computers, but not excluding automobiles, cranes, tractors, and even locomotives.

They appeared at the vehicle depot like a storm cloud and, rattling their weapons, began to write down and take away the property: tables, chairs, computers, calculators, refrigerators, buses, trucks, without any ceremony and disdaining nothing. They even took the mirror from the women's toilet. To the workers' protests … came the unambiguous reply 'You can complain in court.'[17]

One of the most important management skills was fiddling the books, so as to avoid taxation. Fiddled books also made life easier for fraudsters and embezzlers who, quite often, were themselves part of management. Large-scale embezzlement required experienced helpers, so criminal cooperatives appeared that tended to develop into so-called mafias.

It could be argued that the Russian mafias played an important role in society. They represented a significant provider of employment opportunities. Their protection rackets performed a function that the police were failing to perform. If they enforced contracts by violence they were supplying a deficiency of commercial law. If they mediated disputes, they were again filling a gap. Although they certainly helped to stall the concept of the civil society, it was not they but the state's ineffectiveness that held back the transition to a society firmly based on law.

The death sentence was fully privatized by 1996, that being the year in which the state performed its last civil execution. Henceforth, executions were unconnected with the state, the police, and the law. Already prior to 1996, murder by contract was a large part of criminal business. Men who had learned the arts of violence in the security services, or in the Afghanistan war, were plentiful enough and could offer themselves as professional killers. Contract killings, which more often than not took place as the target was leaving an elevator or building, took the lives of straight businessmen, journalists who knew too much, a handful of brave politicians, as well as of criminals who invaded their rivals' territories, or who failed to carry out agreements, or who decided to fight it out with neighbouring gangs. Killings were sometimes grotesquely accomplished, with excessive butchery. Possibly this was simply a survival of centuries-old rural murder techniques or was intended to teach people a lesson, but the increasing television 'scene-of-the-crime' coverage may have introduced an element of showmanship. Killings were

17. *Gudok*, 10 Aug. 2001, 1.

often concentrated in a particular area, or field of activity. St Petersburg was a notorious hot-spot, with killings on a nightly basis. Among professions, bank managers seem to have had a certain vulnerability; between 1992 and 1996 over 50 of them were murdered.[18]

Criminal activity was also exported. A first step came in Soviet times, with the relaxation of emigration restrictions for Jews. Among the thousands of Russian immigrants to Israel were scores of criminals, and they soon established Israel as a base for worldwide operations. Much of this involved contacts with associates in Russia, so money-laundering was an initial activity. Other things followed; the export and management of Russian and east European prostitutes was a line of business in which these entrepreneurs soon showed unusual depths of cruelty and exploitation. In due course, Russian criminal affiliates spread to the USA, notably to New York but also to Los Angeles and Miami, where they became part of the long-term crime scene.

Crime on a retail basis, inherited from the previous decade, also spread although it was not quite as prevalent as people were led to believe by the media; this newspaper extract gives some idea of the flavour:

The wives of locomotive drivers, seeing their husbands off to work, show as much anxiety as if they were setting off for the front. Will they come back safe and sound? When has it ever been like this before? Only in the Civil War and World War 2, and also in the first post-war years before order had been restored and the crime wave subdued . . . And what should we think of that incident in May, when a suburban train of the Moscow Railway was burned by a group of evil-intentioned people hurling bottles filled with inflammable liquid? It was with bottles like those that their fathers and grandfathers fought fascist tanks, and now their grandsons attack peaceful trains.[19]

Rising crime was one, though not a major, cause of Russia's decreasing population, which began to cause anxiety in the 1990s despite the influx of Russian immigrants from the former Soviet republics. In mid-2001 the population was still falling at the rate of 0.6 per cent annually and was down to 144.4 million, three million less than in 1989. This drastic deterioration was not matched by other countries in transition from Soviet-type societies, although a decline in the birth rate did seem to be characteristic of such countries, including Russia. There was a sharp decline in life expectancy in the early 1990s, with that for males sinking by no less than six years to 57 years. With female life expectancy declining by three years, this implies that over a few years about a million Russians died who would not have died if life expectancy had not fallen. A noticeable rise in the death rate was coming from the category of violent death (accidents, murders, suicides) which tended to hit males most (see table, p. 608).

Half the 'additional' Russian deaths were from cardio-vascular disease, but because Russian doctors were reluctant to name certain diseases as

18. Many, of course, were crooks in bankers' clothing. 19. *Gudok*, 14 July 1992, 1.

cause-of-death precise analysis is impossible. Tuberculosis was causing some worry, and prisons were a notorious source of infection followed, some said, by hospitals. At the turn of the century syphilis and hepatitis were also on the increase. The latter, like HIV, owed its rise largely to the increasing use of injected drugs. The population in general seemed unworried by HIV, and offers by western institutions to help with money and know-how were not always taken up. In 2001, pessimists were forecasting an imminent epidemic of HIV and suggested that there were already a million cases, which was almost ten times more than the officially recorded number. HIV patients and, worse, individuals at risk seemed to regard the disease with a fatalism that was said to be 'typically Russian'.

Another breeding ground for tuberculosis was the homeless. These markedly increased in the 1990s but their number was uncertain (the old Soviet crime of vagrancy had been abolished, so the statistics for those sentenced for this crime were no longer available). In 1996 it was estimated that there were between 200,000 and 300,000 homeless in Moscow alone. Before the dissolution of the USSR, about nine-tenths of the homeless were former prisoners, but in the 1990s these were diluted by refugees, people who had sold their homes, and the psychologically unviable. Not much was done for the homeless, and their numbers were unlikely to decrease in the short term. A few overnight shelters were provided by some cities, however.

By 2000 refugees from the Chechen war, and 'transient' immigrants (real and self-proclaimed refugees who entered Russia in hope of proceeding to a more congenial country of asylum), were adding themselves to the previous wave of immigrants. The latter were those who after 1991 flowed into Russia from former Soviet states. They were not forced immigrants, but they were not quite voluntary either. They came from those new republics where life had been made difficult for them (Tadzhikistan and the Baltic republics, for example). Others had lost, or expected to lose, their jobs as a result of the new national regimes. The federal immigration service did its best to resettle these people, but had few resources for the job. It later redirected its activities towards persuading would-be immigrants to stay and make the best of things in the new republics. Those who did immigrate had a hard time, partly because they could not decide exactly who they were. For at least a century Russian settlers in non-Russian lands had been told, and eagerly accepted, that they were a superior kind of Russian, and when they returned as refugees they kept their pride, regarding the native Russians as 'them' rather than 'us', seeing them as lazy and alcoholic. By 1995 about 3 million had arrived, this number including some who were not ethnic Russians. A few local governments, notably Moscow city, were introducing regulations to limit, or prevent, their settlement.

Immigrants from the Caucasus ('people with swarthy skins' was how newspapers often termed them) were a target for black-jacketed youths wearing the insignia of the Russian National Unity organization, and could be beaten up or murdered. The main nationalist (or chauvinist) magazine *Russian Master* seemed to abhor them. This venom reflected, in part, that Russians, who had so long been regarded as the leading component of the Soviet Union, found it harder than other ex-Soviet peoples to identify themselves precisely as a nation. National feeling there certainly was, but it tended to take the form of a frustrated nostalgia. In 2000, the national anthem reverted to the music of Soviet times. This horrified some, but a survey of adults found that half preferred this tune, as against 15 per cent who wanted Glinka's 'Patriotic Song'. The Russian Orthodox Church assumed a leading stance in the creation of the new Russian nationalism. Even the communist leader Zyuganov said nice things about it. Church weddings and funerals became more fashionable. Non-Orthodox Christian churches and sects, some financed from parent organizations in the USA, were put under heavy pressure by the Orthodox Church and its political friends. Public subscription helped the construction of a new cathedral in central Moscow, erected on the same spot as the cathedral pointedly demolished in 1931. It was a replica of the latter, although containing more concrete, and it symbolized the Orthodox Church's resurrection as a pillar of society.

In August 2000 the Russian Orthodox Church canonized Tsar Nicholas II and his family. For Nicholas this was a kind of second coming, because he had already been elevated to sainthood by the émigré Russian Orthodox Church. In the 2000 ceremony, to make up for lost time, the Church created 860 additional saints, making this by far the biggest cannonade of saints ever set off in Russia. After some controversy Nicholas's remains were interred alongside his ancestors in the Petropavlovsk Cathedral in St Petersburg. No decision had been reached about Lenin, marooned in his mausoleum in Moscow, although there was growing support for a burial next to his mother, as he apparently had wished.

Nicholas and Lenin, both men of narrow good intent and broad evil consequence, had helped to make the twentieth century a time of torment and of sacrifice. Dire hardship had been imposed on Russians in the name of one or other great idea. Millions of deaths had resulted. In the end, those sacrifices had not gained very much, apart from a gigantic industrialization. Soviet industry, inefficient though it might be, was still an accomplishment and an asset in which Russians could take pride as their own achievement and their own possession. It was the remains of this, their industry, that in 1996 their president was selling off for peanuts. But the new possessing class that emerged in the 1990s, having made its fortune, was soon yearning for tranquillity and legality. This urge for stability, together with apparent economic improvement after 1998, were two factors on which optimists could seize.

Bibliography

General

Over the last decade there has been a growing output of books about Russia, coinciding with an upheaval in the country itself and in the organization of its archives. At the same time, in the Anglo-Saxon world, libraries have lacked the funds to keep up with this increased flow, so there are quite a few worthwhile titles that are hard to find. All this presents problems to a bibliographer working with limited space who, for a given subject, may have to choose between a modern but hard-to-obtain book and a reputable older but perhaps dated volume. So the reader is hereby notified that this bibliography does not contain every possible title on a given subject. There are worthy books that have been omitted but which may still be found on library shelves. Studies which showed the way in their time, but whose findings have been absorbed in later books, are among these.[1]

The opening of Russian archives over the last decade has not rendered obsolete what was written before. Western historians already had a sound appreciation of what had been happening in the Soviet Union. The new revelations add detail, sometimes explain why a previously inexplicable decision was made, and indicate certain fields that were previously taken for granted but in fact need more emphasis. For a taste of those archives, there is *Revelations from the Russian Archives: Documents in English Translation* by D. Koenker and R. D. Bachman, published by the Library of Congress in 1997.

For really complete book listings the reader is advised to turn to specialized annual bibliographies like *The American Bibliography of Slavic and East European Studies*, and *European Bibliography of Soviet, East European and Slavonic Studies*. Scholarly journals, mentioned in the next paragraph, review and list new publications.

The *Slavic Review* offers articles and book reviews covering history, politics, economics, and literature. Then there is the *Russian Review*, whose articles tend to be shorter but more varied. *Euro-Asian Studies* (formerly *Soviet Studies*) is especially strong in economics and politics. The *Slavonic and East European Review* devotes relatively little space to modern history, but what is there is good. Also worth reading are a number of more recently established journals, including *Canadian Slavonic Papers*, *California Slavic Studies*, *Canadian-American Slavic Studies*, *Russian History*, *Political History and Culture of Russia*, *Post-Soviet Affairs* (formerly *Soviet Economy*), and *Russian Literature Triquarterly*. There are also the twice-annual organ of the Study Group on the Russian Revolution, *Revolutionary Russia*, and *Journal of Soviet Military Studies*. The *Scottish Slavonic Review* sometimes has had interesting historical pieces, while the *Journal of Ukrainian Studies* devotes considerable space to history. In the Cold War decades the US Information Service published *Problems of Communism* which published useful and accessible articles by fair-minded specialists. This has now metamorphosed into *Problems of Post-communism*.

Most of the books mentioned in this Bibliography contain their own bibliographies. Encyclopedias also sometimes provide suggestions for reading. Among them are *The Cambridge Encyclopedia of Russia and the Soviet Union* (1982), edited by A. Brown and

---

1. A shamefaced footnote in suitably small type seems the best place to confess that, in this edition, the Bibliography contains several titles that the author has not seen, but only read about. He hopes to do better next time.

others. R. Maxwell, *Information USSR* (1962) consists of selective translations from the *Great Soviet Encyclopedia*, and may be regarded as a revealing presentation of the Soviet view of things in the late 1950s. A multi-volume encyclopedia originating in the USA that has been appearing over recent decades is *The Modern Encyclopedia of Russian and Soviet History*. For the quick reference, J. Paxton, *Companion to Russian History* (1984) can be useful. *The Soviet Union: A Biographical Dictionary* (1990), edited by A. Brown, is informative, while M. McCauley's *Who's Who in Russia since 1900* (1997) covers a slightly longer time-span. *The Longman Companion to Imperial Russia, 1689–1917*, edited by D. Longley, covers history, culture, and religion. J. Paxton's *Imperial Russia; A Reference Handbook* (2001) contains all kinds of useful material presented in an accessible manner.

Geography texts include L. Symons and J. Dewdney, *The Soviet Union* (1982) and J. P. Cole, *Geography of the USSR* (1967). Perhaps of more interest to history specialists are the two-volume collection, edited by J. Bater and R. French, *Studies in Russian Historical Geography* (1983) and W. H. Parker, *An Historical Geography of Russia* (1968). There are several historical atlases available, including A. Adams, *An Atlas of Russian and East European History* (1967), A. F. Chew, *An Atlas of Russian History* (1967), and R. N. Taafe, *An Atlas of Soviet Affairs* (1965). An exquisite and enlightening work is R. Milner-Gulland and N. Dejevsky, *A Cultural Atlas of Russia and the Soviet Union* (1989). An informative textbook is edited by M. Bradshaw, *The Soviet Union: A New Regional Geography* (1991). J. P. LeDonne's *The Russian Empire and the World, 1700–1917* (1997) is very good on geopolitics and narrative, but the theorizing seems vulnerable.

Textbooks may be torturesome for their readers and, even more, for their authors, but they are, nevertheless, convenient reference sources. Since each author has his own ideas of what should be included and what omitted, one textbook may usefully supplement another. In the 1950s a succession of blockbuster textbooks were dropped into the US college market. Some of these failed to explode, but two by expatriate Russians deservedly became popular: M. T. Florinsky, *Russia, a History and an Interpretation* (2 vols., 1953) and N. V. Riasanovsky, *A History of Russia* (1969); later editions of the latter have been published. There were others, too, that may still be found on library shelves and for the most part they are reliable, if unexciting, but not always easy to read because so many American printers seem to prefer working with diluted ink. The British historian H. Pares, who lived through so much of what he wrote about, published his *History of Russia* (1949), but this is not good for the post-revolutionary years. H. Seton-Watson, *The Russian Empire 1801–1917* (1967) is of great help, as its 800-odd pages provide space for detailed interpretation as well as dense facts; it is particularly strong on foreign affairs and government. G. Hoskings in *Russia: People and Empire, 1552–1917* (1997) suggests, among many other things, that empire-building took Russians' minds off their own nation-building. An expanded development of this work is the highly recommended *Russia and the Russians* (2001) which takes the story up to the end of the Soviet period, a period in which Hosking concludes that policies did willy-nilly tend to build a Russian nation, in the ethnic if not the civic sense. Two books dealing in fairly popular style with the period from the Decembrist to the 1917 rising are *The Shadow of the Winter Palace* (1976) by E. Crankshaw and *Russia's Failed Revolutions* (1981) by A. B. Ulam. A popularization of a longer period (1613–1917), with sound academic underpinning, is W. B. Lincoln, *The Romanovs* (1981).

Shorter texts include J. M. Thompson's *Russia and the Soviet Union* (1994), moving smoothly from Kievan Russia to Yeltsin's Russia in about 300 pages, J. N. Westwood's *Endurance and Endeavour* (1973), criticized for its excruciating puns, and P. Dukes's *A History of Russia* (1990), which combines a brief narrative from medieval times with very interesting summaries of how different historians interpret the main events. *A History of*

Russia and the Soviet Union (1977) by D. MacKenzie and M. Curran offers very full coverage of the earlier centuries. G. Freeze edited *Russia: A History* (1997) with its specialists' contributions. Earlier, the same author edited *From Supplication to Revolution* (1988), a collection of documents covering social history up to 1906. Two textbooks which make a virtue of brevity are L. Kochan, *The Making of Modern Russia* (1963), which has chapters dealing with the pre-1812 period, and K. Charques, *Twilight of Imperial Russia* (1958). E. Acton's *Russia* (1986) manages to compress ten centuries without sacrificing liveliness; and there is also H. Rogger, *Russia in the Age of Modernisation and Revolution 1881–1917* (1983).

For the Soviet period there are R. G. Suny, *The Soviet Experiment* (1998), which is a very full account, J. M. Thompson, *A Vision Unfulfilled* (1996), M. Kort, *The Soviet Colossus* (1991), M. K. Dziewanowski, *A History of Soviet Russia* (1985), W. McClennan, *Russia: A History of the Soviet Period* (1986), the invariably informative M. McCauley's *The Soviet Union since 1917* (1981), and a very worthwhile paperback, G. Hosking, *A History of the Soviet Union* (1985), as well as some older works: H. Dymytryshin, *USSR: A Concise History* (1965), Ian Grey, *The First Fifty Years* (1967), D. W. Treadgold's exhaustive *Twentieth Century Russia* (1959, but 8th edition in 1994), P. Sorlin's short *The Soviet People and their Society from 1917 to the Present* (1969). J. Keep's *Last of the Empires* (1995) is a very sound treatment of the USSR's last decades, from 1945 to 1991.

Utopia in Power (1986), by M. Heller and A. Nekrich, is halfway between a polemic and a history of the USSR; especially good on the attempt to annihilate public memory by creating a fictitious past, it can be read with caution and enjoyment. H. C. d'Encausse has undertaken a useful, and in places original, two-volume study, *History of the Soviet Union 1917–1953* (1981). Also translated from French are C. Bettelheim. *Class Struggles in the USSR* (4 vols., starting in 1976), and D. Rousset, *A Critical History of the USSR* (vol. i, 1982); both of these are marxist interpretations which seek to show that the Soviet Union was not really marxist at all, Bettelheim preferring to regard it as a final stage of capitalism and Rousset as a bureaucratic aberration. In a rather different class is E. H. Carr's multi-volume study of the first decade of Soviet history, whose individual titles are given in the chapter bibliographies. Although the author can occasionally be detected leaning ever so slightly backwards with one eye half-closed, this work deserves respect as a painstaking and pioneering enterprise. More specialized are M. Sandle, *A Short History of Soviet Socialism* (1998), P. Dukes, *October and the World* (1979), which relates the Revolution to movements in other countries, V. Andrle's *A Social History of Twentieth Century Russia* (1994), and N. Robinson's *Ideology and the Collapse of the Soviet System* (1995), which is a two-for-the-price-of-one offer, surveying Soviet ideology from 1917 to 1985 and then going on to how it reacted with Gorbachev's reorientation. S. F. Cohen, *Rethinking the Soviet Experience* (1985), contains some interesting ideas by an expert on the 1920s and 1930s, while *Reinterpreting Russia* (1999) by G. Hosking and R. Service does a similar job over a longer time-span. O. A. Narkiewicz also has some perceptive ideas in her *Marxism and the Reality of Power 1919–1980* (1981), and so does M. Lewin in *The Making of the Soviet System* (1985). M. Ferro's *The Bolshevik Revolution: A Social History* (1980) is still of value. R. Sakwa's *The Rise and Fall of the Soviet Union 1917–1991* (1999) is particularly strong on political history.

Problems faced by would-be reformers are covered in R. O. Crummy (ed.), *Reform in Russia and the USSR* (1989) and T. Taranovski (ed.), *Reform in Modern Russian History* (1995). Shorter and more factual is D. Saunders, *Russia in the Age of Reaction and Reform* (1992). One of the most intractable problems facing Russian reformers is treated in F. W. Wcislo, *Reforming Rural Russia* (1990), which covers the period 1855–1914.

Two books worth looking at for their well-chosen and well-reproduced illustrations are O. Hoetzch, *The Evolution of Russia* (1966) and I. P. Nettl, *The Soviet Achievement* (1967).

Books which go deeper into Russian history, seeking and proposing plausible explanations of why things turned out the way they did, include T. G. Masaryk, *The Spirit of Russia*
(1918) and I. H. Billington, *The Icon and the Axe* (1966), both of these are still interesting,
and stress permanent factors like religion, geography, and western contacts. More recently,
the perennial discussion about Russia and the west has been diversified by I. B. Neumann's
Russia and the Idea of Europe: A Study of Identity and International Relations (1996) and
M. Malia's *Russia under Western Eyes* (1999), which seeks to explain why the west sometimes
demonized, occasionally enthused. Meanwhile, E. Kingston-Mann offers some guidance on
why Russia so often borrowed the wrong things from the west in his *In Search of the True
West* (1999). N. Berdiaev's *The Russian Idea* (1947) is nowadays not just an exploration of
Russian culture and attitudes, but also an introduction to its celebrated author (the philosopher N. Berdyaev, ex-marxist, ex-professor of philosophy at Moscow University, and
expatriate). W. Weidlé, in *Russia Absent and Present* (1961), also emerged with interesting
though not incontrovertible conclusions. In the mid-1970s there appeared T. Szamuely, *The
Russian Tradition* (1974) and R. Pipes, *Russia under the Old Regime* (1974). These two were
praised most highly by those reviewers least familiar with Russian history, but that is a
common phenomenon and should not be held against them. Later, R. V. Daniels produced
Russia: The Roots of Confrontation (1985), which describes how history, rather than marxism, made communist Russia what it was. There are some interesting ideas, sometimes
arguable, in M. Raeff, *Understanding Imperial Russia: State and Society in the Old Regime*
(1984), and the same can be said of J. Cracraft's *Major Problems in the History of Imperial
Russia* (1994), which deals mainly with domestic history of the eighteenth and nineteenth
centuries. The interacting attitudes of the Russians and their monarch were fascinatingly
studied by M. Cherniavsky in his *Tsar and People* (1961). By no means outdated are the
following studies in intellectual history: *Continuity and Change in Russian and Soviet
Thought* (1955), edited by E. I. Simmons, and *Russian Thought and Society 1800–1917* (1984),
edited by R. Bartlett, the anthology by M. H. Kohn, *The Mind of Modern Russia* (1962), and
M. Raeff's *Russian Intellectual History* (1966), while R. Hare's *Pioneers of Russian Social
Thought* (1951) provides biographies of some of the more notable thinkers. A. Walicki, *A
History of Russian Thought from the Enlightenment to Marxism* (1979) gives, among other
things, brief outlines of the ideas of all the important thinkers, including those, like Pobedonostsev, whose thought was remarkable for the power behind as much as for the power
within. More specialized works in this field include E. C. Thaden, *Conservative Nationalism
in Nineteenth Century Russia* (1964), H. Kohn, *Panslavism* (1953), and N. V. Riasanovsky,
Russia and the West in the Teaching of the Slavophils (1952). Outstanding Slavophils get full
treatment in P. K. Christoff's multi-volume *An Introduction to Nineteenth Century Russian
Slavophilism* (1982, etc.). There is also the very full (600-odd pages) *The Slavophile Controversy* (1975) by A. Walicki. Slavophils, nationalists, and others are covered in P. J. S. Duncan,
Russian Messianism (2000), which goes up to the Yeltsin years. For the intelligentsia as a
whole there is the collection *The Russian Intelligentsia* (1961), edited by the indefatigable
R. Pipes. S. R. Tompkins, *The Russian Intelligentsia: Makers of the Revolutionary State* (1957)
is concerned largely with the radical intelligentsia of the nineteenth century.

A general introduction to Russian life in the nineteenth century is the well-illustrated
Russian Writers and Society 1825–1904 (1967) by R. Hingley, which deals more with society
than with writers. Some of the essays edited by C. E. Black into the long *The Transformation
of Russian Society: Aspects of Social Change since 1861* (1960) are still not outdated.
D. S. Mirsky, *Russia, a Social History* (1952) is also still worth reading. More specialized is
O. Kharkhordin, *The Collective and the Individual in Russia* (1999). Perhaps the best understanding of Russian society, however, would be gained from Russian novels (not necessarily

the best-known ones), and from the innumerable memoirs and autobiographies by former residents in Russia. Some of the latter are mentioned in the chapter bibliographies below, but there are many more and they still appear. In a class of its own is D. Mackenzie-Wallace's unsurpassed *Russia* (1912, but reprinted since), whose author spent several years as *The Times* correspondent in Russia, making a thorough study of Russian life and institutions of the late nineteenth century

Difficult to categorize is S. Boym's *Common Places* (1994), which seeks understanding of the nuances of Russian daily life; it is a rewarding read for those already familiar with Russian social history.

T. Talbot Rice, *Concise History of Russian Art* (1963), illustrates and describes painting, sculpture, and architecture of the tsarist period. There is also the rather bigger work by G. H. Hamilton, *The Art and Architecture of Russia* (1954), and *Art and Culture in Nineteenth Century Russia* (1983), edited by G. V. Stavrou. Books devoted to individual Russian artists can now be found in libraries and specialized bookstores. W. Brumfield's *Reshaping Russian Architecture* (1990) is an interesting account of how tsarist architecture was transformed into Soviet architecture.

For literature there are scores of guides. Among the most useful of these are V. Terras, *A History of Russian Literature* (1991), *The Cambridge History of Russian Literature* (1989), edited by C. Moser, W. Kasack's *Dictionary of Russian Literature since 1917* (1988), *The Cambridge Companion to the Classic Russian Novel* (1998), edited by M. V. Jones and R. F. Miller, *Handbook of Russian Literature* (1985), edited by V. Terras, and *Ideology in Russian Literature* (1990), edited by R. Freeborn and J. Grayson. Slightly older, but still valid, are F. D. Reeve, *The Russian Novel* (1966), M. Baring, *Landmarks in Russian Literature* (1960), H. Gifford, *The Novel in Russia* (1964), and R. Freeborn, *The Russian Revolutionary Novel: Turgenev to Pasternak* (1982). For a detailed who-wrote-what (but not much else) there are M. Slonim's three volumes *The Epic of Russian Literature: To Tolstoy* (1950), *From Chekhov to the Revolution* (1962), and *Modern Russian Literature* (1955). There is also *A History of Soviet Literature* (1963) by V. Alexandrovna. Beginning in 1977, successive volumes of *The Modern Encyclopedia of Russian and Soviet Literature* appeared, edited by H. B. Weber and written by expert contributors. Other interpretative books are E. J. Brown, *Russian Literature since the Revolution* (1963), R. W. Mathewson, *The Positive Hero in Soviet Literature* (1958), and the collection of specialized essays, edited by M. Haward and L. Labedz, *Literature and Revolution in Soviet Russia, 1917–1962* (1963). But it is better to read, rather than read about, the novels; the best are in English translation. In addition, the 'thick' journal *Soviet Literature*, in which many Soviet novels were published for the first time, had an English-language edition. The journal *Russian Literature Triquarterly*, published in the USA, has also offered translations of Russian and Soviet fiction. Contemporary Russian fiction in translation is published in the *Glas New Russian Writing* series. Selected readings are provided by M. Crouch and R. Porter in *Understanding Soviet Politics through Literature* (1984). For poetry, there is E. Bristol, *A History of Russian Poetry* (1991), and for the theatre, M. L. Slonim, *Russian Theatre from the Empire to the Soviets* (1961) is still useful. For music, R. A. Leonard, *A History of Russian Music* (1956) covers, rather thinly perhaps, both the tsarist and Soviet periods. For fuller coverage of the Soviet period there are *Music of the Soviet Age 1917–1987* (1998) by L. Hakobian, *Soviet Composers and the Development of Soviet Music* (1970) by S. D. Krebs, and *Music and Musical Life in Soviet Russia 1957–1981* (1983) by B. Schwarz. Shostakovich's controversial memoirs were published as his *Testimony* in 1979. More specialized books are S. F. Starr, *Red and Hot* (1983), which details the alternating periods of repression and tolerance extended to jazz, culminating in permission to stage an original rock opera in Moscow during one of the happier periods of the Brezhnev regime, and R. C. Ridenour, *Nationalism, Modernism, and Personal Rivalry in Nineteenth Century Russian Music* (1981), a fascinating account of the formative 1860s.

All the arts, including music, are covered in S. Volkov's *St. Petersburg: A Cultural History* (1995), which also touches on other matters, like the Zhdanovite purges. Other cultural studies include *The Cambridge Companion to Modern Russian Culture* (1998), edited by N. Rzhevsky, and *Russian Cultural Studies* (1998), edited by C. Kelly and D. Shephard, which is a good introduction to the 1917–95 period. The same pair are also credited with *Constructing Russian Culture in the Age of Revolution 1881–1940* (1998). V. Brovkin in *Russia after Lenin* (1998) studies how Russian life and culture fitted in, or were fitted up, in the earlier Soviet decades. *Russian Popular Culture* (1992) by R. Stites deals with popular entertainment in the twentieth century.

For a study of nineteenth-century publishing, the rise of newspapers, and the increased demand for reading matter, C. A. Ruud, *Fighting Words* (1982) is very good, and it also makes considerable though patchy reference to the subject of its title, the censorship. For censorship in Soviet times see M. Dewhirst and R. Farrell, *The Soviet Censorship* (1973). *The Red Pencil* (1989), edited by M. Choldin and M. Friedburg, includes many examples of the absurdities created by the Soviet censorship.

The standard works on pre-1917 economic history are P. Lyashchenko, *History of the National Economy of Russia* (1949), a translation of the Soviet edition, which is inclined to portray imperial Russia as some kind of colony; J. Mavor, *An Economic History of Russia* (1914); P. W. Gatrell, *The Tsarist Economy, 1850–1917* (1986); and the brief but good *The Industrialisation of Russia 1700–1914* (1972) by M. Falkus. O. Crisp, *Studies in the Russian Economy before 1914* (1976) is a collection of well-thought-out essays. A. Nove, *An Economic History of the USSR* (1969) is a readable introduction to post-1917 economic history, and so is R. W. Davies's *Soviet Economic Development from Lenin to Khrushchev* (1998), which carries the story further. The same author edited *From Tsarism to the New Economic Policy* (1990), which gives much detail about the economy in the 1914 to 1928 period. A longer time-scale, 1860 to 1928, is covered in P. R. Gregory's *Before Command* (1994), which argues that NEP (a regulated market economy) would have performed better than Stalin's five-year plan system. V. E. Bonnell, *The Russian Worker* (1983) consists of translations of five very interesting contemporary accounts of workers' lives under tsarism, while S. P. Turin, *From Peter the Great to Lenin* (1935) is an outdated but sometimes useful study of neither Peter nor Lenin nor the years between, but of the Russian labour movement. The collection edited by D. Lane, *Labour and Employment in the USSR* (1986), contains historical pieces, while A. Pravda and B. Ruble have edited *Trade Unions in Communist States* (1986) which, while not especially historical nor confined to the USSR, does provide a useful summary of the main features. Other titles relating to the workers will be found in the chapter bibliographies. That continuing problem of the Russian economy, the peasantry, receives attention in *The Peasant in Nineteenth Century Russia* (1968), edited by W. S. Vucinich and containing much fascinating detail about peasants' lives. G. Yaney in his *The Urge to Mobilize* (1982) deals with attempts at agrarian reform between 1861 and 1930 and shows how city people seemed to have no doubts about their ability to transform the rural situation, even though they never quite understood it. T. Shanin, *The Awkward Class* (1972) has some illuminating things to say about the peasantry in the years 1910–25. D. Moon's *The Russian Peasantry 1600–1930* (1999) among other things gives the peasants some credit for having minds of their own. That continuing feature, the peasant commune, is featured in the collection *Land Commune and the Peasant Community in Russia* (1990), edited by R. Bartlett and covering the centuries up to 1930; the same subject, on a more concentrated time-scale, is dealt with by D. Atkinson's *The End of the Russian Land Commune 1905–1930*

(1983). Two contributions by D. Christian, *Living Water: Vodka and Russian Society on the Eve of Emancipation* (1990) and *Bread and Salt* (1984), are good reading and throw considerable light on peasant society, among other things. Two very different angles on tsarist trade and commerce are provided by A. Fitzpatrick's many-faceted *The Great Russian Fair* (1990), which surveys the major trade fair of Nizhnii Novgorod from 1840 to 1890, and the somewhat legalistic but illuminating *The Corporation under Russian Law 1800–1917* (1991), by T. Owen. The same author went on to extend his coverage with *Russian Corporate Capitalism from Peter the Great to Perestroika* (1995). J. N. Westwood's *A History of Russian Railways* (1964) is useful, although its author seems to be more interested in railways than in history. Books about nineteenth-century capitalists, big and small, were until recently very rare, but much can now be learned from A. J. Rieber, *Merchants and Entrepreneurs in Imperial Russia* (1982), T. Owen, *Capitalism and Politics in Russia: A Social History of the Moscow Merchants 1855–1905* (1981), and J. A. Ruckman, *The Moscow Business Elite: A Social and Cultural Portait of Two Generations, 1840–1905* (1984). F. V. Carstensen, *American Enterprise in Foreign Markets* (1984) deals with the operations of the Singer and International Harvester companies, both of which proved that there was a latent consumer demand in Russia by offering their customers generous credit, something which native companies rarely did. This throws light on the still unsettled question of precisely why the tsarist economy was backward. T. Shanin, in *Russia as a 'Developing Society'* (1985), deals with the late tsarist period.

P. Juvilier, *Revolutionary Law and Order* (1976) is a useful survey of the relationship between law and society, mainly but not exclusively in Soviet times. *Reforming Justice in Russia* (1997) edited by P. H. Solomon, contains fifteen essays covering 1864 to 1996.

Many competent books were published, usually in successive editions, to describe the Soviet political system. Among them were D. J. R. Scott, *Russian Political Institutions* (1969) and an excellent paperback, M. McAuley, *Politics and the Soviet Union* (1977), which takes a historical approach. Later developments are included in L. G. Churchward, *Soviet Socialism: Social and Political Essays* (1987). An associated topic is covered by J. N. Hazard in his *The Soviet Legal System* (1977).

G. Porton's *The Soviet Era* (1993) is a text covering politics over the communist period. R. Sakwa's *Soviet Politics* (1989) included the changes of the early Gorbachev years, and there are other books by the same author. G. Smith's *Soviet Politics* (1992) is very useful. R. C. Tucker, *The Soviet Political Mind* (1972) exhibits a good part of its author's political mind as well; it examines the attitudes underlying the system. Histories of the communist party from before 1917 include L. B. Shapiro, *The Communist Party of the Soviet Union* (1960), B. Meissner, *The Communist Party of the Soviet Union* (1956), and I. S. Reshetar, *A Concise History of the Communist Party of the Soviet Union* (1960). The Soviet textbook *History of the Communist Party of the USSR, Short Course* exists in many languages and editions; the pre-1956 and post-1956 editions are easily distinguished and both are fascinatingly tendentious. For a statistical analysis of the party's membership over the years, there is the still valid T. H. Rigby, *Communist Party Membership in the USSR 1917–1967* (1968). Differences inside the communist party from 1903 to 1939 are examined in R. V. Daniel, *The Conscience of the Revolution* (1960). For marxism as such there are many books, some of which are tedious. Perhaps I. Berlin, *Karl Marx* (1948) would make the most palatable beginning. A translation of the multi-volume post-Stalin version of Lenin's *Collected Works* has been published. Stalin's *Collected Works* also exist in English, as do earlier versions of Lenin's. They all make good bedtime reading.

A useful but inevitably incomplete account of the security organs is in R. Hingley, *The*

Russian Secret Police 1565–1970 (1970), a book which will be enjoyed especially by Russophobes. The chapter bibliographies list other titles about the secret police.

Descriptions of how the tsarist government worked are still scarce, although that much-reviled institution, the bureaucracy, has recently received more detailed study, which tends to suggest that it has been a little misjudged, in so far as it did contain competent, hard-working men who had some sensible ideas for reform. W. M. Pintner and D. K. Rowney have edited a volume, *Russian Officialdom* (1980), which takes a look at the institution from the seventeenth century to the 1920s. W. B. Lincoln, *In the Vanguard of Reform* (1982), praises the officials who, in Nicholas I's time, quietly laid the foundations for the great reforms of his successor, D. Lieven's *Russia's Rulers under the Old Regime* (1989) consists largely of very informative biographies of those who rose to the top of the bureaucracy in the final tsarist decades, while D. T. Orlovsky in his *The Limits of Reform* (1981) looks at the structure and personnel of just one powerful ministry, the ministry of the interior, from Alexander I to Alexander II. S. Utechin, *Russian Political Thought* (1964) casts light on tsarist government and its spirit, as does, indirectly, M. Raeff's documentary survey of unsuccessful reform proposals, *Plans for Political Reform in Imperial Russia 1730–1905* (1966). J. Walkin, in *The Rise of Democracy in Prerevolutionary Russia* (1962), looks at political institutions over the last sixty years of the Romanov regime and believes that participatory democracy had, possibly, a viable future. Memoirs by, and biographies of, Russian statesmen and politicians mentioned in the chapter bibliographies below are another source of information, while P. P. Gronsky and N. Astrov, in a posthumous kind of way, are quite informative in their *The War and the Russian Government* (1929).

A short but reliable guide to tsarist foreign policy is B. Jelavich, *A Century of Russian Foreign Policy 1814–1914* (1964). Her later *St Petersburg and Moscow* (1974) covers similar ground but carries on up to the Brezhnev years. For the Soviet period as a whole, A. B. Ulam, *Expansion and Coexistence 1917–1967* (1968) and M. Beloff's two-volume *The Foreign Policy of Soviet Russia 1929–1941* (1947) are still worth reading, although some of their Cold War era assumptions might be questioned. *Russian Foreign Policy* (1962), edited by I. J. Lederer, has essays covering the nineteenth and twentieth centuries. Other useful books include R. Quested, *Sino-Russian Relations* (1984), which goes from Genghis Khan to Gromyko; L. Fischer, *The Soviets in World Affairs 1917–1929* (1951); E. H. Carr, *German–Soviet Relations between the Two World Wars 1919–1939* (1952); G. F. Kennan, *Russia and the West under Lenin and Stalin* (1961); R. C. North, *Moscow and Chinese Communists* (1953); and W. A. Williams, *American–Russian Relations 1781–1947* (1952). M. M. Laserson, *The American Impact on Russia* (1950) is rather more than a study in foreign policies. The critical period of Soviet foreign policy leading to the Second World War has been examined by a dissident Czech, J. Hochman, in his *The Soviet Union and the Failure of Collective Security 1934–1938* (1984). The same subject is covered by *The Soviet Union and the Struggle for Collective Security in Europe 1933–1939* (1984) by J. Haslam, one of his several volumes covering inter-war foreign policy. *The Fifty Years War* (1995) by R. Crockatt deals with US–Soviet relations between 1941 and 1991.

N. Hans, who worked in the tsarist educational system, dealt thoroughly with its history in his *History of Russian Educational Policy 1701–1917* (1931), while his *The Russian Tradition in Education* (1963) consists of biographies of leading tsarist educationists. W. H. E. Johnson, *Russia's Educational Heritage* (1950) is also useful, and so is P. L. Alston, *Education and the State in Tsarist Russia* (1969). The development of Soviet education can be followed in several books by John Dunstan, and in *The Changing Soviet School* (1960) by G. Z. F. Bereday, while N. Grant, *Soviet Education* (1964) describes how it was in Khrushchev's time. The story is carried further in M. Matthews, *Education in the Soviet*

Union (1982), which runs from the 1950s to 1979. A more specialized study is S. Fitzpatrick, *Education and Social Mobility in the Soviet Union 1921–1934* (1979), which explains, implicitly at least, how the carrot of promotion brought forth a multitude of new Soviet men and women, educated but not imaginative. In a related field, J. Brooks, in *When Russia Learned to Read* (1985), describes the linked growth of literacy and popular literature in the final tsarist decades. The peak of the Soviet academic system, the Academy of Sciences, is treated by A. Vucinich in his *Empire of Knowledge* (1984), which concentrates on the relationship of science to ideology in the Soviet period. A very informative and readable book is L. Graham, *Science in Russia and the Soviet Union* (1993). One branch of learning, medicine, makes an interesting story, as is proved by N. M. Frieden, *Russian Physicians in an Era of Reform and Revolution 1856–1905* (1981).

Related to the latter is J. E. Tuve's *The First Russian Women Physicians* (1984). The 1970s saw the beginning of a steady flow of books inspired by interest in the 'woman question'. The period from 1860 to 1930 is well covered in R. Stites, *The Women's Liberation Movement in Russia* (1978), while the Soviet period gets good coverage in a collection edited by D. Atkinson, A. Dallin, and G. W. Lapidus, *Women in Russia* (1977). B. A. Engel wrote *Mothers and Daughters* (1983), which is also quite informative about the nineteenth-century intelligentsia in general. N. Pushkareva, in *Women in History from the Tenth to the Twentieth Century* (1997), does not neglect the daily, family, routines. L. H. Edmondson, in *Feminism in Russia 1900–1917* (1984), has written a readable book, but also a sad one, for it shows how participation in the liberation movement was followed by a loss, after October 1917, of most of the gains made. *Russia through Women's Eyes* (1996), edited by T. W. Clyman and T. Vowles, presents the autobiographies of eleven nineteenth century women. In *Women in Russia and Ukraine* (1996), edited by R. Marsh, there are twenty-one essays covering the seventeenth century to the late twentieth. Also concerned with women, but throwing sidelights on industry, is R. L. Glickman, *Russian Factory Women: Workplace and Society 1880–1914* (1984). A new biography of a prominent liberated woman is B. Clements, *Bolshevik Feminist* (1979). This is about Alexandra Kollontai, a rather different kettle of fish from her contemporary Krupskaya, who has been given sensible treatment in R. McNeal's *Bride of the Revolution* (1973). The volume of essays edited by L. H. Edmondson, *Women and Society in Russia and the Soviet Union* (1991), covers a number of topics in the late tsarist and Soviet periods; she has also edited *Gender in Russian History and Culture* (2001). Much more specialized but of relevance to several topics is S. Bridger's *Women in the Soviet Countryside* (1987), while G. Browning's *Women in Politics in the USSR* (1987) is a useful summary. M. Ilic has written *Women Workers in the Soviet Interwar Economy* (1999) and edited *Women in the Stalin Era* (2001).

Religion is well covered in *The Modern Encyclopedia of Religions in Russia and the Soviet Union* (1988) by P. Steeves, and D. Pospielovsky's two-volume *The Russian Church under the Soviet Regime* (1984). There is also the collection edited by G. Hosking, *Church, Nation and State in Russia and Ukraine* (1991). Other books on religion can be found in the chapter bibliographies, as can books on the Russian Jews. W. Korey's history *Russian Anti-Semitism* (1995) ends by asking why Gorbachev and Yeltsin failed to speak out against that phenomenon (one explanation might be that anti-Semitism is not quite so strong as the author imagines; but this is a very good study). A. Bennigsen and S. Wimbush, *Muslims of the Soviet Empire* (1986) sets out to be a useful guide to the nationalities and covers their religion in doing so. For the Russian army, as opposed to its campaigns, J. Keep's *Soldiers of the Tsar* (1985) has a long span (fifteenth century to Alexander II's reform) and relates the army to society. A. Wildman's books (see the bibliography of Chapter 10) also have historical background. W. C. Fuller's long *Strategy and Power in Russia 1600–1914* (1992) is a sound history of the Russian military, while B. W. Menning's *Bayonets before Bullets* (1992) studies the army in the reforming period of 1861–1914. For the Soviet period, R. C. Nation's *Black Earth, Red Star* (1991) is a good blend of diplomatic and military history directed at security concerns. Memoirs and biographies fill some of the gaps. For the Soviet army, J. Erickson, *The Soviet High Command* (1962) is virtually a history of the armed forces from 1918 to 1941 and is only partially outdated. The same might be said of the shorter M. Mackintosh, *Juggernaut* (1967) and E. O'Ballance, *The Red Army* (1964). For the navy, D. Mitchell, *A History of Russian and Soviet Sea Power* (1974) ploughs wide but shallow waters. D. Woodward, *The Russians at Sea* (1965) starts around 1700 and is a reasonable, short account. Some libraries still have M. Mitchell's long *The Maritime History of Russia 1848–1948* (1949), which covers exploration and commercial as well as naval matters. J. N. Westwood's *Russian Naval Construction 1905–1945* (1994) has been described as naval history with the interesting bits left out, but it does half-explain the apparent boneheadedness of Russian naval policies. C. Benckendorff's attractive autobiography *Half a Life* (1955) includes its author's experiences in the tsarist navy, as does D. Fedotov White, *Survival through War and Revolution in Russia* (1939). For the air force there is an abundance of plane-spotters' guides, but few deeper works. R. Kilmarx, *A History of Soviet Air Power* (1962) is still valuable.

For coverage of the nationalities within Russia and the USSR, R. J. Kaiser's *The Geography of Nationalism in Russia and the USSR* (1994) is a very good start, covering the national peoples over the last two centuries, and a useful general history is B. Nahylo and V. Swoboda's *Soviet Disunion* (1990). J. Morison (ed.), *Ethnic and National Issues in Russian and East European History* (2000) is also a useful contribution. Readings and documents are presented in M. B. Olcott's *The Soviet Multinational State* (1990). A historical base is provided by D. Brower and E. Lazzerini, *Russia's Orient: Imperial Borderlands and Peoples, 1700–1917* (1997). D. Lieven's *Empire* (2000) deals with the Russian Empire as an empire, and makes interesting comparisons with other empires. Since the break-up of the USSR a succession of books has appeared covering the history of one or another of the new states. Few of these works could be termed Russophile, but there are some good ones among them, and more are on the way.

Among books difficult to place in broad categories are A. Chandler's *Border Controls* (1998), about the various ways the Soviet Union controlled its frontier crossings; A. M. Etkind's *Eros of the Impossible* (1997), a history of psychoanalysis in Russia; and *The Soviet Germans: Past and Present* (1986) by I. Fleischauer and B. Pinkus and dealing with that small ethnic minority (about 2 million in 1990).

Chapter 1

There are many books about Catherine the Great, most of which concentrate on her sex life, which was not really the centre of her own attention or of her importance. Good studies include J. Alexander's *Catherine the Great: Crises and Conquests* (1988), and S. de Madariaga's *Catherine the Great* (1990), and there are more coming. *Life in Russia under Catherine the Great* (1969) by M. Kochan gives a brief, readable, and well-illustrated description of the Russian society in which Alexander I grew up. The more ambitious student might like to tackle the 2,000-odd pages of W. Tooke, *View of the Russian Empire during the Reign of Catherine the Second, and to the Close of the Eighteenth Century* (1800),[2] the result of its author's long residence and research in St Petersburg. A good account of Alexander's

---

2. Almost all of the 19th-century publications mentioned in this bibliography have been reprinted since the 1960s.

Russia, particularly in its institutional aspects, is conveyed by M. Raeff's biography *Michael Speransky* (1961). Similarly, P. K. Grimsted, *The Foreign Ministers of Alexander I* (1969) reveals more than the title indicates, notably the Tsar's deviousness in dealing with his advisers. Alexander's friend Arakcheyev is described, readably and without an excess of profundity, in M. Jenkin, *Arakcheev* (1969). Another useful biography, by M. and D. Josselson, is *The Commander: A Life of Barclay de Tolly* (1980). Magnitsky's tumultuous going-over of Kazan University is one of the matters covered in C. H. Whittaker's *The Origins of Modern Russian Education* (1984), which is devoted to the life and thought of the talented Count Uvarov. As for the Tsar himself, a good short study is A. McConnell, *Tsar Alexander I* (1970), and A. Palmer has written the longer, but popular in style, *Alexander I* (1974). J. M. Hartley's *Alexander I* (1994) has a lot to recommend it, being clear and of moderate length.

The war of 1812 is described by various eyewitnesses in A. Brett-James's collection *1812: Napoleon's Defeat in Russia* (1966). L. Cooper, *Many Roads to Moscow* (1968) compares Napoleon's invasion with those of the Swedes and Nazis. An interesting post-mortem on the fire of Moscow is D. Olivier, *The Burning of Moscow* (1966). The *Memoirs* of John Quincy Adams (1874) contain in their second volume the US representative's impressions from on high, during his stay in St Petersburg in 1809–14. An intelligent British observer's account of conditions in 1814 along the route of Napoleon's invasion is *Travels through Part of the Russian Empire and the Country of Poland, Along the Southern Shores of the Baltic* (1816) by Robert Johnston. A specialized book, interestingly written, is *The Cossacks* (1969) by P. Longworth. The classic account of the Decembrist Revolt was A. G. Mazour, *The First Russian Revolution, 1825* (1937). There is also M. Zetlin, *The Decembrists* (1958), while M. Raeff, in his *The Decembrist Movement* (1966), presents key documents, including the constitutional schemes composed by the plotters.

An offbeat memoir by an offbeat character is N. Durova's *Cavalry Maiden* (1988), whose author was a gentlewoman who managed to serve as an officer in Alexander's hussars during the Napoleonic Wars. She did this without any help from the Skoptsy who, according to L. Engelstein's restrained *Castration and the Heavenly Kingdom* (2001), not only practised castration but also favoured the mutilation of both sexes in order to eliminate the distinction of male and female. A. Nikitenko's *Up from Serfdom: My Childhood and Youth in Russia 1804–1824* (2001) is a conservative memoir by a professor and censor about his serf childhood, and how his talents brought him freedom.

Chapter 2

Probably the most useful view of Nicholas and his Russia is provided by N. V. Riasanovsky, *Nicholas I and Official Nationality in Russia 1825–1855* (1959): this deals not only with ideology but also with the Tsar and his entourage. For a straight biography, there are C. de Grunwald, *Tsar Nicholas I* (1954) and W. B. Lincoln, *Nicholas I* (1978); the latter is patchy but well researched and readable. One of the most enjoyable books about the reign is J. S. Curtiss, *The Russian Army under Nicholas I 1825–1855* (1965), which conveys useful impressions of Nicholas and his generals, as well as information about the army and its campaigns. Nicholas actually embarked on military reform in the first part of his reign, endeavouring to cut through the mass of complex and impenetrable army laws. This effort gets its due reward in F. W. Kagan's *The Military Reforms of Nicholas I* (2000). The life of the ordinary Russian soldier in the first half of the nineteenth century is studied in E. Wirtschafter's *From Serf to Russian Soldier* (1990). For the Crimean War, there are W. Baumgart, *The Crimean War* (1999), scholarly and brief, and T. Royle, *Crimea* (1999), which is longer, while J. S. Curtiss looks at things from the Russian side in *Russia's Crimean War* (1979). The Third

Section is studied in two excellent and partly complementary monographs: *The Third Section* (1961) by S. Monas and *The Third Department* (1968) by P. S. Squire.

Studies of individual writers are too numerous to mention in these bibliographies; the surveys of art and literature mentioned in the General Bibliography, which themselves are only a selection, contain suggestions for further reading. For the radical thinkers, a good start is E. Lampert, *Studies in Rebellion* (1957), which centres around the lives and times of Belinsky, Herzen, and Bakunin. For a full-length study of Bakunin there is G. Maximov, *Bakunin* (1953), and for Herzen, M. Malia, *Alexander Herzen and the Birth of Russian Socialism* (1961). J. Seddon's *The Petrashevtsy* (1985) seems still to be the only English-language book on this subject.

Two very detailed accounts by foreign observers who in their time did much to illuminate Russia for the serious western reader are Baron von Haxthausen, *The Russian Empire, its Peoples, Institutions and Resources* (1856) and J. G. Kohl, *Russia: St Petersburg, Moscow, Kharkoff Riga, Odessa, the German Provinces on the Baltic, the Steppes, the Crimea, and the Interior of the Empire* (1844). With their Teutonic thoroughness these works stand favourable comparison with the rather poor travellers' tales of de Custine and A. Dumas.

Chapter 3

The essence of Alexander II's reforms is conveyed in the varied pieces edited by B. Eklof, J. Bushnell, and L. Zakharova: *Russia's Great Reforms* (1994). Two reliable, though not over-critical, biographies of Alexander II are S. Graham, *Tsar of Freedom* (1935) and E. Almedingen, *The Emperor Alexander II* (1962). W. B. Lincoln's *The Great Reforms* (1990) provides useful summaries of the reforms but is primarily, and interestingly, concerned with how the reforms were arrived at. For a very full history of the peasants up to 1861, J. Blum, *Lord and Peasant in Russia* (1961) is still worth consulting. For finding answers to questions that many historians skate around, G. T. Robinson's *Rural Russia under the Old Regime* (1929) was admirable and remains useful, although not easy, reading. There are also the books already mentioned in the General Bibliography. D. Field, *The End of Serfdom* (1976) details the debates of 1855–61 which preceded and shaped the great liberation. T. Emmons, in his *The Russian Landed Gentry and the Peasant Emancipation of 1861* (1968), deals with an important aspect of the Emancipation, and the same author edited the short but useful collection of Russian and Western opinions *The Emancipation of the Russian Serfs* (1970). Some of the books mentioned in the bibliography for Chapter 7 throw light on the results of the reform. A very detailed study of one Russian village is the basis of S. Hock's *Serfdom and Social Control in Russia* (1986). D. Moon, *Russian Peasants and Tsarism on the Eve of Reform* (1992) is another contribution, while the peasants' lot after the Emancipation is studied in B. Eklof and S. Frank, *The World of the Russian Peasant* (1990) and in D. Macey, *Government and Peasant in Russia 1861–1906* (1987). For the landowners, there is B. Seymour, *Nobility and Privilege in Late Imperial Russia* (1985).

An account of Kankrin and his economic policies is given in W. M. Pintner, *Russian Economic Policy under Nicholas I* (1967). Early Russian industrialization and technology is detailed in W. L. Blackwell, *The Beginnings of Russian Industrialization, 1800–1860* (1968), while *The Beginnings of Railway Development in Russia* (1969) by R. M. Haywood not only deals with railway policy between 1835 and 1842 but also summarizes the development of pre-rail transport and incidentally throws some light on how decisions were reached in Nicholas's Russia. Likewise, the same author's *Russia Enters the Railway Age* (1998), a long book about a massive project (the St Petersburg to Moscow Railway), reaches widely, and portrays Nicholas at his best. It also describes a near-accident to the imperial train in which both the future Alexander II and Alexander III were lucky to escape with their lives. A. Parry, *Whistler's Father* (1939) is about the husband of Whistler's mother, and describes how he helped to build the St Petersburg to Moscow Railway, dying in the process, while she attempted to convert Russians to her own brand of Christianity. *Labour and Society in Tsarist Russia: The Factory Workers of St. Petersburg 1855–1870* (1971) by R. E. Zelnik deals with the rise of industrial labour during Alexander's reign. M. Tugan-Baranovsky's nineteenth century classic appeared in an edited translation in 1970, entitled *The Russian Factory in the Nineteenth Century*.

Chapter 4

Much of the work put into Alexander's reforms was actually carried out during the reign of his father, as is well brought out in R. Wortman, *The Development of a Russian Legal Consciousness* (1976), which describes how, in one department of state, competent bureaucrats developed useful ideas. In relation to their importance, the reforms of Alexander II have received meagre treatment by western scholars, but some of the books listed in later chapter bibliographies may also be consulted as they often deal with the consequences of what happened in the 1860s and 1870s. For the judicial reform, its antecedents and consequences, a former member of the Russian Bar, S. Kucherov, wrote the very readable *Courts, Lawyers, and Trials under the Last Three Tsars* (1953). Law in the rural areas, where the reforms were less felt, is dealt with by S. P. Frank in *Crime, Cultural Conflict, and Justice in Rural Russia 1856–1914* (1999), which uses the records of one province and argues, for example, that much of peasant violence was simply peasants taking justice into their own hands. For the military reform, F. Miller, *Dmitri Miliutin and the Reform Era in Russia* (1968) is very useful and touches on other personalities and problems of the time, including education. It could be followed by D. A. Rich's *The Tsar's Colonels* (1998), which deals with the part that Milyutin did not reach, the general staff and its need for modernization. For local government there is P. Vinogradoff, *Self-Government in Russia* (1915) and G. Fischer, *Russian Liberalism from Gentry to Intelligentsia* (1958). Aspects of the *zemstva* are covered in *The Zemstvo in Russia* (1982), edited by T. Emmons and W. Vucinich. All these reforms are, of course, dealt with by the textbooks, and H. Seton-Watson, *The Russian Empire 1801–1917* (1967) is particularly useful. W. Mosse, *Alexander II and the Modernization of Russia* (1958) gives a clear but brief account. See also the above-mentioned *Russia's Great Reforms*. M. McCauley and P. Waldron, *The Emergence of the Modern Russian State 1855–81* (1988) deals with Alexander's reign as a development period. A major participant in the reforms was the interior ministry, whose history from 1802 to 1881 is detailed in D. T. Orlovsky's *The Limits of Reform* (1981). D. Mackenzie-Wallace, *Russia* (1877), provides commentary on how the judicial and local government reforms worked out in practice and entirely refutes the Russian expression 'to lie like an eyewitness'. Also good is A. Leroy-Beaulieu, *Empire of the Tsars and the Russians* (3 vols., 1899–93). *The Politics of Autocracy: Letters of Alexander II to Prince A. I. Bariatinskii, 1857–1864* (1966) is illuminating, especially the introduction by its editor A. J. Rieber. Books on the individual writers and musicians of the period are too numerous to mention; the works mentioned in the General Bibliography contain useful book-lists. Perhaps N. Rimsky-Korsakov, *My Musical Life* (1924) deserves special mention, for it deals not only with music but also with life in the navy and St Petersburg.

Volume i of A. S. Vucinich, *Science in Russian Culture* (1963), has something to say about technology but is largely, and interestingly, concerned with Russian scientists up to 1860, their thoughts and their opportunities. Relaxed censorship was one circumstance favouring thought and opportunity; the edited memoirs of A. Nikitenko, *Diary of a Russian Censor*

(1974), additionally illuminate a range of social topics rather wider than censorship, under Nicholas and Alexander, although he is rather an endearing stick-in-the-mud. For education, A. Sinel's study of Dmitri Tolstoy's policies, *The Classroom and the Chancellery* (1973), provides a clear picture.

The intellectual background of the revolutionary movement is covered by E. Lampert in *Sons against Fathers* (1965), which centres around Chernyshevsky, Dobroliubov, and Pisarev. There is also P. Pomper, *Peter Lavrov and the Russian Revolutionary Movement* (1972). A readable general picture of revolutionary activity from 1825 to 1887 is provided by A. Yarmolinsky, *Road to Revolution* (1957). A pioneering detailed study of the Populists was F. Venturi, *Roots of Revolution* (1960). D. Hardy's *Land and Freedom* (1987) studies the break-up of Land and Liberty in 1879. A. Gleason's *Young Russia* (1980) examines the birth of radicalism from the 1860s and suggests how idealism was squeezed out by revolutionism, while V. Nahirny's *The Russian Intelligentsia* (1983) occasionally gives the impression that if psychiatry had been better developed many young people would not have needed to sublimate their hang-ups in revolutionary activity. D. Brower, *Training the Nihilists* (1975) studies the link between education and radicalism and supports the belief that students from the lower social classes were less likely than noble students to become revolutionaries. M. Maxwell's *Narodniki Women* (1990) contains biographies of celebrated women revolutionaries including Vera Zasulich. What happened to revolutionaries in emigration is studied by M. Miller in *The Russian Revolutionary Émigrés 1825–1870* (1986), and by W. McClennan in *Revolutionary Exiles* (1979). I. Slatter, in *From the Other Shore* (1984), deals with the Russian emigrants who came to Britain in 1880–1917. Vera Zasulich at last received perceptive treatment in *Vera Zasulich* (1983) by J. Bergman, who concludes that she was too decent to be a truly effective revolutionary; her attack on Trepov was intended to be an act of self-sacrifice, not an incentive for a wave of bilateral terrorism. The assassination of the Emperor and its antecedents is covered in D. I. Footman's life of the leading conspirator, Zhelyabov, in *Red Prelude* (1944). R. Hingley, *Nihilists: Russian Radicals and Revolutionaries in the Reign of Alexander II* (1967) covers the same ground differently. In *The Unmentionable Nechayev* (1961), M. Prawdin handled his subject well, apart from a laboured attempt to portray Lenin as some kind of Nechayevite Second Coming. Other biographies are J. H. Billington, *Mikhailovsky and Russian Populism* (1958), and S. H. Baron, *Plekhanov, the Father of Russian Marxism* (1963). Those who prefer the horse's mouth would enjoy *Underground Russia* (1883) by the celebrated assassin S. Stepnyak, *Memoirs of a Revolutionist* (1968) by Vera Figner (one of the last of the leading members of the People's Will to remain at large, being arrested in 1884 and sent to gaol for twenty years), and another *Memoirs of a Revolutionist* (2 vols., 1899, 1906) by Prince P. A. Kropotkin. The latter, an anarchist so widely respected that Lenin allowed him a state funeral in 1921, was one of those who 'went to the people'. An edition of these memoirs, with commentary, was published in 1962 (ed. I. A. Rogers). Turgenev's *Virgin Soil* (1877, now in paperback), while not the best of his novels, does convey how very varied in temperament and intentions were the young individuals who went to the peasants and workers.

Another cross borne by Alexander II is studied in R. F. Leslie, *Reform and Insurrection in Russian Poland* (1963), which is devoted mainly to the 1863 rebellion.

Chapter 5

An agreeable way of making acquaintance with this period is by reading R. Hare, *Portraits of Russian Personalities between Reform and Revolution* (1959), which includes writers, revolutionaries, Stolypin, Witte, and Pobedonostsev among its subjects. For another angle,

D. Offord's *Nineteenth Century Russia* (1999) is largely about the radicals. The same author's *The Russian Revolutionary Movement in the 1880s* (1986) describes, analyses, and interprets the several groups of that decade. N. Naimark, *Terrorists and Social Democrats* (1983) deals mainly with 1881–1895 and how the Narodniks mutated and merged. It contains much background information about the life of students and workers and also has an account of Narodnik activity within the imperial army. The 1887 attempt to bomb Alexander III is one of several episodes interestingly described in I. Deutscher, *Lenin's Childhood* (1970): the *de facto* leader of the conspiracy, Lenin's brother, is revealed as a young man with a nobility of character that led to his downfall. *Thou Shalt Kill* (1993) by A. Geifman deals with the causes and effects of revolutionary violence between 1894 and 1917.

How the state developed countermeasures in the form of security policing is described in J. W. Daly's *Autocracy under Siege* (1998) covering the interaction between security police and opposition up to 1905. Zubatov gets a high mark for talent and sympathy. Zubatov similarly receives praise in F. S. Zuckerman's *The Tsarist Secret Police in Russian Society 1880–1917* (1996). *Fontanka 16* (1999) by C. A. Ruud and S. A. Stepanov provides a good account, too, ending with the Malinovsky affair.

There is a scarcity of material about the reign of Alexander III, although much may be gleaned from *The Memoirs of Count Witte* (1921) by S. I. Witte. This English version is abridged from the original and should be read with an awareness of the several axes which its author was grinding. R. Byrnes's study *Pobedonostsev* (1968) also conveys much about the reign. K. P. Pobedonostsev, apart from numerous anonymous articles, also expressed his ideals in *Reflections of a Russian Statesman* (1898). How a bureaucracy aligned towards liberalization in the previous reign adjusted to the new atmosphere can be studied with H. W. Whelan, *Alexander III and the State Council: Bureaucracy and Counter-reform in Late Imperial Russia* (1982). The collection edited by W. Gurian, *Soviet Imperialism* (1953), contains much information on Russification and tsarist policies towards the nationalities. Russification is also covered in E. C. Thaden (ed.), *Russification in the Baltic Provinces and Finland, 1855–1914* (1981), and S. A. Zenkovsky, *Pan-Turkism and Islam in Russia* (1960); the latter deals with 1905–21, and hence includes the Central Asian revolt of 1916. Provincial governors in the last tsarist decades are studied in *The Tsar's Viceroys* (1987) by R. G. Robbins. The enlightened governor of Bessarabia, S. D. Urussov, in his *Memoirs of a Russian Governor* (1908), has interesting comments on the pogroms, and much else besides.

Pogroms were a feature of Alexander III's reign, and much has been written about the condition of the Tsar's Jewish subjects. This paragraph includes works which may relate to the whole of the tsarist period. S. W. Baron, *The Russian Jew under Tsars and Soviets* (1964) and S. Dubnow, *History of the Jews in Russia and Poland* (1920) are useful, as is the collection edited by J. Frumkin and others, *Russian Jewry, 1860–1917* (1966). J. D. Klier's *Imperial Russia's Jewish Question 1855–1881* (1995) is largely about how the Jews were viewed at that time. More specialized books include Y. Peled's *Class and Ethnicity in the Pale* (1989); J. Klier and S. Lamboza (eds.), *Pogroms* (1991); E. Mendelsohn, *Class Struggle in the Pale* (1970), describing the growth of the Jewish socialist movement up to 1905; I. Frankel's very carefully researched *Prophecy and Politics: Socialism, Nationalism, and the Russian Jews, 1862–1917* (1981); and H. Rogger, *Jewish Policies and Right-Wing Politics in Imperial Russia* (1986). The latter touches on the Black Hundred and provides material for discussing whether there was anything that might later be described as a fascist movement in tsarist Russia. One of the interesting points made by M. Stanislawski in his *Tsar Nicholas I and the Jews* (1983) is that because most writing about this subject was done in the reign of Nicholas II, it projects the contemporary feeling that Jewish policy was deliberately vicious back to

Nicholas I's time, thereby distorting the view. E. H. Judge, in *Easter in Kishinev* (1992) attributes that pogrom to local agitation leading to patriotic riots; the rest followed.

Chapter 6

G. Wheeler, *The Modern History of Soviet Central Asia* (1964) is still a good introduction to that area, dealing with both nineteenth- and twentieth-century developments. M. Rywkin, *Russia in Central Asia* (1963) is mainly about the Soviet period but has a chapter on tsarist policies. *Russian Central Asia 1867–1917* (1960), by R. A. Pierce, concentrates on those forty important years. The alleged Russian threat to India called forth a host of books in the second half of the nineteenth century about Russian intentions in the area, but the less alarming *Tsarism and Imperialism in the Middle and Far East* (1940) by B. H. Sumner is preferable. D. Geyer's *Russian Imperialism* (1987) shows how foreign and domestic requirements clashed in the last half-century of tsarist Russia.

An agreeable introduction to the history of Siberia is G. Lensen, *Russia's Eastward Expansion* (1964), consisting of extracts, with commentary, from the writings of those who over the centuries had experience of that region. Two good histories of Siberia are V. L. Mote, *Siberia: Worlds Apart* (1998) and A. Wood (ed.), *The History of Siberia* (1991). J. J. Stephan's *The Russian Far East* (1994) is well written. *The Great Siberian Migration* (1957) by D. W. Treadgold is an exhaustive study of the government's development policies. S. Marks, *Road to Power* (1991) is a very good account of how the Trans-Siberian Railway was pushed forward by Witte and others. Siberian development, from the seventeenth to the twentieth century, is covered in various aspects by the collection edited by A. Wood and R. French, *The Development of Siberia* (1989). G. Kennan, *Siberia and the Exile System* (1891), is a classic exposé which greatly irritated the government. Asian Russia has always attracted western travellers with literary ambitions; three works which are useful and deserve prizes for endurance are: *Narrative of a Pedestrian Journey through Russia and Siberian Tartary, from the Frontier of China to the Sea and Kamchatka* (1825) by Captain John Dundas Cochrane, RN (this was a pedestrian journey indeed, for the author set out from Dieppe on foot and covered about 30,000 miles); *Oriental and Western Siberia* (1858) by Mr Thomas W. Atkinson and *Recollections of Tartar Steppes and their Inhabitants* (1863) by Mrs Thomas W. Atkinson. The indefatigable Atkinsons covered nearly 40,000 miles, largely on horseback. Mr was an artist and included his landscapes in the book. Mrs was formerly a governess in a Russian family and a high point of her book is her conversations with wives of the Decembrists who were still in exile at mid-century. For a synthesis of travellers' tales, railway-building, and official policies, Harmon Tupper, *To the Great Ocean: Siberia and the Trans Siberian Railway* (1965) is comprehensive.

'*Matey' Imperialists* (1982) by R. K. I. Quested has a title which is not as out of place as it might seem at first sight, for it describes how the Russians behaved in Manchuria from 1895 to 1917. *The Russo-Chinese War* (1967), by the late and very lamented George Lensen, describes Russia's involvement in the Boxer Rebellion. There are too many books about the Russo-Japanese War in English. J. N. Westwood, *Russia against Japan* (1986) aimed to eliminate the accretion of myths and misapprehensions that were bred in eight decades of narratives; it is therefore a rather slim volume. The non-military side of the war is well handled by J. A. White in his *Diplomacy of the Russo-Japanese War* (1964). For the military side, the fullest account is the multi-volume *Official History of the Russo-Japanese War* (1910), compiled by the British Committee of Imperial Defence. Of the scores of eyewitness accounts of the fighting, two are especially illuminating; Sir Ian Hamilton, *A Staff-Officer's Scrapbook* (1907) and A. N. Kuropatkin's explanation of his lack of success, *The Russian*

Army and the Japanese War (1909). For the naval side, J. N. Westwood, *Witnesses of Tsushima* (1970) will gratify addicts of blood and thunder; the squeamish should content themselves with the introduction, which deals with Russian naval policy in the Far East. A good history of the war which usefully blends both Russian and Japanese sources is D. Warner, P. Warner, *The Tide at Sunset* (2002). An offbeat collection, edited by D. Wells and S. Watson, is *The Russo-Japanese War in Cultural Perspective, 1904–05* (1999). Although the Russians lost the military war they triumphed on the literary side, having had centuries of experience in writing about war, from *Prince Igor* to *War and Peace*, so their accounts of the war vastly surpassed the ludicrous samurai-style narratives of the Japanese, who for centuries had had no international conflicts to write about.

Chapter 7

Nicholas II (1994), by D. Lieven, is a very good biography, sympathetic but critical. M. Ferro's *Nicholas II* (1991) is a manageable account of the Emperor's life by an experienced practitioner. Of R. Massie's blockbusting *Nicholas and Alexandra* (1968), it may at least be said that the book is better than the film. It treats very well the nature of haemophilia and is very readable. Another popular but not negligible biography is E. M. Almedingen, *The Empress Alexandra 1872–1918* (1961). Of the several books on Social Democracy, J. H. L. Keep, *The Rise of Social Democracy in Russia* (1963) takes the story up to 1905, as does the somewhat shorter *The Russian Marxists and the Origins of Bolshevism* (1955) by L. Haimson. R. Brym in *The Jewish Intelligentsia and Russian Marxism* (1978) makes the point that many Jews became revolutionaries out of the sheer frustration of being denied jobs appropriate to their abilities. D. W. Treadgold, *Lenin and his Rivals* (1955) treats the ideological struggles of 1898–1906 and includes useful accounts of the non-Bolshevik socialists and liberals. N. Valentinov, *Encounters with Lenin* (1968) is by a gifted and perceptive author who was a colleague of Lenin in exile, before breaking with him. Other views of Lenin's ideological critics are contained in R. Williams, *The Other Bolsheviks* (1986), which apart from dealing with the misgivings of Gorki and Lunarcharsky in 1904–14 also deals with Bogdanov, possibly the most original of the Bolshevik thinkers and not loved by Lenin. The argument between these two is elaborated by Z. Sochor in *Revolution and Culture* (1988). R. Stites, in *Revolutionary Dreams* (1989), gives a quite touching account of how utopian ideas influenced Bolshevik behaviour. A. Besancon, in *The Intellectual Origins of Leninism* (1981), among other things gives the impression that Lenin's ideology squeezed out his humanity. D. Lane's *The Roots of Russian Communism* (1969) is very informative. For a general view of intellectual currents C. Read's *Religion, Revolution, and the Russian Intelligentsia* (1979) is quite interesting. Some of the writings of the most percipient 'Economists' are available in translation in J. Frankel, *Vladimir Akimov on the Dilemmas of Russian Marxism, 1895–1903* (1969); the introduction of this volume is an excellent summary of Russian marxist theory. R. Pipes, *Social Democracy and the St. Petersburg Labour Movement* (1963) attempts to correct exaggerated accounts of Lenin's significance in the early years of the social democratic movement. A. B. Ulam, *Lenin and the Bolsheviks* (US title *The Bolsheviks*: 1965) takes the story from the early days to Lenin's death. In *Octobrists to Bolsheviks* (1984), M. McCauley presents an interesting collection of documents from 1905–17, while R. Pipes in *The Unknown Lenin* (1996) uses material freshly released from the archives. Among the best of the older biographies of Lenin are D. Shub, *Lenin* (1966) and H. Shukman, *Lenin and the Russian Revolution* (1966). These might be supplemented by the collection of essays by various specialists on aspects of Lenin's life edited by L. Shapiro and P. Reddaway, *Lenin: The Man, the Theorist, the Leader* (1967). The first of three volumes of R. Service, *Lenin: A*

Political Life appeared in 1985 and takes him as far as 1910. Vol. ii (1991) continues the story to 1918. The same author's *Lenin: A Biography* (2000) describes the man himself. Another multi-volume biography, absolutely devoid of convoluted language and with a definite viewpoint, is T. Cliff's *Lenin*, the three volumes of which appeared in 1975, 1976, and 1978. C. Rice's *Lenin* (1990) and B. Williams's *Lenin* (2000) are succinct. Lenin's own works are available in a multiplicity of editions. What 'Leninism' consisted of is still drably argued; a good commentary is N. Harding, *Leninism* (1996). The same author produced *Lenin's Political Thought* (1977). Whereas Pipes sees Lenin as using marxism to cloak his quest for power, Harding views him as basing his policies on marxism. (Service seems to have it both ways, quite plausibly too, seeing Lenin as a devoted marxist willing to modify the doctrine in light of experience.)

A. P. Mendel, *Dilemmas of Progress in Tsarist Russia* (1961), explains why movements such as Legal Populism and Legal Marxism split away from their parent movements, while R. Kindersley, *The First Russian Revisionists* (1962) concentrates on Legal Marxism. G. Swain, in his *Russian Social Democracy and the Legal Labour Movement 1906–14* (1983) reveals the gap, in those years, between Lenin's perceptions and reality.

P. Pomper gives the Bolsheviks a hard time in *The Russian Revolutionary Intelligentsia* (1970). The Socialist Revolutionaries are seen in action in C. Rice's *Russian Workers and the Socialist Revolutionary Party through the Revolution of 1905–07* (1988).

The Crisis of Russian Populism (1967) by R. Wortman examines the ideas and difficulties of three leading Populists. The politics of the rural situation are also covered by R. Hennesey in *The Agrarian Question in Russia 1905–1907* (1977), by L. Haimson's collection, *The Politics of Rural Russia 1905–1914* (1979), and by M. Perrie in *The Agrarian Policy of the Russian Socialist-Revolutionary Party* (1976). R. G. Robbins, *Famine in Russia 1891–1892* (1975) is about the previous reign, but helps to explain how peasants felt in the early twentieth century. Those of them who decided to move to Moscow and become workers are observed in *Peasants and Proletarians* (1979) by R. F. Johnson. *Radical Worker in Tsarist Russia* (1986), edited by R. Zelnik, is a fascinating autobiography of a Russian worker in the period up to 1905. How student activists viewed themselves, both before and after 1905, is conveyed in S. K. Morrissey's *Heralds of Revolution* (1998).

For Russian liberalism, whatever that might be, G. Fischer, *Russian Liberalism* (1958) goes up to about 1905, by which year T. Riha's biography of Milyukov, *A Russian European* (1969), is in full flow and takes the story up to the fiasco of 1917. A newer biography of Milyukov is M. K. Stockdale's *Paul Miliukov and the Quest for a Liberal Russia 1880–1918* (1996). Milyukov's explanation of his failure, among other more useful information, is conveyed by his autobiography *Political Memoirs, 1905–1917* (1967 edn., ed. A. P. Mendel). Another liberal is given generous two-volume treatment in R. F. Pipes, *Struve* (1970, 1980). A reliable guide to a more cheerful period for the liberals is S. Galai, *The Liberation Movement in Russia 1900–1905* (1973).

Many of the multitude of memoirs by revolutionaries begin their story around 1900. They should all be treated with caution (especially Trotsky's, whose deceptions and self-deceptions are superbly concealed by his fine style). Worth mentioning are V. Serge, *Memoirs of a Revolutionary, 1901–1941* (1963), B. Savinkov, *Memoirs of a Terrorist* (1931), the Menshevik Eva Broido, *Memoirs of a Revolutionary* (1967), and L. Trotsky, *My Life* (1930). The first volume of I. Deutscher's trilogy on Trotsky, *The Prophet Armed: Trotsky 1897–1921* (1954), is an advantageous substitute for Trotsky's autobiography. A useful biography covering the Mensheviks is I. Getzler's painstaking *Martov* (1967).

The immediate antecedents of 1905 are among the topics covered in E. H. Judge, *Plehve: Repression and Reform in Imperial Russia, 1902–1904* (1983), in which the subject appears as something of a pragmatist. This book might well be read concurrently with K. Frohlich, *The Emergence of Russian Constitutionalism 1900–1904* (1981).

As for the 1905 rebellion, J. Morison's *The 1905 Revolution in Russia* (1999) is concise. A. M. Verner's *The Crisis of Russian Autocracy* (1990) emphasizes the importance of Nicholas's role in 1905. S. Harcave, *First Blood: The Russian Revolution of 1905* (1965; in some editions the subtitle becomes the main title) is readable. Vol. ii of T. Shanin's *The Roots of Otherness* (1986) deals, quite deeply and sociologically, with 1905–7, while A. Ascher's *The Revolution of 1905* (1988) is a good straightforward treatment, and the same author's *The Revolution of 1905: Authority Restored* (1992) deals mainly with 1906. D. C. Rawson's *Russian Rightists and the Revolution of 1905* (1995) has the virtue of covering places in addition to St Petersburg and Moscow. Studies like these make books like G. Gapon, *The Story of my Life* (1905) and G. Hough, *The Potemkin Mutiny* (1960) look quite flimsy. W. Sablinsky, in his *Road to Bloody Sunday* (1976), deals with Father Gapon and seems to suggest that Bloody Sunday occurred because nobody expected it to occur and because the authorities could think of no other way to deal with the situation that Gapon had created. Police socialism gets good treatment in J. Schneiderman, *Sergei Zubatov and Revolutionary Marxism* (1976) and D. Pospielovsky, *Russian Police Trade Unionism* (1970). Some perceptive studies of this stormy period of Russian history are contained in J. Maynard, *Russia in Flux* (1948). Aspects of the rebellious workers are treated in L. Engelstein, *Moscow 1905* (1982) and V. F. Bonnell, *Roots of Rebellion* (1983); both of these concentrate on working-class organization. H. Reichman's *Railwaymen and Revolution* (1987), apart from having the rare virtue of depicting 1905 away from St Petersburg and Moscow, also implies that the most rebellious railwaymen were those who had the closest ties with their villages. A. Verner's *The Crisis of Russian Autocracy* (1990) looks at the role, or non-role, of Nicholas II in 1905. A general picture of society is provided by G. Surh's *1905 in St. Petersburg* (1989), which is especially good on Gapon's 'Assembly of Russian Mill and Factory Workers'. Civil rights came into the foreground in 1905 and these are looked at from several different historical points of view in the collection edited by O. Crisp and L. Edmonson, *Civil Rights in Imperial Russia* (1989). Another collection, this time on varying historical topics between 1881 and 1917, is edited by R. McKean: *New Perspectives in Modern Russian History* (1991). A rare view of the 1905 events in the provinces and villages is an incidental benefit of S. Seregny's *Russian Teachers and Peasant Revolution* (1989), which is about educational politics in that year. The countryside is also involved in I. Bushnell's *Mutiny among Repression* (1985), which shows how in 1905–7 peasant soldiers would solve their internal conflict between loyalty and humanity by the desperate expedient of mutiny.

The post-1905 situation has been studied in several recent publications. P. Waldron, in *Between Two Revolutions* (1998), studies Stolypin's various reforms. A biography of the man is A. Ascher, *Stolypin* (2001). A. Levin, who published *The Second Duma* in 1940, returned with *The Third Duma: Election and Profile* in 1973. The same period is covered differently in B. Pinchuk, *The Octobrists in the Third Duma, 1907–1912* (1974). T. Emmons adds to knowledge of the First Duma with *The Formation of Political Parties and the First National Elections in Russia* (1983), although it is mainly concerned with its immediate antecedents. How Stolypin tackled three main issues (agriculture, Finland, zemstvo extension) is the substance of G. Tokmakoff, *P. A. Stolypin and the Third Duma* (1981). G. A. Hosking, *The Russian Constitutional Experiment* (1973) is devoted to the interaction between government and Duma up to 1914, thereby throwing much light on Stolypin's problems. The Stolypin peasant reform is additionally treated in the already-mentioned book by G. T. Robinson and in L. Owen, *The Russian Peasant Movement, 1906–1917* (1937). D. Atkinson, *The End of the Russian Land Commune, 1905–1930* (1983) is an important contribution. J. Pallot in *Land*

Reform in Russia 1906–1917 (1999) suggests that the Stolypin Reform failed because it showed no understanding either of peasants' attachment to the commune or of the degree of opposition it would arouse. The unsuccessful efforts to reform local government are related by N. B. Weissman in his *Reform in Tsarist Russia* (1981). In both agriculture and local government the role of the landowning gentry was sometimes decisive, and aspects of this situation are covered in R. T. Manning, *The Crisis of the Old Order in Russia* (1982), detailing relations between landowners and the government around 1905 and observing the importance of class antagonisms between the nobles and peasantry, G. M. Hamburg, *Politics of the Russian Nobility, 1881–1905* (1984), and D. Edelman, *Gentry Politics on the Eve of the Russian Revolution: The Nationalist Party, 1907–1917*. T. Pearson, in *Russian Officialdom in Crisis* (1989), deals with the problem of distributing authority in the countryside, and accordingly has much to say about *zemstva*, land captains, the traditional nobility, and the bureaucracy. L. Haimson's collection *The Politics of Rural Russia 1905–1914* (1979) contains specialized essays that, for the most part, are still valid.

Chapter 8

Textbook coverage of Nicholas's reign used to be marked by the division between 'pessimistic' and 'optimistic' assessments of the regime's prospects on the eve of the war. Most historians, and probably all Soviet historians allowed to publish, were pessimists, arguing that the regime could not have survived, war or no war. Nowadays there is less of a debate, with writers tending to allow the readers themselves to make up their minds, if they see a need to do so. For reliable coverage of Nicholas's unhappy reign, in addition to titles mentioned in the previous chapter bibliography there are W. B. Lincoln, *In War's Dark Shadow* (1983), L. Kochan, *Russia in Revolution, 1890–1918* (1966), and R. Charques, *Twilight of Imperial Russia* (1958). A useful collection of essays is *Russia under the Last Tsar* (1969), edited by T. G. Stavrou. A short collection of extracts from the writings of western and Soviet historians, *Russia in Transition, 1905–1914* (1970), edited by R. H. McNeal, presents opposing views on such themes as Russia's economic and political prospects, and on Stolypin.

Day-to-day life is agreeably presented by H. Troyat in *Daily Life in Russia under the Last Tsar* (1961). M. Kovalevsky's *Modern Customs and Ancient Laws of Russia* (1891) is fascinating for a reader already familiar with the period. W. H. Bruford, in his *Chekhov and his Russia* (1947), makes a kind of social survey of early twentieth-century Russia, using the writer's works as his raw material. F. H. F. Palmer, *Russian Life in Town and Country* (1901), is a reliable account, by the secretary of one of Nicholas's equerries, of what it was like to be a Russian under the last Romanov. Further sociological insight may be found in A. Kuprin's novel *Yama* (sometimes entitled *The Pit*), which is largely concerned with prostitution, and in his *The Duel*, which is about army life. A good account of the tsarist army's political influence is contained in the already-mentioned W. C. Fuller, *Civil–Military Conflict in Imperial Russia 1881–1914* (1985), which shows that the war ministry did not always get its own way. Another study is R. H. McNeal, *Tsar and Cossack 1855–1914* (1986), dealing with a unique military society. V. T. Bill's aptly titled *The Forgotten Class* (1959) describes the Russian industrialists and merchants adequately enough, and has a useful section about the Old Believers. Both education and the 'woman question' are dealt with in A. H. Koblitz, *A Convergence of Lives* (1983), which is about Sofia Kovalevskaya, who, like so many other intelligent women, had to 'choose between knowledge and revolution'.

For the economy, there is T. H. von Laue, *Sergei Witte and the Industrialization of Russia* (1963), which is good but would have been better if its author had done some more homework in economics. M. Miller, *The Economic Development of Russia 1905–1914* (1926, 1968) is useful but patchy, and offers the rare courtesy of a conversion table for the old Russian weights and measures. The role of foreign capital and technology is described in J. P. McKay, *Pioneers for Profit: Foreign Entrepreneurship and Russian Industrialization 1885–1913* (1970). The professional life of the engineer-managers in the southern steel and coal industries is interestingly described in S. P. McCaffray's *The Politics of Industrialization in Tsarist Russia* (1996). Two of that class of book which, ostensibly aimed at a very narrow subject, touches on a very broad spectrum of topics are A. Fenin, *Coal and Politics in Late Imperial Russia* (1990), which is the memoirs of an engineer, and J. Coppersmith, *The Electrification of Russia 1880–1926* (1991). J. A. Grant's *Big Business in Russia* (1999) provides a history of the famous and infamous Putilov engineering company from its 1868 foundation to modern times. Nicholas's rearmament drive is well covered in P. W. Gatrell, *Government, Industry and Rearmament in Russia, 1900–1914* (1994). The working class at this time receives attention in R. McKean, *St. Petersburg between the Revolutions* (1990), about the labour movement. L. I. Phillips, *Bolsheviks and the Bottle* (2000) is better than its title might suggest, dealing essentially with drink and the working class over the first third of the twentieth century; unsurprisingly, the role of drink in the assertion of masculine identity seems to have been as important in Russia as elsewhere. Urbanization is dealt with by J. Bradley in *Muzhik and Muscovite* (1985), and other books covering the cities are the collection edited by M. Hamm, *The City in Late Imperial Russia* (1986), which details the situation in eight large cities, and R. Thurston's *Liberal City, Conservative State* (1987). The latter is about Moscow's critical situation in 1906–14 and suggests that half the problem was that a liberal city government had difficulty in cooperating with a conservative state. These difficulties are also illustrated in J. Hutchinson's *Politics and Public Health in Revolutionary Russia* (1990). Education is studied in J. McClelland, *Autocrats and Academics: Education, Culture and Society in Tsarist Russia* (1987), J. Johanson, *Women's Struggle for Higher Education in Russia 1855–1900* (1987), which is as much about inter-ministerial struggles as about women, and S. Kassow, *Students, Professors and the State in Tsarist Russia* (1989), which shows how universities formed a self-contained world in which radical ideas had more freedom to develop than elsewhere. The universities' role in the post-1905 ferment is described in D. Wartenweiler's *Civil Society and Academic Debate in Russia 1905–1914* (1999).

When Russia Learned to Read (1985), by J. Brooks, is about the spread of literacy in the last half-century of tsarist Russia. A related topic, the rise of a mass-circulation press after 1855, is covered by L. Reynolds in *The News under Russia's Old Regime* (1991), while C. Ruud in *Russian Entrepreneur* (1990) gives a biography of Ivan Sytin, the publisher responsible for the progressive popular newspaper *Russkoye slovo* (which eventually was metamorphosed into *Izvestiya*). A collection about women in journalism in the last Romanov years, edited by B. T. Norton and J. M. Gheith, is titled *An Improper Profession* (2001).

The Tsar's Viceroys (1987), by R. Robbins, deals with the provincial governors, and their quite hard-working lives are illustrated with many examples. At the opposite end of the scale were the Social Democrats, of whom some Ukrainian examples, cut off from their leadership and harried by the police, are studied by R. Elwood in *Russian Social Democracy in the Underground* (1974). N. Schleifman's *Undercover Agents in the Russian Revolutionary Movement* (1988) is involved with the travails of the Socialist Revolutionaries in 1902–14; Azeff is well covered, but still remains much of a mystery. Books on the Okhrana have already been mentioned; B. Nikolaevsky, *Azeff the Russian Judas* (1934) is not as bad as its title suggests. Of memoirs so far unmentioned, those by V. N. Kokovtsov, Stolypin's successor as prime minister, are quite valuable: *Out of my Past* (1935). Also worth reading are

V. I. Gurko's recollections, *Features and Figures of the Past: Government and Opinion in the Reign of Nicholas II* (1939) and, especially, B. Pares, *My Russian Memoirs* (1931), which describes its author's experiences between 1898 and 1919. V. V. Shulgin, *Days of the Russian Revolution* (1984) is a memoir of a right-wing Duma member covering 1905–17.

Chapter 9

Patriotic Culture in Russia during World War I (1995) by H. F. Jahn deals not only with the uplifting endeavours of plays, posters, and films but also those of picture postcards and nightclubs. D. C. B. Lieven's *Russia and the Origins of the First World War* (1983) is a succinct account of how Russia was dragged into the war. Still very useful for a study of Russia at war are the several works published by the Carnegie Foundation, which also took care to ensure that most major libraries acquired them; most of them also provide the pre-war background for their topics. These books are: *Russian Public Finance during the War* (1928) by A. M. Michelson and others; *Russia in the Economic War* (1928) by B. E. Nolde; *State Control of Industry during the War* (1928) by S. O. Zagorsky; *The War and the Russian Government* (1929) by P. P. Gronsky and N. J. Astrov; *Russian Schools and Universities in the World War* (1929) by N. Ignatiev and others; *The Cooperative Movement in Russia during the War* (1929) by F. M. Kayden and A. N. Antsiferov; *Russian Agriculture during the War* (1930) by A. N. Antsiferov and others; *Food Supply in Russia during the World War* (1930) by P. B. Struve and others; *Russian Local Government during the War and the Union of Zemstvos* (1930) by T. J. Polner and others; *The Russian Army in the World War* (1931) by N. N. Golovine; *The Cost of the War to Russia* (1932) by S. Kohn and A. F. Meyendorff; and *The End of the Russian Empire* (1931) by M. T. Florinsky. The last describes the disintegration of society and bureaucracy, and has been reprinted as a paperback. A more detailed account by one who was there is B. Pares, *Fall of the Russian Monarchy* (1939). The inside story is conveyed by A. N. Iakhontov's notes, taken at meetings of the Council of Ministers in 1915, edited by M. Cherniavsky and entitled *Prologue to Revolution* (1967). The same kind of inside story is conveyed by C. F. Vulliamy, *From the Red Archives* (1929), an edited translation of documents relating to the last pre-revolutionary years. The Rasputin episode is described, not always convincingly, by one of his murderers, F. F. Yusupov, in *Lost Splendour* (1953), and by J. T. Fuhrmann, in *Rasputin: A Life* (1990) and A. de Jonge in *Life and Times of Rasputin* (1982). E. Radzinsky subtitles his *Rasputin* (2000) 'The Last Word'; at almost 700 pages this is a massive last word, but the book does seem to say everything it is possible to say. F. A. Golder, *Documents of Russian History 1914–1917* (1969) is exactly what its title describes. C. J. Smith, *The Russian Struggle for Power 1914–1917* (1956) is actually an account of Russia's foreign relations, especially with the Allies. More recent titles include L. H. Siegelbaum's study of the war industries committees, *The Politics of Industrial Mobilization in Russia 1914–17* (1983), K. Neilson, *Strategy and Supply: The Anglo-Russian Alliance 1914–17* (1984), and R. Pearson's study of liberal travails, *The Russian Moderates and the Crisis of Tsarism 1914–17* (1977). A very good history of the regime's performance in the wartime years is N. Stone, *The Eastern Front* (1975).

What the generals saw is conveyed in A. I. Denikin, *The Russian Turmoil* (1922), A. A. Brusilov, *A Soldier's Notebook* (1930), and B. Gourko, *Memories and Impressions of War and Revolution in Russia 1914–1917* (1918), among many others. Three commendable accounts (and there are others) from a less exalted viewpoint are G. P. Tschebotarioff, *Russia my Native Land* (1964), by a former Cossack artillery officer who participated in the Great and Civil wars; *The Grinding Mill* (1935) by another junior officer, A. Lobanov-Rostovsky; and *A Subaltern in Old Russia* (1944) by a Red Army general, A. A. Ignatiev. W. B. Steveni, *The*

Russian Army from Within (1914) gives a westerner's observations. For the adventures of a Prussian pachyderm on the Eastern Front, see General Ludendorff, *My War Memories 1914–1918* (2 vols., n.d.). W. B. Lincoln's *Passage through Armageddon* (1986) is a readable general history of Russia's war years. The massive refugee problem inside wartime Russia is covered by P. Gatrell in his *A Whole Empire Walking* (1999).

Chapter 10

O. Figes's *A People's Tragedy* (1996) is very informative and readable, covering the years before and after 1917 with a good balance of fundamentals and details. Very useful sources, especially as they integrate much recent research, are *The Blackwell Encyclopedia of the Russian Revolution* (1988), edited by H. Shukman, and *The Critical Companion to the Russian Revolution 1914–1921* (1997), edited by E. Acton, V. Cherniaev, and W. G. Rosenburg and containing almost 800 pages and 65 pieces. A good account of the first revolution is T. Hasegawa, *The February Revolution: Petrograd 1917* (1981), which, among other things, suggests that the soviets were more symbolic than powerful, the Duma's provisional committee (which controlled the railways and had the confidence of both army and soviets) being the effective authority. M. Ferro has also written ground-breaking studies of the Revolution: *The Russian Revolution of February 1917* (1972) and *October 1917: A Social History of the Russian Revolution* (1980). Some critics regard the book by the Russian historian E. N. Burdzhalov, *Russia's Second Revolution* (1987), as the best book about the February Revolution; the author raised a hornets' nest among his Soviet colleagues when he first revealed this work. G. Katkov, *Russia 1917* (1967) is still useful, especially for the immediate antecedents. Another good account, with some emphasis on society, is S. Fitzpatrick, *The Russian Revolution* (1982). L. Shapiro, *1917: The Russian Revolutions* (1984) emphasizes the importance of power, its grasp and retention. An excellent short account is J. D. White's *The Russian Revolution 1917–1921* (1994). A very brief account, but incorporating new research, is R. Service, *The Russian Revolution* (1986). The same author edited *Society and Politics in the Russian Revolution* (1992). Shorter treatments include B. Williams, *The Russian Revolution 1917–1921* (1987) and D. Marples, *Lenin's Revolution* (2000). R. A. Wade's *The Russian Revolution: 1917* (2000) is very well done, and additionally does not downplay the nationalities. A source book, covering 1917–21, is available in the form of R. Kowalski's *The Russian Revolution* (1997). Documents and commentary figure in *The Fall of the Romanovs* (1995), covering the atmosphere of the last months of the regime, and presented by M. D. Sternberg and V. Khrustalev. J. Burbank's *Intelligentsia and Revolution* (1986) deals with the polemics exchanged between the Bolsheviks and their critics in 1917–21. How the Bolsheviks succeeded in taking over the leadership of the mass organizations after spring 1917, without those organizations' rank and file quite knowing what was going on, is described by J. Keep in his *The Russian Revolution: A Study in Mass Mobilisation* (1977). However, this book, like several others, needs to be read in conjunction with later books resulting from easier research conditions over recent years. Several of these concentrate on a particular area or group and collectively they demonstrate that there was no single pattern for the events that unrolled in 1917. Among them are: R. Suny, *The Baku Commune 1917–1918* (1972), G. Gill, *Peasants and Government in the Russian Revolution* (1979), O. Figes, *Peasant Russia, Civil War: The Volga Countryside in Revolution 1917–1921* (1989), D. Raleigh, *Revolution on the Volga* (1985), about Saratov in 1917, and R. Snow, *The Bolsheviks in Siberia 1917–1918* (1977). A still useful commentary is presented by E. Acton in his *Rethinking the Russian Revolution* (1990). The period between February and October is well detailed by several of the main participants, each grinding his own particular axe; Milyukov has already been mentioned. A. F. Kerensky published *The Catastrophe* (1927), *Crucifixion of Liberty* (1934), and *The Kerensky Memoirs* (1966): it is interesting to note which of his views are changed or unchanged, as not only time, but current events, influence his perspective, and it could be argued that his memoirs do not show him at his best. Kerensky also collaborated with R. P. Browder in *The Russian Provisional Government 1917: Documents* (1961), which is too selective, but useful. A sound biography of Kerensky was late in coming, but arrived with R. Abraham's *Alexander Kerensky* (1987). Among other biographies are a study of *Tseretelli* (1976) by W. Roobol, and R. Slusser's *Stalin in October* (1987), whose subtitle 'The Man who Missed the Revolution' seems a trifle unkind. For the Socialist Revolutionaries, V. M. Chernov, *The Great Russian Revolution* (1936) is sometimes revealing, and I. Sternberg, who was a Left SR and became a member of Lenin's original coalition government, lets a few cats out of various bags in his *In the Workshop of the Revolution* (1953). Another absorbing memoir is *Stormy Passage* (1961) by W. S. Woytinsky, who was a revolutionary student in 1905, broke with Lenin in 1917, and became an editor of *Izvestiya* and a member of the Petrograd Soviet. *On the Eve of 1917* (1982) is by A. Shlyapnikov, who later led the Workers' Opposition. What the Bolsheviks were doing, or not doing, before 1917 is described, not always sympathetically, by the prominent Menshevik T. Dan in his *The Origins of Bolshevism* (written 1940, published 1964). What Dan and his friends were doing, or not doing, in 1917, is covered in J. D. Basil, *The Mensheviks in the Revolution of 1917* (1983), but some of the author's interpretations are hard to swallow. Another bite at the same cherry is Z. Galili y Garcia's *The Menshevik Leaders in the Russian Revolution* (1989). The failure of the Kadets is chronicled in W. Rosenberg's *Liberals in the Russian Revolution* (1974), which takes their story up to 1921. The collection edited by C. Timberlake, *Essays on Russian Liberalism* (1972), likewise covers an extended period. What the SRs were doing in 1917 is sympathetically examined by O. H. Radkey in *The Agrarian Foes of Bolshevism* (1958). The anarchists are covered, from 1905 to their suppression during the Civil War, by P. Avrich in *The Russian Anarchists* (1967). A sad story which examines one of the reasons for the failure of the Provisional Government is R. A. Wade, *The Russian Search for Peace February–October 1917* (1969). Equally melancholy is the more extensive *The Allies and the Russian Revolution, from the Fall of the Monarchy to the Peace of Brest-Litovsk* (1954) by R. D. Warth. L. Heenan's *Russian Democracy's Fatal Blunder* (1987) is about the summer offensive and seems to suggest that domestic considerations (like finding gainful employment at the front for the Petrograd garrison) were more important than military.

Much recent research has been devoted to the grass roots of the revolutions. O. Anweiler has studied the soviets from 1905 to 1921 in *The Soviets* (1974). D. Koenker, *Moscow Workers and the 1917 Revolution* (1981) is very informative, even though its strong statistical under-pinning tends to reduce people to digits. D. Mandel has studied the Petrograd workers in *The Petrograd Workers and the Fall of the Old Regime* (1983) and *The Petrograd Workers and the Soviet Seizure of Power* (1984). D. Kaiser has edited *The Workers Revolution in Russia 1917: The View from Below* (1987). A statistically based study of strikes between the two revolutions in D. Koenker and W. Rosenberg, *Strikes and Revolution in Russia 1917* (1989), suggests that violence was rare and that the workers were well capable of organizing themselves without the help of outsiders. R. A. Wade treats another important topic in his *Red Guards and Workers' Militias in the Russian Revolution* (1984). S. A. Smith, in his *Red Petrograd: Revolution in the Factories 1917–1918* (1983), suggests that workers took over their factories to protect their jobs rather than their revolution, and failed not because of managerial resistance or sabotage but simply because they had no idea what to do next.

A. Wildman, *The End of the Russian Army* (1980) is mainly concerned with the soldiers' revolts of spring 1917, but includes useful historical background for the tsarist army. The second volume (1987) continues the story. The role of the sailors in the Revolution is competently handled by F. Mawdsley in *The Russian Revolution and the Baltic Fleet* (1978) and by N. Saul in *Sailors in Revolt* (1978).

Outside the Soviet Union the best detailed account of the October Revolution and its time was deemed to be the first volume of W. H. Chamberlin, *The Russian Revolution* (1935); inside Soviet Russia the party leadership loved John Reed's enthusiastic *Ten Days that Shook the World* (1919). There are many others, some of which are usefully anthologized in R. Pethybridge, *Witnesses to the Russian Revolution* (1964). In *Memories of Revolution* (1993), A. Horsborough-Porter presents interviews with Russian women remembering 1917. Another revealing anthology, including the accounts of relatively humble participants, is D. von Mohrenschildt, *The Russian Revolution of 1917* (1971). Trotsky very skilfully combines personal experience with interpretation and narrative in his *History of the Russian Revolution* (1936), which is as reliable as one can expect from so committed a participant. For more serious history, the first volume of F. H. Carr's multi-volume history was *The Bolshevik Revolution 1917–1923* (1950), which carries the signs of its time. Two other books are *Red October* (1967) by R. V. Daniels, and *The Russian Revolution* (1970) by M. Liebman, which stresses the significance of the Revolution for socialism. A collection of documents was edited by I. Bunyan and H. H. Fisher in 1934: *The Bolshevik Revolution 1917–1918*. Other documents can be found in M. McCauley's collection, listed later. *Revolution in Russia: Reassessments of 1917* (1992) is a collection edited by E. Frankel, J. Frankel, and B. Knei-paz. O. Figes and B. Kolonitskii discuss how language and symbols were changed to support the new regime in their *Interpreting the Revolution* (1999).

Chapter 11

An up-to-date, manageable, history of 1917–21 is C. Read's *From Tsar to Soviets* (1996), which gives good coverage to ordinary people. Two excellent books on the Civil War are W. B. Lincoln's *Red Victory* (1989) and C. Mawdsley's *The Russian Civil War* (1987). Among older but still useful accounts of the Civil War are the second volume of W. H. Chamberlin, *The Russian Revolution* (1935), and D. Footman, *Civil War in Russia* (1961). The first volume of P. Kenez, *Civil War in South Russia* (1971) deals with 1918 and the second volume with 1919–20. Both cover mainly the White Army and show that its failure was really due to non-military reasons. In *Civil War in Siberia* (1996), J. D. Smele suggests that Kolchak failed largely because he did not act like a dictator. Another work on Kolchak and the intervention in Siberia is R. M. Connaughton's *The Republic of the Ushakovka* (1990). An edited transcript of Kolchak's eve-of-execution interrogation is the main item in F. Varneck and H. H. Fisher's collection, *The Testimony of Admiral Kolchak and Other Siberian Materials* (1953). *The Fate of Admiral Kolchak* (1963) by P. Fleming is readable but not searching. A soldier-participant in struggles against both Whites and Reds in Siberia, P. Dotsenko, has written the idiosyncratic *The Struggle for Democracy in Siberia* (1983). A. I. Denikin wrote five volumes of memoirs, which are summarized in English in his *The White Army* (1930). General P. N. Wrangel also had his say, in *Always with Honour* (1957). On foreign intervention there are: G. A. Brinkley, *The Volunteer Army and Allied Intervention in South Russia 1917–1921* (1966), J. A. White, *The Siberian Intervention* (1950), R. H. Ullman, *Britain and the Russian Civil War* (1968), J. F. C. Bradley, *Allied Intervention in Russia* (1968), and J. Silverlight, *The Victors' Dilemma* (1970). The latter is based mainly on British sources. Other sideshows are covered in M. Malet, *Nestor Makhno in the Russian Civil War* (1982), P. Arshinov's *History of the Makhnovist Movement* (1987), and O. H. Radkey's study of the Greens and the Tambov Revolt, *The Unknown Civil War in Soviet Russia* (1976). *The Day We*

Almost Bombed Moscow (1986) by C. Dobson and J. Miller is a very readable account of the British participation, covert and overt, in the Russian Civil War. Its somewhat catchpenny title derives from an incident when British aircraft, transported by rail, were placed on airfields close enough to bomb Moscow, an idea that was soon squashed by the British war minister, Churchill. *Russia's Retreat from Poland 1920* (1990), by T. Fiddick, is a well-rounded view of the Bolsheviks' ill-judged and ill-fated march on Warsaw.

Political life in these troubled years is well covered by the third volume of R. Service's *Lenin: A Political Life* (1995), and by *Party, State and Society in the Russian Civil War* (1989), edited by D. Koenker, W. Rosenberg, and R. Suny, which, like most such collections, is patchy but goes into enough detail to show the danger of simplifying the issues. How the Mensheviks, their leadership split, lost influence in 1918 is discussed by V. Brovkin in *The Mensheviks after October* (1987). O. Radkey wrote *The Election to the Russian Constituent Assembly of 1917* (1950), which tells of the true state of public opinion, and much else besides. L. Shapiro, in *The Origin of Communist Autocracy* (1955), claims that it was in the Civil War years that the rot set in inside the party, an idea that can be examined with the help of T. H. Rigby, *Lenin's Government* (1979), R. Service, *The Bolshevik Party in Revolution* (1979), and the collection of documents edited by M. McCauley, *The Russian Revolution and the Soviet State 1917–1921* (1975). The fate of Soviet democracy between 1917 and 1924 is covered by S. Farber in *Before Stalinism* (1990). How the Bolsheviks reacted with Moscow, and vice versa, in the Civil War years is recounted by R. Sakwa in *Soviet Communists in Power* (1988), while the opposition of the 'Left Communists' is covered by R. Kowalski in *The Bolshevik Party in Conflict* (1991). Lenin's responsibility for some of the unpleasant things that happened after his death is implied in M. Liebman, *Leninism under Lenin* (1975) and L. Gerson, *The Secret Police in Lenin's Russia* (1976). G. Leggett's well-researched *The Cheka* (1981) adds considerably to knowledge of this topic.

M. McAuley in *Bread and Justice* (1991) describes what it was like to live in St Petersburg in 1917–22. The politics and society of this period are also treated in V. N. Brovkin's *Behind the Front Lines of the Civil War* (1994). F. Benuventi's *The Bolsheviks and the Red Army 1918–1922* (1988) and M. von Hagen's *Soldiers in the Proletarian Dictatorship: The Red Army and the Soviet Socialist State 1917–1930* (1990) together present a well-rounded picture of the army's changing place in society. The fate of the émigrés is detailed in M. Raeff, *Russia Abroad: A Cultural History of the Russian Emigration 1919–1939* (1990), and in the first-hand accounts of several generations edited by M. Glenny and N. Stone, *The Other Russia* (1990). Two other, very different, first-hand accounts come in *The Memoirs of Anastas Mikoyan* (vol. i, 1988) edited by S. Mikoyan, no more embellished than the memoirs of a typical western minister and dealing largely with revolution and civil war in the Caucasus, and *Alexis Babine in Saratov 1917–1922* (1988), edited by the enterprising D. Raleigh. Babine's first claim to distinction was shooting a pine-cone off a friend's head, with fatal results, and his second was this diary. In between he was a grey, narrow-minded librarian interested in the small things of provincial life—which is why his diary is so valuable.

Economics and foreign relations are treated by E. H. Carr in the second and third volumes, respectively, of his *The Bolshevik Revolution* (1952, 1954), and the Bolsheviks' first major foreign affairs problem is dealt with by J. Wheeler-Bennett in *Brest-Litovsk: The Forgotten Peace* (1938). What went on inside the factories can be discerned from T. F. Remington, *Building Socialism in Soviet Russia: Ideology and Industrial Organization 1917–1921* (1984) and C. Sirianni, *Workers Control and Socialist Democracy: The Soviet Experience* (1982), although both books have broader ambitions: Remington seeks to show that the socialist state mobilized new elements of society to support it and thereby destroyed its own social base, while Sirianni argues that what happened to the Bolsheviks in these years was not simply a result of circumstances beyond their control, because they did make choices, and those choices were determined not by external circumstances but by their ideology. W. Husband's *Revolution in the Factory* (1990) is about the textile industry from 1917 to 1920. The life and thought of the workers on the eve of the Kronstadt rising are detailed in J. Aves, *Workers against Lenin* (1996).

J. E. Mace, *Communism and the Dilemmas of National Liberation* (1983) is about the problems caused by the ungrateful Ukrainians in 1918–33. This covers just one facet of the nationalities problem, which occupied so much of the communist leaders' thoughts at this period. Two books dealing with this preoccupation are S. Blank's *The Sorcerer's Apprentice* (1994), a nicely titled study of Stalin as commissar for nationalities, and J. Smith's *The Bolsheviks and the National Question 1917–23* (1999), which emphasizes the role of nationally conscious people in the evolution of Bolshevik nationalities policy. It is rather more sympathtic than R. Pipes's earlier *Formation of the Soviet Union: Communism and Nationalism 1917–23* (1964). Other books relating to this period are T. E. O'Connor, *The Politics of Soviet Culture* (1983), which is largely a study of Lunacharsky; *Bolshevik Culture* (1985), edited by A. Gleason, P. Kenez, and R. Stites, which deals with the first decade of Soviet culture; A. Tuominen, *The Bells of the Kremlin* (1982), which is by a Finnish member of the Comintern in Lenin's time; and two books about British reactions, S. White, *Britain and the Bolshevik Revolution: A Study in the Politics of Diplomacy, 1920–1924* (1979), and M. H. Cowden, *Russian Bolshevism and British Labour 1917–1921* (1984). A useful biography of Trotsky is I. Howe, *Leon Trotsky* (1978) but this is largely superseded by D. Volkogonov's *Trotsky* (1996). Trotsky, of course, was the originator of the breathtaking lies about the Kronstadt Revolt that remained embedded in Soviet accounts. The western reader was lucky, for there were two good studies of this outbreak, J. Avrich, *Kronstadt 1921* (1970) having been followed by I. Getzler, *Kronstadt 1917–1921* (1983), which dealt with the Revolution as well as the Revolt.

Another Bolshevik's biography is W. Lerner's *Karl Radek: The Last Internationalist* (1970). For the Comintern, over its entire history, there is K. McDermott and J. Agnew's *The Comintern* (1997).

Chapter 12

A prominent participant in the arguments of what to do next was Bukharin, who receives superb biographical treatment in S. Cohen, *Bukharin and the Bolshevik Revolution* (1973). His thought on these matters is well set out in M. Haynes, *Nikolai Bukharin and the Transition from Capitalism to Socialism* (1985). R. B. Day, *Leon Trotsky and the Politics of Economic Isolation* (1973) gives the views of another participant. R. Pethybridge, *The Social Prelude to Stalinism* (1974) is a thoughtful attempt to explain how the emergence of alternatives to Stalin's way was stifled by social influences. The general political atmosphere of 1924–6 is well conveyed in the memoirs of N. Valentinov, *The New Economic Policy and the Party Crisis after the Death of Lenin* (1971). More of the flavour of the NEP period can be enjoyed in A. Banerji's *Merchants and Markets in Revolutionary Russia 1917–30* (1997) and A. Ball's *Russia's Last Capitalists: The Nepmen 1921–1929* (1987), the collection largely concerned with culture edited by S. Fitzpatrick, A. Rabinovitch, and R. Stites, *Russia in the Era of NEP* (1991), W. Chase's *Workers, Society, and the Soviet State: Labor and Life in Moscow 1918–1929* (1987), C. Ward's *Russia's Cotton Workers and the New Economic Policy* (1990), and P. Kenez's *The Birth of the Propaganda State* (1986), which deals with how the people were influenced by the mass mobilizations of 1917–29. Much detail about industry and agriculture can be derived from the collection edited by R. W. Davies, *From Tsarism to the*

New Economic Policy (1990). E. C. Reiman's *The Birth of Stalinism* (1987) provides an excellent description of the USSR towards the end of NEP.

How the regime hoped to create a new, improved, human being is covered by L. Attwood, *The New Soviet Man and Woman* (1990). The particularities of the woman's situation are detailed in E. A. Wood, *The Baba and the Comrade* (1997) and in L. Attwood, *Creating the New Soviet Woman* (1999). A. Gorsuch's *Youth in Revolutionary Russia* (2001) covers young women, and their consorts too.

Of the older accounts, E. H. Carr, *The Interregnum 1923–1924* (1954) bridges the gap between his three volumes on the Bolshevik Revolution and his three-volume *Socialism in One Country*. The first volume of the latter (1958) deals with the economy and with the main party personalities, the second (1959) with the party and government, and the third (1964) with foreign relations, from 1924 to 1926. A somewhat different perspective is offered by I. Deutscher in *The Prophet Armed: Trotsky 1921–1929* (1959). Volkogonov's biography offers yet another version, and has the benefit of greater archival access. Deutscher's *Stalin* (1961) was once regarded as a standard work on the subject, and still has its uses. Other middle-aged biographies of Stalin should not be scorned. They include R. Hingley, *Joseph Stalin* (1974) and A. B. Ulam, *Stalin* (1974). A. Bullock's *Hitler and Stalin: Parallel Lives* (1991) is full and reliable; the two tyrants differed in one fundamental: Stalin, unlike Hitler, knew when to stop. R. Conquest's *Stalin: Breaker of Nations* (1991) is a good and not overlong synthesis but, like Bullock's book, almost ignores the five-year plans. R. McNeal's *Stalin: Man and Ruler* (1988) can be recommended. The subject of Stalin as a person is by no means exhausted, and new books will inevitably appear, either to go deeper into his psychology or to use materials that hitherto have been under lock and key. In the latter category is D. Volkogonov's *Stalin: Triumph and Tragedy* (1991), which is illuminating but not definitive. One of the earlier attempts to take a closer look at Stalin was F. Smith's *The Young Stalin* (1967), which is quite useful, although its attractive proposition that Stalin was once a police informer lacks proof, as opposed to probability. In a class by itself is R. Tucker's two-volume work. In his first volume, *Stalin as Revolutionary* (1973), he puts forward the proposition that the root cause of Stalin's neurosis (or whatever it was) was the childhood hammering he received from his drunken, violent father; this is plausible, but far from proven. In his second volume, *Stalin in Power* (1990), the author goes further and suggests that Stalin consciously and carefully followed in the footsteps of Peter the Great and Ivan the Terrible, a suggestion that, again, is plausible but not proven. Russian researchers have noted that Stalin's personal library provides evidence of greater interest in the Roman emperors, especially Augustus Caesar, than in Ivan and Peter.

Whether Stalin was anti-Semitic is a question that biographers have not yet dealt with in a convincing way. L. Rappoport in his informative *Stalin's War against the Jews* (1991) considers that the Doctors' Plot was final proof of Stalin's anti-Semitism, but this seems simplistic. When dealing with a probable case of paranoia (and Stalin's would have been inflamed by a feeling, quite justified, that he was surrounded by colleagues who did not like him) it is unhelpful to ascribe aggression to hatred of a particular group. As many Jews did well under Stalin as perished.

For Stalin's activities while Lenin was writing his 'Testament', M. Lewin, *Lenin's Last Struggle* (1968) is very well done. What he was doing after Lenin died forms part of N. Tumarkin's fascinating *Lenin Lives!* (1983), which is about how Lenin was canonized to become cult-fodder. The problem of what to do with political enemies was solved violently, as can be illustrated by the 1922 show trial of SRs, described by M. Jansen in *A Show Trial under Lenin* (1982). The interaction between the grass roots and political developments in this period is studied by O. A. Narkiewicz in *The Making of the Soviet State Apparatus* (1970).

The industrialization debate is fully discussed in the two volumes of *Foundations of a Planned Economy 1926–1929* (1969), a further instalment from E. H. Carr, this time assisted by R. W. Davies. *The Famine in Soviet Russia* (1927) by H. H. Fisher is a detailed study of this tragedy from the viewpoint of the American relief organization. Lenin's internal contradictions on the subject of the peasantry (that is, his constant need, not always recognized, to reconcile his marxist analysis with the realities of Russian peasant life) are treated by F. Kingston-Mann in *Lenin and the Problem of Marxist Peasant Revolution* (1983). A useful background guide to collectivization, still worth reading, is J. Maynard, *The Russian Peasant and Other Studies* (1942), which deals with the fundamental issues of peasant life from Nicholas I to Stalin. *Village Life under the Soviets* (1927) by K. Borders conveys the feel of rural Russia on the eve of collectivization. The events leading up to collectivization are analysed in J. Hughes, *Stalin, Siberia and the Crisis of the New Economic Policy* (1991), which makes the point that Stalin thought the dire state of grain supply in Siberia was typical of the whole country, and acted accordingly. J. Hughes went on to produce *Stalinism in a Russian Province* (1996), which deals with collectivization and dekulakization in Siberia. How far collectivization was a manifestation of town-versus-country antagonism may be gauged, among many other things, from V. Lynne's *The Best Sons of the Fatherland: Workers in the Vanguard of Soviet Collectivization* (1987). For the still uncertain history of the collectivization itself, a good guide is M. Lewin, *Russian Peasants and Soviet Power* (1968). For a description of how peasants resisted collectivization, see L. Viola, *Peasant Rebels under Stalin* (1996).

The Soviet Academy of Sciences prepared a massively researched study of collectivization which, had not Khrushchev been dethroned in 1964, might actually have been published earlier. As it was, V. Danilov's 1977 work appeared only in 1988, as *Rural Russia under the New Regime*. An alternative is R. W. Davies's first two volumes under the general title of *The Industrialisation of Soviet Russia*: volume i is *The Socialist Offensive: The Collectivisation of Soviet Agriculture 1929–1930* (1980) and volume ii is *The Soviet Collective Farm* (1980). *The History of a Soviet Collective Farm* (1955) is by a former collective farm chairman, F. Belov, who left Russia in the 1940s; its conclusions are expectedly negative, but it provides useful first-hand details of how things really were. A collection of research papers, *The Soviet Rural Community* (1970), edited by J. R. Millar, has some useful and original information on various aspects of Russian agriculture from Stalin to Brezhnev.

Chapter 13

'Every time you talk to one Russian you feel as if you were talking to them all. Not exactly that everyone obeys a word of command; but everything is so arranged that nobody can differ from anybody else.' These are a few lines from André Gide, *Back from the USSR* (1937). In the 1930s (and after 1953), a procession of foreigners visited the USSR for a few weeks and later published their revelations. Few of these are worth listing here, although few were totally bad. The impressions of brainy characters like Bernard Shaw and Gide could hardly fail to yield something, while the travel writers and journalists, beaming their professional insight onto the superficial to cook up semi-baked profundities, probably did little harm. The better first-person account is often by the unpretentious specialist who simply records what he sees without trying to make fancy interpretations. Perhaps a model of this kind of book is A. Monkhouse, *Moscow 1911–1933* (1934); the author was a British electrical engineer working in Russia most of his life, and had the additional distinction of being a defendant in the Metrovick Trial. Foreign technology was to play an important part in the five-year plans, but native technology was expected to learn fast. Technological aspects of Stalinist society are dealt with by K. F. Bailes in *Technology and Society under Lenin and Stalin* (1978). By the same author, *Science in Russian Culture* (1990), vol. i, is also good. Various cultural topics are dealt with, sometimes heavily, in *The Culture of the Stalin Period* (1990), edited by H. Gunther, and there is also S. Fitzpatrick's *Cultural Revolution in Russia 1928–1932* (1978). Somewhat more specialized topics are dealt with in books emanating from the Centre for Russian and East European Studies at Birmingham University: N. Lampert, *The Technical Intelligentsia and the Soviet State* (1979), dealing with the life and work of managers and technicians in 1928–35; R. Lewis, *Science and Industrialisation in the USSR* (1979), describing the organization of scientific research 1917–40; E. A. Rees (ed.), *Decision-Making in the Stalinist Command Economy* (1997), covering the second Five-Year Plan; and J. N. Westwood, *Soviet Locomotive Technology during Industrialization 1928–1952* (1982). As for economic progress in general, this is best reviewed in Nove's book, mentioned earlier, or with some of the titles listed on later pages. M. Lewin, *Political Undercurrents in Soviet Economic Debates* (1974), throws some light on the economic problems of the 1930s and later decades.

R. W. Davies presents the third volume of his *Industrialisation of Soviet Russia* (1989), which contains some mind-boggling examples of the chaos that attended the first five-year plan. Volume iv is devoted to *Crisis and Progress in the Soviet Economy 1931–1933* (1996); like the other volumes this is a big and well-packed book, this time featuring the leadership's descent from ludicrous overconfidence to serious debates about what to do next (or, as one reviewer put it, arguing about which banana skin to tread on next). Other books about the economy include D. Filtzer's *Soviet Workers and Stalinist Industrialization* (1986), which is challenging both in the profusion of ideas and in the scarcity of commas. L. Siegelbaum's *Stakhanovism and the Politics of Productivity in the USSR* (1988) concentrates on that one aspect of the labour scene, incidentally suggesting that the need for an efficient industrial management was hard to reconcile with the party's hegemony. Workers in the first plan are the subject of H. Kuromiya's *Stalin's Industrial Revolution: Politics and Workers* (1988). There is also D. R. Shearer, *Industry, State, and Society in Stalin's Russia 1926–1934* (1996). Particular projects are covered by the eyewitness *Behind the Urals* (1942) by J. Scott, which is about Magnitogorsk, and A. Rassweiler's *The Generation of Power* (1988). The latter is about the Dnieper hydroelectric scheme and especially the party's role; Stalin was not very keen on it, saying it reminded him of a peasant who bought a gramophone instead of mending his plough. Another big project was the Baltic–White Sea Canal ('Belomor'); C. A. Ruder, *Making History for Stalin* (1998) describes how celebrated artistic figures were persuaded to contribute to the propagandistic book about this forced labour enterprise (several wriggled out of this honour). J. McCannon in *Red Arctic* (1998) deals with the Northern Sea Route, and Arctic development, a highly publicized endeavour throughout the Soviet period.

How the party fitted into the upheaval of the 1930s is looked at from various angles by N. Shimotomai's *Moscow under Stalinist Rule 1931–1934* (1992), C. Merridale's *Moscow Politics and the Rise of Stalin* (1990) which covers 1925–32, and D. Thorniley's *The Rise and Fall of the Soviet Rural Communist Party 1927–1939* (1988). The party's weapon against bureaucracy, the Workers' and Peasants' Inspectorate, lasted from 1924 to 1934, and its changing functions and influence are described by A. Rees in *State Control in Soviet Russia* (1987). *Mechanism of Power in the Soviet Union* (2000), edited by N. E. Rosenfeldt, B. Jensen, and E. Kulavig, discusses communication and decision-making, especially under Stalin.

There are many books about the purges, not all of which can be recommended. A very complete (for its time) study was R. Conquest, *The Great Terror* (1968), but much more is known now, which is why this book was revised for publication in 1990 with the subtitle 'A Reassessment'. A Russian historian, V. Rogovin, produced *1937: Stalin's Year of Terror* in 1998. G. Katkov wrote *The Trial of Bukharin* (1969), while former Red Army General Gorbatov's memoirs, which include his arrest, torture, and incarceration before the war, were translated as *Years of my Life* (1965). N. Mandelstam, widow of a talented and purged poet, revealed much about life during the purges and, unwittingly perhaps, about Russian spirituality, in her *Hope against Hope* (1970) and *Hope Abandoned* (1974). A scientist and a historian, F. Beck and W. Godin, after quitting the USSR, published their own analysis, based on their personal experiences, in *Russian Purge and the Extraction of Confession* (1951). Also still relevant is the collection edited by S. Wolin and R. M. Slusser, *The Soviet Secret Police* (1957), while R. Conquest, *The Soviet Police System* (1968) is a succinct account covering the fifty years after 1917. A. Knight, *Beria* (1993) deals with someone closely involved in the purgings while S. Beria's *Beria* (2001) is a study from a completely different angle, that of his son, resulting in a sometimes puzzling, but not negligible, book.

D. Gluckstein, *The Tragedy of Bukharin* (1994) points out that Bukharin supported the early show trials and helped Stalin's rise. There is also an above-average documentary film, featuring Bukharin's wife: *Widow of the Revolution* (1999). O. V. Khlevniuk edited *In Stalin's Shadow* (1995), a biography of Ordzhonikidze, a strong industrializer, uneasy about the purges, and committing suicide when he realized he was next on the list. F. I. Chuev, *Molotov Remembers* (1993) presents very pro-Stalin interviews with the aged Molotov. Molotov is also well covered in D. Watson, *Molotov and Soviet Government* (1996).

R. W. Thurston, *Life and Terror in Stalin's Russia 1934–1941* (1996) conveys the feel of that period, as do V. Garros, N. Korenevskaya, and T. Lakusen (eds.), *Intimacy and Terror* (1995), which contains excerpts from ten mid-1930s diaries, including one by a self-disgusted informer, and G. Andreev-Khomiakov, *Bitter Waters* (1997), an amusing and down-to-earth memoir beginning in mid-1930s, when the author was released from his penal colony. S. Fitzpatrick, *Stalin's Peasants* (1994) shows how the peasants coped with living under Stalinism, and her *Everyday Stalinism* (1999) shows how citizens adjusted and adapted. In *A Revolution of their Own* (1997), edited by B. A. Engel and A. Posadskaya-Vanderbeck, eight women are interviewed about their life in the Soviet period.

Of the several defectors from the NKVD, W. G. Krivitsky was sufficiently important to be murdered by his former colleagues, but not before he had written his *In Stalin's Secret Service* (1939). In *Origins of the Great Purges* (1985), J. A. Getty proposes that the earlier purges were for the sake of efficiency, and in particular aimed to ensure that distant party officials actually did what they were told by the centre. Much of the evidence comes from the Smolensk Archives. The latter provided the raw material for M. Fainsod, *Smolensk under Soviet Rule* (1958), which even in this abridged form reveals quite a lot about the NKVD's activities. A new edition of this, with some of its conclusions revised, appeared in 1979 as J. Hough and M. Fainsod, *How the Soviet Union is Governed*. A. Solzhenitsyn's multi-volume *The Gulag Archipelago 1918–1956* (1974–8) is a major literary and historical work. V. M. Petrov and E. Petrov published their *Empire of Fear* in 1956. M. Popovsky, once a Soviet science journalist, confirms in his *The Vavilov Affair* (1984) that Lysenko's hostility was the cause of the great biologist's downfall. S. Swianiewicz in *Forced Labour and Economic Development* (1965) examines the industrial significance of the labour camps. Two of the biggest NKVD complexes receive individual treatment in *Vorkuta* (1976) by a former Polish inmate, V. Buca, and *Kolyma* (1978) by R. Conquest. *Till my Tale Is Told* (2000), edited by S. Vilensky, contains women's memoirs of the Gulag. A serious history making use of newly released material is G. Mikhailovna Ivanova, *Labor Camp Socialism* (2000).

Recent books about the triumphs (few) and travails (many) of the Orthodox Church include: W. B. Husband, *'Godless Communists'* (2000) about atheism in 1917–32, G. Young, *Power and the Sacred in Revolutionary Russia* (1997), which is about religious activists in the village in the 1920s, A. Luukkanen, *The Religious Policy of the Stalinist State* (1977), and K. R. Hill, *The Puzzle of the Soviet Church* (1989). In *Storming the Heavens* (1998), D. Peris deals with the Godless League and its highly bureaucratic structure and impecunious, short-lived cells. Older works include J. S. Curtiss, *The Russian Church and the Soviet State 1917–1950* (1953), W. Kolarz, *Religion in the Soviet Union* (1961), which is especially good on the sects and the non-Christians, and J. Thrower, *Marxist-Leninist 'Scientific Atheism' and the Study of Religion and Atheism in the USSR* (1983), which is itself a marxist analysis. W. C. Fletcher, *The Russian Orthodox Church Underground 1917–1970* (1971) concentrates on unofficial and illegal activities.

The ever-debatable general nature of Stalinism is dealt with by G. Gill's *Stalinism* (1990), a short book which quite successfully comes to grips with the problem of defining that phenomenon, and his somewhat longer *The Origins of the Stalinist Political System* (1990), and there is also *Stalinism: Its Nature and Aftermath* (1991), edited by N. Lampert. S. Fitzpatrick edited *Stalinism – New Directions* (2000). C. Ward wrote *Stalin's Russia* (1993) and edited *The Stalinist Dictatorship* (1998). For general labour questions, in addition to the specialized titles mentioned earlier, there are S. Schwartz, *Labour in the Soviet Union* (1953), which is becoming dated although it was good in its time, and F. C. Brown, *Soviet Trade Unions and Labour Relations* (1960). K. M. Straus, *Factory and Community in Stalin's Russia* (1997) discusses the emergence of a Stalinist working class.

Soviet law (and not just Stalinist law) is dealt with by S. Kucherov in *The Organs of Soviet Administration of Justice: Their History and Operation* (1970); by J. N. Hazard, *Law and Social Change in the USSR* (1953); and H. J. Berman, *Justice in the USSR* (rev. edn., 1963). F. L. Johnson, *An Introduction to the Soviet Legal System* (1969) is short and clear. F. Huskey's *Russian Lawyers and the Soviet State* (1986) deals with the Soviet Bar from 1917 to 1939. A more recent work is A. Solomon, *Soviet Criminal Justice under Stalin (1996)*.

J. Brooks, *Thank You, Comrade Stalin!* (2000) studies official Soviet values as expressed in the press over thirty-five years. One theme was that people were to be grateful to Stalin. The sad story of the abandoned orphans of the 1920s is recounted, not impeccably, in V. M. Zenzinov, *Deserted* (1931), while A. S. Makarenko's rehabilitation of some of these is described in his once-celebrated *Road to Life* (1953). Makarenko's ideas are competently examined in *Soviet Education: Anton Makarenko and the Years of Experiment* (1962) by I. Bowen. A. K. Geiger, *The Family in Soviet Russia* (1968) is mainly but not exclusively devoted to the Stalinist years. The shaping of Soviet minds is discussed in A. Inkeles, *Public Opinion in Soviet Russia* (1950). Another kind of mind-shaping, accompanied by banging of heads, figures in *Soviet Historians in Crisis 1928–1932* (1980) by J. Barber.

S. Davies, in *Popular Opinion in Stalin's Russia* (1997) uses officials' secret reports to tease out what people were really thinking in Stalinist Russia. One person's opinion, expressed by an American woman living in Russia, is to be found in M. Leder, *My Life in Stalinist Russia* (2001).

Chapter 14

In 1940, the Soviet leadership foresaw that the other European powers could tear each other to pieces, after which the Red Army might be very useful. This wishful thinking, plus the Soviet military ideology of the offensive, and the habit of general staffs of making plans for all kinds of military contingency, including attacks on their neighbours, provided a basis for V. Suvorov's *Ice-breaker* (1990), which claimed that when Hitler attacked in 1941 it was just in time to forestall a Red Army offensive against Germany. This book became popular and was several times translated. Historians did not show much respect for it, although some

German historians decided to take it seriously. What is notable is that a number of reputable western historians dignified the book by refuting it (and another is dignifying it by including it in this Bibliography). Even D. Glantz, in his excellent *Stumbling Colossus* (1998) about the Red Army in 1941, was diverted into attacking the so-called 'revisionist' argument. For Soviet strategy as a whole Glantz also wrote *The Military Strategy of the Soviet Union* (1991), which covers several decades.

To what extent Stalin and his generals were surprised by Hitler's invasion is a question that needs further research, which is now becoming possible. In 1965 the Soviet historian A. Nekrich published a study on this matter, causing a dispute among historians which ended with Nekrich's expulsion from the party; the course of this dispute is described in V. Petrov, *June 22 1941* (1968). Nekrich had been unlucky, because his book was accepted before the fall of Khrushchev but published after that atmosphere-changing event. Nekrich, who seems to have refused to recant, eventually found himself in exile and wrote his autobiographical *Forsake Fear* (1991). N. Tolstoy, in *Stalin's Secret War* (1981), goes into this question, too. G. Gorodetsky, *Grand Delusion* (1999) is a well-sourced narrative of the road to June 1941. The studies on foreign policy by Haslam and Hochman, listed earlier, also provide material for thought. To this period of Soviet foreign affairs also belongs E. H. Carr, *The Twilight of the Comintern* (1982). An eyewitness account of the Soviet takeover of Latvia is in P. Benton, *Baltic Countdown* (1984). Soviet foreign relations during the war itself are well chronicled in V. Mastny, *Russia's Road to the Cold War* (1979).

A readable book about the war is A. Werth, *Russia at War* (1964), a product of its author's stay there during the period. For the campaigns, J. Erickson's highly detailed *The Road to Stalingrad* (1975) and *The Road to Berlin* (1983) are very complete, and as a consequence rather heavy going except for ardent war-gamers. R. Overy's *Russia's War* (1999) goes into social and economic questions among other things. *The Russo-German War* (1971) by A. Seaton is a workmanlike account. J. N. Westwood's short *Eastern Front* (1984) is redeemed by the illustrations. Readable but not especially perceptive are A. Clark, *Barbarossa* (1965), and P. Carell, *Hitler's War on Russia* (1964) and *Scorched Earth* (1970). G. Deborin, in *The Second World War* (1964), gave the Soviet view as it was in Khrushchev's time. A very exhaustive study of the Russian partisans is contained in the collection edited by J. A. Armstrong, *Soviet Partisans in World War II* (1964). For those unwilling to plough through H. Salisbury's long best-seller about Leningrad at war, there is L. Goure, *The Siege of Leningrad* (1962). The battle of Stalingrad reached best-seller status with A. Beevor's *Stalingrad* (1998), a highly readable book; some reviewers claimed that it contained a major strategical misapprehension, but this should not deter the reader. German occupation policies are discussed in A. Dallin, *German Rule in Russia 1941–1945* (1957). The Vlasov movement is covered in G. Fischer, *Soviet Opposition to Stalin* (1952); W. Strik-Strikfeldt, *Against Stalin and Hitler* (1970), covers the same ground differently. A more recent study is C. Andreyev, *Vlasov and the Russian Liberation Movement* (1987), while *Cossacks in the German Army 1941–1945* (1991), by S. Newland, looks at part of the Russian anti-Soviet forces. How the Soviet planning system coped with the demands of war is described in M. Harrison, *Soviet Planning in Peace and War 1938–1945* (1985). There is also J. Barber and M. Harrison, *The Soviet Home Front 1941–1945* (1992). One important part of this topic is exhaustively examined in W. Moskoff, *The Bread of Affliction* (1990), which is about the rationing system. R. J. Brody, *Ideology and Political Mobilization* (1994) is a brief but good account of how the party transmitted its propaganda to a population that had handed in its radios and did not have good access to newspapers.

The inter-war development of the Soviet Army is treated in several recent works. L. Samuelson, *Plans for Stalin's War Machine* (2000) covers 1925–41, suggesting that until

Hitler became a threat the Red Army was simply a reflection of the supposed needs of 'socialism in one country'. R. R. Reese, *Stalin's Reluctant Soldiers* (1996) is more of a social history for 1925–41. It suggests that the low quality of officers in 1941 was less connected with the purges than is sometimes claimed. The same author's *The Soviet Military Experience* (2000) covers the entire Soviet period. S. W. Stoecker's *Forging Stalin's Army* (1998) is mainly about Tukhachevsky's reforms.

Many Red Army generals have written memoirs that have appeared in translated editions. An excellent and highly illuminating selection from the best of about fifty of such memoirs has been translated and included in S. Bialer, *Stalin and his Generals* (1969); most of these were published in Khrushchev's time and relate to the war, but some include comments on the army purge. Marshal Zhukov's memoirs have been published in several editions; the more recent the edition, the fewer the expurgations.

R. Pennington, *Wings, Women, and War* (2002) and A. Noggle, *A Dance with Death* (1994) are about Soviet airwomen, including the all-women fighter and bomber squadrons of the Red Air Force and their exploits. Apparently they were not issued with parachutes until 1943; A. Sella, who wrote *The Value of Human Life in Soviet Warfare* (1992), might have some comment to make about that.

Chapter 15

S. Zubkova, *Russia after the War: Hopes, Illusions and Disappointments 1945–1957* (1998) shows how people felt, using interviews, letters, and party records. One aspect of their society is detailed in M. Parrish, *The Lesser Terror: Soviet State Security 1939–1953* (1996). Another view of what Stalinism was like on the ground can be found in S. Kotkin, *Magnetic Mountain: Stalinism as a Civilization* (1995).

Apart from the biographies already mentioned, Stalin is discussed from several angles in T. H. Rigby, *Stalin* (1966), which is a collection of comments and quotations. Stalin's daughter, Svetlana Allilueva, whom Brezhnev allowed to emigrate, published *Twenty Letters to a Friend* (1967) and *Only One Year* (1969); these are both sensitive, subjective, yet honest accounts of her life, her father, and his associates. Sergo Beria's book, already mentioned, also shows what it was like to be in the inner circle. For a taste of the idolatry that was served up to the ordinary Soviet citizen, E. Yaroslavsky, *Landmarks in the Life of Stalin* (1942) is interesting, if only because it is something of a landmark in lying.

T. Dunmore surveys the political history of the period in *Soviet Politics 1945–1953* (1984). The same author in *The Stalinist Control Economy* (1980) suggests that after the war the bureaucracy had enhanced power, and that Stalin could not be sure that it would carry out his wishes. This thesis does not contradict the feeling that post-war politics were dominated by a struggle for influence over Stalin, with Zhdanov on the one side and an alliance of Malenkov and Beria on the other. W. G. Hahn, in his *Post-war Soviet Politics: The Fall of Zhdanov and the Defeat of Moderation 1946–53* (1982), proposed that Zhdanov was a moderate whose views were rejected by Stalin, at Malenkov's prompting, and that the Leningrad affair was intended to wipe out his supporters. W. O. McCagg, *Stalin Embattled, 1943–1948* (1978) suggests that Stalin had less control after the war than before, and that his policies were often manoeuvres designed to deal with particular interest groups. In *International Policy Formation in the USSR* (1983), G. D. Ra'anan argues that there were two competing foreign policies at this time. Zhdanov's more aggressive policy, favourable perhaps to Tito, and the Beria–Malenkov line, which was very cautious. The origins and course of the Cold War over a long time-span are discussed in the collection edited by D. Armstrong and E. Goldstein, *The End of the Cold War* (1991). V. Zubok, *Inside the Kremlin's Cold War* (1996) is a well-researched account paying attention to the personalities of the Soviet leadership; Stalin could be panicky although in complete control, Malenkov wanted détente while Khrushchev wanted incompatibles—friendship with the USA plus revolutionary assertiveness. V. Mastny, *The Cold War and Soviet Insecurity: The Stalin Years* (1996) again emphasizes Stalin's personality, especially his fears.

Post-war Ukraine, and particularly the collectivization campaign in the western Ukraine, is the subject of *Stalinism in the 1940s* (1991) by D. Marples. Agriculture is also involved in C. Kaplan's *The Party and Agricultural Crisis Management in the USSR* (1987) which has much to say about the lot of local party secretaries in the last Stalin years. The nature of Stalinism is condemned by R. A. Medvedev in *On Stalin and Stalinism* (1979), which is a kind of addendum to his celebrated *Let History Judge* (1972) and makes the same use of inside knowledge acquired by the author as a Soviet citizen and self-professed loyal Leninist. He also wrote *All Stalin's Men* (1983), consisting of biographies of Voroshilov, Mikoyan, Suslov, Molotov, Kaganovich, and Malenkov. His brother Z. A. Medvedev, a scientist, wrote *The Rise and Fall of T. D. Lysenko* (1969) and *Soviet Science* (1979). The latter is especially good on what it was like to be a Soviet scientist in Khrushchev's time, and also shows how political pressures could lower the quality of scientific work. P. R. Josephson, *Physics and Politics in Revolutionary Russia* (1991) deals mainly with the 1920s and 1930s while L. Badshah, in *Kapitsa, Rutherford, and the Kremlin* (1985), also has much to say about Stalinist science, making it clear that Kapitsa's stay in the USSR from the mid-1930s was involuntary. D. Holloway, *Stalin and the Bomb* (1994) deals with one aspect of Soviet physics, while L. R. Graham, in *What Have We Learned about Science and Technology from the Russian Experience?* (1998), hints that Russian science was hurt more by underfunding in the 1990s than by Stalinism.

Aspects of Zhdanovism and propaganda are dealt with by F. C. Barghoorn, *The Soviet Image of the United States* (1950), H. Swayze, *Political Control of Literature in the USSR 1946–1959* (1962), J. Keep's collection *Contemporary History in the Soviet Mirror* (1964), and C. E. Black, *Rewriting Russian History* (1956). M. Pundeff, *History in the USSR* (1967) is a collection of translated decrees, exhortations, and instructions relating to the tasks of the Soviet historian. Those who prefer to get their information straight from the donkey's mouth should refer to A. A. Zhdanov, *Essays on Literature, Philosophy and Music* (1950). For a scholarly work on the tools of propaganda, see M. W. Hopkins, *Mass Media in the Soviet Union* (1970). A sensitive account of one woman's life under Stalin is E. S. Ginzburg, *Into the Whirlwind* (1967), which begins with the murder of Kirov and continues with the arrest and imprisonment of the author. The satirical sketches by M. M. Zoshchenko, *Scenes from the Bath-House* (1961), are amusing and often perceptive in their views of the ordinary Soviet citizen. Of good foreigners' accounts, which are rare because visas were scarce, and more often than not issued to visitors who could be relied on not to write too perceptively, the best may be M. Gordey, *Visa to Moscow* (1952), written by a Russian-speaking Frenchman. M. Granick, *The Red Executive* (1960) is a study of factory management as it had developed by the 1950s. The Soviet health services received professional treatment from M. G. Field in *Doctor and Patient in Soviet Russia* (1957).

Nationalities were discussed extensively in W. Kolarz, *Russia and her Colonies* (1953), and succinctly in R. Conquest, *Soviet Nationality Policy in Practice* (1967). More specialized were O. Caroe, *Soviet Empire* (1953), which studied what used to be called Turkestan but which was divided into union republics by the Soviet Constitution; G. Wheeler's brief *The Peoples of Soviet Central Asia* (1966); and *The Soviet Middle East* (1968), also about Central Asia, by A. Nove and J. A. Newth. The life of Soviet Jews is covered in the collection edited by L. Kochan, *The Jews in Soviet Russia since 1917* (1970); and *The Soviet Government and the*

Jews, 1948–1967 (1984) by B. Pinkus. The same author has produced *The Jews of the Soviet Union* (1988), covering seven decades. R. Weinberg, *Stalin's Forgotten Zion* (1998) is about Birobidzhan and its propaganda uses. L. Rapoport, *Stalin's War against the Jews* (1991) is mainly about the Doctors' Plot. Y. Rapoport, no relation but one of the doctors involved, wrote *The Doctors' Plot* (1990).

Apart from the general studies already mentioned, literature is discussed from various angles in E. J. Brown, *Russian Literature since the Revolution* (1961), A. Kemp-Welsh, *Stalin and the Literary Intelligentsia 1928–1939* (1991), while the title of E. J. Simmons, *Through the Looking Glass of Soviet Literature: Views of Russian Society* (1961) is self-explanatory. H. Ermolaev, *Censorship in Soviet Literature 1917–1991* (1997) gives good coverage to a fascinating subject. D. Youngblood, *The Magic Mirror* (1999) is about film-making before 1917. R. Taylor and D. Spring (eds.), *Stalinism and Soviet Cinema* (1993) is patchy but generally good. R. Taylor also edited *Inside the Film Factory* (1991). A good reference for the Russian film, from the beginnings to 1958, is J. Leyda, *Kino* (1960). For extracts from films, plays, songs, and folklore during the Soviet period, see J. van Geldern and R. Stites (eds.), *Mass Culture in Soviet Russia* (1995).

The 'Khrushchev Memoirs' (N. S. Khrushchev, *Khrushchev Remembers*, 1971), which first arrived in the west in 1970, say a lot about their subject's experiences with and under Stalin. Written by an accomplished polemicist, they need to be taken with a pinch of salt.

Chapter 16

W. J. Tompson, *Khrushchev: A Political Life* (1994) is a recent and competent biography. *Khrushchev: The Years in Power* (1977) by R. A. and Z. A. Medvedev is also good and is supplemented by R. A. Medvedev, *Khrushchev* (1984), in which the author exhibits his characteristic mix of blind-spots and inside information. Interesting essays about Khrushchev are contained in *Nikita Khrushchev* (2000), edited by W. Taubman, S. Khrushchev, and A. Gleason. Most biographers are agreed on their subject's courage but differ about his role in the purges, although they implicitly or explicitly accept that he had a guilty conscience. The collection edited by M. McCauley, *Khrushchev and Khrushchevism* (1988), sheds some useful light. Some filial comments come from S. Khrushchev's *Khrushchev on Khrushchev* (1990). Khrushchev's denunciation of Stalin is quoted and discussed in B. D. Wolfe, *Khrushchev and Stalin's Ghost* (1956) and T. H. Rigby, *The Stalin Dictatorship: Khrushchev's Secret Speech and Other Documents* (1968). Khrushchev's manoeuvrings inside the party are discussed in C. A. Linden, *Khrushchev and the Soviet Leadership 1957–1964* (1967), and also in R. Pethybridge's general survey, *A History of Post-war Russia* (1966). His uneasy relations with his generals are examined in R. Kolkowicz, *The Soviet Military and the Communist Party* (1967). His part in negotiating the Test-Ban Treaty is covered by G. T. Seaborg, *Kennedy, Khrushchev, and the Test Ban* (1981), which also suggests that one of the obstacles to better understanding was that although the USA and USSR often developed similar views, they rarely held them at the same time. *Khrushchev and the Development of Soviet Agriculture: The Virgin Land Programme, 1953–1964* (1967) by M. McCauley deals with a favourite and grandiose project. Many of Khrushchev's colleagues are included in the forty-two biographical essays in *Soviet Leaders* (1967), edited by G. W. Simmonds. The easier atmosphere in the arts is treated in the collection of essays edited by M. Hayward, *Soviet Literature in the Sixties* (1965), and in G. Gibian, *Interval of Freedom* (1960), which discusses literature between 1954 and 1957. D. Brown, *Soviet Russian Literature since Stalin* (1978) covers a slightly longer period.

Soviet law is brought to fascinating life in G. Feiffer, *Justice in Moscow* (1964), and in

B. A. Konstantinovsky, *Soviet Law in Action: The Recollected Cases of a Soviet Lawyer* (1953). Other books on law, not confined to the Khrushchev period, are G. van den Berg's *The Soviet System of Justice* (1985) and F. Feldbrugge (ed.), *The Distinctiveness of Soviet Law* (1987), which includes a study of the Stalinist legal system. Housing, which received a boost in the Khrushchev period, is discussed in G. Andrusz, *Housing and Urban Development in the USSR* (1984), which also deals with the post-Khrushchev years and throws much incidental light on Soviet society. Other books which cover more than the Khrushchev years are S. Fortescue, *The Communist Party and Soviet Science* (1986), P. Kneen, *Soviet Scientists and the State* (1984), and R. Humble, *The Soviet Space Programme* (1988). The uproarious memoir by an astronomer who lived through the Stalin, Khrushchev, and Brezhnev years also comes into this category: *Five Billion Vodka Bottles to the Moon* (1991), by I. Shklovsky. An original and sometimes irreverent comment on the theory of convergence is provided by Mervyn Jones, *Big Two* (US title, *The Antagonists*: 1962), which compares the USA and USSR and seems to have a high opinion of neither. Two books by western students who spent a year in Russia are W. Taubman, *The View from Lenin Hills* (1968) and H. Pitcher, *Understanding the Russians* (1964); both of these are good and informative. *Life in Russia Today* (1969) by J. Miller, *The Russian* (1968) by L. Vladimirov, and *Russians Observed* (1969) by J. W. Lawrence can also be recommended for portrayals of Soviet life in the 1960s.

Soviet sociology was slow to recover from the Stalinist years, but some of its products appeared in English as *Studies in Soviet Society*. No. 1 of this series was *Industry and Labour in the USSR*. No. 2, edited by G. V. Osipov, was *Town, Country and People* (1969). S. F. and F. Dunn made good use of Soviet sociological and ethnographical research in their *The Peasants of Soviet Russia* (1967), while another, offbeat but enjoyable, description of rural Russia as it really was in the 1960s is V. Soloukhin, *A Walk in Rural Russia* (1966). *The Soviet Family* (1963) by D. and V. Mace is another contribution. The experience of Russian Christianity in the 1950s and 1960s is included in M. Bourdeaux, *Opium of the People* (1965). K. C. Farmer, in *The Soviet Administrative Elite* (1992), deals with recruitment, the unusual party education system, and other matters.

The USSR's relations with individual states have been dealt with by works too numerous to mention in these bibliographies. S. Galai's *The Soviet Union and National Liberation Movements in the Third World* (1988) deals with a subject that became important in the Khrushchev years. The friction between Russia and China which began in 1945 and came to a head in Khrushchev's time is detailed in O. A. Wested (ed.) *Brothers in Arms* (1998).

Chapter 17

Books illuminating the mechanism, or messiness, of party leadership changes include: O. Narciewicz, *Soviet Leaders* (1986); D. Doder, *Shadows and Whispers* (1986); A. D'Agostino, *Soviet Succession Struggles* (1987); and R. Owen, *Crisis in the Kremlin* (1986). Biographies of the post-Khrushchev leaders tended to be written while they were in office and are therefore incomplete. J. Dornberg's *Brezhnev*, for example, was published in 1974. Z. A. Medvedev, *Andropov* (1983) says as much about Brezhnev's last years as it does about its ostensible subject. Inevitably it also deals with the KGB, a topic more fully explored in A. Myagkov, *Inside the KGB* (1976). Another book about Andropov is *Andropov in Power* (1983) by J. Steele and F. Abraham. I. Zemtsov's *Chernenko: The Last Bolshevik* (1989) shares some of the characteristics of its subject. G. W. Breslauer, *Khrushchev and Brezhnev as Leaders* (1982), is especially good on authority-building. Of related interest is the psychology of leaders and led examined in *The Russian Mind since Stalin's Death* (1985) by Y. Glazov. Several collections were published after Brezhnev's death, looking forward to the future. If their speculative parts are disregarded, they are good guides to the problems faced, or not faced, under Brezhnev. Two of them are R. F. Byrnes (ed.), *After Brezhnev: Sources of Soviet Conduct in the 1980s* (1983), and H. Sonnenfeldt (ed.), *Soviet Politics in the 1980s* (1985). A good textbook on the party as it then was is R. I. Hill and P. Frank, *The Soviet Communist Party* (1983), while a political perspective for the period is provided by A. Nove, *Stalinism and After* (1981).

Brezhnev Reconsidered, edited by E. Bacon and M. Sandle, was anticipated in 2003 and was expected to raise the possibility that the Brezhnev period was not just a time of stagnation. Aspects of Soviet society are dealt with in M. Dewhirst and W. Farrell (eds.), *The Soviet Censorship* (1973); D. Powell, *Antireligious Propaganda in the Soviet Union* (1975), which suggests that this propaganda was clumsy and ineffective, continuing only because nobody wanted to admit that it was useless; M. Matthews, *Class and Society in Soviet Russia* (1972) and the same author's *Privilege in the Soviet Union: A Study of Elite Life-Styles under Communism* (1978); D. Lane, *The End of Social Inequality? Class, Status and Power under State Socialism* (1982); A. McAuley, *Women's Work and Wages in the Soviet Union* (1981); G. Littlejohn, *A Sociology of the Soviet Union* (1984); J. Brine, M. Perrie and A. Sutton (eds.), *Home, School and Leisure in the Soviet Union* (1980); Ellen Jones, *Red Army and Society* (1985); T. Colton and T. Gustafson (eds.), *Soldiers and the Soviet State* (1990), which deals with civil–military relations from Brezhnev to Gorbachev; M. Kaser, *Health Care in the Soviet Union and Eastern Europe* (1976); J. Dunstan, *Paths to Excellence and the Soviet School* (1978); M. Matthews, *Education in the Soviet Union* (1983); J. Riordan, *Sport in Soviet Society* (1977); and A. McAuley, *Economic Welfare in the Soviet Union: Poverty, Living Standards, and Inequality* (1979). A. Roxburgh's *Pravda: Inside the Soviet News Machine* (1988) includes a history of the paper and is uniquely structured, short, and admirable. J. Riordan added to his studies of Soviet people a collection titled *Soviet Youth Culture* (1989). A study of Soviet emigrants from this and preceding periods led to J. R. Miller's *Politics, Work and Daily Life in the USSR* (1987). Fiction, in the form of J. Voznesenskaya's *The Women's Decameron* (1986), tells a lot about the tribulations of young women in the USSR at this period, while N. Lampert's *Whistleblowing in the Soviet Union* (1985) is about tribulation in general and the problem of making complaints. D. Kaminskaya, in *A Final Judgement* (1982), describes what it is like to walk the tightrope between ideology and justice as a Soviet defence lawyer. Some recommended first-hand impressions of life in the Soviet Union are: R. Kaiser, *Russia, the People and the Power* (1976), Hedrick Smith, *The Russians* (1976), M. Binyon, *Life in Russia* (1983), and A. Lee, *Russian Journal* (1981). In *Who are the Russians?* (1973), W. Miller gave his interpretation of the forces which made Russians what they are. The seamy side of Soviet life is revealed by K. M. Simis and V. G. Treml. The former, in *USSR: The Corrupt Society* (1982), discusses and condemns corruption, incidentally viewing the KGB as a sanitary and useful institution because it tried to improve matters. Treml had been taking his statistical breathalyser to Soviet society for some years, and produced *Alcohol in the USSR* (1982). S. White, *Russia Goes Dry* (1996) is about the campaign against alcohol. In her *The KGB* (1988), A. Knight wrote a book more sensible than some on that subject. For day-to-day police activity, see L. I. Shelley's *Policing Soviet Society* (1996), which is about the militia, and shows how a low crime rate was balanced by a deficiency of civil liberties.

A. V. Ledeneva, *Russia's Economy of Favours* (1998) deals with one of the most enduring and significant features of Russian society, its interpersonal transactions and *blat*, the access to, or exchange of, favours. *Blat* has sometimes kept society going; it has also ruined many friendships.

Problems faced by a multinational state include nationalisms, and these received partial coverage in: Y. Ro'i (ed.), *The USSR and the Muslim World* (1984), M. Rywkin, *Moscow's*

Muslim Challenge (1982), R. Karklins, *Ethnic Relations in the USSR* (1985), V. Zaslavsky and R. J. Bryan, *Soviet-Jewish Emigration and Soviet Nationality Policy* (1983), and J. Dunlop, *The Faces of Contemporary Russian Nationalism* (1983). Rywkin's book goes back to tsarist times; Dunlop was fairly optimistic, seeing no inevitable conflict. C. Barner-Barry and C. Hody discuss the nationalities both before and after the dissolution of the USSR in *The Politics of Change* (1995).

Books by or about the dissident movement include N. Gorbanevskaya, *Red Square at Noon* (1972); A. Brumberg, *In Quest of Justice* (1970); P. Reddaway, *Uncensored Russia: The Human Rights Movement in the Soviet Union* (1972); A. Sakharov, *Sakharov Speaks* (1974) (Sakharov's *Memoirs* (1990) cover a wider field); S. Bloch and P. Reddaway, *Russia's Political Hospitals* (1977); M. S. Shats, *Soviet Dissent in Historical Perspective* (1980); V. Bukovsky, *To Build a Castle* (1978); R. L. Tökes, *Dissent in the USSR* (1975); and M. Hopkins, *Russia's Underground Press* (1983). The latter is about *Chronicle of Current Events*, from its beginnings in 1968. Translations from dissident writings are to be found in R. A. Medvedev, *Samizdat Register 11* (1981). The Nekrich affair is among the topics covered in R. D. Markwick's *Rewriting History in Soviet Russia* (2001), which covers 1956–74. Of the several novels that were published in the west but not in the Soviet Union, G. Maximov, *Faithful Ruslan* (1975), is recommended for the skill with which the author has fixed specific characteristics of the Stalinist personality in a series of individual dog characters, V. Voinovich, *The Life and Extraordinary Adventures of Private Ivan Chonkin* (1976), for its comedy, and A. Zinoviev, *The Yawning Heights* (1979), for its amusing perception. N. Shneidman's *Soviet Literature in the 1980s* (1989) is partly a social commentary. D. Brown, *The Last Years of Soviet Russian Literature* (1993) is about fiction 1975–91.

General books on the Soviet economy include A. Nove, *The Soviet Economic System* (1977), D. Dyker, *The Soviet Economy* (1976), and M. Kaser, *Soviet Economics* (1970). Science and technology is covered in: R. Hutchings, *Soviet Science, Technology, Design* (1976), R. Amann, J. Cooper and R. W. Davies, *The Technological Level of Soviet Industry* (1977), which is a massive collection of case studies, and J. Thomas and U. Kruse-Vaucienne (eds.), *Soviet Science and Technology* (1977). How new technology works in practice is one of the topics in V. Lysenko, *A Crime against the World* (1983), whose author, a defecting sea captain, describes how the urge to meet high targets in the fishing fleet resulted in misuse of men and equipment, waste, and destruction of fish stocks all over the world. Environmental issues are covered by P. R. Pryde in *Conservation in the Soviet Union* (1972), M. Goldman in *The Spoils of Progress* (1972), and F. Singleton (ed.), *Environmental Misuse in the Soviet Union* (1976). Later books include P. R. Pryde, *Environmental Resources and Constraints in the Former Soviet Republics* (1995), the same author's *Environmental Management in the Soviet Union* (1991), D. Weiner's *Models of Nature* (1988), and a collection edited by J. Massey Stewart, *The Soviet Environment* (1992). D. J. Petersen in *Troubled Lands* (1993) details the accumulated destruction. Equally troubled are M. Feshbach and A. Friendly, *Ecocide in the USSR* (1992), and M. Feshbach, *Ecological Disaster* (1995).

Local government is concerned in environmental issues, and some hints of its power and powerlessness are given by C. Ross, *Local Government in the Soviet Union* (1987).

A comprehensive survey of relations with eastern Europe is *Soviet Policy in Eastern Europe* (1984), edited by S. M. Terry. There is also K. Gerner, *The Soviet Union and Central Europe in the Post-war Era* (1985). R. F. Miller and F. Feher have edited *Khrushchev and the Communist World* (1984). For the situation in Brezhnev's time there is R. L. Hutching, *Soviet–East European Relations: Consolidation and Conflict 1968–1980* (1983), which naturally has a lot to say about Czechoslovakia and Poland in particular. Czechoslovakia in 1968 gets full treatment in *The Kremlin and Prague Spring* (1985) by K. Dawisha, and by J. Valenta in *Soviet Intervention in Czechoslovakia 1968* (1979); both portray the Soviet leadership as divided and uncertain until the eleventh hour. Dawisha stresses the fear of ideological infection, both in eastern Europe and in the USSR itself, as a main motivation for the Soviet intervention. Also worth consulting are R. Remington, *The Warsaw Pact* (1971) and T. Wolfe, *Soviet Power and Europe 1945–1970* (1970).

Relations with other countries are covered in A. B. Ulam, *Dangerous Relations: The Soviet Union in World Politics 1970–1982* (1983). Much of this excellent volume is spent detailing the mismanagement by both the USA and the USSR of the opportunities presented to them. J. L. Gaddis, *We Now Know* (1997) is, despite its title, a good, serious account of the Cold War. There is also R. Edmonds, *Soviet Foreign Policy: The Brezhnev Years* (1983). A. N. Shevchenko, *Breaking with Moscow* (1985), by a defecting foreign affairs adviser, says much about the inside workings of Soviet diplomacy, while C. Keeble (ed.) in *The Soviet State: The Domestic Roots of Foreign Policy* (1985) sets forth some of the links between the internal situation and foreign policies. Policies towards the Third World and their results are described in R. Kanet (ed.), *The Soviet Union and the Developing Nations* (1974); C. Stevens, *The Soviet Union and Black Africa* (1976); A. Rubinstein, *Red Star over the Nile* (1977); B. D. Porter, *The USSR in Third World Conflicts: Soviet Arms and Diplomacy in Local Wars 1945–1980*, which is good at facts although some may question its opinions; and S. T. Hosmer and T. W. Wolfe, *Soviet Policy and Practice towards Third World Conflicts* (1983). The application of naval power is dealt with by M. McGwire and J. McDonnell (eds.), *Soviet Naval Influence* (1977); M. McGwire (ed.), *Soviet Naval Policy* (1975); and B. Dismukes and J. McDonnell (eds.), *Soviet Naval Diplomacy* (1979). An excellent, very full analysis of armament, disarmament, and foreign relations is D. Holloway, *The Soviet Union and the Arms Race* (1983), while S. Talbott, *Endgame* (1979) chronicles one complex set of arms negotiations, that involving SALT-1. A brief look at the nuclear weapons problem is contained in J. Haslam's *The Soviet Union and the Politics of Nuclear Weapons in Europe 1969–1987* (1989), and there are also J. G. Mathers, *The Russian Nuclear Shield from Stalin to Yeltsin* (2000), and D. R. Marples (ed.), *Nuclear Energy and Security in the Former Soviet Union* (1997). The Soviet defence industry is studied in P. Almquist, *Red Forge* (1990) and J. Cooper, *The Soviet Defence Industry* (1991). J. Harford, *Korolev* (1997) is about the scientist who was the life and soul of the Soviet space effort. Other books on Soviet science include S. Fortescue, *Science Policy in the Soviet Union* (1990) and *New Atlantis Revisited* (1997) by P. R. Josephson, which is about Akademogorodok, the research town founded in Khrushchev's time. J. L. Roberg, *Soviet Science under Control* (1998) shows the influence scientists had and is a good brief summary.

M. Galeotti, *Afghanistan, the Soviet Union's Last War* (1995) is a workmanlike account of that tragedy, and so is M. Urban, *War in Afghanistan* (1990). A. Heinämaa's *The Soldiers' Story* (1994) contains interviews with soldiers returning from that campaign, showing how the war affected minds.

Chapter 18

A. Brown's *The Gorbachev Factor* (1996) and J. Hough's *Democratization and Revolution in the USSR 1985–1991* (1997) are both excellent treatments of the Gorbachev period. For a shorter but well-informed view M. McCauley's *Gorbachev* (1998) is recommended. Brown's view may also be found in his *Perestroika in Perspective* (1997). J. Gibbs, *Gorbachev's Glasnost* (1999) deals with the most crucial of the changes, and this might be read in conjunction with J. Murray, *The Russian Press from Brezhnev to Yeltsin* (1994), which covers the *glasnost'* liberation.

The horse's mouth has sometimes proved unrewarding; Gorbachev, Shevardnadze, and Yeltsin, together with Gorbachev's high-profile wife Raisa, have all published their memoirs, but they are not very revealing. A. Sobchak's *For a New Russia* (1991) is better, and so is *Moscow and Beyond 1986–1989* (1991), by the celebrated A. Sakharov. Another first-person account, covering previous decades of poetic and political activity also, is Yu. Yevtushenko's *Fatal Half-Measures: The Allure of Democracy in the Soviet Union* (1991). Other, later, memoirs include A. S. Chernyaev, *My Six Years with Gorbachev* (2000) and Y. Ligachev, *Inside Gorbachev's Kremlin* (1996). *My Years with Gorbachev and Shevardnadze* (1997), by their interpreter P. Palazchenko, sees things from a different, and rewarding, angle.

G. Hosking's thoughtful *The Awakening of the Soviet Union* (1990) was largely concerned with the social forces behind the urge for a 'civil society'. *Glasnost'*, which brought quick results by 1989, is well covered by A. Nove in *Glasnost' in Action* (1989) and R. W. Davies in *Soviet History in the Gorbachev Revolution* (1989). Davies continues his story in *Soviet History in the Yeltsin Era* (1997). Other fruits of *glasnost'* can be tasted in *Dear Comrade Editor* (1992), edited by J. Riordan and S. Bridger, which presents readers' letters to the weekly *Ogonyok* in the Gorbachev period, and in H. Goscilo and B. Lindsay (eds.), *Glasnost: An Anthology of Russian Literature under Gorbachev* (1990). The collection edited by J. Graffy and G. Hosking, *Culture and the Media in the USSR Today* (1989), also touches on this theme. G. Faraday, *Revolt of the Film-Makers* (2000) deals with the upheaval in the film industry.

The political machinations attending Gorbachev's ascent were ably dissected with the aid of influential participants in A. Roxburgh's *The Second Russian Revolution* (1991). Some very necessary background information about the value of personal connections is conveyed in *Patronage and Politics in the USSR* (1992) by J. Willerton. One of the pivotal moments in *perestroika*, the 28th Party Congress, is covered by the collection edited by A. Rees: *The Soviet Communist Party in Disarray* (1992). A. D'Agostino in *Gorbachev's Revolution* (1998) propounds the view that Gorbachev was not using his power to obtain radical reform but using reform to amass power. V. Sergeyev and N. Biryukov, *Russia's Road to Democracy: Parliament, Communism and Traditional Culture* (1993) covers essentially 1988–9.

W. E. Odom, *The Collapse of the Soviet Military* (1998) suggests that the military, being so intermingled in the party elite, were not well placed to mount a revolt against Gorbachev's innovations, whose consequences they were slow to see. Another good book about the military, under Yeltsin as well as Gorbachev, is R. V. Barylski, *The Soldier in Russian Politics* (1998).

Some of the problems faced by the leadership are covered in P. Gregory's *Restructuring the Soviet Economic Bureaucracy* (1990), while *The Destruction of the Soviet Economic System* (1998), edited by M. Ellman and V. Kontorovich, attributes much of the trouble to Gorbachev's tinkering. T. Cox, *From Perestroika to Privatisation* (1996) deals with the 1985–91 economic reforms, such as they were.

S. Carter's *Russian Nationalism Yesterday, Today and Tomorrow* (1990) remains a useful foundation for this topic. Nationalism is treated from several angles also in A. McAuley (ed.), *Soviet Federalism, Nationalism, and Decentralisation* (1991). How the nationalities problem was tackled, or not tackled, in the Gorbachev years is detailed in N. Diuk and N. Karatnycky, *The People Challenge* (1990). Gorbachev was caught off his guard by nationalism and R. G. Suny in *The Revenge of the Past* (1993) takes a historical approach in his explanation of how ethnicity broke up the USSR. B. Fowkes in *The Disintegration of the Soviet Union* (1997) also sees nationalism as the prime destabilizing factor. Y. M. Brudny, in

Reinventing Russia (1998), discusses the nationalism of Great Russians as it manifested itself in 1953–91.

Other factors contributing to the petering-out of Gorbachev's USSR are studied in J. Miller, *Mikhail Gorbachev and the End of Soviet Power* (1993), N. Robinson, *Ideology and the Collapse of the Soviet System* (1994), and G. M. Easter, *Reconstructing the State* (2000), which emphasizes personal networks and their part in destabilizing the USSR. D. Lane, in *The Rise and Fall of State Socialism* (1996), interprets what went wrong with the communist system as a whole, and R. V. Daniels presents documents and comment in *Soviet Communism from Reform to Collapse* (1995).

V. Vitaliev tells all one needs to know about prostitution, racketeering, Nazism, and privilege in *Special Correspondent* (1990). On a higher plane, D. S. Likhachev, a scholar regarded as the 'guardian' of Russian culture, set forth his comments in *Reflections on Russia* (1991). H. Pilkington, *Russia's Youth and its Culture* (1994) is mainly but not exclusively about the 1980s. S. I. Webber, *School, Reform and Society in the New Russia* (2000) deals with the post-1985 period. R. W. Ortung in *From Leningrad to St. Petersburg* (1995) shows how democratization proceeded in this city. A. White, *Democratization in Russia under Gorbachev 1985–91* (1999) deals with the thousands of unofficial organizations, including charities, that were set up. Among those who benefited from these were the disabled, who had little state support.

Three quite specialized books are T. Ryback's *Rock around the Bloc* (1990), about the fate of rock music in the USSR and eastern Europe in Gorbachev and pre-Gorbachev times, R. Rand's *Comrade Lawyer* (1991), based on first-hand experience of the work of defence lawyers in Gorbachev's time, and M. Bourdeaux's *Gorbachev, Glasnost and the Gospel* (1991), about the new situation with religion. The collection edited by E. Shirley and M. Rowe, *Candle in the Wind* (1989), also covers religion.

A. Aslund's *Gorbachev's Struggle for Economic Reform* (1991) is a highly critical commentary on the biggest failure of Gorbachev.

V. Tolz, in *The USSR's Emerging Multiparty System* (1991), steers the reader through a complex process. *Steeltown, USSR* (1991) is a very interesting impression of life in one of Russia's least salubrious cities by S. Kotkin, who endured several months there in the late 1980s.

Commentaries on the Gorbachev years as they unfolded include R. Sakwa's *Gorbachev and his Reforms* (1990) and S. White's *Gorbachev and After* (1991), both of which go quite deep. Then there are: *Gorbachev: Heretic in the Kremlin* (1991) by D. Doder and L. Branson, *Revolution and Evolution* (1989) by M. Crouch, *Why Gorbachev Happened: His Triumphs and his Failure* (1991) by R. Kaiser, *What Went Wrong with Perestroika* (1991) by M. Goldman, M. Sixsmith's *Moscow Coup* (1991), and J. Parker's *Kremlin in Transition* (vol. ii, 1991). There are also two collections edited respectively by D. Spring and M. McCauley, *The Impact of Gorbachev* (1991), and *Gorbachev and Perestroika* (1990), and another is edited by C. Merridale and C. Ward: *Perestroika* (1991).

Among the more interesting books on foreign policy are S. Woodby's *Gorbachev and the Decline of Ideology in Soviet Foreign Policy* (1989), A. E. Stent, *Russia and Germany Reborn* (1999), which suggests that the German reunification of 1989 was largely the result of Gorbachev and Shevardnadze pushing hard against opposition, and *Witnesses to the End of the Cold War* (1996), edited by W. C. Wohlforth, which features the reminiscences of US and Russian officials who had been actively involved at the time.

Chapter 19

Many of the books about this so-called transitional period are themselves transitional, being contemporary studies that will be replaced by deeper and more informed works. Many more books are on the way, so this chapter bibliography, likewise, can only be transitional.

J. Morisson's *Boris Yeltsin* (1991) is still adequate for the president's climb to power. L. Shevtsova's *Yeltsin's Russia* (1999) examines, not uncritically, his path up to 1998. Boris Yeltsin, *Midnight Diaries* (2001) is candid, like the memoirs dashed off by his cronies Korzhakov and Kostikov, but only within limits. These three memoirs are a long way short of providing a consistent and complete narrative. L. Aron, *Yeltsin* (2000) is good.

R. Medvedev, still a socialist, wrote *Post-Soviet Russia* (2000), which has a flavour of its own and is worthy of attention. Also informative is E. Bacon and M. Wyman, *Contemporary Russia* (2001). M. Wyman has also written *Public Opinion in Post-communist Russia* (1997). Eyewitness commentary on Russia in the early 1990s, not neglecting the provinces, is to be found in M. McAuley's *Russia's Politics of Uncertainty* (1999). *Rebirth of a Nation* (1998) by J. Lloyd is a detailed commentary by an assiduous journalist.

Books on political development include S. White, A. Pravda and Z. Gitelman (eds.), *Developments in Russian Politics* (2001), G. Gill and R. D. Markwick, *Russia's Stillborn Democracy?* (2000), which covers the Yeltsin and Gorbachev years, N. Robinson (ed.), *Institutions and Political Change in Russia* (2000), V. Sperling (ed.), *Building the Russian State* (2000), P. Kirkow, *Russia's Provinces* (1998), which is two case studies about how provinces related to each other and to the centre, and V. Edwards, G. Polonsky and A. Polonsky, *The Russian Province after Communism* (2000). J. W. Hahn (ed.), *Democratization in Russia* (1996) is about the development of legislative institutions in 1990–2. V. Tikhomirov (ed.), *Russia after Yeltsin* (2001) is mainly about the state of the country in 2000 and is a good introduction.

Moving to less salubrious topics, S. Handelman's *Comrade Criminal: Russia's New Mafiya* (1995) is very good, and includes the 'theft' of industry. The author interviewed sundry shady characters. Other books on crime include M. Galeotti (ed.), *Russian and Post-Soviet Organized Crime* (2001). R. W. Lee, *Smuggling Armageddon* (1998) examines the possible smuggling of nuclear material out of Russia

A. Lieven, *Chechnya: Tombstone of Russian Power* (1999) is a very fair account of the first stages of this conflict. J. B. Dunlop, *Russia Confronts Chechnya* (1998) gives good background, starting in the eighteenth century, and a horrified Russian's account is A. Politkovskaya, *A Dirty War: A Russian Reporter in Chechnya* (2001).

V. Sperling, *Organizing Women in Contemporary Russia* (1999) shows why women were slow to organize in the transition period, while L. Racioppi and K. O'Sullivan See, in *Women's Activism in Contemporary Russia* (1997), present nine case studies.

Two books about the resurgent KGB are J. M. Waller's *Secret Empire* (1994) and Y. Albat's *The State within a State* (1994). The problems faced by Russians in the new post-Soviet republics are treated in H. Pilkington, *Migration, Displacement and Identity in Post-Soviet Russia* (1998), P. Kolstoe, *Russians in the Former Soviet Republics* (1995), and J. Chinn and R. Kaiser, *Russians as the New Minority* (1996).

The deteriorating situation of most workers can be grasped from N. Manning, O. Shkaraton and N. Tikhonova, *Work and Welfare in the New Russia* (2000), which is informative about unemployment and poverty and could be supplemented by M. G. Field and J. L. Twigg, *Russia's Safety Nets* (2000), which discusses the deterioration of health and social welfare provision. Other books on labour matters are S. Clarke, *The Formation of a Labour Market in Russia* (1999), and S. Ashwin, *Russian Workers; The Anatomy of Patience* (1999).

Labour politics in the Yeltsin years are discussed in *Tattered Banners* (1996) by W. D. Connor, and S. Clarke, P. Fairbrother and V. Borisov, *The Workers' Movement in Russia* (1995) is about the new independent labour unions. The state of industry is revealed in P. Rutland, *Business and the State in Contemporary Russia* (2000), and S. Clarke (ed.), *Management and Industry in Russia* (1995), which studies a dozen enterprises in 1991–3 in depth, and incidentally reveals much about the 'black economy'. V. Tikhomirov, *The Political Economy of Post-Soviet Russia* (2000) is very detailed. The real saviour of the Russian economy is discussed in D. Lane (ed.), *The Political Economy of Russian Oil* (1999).

S. Braginsky and G. Yarlinsky, *Incentives and Institutions* (2000) has some interesting ideas about the transition to a market economy, and so does T. Gustafson, *Capitalism Russian Style* (1999), which is critical. J. R. Blasi, M. Kroumova and D. Kruse, *Kremlin Capitalism* (1996) is also about the privatization of the economy. A brave man, P. Klebnikov, wrote a scathing book about Berezovsky, one of the 'oligarchs', *Godfather of the Kremlin* (2000), and C. Freeland in *Sale of the Century* (2000) is equally scathing about this process although a mite less personal. D. Woodruff, *Money Unmade: Barter and the Fate of Russian Capitalism* (1999) deals with one of the phenomena of that time, the near-disappearance of ready money.

S. Cohen's *Failed Gamble* (2000) recounts how the USA missed its chance to set Russia in the right direction; the book is bitter, but well argued. On a parallel track is P. Reddaway's *The Tragedy of Russia's Reforms* (2001).

A. M. Barker (ed.) deals with offbeat topics like tattooing, keeping pets, and the MMM 'pyramid' financial scam in *Consuming Russia: Popular Culture, Sex, and Society since Gorbachev* (1999).

Maps and Tables

Map 1 Russia's place in the world, as Russians saw it. This map is based on the projection used for Soviet school atlases.

Map 2 Union of Soviet Socialist Republics, 1950.

Based on J. N. Westwood: *Russia 1917–64* (Batsford 1966).

Map 3 Changing Frontiers.
Based on J. N. Westwood: *Russia 1917–64* (Batsford 1966).

Map 4 The Conquest of Turkestan and Turkmenia.
Based on Seton-Watson: *The Russian Empire 1801–1917* (OUP 1967).

	Treaty of Peking 1860
	Treaty of St Petersburg
	Treaty of St Petersburg 1875
	To Japan 1905–46
✕	Soviet-Japanese frontier battles 1938–39

0 100 200 300 400 500 miles

0   200   400   600 km

Okhotsk

Yakutsk

SEA OF OKHOTSK

R   U   S   S   I   A

Lena

Lena Goldfields

Kamchatka Bay

KAMCHATKA

(To USSR 1946)

Kurile Islands

BAM Rly. (2000)

Amur

Nikolayevsk

Sakhalin

Khabarovsk

Lake Baikal

Aigun

Irkutsk

Chita   Nerchinsk

Hakodate

Kharbin

SEA OF

Kyakhta   *Chinese Eastern Rly.*

Vladivostok

Lake Khasan   JAPAN

S. Manchurian Rly.

Ulan Bator

✕ Khalkin Gol

JAPAN

Tokio (Edu)

OUTER MONGOLIA
(Mongolian People's Republic from 1925)

Mukden

KOREA

Shimoda

C   H   I   N   A

Seoul

Peking

Port Arthur   Yalu   Inchon   Pusan

Nagasaki

Tsushima Str.

Shanghai

EAST CHINA SEA

Map 5 Russia as a Pacific Power.
Based on Seton-Watson: *The Russian Empire 1801–1917* (OUP 1967).

Map 6 Russia and its republics.

Based on Sakwa: *Russian Politics and Society* (Routledge 1993), 40.

Table 1 Population (in millions)

(a) Pre-reform Russian Empire

	Total	Percentage in towns	Percentage of serfs	Male serfs	Male state peasants
1812	41	4	46	10	7
1835	60	5	36	11	10
1858	74	6	31[a]	11	13

(b) Post-reform Empire and USSR

		Total	Percentage in towns
1870	Empire	86	11
1897	Empire (22.4 million sq. km.)	125	15
1913	Empire (22.3 million sq. km.)	166	18
1913	post-1945 frontiers (22.4 million sq. km.)	159	18
1920	inter-war frontiers (21.7 million sq. km.)	137	15
1926	inter-war frontiers (21.7 million sq. km.)	147	18
1939	inter-war frontiers (21.7 million sq. km.)	171	33
1939	post-September frontiers (22.1 million sq. km.)	191	32
1950	post-1945 frontiers (22.4 million sq. km.)	178	39
1960	post-1945 frontiers (22.4 million sq. km.)	212	49
1980	post-1945 frontiers (22.4 million sq. km.)	265	63
1991	post-1945 frontiers (22.4 million sq. km.)	290	66

(c) Within frontiers of post-1991 Russia

	Total	Below working age	Above working age	Percentage in towns
1897	68			
1939	108			
1970	130	37	19	62
1991	149	35	28	74
2000	146	29	30	73

Note: Pre-1897 figures based on 'revisions' for tax purposes, and only approximate. There were published censuses for 1897, 1926, 1939, 1959, 1970, 1979, and 1989.

[a] The percentage of serfs in European Russia in 1858 was 38.

Table 2 Average expectation of life (at birth)

		Years	Child mortality	
			(Deaths in the age group 0–9 years as percentage of total deaths)	
1897	(European Russia)	32	1910	64
1926	(European Russia)	44	1926	61
1955	(USSR)	67	1960	11
1972	(USSR)	70		
1990	(USSR)	69		
			(Deaths up to 1 year, per thousand births)	
1970	(Post-1991 Russia)	69	1970	23
1991	(Post-1991 Russia)	69	1991	18
1999	(Post-1991 Russia)	66	1999	17

Table 3 Birth and death rates

	Births per thousand		Deaths per thousand
1868–72 (European Russia)	50	1871–75 (European Russia)	37
1908–12 (European Russia)	45	1906–10 (European Russia)	29
1913 (all territory)	47	1913 (European Russia)	27
1916 (all territory)	30	1913 (all territory)	29
1917 (all territory)	24	1916 (all territory)	29
1924 (all territory)	43	1917 (all territory)	28
1928 (all territory)	42	1919 (European Russia	
1930 (all territory)	39	excluding Caucasus)	47
1932 (all territory)	31	1924 (all territory)	22
1935 (all territory)	29	1929 (all territory)	20
(Abortion restricted June 1936)		1940 (all territory)	18
1937 (all territory)	39	1950 (all territory)	10
1939 (all territory)	36	1960 (all territory)	7
1940 (all territory)	31	1980 (all territory)	10
1950 (all territory)	27	1990 (all territory)	10
(Abortion de-restricted 1955)			
1960 (all territory)	25		
1980 (all territory)	18		
1990 (all territory)	17		
1970 (Post-1991 Russia)	15	1970 (Post-1991 Russia)	9
1991 (Post-1991 Russia)	18	1991 (Post-1991 Russia)	11
2000 (Post-1991 Russia)	8	2000 (Post-1991 Russia)	15

Note: Relatively low death rates in First World War are partly a consequence of lower birth rates.

Table 4 Premeditated deaths (thousands) within post-1991 Russian frontiers

	Suicides	Murders
1970	38.9	9.4
1991	39.4	22.6
2000	57.3	38.2

Table 5 The major nationalities; Russian Empire and USSR (millions)

	1897	1959	1979
Great Russian	55.6	113.9	137.4
Ukrainian	22.4	32.7	42.3
White Russian	5.8	6.6	9.4
Polish	7.9	0.6	1.1
Jewish [a]	5.0	0.5	1.8
Kirgiz/Kaisats [b]	4.0	0.9	1.9
Tatar	3.4	4.6	6.3
Azerbaizhani	[c]	2.9	5.4
Uzbek [b]	0.7	5.9	12.5
Kazakh	[c]	3.6	6.5
German	1.8	1.2	1.9
Latvian	1.4	1.3	1.4
Bashkir	1.3	0.6	1.3
Lithuanian	1.2	2.3	2.8
Armenian	1.2	2.5	4.1
Romanian/Moldavian	1.1	2.2	2.9
Estonian	1.0	0.9	1.0
Mordvinian	1.0	1.0	1.2
Georgian	0.8	2.6	3.5
Tadzhik	0.3	1.4	2.9
Turkmenian	0.3	1.4	2.0
Greek	0.2	0.1	0.3
Bulgarian	0.2	0.3	0.3

Note: 1897 and 1959 populations are defined according to language, but 1979 census figures are based on self-definition. In the case of Great Russians, the Baltic nationalities, and the Asian and Caucasian nations there is little difference between nationality by language and by self-definition, but in 1979 only 14% of self-defined Jews spoke their national language, 29% of Poles, 38% of Greeks, 57% of Germans, 67% of Bashkirs, 68% of Bulgarians, 72% of Mordvinians, 74% of White Russians, 83% of Ukrainians, and 86% of Tatars. In the 1979 census 153 million gave Russian as their mother tongue. However, some doubts have been expressed about the precision of the language question asked by the census.

[a] Jews by faith were 5.2 million in 1897. By self-definition, as opposed to language, they were 2.3 million in 1959.
[b] Redefined in the Soviet period.
[c] Not separately defined in 1897.

Table 6 Class structure according to official categories (per cent)

	1897
Hereditary nobles	1.0
Non-hereditary nobles, and non-noble bureaucrats	0.5
Christian priests	0.5
Hereditary and non-hereditary 'honoured citizens'	0.3
Merchants	0.2
Petty commercial classes	10.6
Peasants in rural areas	70.1
Peasants in towns	7.0
Cossacks	2.3
Settlers	6.6
Foreigners	0.5
Others (unclassifiable)	0.4

Other years	1913	1928	1939	1978	1981
Workers, white-collar included	17	18	50	85	86
Workers, excluding white-collar	14	12	32	62	61
Collective/state farmers and workers in cooperative workshops	—	3	47	15	14
Independent peasants (excluding kulaks), independent artisans and handicraft workers	67	75	3	0.01	0.01
Landowners, merchants, bourgeoisie, kulaks	16	5	—	—	—

Table 7 Urbanization

The twenty biggest cities 1978

	Million inhabitants
St Petersburg	1.26
Moscow	1.04
Warsaw	0.68
Odessa	0.40
Lodz	0.31
Riga	0.28
Kiev	0.25
Kharkov	0.17
Tiflis (Tbilisi)	0.16
Tashkent	0.16
Vilna (Vilno)	0.15
Saratov	0.14
Kazan	0.13
Rostov on Don	0.12
Tula	0.12
Astrakhan	0.11
Ekaterinoslav (Dnepropetrovsk)	0.11
Baku	0.11
Kishinev	0.10
Helsinki	0.10

continued

The twenty biggest cities 1989

	Million inhabitants
Moscow	8.77
Leningrad (St Petersburg)	5.02
Kiev	2.59
Tashkent	2.07
Baku	1.76
Kharkov	1.61
Minsk	1.59
Gorki (Nizhnii Novgorod)	1.44
Novosibirsk	1.44
Sverdlovsk (Ekaterinburg)	1.37
Tbilisi	1.26
Kuibyshev (Samara)	1.26
Erevan	1.12
Dnepropetrovsk	1.18
Omsk	1.15
Chelyabinsk	1.14
Alma Ata	1.13
Odessa	1.12
Donetsk (Stalino, Yuzovka)	1.10
Kazan	1.09

The twelve biggest Russian cities 2000

	Million inhabitants
Moscow	8.39
St Petersburg	4.69
Novosibirsk	1.40
Nizhnii Novgorod	1.36
Ekaterinburg	1.27
Samara	1.16
Omsk	1.15
Kazan	1.01
Ufa	1.10
Chelyabinsk	1.08
Rostov on Don	1.01
Perm	1.01

Table 8 Growth of St Petersburg/Petrograd/Leningrad
(million inhabitants)

1800	0.220	1914	2.20
1812	0.308	1920	0.60
1830	0.435	1939	3.38
1863	0.539	1959	3.32
1869	0.667	1970	3.95
1881	0.861	1989	5.02
1897	1.260	2000	4.69

Note: Of the 1897 inhabitants, 58% were classified as peasants.

Table 9 The Tsarist economy: annual production (million tonnes)

	Coal	Pig iron	Oil	Grain
1860	0.29	0.31	—	[a]
1870	0.68	0.33	0.03	[a]
1880	3.24	0.42	0.5	[a]
1890	5.90	0.89	3.9	[a]
1900	16.10	2.66	10.2	56
1910	26.80	2.99	9.4	74
1913	35.40	4.12	9.1	90
1916	33.80	3.72	9.7	64

[a] For European Russia only, grain production averaged 220 million *chetverts* 1857–63, and 179 million *chetverts* 1834–40 (a chetvert approximated 6 bushels). Average annual production in European Russia 1886–90 was 36 million tons.

Table 10 The Soviet economy: annual production

	1913 inter-war frontiers	1928	1940	1945	1960	1990	
Electricity	1.9	5.0	48.3	43.3	292	1,726[b]	milliard KWH
Oil	9.1	11.6	31.1	19.4	148	571	million tonnes
Coal	29.1	35.5	166	150	510	703	million tonnes
Gas	0.0	0.3	3.4	3.4	47.2	815	milliard cu. metres
Steel	4.2	4.3	18.3	12.3	65.3	154	million tonnes
Mineral fertilizers	0.0	0.1	3.2	1.1	13.9	32	million tonnes (hypothetical units)
Tractors	—	1.3	31.6	7.7	238	495	thousand units
Plastics and synthetic materials	—	—	10.9	21.3	312	5,536	thousand tonnes
Clocks and watches	0.7	0.9	2.8	0.3	26	77	million units
Cement	1.5	1.8	5.7	1.8	46	137	million tonnes
Leather footwear[a]	60	58	211	63	419	843	million pairs
Grain[a]	76	69	77	47	125	218	million tonnes
Meat[a]	4.1	4.2	4.0	2.6	8.7	20	million deadweight tonnes
Eggs[a]	10.2	9.2	9.6	4.9	27.4	81.7	milliard
Milk[a]	24.8	29.3	26.5	26.4	61.7	108.4	million tonnes

[a] Agricultural produce figures quoted for 1928 are annual averages for 1924–8, those for 1940 annual averages for 1936–41. The 1913 figure for footwear may be understated. The larger figures have been rounded off to eliminate decimal points.
[b] Of the 1990 electricity output, 233 milliard KWH was hydro and 212 milliard was nuclear.

Table 11 Annual production within post-1991 Russian frontiers

	1980	1991	1999
Electricity (milliard KWH)[a]	805	1,068	846
Oil (million tonnes)	547	462	305
Natural gas (milliard cu. m.)	254	643	592
Coal, all types (million tonnes)	391	353	250
Steel (million tonnes)	84	77	52
Chemical fertilizer (million tonnes at 100%)	11.7	15.0	11.5
Cement (million tonnes)	76	78	29
Tractors (thousands)	249	178	15
Clocks and watches (millions)	54	62	6
Personal computers (thousands)	9	137	28
Passenger automobiles (thousands)	1,166	1,030	954
Leather footwear (million pairs)	351	336	30
Cigarettes (milliard)	181	144	283
Vodka and similar (million dcl.)	208	154	134
Grain, harvested (million tonnes) (Grain yield	95	84	48
quintal/hectare)	14	15	14
Eggs (milliard)	28	34	23
Milk (million tonnes)	33	36	16
Meat and fowl; (million tonnes DWT)	5	6	2

[a] Includes small amount of imported power (8.4 milliard KWT in 1999).

Sources: The tables in this section are mainly composite, being assembled, and sometimes calculated, from a number of sources. For the tsarist period, figures have been taken from the major Russian pre-1917 encyclopedia, F. Brokgaus and I. Efron, *Entsiklopedicheskii slovar* (dopolnitelnyi tom, 1907); P. Khromov, *Ekonomicheskoye razvitiye Rossli* (1967): P. Lyashehenko, *Istoriya narodnogo khozyaistva SSSR* (1956); and B. Urlanis, *Rozdaemost i prodolzhitelnost zhizni v SSSR*(1963). The last named was also used for the Soviet period. However, the basic sources for post-1917 figures (and many for the Soviet period. However, the basic sources for post-1917 figures (and many 1913 figures) were the statistical annual *Nfarodnoye Klhozyaistvo SSSR* and the 1959, 1979, and 1989 censuses. Figures for post-1991 Russia are from *Rossiiskii statisticheskii ezhegodnik 2000*.

Index

There are several conventions for transliterating the Cyrillic alphabet, but throughout this book such conventions have not always been followed. Common usage, convenience, and even personal taste have had their influence. For example, Tchaikovsky could be rendered as Chaikovskii, and there are grounds for preferring Gorbachov to Gorbachev. As for Trotsky, Trotskii, and Trotski . . .